Managing Employment Relations

Eighth Edition

Managing Employment Relations

Theory, Policies and Practice

Tony Bennett, Richard Saundry, Margaret Prior

Publisher's note

Every possible effort has been made to ensure that the information contained in this book is accurate at the time of going to press, and the publishers and authors cannot accept responsibility for any errors or omissions, however caused. No responsibility for loss or damage occasioned to any person acting, or refraining from action, as a result of the material in this publication can be accepted by the editor, the publisher or the author.

First published in Great Britain and the United States in 2024 by Kogan Page Limited

2nd Floor, 45 Gee Street
London
EC1V 3RS
United Kingdom

c/o Martin P Hill Consulting
122 W 27th St, 10th Floor
New York, NY 10001
USA

www.koganpage.com

Kogan Page books are printed on paper from sustainable forests.

ISBNs

Hardback 978 1 3986 1814 5
Paperback 978 1 3986 1812 1
Ebook 978 1 3986 1813 8

British Library Cataloguing-in-Publication Data

A CIP record for this book is available from the British Library.

Library of Congress Cataloging-in-Publication Data

Names: Bennett, Tony (Anthony), author. | Saundry, Richard, author. | Prior, Margaret (Lecturer in human resources management), author.
Title: Managing employment relations : theory, policies and practice / Tony Bennett, Richard Saundry, Margaret Prior.
Description: Eighth edition. | London ; New York, NY : Kogan Page, 2024. | Includes bibliographical references and index.
Identifiers: LCCN 2024043926 | ISBN 9781398618121 (paperback) | ISBN 9781398618145 (hardback) | ISBN 9781398618138 (ebook)
Subjects: LCSH: Personnel management. | Industrial relations.
Classification: LCC HF5549 .B436 2024 | DDC 658.3/15–dc23/eng/20241011
LC record available at https://lccn.loc.gov/2024043926

Typeset by Integra Software Services, Pondicherry
Print production managed by Jellyfish
Printed and bound by CPI Group (UK) Ltd, Croydon CR0 4YY

CONTENTS

LIST OF FIGURES AND TABLES

Figures

Tables

ACKNOWLEDGEMENTS

We would like to thank and acknowledge the previous work of John Gennard, Graham Judge and Virginia Fisher. We would also like to thank Lucy Carter for her guidance and the support of Michelle Nicholson, Rosey Bennett and Christine Crocker. This edition of the book is dedicated to the memories of Tim Bennett, Pat Prior and Frank Saundry.

01
Introduction

Overview

This book is underpinned by the following key themes:

- Changes in the political, economic and social environment of all organisations which impact on the balance of bargaining power between employers and employees and on the policies and practices that regulate employment relations.
- If employers are to engage their employees and improve organisational performance, management approaches to employment relations need to reflect and promote fairness, equity and trust.
- Line managers, in particular, need support in developing people management skills.
- There is a growing imperative to devise coherent strategies and practices for managing workplace conflict.
- A strategy for greater equality, diversity and inclusion should underpin all employee relations policy and practice.
- There is a need for 'good work' for all employees that protects their physical and psychological well-being while delivering organisational objectives.

If the aspirations implied by these themes are to be realised, it must be understood that the management of power and conflict in the workplace is central to effective employment relations policy and practice. For three decades, employment relations has undergone significant change. Union membership has declined rapidly, collective bargaining has contracted and there has been a significant and seemingly permanent reduction in the incidence of strikes and other forms of industrial action. At the same time, the development of human resource management has put an emphasis on communication, employee engagement and business performance. In this context, students sometimes question the relevance of employment relations for the contemporary HR practitioner. This book challenges this narrative and argues that the

CIPD's mission to 'champion better work and working lives' can only be delivered if employment relations lies at the heart of HR practice. To this end, in this opening chapter we set out the case for acquiring the knowledge, skills and insight that underpin employment relations. Furthermore, we outline how this book relates to the latest CIPD Profession Map.

1.1 The relevance of employment relations

For some HR practitioners, the relevance of employment relations faded as the influence of trade unions declined. However, employment relations is not only relevant to the management of people in unionised organisations. On the contrary, its fundamental objective is to understand and, therefore, more effectively manage the employment relationship between employer and employee, irrespective of whether individuals belong to a trade union or any other representative organisation. Furthermore, despite the individualisation of employment relations, collective relationships still exist in all organisations, which require appropriate channels of voice. It is also important to remember that, in both unionised and non-unionised environments, employee grievances have to be resolved, disciplinary matters processed, and procedures devised, implemented, operated, reviewed and monitored.

The study of employment relations also provides practitioners with insights that are largely missing in other management disciplines. A core objective of this book is to broaden our readers' understanding of the management of power and conflict in the workplace. The interests of different parties within any organisation do not always align. This book is designed to help you to identify the causes of conflict and to develop responses and strategies to the benefit of employees and their organisations. For instance, a fundamental employment relations concept is the relative balance of bargaining power between the buyers and sellers of labour services. If certain knowledge and skills are scarce in the labour market, or unions are strong in a particular sector, employees are more likely to be able to negotiate improved terms and conditions. Conversely, if labour is cheap and easily replaceable, or unions are less strong or absent from a workplace, the employer is more likely to be able to set the agenda for any discussion on the terms and conditions of employment for its workforce.

The context within which organisations operate is central to the study and practice of employment relations. Bargaining power is shaped by the external environment and therefore changes in product and markets, government economic policy or employment legislation fundamentally shift the terms on which employers and employees interact. For example, the financial crash and subsequent recession of 2008 radically reduced the bargaining power of labour, while the Trade Union Act 2016 introduced a level of restriction on trade union activity which would have been seen as unthinkable in previous decades. Brexit, the Covid-19 pandemic and the war in Ukraine contributed to labour shortages and rising living costs in 2022 and 2023, which led to workers taking collective action to defend their interests. At the same time concern over the negative impacts of employment insecurity, pay inequality and automation has deepened. This has made issues of 'good work', equity and fairness increasingly relevant. Most recently, a Labour government was elected in July 2024 promising to promote collective bargaining, extend worker representation and strengthen employment rights.

It perhaps goes without saying that employment relations practitioners should always act in a fair and reasonable manner and promote this approach among all management colleagues. However, as we discuss later in the book, this is often not straightforward given the status of HR in many organisations and the increased devolution of people management to line and operational managers. Nonetheless, an understanding and appreciation of organisational justice and how this is reflected in policy and procedure does provide HR practitioners with a chance to shape the management of employment relations. For example, as we explain in Chapter 10, when handling a disciplinary matter, it is crucial that: the employee concerned is aware of the details of the allegation against them; they are given the opportunity to respond to this; they are provided with the opportunity to be accompanied to a disciplinary hearing; and they can appeal against any decision that is made. However, practitioners must also appreciate why such 'good practice' is essential to protecting and advancing the interests of the organisation – namely, the avoidance of costly and damaging litigation, but also, and perhaps more importantly, establishing a degree of workplace justice that can in turn secure the trust and engagement of employees. In short, good employment relations practice also helps to underpin high levels of productivity and performance.

This is particularly challenging when managing during a crisis, such as the Covid pandemic (Wakeling, 2020). Subsequent changes in the nature of the employment relationship and its management, such as the growth in home and hybrid working, have highlighted the importance of innovation in employment relations policies and practices. This involves being able to analyse the suitability of new processes and practices and anticipating any problems with implementation. However, this also requires employment relations professionals to be able to identify and develop the relevant skills required for themselves – for instance in terms of negotiation, communication and ICT skills – and managers in the face of continuing development of many HR tasks to the line.

More broadly, a fundamental objective of this book is to equip our readers with the key knowledge, skills and insight to successfully satisfy the requirements of the CIPD Professional Standards. We understand that many students who study employment relations have very little prior knowledge or understanding of the subject and have often graduated in other disciplines or perhaps come to study through their managerial experience. For this reason, we try to provide the necessary basic knowledge to understand employment relations and also the perspectives to allow for a more critical and nuanced analysis of the subject.

Reflective activity 1.1

What are your initial thoughts on the study and practice of employment relations? Which areas have you had experience of already in your professional work? Which areas appear challenging and why? What strategy might you adopt to overcome these challenges in your study and practice?

1.2 The CIPD HR Profession Map

In the last two decades or more there has been a shift in the focus of the HR profession. The rise of HRM brought with it a new emphasis on the role of practitioners in improving the performance of the organisation by building sustainable organisational capability – not just delivering on the day-to-day people management role, although this remains important. However, in the last decade, the radical changes to the environment of work and employment that we just discussed provide a new set of challenges for HR practitioners. Consequently, the CIPD has developed standards designed to set 'the international benchmark for the people profession' (CIPD, 2024a: 1). The 'Profession Map' charts the role, influence and responsibilities of professionals across the three main dimensions:

- the core knowledge needed to deliver effective human relations strategy and practice;
- the core behaviours expected from all HR professionals to achieve those aims;
- the specialist knowledge – for instance, that of employee relations – that informs the efficacy of the sub-disciplines that make up the policy and practice of human resource management and development.

Table 1.1 sets out how these dimensions relate to specific modules and areas of study. These three key dimensions are underpinned by the overall common purpose and 'professional values' of the HR international community (CIPD, 2024b).

The first of these core values – **being principles-led** – is articulated through three key principles for making good decisions and clearly reflects a renewed focus on the role of HR in delivering 'good work' (See also Figure 1.1).

Table 1.1 The three key dimensions

Core knowledge	Core behaviours	Specialist knowledge
People practice	Ethical practice	Employee experience
Culture and behaviour	Professional courage and influence	Employee relations
Business acumen	Valuing people	Diversity and inclusion
Analytics and creating value	Working inclusively	Learning and development
Digital working	Commercial drive	Reward
Change	Passion for learning	Talent management
	Situational decision-making	Resourcing
	Insights-focused	Organisation development and design
		People analytics
		Well-being

Figure 1.1 The new Profession Map

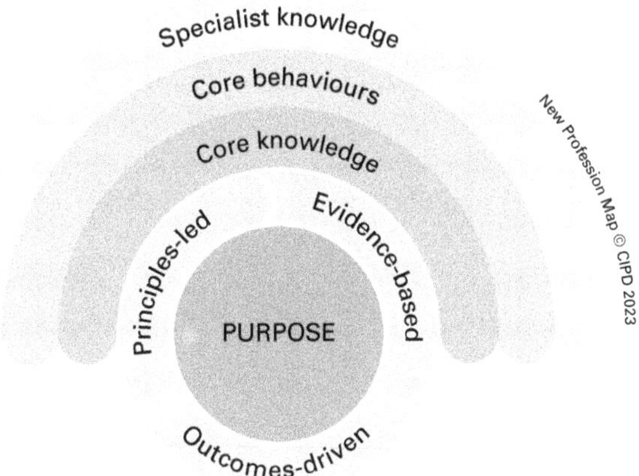

1 Work matters
    - Work can and should be a force for good and it 'exists for the long-term benefit of individuals, organisations and society, balancing economic sustainability with social accountability'.
    - 'Good work' should be safe and inclusive. It should allow everyone to fully use their skills and talents and find 'personal meaning' in what they do and be fairly recognised for that contribution.
2 People matter
    - They are a 'unique' resource of the organisation to be supported and developed to the full.
    - People deserve to be treated fairly and have a meaningful voice on matters that affect them, in addition to their rights and protection under law.
3 Professionalism matters in terms of integrity, being aware of the impact of our actions, continuous development of our people management expertise and in 'championing better work and working lives'.

The second core value is that **decision-making should be evidence-based,** where those sources of evidence are a combination of:

1 Behavioural science and academic research
    - the theory underpinning our profession
    - the psychology of human behaviour
    - independent surveys, reviews and benchmarks
2 Organisational data
    - People analytics can help us to get to know our workforce better, for instance in terms of employee well-being and engagement.
3 Stakeholder concerns by drawing on our own experiences and conversation
4 Practitioner expertise.

The third core value is that the **HR practitioners should be outcomes-driven** in terms of their impact on:

1. work and the collective well-being, success and productivity of organisations, the people within them and the society to which we all belong;
2. people and building inclusive organisations that treat people fairly, respond to diverse voices and develop people for improved personal employability and organisational sustainability, and improve skills in the wider workforce and society;
3. professionalism through building the strength, credibility and integrity of the people profession, leading to better decision-making on matters that affect people, work and change.

The degree of impact that practitioners will have will inevitably depend on the stage of their career and the context in which they are working. Nonetheless, it is important to strive towards positive outcomes for people (such as well-being) as well as business imperatives. Of course, that is not an easy balance to strike (CIPD, 2024b).

1.3 Applying the Profession Map in practice

Having considered an overview of the new standards, how might these new professional guidelines be put into practice? And where might this textbook fit into this process?

About the levels

The Profession Map outlines four different levels at which HR practitioners can have an impact and sets out the knowledge and behaviours they need to excel at each. This allows practitioners to identify what they need to make a positive contribution, irrespective of their experience, seniority or current position.

WHICH LEVEL ARE YOU?

Fundamental level

Your work is likely to be tactical and focused on the day-to-day delivery of tasks. You'll gather information to use in your role, and use information to understand your work, organisation and profession. You'll work with and deliver immediate and short-term outcomes for your manager, colleagues and customers. The fundamental level is not aligned to any grade of CIPD professional membership.

Associate level

Your work will usually be operational, with some complexity. You'll contribute to the thinking around your work, and analyse information to inform your choices and actions. You'll work with and influence immediate colleagues and customers, though your work will create short-term value for a wider audience. Associate level is equivalent to Associate Member (Assoc CIPD).

Chartered Member level

Your work will require thinking at a strategic level and have complexity in the thinking and/or delivery. You'll critically question information and evaluate it to make judgements and decisions. You'll work with and influence a range of stakeholders, creating medium- to long-term value for a wide audience. Chartered Member level is equivalent to Chartered Member (Chartered MCIPD).

Chartered Fellow level

Your work is likely to be entirely strategic in thinking and/or delivery, with a significant level of complexity. You'll develop evidence-based thinking to shape the profession or drive people change. You'll influence stakeholders across the profession and create long-term value for significant numbers of people. Chartered Fellow level is equivalent to Chartered Fellow (Chartered FCIPD).

SOURCE: CIPD: The Profession Map (2024a: 2)

Now let us consider how the different levels work in relation to the specialist knowledge for employee relations as set out in the standards. This is set out in Table 1.2.

Table 1.2 Specific knowledge for employment relations

Level	Fundamental	Associate	Chartered Member	Chartered Fellow
Employee relations culture	The culture and approach to employee relations in your organisation	How the employee relations culture impacts the way people work	How to develop and review your employee relations culture to be resolution-focused and improve business outcomes	How to drive an employment culture that improves performance and reputation, whilst mitigating risk

(continued)

Table 1.2 (Continued)

Level	Fundamental	Associate	Chartered Member	Chartered Fellow
People policies	What people policies are in place in your organisation and how they support employee relations practices	How to apply your organisation's people policies in a wide range of situations to support effective case management and employee relations practice	How to develop and apply people policies which improve the worker experience and employer brand, and mitigate risk	How to develop an employee relations strategy which positively impacts the business, and the way people work
Employment law	Key employment law	How to apply employment law in a wide range of work situations	How to apply and interpret employment law in a range of complex work situations and mitigate risk	How to manage the impact and risk to the organisation of employment law and regulation
Legal systems	The legal system which deals with employment disputes (eg employment tribunals, arbitration)	The evidence needed to support employment legal cases/ labour disputes	How the employment legal system works, and how to prepare for and manage cases/labour disputes	How to lead complex legal cases/labour disputes and manage organisation risks associated with legal action
Dispute resolution	What workplace conflict is and a range of dispute resolution techniques (eg mediation, conciliation, negotiation, settlement agreements)	How to apply different dispute resolution techniques to resolve workplace conflict	How to manage high-risk and complex disputes, and when to use legal routes	How to create a culture which mitigates workplace conflict

(continued)

Table 1.2 (Continued)

Level	Fundamental	Associate	Chartered Member	Chartered Fellow
Collective employment law	What collective employment law and collective bargaining are (if applicable in your region)	Collective employment law, and how to work with formal representative bodies such as Trade Unions and Works Councils (if applicable in your region)	Collective employment law and how to manage collective bargaining relationships (if applicable in your region)	How to develop strategies and frameworks that support collective bargaining and collaborative relationships (if applicable in your region)
Consultation and negotiation	The importance of consultation and negotiation with individuals and groups	Different approaches and models of consultation and negotiation	How to drive effective working relationships through consultation and negotiation	How to establish frameworks and mechanisms to support a culture of effective consultation and negotiation
Voice and engagement	The different ways by which employees' voices can be heard	Why employee voice is important, and the role of employee groups in engaging workers (eg employee councils, staff forums)	How to use employee voice insights to positively impact the way people work	How to use employee voice insight to shape the organisation's culture
Employee and worker relationship	The different types of employees/ workers in your organisation (eg employed, gig worker, contractor, consultant)	The impact of different employee/worker relationships on the organisation	How to balance individual and business expectations regarding employee/worker relationships	How to maximise the individual and organisation benefits of different employee/ worker relationships

SOURCE: CIPD (2024a: 21)

One of the many strengths of the Profession Map is that it is reviewed and revised on a regular basis. For instance, recently, evidence-based practice, staff well-being and the influence of artificial intelligence have all gained greater prominence and will figure in the discussions later in the book. Usefully, in an earlier iteration, the CIPD (2024a) also offered some useful guidance for 'things to think about with respect to the standards', and categories just outlined, by asking practitioners to use the following prompts 'to reflect on your understanding of **employee relations** and uncover areas for future professional development':

- Do your people policies reflect the core values of your organisation?
- When did you last work with unions and employee representative bodies to develop your people practices?
- Do you understand how employment law is created and developed?
- What proactive resolution processes do you regularly use and what alternative options could be used?

Let us focus on this last prompt in a little more detail to see how this might work in practice and be supported by this book. As we can see from Table 1.2, in addition to the four levels of professional competence and the nine elements of specialist knowledge, the HR Profession Map also sets out six aspects of core knowledge and eight core behaviours corresponding to what HR practitioners need in order to be effective. One of these core behaviours is 'professional courage and influence'. How this applies across the four competence levels is set out in Table 1.3.

In broad terms, one might suggest that someone exhibiting this behaviour of 'showing courage to speak up and skilfully influencing others to gain buy-in' will be able to speak up and challenge others, often when confronted with resistance or unfamiliar circumstances. This is particularly important at a time when many organisations are faced with intense pressures to reduce costs and increase efficiency. In these contexts, managers may prioritise short-term operational objectives while neglecting the potential impact on their staff. Therefore, effective HR practitioners may need the confidence to challenge existing managerial approaches to ensure fairness and equity and drive 'good work'.

We can also examine how this element of courage and influence applies to the four impact levels of the standards by using the example of workplace mediation, one of the areas of knowledge outlined in Table 1.2 and discussed in detail in Chapter 13 of this book.

Table 1.3 An extract from the professional courage and influence behaviour standards

Fundamental level	Associate level	Chartered Member level	Chartered Fellow level
Contribute views and opinions clearly	Contribute to discussions and respond to questions in an informed and confident way	Challenge constructively and confidently in the face of opposition	Take a stand with senior colleagues when it is the right thing to do despite significant opposition or challenge

SOURCE: CIPD (2024a: 12)

- Chartered Fellow level
  - At this level, it may be argued that using the strategic and practical arguments, and evidence-based thinking, embedded in this book can allow the reader to better influence changes in organisational culture that sees conflict management as a strategic employee relations and business issue – even in the face of the possible 'significant opposition' with respect to perceptions of efficacy and cost of such an HR decision, thereby helping to 'shape the profession' in terms of gaining greater support for alternative dispute resolution as part of the conflict management strategy for all organisations.
- Chartered Member level
  - At this level, the knowledge derived particularly from Chapter 10 on managing conflict and from Chapter 13 on mediation will equip the reader with the knowledge to 'critically question information and evaluate it to make judgements and decisions' in relation to the appropriateness and the type of workplace mediation scheme for their organisation, and then 'constructively and confidently' present that case to a range of stakeholders.
- Associate level
  - At this level, the in-depth knowledge, techniques and rationale for workplace mediation covered within Chapter 13 will equip the reader from an 'operational' perspective to 'confidently contribute to discussions', and make judgements on 'when to use workplace mediation to resolve disputes'.
- Fundamental level
  - Finally, at this level, it may be argued that in terms of the 'day-to-day delivery of tasks', such as successfully managing workplace disputes, knowledge derived from Chapter 13 provides the reader with the ability to effectively 'contribute their views clearly' on how mediation works and its potential for assisting in managing that conflict effectively.

The efficacy of alternative dispute resolution is covered in depth in the final part of the book. In relation to the book's contribution as part of a course of study, a key objective outlined in the Profession Map is that an individual with the CIPD Associate membership qualification should be capable of adding value to their organisation. They cannot do this on their own – they need to collaborate with others both within and outside the organisation. These outcomes are not necessarily what an academic would emphasise in a master's degree programme. Here students would be expected to be aware of the plurality of perspectives on employment relations issues and be able to critically evaluate competing theories and perspectives. Skills development to solve employment relations problems would have much less emphasis. In this edition of *Managing Employment Relations*, we have sought to integrate the rigour of critical analysis of competing theories and concepts of employment relations with the tangible application of that knowledge in the day-to-day practice of the discipline.

Reflective activity 1.2

Reflecting on the requirements needed to attain the Professional Standards, through our discussion so far and by visiting the CIPD website, how might you begin to plan the achievement of the employment relations elements of the Profession Map? In what way will you utilise the book to this end?

The influential HR practitioner

If HR practitioners, at any point in their career journey, are to be proactive and to have influence in an organisation, they must demonstrate certain abilities (see Figure 1.2). First, they require a successful record of professional competence in the HRM field which is recognised by their colleagues both within and outside the HR function. Second, they must demonstrate an understanding of the HR function as a whole and how its separate components integrate. Third, they must understand the interests of the organisation. Fourth, they must develop a network of contacts, both within and outside the HR profession, including employers' associations and professional bodies such as the CIPD, government agencies such as Acas and also trade unions that may represent staff in their sector. Finally, but perhaps most importantly, they need to build positive high-trust relationships within their organisations, including with senior management, trade union representatives and the line managers who they support and advise. This will not only help to maximise the influence of the HR function, but will facilitate creative solutions to the problems that will inevitably arise. Each of these five abilities is a necessary condition for an effective and influential personnel/HRM professional practitioner – and each is insufficient on its own.

Figure 1.2 The abilities required of an HR practitioner

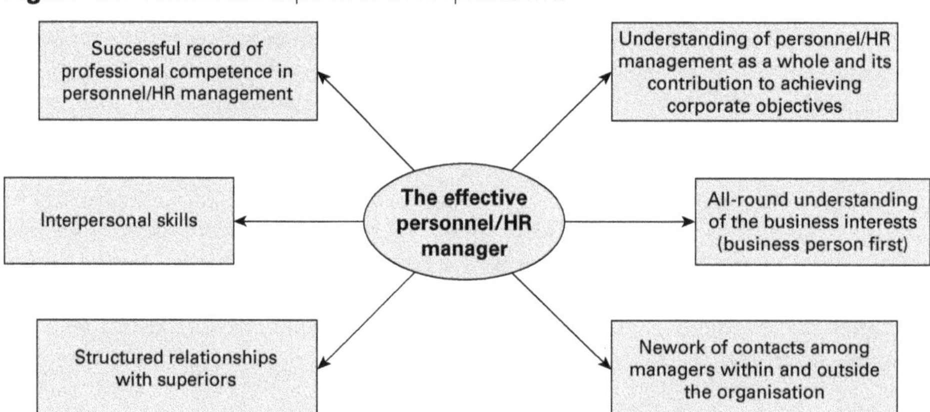

All people managers, regardless of their seniority, need to understand the nature of business in the organisation in which they manage in terms of its mission, objectives, strategies and policies. In the private sector, effective and influential HR practitioners will understand the 'bottom line' for the business and be able to contribute constructively, at the appropriate level of decision-making, to discussions on how the business might be developed and expanded. In the public sector, the effective and influential HR practitioner will understand how employment relations are linked to the quality of service delivery, efficiency and value for money. The effective HR practitioner can also explain how the various components of resourcing, development, reward and relations contribute to the achievement of the objectives of the HR function. This means that they must fully understand how HR strategies and policies combine to achieve the goals of the function.

A key theme of this book is the devolution of responsibility for HR across management teams and the consequent implications for employment relations. Devolution often means that the services of an HR practitioner with a specialism will not always be requested. However, the activities of the employment relations function must nevertheless be delivered to the management team. Generalist HR practitioners with employment relations skills are essential to any management team. This book therefore aims to provide the generalist HR practitioner – and *crucially* any other managers who have to manage people – with the appropriate employment relations knowledge and skills necessary to successfully solve people management problems.

1.4 The structure of the book

The CIPD employment relations specialism centres on understanding, analysing and critically evaluating:

- different theories and perspectives on employment relations;
- the impact of local, national and global contexts in shaping employment relations;
- the roles and functions of the different parties in the control and management of the employment relationship;
- the strategic integration of employment relations processes and how they impact on key people management policy, practice and organisational outcomes, such as employee engagement and employee performance;
- the strategic importance of involving employees in decision-making through employee voice mechanisms, such as communications, consultation and collective negotiation;
- the need to develop and deliver coherent policies, practices and procedures for effectively managing all elements of conflict in the workplace.

To facilitate the acquisition of the key knowledge and skills set out in the Profession Map, and to reflect the emergence of new issues and arguments in the field of employment relations, the contents of this book have again been significantly revised for this eighth edition. In particular, we welcome the continuing significance in the Standards of the knowledge area of equality and diversity, and the increased focus on employee well-being. A critical discussion on current research and practice in both these fields figures prominently in the chapters that follow. More broadly, the notion of intersectionality emerges as an important theme that runs throughout the book. In Chapter 5, for example, a critical awareness of this concept allows us to consider the many dimensions of 'hidden voices'. We suggest that employee voice does not merely serve a homogeneous set of workers. Instead, HR practitioners need to design communication channels within the organisation that meet the needs of less-heard groups, for example, disabled workers, young or older workers, and 'blue-collar' workers.

In response to the new emphasis on people analytics in the Profession Map, we have strengthened the evidence base of the book throughout by using a wide range of publicly available statistical data and peer-reviewed research. We have also drawn extensively on original research conducted by the writers, with a specific focus on the management of workplace conflict and mediation. Furthermore, given the increased focus on 'good work', reflected in the Profession Map, we have further integrated this key concept across chapters. For example, in Chapter 8 we critically analyse trends, concepts and research findings on health and well-being in the workplace. We have also substantially reworked our examination of the context of employment relations to reflect increased policy interest in this area and the particular challenges of automation. Finally, we recognise the implications of the continuing devolution of many HR tasks to the line and therefore the challenges of developing managerial competence and capability is a recurring theme of the eighth edition.

The new edition of *Managing Employment Relations* is structured as follows. Following this introductory chapter, the book is set out in three interlinked sections. In the first section, we aim in Chapter 2 to equip the reader with a knowledge and understanding of the main concepts and models of employment relations needed to critically analyse the themes and debates developed in the book and to be able then to apply that understanding in practical situations. Chapter 3 then offers the reader an up-to-date understanding of the environment within which employment relations takes place. This considers the impact of changes in government strategy on employment policy and practice in the UK, the globalisation of economic activity and the continuing 'puzzle' of low productivity in the UK. In particular, it considers the implications of the Covid pandemic, labour market fragmentation and accelerating technological change.

The second section opens with Chapter 4 exploring the crucial role of the line manager, which, given the continuing devolution of people management, is increasingly important in shaping employment relations. Building on this theme, Chapter 5 commences with a review of the role of strategy, before turning to a discussion on the key drivers of employee engagement. Given that the theory and practice of employee voice underpins effective workforce engagement, the chapter then considers the nature and impact of processes designed to facilitate employee involvement and participation. Chapter 5 closes with a model that incorporates and summarises all the key concepts covered in the first five chapters and acts as a conceptual bridge to the later discussions in the rest of the book.

In Chapter 6 we critically review the development of employee representation in UK workplaces, highlighting its key role in effective employment relations. Chapter 7 then critically and extensively considers the challenges for the HR practitioner in ensuring that the modern workplace recognises its responsibilities to an increasingly diverse workforce. Chapter 8 maps the development of legislation and good practice around health and safety in the UK and explores more recent arguments regarding the potential benefits for business, society and individual workers of a more holistic approach to ensuring the well-being of employees.

The third section of the book focuses on all the key aspects of managing organisational disputes. Chapter 9 offers a conceptual framework for understanding the notion of workplace conflict and also contextualising the debates that take place in the subsequent chapters. This final section of the book reflects the growing recognition by both practitioners and writers of the need for the HR professional, and indeed all managers, to strategically address, through policy and practice, the causes and consequences of conflict in the workplace. To this end, Chapters 10 to 13 cover in detail each of the key areas of conflict management: discipline and performance management, responding to employee grievances, managing redundancies and, a more contemporary development, workplace mediation.

In this way, this text is designed to fully support the CIPD-accredited employment relations specialist module by also covering the skills required by an employment relations professional practitioner in handling employee complaints against management behaviour (commonly referred to as grievances), in handling disciplinary proceedings, in managing a redundancy situation and in managing health and safety. In addition, it covers the management skills, knowledge and understanding required to devise, review and monitor policy and procedure. We have also sought to integrate areas of key legal knowledge within each chapter to avoid an artificial separation between the law and its application within HR practice. The book closes with a concluding chapter that reflects on the future of employment relations, and the opportunities and challenges this may present to organisations and HR practitioners.

We hope you enjoy reading this book. If you can acquire and develop a deep understanding and appreciation of its contents, you will have an excellent chance of reaching the CIPD practitioner Professional Standards in Employment Relations.

Tony Bennett

Richard Saundry

Margaret Prior

Explore further

CIPD (2024a) *The Profession Map*. https://www.cipd.org/uk/the-people-profession/the-profession-map/ (archived at https://perma.cc/E6FT-WCTM).

CIPD (2024b) *The Core Purpose*. https://peopleprofession.cipd.org/profession-map/core-purpose (archived at https://perma.cc/5YHL-WA2P).

02 The concepts and processes of employment relations

Overview

This chapter is in three parts. First, we explain and define employment relations, which we argue is fundamentally concerned with the way that employers, employees, government and other third parties use a range of rules and processes to negotiate and regulate behaviour at the level of the workplace and the work community. We then outline the roles played by the key employment relations actors and examine their differing interests with reference to key theories and perspectives. We explore systems theory and the main frames of reference before going on to discuss more radical approaches such as labour process theory and feminist approaches to employment relations. Finally, we identify and examine the core processes used to regulate the employment relationship.

LEARNING OUTCOMES

When you have completed this chapter, you should be able to:

- understand and analyse the nature of the employment relationship;
- describe the key actors (the participants) in employment relations and critically evaluate the roles that they play and their interests;

- critically assess competing theoretical approaches to employment relations;
- understand the main processes available to employers and employees through which the employment relationship is regulated and conflict is mediated and accommodated;
- assess different perspectives on the role and implications of employment relations processes.

2.1 Introduction

Forty years ago, the conventional approach to employment relations centred on the collective regulation of labour through bargaining between trade unions and employers. This was underpinned by a legal and policy framework developed by government, which also intervened in its role as employer to influence the negotiation of pay and conditions. The relationship between employers and individual employees was generally seen as peripheral. However, the role and significance of employment relations has been progressively marginalised, as demonstrated by the closure of the Workplace Employment Relations Survey (WERS) series, which started in 1980 and was repeated every six to eight years. A comprehensive study that gathered data from large numbers of managers, employees and worker representatives, WERS provided invaluable data on employment relations processes and experiences and allowed in-depth comparisons over time. Following the sixth study, carried out in 2011 (van Wanrooy et al, 2013), the series was discontinued, leaving substantial gaps in information about key aspects of employment relations, especially collective matters.

The driving force behind the erosion of collective employment relations has been a marked change in the political and economic context. As we explore in Chapter 3, the election of the Conservative government in 1979 under Margaret Thatcher and its commitment to free market economics and hostility to organised labour was a seminal moment in British employment relations. However, a global process of de-industrialisation was already well under way by the end of the 1970s, with the consequent decline of industries, which epitomised collective institutional approaches to employment relations. Furthermore, the growing dominance of the service sector, economic globalisation and rapid technological change have had a profound impact on the composition of the labour market, the nature of product market competition and the demand for knowledge and skills.

In this very different environment, the balance of workplace bargaining power and the focus of employment relations has shifted towards a greater emphasis on the relationship between the individual employee and the employer. The day-to-day preoccupation with the negotiation of wages and other terms and conditions through trade unions has been replaced by an emphasis on the management of performance and attempts to secure employee engagement. In practice, employment relations specialists in most organisations are less concerned with collective industrial action than with individual expressions of conflict (Dix et al, 2009). Nonetheless, despite these significant changes, we would argue the basic purpose of employment relations remains the same: to establish rules, agreements and processes to regulate the employment relationship while securing the commitment of employees to organisational goals and objectives.

2.2 What is employment relations?

To answer this question, we first have to understand the nature of the employment relationship. At a superficial level this is a simple economic transaction, an exchange of labour for pay. However, it is much more complex than, for example, buying a house or a car. First, the terms of the transaction and the relationship are shaped by the bargaining power of the parties and, in most cases, this is unequal, with the employer enjoying the more powerful position. This is because, in most circumstances, the employer can replace the employee much more easily than the employee can find work. The employer does not have to employ a specific worker, but the worker needs to be employed (and to be paid) in order to provide themselves and their family with a reasonable standard of living. Second, and partly as a result of this, there is an authority relationship between employer and employee. By agreeing to work for the employer, the employee undertakes to 'obey' any reasonable instructions that they are given. This notion of the employment contract as one made between master (employer) and servant (employee) is one that has become enshrined within UK law. Third, the employment contract is open-ended and indeterminate. While the employer can buy the employee's capacity to work, how that work is performed cannot be set out in sufficient detail in a contract of employment. It is this gap in the contract of employment that employment relations has to fill.

Therefore, employment relations is concerned with developing, applying and negotiating processes and rules through which the employment relationship is conducted and regulated. It also involves the development and maintenance of trust and confidence between employers and employees. When an individual accepts a job, they also accept the wage that is offered or negotiated at the time. However, as the job progresses and the situation and contexts change, that wage (or the other elements of the employment package) may not be enough to maintain commitment, effort and performance. For example, as we discuss later in this book, key antecedents of employee engagement are trust and perceptions of procedural and distributional justice (Purcell, 2012a; Saks, 2006). In short, if people feel their efforts are properly recognised and they are being rewarded fairly, they are likely to be committed to the organisation. In this way there is an ongoing negotiation and renegotiation of what Behrend (1957) termed the 'wage–effort bargain'.

However, as Watson (1995) argues, this approach emphasises the material rewards of work. Instead, he suggests that there is an 'implicit contract' between employers and employees which reflects the broad range of issues that shape the nature of the employment relationship. These include autonomy, control, security, satisfaction, status and power, and the balance of these issues will affect employees' attitudes to both work and employment. In recent years, the notion of the 'psychological contract' has become increasingly fashionable and influential. While in its original form the psychological contract refers to the mutual expectations of employer and employee (see for example Schein, 1978), more contemporary iterations (see for example Rousseau, 1995) have tended to focus on the obligations of the individual employee and neglected reciprocal obligations on the part of the employer (Guest, 2004). Moreover, as Cullinane and Dundon (2006) point out, it provides a singularly individualised account of the employment relationship, which is relegated to an exercise in the securing of organisational engagement. They argue that the employment relationship is not only unequal but is formed and reformed within a complex and dynamic set of social, economic and institutional relationships, and it is to this that we now turn.

2.3 Actors and interests in employment relations

The nature and quality of employment relations is ultimately defined by the interaction between three main 'actors': employers, employees (and their representatives) and the state.

Employers and managers

Over 82 per cent of employees (27.2 million) work in the private sector (Office for National Statistics, 2024a). Of these, 16.7 million work in small and medium-sized enterprises (SMEs) which employ 250 workers or fewer and make up over 99 per cent of all private businesses (Federation of Small Businesses, 2024). Many SMEs are owned and managed by either an individual or family and have no shareholders. Employment relations in SMEs tend to be highly personal and informal, and only a small number will have a specialist HR function, often relying on consultants, lawyers, employers' associations or Acas for HR and employment relations advice (Forth et al, 2006).

In SMEs there is often little or no distinction between the employer and the manager. In contrast, many larger private companies are owned by shareholders but controlled by a professional cadre of managers with the support of a specialist HR function. Some commentators have argued that managers and shareholders' interests may diverge, and certainly the way that employment relations are managed may be dictated by the demands of shareholders; for example, shareholder demands for higher profitability may lead to attempts to reduce costs through restricting pay or downsizing. However, research has generally shown that views of managers and owners are similar (Zeitlin, 1989). Larger companies may also establish productive capacity or service provision in other countries or be part of a company owned and controlled outside the UK, which can significantly shape the nature of employment relations, as we discuss in greater detail in the next chapter.

About 1 million workers are employed by not-for-profit organisations, which are usually small and have social rather than economic objectives. They do, however, include some large organisations, such as Oxfam, the Save the Children Fund, the British Heart Foundation, local housing associations and the Red Cross. This sector also contains worker or producer co-operatives where the enterprise is owned and controlled by its members.

The largest single employer in the UK is the government, with 5.9 million public sector employees in December 2023. The majority of public sector workers are employed in the NHS, education and local authorities. In these areas, employment relations are conducted at arm's length from central government, with relatively autonomous and complex managerial structures. The emphasis on the delivery of public services rather than profit maximisation could be argued to affect the attitude of public sector employers towards employment relations. In addition, the government has traditionally used its position as an employer to set an example for others. Partly as a consequence of these factors, public sector employment has tended to be characterised by job stability, long tenure, high levels of union involvement and relatively good pay and conditions. Moreover, public sector workplaces are more likely to have specialist employment relations managers (van Wanrooy et al, 2013). This is also reflected in managerial attitudes: for example, public sector managers have traditionally been more receptive to trade unions than their private sector counterparts (Bach et al, 2009).

However, over the last four decades, the distinction between the approaches of private and public sector employers has become less clear, as the government has demanded what it sees as better 'value for money' and the public sector has been exposed to competitive pressures through the privatisation and marketisation of public services (Bach et al, 2009). Since 2010, under the Conservative–LibDem coalition and the succeeding Conservative governments, there has been a major shift from public to private sector employment and a more hostile approach to the activities of public sector trade unions. This is examined in greater detail in the next chapter.

The interests of employers are also represented by employers' associations. In the private sector, the most well-known of these are the CBI (Confederation of British Industry), FSB (Federation of Small Businesses), BCC (British Chambers of Commerce) and EEF (Engineering Employers' Federation). In the public sector, similar bodies include the LGA (Local Government Association) and NHS Confederation. Although employers' associations, particularly in the public sector, play some role in national-level collective bargaining, one of their main functions is to represent their members through campaigning and lobbying in an attempt to shape public policy (Demougin et al, 2019). In addition, employers' associations increasingly provide their members with specific advice and guidance services on employment relations issues.

Reflective activity 2.1

What do the contents of the CBI website (www.cbi.org.uk) and its X feed (@CBItweets) suggest about its perspective on employment relations and its main priorities?

Employees, representatives and unions

We noted earlier that the employment relationship is inherently unequal. In most situations individual employers have far more bargaining power than individual employees and workers. Consequently, workers can strengthen and enhance their interests by acting collectively, notably in relation to the negotiation of their terms and conditions of employment. The main way they do this is through trade unions. We explore the history, development and function of trade unions in much greater detail in Chapter 6; however, there are two different types of union. First, sectoral, occupational or industrial unions – for example, UCU (university and college lecturers) and ASLEF (train drivers) – focus on recruiting employees who perform certain jobs or work within a specific sector or industry. Second, general unions – such as the GMB or Unite – organise workers across all sectors, industries and occupations. The Trades Union Congress (TUC), established in 1868, acts as the collective voice of the UK trade union movement in relation to government and international trade union bodies (such as the European Trade Union Confederation and the International Confederation of Trade Unions) as well as providing support and advice to its affiliated unions.

Unions are generally structured into local branches. These may be located within regions, certain professions or workplaces, and elected branch officials (union representatives or shop stewards) will usually deal with workplace-level issues. Branches are supported by regional offices, led by elected officials and employing officers or organisers. These officers may be called on to deal with more serious issues, respond to issues that have wider implications and/or co-ordinate activities to recruit members and strengthen the organisation. The union's leadership will be located at the national headquarters, which deals with national bargaining and broader policy issues.

Traditionally, most union representation revolved around collective bargaining and negotiation with the employer or employers' association over terms and conditions. As collective bargaining has declined, though, a significant part of union work is representing individual members in conflict with their employer. This can involve informal discussions, representation at disciplinary, grievance or absence meetings, and in some cases supporting members through employment tribunal action.

Reflective activity 2.2

Have you ever joined a trade union? Why or why not? Why do you think people join trade unions?

In 2022, there were 6.2 million union members in the UK, nearly one-quarter of the workforce. The current membership numbers of the largest UK trade unions are set out in Table 2.1.

This represents a significant reduction from the peak of more than 13 million in 1979, but union membership was increasing slightly until it fell back a little in 2021–2022. In 2023, around one in three workers had their pay and conditions determined by collective bargaining with trade unions (Department for Business and Trade, 2024). Nonetheless, trade unions still play an influential role within employment relations. Almost 90 per cent of public sector workers are employed in workplaces with a union presence and more than two-thirds of workers employed in workplaces with 50 employees or more work alongside trade union members.

Table 2.1 Trade union membership, 2022–2023

UNISON: The Public Service Union	1,394,892
Unite the Union (2021)	1,246,429
GMB	571,127
Royal College of Nursing	498,638
National Education Union	445,601
Union of Shop Distributive and Allied Workers	369,437
National Association of Schoolmasters Union of Women Teachers	302,407
Communication Workers Union	184,083
Public and Commercial Services Union	183,422
British Medical Association	162,346
Prospect	149,367
University and College Union	122,104

SOURCE: Certification Office for Trades Unions and Employers' Associations: *Annual Report of the Certification Officer, 2022–2023*

Although trade union membership has declined significantly in recent years, there has not been a corresponding growth in non-union forms of representation. As we discuss in Chapter 6, despite some high-profile examples, non-union representatives are found in just 7 per cent of workplaces. Furthermore, non-union representatives play a very different role and are much less likely to be involved with negotiation of terms and conditions or the representation of workers in disciplinary and grievance hearings (van Wanrooy et al, 2013).

The state

As we noted earlier, the state plays a substantial role in shaping the way that employment relations are conducted, through its role as an employer. However, it has an important influence in two other key respects. First, through legislation, it provides a regulatory framework within which employment relations is conducted. It is also responsible for the machinery through which these laws are enforced: the system of employment tribunals and the wider judicial system, including the Court of Appeal and the Supreme Court. Second, as we explore in the next chapter, the government has a significant impact on employment relations through its management of the economy and the consequent effects on economic growth, unemployment, interest rates and inflation.

State as legislator

For many readers, and particularly HR practitioners, employment legislation has a major influence on their working lives. However, our existing legal framework is a relatively recent development. Up until the 1960s, the government did little to intervene directly in employment relations, instead pursuing a 'voluntarist' approach whereby employers were largely left to manage their workplaces relatively free of regulation and trade unions were the main source of protection for workers.

THE LEGISLATIVE PROCESS

The government of the day might issue what has traditionally been called a Green Paper, followed by a White Paper, followed by a Bill, which, after the parliamentary process has been exhausted, becomes an Act of Parliament. The first two stages are not obligatory and governments can bypass them if they so wish. A Green Paper is a consultative document and is used by the government to obtain the views of interested parties to proposed legislation. It also provides an important opportunity for employers' organisations, trade unions and bodies such as the CIPD to influence the detail of legal changes. Recent examples on which the government has entered into consultation include shared parental leave and zero-hours contracts. Once the consultation is complete, the government will usually issue a White Paper setting out its policy and intentions. This provides an opportunity for a further round of lobbying and public debate where interested parties seek to petition MPs and government to recognise their specific interests in terms of the implications of the law being enacted. A Bill is then introduced into Parliament and, assuming it survives the scrutiny of both the House of Commons and the House of Lords, the agreed Bill becomes an Act – for example, the Employment Rights Act (1996). Once this receives royal assent, it becomes law. In addition, Acts of Parliament can give government ministers powers to make detailed orders, rules and regulations without Parliament having to pass a new Act. These are known as Statutory Instruments (SIs) and are used to provide detail and make minor changes that would be too complex to include in primary legislation. For example, although the primary legislation providing for the national minimum wage is contained in the National Minimum Wage Act 1998, changes to the level of the minimum wage are enacted by Statutory Instrument.

However, over the last half century, this has gradually changed, with three critical developments defining the role of the government as a legislator. First, the 1970s saw the development of a framework of individual employment rights, including the right to claim unfair dismissal, equal pay and protection against sex and race discrimination. Alongside this, the employment tribunal system was developed and, in 1975, Acas was established. Second, between 1979 and 1993, successive Conservative governments introduced seven separate pieces of legislation designed to regulate and restrict industrial action by trade unions. This included making secret postal ballots mandatory for lawful industrial action and the outlawing of strike action taken by one group of workers in support of another (secondary action). Finally, following its election in 1997, the Labour government signed the Social Chapter of the 1992 Maastricht Treaty on European Union, which led to EU employment legislation being transposed into UK law and a significant extension of the existing framework of employment protection. However, following the 2016 referendum, the UK left the

EU in January 2020. At the time of writing, no EU measures have been repealed and it is not yet clear what will happen to these elements of employment law.

The framework of employment legislation and policy is also supported by a number of state agencies that have a statutory role in employment relations, whether that role is in respect of individual or of collective issues. In the UK, there are three major agencies of this kind: the Advisory, Conciliation and Arbitration Service (Acas), the Central Arbitration Committee (CAC) and the Certification Office for Trade Unions and Employers' Associations.

Acas was established in 1975 in order to foster good employment relations practice and, at the time, to promote collective bargaining, although this element of its remit was removed by the Conservative government in 1993. Acas provides advice to employers, employees and trade unions on employment relations issues and offers a range of training services. It is responsible for the development of a series of statutory codes of practice, not least the Code of Practice on Disciplinary and Grievance Procedures, and authoritative guidance. Perhaps most importantly, Acas offers mediation, arbitration and conciliation in both individual and collective disputes (see Chapter 9 for further details). Acas is independent of direct government intervention, although its sponsoring ministry is the Department for Business and Trade (DBT). It is governed by an independent council which sets strategic direction, policies and priorities; this consists of a chairperson and 11 other members drawn from trade unions, employers' bodies, small business organisations and academia.

ACAS – PROMOTING BEST PRACTICE AND GOOD EMPLOYMENT RELATIONS

The main duties of Acas are to:

1. Promote good practice through the issuing of codes of practice on discipline and grievance procedures, on the disclosure of information to trade unions for collective bargaining purposes and on time off for trade union duties and activities.
2. Provide information and advice and guidance on a wide range of employment relations matters through its helpline, which can be contacted by anyone and is free, confidential and impartial.
3. Conciliate in complaints to employment tribunals. It has a statutory duty to act as conciliator in a wide range of individual employment rights complaints, including alleged unfair dismissal, alleged discrimination and equal pay claims.
4. Conciliate and mediate in the case of collective disputes.
5. Resolve employment disputes by facilitating arbitration by which the parties to a dispute agree of their own volition that a jointly agreed arbitrator consider the dispute and make a decision to resolve it.

The Central Arbitration Committee (CAC) is a permanent independent body with statutory powers whose role is to resolve disputes in England, Scotland and Wales under legislation relating to recognition and de-recognition of trade unions, disclosure of information for collective bargaining, information and consultation of employees, European works councils, and European companies, co-operative societies and cross-border mergers. It also offers voluntary arbitration in trade disputes, but this has not been used for some years. The committee itself has 34 members: a chair, 7 deputy chairs, 15 members experienced as representatives of workers and 11 representatives of employers. All members of the Committee are appointed by the Department for Business and Trade after consultation with Acas. CAC decisions are made by panels of three committee members appointed by the chair and consisting of either the chair or a deputy chair, one member whose experience is representative of employers and one member whose experience reflects that of workers and employees.

The post of Certification Officer was established in 1975. Its main responsibilities are to maintain records of independent trade unions, staff associations and employers' associations. This is important, as only trade unions that are independent from employer influence and domination enjoy specific rights and responsibilities under UK employment law. The Certification Officer also deals with complaints by trade union members over a range of issues, including financial matters, member registrations, the conduct of internal elections and the management of union political funds. The Certification Officer works with the Department for Business and Trade, but since April 2022 trade unions and employers' associations have been required to pay a levy to fund the office.

Government as economic manager

The development of economic policy and how this has shaped employment relations over time is a major theme of the following chapter. However, for our purposes here, it is important to set out the role the government plays. The economic goals of government tend to be relatively uniform, generally due to the fact that they are central to whether the governing party is re-elected at the subsequent general election. Therefore, most governments will aim to maximise economic growth, employment and prosperity, or at least the prosperity of those groups who will deliver electoral success. The main tools available to government relate to fiscal policy – put crudely, how the government decides to raise tax revenues, how it spends those revenues, and the extent to which it relies on borrowing additional funds to finance further expenditure. Monetary policy in the UK is directed by the Bank of England, which has a remit to control inflation, which it does through interest rates and controlling the supply of money within the economic system. While the Bank of England is nominally independent, there is little doubt that government policy and direction have a significant influence on its strategy and operations.

The key differences between the main political parties are the ways in which those goals are achieved. Traditionally, there is a relatively clear divide between the two main parties, Labour and Conservative. The Labour Party attempts to achieve economic growth through a greater emphasis on investment (both public and private) in transport, housing, education and health. Priority is also given to reducing income inequality, and additional investment is financed by a more redistributive approach to taxation, for example maintaining higher tax rates for high earners.

The traditional focus of the Conservative Party, on the other hand, is on minimising both the tax burden (especially on business) and public expenditure in a belief that this will stimulate private business activity, which will in turn lead to high levels of employment. For Conservatives, the prosperity of those at the lower end of the income 'ladder' is more likely to be enhanced by providing a framework within which private enterprises can flourish and create wealth. The change of government from Conservative to Labour following the general election of 4 July 2024 will therefore have an impact on employment relations. Labour's greater emphasis on spending to maintain public services supports employment in parts of the economy with higher levels of unionisation. In addition, traditional Labour policy sees a much larger role for trade unions in organisational life and supports both an extension of collective bargaining and changes to the legislation relating to trade unions and their activities. This is clearly illustrated by the Labour government's proposals (as outlined in their 2024 election manifesto) to significantly strengthen workers' rights and weaken restrictions on trade union activity and organisation.

Interests – conflict, co-operation and contradiction

How the interests of the different employment relations actors interact will inevitably shape the nature, conduct and outcomes of employment relations. These interests are set out in Table 2.2, and while this list is not exhaustive, it seeks to provide some insight into the relationship between the goals and objectives of employers, employees and government.

Employee interests

In the labour market, employees are generally looking for the best possible available employment conditions. At one level, income and employment are needed to survive and pay for the basic necessities of life; however, some individuals will be driven to maximise income, both to improve their living standards and also to secure a degree of recognition of their value or contribution to the organisation. Therefore, notions of fairness and equity become important for many workers (see for instance

Table 2.2 Interests in employment relations

Employee	Employer	The state
Employment	Profit maximisation	Power
Income	Shareholder value	Economic growth
Fairness	Stakeholder interests	Ideology
Voice	Quality and service	Continuity
Job satisfaction	Employee engagement	
Occupational identity	Creation of employment	
Autonomy	Control	

SOURCE: Adapted from Budd and Bhave (2008)

Dundon et al, 2020); this may be based on comparison with colleagues within the organisation or across the sector, or simply related to an individual's perceptions of whether they are being rewarded and treated fairly.

Employees may also be looking for job satisfaction and sometimes this can compensate for lower levels of financial remuneration. For example, research suggests that care workers have high levels of job satisfaction despite often very poor pay and conditions. To some extent this relates to their relationships with, and the impact of their work on, those that they care for; however, it can also be argued that this also embeds low pay and encourages work intensification (Hebson et al, 2015). Employees' interests might also reflect the need for solidarity and friendship with work colleagues, and for opportunities to have a say in the decisions that shape the nature and conditions of work – that is, employee voice. Similarly, workers may value a degree of autonomy and the freedom and discretion to exert control over their own work. Finally, workers may get significant utility from their identity at work, for instance as a teacher, engineer, skilled craftsperson, nurse or doctor. Crucially, the balance of these different interests is dynamic and will be shaped by the changing external context. For example, in times of recession, employees may prioritise employment security above other issues and be prepared to sacrifice higher levels of pay or a degree of control and autonomy over their work.

Reflective activity 2.3

What is your monetary and non-monetary package of employment conditions? Which elements of this are the most important to you and why?

Employer interests

The interests of the employer will vary depending on the nature of the organisation, but in private enterprises the key objective will be to maximise profitability. This is accentuated in companies whose shares are publicly traded (for example on the London Stock Exchange) and who are therefore answerable to the short-term demands of shareholders who seek increased stock prices and dividends. In family-owned private enterprises, the focus on profitability may be balanced against other objectives such as preserving employment, reputation in the local community and the longevity of the organisation. Publicly owned and not-for-profit organisations do not have a profit motive and may be driven by concerns over service delivery, but cost minimisation will still be a central objective, particularly if they are subject to constraints on government funding.

The fundamental drive for employers to control or minimise staff costs and the central desire of employees to maximise pay – or at least ensure a reasonable level of it – points to an inevitable and inherent conflict at the heart of the employment relationship. However, as Edwards (2003) has argued, employers must try to balance the need to exert control over employees with securing their co-operation. In short, work rules may ensure that workers adhere to certain organisational norms and expectations, but if the employer wants to improve organisational performance, they must also secure the commitment of employees. Intensifying work, adopting a hire and fire approach and/or using zero-hours contracts or (bogus) self-employment may minimise costs, but whether this is sustainable in the long term is more questionable.

The precise balance between control and co-operation is likely to be shaped by a number of different factors. First, the nature of the job: if the job is relatively unskilled and employees are seen as replaceable, employers may take the view that job satisfaction and commitment to the organisation is not necessary and is less important than keeping costs as low as possible. Second, the nature of the labour process and, in particular, the degree of autonomy afforded to employees, will affect the stance taken by the employer. As Real-world example 2.1 demonstrates, where tasks are repetitive, automated and measurable, control, for example through the application of rules, is likely to be much more direct than where job roles are less well defined and there is an emphasis on creativity.

REAL-WORLD EXAMPLE 2.1

A tale of two workplaces

Research conducted by Saundry and Wibberley (2012) into the way that the online fashion retailer Shop Direct Group (SDG) managed workplace conflict highlighted the link between the nature of the labour process and the different approaches adopted by management. SDG, at the time, operated a number of call centres and warehouses that generally dealt with the retail elements of its operation. It also had a large headquarters, which housed its administration and management, and also its creative teams involved with design and buying. Head office staff generally enjoyed a significant amount of discretion, both in terms of how they completed their tasks and the management of working time. Work there was seen to be more creative and staff tended to be more highly paid. Therefore, work was not tightly controlled as it was felt that this would hamper performance. Consequently, working hours and performance were not closely monitored and strict application of procedure was seen as inconsistent with creating a creative culture. The approach was very different within the call centre and warehousing environments. Here, work was routinised, pay was relatively low and key performance indicators were examined by managers on an ongoing basis. A trade union representative interviewed by the researchers explained that managers could 'press a button and for the eight hours [an individual worked]... that'll show every key stroke you've done, every number you've dialled... everything'.

Third, the nature of the labour market shapes the balance between control and co-operation. If the labour market is tight and skills are scarce, the employer will be forced to find ways of increasing engagement by improving terms and conditions or allowing greater degrees of autonomy. Where there is an available supply of labour, employers may be able to adopt a much closer focus on cost reduction.

Reflective activity 2.4

Thinking about the organisation you currently work in, or have previously worked in, consider how the pay and other conditions vary between different roles or departments. What is the rationale for differences in pay and conditions? Do you think this is justified?

The interests of the state

So far in this chapter we have tended to use the terms 'government' and 'state' interchangeably. However, when we are examining the interests of the state, we need to be more precise. 'Government' essentially refers to the ruling political party, which sets out a political programme, enacts legislation, and implements economic, social and foreign policy during its term of office. In addition to the government, however, the state is made up of a variety of institutions. These institutions may be shaped by, but are in theory independent of, government: they include the civil service, the judiciary and the armed forces. Although the government has a clear interest in employment relations as an element in managing the economy, it is also focused on winning and retaining political power. Naturally, these matters are closely related, since economic policies that successfully secure economic growth and rising living standards are likely to lead to positive political results. It is widely accepted that economic competence is a key factor in voting behaviour at general elections.

This has two main implications for employment relations. First, the government will adopt economic policies that inevitably shape the nature of work and the relationships between employers, employees and trade unions. Second, the government may take certain stances towards its own employees and/or towards trade unions to try to signal its priorities to the electorate. In general, both Conservative and Labour administrations have sought to persuade the public that they are economically 'competent', and this has involved being seen to be 'pro-business'. In the case of Conservative governments, this has meant introducing legislation designed to restrict union power and provide employers with much greater freedom and discretion. The Labour government that was in power between 1997 and 2010 weakened its links with the trade union movement and rebuffed union calls to repeal the legislation introduced by the Conservatives. Interestingly, the current Labour government (2024–) was elected on a more radical platform, which was aimed at promoting collective bargaining, worker representation and providing employees with greater legal safeguards. Nonetheless, this policy was justified on the basis of its potential to boost labour productivity and create sustainable economic growth.

While governments come and go, the apparatus of the state continues to function, and again there is a range of different interests that can be identified. As we note in the following, some would argue that the state in the form of the civil service and judiciary provides a degree of neutrality, where the state effectively acts to balance the competing interests within the labour market (Budd and Bhave, 2008). However, the make-up of the British judiciary also reflects the senior echelons of government and business. For instance, in 2022 women made up only one-third of senior judges (serving in the High Court and above) and just 5 per cent of those roles were filled by people from ethnic minorities; neither of these reflected the proportions in the legal profession generally. Moreover, people who were privately educated dominated at all levels. Therefore, it has been argued that the state and particularly the judiciary tend to act in a way which reinforces managerial authority and preserves the 'status quo'.

2.4 Key concepts and perspectives

How we explain, understand and interpret the processes of employment relations depends on our perspective and conceptual approach. In what follows, we examine the main approaches that have been developed to help us make sense of the complexities.

Systems theory

The first concerted attempt to formulate a theoretical framework of employment relations was Dunlop (1958). Drawing on Parsons' theory of social systems, Dunlop defined the 'industrial relations system' as an analytical subsystem of industrial societies and located it on the same logical plane as an economic system. Dunlop's work had the advantage of positioning the core components of an industrial relations system and made the rules and norms of the workplace the centrepiece of analysis, as opposed to the then accepted orthodoxy of industrial conflict or collective bargaining.

Dunlop saw the industrial relations system as a web of rules. The basic components of Dunlop's system are actors, context and ideology. The actors are employers and their associations, workers and their organisations, government and the state. The context within which the system operates incorporates technology, markets and the distribution of power, including economic power. Ideology refers to the common beliefs of the actors, which binds the system together.

Dunlop's approach has been subject to a number of criticisms:

1. It is simply a statement, or general framework, illustrating how rules are made and cannot be presented as a general theory of industrial relations (Meltz, 1991). It just identifies the key elements and components that have to be taken into account when analysing industrial relations.
2. It pays little attention to the employment relationship, which is central to employment relations. Dunlop regarded industrial relations as including all relations between the actors, with the 'web of rules' the central concern.

3 There is no account (let alone an analysis) of the processes by which the rules of the industrial relations system are determined, and only fleeting attention is given to the role of the state in this regard (Marsden, 1982).
4 The centrality of conflict to the employment relationship is underplayed (Muller-Jenstch, 2004). Instead, the essential focus of the systems model is stability as the central purpose of the industrial relations system rather than industrial disputes or wage-setting through collective bargaining (Hyman, 1975).

Critical approaches to the employment relationship

Critical – radical or Marxist – approaches to the employment relationship point to the inherent nature of conflict. Karl Marx argued that the capitalist system of production was inherently exploitative, since the owners of capital maximise profit by appropriating part of the value created by workers. Therefore, within capitalist employment relations, the interests of capital and labour are in direct conflict with each other: workers will seek to increase wages and improve conditions, but this eats into profit and so will be opposed by employers. Furthermore, the employment relationship is characterised by an asymmetry of power: while workers must work to make a living, an employer can simply replace one worker with someone who is unemployed, drawn from what Marx referred to as the 'reserve army of labour'. This power imbalance allows employers to maintain authority and control over workers.

The political economy of industrial relations

Perhaps the best known and most influential Marxist analysis of employment relations is set out by Hyman in his book *Industrial Relations: A Marxist introduction* (1975). Hyman argued that defining industrial relations in terms of a web of rules was far too narrow and that employment relations are concerned with the maintenance of stability and the regulation and control of industrial conflict. He argued that systems theory ignored the processes through which disagreement and disputes between employers and employees are generated and the role played by existing structures of ownership and control. Therefore, 'order' and 'regulation' were only one side of employment relations: instability and disorder must be given equal weight. This led Hyman to conclude that the study of industrial relations was not that of job regulation but rather 'the study of processes of control over work relations'. Moreover, he claimed that those processes could be explained only with reference to class structure and the nature of the political, social and ideological power relations generated by the capitalist system of production.

The political economy of industrial relations developed by Hyman has formed the basis for a number of theoretical contributions. Perhaps the most widely used in contemporary employment relations research is John Kelly's work. In his book, *Rethinking Industrial Relations* (1998), he developed our understanding of patterns of industrial conflict by linking 'mobilisation' theory (Tilly, 1978) to an analysis of economic long-wave trade cycles. He argued that exploitation and domination by employers within capitalism inevitably leads to perceptions of injustice among workers and consequently to shared collective grievances. However, whether such grievances are 'mobilised' into resistance, for example in the form of strike action, depends on a number of factors: interests, organisation, mobilisation, opportunity and counter-mobilisation. Whether grievances are defined collectively, and the ability of unions to organise, is partly a function of the economic context, and Kelly claims that each turning point between upswing and downswing is associated with an upsurge of mobilisation expressed by increased strike activity. At such turning points, workers are likely to see their living standards eroded by rising inflation and to be subject to managerial attempts to reduce costs, providing issues around which collective grievances can be clearly framed. At the same time, union organisation is more likely to be robust given high levels of employment. Nonetheless, converting this sense of grievance into concrete action requires leaders who are able to spread the feeling of injustice and to elevate the collective identity of workers. This is made easier when unemployment is relatively low and consequently workers feel secure and are in a stronger bargaining position. However, employers do not sit back and let this happen. They counter-mobilise against trade unions with the support of the capitalist state.

MOBILISATION THEORY: THE CASE OF THE RMT

In recent years, trade unions have generally become more quiescent in the face of rapid membership decline, the erosion of workplace organisations and an increasingly hostile political and legislative environment. In this context, levels of industrial action have fallen steadily, although there was a resurgence in 2022–2023. One exception to this trend has been the rail transport industry, where the largest union, the RMT (Rail, Maritime and Transport Union), has consistently used industrial action – and the threat of industrial action – over a wide range of issues, including pay, health and safety, pensions, job losses and the impact of privatisation (Darlington, 2009). Applying mobilisation theory, the railways have long tended to have high levels of union density and a fairly healthy demand for the service they offer, giving rail workers a high degree of bargaining power. However, growing competition following privatisation, together with a drive by employers to increase efficiency has led to attempts to restrict pay increases and make other changes to terms and conditions. This has provided a number of shared grievances around which collective resistance can be organised. A key role has also been played by two charismatic leaders of the RMT: the late Bob Crow, who was general secretary from 2001 until his death in 2014, and more recently Mick Lynch, who was elected in 2021. Supported by a network of active, committed and militant local representatives, both have won strong support for industrial action. Darlington (2009) highlighted the effectiveness of the RMT in winning demonstrable gains for members, gains which have continued into the 2020s. As a result, however, both leaders and union members have also been heavily criticised – even demonised – by politicians and the media. Moreover, the Conservative government counter-mobilised in the form of the 2016 Trade Union Act, which further restricted the ability to take industrial action, and the Strikes (Minimum Service Levels) Act 2023, which was aimed at preventing some of those who voted for a strike from taking part in it.

Labour process theory

Another strand of theory underpinned by a Marxist approach to work and employment is the debate on the character of the labour process. The focus of the discussion is the so-called transformation problem, which Marx had already defined as the transformation of (bought) labour power into performed work, or expressed more simply, the problem of managerial control of labour. The labour process debate stems from Braverman's *Labour and Monopoly Capital* (1974), in which he argued that the key task of capitalist management is the continual control of the labour process in order to extract maximum value by transforming labour power into work performance.

At the heart of labour process theory is the understanding that the employer (capital) controls technology and uses it to increase capitalist power and exploitation. In short, technology, machinery and equipment are used by management to systematically deprive workers of their control over the job. For example, the development of the production line and the consequent division of labour not only reduced the level of skill needed but also provided management with greater power and control over the pace and nature of work. Today, the prospect of the greater use of artificial intelligence (AI) and automation also threatens to radically reduce the requirement for certain types of work and skill, while providing organisations with the ability to monitor the activities of their workers much more closely.

REAL-WORLD EXAMPLE 2.2

Amazon warehouses

Global e-commerce company Amazon uses a range of tools to promote high performance in their warehouses, known as fulfilment centres. These include scanners which log every item picked, the time spent on each task and any periods of inactivity. Those who do not reach their targets often lose their jobs. Workers have called the warehouses 'sweatshops' and complained that they might have to walk up to 12 miles during a shift in one of the larger sites. Bloodworth (2019) and others have reported workers being scared to go to the toilet for fear of being penalised, while strict security measures have led to 'associates' losing time on their breaks and effectively working unpaid while going through security at the beginning and end of shifts. The company has strongly resisted unionisation, although there have been some breakthroughs in the US, and many UK workers have joined a union and staged stoppages. Early in 2024, Amazon's French arm was fined £27 million for 'excessive monitoring' of staff.

Reflective activity 2.5

How much should employees be monitored and how much should they have autonomy?

What does labour process theory tell us about this?

Given the dynamics of exploitation and control, the relationship between capital (employer) and labour (workers) is one of 'structured antagonism' (Edwards, 1986). That is, as employers seek to maximise profit at the expense of employees, they also need some level of co-operation from the workforce. Employees might comply, accommodate, consent – or resist.

Feminist perspectives on employment relations

An important contribution to the conceptual debate over employment relations has come from feminist scholars who have criticised research for ignoring the gendered nature of employment relations, despite the feminisation of the UK labour market. In particular, it is argued that the key employment relations actors, such as trade unions, the state and employing organisations, are portrayed as gender-neutral when the opposite is the case (Wajcman, 2000).

In addition to highlighting the asymmetrical power relations referred to earlier, feminist scholars also argue that power inequalities based on gender shape employment relations processes and outcomes. Moreover, the key actors of employment relations have traditionally acted to reinforce gender divisions in work and employment. For example, trade unions were still negotiating separate pay scales for men and women doing the same work right up to the introduction of the Equal Pay Act in 1970, while progress on closing the gender pay gap and countering occupational segregation has been tortuously slow. Furthermore, as Kirton and Healy (2013) have argued, despite the fact that women now form a majority of trade union members, there have been significant barriers preventing this being fully reflected in the leadership of trade unions. There are, however, signs of change in this regard: women are now general secretaries of the two largest trade unions (UNISON and Unite), and the TUC's first woman general secretary, Frances O'Grady, served from 2013 until her retirement in 2022.

Employment relations research has also tended to focus on masculine settings and environments where trade unions have traditionally been strong, despite the fact that these represent a small and decreasing part of the labour market. Areas in which women are more likely to work are less likely to be explored by researchers and so their importance and significance tends to be underplayed. This is beginning to change; however, Wajcman (2000) argues that existing theorisation of the employment relationship still separates work from the household, despite the fact that the sexual division of labour underpins the way that work is organised. Therefore, gender should be an integral part of the analysis of employment relations. We discuss this in greater depth in Chapter 7.

2.5 Frames of reference

Industrial sociologist Alan Fox developed the view that employment relations can be understood, explained and conceptualised in terms of three frames of reference: unitary, pluralist and radical (Fox, 1974, and see Heery, 2016 for a detailed examination). It is important to note that these are not 'models' or 'management styles', but perspectives: that is, different ways of looking at the employment relationship.

A pluralist perspective recognises the differing interests in the employment relationship and acknowledges that conflict is an inevitable part of organisational life. However, it assumes that conflict can be managed and resolved through the institutions of employment relations: trade unions, collective bargaining and dispute resolution procedures. The state is seen as playing a neutral role, facilitating bargaining, negotiation and good employment relations.

Pluralists see the organisation as a coalition of interest groups. However, they fundamentally accept the legitimacy of managerial authority to promote the long-term needs of the organisation as a whole by paying due concern to all the interests affected – employees, shareholders, customers, the community and the national interest. This involves management holding the 'right' balance between the divergent claims of all these participant interests. Trade unions are also seen as an essential way of correcting the unequal power balance in the employment relationship, allowing negotiation to take place on more equal terms. Pluralists do not claim anything approaching perfection for this system. They accept that in some situations imbalances in the relative bargaining power between employers and employees (unions), or between management and a particular group of employees, may be such that for one side or the other, justice (the outcome) is distinctly rough. Such situations, however, are not so numerous or unfair as generally to discredit the system, either from the employees' point of view or from that of management.

Pluralism was the dominant paradigm of post-war employment relations, built on the belief that the best way to manage employment relations was through a recognition of conflict and support for the structures through which it could be resolved. Hence governments of all political persuasions supported the idea of collective bargaining and encouraged the use of systematic procedural approaches to discipline and grievance.

A radical perspective takes as its starting point the unequal distribution of power between the employer and the individual employee. Lacking property or command over resources, the employee is seen as totally dependent on being offered employment by the owners or controllers of property. Therefore, the relationship between employer and employee is a power relationship. Employees are viewed simply as a commodity and have little ability to assert their needs and aspirations.

Like pluralists, radicals believe that conflict is inevitable. Unlike pluralists, though, radicals argue that the institutions of employment relations simply mask the reality of the capitalist employment relationship, disguising and accommodating the inequalities of power and exploitation. Trade unions may be seen as supporting a mythical balance of power. In this view, the only way that trade unions can change this is by moving away from an agenda which focuses solely on collective bargaining and terms and conditions and instead encourage worker resistance to challenge the basis of capitalist employment relations. This also involves developing an explicitly political orientation and confronting the state, which is portrayed as acting to support the interests of capital by, for example, introducing legislation to suppress resistance and enhance managerial control over the labour process.

A unitary perspective, in contrast to both pluralism and radicalism, views the enterprise as a harmonious whole, a united team pulling together for the common good. Employers, managers and employees are united by common interests and values, and management is the only legitimate source of authority, control and leadership. Conflict is viewed as the result of poor communication, irrational behaviour and/or the actions of 'troublemakers'. Trade unions are viewed as a self-seeking force imposing itself on an otherwise integrated body, to be resisted and removed from the enterprise.

Reflective activity 2.6

Imagine that you are the HR manager in a large, unionised organisation. In the last year, the turnover of the organisation has fallen and unless costs are reduced there is a possibility that jobs will be lost through redundancy. In an attempt to increase efficiency, the organisation has proposed new working practices. However, these have been opposed by the union and have not been well received by the workforce. What solutions to this problem are implied by the unitary, pluralist and radical perspectives? Which frame of reference most closely resembles your own perspective on employment relations?

A key feature of contemporary employment relations has been the growing dominance of the unitary perspective, and there is substantial evidence that most managers hold unitary views. While such views have traditionally been commonplace in smaller and family-owned businesses, they are now widely found in larger, and sometimes unionised, organisations. For example, in 2011 eight out of every ten managers responded that they would rather consult directly with employees than through trade unions (van Wanrooy et al, 2013).

Moreover, the growing influence of unitarism is reflected in the fundamental building blocks of human resource management (Bratton and Gold, 2015), which in turn has important implications for the role of HR practitioners in the management of employment relations (see Fisher et al, 2017). The development of HRM heralded a unitary orientation for the HR function in delivering improved business and organisational performance (Guest, 1991), while employment relations was seen as a peripheral and transactional activity.

There is also little doubt that the perspectives that have underpinned government policy over the last 50 years have undergone a substantial shift away from pluralism towards unitarism. The Thatcher government elected in 1979 adopted a very clear unitary philosophy in which trade unions were seen as militant agitators and collective bargaining an obstacle to the free market. However, it can be argued that this has also been reflected in the policy orientations of subsequent Labour and Conservative administrations (Howell, 2000).

2.6 Employment relations processes

Employment relations actors use various employment relations processes or mechanisms to make rules: substantive rules, which set matters such as the level of pay, and procedural rules, which dictate the processes by which substantive rules are made, enforced and changed. The most important employment relations processes are:

- collective bargaining: negotiating with trade unions;
- unilateral employer action to set or change terms and conditions of employment;
- employee involvement and participation: individual or collective processes giving employees input in to decision-making;
- employee engagement: securing the support of individual employees for organisational strategies and goals;
- third-party intervention from organisations like Acas;
- industrial sanctions levied by the employer (relocation, shutdown, lock-out or dismissal) and by employees, including employment tribunal claims and industrial action.

Collective bargaining

Collective bargaining is both an employment relations process for jointly determining employment rules and a system of industrial governance whereby unions and employers reach joint decisions concerning the employment relationship. It usually involves employers negotiating with trade unions to set pay and conditions on behalf of the group(s) of workers for whom they are recognised. If a union is recognised to bargain on behalf of a group of workers, any agreement, such as a pay increase, will be applied to workers of that type, whether they are union members or not. (See Chapter 4 for more about trade union recognition.)

Companies that do not recognise unions might also take into account collectively bargained pay rates in their industry or in comparable firms when deciding on their own employees' employment conditions. This may be necessary if they are to remain competitive in the labour market. Many non-union companies also seek to avoid unionisation by paying better than the union-negotiated pay rates and other employment conditions for their industry. However, as we point out in Chapter 6, in general pay tends to be higher when it is subject to collective bargaining, reflecting the increased bargaining power that a collective approach provides to workers. Therefore, collective bargaining can have a significant influence on terms and conditions across the economy.

From a pluralist perspective, collective bargaining is a vital way of accommodating different interests and resolving conflict through negotiation. In addition, it can be argued that the employee 'voice' provided by collective bargaining underpins trust and fairness. One of the key benefits to employers of collective bargaining is in reducing the transaction costs of negotiating terms and conditions. In large workplaces, individual negotiation would be impractical, time-consuming and costly; therefore, collective bargaining is a relatively efficient way of determining pay and other terms of employment.

However, for some employers with a unitary perspective bargaining with trade unions is considered an obstacle to change and a barrier to flexibility. In this context, the scale and scope of collective bargaining has contracted rapidly in the last four decades, mirroring the broader decline in trade union organisation. In 1970, four out of every five employees had their pay determined through collective bargaining (van Wanrooy et al, 2013). It was thought that this figure had declined to around a quarter of the workforce, but a change in the way the Office for National Statistics (ONS) collects data has resulted in estimates being higher than originally thought. A key reason for this was the change from relying on the Labour Force Survey (LFS) to the Annual Survey of Hours and Earnings (ASHE): the LFS is a survey of employees, who might not know how their pay and conditions are determined, but the ASHE collects information from employers. In 2023, then, the revised figures showed that nearly two in five (39.2 per cent) jobs had pay set by collective agreement; of these, 89.9 per cent were in the public sector, 44.5 per cent in the not-for profit sector and 20.6 per cent in the private sector (Department for Business and Trade, 2024). There has also been a significant reduction in the extent to which collective bargaining takes place at national level, with bargaining at the level of the employer or even the workplace much more common. This is particularly noticeable in the private sector, where company-level collective agreements set pay and conditions for around 9 per cent of jobs and 7 per cent of jobs are covered by workplace agreements.

Unilateral action

Given the decline of collective bargaining and the high cost of negotiating with individual employees, most terms and conditions are set unilaterally by the employer. Even in highly unionised organisations (for example, local authorities, universities and NHS trusts) there have been numerous cases where wage increases and changes in working practices have been imposed in the face of disagreement between employer and union, as Real-world example 2.3 illustrates.

REAL-WORLD EXAMPLE 2.3

Imposition of changes to pay and conditions in British Gas

Formerly a state-owned utility, British Gas was privatised in 1986 but, in common with other privatised industries, retained relatively high levels of trade union membership. In the first half of 2020, Centrica, the owner of the company, announced that around 5,000 jobs – a quarter of the UK workforce – would be cut. In addition, thousands more employees were told in July 2020 (during a Covid lockdown) that they would have to accept substantial changes in their pay and other terms and conditions if they wanted to keep their jobs. Gas service engineers were particularly affected by the changes, which their union, the GMB, referred to as a 'fire and rehire' scheme. Working hours were to be increased from 37 to 40 per week; each engineer's working day would only start when they arrived at the first customer's home and higher rates of pay for weekend and public holiday working were to be removed altogether. In all, the new terms and conditions amounted to a 15 per cent reduction in pay, although British Gas disputed this figure, saying it was a cut of less than 2 per cent. The union said the company, which was making a substantial profit was 'bullying' highly skilled, qualified and experienced workers and held a successful ballot for strike action: this started with a five-day strike in January 2021 and continued with several more strikes over the next two months. On 14 April 2021, 460 engineers were dismissed after they refused to accept the new terms.

In some organisations there may be consultation through a staff forum, but ultimately, if employees are dissatisfied with their pay and conditions, they are faced with few alternatives apart from looking for a better deal elsewhere. For managers, this has short-term efficiency benefits and underlines their right to manage. However, it also runs the risk of eroding employee engagement and increasing employee turnover as employees look for alternative ways of improving their working conditions. Furthermore, as we discuss in greater detail in the next chapter, the move away from collective negotiation and bargaining has increased pay inequality, which threatens to erode perceptions of fairness and organisational justice.

Employee involvement and participation

Given the progressive silencing of employee voice through collective bargaining, employee involvement processes have arguably taken on an added significance. Employee involvement (which is examined in greater detail in Chapter 5) is a broad term that covers a range of processes designed to enable employees to voice their views to the employer and, in some cases, to participate in, or contribute to, management decision-making. Employee involvement processes include forms of direct communication such as regular workforce meetings with senior management and team briefings through which management disseminate key information and messages to staff. Other direct processes of involvement provide employees with input into decision-making processes, for example through their role in problem-solving groups that discuss aspects of performance (for example, quality). Managers may also consult with their staff over various matters, inviting their views on proposed changes or innovations.

Interestingly, the use of direct communication appears to be increasing: in 2011, four out of every five workplaces had workplace meetings involving all staff (an increase from 75 per cent in 2004), while two-thirds used team briefings (compared with 60 per cent in 2004). Employers were also more likely to disclose financial information to their staff. However, there was a decrease in the use of problem-solving groups which provide a degree of influence in the decision-making process (van Wanrooy et al, 2013).

Consultation can also take place through a representative forum (such as a works council) or some other form of joint consultative mechanism. In joint consultation, management seek the views of employee representatives prior to making a decision. Although joint consultation may involve discussion of mutual problems, it does not disturb managerial authority or prerogative and there is no commitment to act on the employees' views. Issues dealt with by joint consultation vary from social matters, such as the provision of canteen or sports facilities, to issues such as the scheduling of production. Employers also have a statutory duty to consult over certain issues such as redundancy and transfer of undertakings (see Chapter 12 for more details).

As with collective bargaining, the scale of joint consultative arrangements appears to be reducing. In 2004, 38 per cent of workplaces had a functioning joint consultative committee (JCC) at the workplace, but by 2011, this had fallen to 25 per cent. This fall was not restricted to the private sector, and while JCCs remain in the majority of public sector workplaces, the proportion reduced from 71 per cent in 2004 to 64 per cent in 2011. Taken together with our discussion of collective bargaining earlier, this illustrates the growing problem of a representation gap in British workplaces, with only 35 per cent having any structure for the representation of employees' views (van Wanrooy et al, 2013). Similarly, a survey carried out for the CIPD in 2022 found that less than half of employers consulted with employee representatives, most preferring individual channels (Suff, 2022).

It is therefore not surprising that only one-third of employees rate their managers as good or very good at allowing views of employees and representatives to influence decisions (van Wanrooy et al, 2013). This reflects the shift away from pluralist approaches in which employment relations are jointly regulated towards an emphasis on the provision of information. This in turn is underpinned by unitary assumptions that conflict and discontent can simply be avoided through effective communication.

Employee engagement

The crisis of employee voice within British workplaces is arguably reflected in the emphasis placed on employee engagement by employment relations professionals. However, there is much debate about the nature of engagement and whether it is an attitude, a set of behaviours or an outcome. An employee might feel pride and loyalty (attitude) and/or be a great advocate for the company to customers or go the extra mile to finish a piece of work (behaviour). Outcomes may include lower accident rates, higher productivity, more innovation, lower labour turnover and reduced absence rates.

Advocates of engagement argue it is a workplace approach designed to ensure that employees are committed to their organisation's goals and values, are motivated to contribute to organisational success, and are able, at the same time, to enhance their own sense of well-being. Engaged organisations are said to have strong and authentic values with clear evidence of trust and fairness based on mutual respect, where two-way promises and commitments – between employers and staff – are understood and fulfilled. Employee engagement strategies are said to enable people to be the best they can be at work, recognising that this can only happen if they feel respected, involved, heard, well led and valued by those they work for and with. Employee engagement is explored in more detail in Chapter 5.

 Reflective activity 2.7

How is employment relations managed in your organisation? What processes are in place? To what extent has there been a shift away from collective processes towards more individualised forms of communication and engagement?

Third-party intervention

In situations where employment relations actors are unable to resolve their differences over the making of employment rules and/or over the interpretation and application of existing rules, they may agree voluntarily to seek the assistance of an independent third party. In the UK, third-party intervention can take one of three forms: conciliation, mediation or arbitration. These processes are examined in detail in Chapters 9, 10 and 13.

In relation to collective disputes, the parties generally turn to Acas for help in seeking to resolve the issues between them. When conciliating in collective disputes, the Acas conciliator acts as a link between the parties in dispute by passing on information that the parties will not, for whatever reason, pass directly to each other. This continues until a basis for agreement is identified or both parties conclude that there is no basis for an agreed voluntary settlement to their problem. The arbitration process, on the other hand, removes control from employers and employees over the settlement of their differences. The arbitrator hears the arguments from both sides and decides the solution to the parties' differences by making an award. Both parties, having voluntarily agreed to arbitration, are morally bound, but not legally obliged, to accept the arbitrator's award. While collective conciliation remains an important aspect of Acas's work, its use has reduced significantly, with 621 cases in 2022–2023 compared with 1,245 in 2003–2004; however, 91 per cent of cases resulted in a settlement. Arbitration is less common, with just 12 such requests received in 2022–2023 (Acas, 2023a).

When a dispute is between two individuals, or between an individual and the employer, workplace mediation may be used as a way of repairing the relationship. This normally takes place before employment has been terminated and involves trained mediators engaged from Acas, internal mediators from the organisation's own staff or private mediation providers. The mediator plays an impartial role and the process is confidential and voluntary. Importantly, parties are not accompanied by trade union representatives or any other individual. The mediator will listen to each person individually and then, in a joint meeting, will help them to discuss the issues between them, identify common ground and hopefully develop a mutually agreed resolution. Acas received 220 requests for mediation in 2022–2023 (See Chapter 13 for a full discussion on workplace mediation).

In cases in which the relationship has already broken down and an individual has notified Acas of their intention to make a claim to an employment tribunal (ET), Acas has a statutory duty to intervene and will seek to conciliate. A claim will only go forward if one or both parties refuse this early conciliation. In 2022–2023,

37 per cent of cases were resolved through early conciliation. Acas can also offer conciliation at a later stage of the employment tribunal process and in 2022–2023, 77 per cent of all employment tribunal claims were resolved through Acas conciliation, saving up to £100 million on the costs of the ET service.

On the whole, the use of third-party intervention reflects the changing nature of employment relations and the shift from collective to individual matters. At the same time, there is some evidence of growth in the use of workplace mediation on individual issues, with requests to Acas more than doubling between 2005/06 and 2018/19. Conflict resolution processes such as mediation and conciliation are a classic pluralist response to workplace conflict and consequent employment disputes. Through the intervention of third parties such as Acas, disputants are given an opportunity to voice their concerns and are then helped to identify areas of common ground so that a mutually acceptable settlement can be reached. However, a radical critique would suggest that this is simply a way of helping employers to reassert their control over the labour process and restore order to the employment relationship.

Industrial sanctions

If the processes of employment relations break down, either employers or employees can impose industrial sanctions. Given the structure of UK employment law, the main sanctions open to employers are locking out all or some of the workforce, relocating operations to another site or closing down the organisation. While these sanctions are rarely used in practice, the threat, particularly of closure or job loss, is extremely potent. Indeed, the threat by multinational employers to relocate production has played a significant part in shifting the balance of workplace power towards the employer and forcing trade unions and their members to accept changes in working conditions.

At an individual level, the employer can simply terminate the employment relationship. While employees enjoy protection against unfair dismissal, employees must also know their rights in this regard and overcome the stress of employment litigation to bring a claim, as well as any costs relating to legal representation. Furthermore, only a small minority of claims succeed (Morris, 2012): the most recent statistics available at the time of writing show that 32 per cent of unfair dismissal claims were settled following Acas conciliation; the bulk of the remainder were withdrawn or dismissed and just 5 per cent of claims were successful following a hearing (Ministry of Justice, 2023). Even when claims are successful, compensation (as of 6 April 2024) is limited to one year's salary or £115,115, whichever is the lower. Compensation may be higher if the dismissal involved discrimination related to a protected characteristic (see Chapter 7). In 2022–2023, however, the median compensation for unfair dismissal was £6,201 and the average (mean) award was £11,914. These considerations inevitably shape the ways in which employees and employers respond to employment disputes.

Naturally, employees can also attempt to impose industrial sanctions. Most commonly, this is through industrial action organised by trade unions. In this way, employees can maximise the potential weight of the sanction and therefore their bargaining power. The main industrial sanctions that employees can impose on employers are overtime bans, working to rule (or working to contract), selective stoppages (such as one-day strikes) and/or all-out strikes.

The threat of the imposition of industrial sanctions can be important in bringing about a settlement of the differences between employers and employees. This threat effect can persuade the actors to adjust their position and negotiate a peaceful settlement. Both parties will be reluctant to go ahead and impose industrial sanctions because of their associated costs. However, the very fact that sanctions are possible means that employers and trade unions have to take them into account and adjust their behaviour accordingly.

We examine the changing shape of workplace conflict in some detail in Chapter 9, but there is little doubt that the use of industrial action to influence employment relations outcomes has become much less prevalent. Between 1965 and 1979 there were, on average, well over 2,000 strikes in the UK every year, but in January 2020 there were just seven stoppages. Following the Covid pandemic, however, there was a resurgence in strikes and other forms of industrial action; this frequently involved 'key' public sector workers who had worked as normal throughout the crisis and whose pay was failing to keep up with inflation. Among those taking such action were transport workers, university lecturers and professional staff, nurses, doctors and schoolteachers. By March 2023 there were 683 stoppages in progress; at the time of writing the number of stoppages has declined to around 50, still substantially higher than pre-2020.

When strikes do occur, they tend to take place in the public sector and involve a relatively large number of workers. However, unions are more likely to use one- and two-day stoppages as a way of minimising the impact on their members. The reasons for these changes are linked to the declining influence of trade unions in general, a more hostile legal environment, and, in the private sector, the globalisation of production. In short, the potential sanction of employers relocating operations or downsizing has increasingly carried greater weight than the potential costs incurred through industrial action.

2.7 Summary

This chapter has shown that employment relations is essentially concerned with how the employment relationship is regulated. This is not straightforward because the exchange of labour for pay is not a simple transaction. Critically, the two parties do not come together on equal terms: there are instead asymmetrical power relations. In some cases, individual employees may enjoy a relatively high level of bargaining power; however, employers are normally in a stronger position because they can hire replacement workers and because they own the equipment, premises and often intellectual property that employees need in order to be able to do their job. Furthermore, the employment relationship is open-ended: while the employer can secure labour, securing commitment, knowledge and ability is much more difficult and also very difficult to specify in a contract. Therefore, employment relations fills the gap in the contract of employment through rules and processes of negotiation, mediation and accommodation.

The main parties to employment relations have a range of interests, and theory focuses on how these interests are played out. Until relatively recently, the dominant perspective in employment relations was pluralism, which accepts that there are differing interests but that these interests can be accommodated, and conflict managed and avoided, through a range of processes and structures. This approach has been criticised by radical commentators who focus on the inequalities inherent within the employment relationship. From this perspective the pluralist processes of conflict resolution, including the role played by the state, are simply ways through which employers cement their control over the labour process and preserve the status quo, whether this is in terms of gender, economic power or social status.

In terms of the practice of employment relations, it is the unitary perspective that appears to be in the ascendancy. This views conflict as an aberration or a function of miscommunication or militant agitation. It also assumes that employers and employees have the same interests, a view that appears to be increasingly held by managers and one which is reflected in contemporary debates over HRM, partnership and employee engagement and the decline of collective employment relations. However, while these remain the key themes of contemporary employment relations, more recent developments have again shone a light on the inequalities within the employment relationship.

KEY LEARNING POINTS

- The employment relationship has a number of distinct characteristics: the parties do not enter the relationship on equal terms; there is an authority relationship between employer and employee; it is incomplete and open-ended.
- Employment relations are primarily concerned with regulating this relationship through rules, processes and institutions. These include collective bargaining, employee involvement and participation, and third-party processes, such as mediation and conciliation.
- Dunlop saw the industrial relations system as a web of rules. He identified the basic components of an industrial relations system as the actors (employers, employees and the state), the environmental context and an ideology that consists of the common beliefs of the actors and that binds the industrial relations system together.
- The systems approach, however, says little about the social processes through which rules are created and negotiated, and ignores the role of conflict within the employment relationship.
- Pluralist perspectives on the employment relationship accept that conflict is inevitable; however, it can be managed and regulated through the development of workplace institutions and processes of negotiation and mediation. The state is seen to play a neutral facilitating role.
- Radical perspectives focus on the inequality inherent within capitalist employment relations. Conflict is inherent and employment relations processes simply reinforce managerial control over labour. This is underpinned by the institutions of the state.

- Unitary perspectives see conflict as a result of either misunderstanding or militant agitation. It assumes that employees and employers have shared interests and goals. Accordingly, the collective institutions of employment relations have little value.
- Employment relations practice in the post-war period was dominated by pluralist approaches, with an emphasis on supporting processes of negotiation and mediation. Since the 1980s, however, managerial perspectives have become increasingly unitary, reflected in the development of HRM and the increased emphasis on employee engagement.

Review Questions

1 To what extent do you agree that employers hold the balance of power within the employment relationship?

2 Considering your own job, to what extent do you share the interests of your employer? Which interests are different and how does this shape your attitude to work?

3 What role do you think gender plays in the way that employment relations are perceived and managed in your organisation?

4 Looking at the employment relations policies of the Conservative, Labour and Liberal Democrat Parties, to what extent are they underpinned by a unitary perspective?

5 What are the limitations of the theoretical perspectives outlined in this chapter? Are theoretical approaches from other disciplines useful in exploring employment relations?

Explore further

Budd, J and Bhave, D (2008) Values, ideologies, and frames of reference in industrial relations, in *The SAGE Handbook of Industrial Relations*, eds P Blyton et al, pp 92–113, Sage Publications, London

Cullinane, N and Dundon, T (2006) The psychological contract: a critical review, *International Journal of Management Reviews*, 8 (2), pp 113–29

Dundon, T, Martinez Lucio, M, Hughes, E, Howcroft, D, Keizer, A and Walden, R (2020) *Power, Politics and Influence at Work*, Manchester University Press, Manchester

Dunlop, JT (1958) *Industrial Relations Systems*, Holt, New York

Edwards, P (2003) The employment relationship and the field of industrial relations, in *Industrial Relations*, 2nd edn, ed P Edwards, pp 1–36, Blackwell, Oxford

Fox, A (1974) *Beyond Contract: Work, power and trust relations*, Faber, London

Guest, D (1987) Human resource management and industrial relations, *Journal of Management Studies*, 24 (5), pp 503–21
Heery, E (2016) *Framing Work: Unitary, Pluralist and Critical Perspectives in the 21st Century*, Oxford University Press, Oxford
Hyman, R (1975) *Industrial Relations: A Marxist introduction*, Macmillan, Basingstoke
Kaufman, R (ed.) (2004) *Theoretical Perspectives on Work and Employment Relationships*, Cornell University Press, Ithaca, NY
Kelly, J (1998) *Rethinking Industrial Relations: Mobilization, collectivism and long waves*, Routledge, London

Websites

www.acas.org.uk (archived at https://perma.cc/TKH4-NZFF) is the official website of the Advisory, Conciliation and Arbitration Service.
www.gov.uk/government/organisations/department-for-business-and-trade (archived at https://perma.cc/7LVK-R8T6) is the website of the Department for Business and Trade and outlines the main provisions of employment legislation.
www.cac.gov.uk (archived at https://perma.cc/C5VU-JNSW) is the website of the Central Arbitration Committee.
www.cbi.org.uk (archived at https://perma.cc/TQ8W-3XHC) is the website of the CBI, the central employers' organisation in the UK.
www.cipd.co.uk (archived at https://perma.cc/ZXM9-Q5XH) is the official website of the Chartered Institute of Personnel and Development.
www.tuc.org.uk (archived at https://perma.cc/HSS3-38UT) is the official website of the Trades Union Congress.

03 The dynamic context of employment relations

Overview

The purpose of this chapter is to examine the factors external to the organisation – political, economic, social and technological – that influence the nature of work and employment relations. We explore how the state shapes the corporate environment in its role as an economic manager, lawmaker and the UK's largest employer. In particular, we focus on related contemporary issues – the problem of low British productivity, the globalisation of economic activity and the impact of the Covid pandemic. Next, we explore changing social attitudes towards work, gender and trade unions. This is followed by an examination of the impact of rapid technological change on the way we work now and may work in the future. Finally, we provide an analysis of contemporary developments in the UK labour market, exploring the splintering of traditional modes of employment and the increased emphasis on 'good work'.

LEARNING OUTCOMES

When you have completed this chapter, you should be able to:

- assess the way in which government policy has influenced employment relations;
- discuss the potential implications of the UK's productivity 'puzzle';

- explain and evaluate the impact of increased globalisation and the consequent challenges for employment regulation;
- critically analyse the impact of new technology and automation on the nature of work and employment;
- describe key changes to the UK labour market and assess the significance of these for employment relations.

3.1 Introduction

The business and organisational environment in which employment relations professionals operate is constantly changing. Over the last 50 years we have seen a radical shift in the nature of the labour market, with a rapid increase in the number of women in work, a growth in part-time and temporary forms of working, the growing domination of employment in services and concerns over job security and income inequality. These changes have been driven by de-industrialisation in developed economies, the globalisation of production and competition and, in the UK, the growing dominance of neo-liberal economic policies based on privatisation and marketisation. At the time of writing, organisations are still dealing with some of the effects of the Covid-19 pandemic, not least in changing attitudes to work. In addition, the acceleration of new technology and the rise of artificial intelligence (AI) threatens to transform the way we work and live. Moreover, the Labour government was elected in July 2024 on a radical platform designed to strengthen workers' rights and create a more conducive environment for trade union organisation and collective bargaining. Therefore, the dynamic context of employment relations presents practitioners with considerable and complex challenges, which we examine in the rest of this chapter.

3.2 The changing political and economic environment

As we saw in Chapter 2, the role played by the state in employment relations can be interpreted in different ways. For radicals, the state always acts to support capital, whether by restricting trade union activity or exposing public services to competition and encouraging private sector investment. In contrast, a pluralist perspective characterises the government as a neutral referee providing a framework which helps employers and employees to accommodate their differing interests. The historic attitudes of governments towards employment relations and its consequent place within national politics have been shaped by two main influences. First, the climate of employment relations has an important impact on key economic outcomes. For example, we would argue that high-trust relationships between employers, trade unions and employees are key ingredients in ensuring effective and productive workplaces, which in turn underpins economic growth and prosperity.

Second, and arguably more important, the stance of the government towards employment relations reflects its origins and the interests of its key stakeholders and supporters. The Conservative Party has traditionally received the bulk of its financial support from individuals with significant business interests. In 2023, £31.3 million out of a total of £44.5 million in donations came from seven prominent business leaders. At the same time, the Labour Party has generally relied on financial support from trade unions. In 2020, unions donated nearly £7 million compared to just £2.3 million from companies and private individuals. However, in the months preceding the 2024 general election, and with Labour looking likely to form the next government, this changed significantly with businesses and individuals donating £14.5 million in 2023 compared to £6 million coming from unions (Shone, 2024).

However, the extent to which these interests are reflected in government policy also depends on wider public opinion and the constraints of international economic conditions. This was illustrated in the run up to the 2024 election by the Labour Party's 'charm offensive' with UK businesses. This is driven by short-term considerations of financial support but perhaps more importantly by a view that business confidence boosts public perceptions of economic competence which is seen as a key ingredient of electoral success. Nonetheless, this is balanced against needing to retain Labour's core support, including the trade unions. As we will see later in this chapter, this inevitably creates a tension over policy development, particularly in relation to workers' rights and trade union legislation.

Reflective activity 3.1

What are the main economic, legal/political and technological factors that have impacted on your organisation in the last five years? How have these affected the balance of power between the employer and employees?

Government intervention – the end of voluntarism

It could be argued that, as a rule, governments have preferred to stay out of employment relations. Certainly, employment relations in the UK was traditionally characterised by 'voluntarism' in which the role of the state was to provide a basic legal framework which supported 'free' collective bargaining between employers and trade unions, and 'plugged gaps' in collective regulation (Dickens and Hall, 2010). This began to break down in the late 1960s as high inflation, low productivity and declining competitiveness were seen by many as a direct consequence of poor workplace industrial relations and high levels of industrial action in particular.

This led the then Labour government to establish the Royal Commission on Trade Unions and Employers' Associations in 1965 under the chairmanship of Lord Donovan. The recommendations of the Donovan Commission are still reflected in the system we work in today. Essentially Donovan concluded that the root cause of the large number of strikes was the fragmented and informal nature of workplace bargaining. His solution to this problem was to 'institutionalise' conflict by encouraging the development of national structures of collective bargaining with specific mechanisms for dispute resolution, such as conciliation and arbitration. In addition, the Commission recommended the introduction of a distinct set of employment rights, including the right to claim unfair dismissal and the development of a system of tribunals to provide workers with a speedy and accessible route to justice. In this way, Donovan sought to create a system for adjudicating and resolving issues which negated the use of industrial action.

In many respects, the establishment of Acas in 1975 epitomised this approach. Acas was charged with encouraging the development of collective bargaining structures as well as acting as an arbitrator and conciliator where such bargaining broke down. At the same time, the first Acas Code of Practice on Disciplinary Practice and Procedures, introduced in 1977, set out guidance on how employers, employees and trade unions should deal with disciplinary matters. Although the actions of the government in implementing the recommendations of the Donovan Commission signalled the beginning of the end of voluntarism, it reflected a pluralist perspective which was dominant at the time. This saw the state as having a clear role in setting the rules and creating an institutional framework through which employers, trade unions and employees could resolve their differences and so minimise the extent and impact of industrial conflict.

Thatcherism and the supremacy of the market

Unfortunately, the problems that Donovan sought to address persisted and, in the winter of 1978/79, in the face of inflation rates of around 8 per cent, low-paid public sector employees took strike action in protest at a 5 per cent pay limit set by the then Labour government. This led to widespread disruption of public services and formed the backdrop to the election of the Conservative government under Prime Minister Margaret Thatcher. Thatcher campaigned on the promise of better management of the economy, lower income taxes, less government expenditure and curtailing union power – all of which were claimed to help the UK economy regain competitiveness. Her commitment to introducing legislation designed to restrict union influence was not simply based on an emotional aversion to trade unionism, but on a fundamental belief that unions represented an obstacle to the working of the free market. Trade unions, it was argued, priced workers out of a job, causing unemployment by increasing wages above the market clearing level through collective bargaining. The Thatcher government argued that removing trade union influence and unnecessary employment regulation would allow labour markets to operate freely and wages to fall to the level at which employers were able and prepared to employ workers.

This was related to a broader monetarist economic philosophy, which rejected the prevailing orthodoxy that governments could maintain full employment through public expenditure and investment. Instead, it held that the key to reducing unemployment and controlling inflation was to enhance the ability of the economy to increase the supply of goods and services to the market more efficiently by:

- creating an environment conducive to private enterprise;
- liberalising product markets;
- privatising public-owned enterprises;

- reducing taxation and cutting public expenditure;
- de-regulating labour markets.

The initial impact of this policy agenda was a large and rapid increase in unemployment, especially in the country's manufacturing industries such as shipbuilding, car manufacture and steel production. Furthermore, many of these traditional industries, which had been owned and controlled by the state and heavily subsidised, were privatised on the basis that the exposure to market forces would force them to become more efficient in order to survive.

The size of the welfare safety net was progressively reduced and it was made easier to hire and fire staff by increasing the qualifying period before employees could claim unfair dismissal to two years. Regulations that maintained minimum wages in occupations which were unprotected by unions and bargaining, such as hairdressing, were also abolished in 1986. All these measures undermined the bargaining power of labour and the ability of workers to challenge their employers. At the same time, the government ceased to encourage trade union membership or support the extension of collective bargaining. To this end an important step was the establishment of pay review bodies for nurses and midwives in 1983, and for schoolteachers in 1991, taking groups of highly unionised public sector workers out of collective bargaining. Furthermore, the duty of Acas to promote collective bargaining was removed in 1993. These reforms, together with the introduction of legislation to restrict the ability of trade unions to mount effective industrial action and the defeat of trade unions in two major industrial disputes (the Miners' Strike of 1984/85 and the strike by print workers employed by News International in 1986) cemented the supremacy of managerial prerogative.

REAL-WORLD EXAMPLE 3.1

British Coal – context, conflict and crisis

In 1984, there were 173 underground coal mines in the UK employing 231,000 people, most of whom were members of the National Union of Mineworkers (NUM). The industry was state-owned and operated by the National Coal Board (NCB). The NUM was a well-organised trade union with high levels of bargaining power, due to the fact that the UK economy relied heavily on domestically produced coal for power generation. However, this masked a downward trend in employment in the industry as a result of improved technology, cheaper coal imports and alternative sources of electricity generation. Although employment relations in the industry were often challenging, the approach of successive governments had been to try to resolve issues and problems through negotiation. Nonetheless, the power of the NUM was reflected in the success of the union in winning significant pay increases following two national strikes in 1972 and 1974.

Margaret Thatcher was elected Prime Minister of the UK in 1979 on an explicit platform of reducing union power, which Thatcher saw as having a negative impact on economic performance. During the early 1980s, the UK government avoided direct confrontation with the NUM knowing that strike action could have a major impact on electricity supplies. However, it was determined to close down coal mines that it believed to be uneconomic and knew this would result in strike action. It built up stockpiles of coal at power stations and made additional plans to ensure that it could minimise the impact of a strike. In March 1984, a series of coal mine closures was announced. In response miners took strike action. Although this spread across the UK, miners in some parts of the country who were less affected by the closures continued to work. Miners who continued to work were supported by the government and protected by a massive police operation, which limited the effectiveness of union picketing. Approximately 9,000 miners who were arrested by police during picketing were dismissed. Existing coal stockpiles and the government's timing of the closure announcements at a time when demand was lower also meant that the strike failed to have a significant impact on electricity generation. A number of court judgements questioned the legality of the union's actions, limiting its activity and imposing severe financial penalties.

In March 1985, after a year on strike, miners voted to return to work without an agreement or having secured any substantive concessions. By 1990, there were fewer than 50,000 coal miners working in the UK and the last underground coal mine, Kellingley Colliery, closed down on 18 December 2015.

Reflective activity 3.2

In what ways do you think that Thatcherism changed society? What implications does this have for the management of employment relations today?

The influence of this seismic shift in policy towards employment relations neither ended with Margaret Thatcher leaving Downing Street in 1990 nor with the landslide election of a Labour government led by Tony Blair in 1997. The Blair government accepted key elements of 'Thatcherism' and made it clear that it was not going to provide 'favours' to trade unions, instead adopting an unambiguous pro-business message. Labour rebuffed calls from trade unions to roll back union legislation and extended programmes of privatisation and marketisation. In 2016, the Conservative government with Theresa May as prime minister went further than even the Thatcher administration would have dared by introducing the Trade Union Act 2016. This included a threshold whereby 50 per cent of eligible members had to vote in an industrial action ballot for the result to stand. In certain public services, unions also had to win the support of 40 per cent of those able to vote. Given that such restrictions are not seen in any other area of public life or democracy, it is difficult to disagree with the TUC that the legislation came close to effectively outlawing strike action in the UK.

It is important to note that the newly elected Labour government has promised to repeal the 2016 Act, along with a range of other measures, which it argues have unfairly restricted the ability of trade unions to organise workers and represent their members. In addition, it is likely that unions will be allowed to use electronic forms of balloting to increase participation. If enacted, this will represent a significant change in the attitude of government to collective action. However, the key elements of trade union legislation introduced by the Thatcher government in the 1980s will remain on the statute book, underlining the degree to which the regulation of trade unions has become an accepted part of mainstream policy.

Reflective activity 3.3

How would you describe the attitude of the current government to trade unions? Why do you think it holds this view and do you think that it is justified?

Fairness and individual rights

While government policy over the last four decades has contributed to a fundamental decline in collective employment relations, it could be argued that some degree of consensus has developed around the importance of individual employment rights and the notion of workplace fairness. Despite its reluctance to reverse legislation restricting trade union activity, the Labour government elected in 1997 took the view that 'fairness' at work was a key driver of improved performance and competitive advantage. This provided the rationale for the introduction of the national minimum wage, the signing of the Social Chapter of the EU Treaty, an extension of individual employment rights and a new union recognition procedure. Importantly, the strengthened framework of employment protection developed between 1997 and 2010 has proved remarkably resilient. Interestingly, successive Conservative-led governments seem to have accepted that certain areas of employment rights such as the national minimum wage, parental rights and equality law have become a settled part of the landscape of work and employment.

Nonetheless, a central theme of policy between 2010 and 2024 was to (as far as possible) reduce what governments have seen as the regulatory burden being placed on business and further restrict the powers of trade unions. This included the introduction of employment tribunal fees in 2013 and an increase in the qualifying period for claiming unfair dismissal from one to two years. For employers, these changes were a necessary deterrent to weak and speculative claims (see for example CBI, 2013); however, others argued that this was supported by little hard evidence and the new regime was simply a barrier to justice (Ewing and Hendy, 2012; Hepple, 2013). Tribunal fees were subsequently removed in 2017 following a legal challenge from the trade union UNISON. The Conservative government led by Rishi Sunak (2022–2024) proposed to reintroduce fees, albeit at a much lower level and, in concert with previous Conservative governments, continued to seek to further restrict trade union activity. We look at this in more detail in Chapter 9. In particular, this included new legislation giving employers in certain sectors the ability to impose minimum service levels during strikes.

Figure 3.1 Strictness of employment protection – individual and collective dismissals (OECD)

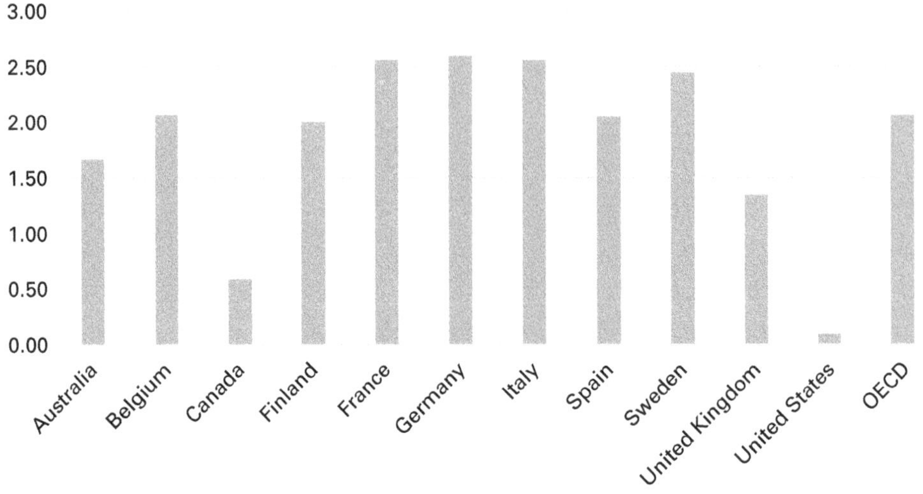

SOURCE: OECD

Although much of the media commentary and government rhetoric tends to emphasise the regulatory hurdles faced by employers, in reality the UK remains a low-regulation economy. The OECD maintains a strictness of employment protection index, which compares legislation relating to individual and collective dismissals across international economies. As Figure 3.1 shows, among developed economies, the UK has one of the weakest regimes and is well below the OECD average and those of other European nations such as Germany, France, Spain and Sweden. Moreover, as Dickens (2012a: 206) has argued:

> The approach to enforcement in Britain is flawed in that too much reliance is placed on individuals having to assert and pursue their statutory employment rights, which generally require only passive compliance from employers.

In short, relying on individual complaints does little to address structural and institutional inequalities (Fredman, 2011). There is a clear danger that organisations subject to litigation defend such cases in isolation rather than using this as a trigger for reviewing their broader organisational policies and practices. It is therefore notable that the manifesto on which the Labour government was elected in July 2024 included pledges to not only extend individual employment rights but also create a Single Enforcement Body, which it claims will 'undertake targeted and proactive enforcement work and bring civil proceedings upholding employment rights' (Labour Party, 2024: 16). We discuss the Labour Party's proposals in more detail later in the chapter and in the rest of the book. While it is unclear how these manifesto commitments will be translated into policy, they go significantly further than the previous Labour administration led by Tony Blair. Furthermore, they reflect a belief that employment security, fairness and equity are key foundations of sustainable economic growth.

Reflective activity 3.4

To what extent do you agree with the argument that employment rights are critical to creating productive and effective workplaces? Should the government try to promote fairness as an end in itself or is fairness only important if it underpins organisational performance and efficiency?

Unpicking the productivity puzzle

There is one thing that has united the different policy prescriptions outlined so far in this chapter: a desire to solve the UK's historic problem of low productivity. As Figure 3.2 illustrates, the UK still lags behind its main competitors, such as the US, but also Germany and France, both of which have much more regulated labour markets in which trade unions play a significant role.

The UK's productivity puzzle remains a major priority for the UK government. While low productivity may have many causes, it has been increasingly argued that a key factor is the relatively low quality of management in UK workplaces (Bloom and Van Reenen, 2007). Speaking in 2018, Andrew Haldane (2018), chief economist of the Bank of England, explained that:

> there is a statistically significant link between the quality of firms' management processes and practices and their productivity. And the effect is large. A one standard deviation improvement in the quality of management raises productivity by, on average, around 10%. This suggests potentially high returns to policies which improve the quality of management within companies.

Figure 3.2 GDP per hour worked, G7 countries, 2022

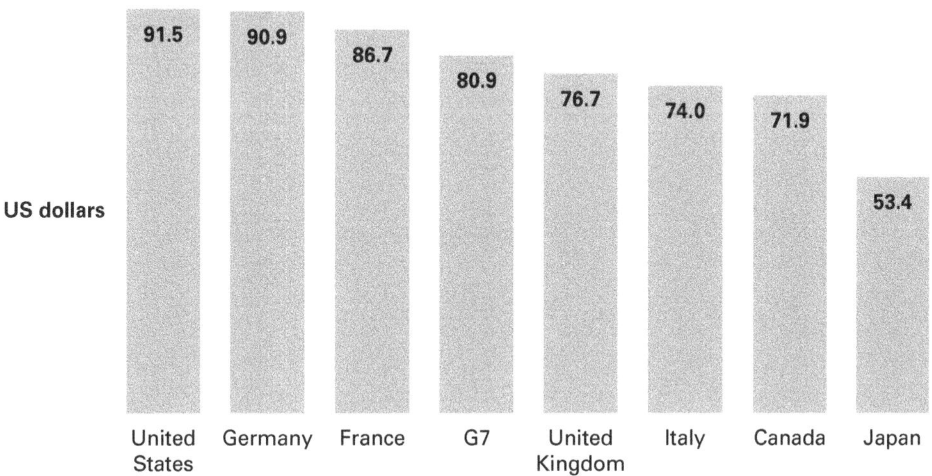

SOURCE: OECD

Figure 3.3 Acas's seven levers of productivity

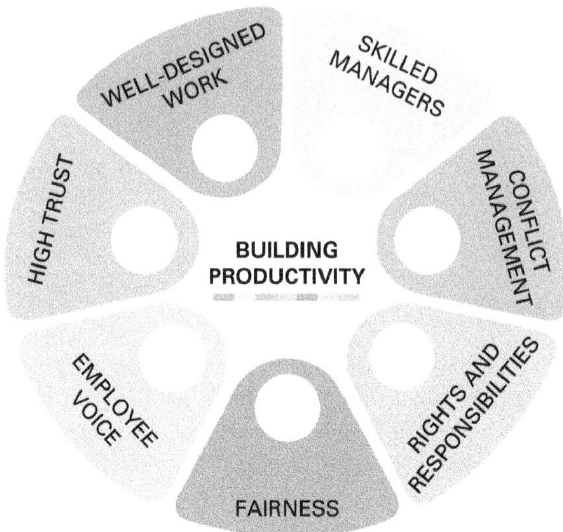

SOURCE: Acas (www.acas.org.uk/index.aspx?articleid=5283). Contains public sector information licensed under the Open Government Licence v3.0.

Indeed, the government has accepted 'that people, and the skills they have, are a key driver of productivity' (HM Government, 2017: 95) and that 'our managers are, on average, less proficient than many competitors' (ibid: 164). This has led to a focus on 'good work', which we will examine in greater depth at the end of this chapter. However, in our view, a broader commitment to workplace fairness and equity is a vital part of the solution, as encapsulated in Acas's seven levers of productivity (Figure 3.3).

The model picks out the importance of skilled managers, a theme that runs through the rest of this book. However, effective management of conflict, employee voice and the maintenance of trust and fairness is also dependent on managers having the necessary capabilities and working within a supportive organisational context. This is discussed in more detail in the next chapter.

Pandemic and politics

The Covid pandemic arguably triggered the most significant shift in the context of employment relations in recent years. At a basic level it represented a huge global economic shock and led to a wave of redundancies. According to the ONS, GDP fell by almost 10 per cent in 2020, the largest annual fall on record. Redundancies increased faster during the pandemic than at the time of the 2008/09 global recession (Office for National Statistics, 2021). Between September and November 2020, 402,000 workers were made redundant, the highest level in any quarter since records began in 1995 (Powell et al, 2022).

However, it could be argued that the pandemic has had a more fundamental and lasting impact on work and employment relations in four key respects. First, it has shaped attitudes to work, as large numbers of front-line workers were forced to operate in an extremely challenging environment. Moreover, 11.7 million jobs were furloughed through the Coronavirus Job Retention Scheme, which arguably provided a space in which large numbers of people reassessed their careers and work–life balance. This arguably led to the 'great resignation', with job-to-job resignations in the UK reaching their highest level this century in the second quarter of 2022. Some have questioned whether these changes represented a substantial reassessment of work as opposed to an expected reaction to a significant labour market shock (Boys, 2022). Across the economy as a whole, resignations returned to more normal levels relatively quickly. Nonetheless, the pandemic has had a lasting legacy in exacerbating a crisis in staff retention among front-line workers as Real-world example 3.2 clearly demonstrates.

REAL-WORLD EXAMPLE 3.2

Covid, crisis and the NHS

Researchers from the University of Bath (Weyman et al, 2023) analysed data from the NHS employee survey between December 2020 and April 2022. Their findings paint a stark picture of the impact of the pandemic and the consequent challenges of retaining a motivated and skilled workforce.

- Only half of NHS staff who were surveyed thought that they would still be working in the NHS in 2027, while around one-third were looking to find other employment or retire over the same period. The research team identified a rising trend of NHS staff looking for work outside the NHS.
- A large majority of respondents felt that staffing levels had fallen in six months prior to the survey in April 2022 – half reported deteriorating morale, increased stress and higher workloads.
- There was evidence of staff feeling tired and exhausted. Around 25 per cent of respondents agreed that they felt 'overwhelmed most days or every day' with a half of these respondents putting it down to their job.
- Mental health problems and staff concerns were not being reported to line managers.
- Between 2020 and 2022, the proportion of staff who would recommend working for the NHS to others fell by 10 per cent with particularly low levels (two out of five) among nurses.
- There was relatively little confidence that working conditions would improve over the next 12 months.

In addition, there has been a sustained increase in work inactivity since the end of the pandemic. In part this has been caused by older workers deciding not to return to the labour market, but also by a steep increase in those aged 16–34 not working, often due to ill health. Research conducted by the Resolution Foundation found that 5 per cent of young people aged between 18 and 24 were economically inactive due to ill health, double the level a decade earlier (McCurdy and Murphy, 2024). While this increase cannot be solely attributed to the pandemic, there is little doubt that it has been an aggravating factor. Whatever the explanation, this creates significant challenges for management of people.

Reflective activity 3.5

What has been the long-term impact of the pandemic in your experience? How has this shaped your experiences of work and the attitudes of those people you know and work alongside?

The second, and perhaps most obvious, legacy of the pandemic has been the spread of remote and hybrid forms of working. Prior to the onset of Covid, 12 per cent of the workforce reported working from home to some extent – this increased to just under half at the height of the pandemic. While the extent of homeworking has varied since the end of the pandemic, the evidence suggests that it has now become a very significant feature of work and employment in the UK with around 4 in 10 UK workers doing some work remotely (Office for National Statistics, 2023a). Within this figure, hybrid working is more common, with workers over 25 and in higher income brackets more likely to do some degree of homeworking. For workers, remote and hybrid working has a range of benefits. Most specifically, it saves on costs associated with commuting and office-based working. The Hybrid Work Commission estimated that hybrid working was worth £13.5 billion annually, equivalent to £1,634 per hybrid worker (Ali et al, 2023: 6). The Commission's own research also found that the majority of hybrid workers felt that it had a positive impact on their work–life balance and made coping with parenting responsibilities easier. However, there was some evidence that mothers were likely to be less positive than fathers about the impact of hybrid working on childcare.

A key issue is the impact of increased remote working on the management of people. The Hybrid Work Commission's research found that the majority of employers whose teams were fully remote believed that this aided productivity. However, employers with hybrid teams or those whose staff worked face-to-face were much less positive about the benefits of working from home. This possibly explains why some organisations have opted for a return to 'the office'. This is potentially driven by a view that remote working can hamper collaboration, teamworking and creativity. For instance, a study of more than 60,000 Microsoft employees found that remote working across the organisation encouraged more siloed working and increased asynchronous communication. Overall, the research suggested that remote working could have a negative impact on information sharing across organisations (Yang et al, 2022). It may also be more difficult for managers to spot potential issues and problems at an early point, while managing conflict remotely may bring additional challenges (Saundry et al, 2024).

Reflective activity 3.6

What do you think are the main challenges when managing people who are working remotely? What advice would you give a new manager on how to manage the performance of a remote team?

It could also be argued that the Covid pandemic has been one of the main factors in potentially creating a more fundamental break with the employment relations of the 1990s and 2000s. This was largely characterised by union decline, low levels of conflict and, in terms of the models outlined in Chapter 2, an increasing domination of unitarist perspectives. In short, many organisations did not see employment relations as a priority, if they even thought about it at all. However, the pandemic exposed the inadequacies of this approach. In the UK, the return to some sort of normality was in combination with rapid increases in the cost of living and tighter labour markets. Consequently, workers in 2022 and 2023 had more bargaining power than at any time since the late 1970s. Moreover, having experienced the trauma of the pandemic, they were now seeing their real wages eroded. This resulted in a palpable sense of anger and frustration, which, as we discuss later, has manifested itself in a spike in industrial conflict and wider demands for greater fairness and equality.

3.3 Globalisation and employment relations

An important feature of contemporary employment relations has been the growing importance of the international context. The greater reach of global markets, the increased mobility of labour and capital, and the extension of European employment regulation means that anyone working in employment relations needs to have a broader perspective and a clear understanding of how this shapes practices in UK workplaces. Multinational corporations have the potential to influence the conduct of employment relations by exporting particular approaches, while the threat of disinvestment can have a fundamental impact on government policy and the balance of workplace bargaining power. In addition, UK governments have sought to attract investment by emphasising the relative lack of regulatory constraints in the UK. For some, this suggests a convergence of national systems of employment relations around a neo-liberal model with an emphasis on de-regulation and labour flexibility. Indeed, the perceived impact of globalisation on job security and working conditions for British workers has been argued to be one of the drivers behind the referendum vote to leave the EU in 2016.

International systems of employment regulation have been developed to provide some protection against the harmful impacts of globalisation. In recent years, EU legislation has played an important role in defining the framework of employment rights within which HR practitioners in the UK operate. However, here again, irrespective of Brexit, there are some signs that the threat of competition from emerging economies has placed pressure on EU countries to dilute their commitment to a social dimension.

In this context, international standards such as those set by the International Labour Organization (ILO) are one way of trying to prevent workers becoming victims of global market forces. More recently, greater emphasis has been placed on the growing role of voluntary labour standards and ethical training initiatives.

The importance of international trade

Since the Second World War, there has been a rapid expansion in international trade and economies have become increasingly interdependent. In 2018, the OECD estimated that the operations of multinational corporations accounted for around half of global exports, one-third of output and about one-quarter of employment (OECD, 2018). There are a number of reasons for this: first, technical advances in communication, transportation and the development of the internet have increased the mobility of labour and capital; second, both labour and capital markets have been liberalised with the removal of tariffs and barriers to trade; third, these developments have, in part, led to rapid growth in less developed economies. For example, China is the leading global economy in terms of purchasing power and second only to the US in terms of output. The International Monetary Fund (IMF) has forecast that emerging and developing countries will grow by more than 4 per cent between 2023 and 2025 compared to advanced economies, which will grow by less than 2 per cent. In the same period, India's GDP is set to increase by just over 7 per cent while growth in the UK will be below 1 per cent (IMF, 2024). These developments have significant implications for the UK, as emerging economies provide new markets and are also both a source of, and destination for, new investment.

The role of multinational corporations (MNCs)

Foreign-owned multinational corporations play an increasingly important role in the UK economy, while UK-owned MNCs have significant influence on economies overseas. MNCs are defined by Leat (2006) as: 'enterprises which in more than one country own or control production or service facilities that add value'. Investment by MNCs in the UK creates jobs both in the organisations directly and in the supply chain and the local economy. Furthermore, MNCs have the potential to influence the way that employment relations are conducted in host countries. For example, research (Edwards and Walsh, 2009; Marginson and Meardi, 2010) has found that foreign-owned MNCs are more likely than their UK counterparts to introduce direct communication and employee involvement strategies, have centralised HR functions and operate single-union bargaining approaches. Accordingly, it has long been argued that the growing influence of MNCs will contribute to the convergence of national industrial relations systems as countries develop the kind of rules and institutions necessary to support large-scale industrial development (Kerr et al, 1960). As Turner and Windmuller (1998) point out, the 1970s saw some evidence of this; US and European systems coalesced around greater direct intervention in the conduct of employment relations in the establishment of individual employment rights, the development of state-sponsored dispute resolution processes and the greater decentralisation and fragmentation of collective bargaining.

It has also been suggested that MNCs facilitate convergence by encouraging different 'regimes' to compete with each other as to who can offer the most conducive environment for profitability (Streeck, 1997). The political pressure on governments to retain employment and attract investment arguably forces different employment relations systems to move towards a de-regulated and neo-liberal model characterised by high levels of flexibility, limited employment protection and weak trade union organisation (see for example Eaton, 2000). Successive UK governments have sought to attract investment on the grounds that the UK has a relatively light-touch approach to labour regulation in comparison with other developed economies, particularly those in Europe.

However, a range of studies in the early 2000s (see for example Hall and Soskice, 2001; Marginson and Sisson, 2004) suggested that national systems of employment relations were relatively resilient in the face of globalisation. The forces of convergence are not necessarily unidirectional and, while increasing international competition and the diffusion of new technology might be expected to lead to pressures towards more de-regulated and flexible systems, the further development of international networks of trade unions and employers and the development of international and regional regulation through bodies such as the EU produce a very different dynamic. However, the increased mobility of capital and productive resources and the consequent threat of multinationals relocating operations to lower-cost economies have reduced the bargaining power of labour. This practice, known as whipsawing (Greer and Hauptmeier, 2016), essentially involves management making coercive comparisons (Muller and Purcell, 1992) between different factories, plants or outlets whereby there is an explicit or implicit threat to move production unless workers (and normally trade unions) make concessions in terms of wages, conditions and/or working practices.

Of course, this is nothing new; as Greer and Hauptmeier point out, such tactics were used by large international corporations such as the Ford Motor Company in the 1970s. However, at that time, the strength of trade unions and institutions of employment relations in the UK limited the power of such threats. In more recent times, the intensification of global competition, the reduction in union bargaining power and the greater mobility of productive resources has accentuated the threat of disinvestment. The case of GM Vauxhall (see Real-world example 3.3) is an excellent example of this, with trade unions adopting pragmatic approaches and even working in co-operation with politicians with whom they share little in common in order to protect employment. While such agreements may be seen as examples of partnership working, they also reflect in stark terms the relative fragility of union influence in the face of international capital.

REAL-WORLD EXAMPLE 3.3

GM Vauxhall – labour agreement saves jobs

In 2012, the Vauxhall car plant at Ellesmere Port was rescued from closure, saving more than 2,000 jobs, when the company announced that the new model of the Vauxhall Astra would be made at the factory. The company had made it clear that the work would go to either Ellesmere Port or its plant at Bochum in Germany. This represented an investment of £125 million.

Securing the future of the plant depended on a new agreement on pay and conditions, which included:

- a four-year pay deal (including a two-year freeze);
- a new shift system to enable 24-hour production;
- an end to the traditional summer shutdown;
- a 37-hour week expandable to 40 hours at times of high demand;
- reform of the pension scheme.

For Vauxhall, the 'responsible labour agreement' was central to its decision to stay, alongside a commitment from government to support supply chain initiatives and apprenticeships.

Globalisation and developing economies – a race to the bottom?

There is significant debate about the impact of globalisation on employment within emerging economies. There is little doubt that foreign direct investment from MNCs has created large numbers of jobs; however, the nature of these jobs and the conditions under which the new global workforce are employed has become a source of increasing concern. An authoritative review of this area, commissioned by the WTO and ILO, summed this up as follows (Bacchetta et al, 2009: 9):

> Few would contest that increased trade has contributed to global growth and job creation... Nevertheless, in many instances, labour market conditions and the quality of employment have not improved to the same degree. In many developing economies job creation has mainly taken place in the informal economy... However, the informal economy is characterized by less job security, lower incomes, an absence of access to a range of social benefits and fewer possibilities to participate in formal education and training programmes – in short, the absence of key ingredients of decent work opportunities.

It could be argued that the development of national and supranational systems of employment regulation may lead multinational organisations to move more labour-intensive parts of their operations to relatively low-wage economies. Writing in the early 1980s, Frobel et al (1980) pointed to the existence of a 'new international division of labour', whereby manufacturing processes that required relatively low-skilled labour were outsourced to countries in which pay was low, union organisation was weak and in which there was little regulation to protect workers. At the same time, high-value processes such as research and development (R&D) and those which require high levels of skills and training were retained within developed economies. The case of Dyson outlined in Real-world example 3.4 is a classic example of this process, whereby many of the technically advanced functions of research and design have been kept in the UK while production has been focused overseas.

REAL-WORLD EXAMPLE 3.4

Dyson disinvests... and invests

In 2002, Dyson, which makes a range of domestic appliances, attracted considerable publicity with its decision to move production of its vacuum cleaners from the UK to Malaysia at the cost of 800 jobs. James Dyson, the owner and founder of the company, claimed that rising labour costs made production unviable. He argued that direct labour costs had doubled in 10 years. Production costs in Malaysia were 30 per cent lower, while wages were around one-third of those in the UK. Dyson told the BBC:

> I don't think I can [see an alternative]... It's been an agonising decision and very much a change of mind... Increasingly in the past two to three years our suppliers are Far East based and not over here.... And our markets are there too. We're the best-selling vacuum cleaner in Australia and New Zealand, we're doing well in Japan and we're about to enter the US. And we see other Far Eastern countries as big markets as well.

At the time, the company decided to keep its headquarters at Malmesbury in Wiltshire along with its R&D department, employing around 1,300 staff. Speaking two years later to the *Guardian*, Dyson claimed that: 'we are a much more flourishing company now because of what we did and it's doubtful if we could have survived in the long term if we had not done so'. In late 2018, Dyson announced a significant investment in a new plant in Singapore to build a range of electric cars, and then, in early 2019, the company announced that its headquarters would also move from the UK to Singapore. The company claimed that this was part of 'future-proofing' and developing Dyson as a 'global technology company'.

In 2023, the company announced its largest-ever investment in manufacturing in Singapore, which would develop a new battery plant. There were also smaller investments in the UK and the Philippines. In the UK, the company will develop a new centre in Bristol employing software and AI engineers. The plan essentially consolidates its strategy of locating research and development within the UK while manufacturing overseas.

SOURCES: *Guardian*; *Daily Telegraph*; BBC

MNCs not only organise their global production chains on the basis of the relative labour costs of developed and less developed economies, but also encourage competition between less developed countries over which governments can offer the cheapest labour and the least regulated labour markets. This 'race to the bottom' is a matter of debate. Some commentators argue that investment from multinationals has a broadly positive impact, not only increasing employment but generally paying wages which are higher than in domestically owned businesses. Moreover, as Williams and Adam-Smith (2010) claim, MNC investment can improve equality of opportunity, opening up employment opportunities for women in particular. MNC activity in developing and emerging economies may also speed up the process of industrialisation and improve the transfer of new technology and knowledge.

While millions of jobs have been created in developing economies, a 2024 Oxfam report (Riddell et al, 2024) argues that this has done little to reduce economic inequality. The report cites research from the ILO that the gap between wage growth and labour productivity has grown in the last two decades. Low wages and long hours are commonplace in many economies and over 17 million workers are in forced labour. Furthermore, attempts by workers to organise collectively are often suppressed, sometimes through violence (see also International Trade Union Confederation, 2023).

Reflective activity 3.7

At the World Economic Forum at Davos in 2019, Winnie Byanyima, the executive director of Oxfam International, argued during a panel discussion that job quality rather than just levels of employment in both developing and developed countries is vital and that this in turn is linked to employment rights and employee voice. The clip of this discussion went viral. Watch this clip, which you can find by searching on the internet. What do you think of this argument? What can governments and employers do to improve the situation?

Therefore, it can be argued that without greater regulation and the development of effective trade union organisation, any benefits of globalisation will feed into extreme inequality (Jaumotte and Osorio Buitron, 2015). Moreover, the prevalence of poor employment conditions has consequences for both employers and their customers. First, growing international concern over labour standards may have an adverse effect on brand reputation. This may also have a negative impact on the commitment and engagement of staff working in the UK and other developed economies. Second, in host countries, continuing employment and income insecurity will make it difficult to sustain and improve productivity, performance and quality. Meanwhile, there are clear signs of growing conflict as workers seek to improve pay and conditions.

REAL-WORLD EXAMPLE 3.5

Globalisation, AI and union organisation – the case of content moderation

Facebook contracts around 15,000 content moderators across the world. Content moderators are tasked with identifying and taking down problematic content, undoubtedly a difficult and challenging job. In 2020, Facebook was reported to have settled a lawsuit filed by moderators based in the US, who claimed that their work had caused PTSD.

In 2019, Facebook content moderation for Sub-Saharan Africa was undertaken by Sama, an AI outsourcing company based in California with contracts working for Microsoft, Google and Meta. Sama employed content moderators based in Nairobi, Kenya. Around 100 content moderators employed by Sama who were concerned about pay and conditions started to organise via a WhatsApp group, which came to be known as the Alliance. An investigation by *Time* magazine (Perrigo, 2022) alleged that some operators took home 'as little as $1.50 per hour'. A petition outlined a series of demands and threatened strike action if the company did not engage with the petition. Sama managers argued that wages and conditions were high compared to typical jobs available in the area.

The main organiser of the action, Daniel Motaung, was suspended and Sama allegedly claimed that he had bullied his colleagues into signing the petition. Others who were active in organising the petition told *Time* that they had to choose between their jobs and the Alliance. A large number of workers began to rescind their support for the protest. In the meantime, Motaung was preparing to apply for the Alliance to be recognised as a trade union under Kenyan law, which would have protected employees who engaged in trade union activity. However, Motaung was dismissed by Sama who claimed that he had bullied and harassed workers into taking action that disrupted the business and put the relationship between Sama and Facebook at risk.

In 2023, Sama ended its relationship with Facebook; however, both companies have faced legal claims from more than 100 workers in relation to unpaid wages and the impact of the work on the mental health of moderators. Moreover, content moderators working for a number of different social media and AI businesses formed the African Content Moderators Union (Nondo, 2023).

International regulation of labour standards

Attempts have also been made to improve and harmonise global labour standards through the International Labour Organization. The ILO is an agency of the United Nations and was set up in 1919 in the wake of the First World War, and all but 8 of the 193 member states of the UN are members of the ILO. The main way in which international labour standards are expressed is through conventions. If conventions are ratified by member states, they have a legal obligation to apply their provisions. Recommendations supplement conventions but do not have binding authority.

The ILO's Declaration on Fundamental Principles and Rights at Work contains five fundamental policies:

- The right of workers to associate freely and bargain collectively:
    - C87 Freedom of Association and Protection of the Right to Organise Convention, 1948
    - C98 Right to Organise and Collective Bargaining Convention, 1949
- The end of forced and compulsory labour:
    - C29 Forced Labour Convention, 1930 and Protocol (2014)
    - C105 Abolition of Forced Labour Convention, 1957
- The end of child labour:
    - C138 Minimum Age Convention, 1973
    - C182 Worst Forms of Child Labour Convention, 1999
- The elimination of unfair discrimination:
    - C100 Equal Remuneration Convention, 1951
    - C111 Discrimination (Employment and Occupation) Convention, 1958
- Protection for workers' health, safety and welfare:
    - C155 Occupational Safety and Health Convention, 1981
    - C187 Promotional Framework for Occupational Safety and Health Convention, 2006.

While all member states are obliged to uphold the principles and conventions outlined above, the ILO has very few powers through which this can be enforced and tends instead to rely on working collaboratively with countries to encourage compliance. In addition to ILO standards, another approach has been to include social and labour clauses in multilateral trade agreements, although these have met with little success (Hepple, 2005). There has been more progress in providing for labour standards in bi-lateral agreements, particularly between developed and emerging economies (Kuruvilla and Verma, 2006). Such clauses often draw on ILO standards.

More recently, there has been significant emphasis placed on the development of 'soft regulation' through voluntary codes of practice (Ngai, 2005). These have become increasingly common as organisations have responded to increasing concern over labour standards. In addition, they have been driven by initiatives and campaigns often involving trade unions and charities. In the UK, the Ethical Trading Initiative (ETI) describes itself as 'a leading alliance of trade unions, NGOs, and companies, working together to advance human rights in global supply chains'. Moreover, it defines its vision as 'a world of work that protects human rights, ensures dignity for all, provides opportunity and is free of exploitation and abuse'. Members of the ETI include well-known retailers such as Lidl, Primark, Marks & Spencer and Asda alongside the TUC, Fairtrade and charities such as CAFOD. The ETI also has a base code of practice, which has a number of key principles:

- Employment is freely chosen.
- Freedom of association and the right to collective bargaining are respected.
- Working conditions are safe and hygienic.

- Child labour shall not be used.
- Living wages are paid.
- Working hours are not excessive.
- No discrimination is practised.
- Regular employment is provided.
- No harsh or inhumane treatment is allowed.

The code, according to the ETI, helps to 'define best practice', while the ETI also provides training for its members, raises awareness of workers' rights and encourages 'work cultures where workers can confidently negotiate with management about the issues that concern them'. An extract from Primark's Supplier Code of Conduct (Primark, 2023), which derives from the ETI principles, is set out in the following box. Primark points out that the Code is based on the Core Conventions and the Fundamental Principles and Rights at Work of the ILO. The Code forms part of the company's terms and conditions with suppliers and was updated and strengthened in 2020. There is also a new clause requiring suppliers to introduce grievance procedures for their staff.

EXTRACT FROM PRIMARK'S SUPPLIER CODE OF CONDUCT

Employment is freely chosen

1.1 There must be no forced or compulsory labour in any form, including bonded, indentured, trafficked, or prison labour and overtime must be voluntary.

1.2 Any fees associated with the employment of Workers must be paid by the Employer.

1.3 Workers must not be required to lodge any monetary deposits or their identity papers with their Employer.

1.4 Workers must be free to leave their Employer after reasonable notice.

Freedom of association and right to collective bargaining

2.1 All Workers have the right to join or form trade unions of their own choosing and to bargain collectively.

2.2 Employers will adopt an open attitude towards the activities of trade unions and their organisational activities.

2.3 Workers' representatives must not be discriminated against and must have access to carry out their representative functions in the workplace.

2.4 Where the right to freedom of association and collective bargaining is restricted under law, Employers will facilitate, and must not hinder, the development of parallel means for independent and free association and collective bargaining.

2.5 Individuals who represent workers should do so willingly, and be freely and transparently elected, without influence from any other party.

Working conditions are safe and hygienic

3.1 Employers must provide a safe and hygienic working environment, bearing in mind the prevailing knowledge of the industry and of any specific hazards. This includes the physical structure of the buildings and facilities used.

3.2 Through policy and procedure employers must take adequate steps to prevent accidents and injury to health arising out of, associated with, or occurring in the course of work.

3.3 Employers must appoint a senior management representative to be responsible for ensuring a safe and healthy workplace environment.

3.4 Workers must receive regular and recorded health and safety training and such training will be repeated for new or reassigned workers.

3.5 Access must be provided to clean toilet facilities and to clean drinking water. If appropriate, clean and safe facilities for the preparation, consumption and storage of food should be provided.

3.6 Employers must provide access to adequate medical assistance and facilities in the event of illness or injury at work.

3.7 Accommodation, where provided, must be chosen by the worker, be clean, safe and meet their basic needs.

Some writers, such as Wedderburn (1995), are sceptical about the potential of soft regulation, arguing that workers' rights must be based on enforceable statutory provision. But as Kuruvilla and Verma (2006) point out, one of the main reasons for low labour standards is a lack of will on the part of governments to either enact or enforce 'hard' regulation of this type. In many countries, statutory protections are in place, but they are often ignored.

Barrientos and Smith's (2007) survey of the impact of the ETI among companies in South Africa, Vietnam and India found some positive impacts, particularly where supply chains were more integrated and there was a stronger relationship between customer and supplier. However, suppliers tended to focus on commercial imperatives and in some cases saw the codes as a barrier. Furthermore, suppliers found that it was difficult to comply with codes due to pressures being placed upon them by buyers. This points to a central problem with codes of conduct in that buyers may demand improved labour standards but may expect suppliers to absorb these costs rather than accept any reductions in their margins. Therefore, the purchasing practices of MNC buyers are a critical factor in determining whether codes will have any substantive impact. Importantly, Barrientos and Smith also found that there was a greater impact on visible 'technical' outcomes such as health and safety standards but very little effect on building trade union structures, enhancing workers' rights or combatting discrimination. In part, this reflects the role of auditing as a mechanism of enforcement but also questions whether any improvements in standards can be sustained without the development of independent and robust mechanisms of worker representation. Therefore, while 'soft regulation' of this type can have benefits, material and sustainable improvements to the terms and conditions of workers are only likely where robust national systems of employment regulation are in place which underpin strong and independent structures of union representation.

3.4 The social context of employment relations

The radical changes in the political and economic environment discussed so far in this chapter have been accompanied by changing social attitudes which inevitably shape the way we view work and employment. In the UK, social attitudes have been tracked since 1983 by the British Social Attitudes Survey (BSA) (Curtice and Scholes, 2023). The most recent data points to two very interesting and related developments. First, for much of the 1980s and 1990s there was an increase in the proportion of the population who considered themselves to be neither working class nor middle class. This arguably contributed to a narrative of the UK becoming a more classless society. However, recent data suggests that class is increasingly relevant. In fact, between 2015 and 2022, the proportion of people saying that they belonged to no social class plummeted from 55 per cent to 22 per cent with 56 per cent identifying as working class compared to 23 per cent in 2015. Moreover, perceptions that class impacts on opportunity is at its highest since 1983, with perceptions of class mobility also decreasing (Heath and Bennett, 2023).

Second, changes in class identity have been mirrored by perceptions of the role of government in addressing income inequality (see Figure 3.4). This shows the percentage of respondents who agreed with the statement 'it should definitely be the responsibility of the government to reduce income differences between the rich and poor'. Between 1986 and 2006 there was a steady reduction in the proportion who definitely thought that this was the responsibility of the government, from 46 per cent to 25 per cent. This increased sharply following the 2008/09 financial

Figure 3.4 Should government take responsibility to address income inequality?

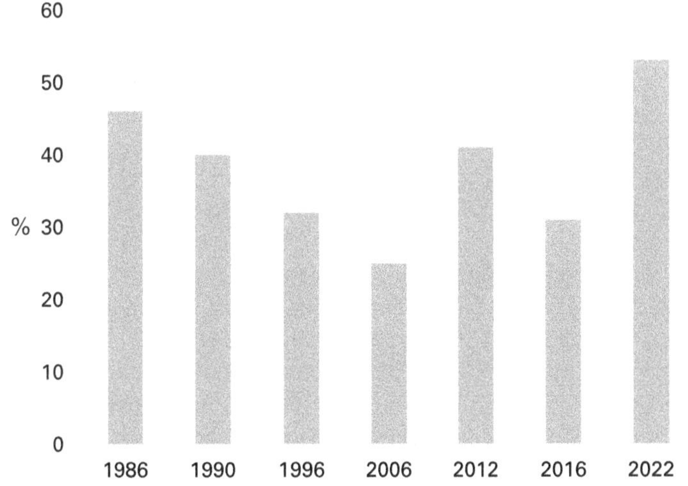

SOURCE: British Social Attitudes Survey

Figure 3.5 Do trade unions play a positive role in Britain today?

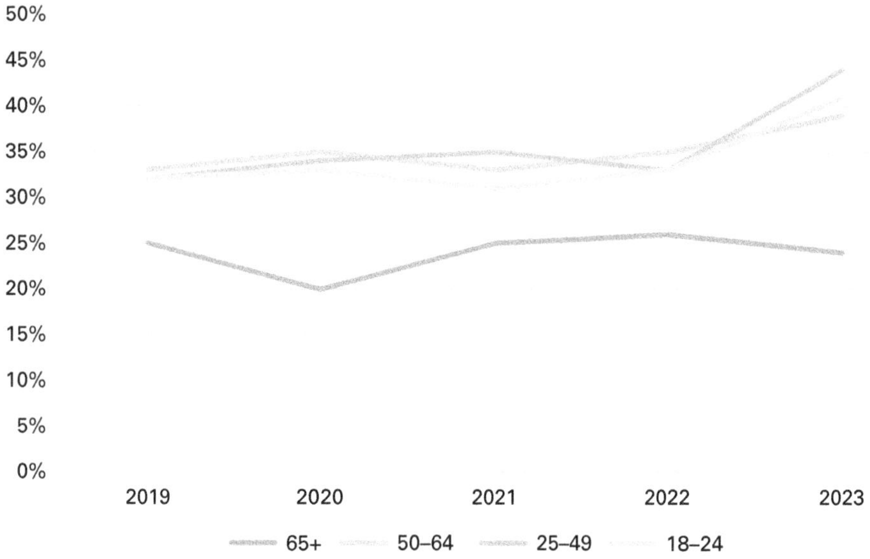

SOURCE: YouGov

crisis only to drop back down again in 2016. However, in 2022, this measure increased to its highest ever level, 53 per cent (Curtice and Scholes, 2023). It is difficult not to conclude that this has been shaped at least to some extent by the Covid pandemic.

Although there is little in the BSA data that relates directly to employment relations, the changes outlined here suggest that the climate is increasingly conducive for collective action and organisation. This is supported by data that explores the attitudes of people in the UK towards trade unions and particularly industrial action. In the UK, the polling organisation YouGov tracks public support for trade unions. As can be seen in Figure 3.5, there is little difference in levels of support for the idea that trade unions play a positive role between people aged 18–24, 25–49 and 50–64.

However, it is also important to note that negative views about trade unions are more common as age increases. The same YouGov poll found that 39 per cent of respondents aged between 50 and 64 felt that unions played a negative role, compared to 24 per cent among those aged 25–49 and just 16 per cent among 18–24-year-olds. Younger workers are also less likely to have a clearly defined opinion, perhaps pointing to a relative lack of awareness. Moreover, it may be expected that although younger workers may have positive attitudes about the idea of trade unionism they may be less supportive of the reality of trade union activity.

However, survey data regarding the wave of strikes in the UK in 2022 and 2023 does not support this, as Figure 3.6 illustrates. In fact, support among people between 18 and 24 years of age was higher in each case than older age groups. Perhaps the real barrier to young people joining trade unions lies in the insecurity and precarity faced by young people entering the labour market. While this creates a basis for activism, younger workers, unlike previous generations, may well find themselves in organisations with little, if any, union presence.

Figure 3.6 Support for strike action by age, UK, 5–6 July 2023

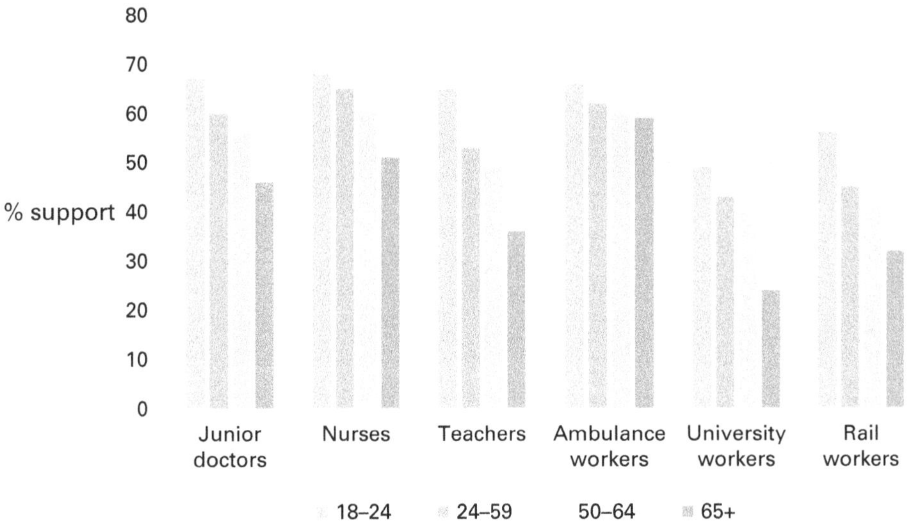

SOURCE: YouGov

Reflective activity 3.8

To what extent and in what ways do you think the attitudes of your family and friends are changing in relation to issues of fairness at work and inequality? Do you think this will have an impact on employment relations and, if so, how?

3.5 New technology and automation – changing the way we work

The impact of new technology on employment relations can be viewed from three different perspectives. One is that new technology, because of its impact on traditional skills, acts as both a de-skilling agent and a creator of unemployment. Second, it can be argued that technology allows managers and employers to increase their control over the labour process by monitoring the activities and performance of their employees. Third, new technology can be a positive force in creating new opportunities for employees who have the chance to learn new skills and can eliminate unpleasant or repetitive tasks.

New technology, bargaining power and the rise of knowledge work

The way in which these factors combine to impact on employment relations is not straightforward. We noted in Chapter 2 that Harry Braverman had argued that technology played a central role in de-skilling workers and allowing managers to gain greater control of the workforce. There is little doubt that in many areas of manufacturing increased automation has both cut jobs and reduced worker autonomy, undermining the power and influence of labour.

However, it could also be argued that for those workers who remain, conditions are often better. For example, in 1970, the UK car manufacturing industry employed around 850,000 workers and produced just over 2 million cars. It was highly unionised and employment relations were poor, with more than 500 stoppages in that year. In 2014, production was just a little lower at 1.6 million cars, but the industry employed 138,000 workers, and while it remains highly unionised, there were only 12 industrial stoppages in 2014 involving approximately 2,000 workers (Rhodes and Sear, 2015; Office for National Statistics, 2015). Improved working environments, as a consequence of automation, may have contributed to more harmonious employment relations. But at the same time, new technology, by eroding employment security, together with the globalisation of competition, critically undermined the bargaining power of car workers and their ability to use industrial action to defend their interests.

It has also been suggested that technological change has heralded the rise of the 'knowledge worker', whereby organisations have a greater requirement for workers with high skill levels, who enjoy greater discretion over their work. However, while it is possible to point to the growth of specific hi-tech sectors and organisations which rely on workers with very highly developed skillsets, the overall picture is one of relatively little change (Williams and Adam-Smith, 2010). Although the shift from manufacturing to service industries has seen a growth in non-manual occupations, work in, for example, call centres is routinised, standardised and offers workers little discretion or autonomy (Taylor and Bain, 1999).

It is also important to acknowledge that technology is not just something that employers can utilise to increase productivity, replace labour or increase their control over the labour process. One of the most significant recent technological developments has been the growth of online social networks such as Facebook, X and Instagram. Although the use of social media is a significant part of many occupations and is actively encouraged by some employers, it has provided managers and HR practitioners with a number of significant challenges (see Broughton et al, 2011, for a review). Employees may use social media for personal reasons during working hours, reducing productivity. In addition, the misuse of social media platforms to denigrate employers and/or their colleagues is becoming an increasingly common reason for disciplinary action in UK workplaces. This reflects the way in which social media is blurring the lines between social and work life, and also potentially reshaping personal and work relations, as individuals discuss work issues in the public gaze and managers and their subordinates become 'Facebook friends'. Research (Saundry et al, 2016) has also suggested that social media provides a 'venue' in which conflict can escalate outside the control of the employer; whereas in the past a disagreement at work would either be forgotten by the next day or could be addressed and resolved by managers, the argument can be carried on through social media so that by the following morning the issue is not only more serious but has potentially spread across a group of colleagues.

 Reflective activity 3.9

To what extent has the use of social media at work influenced the way that people behave in the workplace? Has it had a positive or detrimental effect on your organisation?

Automation, artificial intelligence and the future of work

The current wave of automation and technological development threatens to unleash what some commentators have termed the 'fourth industrial revolution', with profound consequences for the future of work. The use of big data and artificial intelligence means that computers and/or robots can potentially fulfil tasks that need a degree of cognitive ability but are also non-routine. This can include fraud detection, health diagnoses and legal and financial services. A benefit of using computers to perform these tasks is that they don't have the 'frailties' and irrationality associated with the human condition – in short, they don't get tired, they don't need sleep and they are less likely to make mistakes. In total, Frey and Osborne (2013) concluded that almost half (47 per cent) of all jobs in the US will be at risk by the 2030s.

However, there are limits to this, and Frey and Osborne cite the following examples as tasks which are more difficult to replicate:

- **Perception and manipulation** – for example, robots work well in environments that are designed for them, such as a factory or a warehouse, but cleaning a messy house requires quite complex skills of perception and adaptation and a significant degree of manual dexterity.
- **Creative intelligence** – the processes that underpin the creation of knowledge or art are difficult to specify but also relate to a complex and shifting set of values.
- **Social intelligence** – skills such as negotiation, persuasion and care are critical in the workplace but are also difficult for computers to replicate, critically because they require emotional intelligence and a degree of common sense.

From these three bottlenecks it is those related to creativity and social intelligence which are the most difficult to reproduce.

Frey and Osborne went on to calculate the probability of computerisation. Overall, they ranked 702 occupations: the top ranked (least computerisable) were recreational therapists, while the bottom ranked were telemarketers. Table 3.1 selects a number of occupations from the overall rankings. What this illustrates is that people skills and those connected with first line management will be relatively difficult to replace and therefore be increasingly valued as technology develops and is introduced into modern workplaces. Furthermore, it arguably provides a strong case for the strategic importance of employment relations and the skills that underpin it.

In 2017, Patrick Brione conducted research on behalf of Acas into the implications of automation for employment relations (Brione, 2017). He concluded that

Table 3.1 Probability of computerisation (by occupation)

Probability of computerisation	Occupation
0.98	Legal secretaries
0.88	Construction labourers
0.78	Computer operators
0.68	Dental hygienists
0.58	Financial advisors
0.48	Fire inspectors and investigators
0.38	Surveyors
0.31	Human resources specialists
0.25	Managers
0.17	Firefighters
0.08	First line supervisors of personal service workers
0.003	First line supervisors of mechanics, installers and repairers

SOURCE: Frey and Osborne (2013)

while automation may enhance the value of very high-skilled or creative work, it could have a negative impact on those currently working in unskilled work or those working in relatively routine, predictable white-collar jobs. While automation is likely to reduce employment, workers may also face an intensification of control, monitoring and surveillance. However, there will be increasing emphasis on work which relies on highly developed social skills, which could lead to greater value being placed on a range of jobs which are currently low paid and regarded as low status, including those involving social and personal care. Furthermore, Brione suggests that new technology could increase the potential for workplace conflict, underlining the importance of capabilities related to conflict resolution, such as negotiation and persuasion. Moreover, the skills needed to negotiate positive relationships are likely to become more significant in managing people as organisations flatten out hierarchical structures.

At the time of writing, artificial intelligence (AI) is developing rapidly. The introduction of programmes like ChatGPT, which claims to be able to write in a range of styles, is just one example. The debate about the potential threat(s) posed by these forms of AI continues, but there are concerns about the impact on creative work in particular. This was illustrated in 2023 by the five-month strike by members of the Writers' Guild of America, which represents Hollywood screenwriters, and a parallel four-month strike by Hollywood actors. Both groups were concerned about AI being used to replace them (Anguiano and Beckett, 2023).

Reflective activity 3.10

How do you think AI could affect your organisation, or the sector in which you operate, in the next five years? What is the likely impact on levels of employment and workplace relationships?

3.6 The transformation of the UK labour market

One of the main elements of the changing political and economic context has been the radical transformation of the UK labour market. De-industrialisation and the fragmentation of employment have combined to create an increasingly challenging environment for trade union organisation, a more precarious existence for many workers and questions over job quality and the notion of 'good work'.

De-industrialisation and the rise of services

Perhaps the most fundamental change in the UK labour market over the last 50 years has been the shift of employment from manufacturing to service industries. It is important to note that this is not a new phenomenon, and while it accelerated as a result of the election and subsequent policies of the Thatcher government, this process had begun in the early 1960s and affected all developed economies.

As Figure 3.7 clearly shows, this transformation has been part of a long-term trend. In 1911, there was parity between manufacturing and service employment, but the

Figure 3.7 Percentage of working people employed in each industry group, 1911–2011

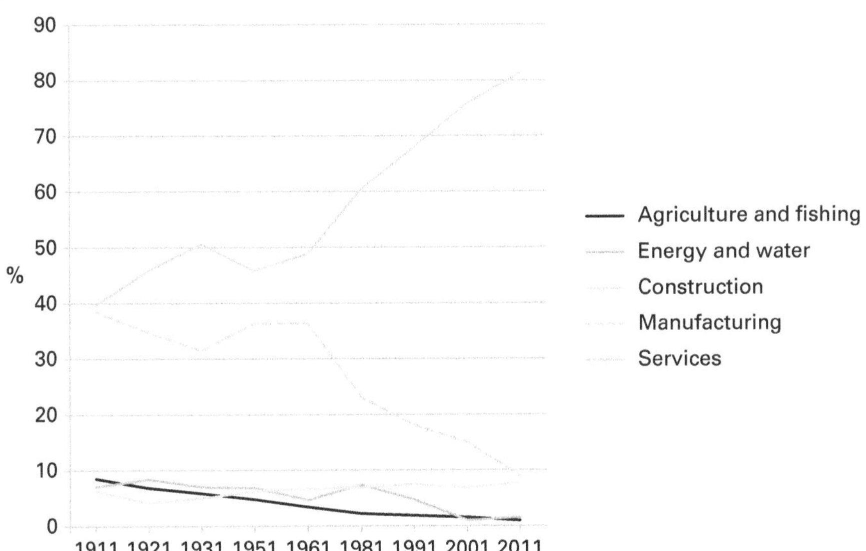

SOURCE: ONS/Census

gulf began to widen from 1960, and by 1981 service employment accounted for six out of every ten jobs. This trend has continued to the point where, in 2023, manufacturing represented just over 8 per cent of the total workforce, with 83 per cent of workers employed in services. This in turn has contributed to a reduction of manual jobs traditionally carried out by men and an increase in the percentage of women in employment, from 53 per cent in 1971 to 72 per cent in 2024. At the same time, the proportion of men in work has fallen from 92 per cent to 77 per cent (Office for National Statistics, 2024b).

Moreover, there has been a change in the nature of employment, with an increased range of different types of employment. Some commentators have argued that the relative growth in jobs in the service sector in comparison with the manufacturing sector has led to an increase in part-time, badly paid and low-status work. While economic growth between 1993 and 2008 had a positive impact on employment stability, this was arguably undermined by the financial crash and consequent recession after 2008 and government policies of austerity.

ZERO-HOURS CONTRACTS

A key feature of the labour market in the last decade has been the increased use of zero-hours contracts. These can be defined as arrangements where the employee is not guaranteed a fixed number of hours – essentially, they are 'on call' and can be asked and are expected to work at short notice and will only be paid for the hours that they work. In the past, similar arrangements were used in industries in which the demand for labour was highly variable, such as dock work. However, they have become increasingly used in jobs in which variability of demand is much more limited. For employers a major benefit is that such contracts are unlikely to accrue employment rights, and if there is a dip in demand, labour costs can easily be reduced. According to the Office for National Statistics, in 2012, 252,000 were employed on a zero-hours contract in the main job, under 1 per cent of the workforce. By 2020, this number had quadrupled and made up 3 per cent of all employment. In subsequent years, this has remained relatively stable. Importantly, there is a significant variation in terms of age in the distribution of zero-hours work – in 2024, 10 per cent of 16–24-year-olds and around one-quarter of workers who were also in full-time education were employed on zero-hours contracts. In addition, the use of zero-hours contracts was much higher in specific industries, including hospitality and social care. The Labour government has pledged to ban what it refers to as 'exploitative zero-hours' contracts by providing workers with a right to a contract that reflects their regular working hours, calculated over a 12-week reference period (Labour Party, 2024: 8).

However, it is important to put the use of 'non-standard' employment contracts into perspective. Between January and March 1997, only 6.3 per cent of those in employment had a main job which was not permanent, while in January to March 2024 the corresponding figure was 5 per cent. One in five of those workers on temporary contracts were unable to find a permanent job (Office for National Statistics, 2024a).

Whatever the statistics, there is no doubt that the ability of managers to adjust the size of their workforces in line with requirements and demand – usually referred to as numerical flexibility – appears to be relatively widespread. The implications of these changes are quite complex. Guy Standing (2011), for example, has argued that globalisation, among other things, has led to the creation of what he has termed the 'precariat' – a new class of workers made up of migrant labour, young people, those on temporary and short-term contracts, and workers displaced from traditional full-time, skilled industrial occupations. These workers not only face job insecurity, but a lack of autonomy and occupational identity. At the same time there has been growing concern that the UK has become an 'hour-glass economy' characterised by a labour market which is polarised between highly paid and highly skilled jobs at one end and low-paid, low-skill jobs at the other – with a significant decline in semi-skilled manufacturing and administrative jobs 'in the middle'. This, it has been argued, will potentially fuel wage inequality (Holmes and Mayhew, 2012).

Atypical work, employment rights and employment status

The fragmentation of employment and increased diversity of contractual forms is particularly significant because of its relationship to individual employment rights. Most importantly, only 'employees' enjoy the full protection of UK employment law. Table 3.2 sets out the rights accorded to different employment modes. This is important because one reason why organisations engage workers on non-traditional contracts is to avoid legal obligations. Furthermore, this implies that a move away from typical employment contracts means a general erosion of employment protection.

Table 3.2 Employment rights by employment status

	Employee	Worker	Self-employed contractor
Right to claim unfair dismissal	✓	×	×
Maternity, paternity, adoption and shared parental leave	✓	×	×
Maternity, paternity, adoption and shared parental pay	✓	✓	×
Statutory Sick Pay	✓	✓	×
Minimum notice periods	✓	×	×
Right to request flexible working	✓	×	×

(continued)

Table 3.2 (Continued)

	Employee	Worker	Self-employed contractor
Time off for emergencies	✓	×	×
Statutory Redundancy Pay	✓	×	×
National Minimum Wage	✓	✓	×
Protection against unlawful deductions from wages	✓	✓	×
Statutory minimum level of paid holiday	✓	✓	×
Protection against unlawful discrimination	✓	✓	✓
Protection under the Working Time Regulations	✓	✓	×
Protection for 'whistleblowing'	✓	✓	×
To not be treated less favourably if they work part-time	✓	✓	×

The determination of employment status is extremely complex and is largely determined through case law. An employee is someone who is engaged under a contract of employment. In broad terms, for a contract of employment to exist, three conditions should apply: first, the employee must be under an *obligation to perform the work personally* – this means that they cannot delegate the work to someone else of their choosing. Second, there must be *mutuality of obligation* between the parties involved. If an individual agrees to provide their own work (i.e. personal service) when the employer requires them to do so, and the employer in return agrees to provide work for the individual and pay a wage or other remuneration for that work, there is a mutuality of obligation. This is more likely to exist where work is relatively regular, and also when the individual cannot delegate their work to another person. Third, the individual should work *under the control of* the employer. Some of the relevant factors to be considered when determining whether an individual is under the control of the employing company are whether the individual:

- is under a duty to obey orders and subject to supervision;
- has control over their hours;
- is subject to the company's disciplinary procedure and rules;
- has to comply with the company's rules on the taking of holidays.

A tribunal will also take a holistic view of the relationship to see whether it is consistent with an employment contract or the individual being self-employed. In doing this they may look at whether they are integrated into the employer's activities – indications of this may be wearing a uniform, attending training and team meetings or having their performance appraised. In short, is the individual treated like any other employee? They will also examine if the individual is in business on their own account. Do they provide their own equipment? Do they work for other clients? Who is responsible for paying tax and National Insurance?

Where none of the three criteria just outlined apply, the individual is likely to be a self-employed independent contractor, running their own business, rather than a worker or employee. However, a 'worker' is someone who undertakes to do or perform personally any work or service for another party, whether under a contract of employment or any other contract. Therefore, while no mutuality of obligation needs to exist, an individual may be judged to be a worker if they are working under a degree of control, and they are unable to delegate their work to another person.

REAL-WORLD EXAMPLE 3.6

Zero-hours contracts and employment status

Pulse Healthcare v Carewatch Care (2012) UKEAT/0123/12/BA

Five care workers were employed by Carewatch under 'zero-hours contracts' and supplied to a primary care trust to provide round-the-clock care for a severely disabled individual. Under the contracts, Carewatch was under no obligation to provide work and the carers were free to work elsewhere. However, the employees worked fixed hours on a regular basis. The contracts made repeated mention of employment and contained clauses related to annual leave, sickness, pension and the provision of uniforms.

However, the Employment Appeal Tribunal (EAT) found that the written contract did not reflect the reality of the situation – while contracts indicated 'zero hours', the care workers worked as part of a team that provided a care package for a client for an agreed number of hours per week. Although they could question working certain shifts when rosters were produced, they worked on regular shifts of 24 or 36 hours per week. They were also not allowed to use a substitute worker to perform their duties. Therefore, the EAT concluded that they worked on global contracts of employment and were 'employees'.

The increased diversity of contractual arrangements and particularly the rise of the so-called gig economy has brought the issue of employment status into stark relief. The CIPD defines the gig economy as 'a way of working that is based on people having temporary jobs or doing separate pieces of work, each paid separately, rather than working for an employer'. More specifically, it usually refers to individuals who 'trade their time and skills through online platforms (websites or apps), providing a service to a third party as a form of paid employment' (CIPD, 2017b: 4). They estimate that around 4 per cent of the working population are employed in the gig economy, amounting to 1.3 million people. Importantly the majority (58 per cent) do 'gig work' in addition to other jobs and overall classify themselves as 'permanent employees'. It is the main job of only one-quarter of gig workers, but for these individuals, only 30 per cent say that they are living comfortably and 20 per cent find life difficult or very difficult (see for instance Cant, 2019). Given the likelihood that technological advances will see these types of work expand, providing adequate safeguards and protection is increasingly important. While a range of legal judgements, including the Uber case outlined in Real-world example 3.7, have extended worker status to many 'gig workers', the situation is still extremely unclear.

REAL-WORLD EXAMPLE 3.7

Uber drivers – workers not contractors

Yaseen Aslam was a taxi driver who worked via the Uber app. To work for Uber, drivers need their own car, which must meet certain conditions. They need a private hire licence, a Disclosure and Barring Service check and a medical. Potential Uber drivers go through an interview process and are required to go through an induction process. The agreement that drivers enter into with Uber specifies that the drivers are self-employed contractors.

Once engaged, drivers receive notifications of potential jobs which they can choose to accept or not. In this sense they can choose when they work or if they work at all and, therefore, it could be argued there is little or no mutuality of obligation. However, they are required to provide the work personally and the driver does not know the identity of the customer. Moreover, the fee and the route are determined by Uber.

The customer pays Uber through the app and Uber then passes this on to the driver minus a commission of 25 per cent. The driver is expected to deal with their own tax and National Insurance. Customers can rate the driver through the app and drivers can be given a warning or dropped altogether if their ratings fall or if they commit serious misconduct. Furthermore, drivers face sanctions if they do not accept or cancel a certain number of trips. However, Uber accepts the risk of fraud and any damages caused by the passenger, and also deals with passenger complaints. Moreover, Uber's marketing implies that it has responsibility for the quality of the service.

Aslam and his colleagues claimed that they were subject to the control of Uber and that they were therefore workers and should be entitled to certain benefits, including the national minimum wage and statutory holidays. Uber argued that the contract is between the passenger and the driver, who can choose how, when and whether to work.

The tribunal looked at the nature of the relationship in practice rather than the letter of the agreement between Uber and its drivers. It decided that Mr Aslam and his colleagues were 'workers', with the judge stating that 'the notion that Uber in London is a mosaic of 30,000 small businesses linked by a common "platform" is to our minds faintly ridiculous. Drivers do not and cannot negotiate with passengers… They are offered and accept trips strictly on Uber's terms'. The decision of the tribunal was subsequently upheld by the Employment Appeal Tribunal, the Court of Appeal and eventually the Supreme Court in 2021.

Two years later the Supreme Court ruled in another key case relating to the employment status of gig workers. However, it judged that Deliveroo riders were self-employed and not workers. The key issue in this case was that the riders could use other drivers to cover their work without any involvement from Deliveroo. The Court ruled that this ability to substitute was 'totally inconsistent with the existence of an obligation to provide personal service which is essential to the existence of an employment relationship'. In addition, Deliveroo riders did not work specific hours, had no fixed place of work and were not required to make themselves available for work. They were therefore free to work for any of Deliveroo's competitors.

Reflective activity 3.11

What are the main characteristics that suggest that an individual is an employee, working under a contract of employment? In your organisation, is there anyone who you think would be considered an employee under the law but who is not treated as such by the employer?

'Good work' – the key to the productivity puzzle?

The rapid changes to the labour market, the potential impact of automation and persistent concerns over poor productivity have seen an increased focus on 'good work'. In an article in the *New Statesman* on 14 August 2017, Peter Cheese, the chief executive of the CIPD, defined 'good work' as:

> work that is engaging, gives people a voice, treats them fairly, is good for their wellbeing, and helps them to progress. It should be positive for individuals, but also lead to wider positive organisational and economic outcomes: higher levels of productivity and output, and greater innovation and adaptability.

This not only places issues like fairness and employee voice centre stage, but suggests that employment relations must be a key element of the strategic thinking of HR professionals if organisations are to meet the challenges of the twenty-first century.

At the end of 2016, the Conservative government appointed Matthew Taylor to lead a review into 'modern working practices'. According to Taylor, the underpinning principle of the review was that 'all work in the UK economy should be fair and decent with realistic scope for development and fulfilment' (BEIS, 2017: 6). While Taylor argued that good work is important for its own sake to ensure that people are treated with decency and respect, he also claimed that:

- The quality of work is vital for the health and well-being of the population.
- Better designed work can 'get the best out of people' and therefore boost productivity.
- The approach to work needs to be responsive but also based on fairness in order to cope with fundamental changes to technology and business models.

Reflective activity 3.12

What does 'good work' mean to you? How important is fairness at work in maximising productivity?

The findings of the review were published in 2017 (BEIS, 2017) and made a series of recommendations with a particular focus on responding to the challenges of 'modern business models'. In particular, it targeted the rise of the 'gig economy' and with it the 3.2 million people that Taylor estimated were then working in insecure jobs. Although it was largely concerned with some of the uncertainties around the legal rights of those working through platforms such as Uber and Deliveroo, the review also had a wider ambition of laying the basis for a new regulatory framework which would encourage the development of 'good work' and with it a more engaged and productive workforce.

THE TAYLOR REVIEW – SEVEN STEPS TOWARDS FAIR AND DECENT WORK

The *Taylor Review of Modern Employment Practices* set out 'seven steps towards fair and decent work with realistic scope for development and fulfilment'. These can be summarised as follows:

1. Our national strategy for work should be directed towards the goal of good work for all, recognising that good work and plentiful work can and should go together.
2. Platform-based working offers welcome opportunities for genuine two-way flexibility and can provide opportunities for those who may not be able to work in more conventional ways. These should be protected while ensuring fairness for those who work through these platforms and those who compete with them.
3. The law and the way it is promulgated and enforced should help firms make the right choices and individuals to know and exercise their rights. We need to provide additional protections for dependent contractors and stronger incentives for firms to treat them fairly.
4. The best way to achieve better work is not national regulation but responsible corporate governance, good management and strong employment relations within the organisation.
5. It is vital that everyone feels they have realistically attainable ways to strengthen their future work prospects.
6. For the benefit for firms, workers and the public interest we need to develop a more proactive approach to workplace health.
7. The Living Wage is a powerful tool to raise the financial base line of low-paid workers.

In reality, little of the Taylor Review was reflected in government policy. In particular there was no immediate progress in either resolving issues around employer status or developing clear policy on extending channels of worker voice.

REAL-WORLD EXAMPLE 3.8

Low pay in the care sector

Prowse et al (2019) explored the working practices and terms and conditions of care workers and focused on the possible promotion and increase in the coverage of the Living Wage Foundation rate in the Sheffield area. The findings of the research highlighted the barriers to improving terms and conditions in this vital sector:

- Pay for care workers who had been transferred from local authority employment to the private sector was under particular pressure. Even those protected by TUPE regulations (see Chapter 12) saw their pay fall eventually as protection was removed.
- Newly recruited care staff, in the past two years (irrespective of age), were paid hourly rates of pay, slightly above the statutory legal rate for the Living Wage.
- Scope for extending the Living Wage Foundation rate in care homes was limited, in part due to the reluctance of employers.
- Younger workers, aged under 21, were particularly vulnerable to lower rates of pay. This was also a barrier to the future recruitment of younger workers into the sector.
- Workers reported increased demands and intensification of work.

Critically the Taylor Review and subsequent government policy failed to address the main failings of the UK's structure of employment regulation. As we argued earlier in this chapter, a legal right is only as strong as the ability of a worker to enforce it. The onus for doing so is on workers themselves – and they are often those who feel most vulnerable and have little access to help. In fact, the focus on the rights of workers in the gig economy has been due, in part at least, to workers being prepared to organise and act collectively, whether that is through Deliveroo riders taking industrial action or trade unions supporting legal cases. While the Taylor Review explicitly acknowledges the role played by trade unions in protecting workers against 'detriment and unfairness', government policy after 2017 was fundamentally focused on reducing union influence.

In this context, it is notable that arguably the most radical element of the Labour government's policy platform at the time of its election was its 'New Deal for Working People' (Labour Party, 2024). The proposals, many of which directly referenced the recommendations of the Taylor Review, included a possible ban on zero-hours contracts, a potential right to 'switch-off', and employment rights from day one. In addition, the government has pledged to 'move towards a single status of worker and transition towards a simpler two-part framework for employment status... that differentiates between workers and the genuinely self-employed' (Labour Party, 2024: 7). However, it is arguably more significant that the proposals represent a very clear argument linking collective employment relations, fairness and economic growth.

A NEW DEAL FOR WORKING PEOPLE – A RETURN TO COLLECTIVE EMPLOYMENT RELATIONS?

The Labour Party's proposals made the following case for collective bargaining:

> When acting alone, workers are often denied their fair share – but when backed by the collective power of their colleagues and trade unions, they can better secure their share of the wealth they helped to create. The labour movement's historic achievements have come through giving people power and a voice at work by means of collective action and collective representation. Labour believes strong collective bargaining rights and institutions at all levels are key to tackling the problems of insecurity, inequality, discrimination, enforcement, low pay, and other issues identified in this Green Paper. Collective bargaining is still the defining feature of industrial relations in some of the most successful economies in Europe, with many having collective bargaining agreements covering well over three-quarters of their workforce.
>
> Unionised workplaces, working hand in hand with employers, are more likely to provide decent pay, good training, and benefits, such as holiday and sick pay, above the statutory minimum. Trade unions have reaffirmed their value throughout the pandemic, from winning the furlough scheme, to agreeing safe working conditions with employers. They have also kept the country going with agreements and campaigns in key sectors. The imbalance of power between individual workers and employers means that it is essential that workers are able to band together to improve their bargaining power. The right of unions to operate effectively in the workplace, in each sector of the economy is vital for achieving fairness, dignity and democracy at work for all.

In order to support this, Labour proposals relating to trade unions and collective bargaining include:

- Repealing the Trade Union Act 2016 and recent legislation to introduce minimum service levels – a Labour government will keep the bulk of previous union legislation but it is likely that ballot thresholds will be removed and unions will be given more freedom to use new technology to ballot their members.
- Simplifying the law to encourage union recognition and introduce a new duty on employers to inform all new employees of their right to join a union, and to inform all staff of this on a regular basis. They are also likely to make it easier for trade unions to enter workplaces in order to organise and recruit new members.
- The development of a fair pay agreement in social care – in essence this represents the development of sectoral collective bargaining, although it will be limited in the first instance to a single sector.

At the time of writing, it is unclear how much of this programme will be carried through into legislation. This reflects the tensions discussed at the start of the chapter between the Labour Party's traditional agenda of fairness and equity and the influence of business interests. Nonetheless, its scale and scope reflect growing public support for greater security at work and a rebalancing of employment relationships.

Reflective activity 3.13

To what extent do you agree with the argument being made by the Labour Party about the benefits of collective bargaining? To what extent is the HR profession prepared for a greater emphasis on collective employment relations?

3.7 Summary

This chapter has examined the dynamic context of employment relations with a particular focus on the UK. Perhaps the most fundamental change has been to the political and economic environment. Here, an increased emphasis on the 'free market' led to the promotion of de-regulation, privatisation and marketisation, which undermined collective approaches to the management and regulation of employment relations. This has been accentuated by the globalisation of economic activity and the ability of multinational corporations to relocate (or threaten to relocate) productive resources to other national economies to take advantage of lower labour costs and weaker regulation. The 2008 recession and the dominance of economic policies of austerity further eroded areas in which trade union organisation was relatively strong and skewed the balance of workplace bargaining power towards the employer.

Alongside the changing political and economic context, we have also seen broader changes to social attitudes and rapid technological change, which will also have profound implications for our attitudes to work and the way in which employment relations are managed in the future. The growing diversity of labour markets means that work–life balance issues and demands for greater equality are likely to become increasingly prominent. At the same time, the increased use of zero-hours contracts and the rise of the gig economy raise important questions of employment security, inequality and organisational performance. These are amplified by the potentially revolutionary impact of increased automation and the rise of artificial intelligence, which not only looks set to radically transform our relationship with work but also to place a premium on human and social skills and capabilities. Concerns over insecurity and inequality were crystallised by the experience of the Covid pandemic, which also had a profound impact on the organisation of, and attitudes to, work.

These issues pose a challenge to the consensus over neo-liberal and market-driven approaches to work and employment which developed in the wake of Thatcherism.

There is growing awareness that 'good work' is an essential component of productive and effective organisations, and this in turn has the potential to refocus attention on workplace fairness and equality. This is not only reflected in public opinion but also in mainstream political discourse, with the Labour government elected in 2024 on a manifesto including a set of employment relations policies which are arguably more radical than anything seen in the last 50 years. Whether a more transformative approach to policy around work and employment comes to pass is likely to become clearer in the coming years.

KEY LEARNING POINTS

- Changes in economic management and reforms to labour law have undermined the organisation and influence of trade unions in the UK and have (in general) reduced the bargaining power of labour.
- The role of the state in employment relations has fundamentally changed – governments have moved away from a pluralist approach through the support of collective bargaining and collective employment relations institutions. However, this could be reversed by the election of the 2024 Labour government.
- The continuing globalisation of markets will be a major influence on organisational change and thus employment relations. The threat of employers moving production to less developed economies further reduces the bargaining power of labour in the UK.
- Social attitudes can have an important impact on employment relations. In the wake of the Covid pandemic, there are some signs of an increased salience of social class, a growing emphasis on state intervention and greater awareness of the positive role of trade unions.
- The rise of automation and artificial intelligence threatens to have a revolutionary impact on the landscape of employment in the next two decades, but also will place greater value on people-related skills.
- The UK labour market has been transformed over the last four decades. There has been a continuing growth in service sector employment and a significant rise in the number and proportion of women employed. Recent increases in the use of zero-hours contracts and the rise of the gig economy threaten to reduce employment security and further reduce the bargaining power of labour.
- The radical transformation of the context of employment relations in the last four decades has led to the idea of 'good work' becoming a central part of mainstream policy discourse, bringing issues of fairness and job quality to the fore.

Review Questions

1 To what extent has the Covid pandemic had lasting consequences for the management of employment relations in the UK?
2 How have changing social attitudes in the UK over the last 40 years shaped the way in which employment relations are conducted? What impact do you think this could have in the next two decades?
3 What impact will the increased use of social media (both inside and outside work) have on employment relations and what challenges does this pose for the management of employment relations?
4 Will the rise of artificial intelligence and computerisation bring positive benefits for workers and employees? What are the consequences of increased automation for the management of employment relations?
5 How important is 'good work' in solving the UK's problem of low productivity? How can this be delivered in UK workplaces?
6 Critically assess the impact of the Labour government's 'New Deal for Working People' on employment relations within the UK.

Explore further

Ali, V, Corfe, S, Norman, A and Wilson, J (2023) *Hybrid Work Commission 2023*, Public First. Available from: https://www.publicfirst.co.uk/wp-content/uploads/2023/08/Hybrid-Work-Commission-report-Embargoed-until-13th-Sept-2023.pdf (archived at https://perma.cc/9AWQ-DBB6) [accessed 17 May 2024].

Boys, J (2022) *The Great Resignation – Fact or fiction?* CIPD. Available from: https://www.cipd.org/uk/views-and-insights/thought-leadership/cipd-voice/great-resignation-fact-fiction/ (archived at https://perma.cc/UZN3-4H65) [accessed 16 May 20204].

Brione, P (2017) *Mind Over Machines: New technology and employment relations*, Acas Research Papers, 02/17

Labour Party (2024) *Labour's Plan to Make Work Pay: Delivering a new deal for working people*. Available from https://labour.org.uk/updates/stories/a-new-deal-for-working-people/ (archived at https://perma.cc/22W3-AM5K) [accessed 28 May 2024]

Riddell, R, Ahmed, N, Maitland, A, Lawson, M and Taneja, A (2024*) Inequality Inc. – How corporate power divides our world and the need for a new era of public action*, Oxfam International. Available from: https://oi-files-d8-prod.s3.eu-west-2.amazonaws.com/s3fs-public/2024-01/Davos%202024%20Report-%20English.pdf (archived at https://perma.cc/2D55-XM65) [accessed 15 May 2024].

Websites

www.natcen.ac.uk/british-social-attitudes (archived at https://perma.cc/ULT6-WG3U) – website containing the results of the British Social Attitudes Survey.

www.ons.gov.uk/ons/index.html (archived at https://perma.cc/A8UH-VEZP) – website of the Office for National Statistics, which contains a wealth of valuable labour market data and analysis.

04 Managing employment relations

Overview

This chapter examines the way in which employment relations are managed. We start by exploring the changing context within which managers operate and the shift from environments which are predominantly regulated through collective institutions to those in which direct relationships with individual employees are the norm. We look at the different issues associated with managing with, and without, trade unions. The changing landscape of employment relations has also reshaped the role of employers' associations and the next section of the chapter briefly explores the way in which they support their members. We then examine the way in which different managerial approaches to employment relations can be conceptualised in terms of management styles, which, in turn, define the roles played by individual managers. The last part of the chapter examines the implications of the continuing trend of devolving HR duties to the line and the challenges and implications of this for the effective and productive management of employment relations.

LEARNING OUTCOMES

When you have completed this chapter, you should be able to:

- understand and describe the main roles undertaken by line managers in the context of employment relations;
- critically assess recent developments in the management of employment relations;

- understand how employers' organisations support managers in their day-to-day work;
- identify different management styles and use these to critically evaluate organisational approaches to the management of employment relations;
- critically analyse the implications for employment relations of the greater devolution of HR duties to front-line managers.

4.1 Introduction

When examining the role of managers in employment relations, it is tempting to see management as a homogeneous entity, with no distinction made between the employer, senior managers, supervisors and practitioners responsible for managing human resources. In some organisations, this is the case; around four out of five workers are employed by SMEs in which the owner, or director, is often also the line manager. However, as organisations expand, there is a need for additional managerial layers and functional specialisms, such as HR. Ultimately, in very large private corporations there is a separation between ownership and management, as the business is often owned by shareholders, with professional managers employed to run the business.

Accordingly, the values and attitudes of managers at different levels and in different parts of the organisation may vary. For example, it might be expected that directors of a company will have values which closely reflect the objectives of major shareholders. This is also likely to be reinforced by the fact that it is common for senior managers to have relatively large shareholdings as part of their remuneration package. However, further down the managerial hierarchy, managers may identify more closely with their 'team'. Quite often line managers are promoted from the 'shopfloor' and this can make it difficult for them to secure the legitimacy and authority they need to manage effectively. In fact, the evidence tends to suggest that managers' values (and therefore their attitudes) tend to align with those of the organisation more generally. Furthermore, while the traditional view of the 'personnel' manager may have been as a neutral referee between employees and employer, HR practitioners increasingly see their role as supporting managerial and organisational strategy.

Consequently, it is possible to discern identifiable organisational approaches to the management of employment relations, whether regarding trade unions, employee involvement and participation, or the determination of pay and conditions. We examine these management 'styles' here. Perhaps more importantly, as Marchington and Wilkinson rightly note, HRM responsibilities do not 'reside solely or even primarily' with specialist HRM staff but rather with the line manager (2012: 165). In this context, this chapter considers the theoretical and practical implications of the increasing trend to devolve HR duties – and therefore the responsibility for the management of the employment relationship – to line managers. Significantly, the choice of management style they adopt is crucial; and for many organisations this will require a fundamental reappraisal of the key knowledge, skills and attitude their managers will need. Furthermore, academic commentators and practitioners alike are increasingly recognising the need to ensure that people with suitable attitude, motivation and abilities are recruited or promoted to the role. This is to avoid 'accidental managers' assuming the role without the necessary capability or for the wrong reasons (Townsend and Hutchinson, 2017; Chartered Management Institute, 2023).

4.2 Who manages employment relations?

Findings from the last full-scale workplace employment relations survey, WERS2011 (van Wanrooy et al, 2013), allow us to paint quite a detailed picture as to who manages employment relations. As we have noted, most organisations are small and do not have specialist managers with responsibility for either HR or employment relations. In fact, van Wanrooy et al found that 86 per cent of the individuals who had responsibility for dealing with employment relations issues were employed in a more general role and had nothing in their job title relating to HR or employment relations. In almost eight out of ten workplaces, issues such as discipline and grievance, health and safety, and pay were handled by a general manager or owner. Therefore, most managers who deal with employment relations do so as part of a wider role within the organisation.

Interestingly, the previous Workplace Employment Relations Survey conducted in 2004 (WERS2004) had found an increase in the use of staff with specialist HR knowledge or who spent a large proportion of their time on such issues (Kersley et al, 2006), perhaps in response to the growing demands of employment legislation in the late 1990s; however, WERS2011 found no evidence of this continuing. Not surprisingly, as Figure 4.1 clearly shows, the presence of employment relations specialists was much greater in larger workplaces; they were found in almost three-quarters of workplaces with 100 employees or more, but in just 15 per cent of those with between 5 and 19 employees.

Figure 4.1 Proportion of workplaces with an employee relations specialist, 2011

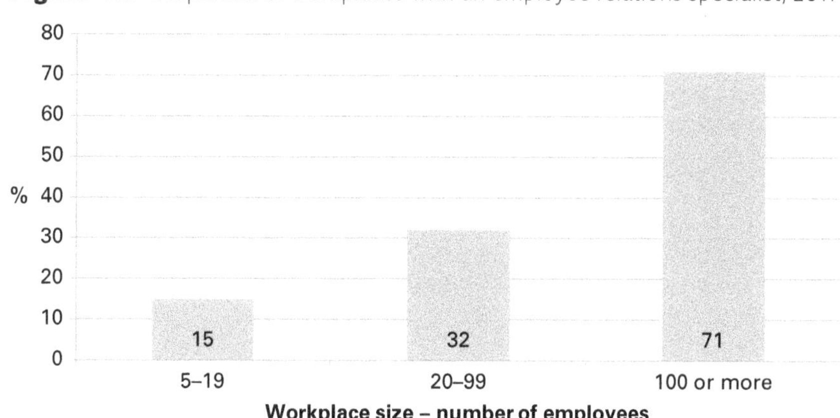

SOURCE: Workplace Employment Relations Survey 2011 (van Wanrooy et al, 2013)

Given that managers with specialist knowledge are much more likely to be found in larger workplaces, more than half of all employees work somewhere that has an employment relations manager with a relevant formal qualification. It should also be noted that van Wanrooy et al's analysis confirmed a longer-term trend of an increasing proportion of female employment relations managers; and this reflects faster progression for women within HR than within other managerial disciplines. This is interesting in two respects: it is arguably an illustration of occupational segregation in that HR is often (inaccurately) stereotyped as the 'caring' side of management; also, regression analysis of WERS2011 conducted by van Wanrooy et al (2013) found that female managers were more likely to adopt a consultative approach to decision-making than their male counterparts.

WERS2011 data also sheds light on the amount of discretion given to managers in terms of employment relations, whether from HR or from more senior managers in the organisation. The main terms and conditions of employment tend to be set centrally at a relatively high level, but line managers often have much more control over the day-to-day handling of issues such as performance and recruitment. Furthermore, this degree of freedom had increased since the 2004 survey in respect of appraisals, grievances and equal opportunities, reflecting the devolution of responsibility for certain HR and employment relations issues.

More than half of British workplaces in the private sector (56 per cent) had an individual on their board of directors who had responsibility for employment relations and there was a notable increase in the likelihood of board representation among medium-sized enterprises between 2004 (39 per cent) and 2011 (60 per cent). However, we need to treat such statistics with some caution; the representation of HR in the boardroom does not necessarily reflect the relative importance of employment relations within the organisation. In most cases, board representation will be through HR directors, and recent research suggests that within HR teams, employment relations is rarely the responsibility of the most senior practitioners (Saundry et al, 2019).

4.3 What do managers do?

This debate can be traced back to Fayol's (1990) classic and highly technical model of the general principles of management, with its emphasis on the notion of chains of command within a hierarchy. This contrasts with Mintzberg's (1990) more revealing exposition of the 'folklore' of the manager's job and the reality of its contingent and episodic nature. Previously writers have focused on the degree to which management has moved from being a traditional bureaucratic function, with tightly defined rules and regulations, to playing a more facilitative role in giving employees more autonomy to carry out their work. However, as critics have argued, this shift can mask the way in which de-layered structures have the potential to subtly reassert control over the labour process and intensify work (see Thompson and McHugh, 2009 for a critical discussion).

In more practical terms, writers like Mullins (2010) suggest that the key functions of the line manager are: clarifying the objectives of their team; planning work; organising activities; directing and guiding; and controlling performance (Figure 4.2).

Figure 4.2 Key functions of a line manager

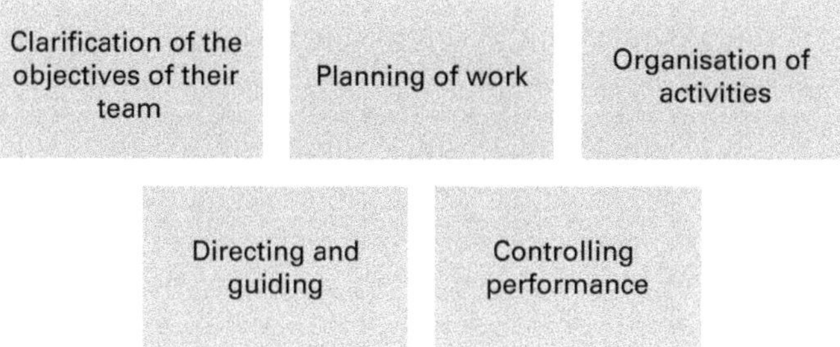

Similarly, Acas (2014), in its guide for line managers, suggested that the key aspects of the role include:

- Managing people
- Managing budgets
- Organising work rotas
- Monitoring quality
- Managing performance
- Ensuring customer care.

From a more contemporary perspective, Frost and Alidina argue that 'management is technical work. It's often essential and without it things wouldn't happen' (2019: 35). However, the execution of that work is also underpinned by the 'norms and parameters' of the organisation. This, as we will consider in Chapter 5, highlights the cultural influences that shape the actions of the line manager.

Reflective activity 4.1

Do you think the list of managerial activities above covers the main tasks that managers should be expected to do? Can you suggest anything that should be added?

Watson (2006: 167) offers a broader perspective of the role of management and argues that management can be understood as three distinct categories:

- Management as the function of shaping the relationships, understanding and processes needed to bring about tasks to achieve the overall objectives of the organisation;
- Managerial work as the activity of bringing about that shaping;
- Managers as the people who have the responsibility to ensure that the tasks are carried out successfully.

Watson implicitly criticises the notion of managing 'human resources'. Instead, the role of the manager is to manage relationships to ensure the achievement of particular tasks of value to the organisation through the facilitation of their team's efforts and other material resources. As Dundon and Rollinson point out, this is in stark contrast to the dominant notion of 'managerial prerogative', which, in turn, is based on a 'property rights' argument of the manager as owner of the necessary competence to decide on issues as a 'professional manager' (2011: 109). Indeed, the employment contract is founded, in part, on the notion of 'obedience' and reflected in organisational rules, the management of performance and ultimately the application of discipline, through which managers seek to enforce a degree of control and compliance.

However, as we discussed in Chapter 2, in most organisations this is insufficient to achieve necessary levels of performance, efficiency and quality. Therefore, managers must also try to secure the commitment and co-operation of their team by adjusting reward and remuneration or by ensuring that they communicate and consult over important decisions. This is not straightforward, particularly as managers often have limited influence on either broader organisational strategy or the changing competitive conditions in which they work. Consequently, attempts to secure the consent of their staff will be compromised by pressures to reduce costs and increase efficiency. It is this basic contradiction at the heart of the capitalist employment relationship (Hyman, 1987) that managers must face daily.

4.4 Working with, and without, unions

The contradiction between control and consent that characterises the management of employment relations is clearly reflected in the historical relationship between managers and trade unions and the scale and scope of collective bargaining.

The erosion of collective bargaining

As we outlined in Chapter 2, the reach of collective bargaining expanded rapidly in the post-war period so that by 1980 almost two-thirds of British workplaces (with 25 or more employees) and half of those in the private sector negotiated pay and conditions with trade unions (Brown et al, 2008). This was partly because collective bargaining offered significant advantages for management in terms of reducing the transaction costs of determining wages and conditions.

However, it was also driven by a desire to maintain managerial prerogative in the face of collective action and organisation by workers. By creating processes and procedures through which pay and other terms could be negotiated, the eventual outcomes had greater legitimacy; therefore more fundamental threats to the existing balance of power in the workplace could be warded off. Relationships with trade unions also enabled managers to handle individual issues more easily. Trade unions played a self-disciplinary role in many workplaces, ensuring that their members adhered to rules in relation to absence and other matters (Edwards, 1994). If disciplinary disputes and employee grievances escalated, managers could work with trade unions to work towards informal resolutions.

However, the extent of union recognition fell rapidly between 1984 and 1998, and then at a slower rate to 2004. By this time, just 38 per cent of workplaces employing

Figure 4.3 Percentage of employees whose pay is set by a collective agreement between employer and trade union, 1996–2023

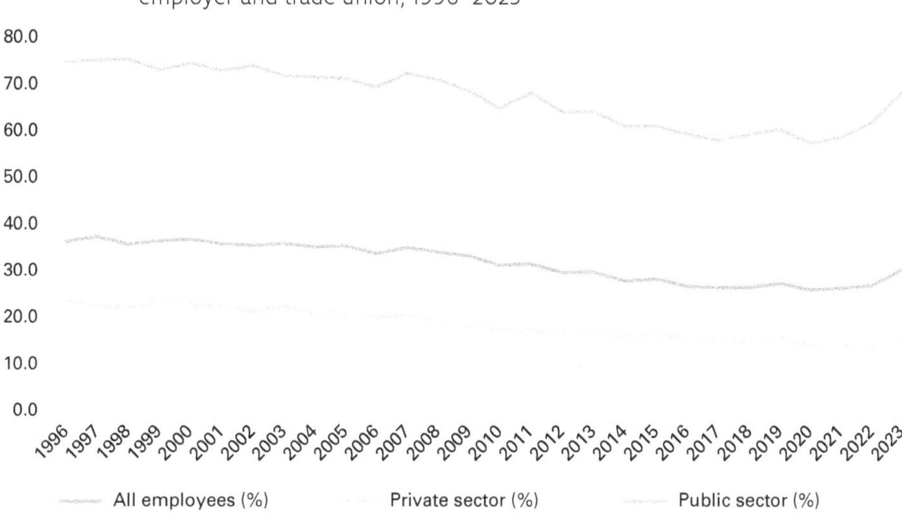

SOURCE: Office for National Statistics

25 or more employees recognised unions, and only 22 per cent in the private sector (Brown et al, 2008). In some respects, this mirrors the decline in union density and organisation during this period, which we discuss in greater detail in the next chapter. But Brown et al have argued that the decline in union recognition and collective bargaining was rooted in decisions made by managers in newly established workplaces not to recognise unions between 1950 and 1960, and again between 1970 and 1980. Of course, after the election of the Thatcher government in 1979, the disappearance of workplaces in highly unionised industries in manufacturing exacerbated this, but 'the demise of collective bargaining was already well-advanced' (Brown et al, 2008: 8). Of perhaps greater importance was the programme of privatisation and wider intensification of competition which created conditions in which managers, faced with the option of working with, or without, unions generally chose to do the latter.

In broad terms the contraction of collective bargaining continued through the 1990s and 2000s, albeit at a slower pace (see Figure 4.3). In 1996, 36 per cent of employees had their pay determined through a collective agreement – this included nearly three-quarters of workers in the public sector. However, by 2020, this had fallen to 26 per cent among all employees: 57 per cent in the public sector and just 14 per cent in the private sector. Interestingly, since the Covid pandemic, the scale of collective bargaining over pay has seen an uptick, particularly in the public sector.

Reflective activity 4.2

Why do you think the scale of collective bargaining increased between 2021 and 2023? What is the attitude of leaders in your organisation to working with unions and has this changed in recent years?

Managerial attitudes to collective employment relations

Traditionally, British managers have had an ambivalent attitude towards the collective regulation of labour in general and trade unions specifically. Clegg's seminal text (1976) on the systems of industrial relations in the UK in the 1970s, for instance, identified the 'philosophical' nature of management as being broadly unitarist. There is some support for this in recent data from WERS2011, with four out of five managers preferring to consult directly with staff rather than through employee representatives (van Wanrooy et al, 2013). In addition, only 23 per cent of managers either actively encouraged or were in favour of union membership, 17 per cent were against and 60 per cent were neutral. However, managerial attitudes towards trade unions do vary in relation to sector and size of workplace. In workplaces with 500 or more employees, 48 per cent had positive attitudes to union membership, which increased to 73 per cent in all public sector workplaces. In the private sector, just 12 per cent were in favour, while 20 per cent held negative views about union membership. Therefore, the attitudes of managers would appear, to some extent, to reflect the organisations in which they work.

Recognition, resistance and continuing individualisation of employment relations

In general, despite some of the potential benefits of working with unions, British managers have only done so when placed under some element of pressure, either by government policy or, perhaps more importantly, by trade unions themselves. Arguably, the most recent attempt to promote collective bargaining through state policy was the introduction of a statutory procedure for union recognition as part of the Employment Relations Act 1999. However, even this was introduced rather reluctantly by a new Labour government, which was forced to keep a pre-election pledge to the trade union movement. As Williams and Adam-Smith (2010) point out, its terms were extremely limited. It did not apply to small workplaces (fewer than 21 employees), where union recognition was traditionally extremely low. In addition, the procedure (summarised in the following box) required trade unions to reach a threshold of support of 40 per cent of the entire 'bargaining unit' before union recognition would be granted.

STATUTORY UNION RECOGNITION PROCEDURE

- Union requests recognition in respect of a group of at least 21 workers.
- Central Arbitration Committee (CAC) determines whether there is sufficient support:
  - If more than 50 per cent of the group are union members, CAC can order recognition.
  - If not, at least 10 per cent of the group must already be union members.
  - There must be a likelihood that a majority of the group would be in favour of recognition.
- CAC can then order a ballot of the relevant group:
  - To win recognition, the union must get a majority of those voting and be supported by 40 per cent of the total constituency.

There is some evidence that new union recognition agreements increased both prior to, and after, the introduction of the procedure. In 2001, there were 685 new deals; however, the number of new agreements fell significantly after this high point, as unions were forced to move into areas of industry that were more difficult to organise, and as Gall (2007) has pointed out, employers have become more active in resisting unionisation. In Real-world example 4.1, we look at a 2024 application for statutory recognition which illustrates how the process works in practice.

REAL-WORLD EXAMPLE 4.1

In February 2024, the Communication Workers Union (CWU) submitted an application to the CAC for recognition in respect of 15 engineers employed by SeeChange Technologies Ltd. The union had previously written to the employer formally requesting recognition, however no response was received within the 10 days set out in the statutory procedure.

The Union claimed that 12 of the 15 engineers were members of the union and that 80 per cent of its members working for SeeChange voted in September 2023 to support recognition for collective bargaining. The CWU argued that it had selected the bargaining unit because the 15 engineers were compensated and managed differently from the other departments. The employer denied this and also contested the number of employees within the bargaining unit.

The CAC had to decide whether at least 10 per cent of the workers in the Union's proposed bargaining unit were members of the union. The CAC found that 75 per cent were members. Therefore, the next test was whether a majority of the workers constituting the agreed bargaining unit would be likely to favour recognition of the Union. The CAC accepted that the level of membership provided 'a legitimate indicator as to the degree of likely support for recognition of the Union for collective bargaining'. Therefore, they found that, on balance, a majority of the workers in the bargaining unit would be likely to support recognition. Consequently, the application for statutory recognition was accepted.

SOURCE: Central Arbitration Committee

Figure 4.4 shows the number of new applications received by the CAC between 2001 and 2023, and while this has remained relatively steady since 2006, the level in 2023 (53) is less than half that of the high point in 2002 (118).

Overall, up until 2020, the introduction of statutory recognition failed to halt the erosion of collective bargaining. Newly established workplaces chose not to work with unions and within unionised workplaces the scope of bargaining continued to shrink. Although there are signs that the use of collective bargaining to determine pay is beginning to increase, it is too early to say whether this will be sustained in the face of a number of barriers.

First, small workplaces are highly resistant to union organisation. Analysis of WERS2004, which covered the period over the introduction of statutory recognition, found that the greatest fall in the incidence of collective bargaining was among workplaces with between 10 and 24 employees. In 1998, 28 per cent of these

Figure 4.4 New applications to the CAC for statutory union recognition, 2001–2023

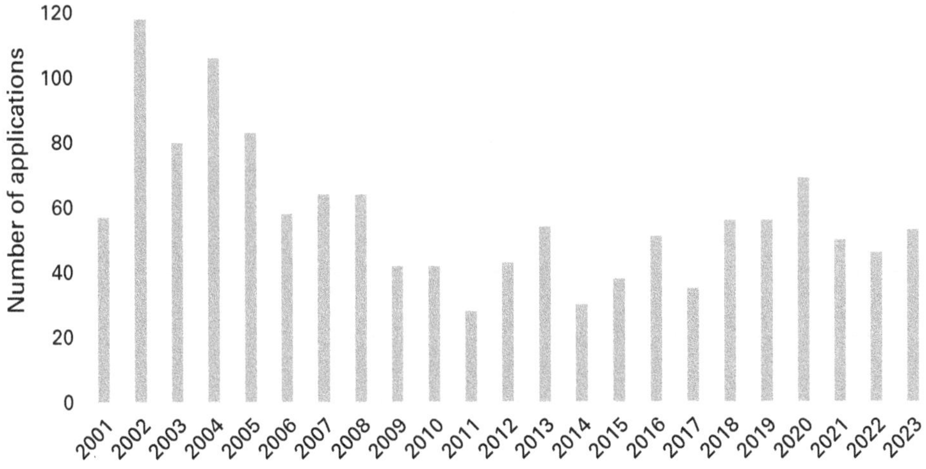

SOURCE: Central Arbitration Committee

workplaces had recognised unions, but by 2004, this was just 18 per cent (Kersley et al, 2006). It has long been acknowledged that owners of small and medium-sized enterprises are generally hostile to union membership and involvement (Rainnie, 1989). Trade unions are perceived to be antithetical to the notion of paternalistic and informal employment relations, based on the close personal ties between employer and employee, that characterise smaller workplaces and organisations (Ram et al, 2001). This does not mean that employment relations are necessarily harmonious. Wood et al's (2017) analysis of WERS2011 found that very small organisations (five to nine employees) had the highest rates of disciplinary sanctions and employment tribunal applications. Furthermore, conflict is also more likely to be suppressed in small business environments, in which employees are less likely to have the protection of formal procedure.

Second, large non-union businesses often adopt a policy of union substitution by offering relatively generous terms and conditions and developing channels of direct employee voice. We provide the example in Chapter 6 of Marks & Spencer, whose employee representatives are, unlike most non-union representatives, trained to accompany colleagues into disciplinary and grievance hearings. Although non-union representation has failed to come even close to filling the gap left by trade union decline, there have been some signs of growth (albeit from a very small base) in large private sector workplaces: from 6 per cent in 2004 to 13 per cent in 2011 (van Wanrooy et al, 2013). In addition, van Wanrooy et al (2013) found that levels of mutual trust between non-union representatives and managers was higher than between managers and union representatives. This may reflect the fact that non-union representatives are less likely to challenge managerial prerogative but could also be explained by a preference among managers for non-union forms of voice.

Third, some organisations are actively hostile and aggressive towards trade unions, using threats and intimidation in an attempt to resist attempts to organise. Perhaps the most prominent example of this is the approach taken by online retail giant Amazon to union recognition (see Real-world example 4.2).

REAL-WORLD EXAMPLE 4.2

One click to quit?

Amazon has consistently resisted union organisation and the robust tactics it has used to defeat attempts to unionise its warehouses in the US have been well documented (Logan, 2021). In the UK, the GMB has attempted to use the statutory recognition procedure to force Amazon to recognise the union for collective bargaining purposes at its BHX4 site in Coventry. According to its submission to the CAC, the GMB claimed that membership in July 2022 was 106 and by March 2024 this had increased to 1263. Amazon refused to accept the application, arguing that it did not believe that voluntary recognition 'was an appropriate path for its business'. The CAC concluded that membership density was just under 36 per cent and that this constituted evidence that there was a likelihood that a majority of workers would be in favour of statutory recognition. As a consequence, a ballot in line with the recognition procedure opened in June 2024, with results expected after this book went to press. However, since this decision was announced the GMB has claimed that Amazon has used a range of strategies to persuade workers to vote against recognition (Smythe, 2024). This has included the introduction of a 'one click to quit tool' whereby a QR code is widely publicised through which workers can automatically email the GMB to end their membership.

Even within those workplaces which recognise trade unions, there has been a clear trend towards more individualised approaches to employment relations. Brown et al (2008: 354) noted in their analysis of the WERS series of surveys (up to 2004) that 'there has been a fundamental shift in attitudes, towards individualism and away from collectivism'. This would appear to be continuing. For example, there was a small but significant reduction in the proportion of employees who felt that their managers were in favour of union membership between 2004 and 2011. Notably, some of the biggest sectoral reductions were in the public sector, in areas such as public administration, health and education (van Wanrooy et al, 2013).

While this does not appear to have been reflected in any reduction in the scope of the issues that managers negotiate with trade unions, the picture is very different in the private sector. In 2013, van Wanrooy et al reported that in private sector workplaces in which trade unions were recognised, the scope of issues that were subject to bargaining had narrowed substantially, with the mean number of items over which they negotiated falling from 1.6 to 1.1. They argued that:

> these findings on the scope of collective bargaining in the private sector are reminiscent of those in earlier WERS studies (for example, Millward et al, 2000) in suggesting that formal recognition of unions for pay bargaining may often resemble a 'hollow shell' in which unions and their members have little influence over the setting of terms and conditions (van Wanrooy et al, 2013: 82).

Reflective activity 4.3

Why do you think that Amazon is fighting against the unionisation of its sites in the UK? Do you think that this is a sustainable strategy and what are the potential risks of responding in this way?

4.5 The changing roles of employers' associations

Employers' associations, like unions, have seen their influence fade in recent years. In 1983 there were 375 employers' associations, but by 2019 this had shrunk to just 54. This is largely a result of mergers but also reflects the contraction of industry-wide, multi-employer bargaining. The individualisation of the management of employment relations has also been reflected in the changing role of employers' associations. Employers' associations are voluntary, private bodies which exist to provide information and co-ordination in areas of common interest.

Nevertheless, employers' associations play a number of key roles in managing employment relations, although the nature and importance of their work in this area has changed significantly in recent years (Gooberman et al, 2018). In particular, a systematic review of the most cited publications on employer associations (Demougin et al, 2019) revealed that their traditional role in collective bargaining with trade unions has fundamentally reduced. This reflects, as we have seen, the commensurate decline in the influence of trade unions and in particular the erosion of multi-employer bargaining.

For employers' associations like the Local Government Association (LGA), which has traditionally negotiated pay at national level in respect of local authority workers, it also represents a major change. The LGA acts as the voice of the local government sector and as an authoritative and effective advocate on its behalf, covering 414 local authorities across England and Wales. Like all employers' associations, a major function of the LGA is to lobby national government over issues relevant to its members. In regard to employment relations, although collective bargaining on behalf of its members is still part of its remit, it now plays a much wider 'consultancy' role. For example, the LGA has an employment relations unit that:

> provides comprehensive advice on all aspects of employment relations and practices. Our employment law and policy advisers keep authorities up-to-date on the human resources implications of new legislation and case law developments (Local Government Association, 2024).

As this suggests, increasingly, employers' associations, rather than bargaining collectively, provide their members with the support and information to bargain individually. Many of them therefore provide a commercial employment relations service which offers members advice and support on wage rates and conditions of employment, disciplinary procedures, redundancy procedures and even representation at employment tribunals. Most employers' organisations also provide employee relations information services. Prominently featured in such information are pay and benefits data, based on regularly conducted surveys, which are useful for salary and pay comparisons and in local negotiations.

As the collective bargaining role of employers' associations has been eroded there has been greater emphasis on political lobbying and representing the interests of their members, for instance, in influencing government in terms of labour and employment legislation. Similarly, employers' associations have continued to expand the provision of services to their members, often relating to individual rather than collective issues and cases. Key provision includes: guidance and providing an industry standard of good practice for equality, diversity and inclusion, legal services, training and development of staff and advice on HRM issues.

The Engineering Employers' Federation, now trading as Make UK, provides a wide range of business support services. The EEF can help members negotiate with unions, respond to recognition demands or mediate in the event of a dispute. Other services include:

- Health and safety
- Legal services
- Discipline, grievance and disputes
- Employee relations
- Mediation
- Organisational change
- Performance management
- Restrictive covenants
- Employee engagement
- HR documentation
- Pay and reward
- Resources and recruitment
- Workforce planning.

In some ways, it could be argued that the growing business consultancy role of employers' associations represents a marketisation of the HR function within the public sector. It is also another potent indication of the erosion of institutional employment relations and its replacement with a fragmented and individualised system dominated by concerns over legal compliance.

REAL-WORLD EXAMPLE 4.3

Employers' association views on trade union legislation

As discussed in Chapter 3, the Trade Union Act 2016 was introduced by the Conservative government and was designed to regulate union activity. It was highly controversial, and employers' groups had a variety of views on the initial proposals contained in the Trade Union Bill.

1. Confederation of British Industry

Business group the CBI welcomed what it called 'a modernisation of our outdated industrial relations laws'. Deputy director-general Katja Hall said:

> The introduction of thresholds is an important, but fair, step to ensure that strikes have the clear support of the workforce.
>
> Placing time limits on ballot mandates is an important measure to ensure industrial action is limited to the original dispute and not extended to other matters.

SOURCE: https://www.personneltoday.com/hr/trade-union-bill-introduced-anger-unions/ [accessed 1 July 2024]

2. Engineering Employers Federation

The EEF was more cautious. In a news release discussing the inclusion of the reforms in the Queen's Speech in 2015, Tim Thomas, head of employment policy, argued for:

> a measured legislative approach. This needs to balance the objectives of ensuring that ballots properly reflect the views of all trade union members, and provide a mandate for timely, specific industrial action, with the unintended potential to undermine the constructive relations that currently exist between trade unions and many employers in the private sector.

3. Welsh Local Government Association

The Welsh Local Government Association, which represents local authority employers in Wales, was highly critical of the trade union reforms, arguing that:

> the Government's proposals were aimed at tackling problems that do not reflect the reality of modern industrial relations in Wales. The number of days lost to strike action has dropped by over 90 per cent in the last twenty years and industrial action today increasingly takes the form of protest action rather than all-out strikes, which makes the legislation even less warranted. As employers, we have disagreements and disputes with the trade unions but we seek to work with them in a mature and responsible manner. The purpose of this Bill however seems to harken back to an outdated 'I'm all right Jack' caricature of the way business is conducted, with a set of proposals on strike laws that are probably unworkable and which represent a deeply unfair curtailing of trade union rights. As such the WLGA is firmly opposed to the introduction of the Trade Union Bill as it is currently drafted.

SOURCE: https://www.wlga.wales/councils-voice-opposition-to-draft-trade-union-bill [accessed 1 October 2019]

 Reflective activity 4.4

Real-world example 4.3 provides the views of three employers' associations on proposals, now contained in the 2016 Trade Union Act, for a threshold for strike ballots. In what way are these views different and what does this suggest about the membership of the three associations and their outlook on employment relations?

4.6 Management styles

In Chapter 5 we discuss the impact that the values and preferences of organisations' dominant management decision-makers can have on strategy formulation. This will in part be determined by whether senior managers approach employment relations with a unitarist or pluralist frame of reference. As we explained in Chapter 2, a unitarist perspective is rooted in the idea that organisations are fundamentally harmonious and integrated, with all employees sharing similar goals and working in a unified way towards a common set of objectives. A pluralist perspective, in contrast, recognises that different groups exist within an organisation and that conflict can, and does, exist between employer and employees (Fox, 1985).

These different perspectives are extremely broad, and it is important to note that an organisation is made up of individuals with a wide variety of complex and nuanced views (Bacon, 2013). That said, organisational philosophies are shaped by the dominant values of its most powerful members. Organisations with a unitarist philosophy can be either authoritarian or paternalistic in their attitudes, and this can have a major impact on management style. Alternatively, organisations that adopt a pluralist approach will tend to embrace collective relationships, and while accepting that conflict will inevitably occur, will emphasise the need to develop co-operative and constructive relations between interest groups. It is this distinction in approach to the management of people that leads to variations in employment relations policies, ranging from the paternalistic non-union approach of Marks & Spencer through to the single-union no-strike philosophy of Japanese firms such as Nissan, or the multi-union sites of companies such as Jaguar Land Rover.

Although external constraints on employment relations policy formulation are an important element, internal limitations are probably of greater significance. Factors that often determine management style are organisational size, ownership and location. Style can be an important determinant in defining employment relations policy and practice and is as much influenced by organisations' leaders as it is by business strategy. In contrast to the notion of leadership traits such as 'paternalistic' or 'autocratic', Dundon and Rollinson usefully define management style as 'a manager's preferred approach to handling employment relations, which reflects the way that he or she exercises authority over subordinates' (2011: 114). From this broad definition, we can (following Purcell and Sisson, 1983), identify different types of styles (see Figure 4.5).

Figure 4.5 Management styles

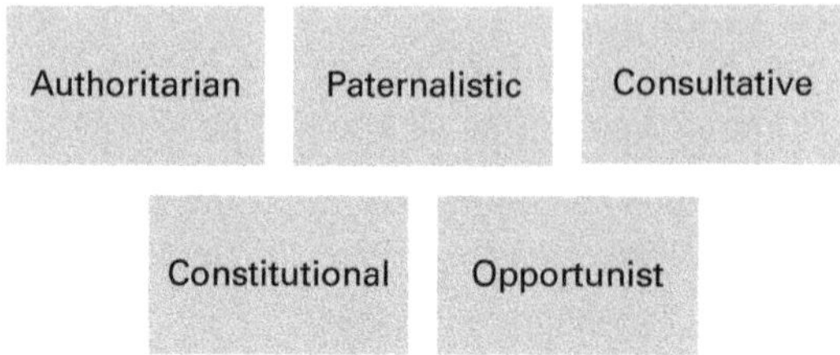

The 'authoritarian' approach sees employment relations as relatively unimportant. Although policies and procedures may exist (for instance, for grievances or discipline), they are often there because of some legislative necessity; as a consequence 'people issues' are not given any priority until something goes wrong. For small firms, the potential for complaints of unfair dismissal (although relatively rare) is a particular concern. This is normally due to the fact that their employment relations processes tend to be less well developed than in larger organisations, who have the luxury of employing HR specialists. As a result they may pay little attention to formally managing the performance of their staff and might be unlikely to record warnings given to a poorly performing employee. They would then find it difficult to defend an employment tribunal claim if that employee was dismissed on the grounds of capability.

'Paternalistic' organisations may share some of the size and ownership characteristics of the authoritarian type, but they tend to have a much more positive attitude towards their employees (as mentioned with respect to Marks & Spencer). Employee consultation is a high priority and staff retention and reward are seen as key issues. The John Lewis Partnership is a good example of an organisation whose constitution includes this type of staff involvement. However, unions will generally be seen as unnecessary as there is a unitarist assumption that the organisation will automatically operate in the best interests of its staff.

'Consultative' organisations may have paternalistic traditions; however, over time they have accepted the development of trade unions and have attempted to develop constructive relationships, working in partnership where possible. Importantly, measures designed to secure employee engagement and individual commitment are emphasised alongside more traditional collective employment relations. In contrast, the type of 'constitutional' organisation described by Purcell and Sisson (1983) assumes an established trade union presence. Managerial approaches are underpinned by a pluralist perspective, but this is often out of necessity rather than design. Strong trade unions mean that managerial prerogative is defended through the negotiation of detailed collective agreements, rules and processes. Consequently, employment relations tend to be adversarial. In the 'opportunist' organisation, management style is determined by local circumstances. These would determine, for example, whether it was appropriate to recognise trade unions or not, or the extent to which employee involvement was encouraged.

Individual and collective dimensions of management style

The traditional focus on types of organisations and associated management styles remains useful but, in reality, managerial approaches rarely fit neatly into the categories of style described here. Purcell (1987: 535) developed a more sophisticated account which suggested that management style has two further dimensions – individualism and collectivism – and that each dimension has three stages. Individualism is concerned with the extent to which policies are directed at individual workers and whether the organisation takes into account the feelings of all its employees and 'seeks to develop and encourage each employee's capacity and role at work'. The three stages in the individual dimension are set out in Figure 4.6.

In the first stage, the employee is treated as a commodity – they are not well regarded and have low job security. As we noted in the previous chapter, this could be seen as reflecting more recent developments in the labour market with the growth of precarity. The second stage sees the employer accepting greater responsibility for the employee and for the development of better working conditions and improved job quality. Finally, the third stage recognises the employee as a valuable resource, requiring investment and nurturing. It could be argued that the current debate about the importance of 'good work' explored in the previous chapter reflects a progression from commodity to resource status.

However, it could also be suggested that experiences of work are also shaped by the orientation of management to the collective. Purcell's collective dimension is set out in Figure 4.7 and reflects the degree to which management policy encourages or discourages employees to have a collective voice.

At the unitary stage, management opposes collective relationships either openly or by covert means. The adversarial stage represents a management focus that is on a stable workplace, where conflict is institutionalised and collective relationships limited to avoiding and resolving disputes. The final, co-operative stage has its focus on constructive relationships and greater openness in the decision-making process. This, it could be argued, is fundamental to delivering sustainable 'good work'.

Dundon and Rollinson (2011: 115) argue that while Fox (1985) better explains 'the attitudes and values of individual managers', the notion of management style 'is a more useful tool to describe an overall approach to employment relations' and thus captures the 'different shades of both unitarism and pluralism within any organisation'. Crucially, management style is both ideological and contingent: managers adopt different styles depending on the wider context and the balance of power that exists within an organisation. Therefore, identifying a particular management style is not just a question of labelling an organisation 'individualist' or 'collectivist'. Purcell

Figure 4.6 Managing the individual

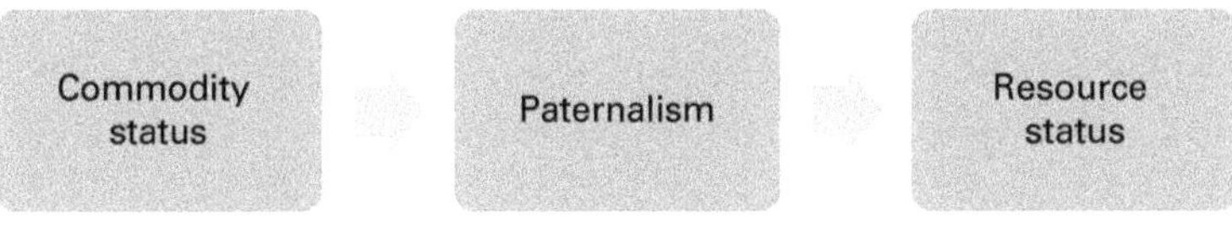

Figure 4.7 Managing the collective

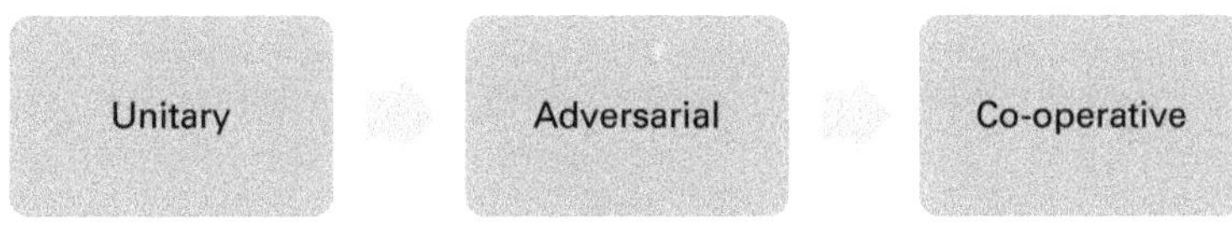

(1987) points out that the interrelationship between the two is complex; simply because an organisation is seen to encourage the rights and capabilities of individuals does not necessarily mean that it is seeking to marginalise any representative group.

Linked to the influence of management style, is the distinction made between management and leadership (Boxall and Purcell, 2022). For instance, Frost and Alidina emphasise that all managers need to understand the importance of inclusivity and their leadership role in its achievement. This means adhering to agreed policy, practice and guidelines. Otherwise, as they further stress, '[if]... those managers don't follow those guidelines – either because they forget or because they actively think they aren't worth it' (2019: 114), then their aims will not be achieved. This shows the key role of the line manager, in this case in relation to equality and diversity.

Conversely, style can be a determinant of how a manager 'manages' an aspect of the people management role. Saundry et al (2022) usefully categorise the different managerial styles or types exhibited when managers handle workplace disputes. Their extensive research suggests that some managers are 'naturals' who have the people skills to effectively manage conflict. Others may seek to 'dodge' the issue, often leading to an escalation of the dispute. 'Rogue' managers are often driven by 'gut feelings' and resist being constrained by policy and procedure. Consequently, HR practitioners often feel a need to restrain their inconsistency. Finally, most new managers, lacking in confidence, are 'dependents', relying heavily on advice and guidance from their HR colleagues. Effective conflict management is a central theme of this book and is revisited in detail in Chapter 9 onwards. Crucially, though, line managers ultimately shape the experiences of work. As the TUC (2019: 4) points out:

> Our line managers, the bosses that we likely have most face-to-face interaction with, have a big impact on our experience of work. We all remember a great line manager who allowed us to be our best. Unfortunately, plenty of us also probably remember a not-so-good line manager who made work miserable, whether intentionally or not. Line management is therefore important whenever we talk about good work.

Reflective activity 4.5

Can you identify the management style that operates within your organisation? What implications does that have for quality of employment relations and the performance of the organisation?

4.7 The growing influence of HRM

In recent years, the approach of many organisations to the management of employment relations has been shaped by the growing influence of human resource management (HRM). It is difficult to see whether the growth of HRM has contributed to a shift away from more pluralistic management styles or whether it is a reflection of the decline of collective employment relations. Either way, there is little doubt that it represents a profound change in the way that organisations consider the management of work and employment. As we discuss in more detail in the next chapter, HRM contends that people management is central to the strategy of the business and consequently implies a re-orientation of practitioners away from a concern with the negotiation and accommodation of collective relationships and towards a closer identification with 'business' objectives and the individual worker or work group.

In this way, people management (and by extension employment relations) is seen as supporting 'bottom-line' objectives by delivering high levels of organisational commitment ('soft' HRM) and cost-efficiency through increased work flexibility ('hard' HRM). While this reflects the contradictory nature of employment relations, the overarching philosophy is essentially a unitarist one; collective relationships and institutions are subordinate to individuals and work groups within the organisation. Therefore, for many employment relations professionals, the onus is on strategies to secure employee engagement rather than to regulate and manage conflict through collective bargaining and consultation.

Of course, within unionised workplaces, HR practitioners and employment relations professionals play a key role in maintaining relationships with union representatives. But for the organisation, as we implied earlier in this chapter, this is often out of necessity rather than choice. Although many employment relations specialists appreciate the importance of positive management–union relations, they may have to convince senior managers and even other colleagues within HR of the benefits. Overall, Williams (2014: 154–55) argues that the predominant model of 'sophisticated HRM and the management of employment relations' is a strategy that seeks to:

- develop a climate where employees feel valued and thus work more effectively;
- put more of a 'fit' between employment policies and the overall business objectives;
- manage employees to enable them to better contribute to overall business goals;
- increase worker commitment through strategies of employee engagement.

It is important to note that this approach is generally based on a preference for weak unions or no unions at all and is, therefore, highly unitarist in nature. If, as it is increasingly argued, more 'people management' tasks are falling within the remit of the line, what then are the implications for effectively managing employment relations in the workplace?

Devolving the management of employment relations

It has been recognised for many years by both employment relations writers and practitioners that a key effect of the rise of HRM has been a transfer of HR duties and responsibilities to the line. In the next chapter we discuss the potential for HR practitioners taking on a more strategic role within the organisation. This in turn is based on the argument that it is more appropriate for first line managers to deal with operational employment relations issues (Ulrich, 1997). Interestingly, it might be suggested that this is nothing new and that managing people has always been a central part of the remit of the line manager (see for example Legge, 2005). Renwick also argues that the people management role of line managers 'seems such a common occurrence in work organisations today that it might be seen as an essential aspect of an HRM-approach to employment relationships' (2013: 264). Line managers have, therefore, played a long-standing role in managing employment relations. The key change, then, is not the centrality of the role played by line managers but the extent to which they undertake these duties without the support of HR specialists or employment relations structures and institutions.

We noted at the start of the chapter that line managers have growing autonomy to make decisions over a range of issues without reference to more senior colleagues or HR. As Table 4.1 shows, there were increases across the board in terms of those duties from 2004 to 2011. Specifically, line managers had increased autonomy in the areas of appraisal, equality issues, grievance, discipline and health and safety. These developments raise several important questions, not least regarding the support available and, in cases where managers lack the knowledge, skills and/or attitude to carry out such duties, how this is addressed (Townsend and Hutchinson, 2017; Bennett et al, 2023).

The degree to which front-line managers themselves have embraced or rather contested this 'new' role is a matter for debate (Whittaker and Marchington, 2003;

Table 4.1 HR issues where decisions can be made at branch sites without consulting managers elsewhere in the organisation

	2004	2011
	%	%
Training of employees	72	78
Performance appraisals	60	74
Staffing plans	66	72
Recruitment and selection	63	68
Health and safety	42	63
Grievances	44	55
Working hours	53	54
Discipline	46	52
Equality and diversity	34	43
Holiday entitlements	25	27
Rates of pay	30	23
Union recognition	17	18
Pensions	12	7
None of these	11	9

SOURCE: van Wanrooy et al (2013)

Renwick, 2013; Townsend and Hutchinson, 2017). Significantly, as Boxall and Purcell (2022) argue, the way in which employees and workers experience and view HR practices is inevitably shaped by the nature of their relationships with their line managers. Furthermore, as we argue in the next chapter, this will influence their engagement and performance. In addition to concerns over the capability of line managers to undertake these tasks, there are questions over their capacity to deliver. Bevan and Cooper (2022) argue that managers face challenges in finding time to manage their teams effectively while also dealing with operational pressure from senior management. As such they represent a 'squeezed middle' in many organisations who need greater support, particularly from HR (Bajorek, 2020).

MANAGERIAL CONFIDENCE – KEY FINDINGS FROM ACAS RESEARCH

Since 2010, Acas has funded a range of projects examining the management of workplace conflict (see Saundry and Wibberley, 2014b; Saundry et al, 2016; Saundry et al, 2019). These have highlighted a lack of managerial confidence and competence in managing people. Findings include:

- Managers tend to be reactive in their approach and are promoted purely for their technical skills and success and not their people management skills – this relates to those that Marchington and Wilkinson term 'reluctant managers' (2012: 171).
- Managers receive inadequate training and development to manage people.
- Lack of confidence, or a propensity linked to their chosen management style, drives many managers to formalise the dispute early rather than to address the issues at an early stage.
- A surface-level informality and collegiality often hides a more autocratic, target-driven and non-empathetic style adopted by the manager.

The management style or strategy of senior managers can have a major influence on the extent to which managers can take time to explore more creative resolutions to problems. Senior management often prioritise short-term targets and objectives at the expense of less tangible goals of good employment relations and effective conflict management.

Purcell and Hutchinson's (2007) research supports these findings, identifying the key link between employee commitment to their organisation and the quality and consistency of HR policy as delivered by their line managers. Boxall et al's (2016) critical review of the literature usefully notes the often-used conceptualisation of the A (ability), M (motivation) and O (opportunity) for line managers to initiate HR policy and practice in the workplace. Despite their observation that the AMO model focuses more on effecting organisational performance than, for instance, employee well-being, this remains a useful framework for us to better understand the role of the first line manager. In sum, this approach emphasises the question of whether all line managers have the time and/or inclination to consistently and effectively implement HR policy. As we have noted, a number of Acas-funded studies have found that operational imperatives can impact negatively on the handling of people issues. In particular, Boxall and Purcell (2022) have highlighted the crucial role that line managers have in the consistent application of HR policy and practice.

Writers have identified several interlinking themes that help inform our understanding of the degree to which 'intended' HRM strategy and policy is implemented (Evans, 2015). For several theorists this turns on the extent to which first line managers have the skills and knowledge, or in the context of AMO, the ability, to successfully enact HR practices (Kellner et al, 2016). For others, effectiveness also depends on the influence of certain 'mediating' factors such as autonomy and opportunity (Boxall et al, 2016).

The conventional wisdom has tended to be that first line managers distrust and dislike HR policy and process. Instead, they prefer less formal ways of dealing with difficult employment relations issues, which provide them with the flexibility to make decisions that reflect the need to meet operational objectives, cultural norms within the workplace or even their own personal beliefs and values (Earnshaw et al, 2000; Rollinson, 2000; Dunn and Wilkinson, 2002; Franklin and Pagan, 2006). For example, a line manager may decide to take a lenient approach with a popular member of their team who is guilty of an act of misconduct because disciplinary action could undermine morale. For HR practitioners this raises the spectre of procedural inconsistency, legal challenge and more fundamental problems of equity, with equally negative implications for engagement and productivity, even to the extent, as suggested from recent survey results, of senior HR specialists fearing 'maverick, lower-level line managers taking unexpected actions [which] creates a pressure for control' (Brookes and Brewster, 2022: 161). This, it can be argued, only serves to deepen the sense among line managers of HR as a bureaucratic constraint (Guest and King, 2004). Thus, they become what Townsend et al (2022) term the 'victim' of HRM implementation. In contrast, when line managers believe that they have sufficient 'agency' and 'policy enactment capacity' they can be 'masters' of that implementation.

Similarly, Evans's (2015) research in the retail sector found that there was a gap between the intended role of first line managers in handling HR issues and the reality. Confusion over the extent of delegation, a lack of monitoring of line managerial activity and the absence of support from more senior managers contributed to this problem. However, this was rooted in the tensions inherent in the role of first line managers, who are often faced with competing demands. For example, a line manager may be under pressure to reduce cost and therefore to adopt a 'hard approach' to the management of HR issues. At the same time, they may be expected to improve service quality, which requires engaged and committed staff. Balancing these priorities, particularly where there are few incentives to implement policies in a consistent way, is particularly challenging. For many line managers the extra burden of people management duties causes 'role overload' when added to their operational tasks and crucially the 'role ambiguity' of seeking to maintain their 'right to manage' while also on occasion needing to seek the support of HR colleagues to achieve that aim (Evans, 2017).

Barriers to devolution – HR and the 'line'

Reporting more than 40 years ago on his research into line managers and employment relations, Smith (1983: 43) argued that managers then, as now, fought to protect their 'right to manage'. He concluded at the time that managers felt that specialist (HR/personnel) colleagues could often wrongly give concessions – certainly to trade unions – that undermined their authority. This illustrates a tension between the approach and the concerns of HR practitioners and operational managers, which remains evident today and represents a substantial barrier to the effective devolution of people management responsibilities.

More recently, Marchington and Wilkinson (2012) have identified a number of criticisms made by many managers of their HR colleagues. It is important here to stress that HR practitioners face the difficult task of reconciling some of the criticisms listed here, rightly or wrongly, while also satisfying the demand for their services still expected by those same managers.

Reflective activity 4.6

Marchington and Wilkinson's (2012) research found that line managers had a number of negative perceptions of HR practitioners:

- HR is out of touch with commercial realities.
- HR constrains the autonomy of line managers to make decisions.
- HR is 'slow to act' and always wanting to check options.
- HR creates procedures that appear sound in theory but are hard to apply in practice.

Do you think that these criticisms are fair? What could HR practitioners do to challenge these perceptions?

Whittaker and Marchington's (2003) study both compounds and, in part, contradicts these criticisms, offering evidence that many line managers actually found it difficult to find sufficient time to carry out HR duties when focusing primarily on more immediate business goals. Perceptions of HR will also be shaped by the outcomes of people management actions and in particular their impact on notions of fairness, efficiency and performance (Evans, 2015; Vermeeren, 2014). In fact, Cunningham and Hyman (1999) found that line managers welcome HR advice and guidance, while other studies have suggested that managers welcome the 'cover' and certainty provided by procedure (Cooke, 2006; Cole, 2008).

It should also be said that HR practitioners are often equally critical of line managers, often pointing to an inability to resolve problems through informal discussion (CIPD, 2007). There is equal scepticism of the capabilities of higher management, with HR practitioners surveyed by the CIPD in 2016 reporting that only 50 per cent of senior leaders were effective in managing difficult conversations and 38 per cent were effective in conflict management (CIPD, 2016). Line managers often do not fully appreciate that HR policy and practice, and employment rights in particular, need to be upheld, particularly when they appear to be in conflict with business goals. Moreover, they may not see, for instance, the importance of recognising the representative rights of trade unions or of acting consistently across the organisation.

Furthermore, the concerns of line managers contain a fundamental paradox; they want to have greater autonomy and flexibility but at the same time they want clearer and more detailed guidance from HR practitioners. In some ways this crystallises the problem of line managerial capability. On one hand, line managers who lack confidence in dealing with difficult issues will inevitably opt to retreat to the safety of process and procedure (Saundry et al, 2016). On the other hand, unless HR practitioners trust line managers to act in a way which is fair and consistent, they will be reluctant to give them the space to use their discretion.

Therefore, there is a need to 'clarify and delineate line management's role in HRM implementation' (Op de Beeck et al, 2016: 1914). Crucially, for Saundry et al (2021) a key moderating factor in this relationship is the degree of 'proximity' of HR. For instance, geographical distance between HR and the line managers and employees they support can lead to HR becoming disconnected, making it much harder to build high-trust relationships with managers. However, the trend towards functional specialisation can also reduce cognitive and social proximity between employment relations specialists and other key stakeholders, resulting in the progressive marginalisation of employment relations.

This disengagement can be further exacerbated by what Op de Beeck et al (2016) term 'perceptual discrepancy' in HR's estimation of the capacity and capability of the managers they advise. From the perspective of the line manager, Kehoe and Han (2020: 112) highlighted a more complex dynamic in the devolution of HR to the line:

> As an alternative to simply acting as implementers of HR practices, line managers may adapt an organization's HR practices – or replace them with entirely different HR practices altogether – to achieve congruence between their capabilities, the surrounding environment, and their management activities. In so doing, line managers may become the source of variance not only in HRM process – but also in the content of HR practices within and across organizations.

Consequently, it is important that HR not only support line managers but also actively develop their skills, knowledge and confidence (Bos-Nehles et al, 2013; Trullen et al, 2016). However, there can be a tendency for HR practitioners to regulate and control managerial actions. Fisher et al (2017) found that scripts, checklists and flowcharts were commonly used in the management of disciplinary and grievance issues to make sure that managers operated in a consistent manner. While this ensured a degree of legal and procedural compliance, it inevitably limited managerial discretion and curtailed informal and creative approaches to conflict resolution.

Contemporary developments in relationships between HR and managers

The relationship between HR practitioners and line managers is also shaped by changing context. Monks and Conway (2022) argued that in the wake of the Covid pandemic, line managers have had to become 'hands-on' in the face of new models of hybrid and remote working, which in turn has added to pressures on their own time.

This has the potential to lead to further tension between line managers and their HR colleagues in relation to the devolution of people tasks. Moreover, the growth of AI and the increasing use of algorithmic HRM control can result in workers feeling even more isolated as such automation replaces the support and feeling of value they seek from their line manager (Duggan et al, 2023). This development could have major implications for devolution, as algorithms reduce the need for decision-making by managers and HR (Monks and Conway, 2022). However, it is also possible that the application of AI tools for more routine people management tasks could free up managers, providing more space to develop a coaching role with a focus on protecting the well-being of staff (Drent et al, 2022).

Reflective activity 4.7

To what degree do first line managers in your organisations have autonomy in the interpretation and delivery of HR policy? To what extent has this been a positive or negative outcome of devolution?

More generally, Kim and Kehoe (2022) assess and conceptualise the degree to which first line managers have the ability, motivation and opportunity (AMO) to implement devolved HR policy. They note that HR duties still play a relatively small part of a manager's recognised workload. Consequently, the role that they play in managing people can be under-appreciated and unrewarded by organisations. To complement this analysis, Roy Bannya and Bainbridge (2022) have usefully applied social exchange theory (SET) to demonstrate that the efficacy of the devolved role of the manager will turn on the relationship between them and their staff. In particular, this reflects how they and their teams assess the level of reciprocity in terms of the two parties' desired outcomes from the employment relationship. Significantly, in their research on the state of employment relations in the NHS, Bennett et al (2023) reach a similar conclusion, emphasising the need for the line manager to have the requisite capability, in terms of skills and knowledge, the capacity, in terms of the time to devote to HR, and therefore the confidence to effectively carry out the role. Crucially, as we stress elsewhere, it is also vital that people management capability becomes central to the recruitment and career development of managers, moving away from a focus on technical or operational expertise.

In closing this section, we note tentative evidence that organisations are beginning to realise the need to give front-line managers the skills to deal with the new tasks they are expected to take on (Kellner et al, 2016). One organisation that has recognised the key role of training and development in equipping its managers with the skills and knowledge to effectively manage the employment relationship is Aspire Technology Solutions, an IT-managed service and cyber security provider in the UK. In 2024, it developed and launched a managers' training programme which is outlined in Real-world example 4.4.

REAL-WORLD EXAMPLE 4.4

The Aspire leadership academy: setting definitive standards of management and leadership

Aspire specialises in cyber security, IT support, cloud management, high-speed connectivity and voice/unified communications. Recognising the central role of the line manager in achieving this mission, the company's Learning and Development team designed a bespoke programme of modules for managers across the organisation focusing on:

- An introduction to management
  - Understanding and utilising appropriate management and leadership styles; delegating tasks; the role and responsibilities of line managers
- Developing self-awareness
  - Communication skills, emotional intelligence; managing difficult conversations
- Building high-performing teams
  - Staff motivation, coaching and team development
- Strategic management
  - Time management, continual improvement and innovation
- Recruitment and resourcing
  - Recruitment good practice; talent development
- Inclusive management
  - Equality, diversity and inclusion, well-being and mental health.

Adopting a blended approach, the training incorporates a combination of pre-learning resources through e-learning and podcasts, monthly two-hour workshops and on-the-job learning with coaching when required.

The key objectives of the programme include:

- Empowering teams and individuals to innovate
- Higher staff retention and better-skilled colleagues
- Highly productive and efficient teams
- Enhanced customer experience leading to business growth.

Reflective activity 4.8

Reflecting on your own experiences, identify the key knowledge, skills and attitude needed for line managers to effectively manage employment relations in your organisation. Justify your choices. To what extent are 'soft' skills – such as emotional intelligence, empathy and listening skills – appropriate for effective line management? As an HR practitioner, how can you ensure that these can be developed?

4.8 Summary

The management of people cannot be seen as a neutral activity and particularly the style adopted by line managers has fundamental implications for the quality of employment relations, engagement and organisational performance. Management style is influenced by many factors, including the nature of the organisation and the sector it is in, the culture of the organisation and the preferences, to a degree, of individual managers.

Managers in the UK have, at best, had an ambivalent attitude towards trade unions and collective regulation of labour. While they have traditionally operated within a system of employment relations informed by a pluralist perspective, their own outlook tends to be unitarist. In recent years, the contextual changes outlined in the first part of this book have provided conditions in which managers have increasingly been able to dictate the terms on which employment relations are conducted. This has seen the progressive erosion of collective bargaining and the joint regulation of pay and conditions and the promotion of direct strategies of communication and involvement. Weak attempts by government to provide a statutory underpinning for union recognition have had limited success and have failed to arrest the charge towards more individualised employment relations.

In this context, the importance of the role played by line managers is brought into stark focus and has been accentuated by attempts to devolve greater responsibility for the management of employment relations. This presents HR practitioners with both conceptual and practical challenges. They have to respect the autonomy of the line manager at the same time as trying to ensure equity and consistency of outcomes across the organisation. Linked to this is the clear need to ensure that all managers have the appropriate knowledge, skills and attitude to effectively manage all aspects of the employment relationship. The evidence suggests that this is not always the case, but there are tentative signs that organisations are realising the importance of the acquisition and utilisation of 'soft' skills such as negotiation, listening, persuasion and questioning.

Nonetheless, if HR is to attain a more strategic role, it should not be seen merely as a means of cost-cutting or outsourcing and/or centralising HR services. Rather, the aim must be for HR to work closely with first line managers to effectively carry out those devolved people management tasks. To this end, we would argue that, in addition to developing frontline management capability, there is also a recognition that the role is impacted by role conflict, culture influences and the identity construction of the holder (Watson, 1995). Therefore, HR needs to acknowledge the aspirations and expectations of the new manager and make clear what the role involves. Fundamentally, in order to avoid what Townsend and Hutchinson (2017) have termed the 'accidental manager', organisations need to ensure that promotion is not based solely on a candidate's operational excellence or that they are merely 'the next person in line'. However, as we go on to explore in the following chapters, developing the employment relations competencies of line managers will have little impact unless broader organisational approaches provide a consistent context in which these newfound skills and attitudes can be utilised.

KEY LEARNING POINTS

- The management of employment relations has been transformed in the last 30 years. We have seen the rapid and progressive erosion of collective bargaining and joint regulation and the growth of individualised approaches and practices designed to secure employee commitment and engagement.
- Attempts by government to provide statutory support for union recognition have been half-hearted and have had limited impact to date.
- Management style is not only shaped by the individual preferences of managers but by the context of the organisation, its culture and the balance of workplace power. Recent years have seen a clear shift from collective to individual styles.
- Responsibility for the management of employment relations has been increasingly devolved to line managers. There are clear tensions between the desire of line managers for flexibility and autonomy and the obligations of HR practitioners to promote consistency and organisational integrity.
- There are significant doubts as to whether line managers have the necessary skills, knowledge and, therefore, confidence to manage employment relations effectively. In addition, they operate in a context in which operational imperatives crowd out less tangible, but nonetheless important, objectives of fairness, equity and trust.

Review Questions

1. Critically explain the concept of management style in the context of employment relations.
2. What have been the main changes to the scale and scope of collective bargaining in the UK? What does this suggest about the way in which management styles have changed, and are changing, in the UK?
3. Your organisation is a small-to-medium-sized firm and has recently been approached by a union that claims that it has over 50 per cent membership in a particular bargaining unit in your organisation. Senior leaders in your organisation are not that keen to recognise a union. However, the union is talking about going to the Central Arbitration Committee. What advice would you give to the leadership team and what actions do you need to take in preparation for the case going to the CAC?
4. You have been invited to give a talk entitled 'avoiding the accidental manager' at a one-day workshop organised by the local branch of the CIPD on the skills, knowledge, capacity and confidence front-line managers need to effectively manage employment relations in the workplace. Outline, with appropriate evidence, what you would include in your talk.
5. What are the main tensions in the relationship between HR practitioners and line managers? What can HR practitioners do to resolve these issues?

Explore further

Chartered Management Institute (2023) *Taking Responsibility – Why UK PLC needs better managers*. Available from: https://www.managers.org.uk/wp-content/uploads/2023/10/CMI_BMB_GoodManagment_Report.pdf (archived at https://perma.cc/XDL8-M85H). [accessed 21 May 2024].

Saundry, R, Fisher, V, and Kinsey, S (2021) Disconnected Human Resource? Proximity and the (mis)management of workplace conflict, *Human Resource Management Journal*, **31** (2), pp 476–92

Townsend, K, Bos-Nehles, A and Jiang, K (2022) *Research Handbook on Line Managers*, Edward Elgar Publishing, Cheltenham.

TUC (2019) *Improving Line Management: Why better line management will help improve work for everyone*, TUC Publications, London.

Websites

www.cbi.org.uk (archived at https://perma.cc/JBE8-43Z2) – the website of the Confederation of British Industry.

www.managers.org.uk (archived at https://perma.cc/M9DA-CUGZ) – the website of the Chartered Management Institute which contains a range of up-to-date policy and research relating to management in the UK.

www.gov.uk/government/organisations/central-arbitration-committee (archived at https://perma.cc/4TVV-NTP6) – the website for the Central Arbitration Committee which provides information on the union recognition process and details of current cases.

05 Employment relations strategy, employee engagement and voice

Overview

The chapter is divided into three parts. The first part deals with the formulation of an organisation's strategy, concentrating on the main elements of business strategy, the levels at which strategic decision-making takes place – the corporate level, the business-unit level and the levels appropriate to the different functions of the business – and the 'fit' between an organisation's activities and its resources. The focus then turns to the associated employment policies necessary to achieve those strategic objectives. The second part of the chapter is concerned with exploring the nature of employee engagement, particularly asking with whom, and in what, employees are engaged. Evidence in relation to the extent of employee engagement is then assessed. A crucial aspect of this chapter is to identify the conditions under which engagement can be developed. MacLeod and Clarke's influential 'enablers of engagement' model is examined, and the factors that they argue underpin employee engagement – leadership, engaging managers, employee voice and organisational integrity – are discussed. Next, we consider the barriers to engagement with a focus on the critical role played by managerial attitudes and behaviours. The third and final part of the chapter discusses the nature and practice of employee voice as a key element of employment relations and engagement strategy.

LEARNING OUTCOMES

When you have completed this chapter, you should be able to:

- understand what strategy is, and analyse the ways in which strategic choices are shaped by the values, preferences and power of those who are the principal decision-makers;
- explain and evaluate the link between organisational, HRM and employment relations strategies;
- examine and critically analyse the link between employee engagement and organisational performance;
- critically assess the techniques and processes designed to secure employee engagement;
- identify and explain specific employee involvement and participation practices and critically assess their importance and impact within the overarching concept of employee voice;
- develop an informed view as to the appropriate employee involvement and participation practices for different organisational contexts;
- describe the main barriers to securing employee engagement.

5.1 Introduction

The link between HR strategy and organisational performance is complex and difficult to define (Marchington and Wilkinson, 2012; Armstrong, 2021). As Keith Sisson and John Purcell (2010) have pointed out, the 'holy grail' of a convincing causal link has been frustratingly elusive. In addition, as Bratton et al (2022: 104) conclude, 'critics argue that the effectiveness of strategic choices in HR is difficult to measure due to the problem of quantifying the HR and performance variables and meeting the criteria of causality'. Some might say, unsurprisingly then, that the take-up of more strategic approaches to HRM and employment relations has been relatively slow. Existing evidence suggests that employment relations is rarely included in formal organisational strategy or even seen as a strategic issue (van Wanrooy et al, 2013; Saundry et al, 2019).

Nevertheless, as we will demonstrate in this chapter, strategy remains crucial for effective employee relations and, despite the plethora of research into the link between HR and performance, one of the most difficult tasks facing HR professionals is opening the minds of their management colleagues to adopting more strategic approaches to managing people. That is why, in this book, great emphasis is laid on the need to gain commitment from senior management colleagues to employment relations initiatives. This often rests on constructing a convincing 'business case', which relates specific policies and practices to quantifiable outcomes. However, this can be challenging, as shown by the difficulties in demonstrating a clear connection between HRM and improved performance. For example, although most practitioners would agree 'good employment relations' underpins high levels of engagement and productivity, this is not easy to evidence.

It is significant that the NHS, the largest employer in the UK, clearly sees 'workforce' issues as a strategic priority. Its long-term workforce plan, published in 2023, is committed to changing the culture of the organisation with a greater focus on well-being to reduce the number of staff leaving the services by up to 130,000 over the next 15 years (NHS England, 2023). However, planned actions like this are made even more difficult by the changing context within which employment relations strategies are framed and delivered. Crucially, that context includes dealing with external crises, such as the Covid pandemic. This had a fundamental impact in reshaping the organisation of work with a continuing growth of home and hybrid working. However, as David Spencer has argued, it created 'new dangers for those in work' with key workers like those in the NHS 'required to work excessive hours and under conditions that present direct harms to their health' (Spencer, 2022: 7).

In addition, although they played a key role during the pandemic, the erosion of trade union organisation and influence means that employer–union relationships are no longer the prime consideration in many workplaces. This may lead some senior managers (including HR practitioners) to consider that employment relations is no longer important and is essentially concerned with transactional as opposed to strategic activities. Therefore, employment relations professionals will need to develop creative, and often patient, approaches to building support for locating employment relations at the heart of organisational strategy. Crucially there is a strong case for this – as we argued in Chapter 3, unions remain the main source of employee voice in many parts of the economy. It is also possible that the election of a Labour government in 2024 could boost union organisation and influence. Consequently, developing high-trust relationships between unions and managers is vital in securing employee engagement and in minimising the damage that can be caused by workplace conflict. However, this does not happen by accident – good employment relations are a function of clear strategic choices and effective implementation.

Reflective activity 5.1

How can employment relations contribute to wider organisational strategies? How would you convince senior managers of the need to locate employment relations at the centre of their strategic priorities?

5.2 What is strategy?

The origin of the concept can be traced back in military history to the Greek word for an army commander, *stratēgos*, and there remain many definitions of strategy. In the context of public or private organisations, it reflects the way that senior managers lead the organisation or business in a particular direction (Boxall and Purcell, 2022). One of the most comprehensive and detailed texts on strategy is the work of Whittington et al (2023), who offer a critical understanding of what corporate strategy is and why strategic decisions are important. They view corporate strategy in two ways – as a matter of economic analysis and planning, and as a matter of organisational decision-making within a social, political and cultural process. Drawing on these key characteristics, we offer the following definition to frame the discussion in the context of this chapter:

> Strategy is the direction and scope of an organisation over the long term, which achieves advantage for the organisation through its configuration of resources within a changing environment, to meet the needs of markets and to fulfil stakeholder expectations.

Functional-level strategy

Functional-level strategy is concerned with how the different functions of the organisation translate corporate-level strategies into operational aims. In HR terms, this suggests that there may be a clear alignment between business and HR strategy. Figure 5.1 shows how this leads to the formulation of an employment relations strategy. That is, business strategy drives HRM strategy, which in turn drives employment relations strategy. Practices and policies that regulate the employment relationship are then derived from this process.

Once we have reached down to this level of strategy, it is important that the various functions (including HRM) consider how they develop their own strategy and how this fits with the rest of the organisation.

Reflective activity 5.2

What external factors over the next five years are likely to impact on corporate strategy within your own organisation? How will these impact specifically on your employment relations strategy?

Figure 5.1 Strategic employment relations management: an overview

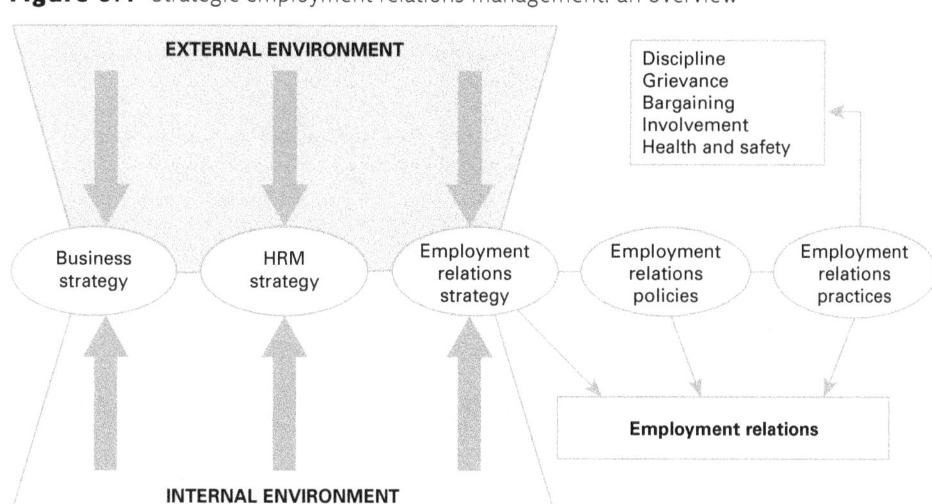

People strategy

One aspect of strategy concerns the match between an organisation's activities and its resources. Those resources may be physical, such as buildings or plant, or people. As seen in Figure 5.1, a key aim of HRM is to achieve strategic integration within the broader objectives of the organisation. However, difficulties exist in making this happen. Some of the main barriers are:

- the size and complexity of large organisations and the different people management needs of their constituent parts;
- the people strategy of most SMEs can and will differ;
- the changing nature of business strategy;
- the absence of a strictly defined business strategy;
- the qualitative nature of HR policies and consequent tensions with the quantifiable objectives of the business;
- the incompatibility between the short-term financial goals of many organisations and HR policies.

Against this backdrop, HRM strategists and writers have sought to capture a model through which HRM can conceptualise and practically address these barriers (Ulrich, 1997; Ulrich and Brockbank, 2005; Boxall and Purcell, 2022; Armstrong, 2021).

'Best fit' and 'best practice'

The first two models, while common in many organisations, differ in their overall approach. Both seek to highlight the central contribution that HR policies can make to business strategy. Best fit, however, is based on a contingent view that the strategic needs of the business can vary and so an 'it depends' perspective should be adopted by practitioners. To this end, best fit is based on:

- a vertical integration between the organisation's strategy and HRM policies and practices;
- the link between business strategy and performance of every individual in the organisation being central to that 'fit';
- the assumption that organisations are more efficient when they achieve fit compared with when there is no fit.

In contrast, best practice is premised on the view that there is a 'bundle' of HRM policies and practices that, when marshalled together in any organisation, can make an effective contribution to its overall business strategy. It offers a common set of practices for all organisations in terms of:

- selective hiring
- employment security
- self-managed teams or teamworking
- high pay, contingent on company performance
- extensive training
- reduction of status differences
- sharing information.

The emphasis in best practice is to achieve both vertical and horizontal integration throughout the organisation, through the framework of an 'internally consistent set of HR practices' (Marchington and Wilkinson, 2012). The issue with best practice, however, is that it implies that there is one best way, in contrast to the other models reviewed in this section which clearly argue that HR strategy, given its many variables, is contingent in nature.

Resource-based strategy

While acknowledging the need to integrate HR policy and practice in the formulation of business strategy, a resource-based view (RBV) focuses more on the specific skills and knowledge of an organisation's workforce, and the added value that 'uniqueness' can bring in terms of competitive advantage. There is little doubt that this approach has become extremely influential (Wright and Ulrich, 2017). For proponents of RBV the focus is on the internal resources of the organisation, rather than analysing performance in terms of external context. In addition, people are viewed as strategic assets, and competitive advantage is gained and sustained through the development of that 'human capital'. Importantly, this is seen as unique – human resources are therefore not only valuable, but they are rare and inimitable. Therefore, the focus is on how organisations can develop strategies which both recognise and make the most of these attributes and build and maintain unique, enviable clusters of human assets (see Chapters 3 and 4 of Boxall and Purcell (2022) for an excellent critical in-depth discussion on the relative merits and limitations of best fit, best practice and RBV).

In contrast to the resource-based approach, an organisation can choose to adopt a 'hard' HRM approach. Rather than focus on the 'inimitability' of the employees, competitive advantage is seen as being better achieved through financial efficiencies, where people are viewed as any other factor of production and as a cost to be minimised wherever possible. Making the business case for a strategy based on an RBV or 'soft' HRM approach, when appropriate, remains a key challenge for all practitioners. Significantly, in this context, a global study by Sadun et al (2017), which examines the link between management practices and productivity, suggests that properly funded and sustained management development and training produces skills and knowledge in line managers that are not easy for competitors to imitate. Moreover, Shaw's (2021) extensive and critical examination of the literature suggests that RBV remains a valuable concept. While HR practices can be imitated by others, the human capital resources that underpin the notion of RBV are far harder to replicate.

Reflective activity 5.3

To what degree does your organisation adopt a best fit, best practice or resource-based view of people management? Which approach are you more persuaded by and why?

Ulrich and the rise of the 'business partner'

Whichever model is adopted, HR functions within organisations are increasingly expected to demonstrate how they can 'add value to the business'. Our final model, driven by writers such as Ulrich (1997) and Ulrich and Brockbank (2005), argues for a greater awareness of the need for clear HR strategies that are aligned to business strategies. Crucially, it calls for HR to transform itself into a more focused 'business partner' that can provide line managers with clear advice and information. The main elements of their model are set out in Table 5.1.

It is notable that this model seeks to capture the key roles that HR practitioners can play, both as a strategic partner to senior management and as an operational support to line managers and staff in terms of the practical achievement of that strategy. With respect to employment relations strategy, Ulrich and Brockbank appear to recognise the key contribution HR practitioners can make in representing the views and interests of employees, through their role as an employee champion or advocate.

According to the CIPD (2013a), the 'business partner' model is the most commonly adopted HR service delivery model. Moreover, it has been argued that the idea of the strategic business partner has become central to the contemporary identity of HR professionals (Wright, 2008; Pritchard, 2010; Keegan and Francis, 2010). However, this is interpreted in very different ways. In some organisations it may simply be a title conferred on senior HR managers, while in others it reflects a more fundamental shift to a more strategic orientation. Furthermore, the notion of business partners and the Ulrich model itself on which they are based have been increasingly challenged (Stephens, 2015). It could be argued that the development of business partner models has been used in some respects to justify a reduction in HR resource, removing 'on-site' practitioners and creating a more centralised HR function on the basis that this will inculcate a more strategic approach and force operational managers to take responsibility for people management.

This has important consequences for the place of employment relations within HR strategy. However the business partner model is enacted, it represents a fundamental shift away from HR professionals balancing the interests of the employer and employees (Francis and Keegan, 2006) towards a singular focus on corporate objectives. Indeed, recent research into the roles played by HR practitioners in the management of workplace conflict has questioned whether practitioners see themselves as 'employee advocates' at all. Furthermore, it suggests that the predominant result of the adoption of business partner models has been to create a more distanced and remote HR function which is less able to develop and maintain the relationships necessary for more nuanced, creative and informal approaches to conflict resolution (Saundry et al, 2021).

Table 5.1 Models of HRM styles

Mid 1990s	Mid 2000s – present day
Admin expert	➢ *Functional expert*
Employee champion	➢ *Employee advocate*
Agent for change	➢ *Human capital developer*
Strategic partner	➢ *Leader*

SOURCE: Ulrich (1997) and Ulrich and Brockbank (2005)

Interestingly, Ulrich (2015) himself subsequently, emphasised that 'the new HR operating model' needs to be more about relationships than partners (see also Balogun et al, 2014). Similarly, Perry Timms (2018: 122) calls for the need to 'transform' the Ulrich model and for HR business partners to become 'neo-generalists', encapsulating 'the brilliance of people who happen to have more than one area of expertise and a range of capability'. The urgency for a change in people management strategy is further evidenced in results from a recent survey of senior HR managers who do not believe that many business partners have the skills needed for the HR challenges of the future (Mitchell, 2023). Interestingly, this presents a parallel to the theme of having the right line managers in place that we discussed in the previous chapter. Similarly, we also need the right business partners in place to effectively support those managers.

To this end, Wright and Ulrich have called for a multi-level approach to strategic HRM, including greater focus on the perception of the individual employee of HRM policy and practice. As they argue:

> Each practice affects individuals who perceive the practice, evaluate the practice, and react to the practice affectively and behaviorally... so the link between the organization-level practice and organization-level performance must take place through individuals (Wright and Ulrich, 2017: 53).

Similarly, Jiang et al (2022) argue that strategic HRM would benefit from the insight realised through the multiple lens of the unitarist, pluralist and radical perspectives we discussed in Chapter 2. They point out that conventional approaches have tended to foreground managerial, and largely unitarist perspectives, marginalising the experiences of employees. It could be argued that one way of reorienting strategy to focus on employee experience is to place employee well-being at the centre (Hesketh and Cooper, 2019). Armstrong also argues that this emphasises the importance of the 'quality of working life of individual employees in terms of their experience of work and how they function there physically, psychologically and socially' (2021: 85). Moreover, Bratton et al (2022) point out that if people are an organisation's most valuable asset their health and wellness must be at the centre of strategy. Of course, it is also important to take a broad view of employee well-being which includes issues of organisational justice – the way in which workers are treated by their managers and the extent to which the organisation embraces both individual and collective voice.

Employment relations strategy

Having examined the nature of strategy formulation, we now turn to look at how employment relations fits within this process. Whatever means organisations choose for devising their strategy, either at corporate or business level, the design and management of employment policies and processes, it can be argued, will figure prominently in delivering and sustaining business improvement. In addition, the process of change, and its impact on the development of strategy, also presents many challenges for the employment relations professional.

As we discuss in Chapters 4 and 6, there is the issue of trade unions and the provisions for recognition. Where trade unions already exist and are recognised within an organisation, the trends towards individualism, as opposed to collectivism, mean that strategic choices will inevitably be made. For instance, what should be the stance of the organisation in relation to unions, and do alternative or complementary voice mechanisms need to be developed? Where unions are not recognised, the organisation may need to consider how it responds to any requests for recognition.

While context is critical in deciding the strategic response to these issues, providing employees with effective channels of individual and collective voice, is also important. As we argue in Chapter 6, effective structures of representation and high-trust relationships with trade unions can be beneficial in terms of developing employee engagement. This is a central element of any employment relations strategy. However, in addition to facilitating collective voice, organisations will need to ensure that individuals have opportunities to be heard and to participate in decision-making processes. Employment relations professionals will also need to decide how engagement is measured and the means through which low engagement is targeted. We examine employee engagement in greater depth in the next part of this chapter.

In terms of the delivery of employment relations strategy, the line manager has a key role to play. However, this is shaped by the nature of their relationship with HR. As Kim and Kehoe (2022) point out, attention has tended to focus on the ways in which line managers implement HR practice and neglect the fact that they are central to enactment of strategy on the front line. Consequently, the development of managerial capability should itself be a core component of HR and organisational strategy.

Overall, it is important to develop an employment relations strategy that is responsive to the needs of the organisation. It must also provide an overall sense of purpose to the employment relations professional and assist employees to understand where they are going, how they are going to get there, why certain things are happening, and most importantly, the contribution they are expected to make towards achieving the organisational goals (see Boxall and Purcell, 2022). We would argue that a clear employment relations strategy is an essential part of any organisation's overall business and HR policy and practice. Its unique focus, in terms of giving voice to employees, effectively managing conflict, ensuring the health and safety of staff and supporting line managers with devolved tasks, makes a real contribution to the effective performance and well-being of the workforce.

Reflective activity 5.4

Reflecting on your understanding of employment relations strategy, what actions and initiatives would you include in such a strategy and why? Who would you consult on its formation?

5.3 Employee engagement

For many commentators, a key component of an effective employment relations strategy is employee engagement (Bratton et al, 2022). Crucially, there is potentially a significant role for human resource management professionals in most workplaces to drive the engagement agenda at senior and line management level and translate it into everyday reality. Although there is growing evidence of the link between management practices and organisational performance (Sadun et al, 2017), the role of employee engagement in this has not yet been firmly established. For example, Truss et al (2013) warn against attributing improved performance solely to engagement initiatives while ignoring the contribution of 'work intensification' and 'worker compliance'. Furthermore, engagement cannot simply be 'imposed' through top-down mechanisms. Instead, as we shall argue, it is dependent on engaging employees through creating an environment characterised by high levels of support, security and trust. This in turn requires the development of front-line managers who have the skills to communicate with and motivate their staff through effective channels of direct and indirect employee voice.

 Reflective activity 5.5

What does the term 'employee engagement' mean to you in the context of your organisation? What do you think are the key factors that maximise your own engagement with your organisation and with your job?

Defining employee engagement – engaged with whom or what?

Defining employee engagement is not straightforward. MacLeod and Clarke, in their highly influential 2009 review of engagement, identified 50 different definitions. Some commentators see employee engagement as a set of approaches or strategies designed to elicit organisational commitment. However, for others, employee engagement is an outcome of managerial actions and activity (see for example Purcell, 2012a). However, to whom, or with what, are employees engaged?

Management consultants who undertake employee engagement surveys give the impression that engagement is mainly or wholly to do with engagement *with the employer and the organisation* for which people work (Dromey, 2014). It is normally measured as the extent to which employees wish to stay with their employer, are proud to work for the firm and are prepared to exert extra effort on behalf of the organisation. This can sometimes be brought together as an 'engagement index'. However, it could be argued that commitment to the job, the team or a particular individual may have a more powerful influence on performance than commitment to the organisation. In reality, employees have multiple loyalties. In some circumstances, employees such as a nurse or a teacher may be indifferent towards an employer but be passionate about their job, patients, pupils or colleagues.

The multi-faceted nature of employee engagement has also been noted by Alfes et al (2010), whose research suggests that engaged employees perform better than others, take less sick leave and are less likely to leave their employer. They point out that central to the concept of employee engagement is the idea that all employees contribute to the successful functioning and continuous improvement of organisational processes. Importantly, Alfes et al argue that engagement is not homogeneous and distinguish between three types (or dimensions) of employee engagement: intellectual engagement, affective engagement and social engagement (Figure 5.2).

Figure 5.2 Dimensions of employee engagement

Intellectual engagement	Affective engagement	Social engagement
The extent to which individuals are absorbed in their work and think about ways in which performance can be improved	The extent to which people feel positive emotional connections to their work experience and thus with the company	The extent to which employees talk to colleagues about work-related improvements and change

SOURCE: Alfes et al (2010)

Similarly, Gourlay et al (2012) identify two types of engagement. If individuals are intrinsically motivated by the love of their job, their relationships with colleagues or the values of the organisation, they are likely to exhibit 'emotional' engagement. In contrast, 'transactional' engagement occurs when an employee is driven to pursue more extrinsic rewards by a fear that if they do not perform, they may lose their job or be unable to afford a certain standard of living. Therefore, this research suggests that employee engagement has several dimensions and that which secures the engagement of one group of employees is likely to differ from another.

The extent of employee engagement

While data on the extent of employee engagement has often been patchy, a 2022 survey conducted on behalf of Engage for Success (Pass et al, 2023) explored employee engagement in reference to the Covid pandemic. It assessed engagement across three components: overall satisfaction with an employee's organisation; whether the employee planned to be working for the same employer in three years' time (loyalty); and whether the employee would recommend their organisation as 'a great place to work' (advocacy). Just over two-thirds of employees (68 per cent) were either satisfied or very satisfied with their organisation as a place to work. Sixty-three per cent of respondents would recommend their organisation, while just over half (55 per cent) planned to be working for the organisation in three years' time. Importantly, levels of engagement were correlated with perceptions of the importance placed on this by managers and organisational leaders. In addition, high levels of engagement were more likely to be found in individuals who found their work meaningful and important.

There was also evidence that there was a significant dip in engagement during the pandemic. Although this had recovered to some extent by August 2022 (when the research was conducted) engagement levels were still below those pre-Covid. Importantly, the drop in engagement during the pandemic was significantly lower for those individuals working in organisations where there had been concerted attempts to involve, and communicate with, employees. In particular, there was a positive relationship between the frequency of face-to-face meetings – both individual meetings with a manager and team meetings. Interestingly, virtual meetings did not have the same impact. The availability of learning and development opportunities was also found to have limited reductions in engagement.

Although a wide range of different measures are used to gauge employee engagement, Pass et al's findings are broadly consistent with other research. For example, in 2024, the CIPD found that seven in ten people were satisfied with their job (CIPD, 2024c). However, this also means that 30 per cent of employees are disengaged and dissatisfied. In fact, the 2024 Gallup *State of the Global Workforce* report revealed that 31 per cent of workers in the UK were watching for or actively seeking a new job. Furthermore, overall employee engagement in the UK was ranked 33 out of 38 countries included in the research (Gallup, 2024). Therefore, it is clear that there is significant scope to improve employee engagement in UK workplaces and address the 'productivity puzzle' that we discussed in Chapter 3.

Reflective activity 5.6

Critically assess the extent of employee engagement at your workplace. What are the main factors that explain this and what could your employer do to secure higher levels of engagement?

Enablers of engagement

MacLeod and Clarke (2009) concluded that there were four main factors which were critical to securing high levels of employee engagement: integrity, leadership, engaging managers and employee voice. We explore the first three of these here before a more detailed examination of employee voice in the final part of this chapter.

Integrity and leadership

MacLeod and Clarke (2009) argued that behaviour throughout the organisation should be consistent with its stated values, leading to trust and a sense of integrity. Most organisations have stated values and accepted behavioural norms. Where there is a gap between the two, the size of the gap is reflected in the degree of mistrust within the organisation. If this gap is closed, high levels of trust usually result. If an employee sees the stated values of the organisation embodied in the leadership and supported by colleagues, a sense of trust in the organisation is more likely to be developed, thereby constituting a powerful enabler of engagement. Ideally, effective leadership defines a clear mission which has widespread ownership and commitment from managers and employees at all levels. A strong narrative provides a shared vision for the organisation at the heart of which lies employee engagement. It is a story which explains the purpose of an organisation and the breadth of its vision and sets out the contributions that individuals can make. Employees must understand not only the goals of the organisation for which they work, but also how they can make a contribution. This can turn on the style of leadership within an organisation. For example, if the workplace culture is 'toxic', employees are less likely to 'speak up' (Acas, 2019b).

The role of managers

Reflecting our discussion in Chapter 4, front-line managers play a critical role in giving local context to that vision and employees' place within it. For MacLeod and Clarke (2009), 'engaging managers' are at the heart of organisational culture. The results of Robinson and Hayday's (2009) study on how managers inspire and engage their teams to perform and behave well in their dealings with people are set out in Figure 5.3.

Robinson and Hayday found that there was a feeling among engaged teams that they were happy and enjoyed their work, and that there was a good atmosphere, compared with other teams. An important feature was teams' openness and ability to discuss a wide range of topics. In contrast, the factors associated with disengagement or low levels of engagement exposed basic failings in employment policy and practices. For example, where people work in jobs with very short task cycle times, where there is high stress related to little autonomy and inflexibility, and where there is a feeling of job insecurity, employees tend to have lower engagement levels. Lower levels of engagement are also more likely to be found where there is perceived unfairness in rewards, where there is bullying and harassment, and where people believe they are stuck in their jobs and feel cut off from open communications.

Furthermore, this is likely to be exacerbated by the external context. For example, van Wanrooy et al (2013) found a clear link between lower levels of engagement and the extent to which workplaces had been affected by recessionary pressures. They argued that there was a clear relationship between employee engagement and workplace conflict, with less effective employee engagement in workplaces where either industrial action had taken place in the previous 12 months, or where respondents felt that there was a poor overall climate of employment relations within their organisation.

HR can play an important role in helping managers to engage their staff – through advice and coaching and also developing effective structures of communication and voice which managers can easily navigate. Where this support is not evident, managers will often 'freestyle', devising their own unit-level voice mechanisms. While these can have positive impacts, they can create an inconsistency of approach which can create wider problems across the organisation (Mowbray et al, 2022).

Figure 5.3 Behaviours of engaging and disengaging managers

Engaging managers	Disengaging managers
Communicate, make clear what is expected	Self-centred – lack empathy and interest in people
Listen, value and involve team	Fail to listen and communicate
Supportive and back up team members	Don't motivate or inspire
Target-focused with clear strategic vision	Don't deliver – blame others, don't take responsibility
Show active interest in others	Aggressive
Display good leadership skills and command respect	Lack awareness

SOURCE: Robinson and Hayday (2009)

5.4 Employee voice

The fourth driver of engagement is the ability for employees to feed their views upwards and to see consequential action taken by management. This may take place on an individual level through the line manager or through collective channels through partnership working between management and unions, or alternatively via team briefings and other representative fora. Dromey's (2014) analysis of WERS2011 also concluded that successful engagement is premised on giving genuine voice to employees in terms of influencing overall decision-making in the organisation. Van Wanrooy et al's (2013) analysis of the same data found that 91 per cent of those employees who were satisfied with their influence over decisions also agreed that they were loyal to their organisations. However, among those who were not satisfied with their influence over decisions, less than half said they were loyal.

Furthermore, the strategic significance of voice was highlighted in the Taylor Review on 'good work' (BEIS 2017) which we discussed in Chapter 3. The review argued that managers needed feedback from staff and individuals needed the chance 'to get together physically or virtually and with or without management to discuss common issues affecting them; to have a safe route for the workforce to raise concerns… and to hear and influence big strategic issues which may have an impact on them' (BEIS 2017: 52). Therefore, the key thread linking different forms of voice is that they provide employees with a chance to influence and participate in the decisions that affect their day-to-day working lives.

It is important to note that voice can be exercised in a variety of ways – both individual and collective, ranging from one-to-ones between managers and staff to formal collective consultation and bargaining between management and trade unions. This will inevitably be shaped by the contextual factors. For example, as Wakeling (2020) has argued, the Covid pandemic provided new opportunities for voice, even in a time of crisis. Social distancing forced organisations to embrace new technology, with the potential for 'more innovative and agile ways of working'. In many organisations, video conferencing made senior leaders more visible and accessible while meetings could be organised more quickly, regularly and efficiently. While remote communication has limitations (as discussed earlier), organisational experiences of working through the pandemic underlined the importance of employee voice and the need to adopt a dynamic and strategic approach to employee engagement. Real-world example 5.1 demonstrates how a constructive approach to collective employee voice can help organisations and their staff navigate severe challenges.

REAL-WORLD EXAMPLE 5.1

'Getting the unions on side'

In 2024, like many local authorities across the UK, Cardiff Council was faced with having to find significant savings in order to stay within the Welsh government's funding settlement. The Council provides more than 700 services and employs around 15,000 people. Therefore, rather than simply reducing staffing levels and cutting services, the Council realised that it needed to work differently. According to Tracey Thomas, the Council's chief HR officer, this required a collaborative approach, particularly with trade unions. Thomas explained that 'we wouldn't be able to do half the things we did without the support of the trade unions'. Through effective engagement and constant dialogue, the Council had worked in partnership with trade union representatives to change policy, avoid formal disputes and introduce better working conditions. This included moving bin collections to a four-day cycle, which created savings for the Council while maintaining working hours for refuse staff and services to residents. A key part of this was increased transparency with monthly meetings with unions to discuss the Council finances and financial projections. Although discussions were often challenging, meaningful involvement and participation helped Thomas to 'bring the trade unions with you so that you're not having to have difficult discussions at the eleventh hour'.

SOURCE: Rowsell (2024)

Reflective activity 5.7

In Real-world example 5.1, what made engaging with unions particularly effective? What challenges do you think the HR leadership at Cardiff Council would face in developing this approach?

The theory and practice of employee voice

Employee 'voice' is typically operationalised within a strategy of 'employee involvement and participation' (EIP) which captures a range of techniques from direct communication with employees to indirect or representative participation through workplace consultative and negotiating committees. These types of EIP vary according to the level of influence they give to employees, the scope of the subject matter for discussion and the level in the organisation at which the mechanisms operate. The amount of influence that employees have in decision-making, in particular, is regarded as important because it is likely to shape broader organisational outcomes (Marchington et al, 1992).

Employee involvement is generally seen as directed towards individual employees. By introducing employee involvement mechanisms, management seeks to gain the consent of the employees to their proposed actions based on shared objectives rather than purely control (Walton, 1985; Hyman and Mason, 1995). These mechanisms are aimed at enabling individual employees to inform management decision-making processes. Typically, they are based on management sharing information directly with individuals or groups of employees in return for their views. Alternatively, employee involvement can also involve 'task-based' control of decision-making for employees at the individual job level of the organisation. This encompasses notions of 'job enlargement' and 'job enrichment' (Dundon and Wilkinson, 2013: 492). Although critics might rightly suggest that these types of initiative remain largely unitarist in design, it can also be argued that they increase job satisfaction by reducing the routinisation of work and allowing greater autonomy. However, employee involvement is not about employees sharing power (jointly regulating the employment relationship) with management; the decision whether to accept, or reject, employees' views rests with management alone.

In contrast, employee participation concerns the extent to which employees play an active role within the decision-making machinery of the organisation. This is generally achieved through indirect collective representation in the form of joint consultation, collective bargaining and board-level worker representation. These systems focus on collectively representative structures (Hyman and Mason, 1995). This approach is often termed 'power-based' control as employees 'have a real say' in the decision-making process across all levels of the organisation. It is also underpinned by legal rights (for example the right to consultation over redundancy) and the bargaining power of labour (Dundon and Wilkinson, 2013: 488–90). Crucially, the context of employment relations and the balance of workplace relations will determine the extent to which involvement and participation exist in an organisation. In general, employers are unlikely to invest in EIP practices unless there is a clear business case.

Reflective activity 5.8

Explain the difference in meaning between the terms 'employee involvement' and 'employee participation'. To what extent do the voice mechanisms in your organisation allow employees to participate in decision-making?

Figure 5.4 shows Marchington and Wilkinson's (2012: 348) conceptualisation of the four key aspects of involvement and participation in the context of employee voice. This suggests that the degree to which employees are able to influence decision-making is a function of the scope and subject matter of EIP, the level in the organisation at which involvement and participation takes place, and the specific form of EIP.

Figure 5.4 Key elements of employee involvement and participation

The degree of involvement indicates the extent to which workers or their representatives are able to influence management decisions		
The **scope** of decisions open to influence by workers relates to the type of subject matter dealt with in the participation arena, ranging from the trivial to the strategic	The **level** in the organisation at which workers (or their representatives) are involved in management decisions	The different **forms** – for instance, from face-to-face meetings to collective bargaining

SOURCE: Marchington and Wilkinson (2012)

Marchington et al (2007) identified the breadth or form of these EIP practices to include:

- direct downward communication from managers to employees:
  - newsletters
  - email
  - intranet
  - noticeboards
- direct two-way communication between management and employees:
  - team briefings
  - workplace meetings
  - staff newsletters
  - cascading of information via the management team
- direct upward feedback from employees:
  - problem-solving groups
  - suggestion schemes
  - employee/staff attitude surveys
- direct financial participation:
  - profit-related bonus schemes
  - deferred profit-sharing schemes
  - employee share ownership schemes
- indirect participation:
  - employee representative structures, e.g. works councils
  - joint consultative committees.

We can further include the 'depth' of EIP as measured by its regularity and the power actually given to employees (Cox et al, 2006) or how 'embedded' the aspect of voice is in the workplace (Cox et al, 2007). As Dundon and Wilkinson note, depth is a crucial concept in analysing the extent to which employees, 'either directly or indirectly, can influence those decisions normally reserved for management' (2013: 489). These levels of distinction are extremely helpful from both a theoretical and practical basis in analysing more completely the type, impact and 'concurrence' (Bennett, 2010) of employee voice initiatives. Using these conceptualisations, we can distinguish more clearly between employee involvement, facilitating employee voice and employee participation.

More latterly, Marchington's (2015) transnational study of 25 organisations, and the embeddedness of EIP within them, offers further insight into the differences in channels used for employee voice. In particular, his analysis suggests that the 'breadth' and 'depth' of EIP is shaped in part by the existence of high-trust relations between management and unions. Where management was willing to work with unions, employee voice had greater breadth and depth, particularly in terms of representative EIP. In contrast, devolution of HRM to line managers was 'associated with greater breadth and depth of direct and informal EIP, especially if "engagement" was a criterion for performance management of line managers' (Marchington, 2015: 15).

 Reflective activity 5.9

What employee involvement and participation practices operate in your organisation (or one with which you are familiar)? How, and why, have the various practices been introduced? Has the distribution of the employee involvement practices changed over time?

EIP in practice

The next section takes a more detailed look at how EIP processes work in practice. Ramsay (1996) usefully divides employee involvement and participation initiatives into four broad types:

- communications and briefing systems – which include downward and upward communications systems;
- task and work-group involvement – which includes teamworking and quality circles;
- financial participation – which embraces profit-sharing, profit-related pay and share ownership schemes;
- representative participation.

Communication

Employee communication involves the provision and exchange of information and instructions which enable an organisation to function effectively and its employees to be properly informed about developments. It covers the information to be provided, the channels along which it passes, and the way it is relayed. This can take the form of 'one-way' communication from management to their workforce, or 'two-way', which while also a form of direct voice, is based on an element of information exchange between the two parties (Dundon and Rollinson, 2011: 284). Significantly, a large-scale, cross-sectional survey of employees revealed that 'upward' employee voice can be a key antecedent for effective engagement when senior management is receptive to those employee views (Ruck et al, 2017). However, effectively facilitating this aspect of employee engagement turns on the communication skills of the leader. Acas (2019b) guidance usefully sets out the key skills needed by organisational leaders across three dimensions: influencing, engaging and listening. These are illustrated in Figure 5.5.

With the trend towards flatter management structures and the devolution of responsibilities to individuals, it is increasingly important that individual employees also have the opportunity to influence what happens to them at work. The mix of methods selected to form a communication strategy will be determined by the size, structure of the organisation, its employment relations perspective and, to a degree, where the relative balance of power lies within that company. Two main methods of

Figure 5.5 Key communication skills for leaders

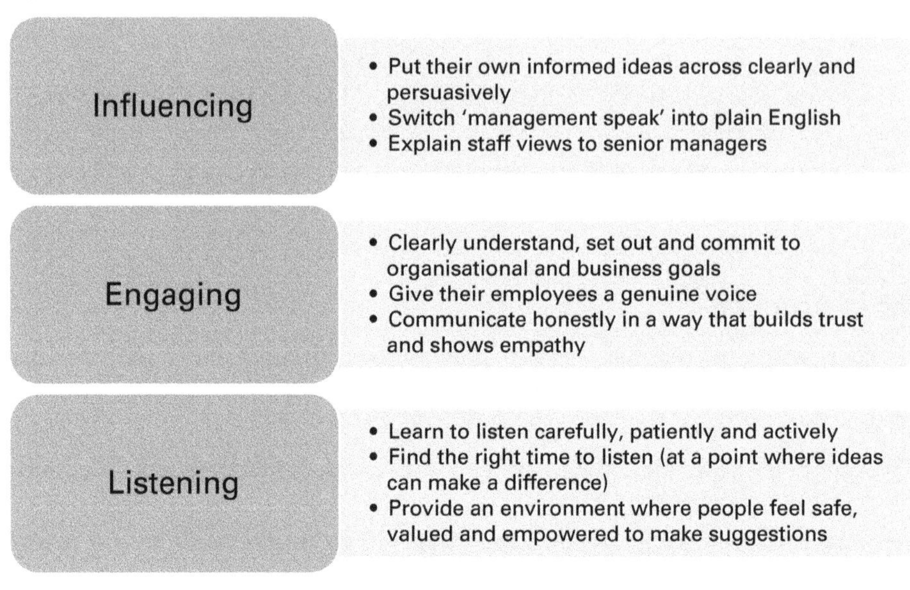

SOURCE: Acas (2019b: 8)

communication can be distinguished. First, there are face-to-face methods that are both direct and swift and they enable discussion, questioning and feedback to take place. The main formal face-to-face methods of communication are:

- **group meetings** – meetings between managers and the employees for whom they are responsible;
- **cascade networks** – a well-defined procedure for passing on information quickly, used mainly in large or disparately widespread organisations;
- **large-scale meetings** – meetings that involve all employees in an organisation or at an establishment, with presentations by a director or senior managers; these are a good channel for presenting the organisation's performance or long-term objectives;
- **inter-departmental briefings** – meetings between managers in different departments that encourage a unified approach and reduce the scope for inconsistent decision-making, particularly in larger organisations.

In the wake of the Covid pandemic, meetings are regularly held using online platforms such as Teams or Zoom. These have a range of benefits in terms of convenience, cost, efficiency and accessibility. However, as we discussed earlier in this chapter, they may not necessarily be the right 'fit' for every situation. In addition, successful online meetings require a slightly different range of skills and techniques. For example, participants cannot rely on body language and non-verbal cues, requiring closer attention to detail and clarity. Therefore, it is important to take these issues into account when deciding on the form of meeting to adopt.

Second, there are written methods. These are most effective where the need for the information is important or permanent, the topic requires detailed explanation, the audience is widespread or large, and there is a need for a permanent record. The chief methods of written communication include company handbooks, employee information notes, house journals and newsletters, departmental bulletins, notices and individual letters to employees. Email is useful for communicating with employees in scattered or isolated locations, and audio-visual aids are particularly useful for explaining technical developments or financial performance. Increasingly organisational intranets are utilised as part of communication strategies.

Crucially, communication strategies, policies and techniques need senior management support, and they require discipline to follow them through. We have noted the potential for social media to be used in HRM practice. It is also being advocated specifically with respect to communication strategy. Silverman et al (2013) identify the potential of blogs and 'discussion fora' to facilitate online communities, through which employees can share their views collectively on issues of interest to them and the organisation. There is an increasing array of social media platforms and apps which managers and organisations can use to facilitate two-way communication. While these can bring significant benefits, there is also a danger that they can help to escalate conflict and provide some more 'reluctant managers' with a way of avoiding face-to-face contact with staff. Therefore, it is important to design an approach to staff communication that fits with the culture of the workplace and does not erode high-trust relationships.

Reflective activity 5.10

What sort of communication strategy has your organisation adopted? Critically assess its effectiveness. How do you think social media could be used in your organisation to enhance EIP? What would be the challenges and potential drawbacks?

Team briefings

Of all the communication methods in use, team briefing is perhaps the most systematic in the provision of top-down information. Briefings work by information cascading down through various management tiers, being conveyed by each immediate supervisor or team leader to a small group of employees, the optimum number being between 4 and 20. This takes place throughout all levels in the organisation; the information eventually being conveyed by supervisors and/or team leaders to shop-floor employees.

On each occasion the information received is supplemented by 'local' news of more immediate relevance to those being briefed. Meetings tend to be short but are designed to help develop the 'togetherness' of a work-group, especially where different grades of employees are involved in the team. Each manager is a member of a briefing group and is also responsible for briefing a team. The system is designed to ensure that all employees from the managing director to the shop floor are fully informed of matters affecting their work. Leaders of each briefing session prepare their own brief, consisting of information that is relevant and task-related to the employees in the group. The brief is then supplemented with information passed down from higher levels of management. Any questions that cannot be dealt with at once are answered in written form within a few days. Although team briefing is not a consultative process, question-and-answer sessions can clarify understanding and give employees the feeling of a measure of input. In terms of the range of topics covered in team briefings, Bennett's research findings on employee voice in the public sector are typical. They included top-down issues, such as company strategy and performance, future plans, organisational finance and new initiatives. There was also discussion on day-to-day issues, such as reaching KPIs, team plans, workloads, and customer and technical issues (Bennett, 2010).

There are, however, practical problems to be borne in mind in introducing team briefings. First, if the organisation operates on a continuous shift-working basis, is it technically feasible for team briefings to take place? Second, management must be confident that it can sustain a flow of relevant and detailed information and managers need the skills and support to deliver information in a coherent and clear manner. Third, if the organisation recognises unions, it is important that management is not seen as undermining their influence. For example, relationships with unions will be damaged if important information comes to them via team briefings rather than through existing consultative channels.

Employee attitude surveys

Employee attitude surveys are typically used to obtain specific data on employee perceptions of fairness, pay systems, training opportunities and employee awareness of an organisation's business strategy and long-term goals. More specifically they can:

- gather staff's views on management proposals for organisational change, ideally to identify and thus pre-empt any unwanted consequences that may lead to major employment relations difficulties;
- help managers make internal comparisons of employee morale and behaviour across a number of departments and sites;
- provide employee views on specific HRM policies such as the operation of the disciplinary and grievance procedures;
- provide data that can be used in problem-solving, planning and decision-making.

However, as Silverman et al note, the traditional employee survey can be tedious to complete, based on 'ticking boxes' and unable to capture real qualitative feedback. In addition, delays in publishing survey results can undermine their relevance and legitimacy (2013: 11). Fundamentally, management must act on the feedback, however critical, which it receives. A failure to respond to negative staff survey data can be counterproductive, eroding faith and trust in the senior leadership of an organisation. It is also important to involve employee and union representatives both in the design of the survey and in formulating actions to address any issues raised.

Reflective activity 5.11

Does the organisation you work for conduct a staff survey? If so, can you identify specific measures that have been taken in response to survey results? With this in mind, how do you think your organisation could improve the way that it gathers data on staff attitudes?

Task and work-group involvement

The objective of task and work-group involvement practices is to tap into employees' knowledge of their jobs, either at the individual level or through the mechanism of small groups. These practices are designed to increase the stock of ideas within the organisation, to encourage co-operative relations at work and to justify change. Task-based involvement encourages employees to extend the range and type of tasks they undertake at work. It involves practices such as job redesign, job enrichment, teamworking and job enlargement. Job enrichment involves the introduction of more elements of responsibility into the work tasks. Job enlargement centres on increasing the number and diversity of tasks carried out by an individual employee, thereby increasing their work experience and skill.

Quality circles

QCs provide an element of 'upward problem-solving' that goes beyond the more limited communications techniques considered earlier, by allowing employees to discuss, identify and put forward as a group their ideas to management for improving working practices (Dundon and Wilkinson, 2013: 291). Typically, employees meet in small groups led by their supervisor on a regular basis for an hour or so to suggest ways of improving productivity and quality and reducing costs. The group meet 'off-line' away from their immediate workplace (Marchington and Wilkinson, 2012: 352) in order to select the issue or problem they wish to address, collect the necessary information and make suggestions to management on ways of overcoming the problem. In some cases, the group itself is given authority to put its proposed solutions into effect, but more often it presents formal recommendations for action, which management then consider. Members of a quality circle are not usually employee representatives but are members of the circle by virtue of their knowledge of the tasks involved in their jobs.

Financial participation

Offering employees a stake in the ownership and prosperity of the business for which they work is one of the most direct and tangible forms of employee involvement and participation. It is argued by its proponents that employees can acquire and develop a greater sense of identity with the business and an appreciation of the business needs. It is suggested that a financial stake gives employees increased enthusiasm for the success of the organisation and often for a voice in its operation. In its most developed form, employee share ownership means that employees become significant shareholders in the business, or even their own employer. Financial employee involvement and participation schemes link specific elements of pay and reward to the performance of the unit or the enterprise as a whole.

Profit-sharing schemes aim to increase employee motivation and commitment by giving employees an interest in the overall performance of the enterprise, by demonstrating that rewards accrue from co-operative effort even more than from individual effort. However, there are practical problems that must be addressed if profit-sharing schemes are to have the desired effect. A scheme has to contain clearly identifiable links between effort and reward. Individuals must not feel that no matter how hard they work in any year, that effort is not reflected in their share of the company's profits. Due account also has to be taken of cross-employee performance, or there is a risk of inter-group dissatisfaction in that some employees might believe other groups have received the same profit-share payment but have made less effort.

Profit-related pay is a mechanism through which employers can reward employees for their contribution to the business. It works by linking a proportion of employees' pay to the profits of the business for which they work.

Reflective activity 5.12

Do you have any financial participation schemes in your organisation? If you do, why were those particular schemes chosen? To what extent and why are they effective? If your organisation does not have any financial participation schemes, do you think that their introduction could deepen engagement and improve performance?

Representative participation

Setting aside the key collective role played by trade unions in facilitating employee voice, discussed in detail in Chapter 6, the other main form of representative participation is consultation. Consultation is a process by which management and employees, or their representatives, jointly examine and discuss issues of mutual concern. It involves seeking acceptable solutions to problems through a genuine exchange of views and information. Unlike negotiation, consultation does not challenge managerial prerogative – management still makes the final decision – but it does impose an obligation that the views of employees will be sought and considered before that final decision is taken. It affects the process through which decisions are made in so far as it commits management first to the disclosure of information at an early stage in the decision-making process, and second to take into account the collective views of the employees.

Consultation does not mean that employees' views always have to be acted upon – there may be good practical or financial reasons for not doing so. However, whenever employees' views are rejected, the reasons for rejection should be explained carefully. Equally, where the views and ideas of employees help to improve a decision, due credit and recognition should be given. Consultation requires a free exchange of ideas and views affecting the interests of employees. Almost any subject is therefore appropriate for discussion. However, both management and employees may wish to place some limits on the range of subjects open to consultation – because of trade confidences, perhaps, or because they are considered more appropriate for a negotiation forum – but whatever issues are agreed upon as being appropriate for discussion, it is important that they are relevant to the group of employees discussing them. Although the subject matters of consultation are a matter for agreement between employer and employees, there are several laws and regulations that specifically require an employer to consult with recognised trade unions and other employee representatives. These include health and safety matters, collective redundancies, transfers of undertaking and certain issues relating to occupational pension schemes.

Joint consultative committees

Joint consultative committees (JCCs) are composed of managers and employee representatives, who may or may not be union representatives, who come together on a regular basis to discuss issues of mutual concern. They may also be referred to as 'works councils' or 'employee forums'. For Bratton et al, they 'tend towards shallower forms of consultation, rather than more consequential negotiating, about workplace change' (2022: 317). Nonetheless, they can build trust and cooperation between employees and management in terms of productivity improvement initiatives (Jirjahn et al, 2024). They usually have a formal constitution which governs their operations, and the number of members on a JCC depends on the size of the organisation. Management in organisations that operate over several different establishments sometimes prefer to consult with employees on a multi-site basis rather than have a consultative committee for each establishment. These are referred to as 'higher-level committees'. While the JCC remains a significant mechanism for consultation in certain parts of the UK economy, it is, like many other forms of collective voice, in steep decline (see also Adam et al, 2014).

From a practical perspective, the JCC should have as its focus a well-prepared agenda and all members should be given an opportunity to contribute to that agenda before it is circulated. The agenda is normally sent out in advance of the meeting so that representatives have a chance to consult with their constituents prior to the committee meeting. Well-run JCCs are chaired effectively. It is important that employee representatives know exactly how much time they will be allowed away from their normal work to undertake their duties as a committee member and the facilities to which they are entitled. Employee representatives should not lose pay as a result of attending committee meetings. If joint consultation is to be effective, the deliberations of the committee must be reported back to employees as soon as possible.

Reflective activity 5.13

Do JCCs exist in your organisation? If so, what forms do they take, and are they successful? If there are no JCCs, what mechanisms are in place to consult with the workforce?

The Information and Consultation of Employees (ICE) Regulations

In addition to the legal obligations to consult set out in the previous section, the Information and Consultation of Employees (ICE) Regulations 2004 provide an obligation on all employers with more than 50 employees to establish consultation mechanisms, where requested to do so by employees. The ICE Regulations introduced an added legal imperative for promoting greater employee involvement in the UK which presented employers with new and specific obligations with respect to managing employment relations. These regulations gave effect to the EU Directive establishing a general framework for informing and consulting employees in the European Union. They came into force on a sliding scale, depending on the number of employees in the organisation.

Only undertakings employing fewer than 50 employees are exempt from the regulations. An 'undertaking' means a legal entity such as an individually incorporated company, whereas an 'establishment' is a physical entity such as a factory, plant, office or retail outlet. A detailed account of the process of managing a staff request for the establishment of an ICE forum is available through Acas. Although there were concerns that the ICE and other regulations that were rooted in EU law could be repealed or watered down after Brexit, they have remained in place. Indeed in 2020, the UK government reduced the threshold for making a legal request to implement information and consultation arrangements from 10 per cent to 2 per cent of the total workforce, subject to a minimum of 15 employees.

However, there is little evidence to suggest that the ICE Regulations have had a significant impact on extending representative collective voice within UK organisations (Hall et al, 2013). While the regulations provide a way of establishing formal arrangements for information and consultation in non-union organisations, they do not (and arguably cannot) determine the quality of the interactions between management and representatives. A study of two organisations that had introduced information and consultation arrangements by Kougiannou et al (2022) found that managers were reluctant to share information and give up their prerogative and control, maintaining a broadly unitarist approach. Moreover, managerial motivations for setting up consultative mechanisms appeared to revolve around the benefits for the business as opposed to a real desire to foreground the interests and experiences of employees. This questions whether relatively weak regulation can really create meaningful voice mechanisms in the absence of strong trade union representation.

The impact of EIP mechanisms

What is the evidence that EIP achieves positive outcomes? Early research undertaken by Marchington et al (2001) demonstrated that employers in the 18 organisations they studied valued the voice of the employee in contributing to management decision-making because they believed it contributed to business performance. Employee voice (through communication systems, project team membership and joint consultation) was perceived to lead to better employee contributions, improved management systems and productivity gains. This was seen to be the result of the number of ideas that emerged through employee feedback and joint problem-solving teams. Marchington et al's (2007) later analysis of WERS2004 data found a strong positive link between the 'breadth' and 'depth' of some information and consultation practices and employee commitment. Employee ratings of the helpfulness of some consultation and communication methods were positively linked to job satisfaction and commitment. Employee ratings of managers' effectiveness in consulting employees and employees' satisfaction with their involvement in decision-making were also positively linked with job satisfaction and commitment, suggesting that the way in which information and consultation are implemented is just as important as the type of practice used.

Interestingly, Marchington et al (2007) found that there was no connection between any single information and consultation method and employee commitment and job satisfaction in workplaces with 25 or more employees. However, significant and positive links were found between the 'breadth' of information and consultation (the number of different practices used together in a workplace) and the 'depth' of direct communication methods and employee commitment. Using a range of complementary EIP practices may be important because a single EIP practice is likely to have less impact on its own than several practices operating together. An individual EIP practice can be more easily dismissed as 'bolted on' or out of line with other HR practices and not be taken seriously by workers. In contrast, a multiplicity of EIP mechanisms may complement each other and provide opportunities for employees to be involved at work in different ways. For example, information received by employees from a team briefing may be useful when they are working in problem-solving groups.

5.5 A conceptual model of employee voice

This final section builds on Marchington and Wilkinson's (2005) model of an 'escalator of participation' to develop an overall framework for the analysis of employee voice, which draws on a number of the central concepts introduced in Chapter 2. The five stages – information, communication, consultation, co-determination and control – are all reflected in our earlier discussion. For instance, information examples include newsletters and noticeboards, 'direct' team briefings are a communication example, and consultation, as we have seen, is epitomised by the workings of the joint consultation committee. The 'indirect' representation of workers by their union falls within the co-determination step, and finally worker ownership, such as co-operatives, captures the practice of control.

However, as Dundon and Wilkinson (2013: 490) rightly state:

> This framework [Marchington and Wilkinson's] allows for a more accurate description not only of the type of involvement or participation [or voice] schemes in use, but the extent to which they may or may not empower employees... [It] is more than a straightforward continuum from no involvement (information) to extensive worker participation (control). It illustrates the point that schemes can overlap and coexist. For example, the use of collective bargaining and joint consultation does not mean that management abandons communication techniques.

Therefore, in Figure 5.6, we have built on this insight, and added the two elements discussed at length in this chapter, EI and EP, to reflect their influence in facilitating employee voice. Furthermore, a third concept of industrial democracy (ID) is located

Figure 5.6 Conceptual framework of employee involvement and participation

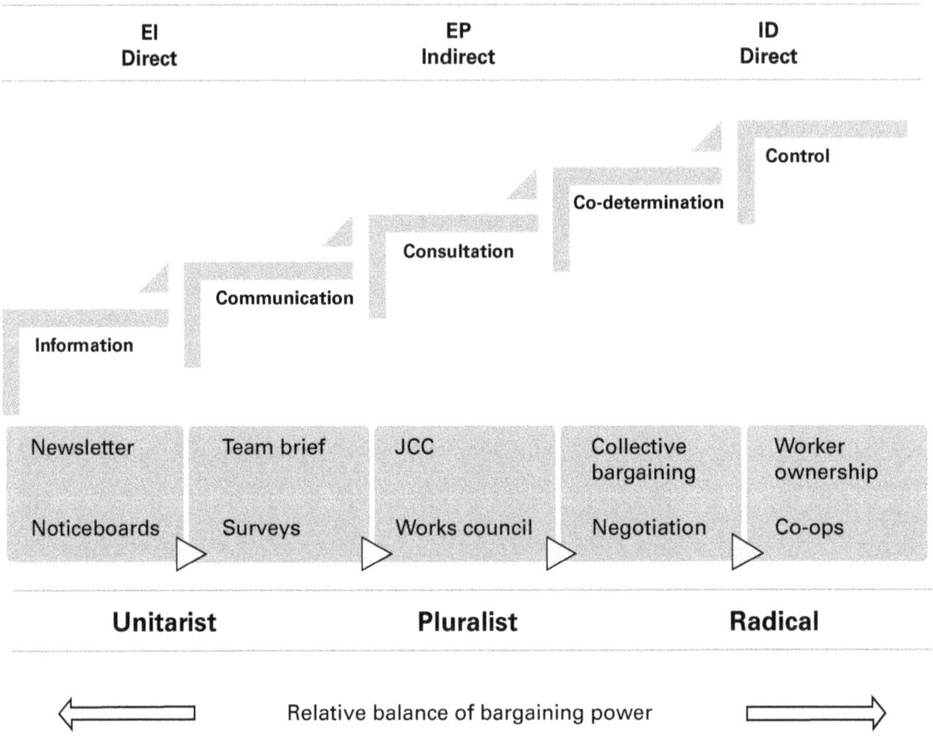

EI Direct	EP Indirect	ID Direct

Information → Communication → Consultation → Co-determination → Control

Newsletter Noticeboards	Team brief Surveys	JCC Works council	Collective bargaining Negotiation	Worker ownership Co-ops

Unitarist	Pluralist	Radical

⇐ Relative balance of bargaining power ⇒

at the control end of the model. Fox's (1974) frames of reference are a valuable analytical tool in our discussions throughout the book. We have introduced them to the model to demonstrate how those perspectives influence the choice and co-existence of EIP initiatives in the workplace. Therefore, in an organisation in which a unitarist perspective of employment relations is dominant, it is likely that employee voice initiatives will be limited to the first two or three stages of the spectrum. In contrast, organisations in which a more pluralist perspective is more evident will tend to use a range of voice initiatives across the spectrum. Finally, by adding the impact of the relative balance of bargaining power to the model, we can see that increasing employer leverage will make it shift the use of EIP towards the lower end of the 'escalator'.

Current debates and new perspectives on employee voice

A recent and significant debate on the nature and efficacy of employee voice centres on the barriers to facilitating voice for all employees, but also specifically recognises the 'missing voices' within organisations. Wilkinson et al (2018: 714, 717) point out the need to 'pay attention to the perspectives, insights and concerns of diverse employees' and identify five categories of 'unheard voices', where:

- there is no structure in place for voice;
- structures exist, but 'no one listens';

- structures exist, grievances are raised, but they are ignored;
- although structures exist, 'they create and perpetuate a climate of silence'.

As Table 5.2 demonstrates, each of the 'voice architectures' leads to different outcomes and explanations. For example, it is possible for voice structures to exist but, because only certain voices are seen as legitimate and credible, no action is taken in response.

Goodwin's (2019) research on the extent to which older workers in local government have real voice also highlights the complexity of ensuring the involvement and participation of all workers in an organisation. Crucially, she argues that not only are the voice structures for older workers in organisations often inadequate for articulating their needs and aspirations, but also there is an assumption that 'the older worker' is part of a homogeneous group within the organisation and society as a whole. In contrast, Goodwin (2019: 25) points out that:

> older workers are heterogeneous but are united in the opinion that employee voice is important and that a means to express it and be heard should be available to all organisational members, which is currently not the case.

While society and to some extent organisations are happy to stereotype the older worker as 'less adaptable' and 'technophobic', there is little recognition that older workers have other needs they wish to articulate. Therefore, the potential contribution of the older worker is negated if no account is taken by employers of specific needs, such as flexibility in hours for caring responsibilities, working beyond retirement age and its implications, and training on new technology. Other commentators

Table 5.2 Unheard voices

Voice architecture	Outcome	Examples
Non-existent	Blackholes	Many SMEs, new firms, precarious employees
Voice structures exist but...	Speaking up is lost to noise	Structural constraints of too much voice, contradictions from different departments/ teams, issues seen as peripheral to leadership
Voice structures exist and...	Voices heard but no action taken	Only certain voices given credence whilst others are discarded or discounted
Voices structures exist but...	Employees are silent because...	They internalise the rules of the game: you tell the boss what they want to hear. They fear the consequences of speaking up
Voice structures exist but...	Assume homogeneity in the workforce	Therefore the tendency or opportunity is often governed by one's gender, race, sexuality or other key heterogeneous characteristics of a individual worker

SOURCE: Wilkinson et al (2018: 715–16)

highlight the roles of gender, sexuality, race and culture in contributing to employees being 'unheard' (see, for example, Ravenswood and Markey, 2018).

Equality of access to being heard is too often mediated by the social position of employees. Wilkinson et al observe that minority groups may 'often opt for silence in the workplace' to 'protect themselves from mistreatment' or in the belief that their voice will not be heard (2018: 717). This in turn relates to intersectionality, where disadvantages endured by many individuals and groups in the workplace can be traced to the multiple social identities they possess. This key element of employment relations is reviewed in detail in Chapter 7, where we consider the context and practice of promoting greater equality, diversity and inclusion in the workplace.

To better understand silence and give greater voice to employees, Nechanska et al (2020) argue that we need to recognise the 'structured antagonism' that mediates the balance of power between workers and the employer, which often result in employee silence when that balance favours the employer. Rather, we should adopt a more pluralist approach to giving voice to workers that embraces both EI and EP channels of engagement simultaneously (Dundon et al, 2023). It could also be argued that this is facilitated by the impact of technology and the increased variety of ways through which employees can make their voices heard, using social media and artificial intelligence (Khan et al, 2023; Prikshat et al, 2021). Dutta et al's (2023) research on the use of chatbots highlights the potential of technology to facilitate direct voice but poses further questions over how this affects the balance of power within the employment relationship. In particular, while this type of approach may help employees share their opinions with their managers, it is debatable whether this can give them a real say in decision-making. Furthermore, there is a danger that these technologies cement employer control over the labour process and can potentially be misused. As Cheese (2021) rightly cautions, the use of AI in all aspects of HR must keep ethical practice 'front and centre' in its design and utilisation.

Reflective activity 5.14

Does your organisation give voice to all workers? Which voices are missing and why? How can employee involvement and participation be effectively 'proofed' to ensure that these missing voices are heard?

5.6 Summary

In recent years, there has been much discussion of the need for HR practitioners to align their role with wider business strategy. The increased prominence of business partner models has been a defining feature of the contemporary HR function. This is seen by some as a way of HR taking on a more strategic role and moving away from transactional activities. In our view, employment relations must be a core component of HR strategy; however, the discussion here has shown that this is no easy task for the HR or the employment relations practitioner. Often, short-term operational considerations crowd out the need to consider the role that effective people management can play. Therefore, it is up to practitioners to develop and demonstrate the relationship between good employment relations and fundamental organisational outcomes. Furthermore, there is evidence that within the HR function itself employment relations has become increasingly stereotyped as a transactional and day-to-day activity.

One of the most powerful arguments for a renewed emphasis on employment relations is its relevance to employee engagement. Although the jury is still out on the existence of a causal relationship between engagement and productivity, there is growing evidence that effective line management is part of the solution to the UK's productivity puzzle. Given the increased role for managing people assigned to line managers, their ability to create a sense of fairness and equity would seem to be vital in building engagement and sustaining improved organisational performance.

Employment relations also highlights the strategic importance of employee voice. This has been widely cited as an essential ingredient of 'good work' but one which has been eroded in recent years. Critically, the discussion in this chapter has demonstrated that for voice mechanisms to underpin increased commitment to the organisation and consequent improvements in performance, employers need to do more than simply inform and communicate with their staff; they need to provide them with a meaningful and genuine voice in the decision-making process. It is therefore concerning that most of the data points to a decline in structured channels of voice and representation, and when employees raise their concerns, these often go unheard. If organisations hope to provide decent and fair work in the future, they must not only place the employment relationship at the core of their strategic thinking, but also seek ways of ensuring that missing voices are listened to.

KEY LEARNING POINTS

- Employment relations has been increasingly marginalised from HR and organisational strategy and characterised as concerned with transactional day-to-day activities. However, a strong case can be made that a focus on employment relations is essential in ensuring good work and driving sustainable improvements in organisational performance.
- Employee engagement is difficult to define; however, it is most accurately seen as an outcome of managerial actions and activity. While it can be secured by specific 'engagement strategies', it is also underpinned by the way in which organisational processes and activities are designed and enacted.
- Employee voice, and particularly having an influence on decision-making, is a key element of any successful engagement strategy. Significant and positive links have been found between the breadth of voice mechanisms and employee commitment.

- While having an open culture – in which there is open and transparent communication between line managers and their staff – is important, robust structures of representation are also vital in ensuring that workers can shape their working lives.
- In many respects, front-line managers play the most critical role in determining levels of employee engagement. 'Engaging managers' have good communication skills and listen to the views of their staff. They provide support and back the judgement of team members where appropriate. They empower rather than control or restrict staff and give them a real say in decision-making.
- Despite their organisational benefits, mechanisms which facilitate employee voice have progressively been eroded. This is particularly true of formal representative structures, but there is also evidence that the voices of specific groups of employees, particularly those that face multiple and connected sources of inequity, are increasingly unheard in UK workplaces.

Review Questions

1. What is your understanding of the different models of HRM strategy? Which one do you think is most suited to your organisation and why?
2. To what extent does the existence of HR business partners imply a strategic approach to the management of people? To what extent is employment relations integrated into HR strategy?
3. Critically assess the challenges of engaging effectively with the increasing number of home- and hybrid - working employees.
4. As part of the organisational plan to review employee procedures and practice, senior management is considering introducing a more systematic approach to employee involvement and participation. You have been asked to produce a briefing paper for the senior management team explaining the likely benefits of this. Drawing on contemporary research, explain and justify the contents of your briefing paper. Include the use of new and existing technology in your assessment.
5. To what extent do all employees in your organisation have access to channels of employee voice? What more could your organisation do to make sure that the voices of potentially marginalised groups are heard?
6. Critically evaluate the potential use of new technology in extending employee voice.

Explore further

Boxall, P and Purcell, J (2022) *Strategy and Human Resource Management*, 5th edn, Bloomsbury, London.

Dundon, T, Wilkinson, A and Ackers, P (2023) Mapping employee involvement and participation in institutional context: Mick Marchington's applied pluralist contributions to human resource management research methods, theory and policy, *Human Resource Management Journal*, **33** (3), pp 551–63

MacLeod, D and Clarke, N (2009) *Engaging for Success: Enhancing performance through employee engagement: a report to government*. Department for Business, Innovation and Skills, London

Sadun, R, Bloom, N and Van Reenen, J (2017) Why do we undervalue competent management? *Harvard Business Review*, **95** (5), pp 120–27

Timms, P (2018) *Transformational HR: How human resources can create value and impact business strategy*, Kogan Page, London

Whittington, R, Angwin, D, Regnér, P, Johnson, G and Scholes, K (2023) *Exploring Strategy*, 13th edn, Pearson Education, Harlow.

Wilkinson, A, Gollan, PJ, Kalfa, S and Xu, Y (2018) Voices unheard: employee voice in the new century. *International Journal of Human Resource Management*, **29** (5), pp 711–24

Websites

www.ipa-involve.com (archived at https://perma.cc/6NDH-9UPL) – the official website of the Involvement and Participation Association, which specialises in assisting both unionised and non-unionised organisations to develop effective information and consultation processes and workplace partnership.

www.acas.org.uk/engagement (archived at https://perma.cc/GSD9-KZJJ) – Acas webpages on employee engagement.

www.engageforsuccess.org (archived at https://perma.cc/FQE7-QWUJ) – the website of Engage for Success, which promotes employee engagement 'as a better way to work that benefits individual employees, teams and whole organisation'.

06 Representation at work

Overview

This chapter examines the way in which employees' and workers' interests are represented in employment relations and in particular focuses on the changing role of trade unions, which, despite their declining influence, still provide the main source of representation in UK workplaces. The chapter begins by outlining the historical development of trade unions and traces their growing power up to the election of the Conservative government in 1979. It then explores, in some detail, the main explanations for the decline in union membership and erosion of union organisation since that time. It goes on to examine the different responses developed by trade unions and their attempts to reorganise UK workplaces. The chapter then discusses the extent to which this gap has been filled by alternative non-union mechanisms and new forms of union organisation. Finally, in summarising, the chapter discusses the future of trade unions and the implications of this for the management of employment relations.

LEARNING OUTCOMES

When you have completed this chapter, you should be able to:

- understand and explain the main purposes, functions and development of trade unions;
- critically assess the key explanations for the decline in trade union membership from 1979;

- describe and critically evaluate the strategies adopted by trade unions to renew and revitalise union organisation;
- discuss the nature and extent of non-union forms of employee representation and critically assess their effectiveness;
- debate the implications of the changing nature of employee representation.

6.1 Introduction

According to section 1 of the Trade Unions and Labour Relations (Consolidation) Act, trade unions are:

> organised groups of employees who: consist wholly or mainly of workers of one or more description and whose principal purposes include the regulation of relations between workers and employers.

Until relatively recently, the management of employment relations was largely conducted between employers and trade unions. In 1979, around seven out of every ten workers were dependent on unions to represent their interests in bargaining pay and conditions. Moreover, over half the workforce were union members. Therefore, in both the public and private sectors, trade unions were not only the primary source of employee representation and voice but played a major role in shaping the life of the nation. However, after the election of the Conservative government in 1979, there was a sharp fall in union membership, and this was accompanied by a significant decline in the scale and scope of collective bargaining. Today, around one-quarter of all workers in the UK are union members and even fewer are covered by collective agreements.

Although it is easy to link trade union decline to the policies of the Thatcher government and subsequent Conservative administrations, the reality is more complex. A number of factors combined to create an increasingly hostile environment for organised labour, including de-industrialisation and the increased globalisation of economic activity. In the UK, while union decline slowed significantly in the late 1990s, the trade unions have not been able to significantly increase membership and density. That is not to say that unions have not responded to the challenges they have faced; they have sought to reshape their approach to employment relations through pursuing workplace partnership and promoting the business case for trade unions. At the same time, recent efforts have focused on rebuilding capacity and influence through grass-roots organisation. The evidence suggests that these strategies have largely enabled unions to consolidate and survive, rather than make any substantial gains.

However, a combination of rising living costs and tight labour markets in 2022 and 2023 boosted union bargaining power, with evidence of unions winning significant pay rises for their members. This was accompanied by the highest levels of industrial action seen in the UK since the late 1980s, and a modest increase in union membership. At the same time, there is little sign of non-union forms of representation filling the 'representation gap' that has opened as a result of union decline. While non-union representation is more common, it is limited to a relatively small minority of workplaces, and research has suggested that it generally fails to provide a strong voice for employees. This chapter looks at these developments in detail and in doing so assesses the future for employee representation in the UK.

6.2 Origins and development of trade unions

The roots of modern trade unions in the UK can be found in the Industrial Revolution of the late eighteenth century and the dramatic migration of workers from the land and from cottage industries into urban centres to work in factories, mills, ironworks and mines. This resulted in the creation of large urban workforces of men, women and children, often working for low wages in extremely poor conditions. It should be remembered that there was no health and safety legislation until the Factory Act of 1833, and no organised system of state welfare support until the introduction of the National Insurance Act of 1911. The power imbalance of employment relationships was stark, and work was a necessary condition for survival. Employers on the other hand could draw their labour from a rapidly growing population. In this context, workers joined together in an attempt to improve conditions; however, such actions were made unlawful by the Combination Acts of 1799 and 1800.

Although this legislation was repealed in 1824, it was not until the 1871 Trade Union Act that unions were recognised under the law. By this time, there were around 1 million trade union members and a number of larger national trade unions had been formed, such as the Amalgamated Society of Engineers (ASE). In addition, the Trades Union Congress (TUC), the representative body of trade unions, was established in 1868. The subsequent years up to the end of the Second World War saw a rapid growth in union membership which coincided with rising industrial militancy and political activism, particularly in the pre-war years. By 1920, there were over 8 million trade union members (see Figure 6.1). Furthermore, this period saw the emergence of general or 'new unions', which extended union membership into semi-skilled and unskilled work. For example, the Gas Workers and General Union (which went on to become what is today the GMB) was formed in 1889, while the Transport and General Workers Union (part of what is today Unite) was formed in 1922.

Economic decline and the Great Depression between 1929 and 1933 saw high levels of unemployment and declining union membership; however, from the mid-1930s, union membership grew, almost unabated, for more than 40 years to a peak of over 13 million in 1979, which represented around 55 per cent of the labour force. The reasons for this growth are complex; however, four key factors can be identified. First, increased industrialisation and high levels of economic growth prior to the Second World War, and full employment in the post-war years, created high levels of demand for labour and, therefore, conditions for unions to grow.

Second, unions themselves became more organised, professional and effective, using their bargaining power in certain industries to make union membership virtually compulsory through what were known as 'closed shops'. Third, post-war governments of different political colours adopted a pluralist approach to employment

Figure 6.1 Trade union membership, 1892–2023

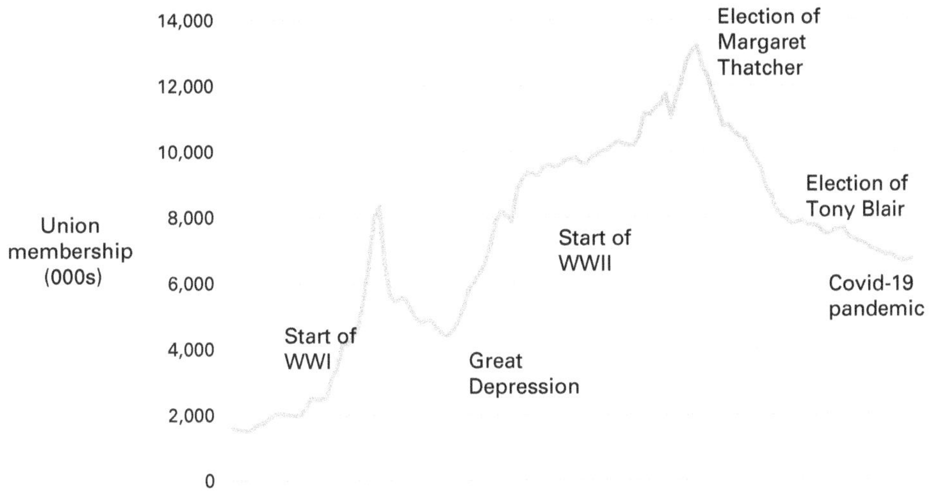

Union membership (000s)
14,000
12,000
10,000
8,000
6,000
4,000
2,000
0
Start of WWI
Great Depression
Start of WWII
Election of Margaret Thatcher
Election of Tony Blair
Covid-19 pandemic

SOURCE: Department for Business and Trade

relations in which trade unions were seen as playing a necessary and important role in establishing stable employment relations. Finally, increasingly well-organised unions were able to win improved terms and conditions for members; this union 'premium' was attractive to workers who had hitherto been unlikely to join. In particular, in the late 1960s and 1970s, in the face of rising inflation and growing economic concerns, membership grew rapidly as workers turned to trade unions to negotiate pay rises that would maintain or increase living standards.

This last point reflects an important contradiction facing trade unions, which, as we shall see later in this chapter, is still very relevant to their current challenges. As we discussed in Chapter 3, industrial militancy was unpopular with many people in the UK and was one reason why Margaret Thatcher's Conservative government was elected in 1979. However, at the same time, the effectiveness of unions in using industrial sanctions (or the threat of them) to win improved pay and conditions was crucial in demonstrating the value of union membership.

Reflective activity 6.1

Do you think that the reasons for the development and growth of trade unions still apply today? To what extent are unions relevant to the issues facing workers today?

6.3 What do unions do?

This question was asked by US academics Richard Freeman and James Medoff in their classic book of the same name in 1984. Their answer was that unions are 'beneficial to organised workers, almost always; beneficial to the economy, in many ways; but harmful to the bottom line of company balance sheets' (1984: 190). In essence, they argued that unions are a vital source of collective voice, which in turn reduces labour turnover, encourages investment in capital and skills and improves managerial decision-making. At the same time, unions are good for members as they are able to negotiate higher wages than would have been paid in their absence. However, while unions may reduce inequality they may also have a negative impact on profitability.

Although Freeman and Medoff's work, and in particular the productivity effects of trade unions, has been a subject of significant debate (see for example Hirsch, 2004), it reflects the fact that the primary purpose of trade unions is to protect and to enhance the living standards of their members. In doing this, they inevitably represent a challenge to managerial prerogative and a source of increased labour costs. The British academic Alan Flanders in 1970 argued that union behaviour was characterised by:

- 'sword of justice' objectives;
- the advancement of job interests and not class interests;
- according the highest priority to delivering their objectives by industrial methods rather than political methods;
- pragmatism – dealing with matters in a sensible, flexible and realistic manner rather than being influenced by fixed theories or ideology.

Flanders argued that throughout their history trade unions have sought to secure more income, more leisure time and more employment stability for their members. They also attempted to enhance and protect their status by establishing employment rights – for example, the right to a certain wage, the right not to have to work long hours, and the right not to be subject to arbitrary dismissal. For this reason, Flanders contended that trade unions can be viewed as a 'sword of justice' seeking fairness of treatment for their members from employers and from the state.

Reflective activity 6.2

What do you think trade unions are for? Would you agree that their main aim should be to act as a 'sword of justice' on behalf of their members?

This 'sword of justice' behaviour is seen in the impact of trade union activity, for example, on pay distribution. The activities of trade unions in negotiating higher wages have a disproportionate effect on groups at the lower end of the pay spectrum. Therefore, this tends to reduce pay inequality, as Freeman and Medoff argued. For example, Metcalf (2005) estimated that if there were no trade unions, the wage differential between male and female employees would be 2.6 per cent higher than its level at the time his study was conducted. The corresponding figures he presented for non-manual/manual worker differentials and between white and black workers were +3.0 per cent and +1.4 per cent respectively. However, as Figure 6.2 shows, the 'gap' between the pay of union and non-union members has decreased significantly

Figure 6.2 Trade union wage premium, 1995–2023

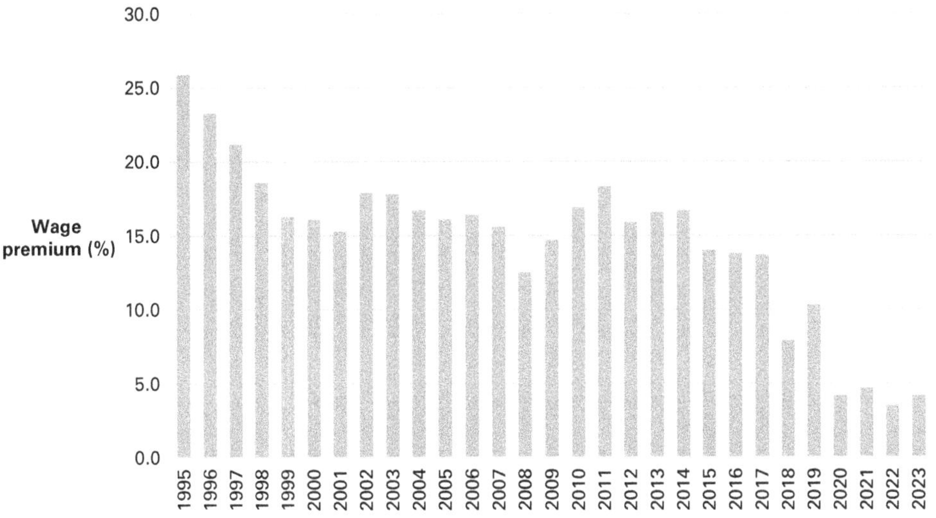

Wage premium (%)
30.0
25.0
20.0
15.0
10.0
5.0
0.0
1995 1996 1997 1998 1999 2000 2001 2002 2003 2004 2005 2006 2007 2008 2009 2010 2011 2012 2013 2014 2015 2016 2017 2018 2019 2020 2021 2022 2023

SOURCE: Department for Business and Trade

over the past two decades. In 1995, the premium was 26 per cent; however in 2023, this was just 4.2 per cent. Notably, this represented an increase on 2022, particularly among private sector workers, reflecting increased union power and activity (Department for Business and Trade, 2024).

This arguably reflects the declining influence and bargaining power of trade unions, even where they still have a presence in the workplace. As we noted in Chapter 2, in 2023, 39.2 per cent of employees had their pay determined through collective agreements while around half of all employees worked in workplaces which have no trade union presence (Department for Business and Trade, 2024). Among others, Dromey (2018: 8) has argued this has important consequences for pay inequality. In particular:

> the period between the 1930s and the late 1970s was characterised both by a significant rise in union membership and by a large decline in inequality, as measured by the share of income going to the top one per cent. Conversely, the period from 1979 until the late 1990s saw a rapid decline in trade union membership and a resurgence in inequality.

Bryson and Forth (2017) have also found that inequality in unionised organisations is lower, while there is extensive international evidence that links labour market inequality with lower levels of collective bargaining (Dabla-Norris et al, 2015).

Although trade unions still play a significant role in setting pay and other conditions, the contraction of collective bargaining since 1979 has seen trade unions revert to strategies based around individual representation and the enforcement of individual rights (Dickens and Hall, 2010). In fact, most shop stewards and workplace representatives spend the majority of their time providing advice to individual members over specific problems at work or providing representation in absence meetings, disciplinary and grievance hearings and redundancy consultations. More than three-quarters of union representatives spend their time representing members on disciplinary and grievance issues, whereas just 61 per cent spend time on rates of pay (van Wanrooy et al, 2013).

Trade unions also attempt to defend and further the interests of their members through political methods, including 'pressure group' activities in relation to the UK government, whether they are conducted by campaigns, delegations, lobbying or sitting on governmental and other advisory committees. At a national level, this role is played by pressurising the UK government to pass legislation favourable to trade unions and is usually co-ordinated by the Trades Union Congress (TUC). The TUC has 48 member unions with a total membership of more than 5.5 million. It performs two broad roles. Its main function is to act as the collective voice of the UK trade union movement to governments, intergovernmental bodies and international trade union bodies. The supreme authority in the TUC is its Annual Congress, which is held in September. Congress policy is decided on the basis of motions, submitted by affiliated unions, being accepted by a majority vote of delegates. The implementation of policy decided at Congress is the responsibility of the General Council, which is serviced by the general secretary.

Individual trade unions are also able to exert an influence over UK policy through their relationship with the Labour Party. Although the links between Labour and the unions have been weakened in recent years, fees from affiliated trade unions and additional donations make up a significant part of Labour Party funding. In addition, many Labour MPs have a trade union background and are union members. However, while the ties between unions and the Labour Party remain close, trade unions have often expressed disappointment that Labour governments have not provided greater support to trade union campaigns over issues such as employment legislation.

Reflective activity 6.3

To what extent do trade unions play a positive role in ensuring effective organisations, and what is the impact of collective bargaining on performance and productivity?

6.4 Trade unions – a declining force?

The defining feature of employment relations over the last five decades has been the decline in trade union membership and density. Total union membership in the UK peaked at an all-time high of 13.2 million members in 1979, but by 2023 this had more than halved to just 6.4 million. The rate of decline slowed markedly with the election of the Labour government in 1997, and between 2016 and 2020, there was a slight increase, but membership dropped again in 2021 and 2022, in the wake of the pandemic, before increasing a little in 2023.

Figure 6.3 provides a breakdown of union density by sector, which clearly shows the concentration of union membership in public services such as health, education and public administration. Trade union density is much larger in the public sector

Figure 6.3 Union density by industry, 2023

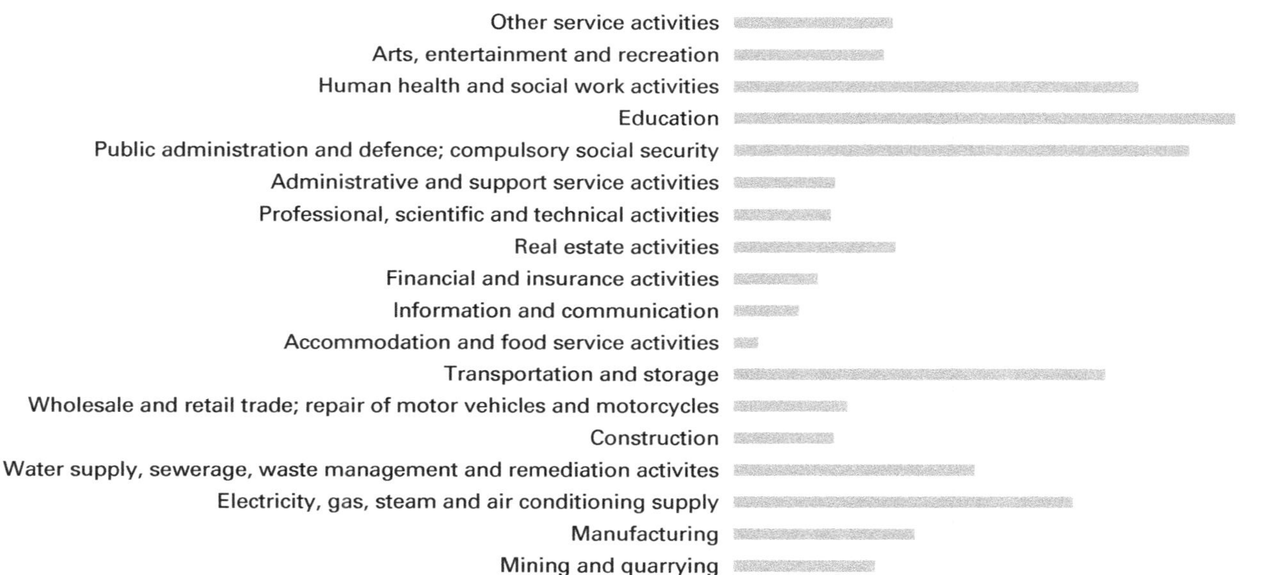

Other service activities
Arts, entertainment and recreation
Human health and social work activities
Education
Public administration and defence; compulsory social security
Administrative and support service activities
Professional, scientific and technical activities
Real estate activities
Financial and insurance activities
Information and communication
Accommodation and food service activities
Transportation and storage
Wholesale and retail trade; repair of motor vehicles and motorcycles
Construction
Water supply, sewerage, waste management and remediation activites
Electricity, gas, steam and air conditioning supply
Manufacturing
Mining and quarrying
0.0 5.0 10.0 15.0 20.0 25.0 30.0 35.0 40.0 45.0 50.0
Membership of trade unions as proportion of total employment (%)

SOURCE: Department for Business and Trade

(49 per cent) than the private sector (12 per cent). Density is particularly low in the private service sector, but even in manufacturing, once a stronghold of union organisation, just 17 per cent of workers were members in 2023. The decline in density has been particularly steep among men – just one in five male employees were union members in 2023. Women are now more likely to be unionised with around one-quarter in membership (Department for Business and Trade, 2024).

In addition, union membership among younger workers is low. In 2023, just over 5 per cent of 16–19-year-olds and 11.5 per cent of workers between the ages of 20 and 24 were union members. Furthermore, the membership of trade unions in the UK has become increasingly 'old'. In 1995, the highest concentration of union membership was in the 35–49 age group, while in 2023, workers aged 50 or over were most likely to be members of a union (40 per cent). While this creates a significant challenge for trade unions, there are tentative signs that recruitment among 16–24-year-olds may be improving.

Moreover, there has been a substantial shift in the personal and job characteristics of trade union members. Workers with degree-level qualifications (or equivalent) or those on middle incomes are more likely to be trade union members. More than one-quarter of those earning between £500 and £999 per week are union members compared to around one in ten of those workers paid less than £250 (Department for Business and Trade, 2024).

Reflective activity 6.4

What are the implications of the data on trade union membership outlined here for employment relations in general? To what extent will the changing composition of union membership shape the bargaining agenda?

However, falling membership and density is only one aspect of trade union decline. Just as important is the erosion of union organisation and representative capacity. Between 1984 and 2004, the estimated number of trade union representatives decreased from 335,000 to 128,000 (Charlwood and Forth, 2009). In 2011, just 7 per cent of all workplaces had an on-site union representative (van Wanrooy et al, 2013). Although there is a lack of reliable contemporary data, it is unlikely that this situation has improved. This not only constrains union effectiveness and influence but makes it more difficult to recruit new members.

6.5 Explaining trade union decline

There are a number of explanations for the progressive decline in trade union membership and density.

Business cycle

Some commentators have argued that trade union decline can be matched to the business cycle with periods of economic growth being associated with increasing union density as workers feel confident but also need their incomes to keep pace with rising prices. However, in times of recession and rising unemployment, unions will lose members who are made redundant while those in work may see union membership as both a risk and a cost, particularly if inflation is relatively low. Certainly, Figure 6.1 shows that the two major reductions in union membership coincided with sustained periods of high unemployment between the 1920s and early 1930s and again in the 1980s. Nonetheless, union membership and density did not recover in the late 1990s despite sustained economic growth and the election of a Labour government. At the time of writing the UK economy is experiencing very sluggish growth, however a combination of increased costs of living and tight labour markets (in the wake of the Covid pandemic, Brexit and the war in Ukraine) has seen trade unions become much more prominent in defending members' interests. Whether this will convert into a sustained increase in union density is yet to be seen.

Role of the state

Many people, particularly those in the labour movement, have blamed hostile government policy for reduced membership and influence. The fact that the decline in union membership coincided with the election of a Conservative government which enacted a programme of legislation designed to restrict union activity has given some credence to such beliefs. The state can influence membership directly through laws on recognition and the closed shop, and indirectly by creating the environment in which employee–management relations are conducted. In this way the state can undermine or promote collectivism. Freeman and Pelletier (1990) calculated a 'legislation index' according to how favourable or unfavourable various strands of labour laws were to unions in each year. They concluded that changes in the law in the 1980s were 'responsible for the entire decline' in union membership. However, this theory fails to explain why there have also been substantial declines in union membership in countries, such as the Republic of Ireland, in which 'anti-union' legislation has not been introduced. Nonetheless, it is likely that the approach of successive governments to industrial action and the marginalisation of trade unions within policy development has sent a clear signal to employers in the private sector that they have complete discretion over how they choose to manage employment relations. This in turn has shifted the balance of power against trade unions, thus reducing their effectiveness in the eyes of potential members.

Reflective activity 6.5

What impact do you think legislation has had on trade union influence? In your view has this legislation been necessary in restraining unreasonable union activity, or has it restricted the legitimate voices of union members?

Benefits of union membership

It has been argued that a key contributing factor to union decline is that for many workers the benefits of trade unions are now less clear than they once were (Fernie and Metcalf, 2005). As we have pointed out, an important advantage to the individual who joins a trade union is the wage premium compared with an equivalent non-member. However, as we have also seen, this gap has been progressively eroded. Therefore, even where unions are recognised there is less incentive for workers to join (Metcalf, 2005). In addition, it is also argued that the extension of employment rights (outlined in Chapter 3) has undermined the rationale for workplace representation and therefore for unions themselves. This has arguably been exacerbated by the expansion of alternative sources of advice, whereby employees with problems at work can ring the Acas helpline, visit the Citizens' Advice Bureau or consult an employment lawyer (sometimes for no initial charge).

Reflective activity 6.6

If you had a serious problem at work and needed advice from a third party, would you go to a union representative or consider joining a trade union? If not, who would you turn to and why?

Changing attitudes

In 2000, Millward et al suggested that workers had lost their taste for belonging to a union, but generally, workers are not negative to the idea of trade unions and what they represent; it is simply that they are unlikely to join up. As Towers (1997) has argued, this represents a 'frustrated demand', but nonetheless trade unions find it increasingly difficult to recruit new members to replace those leaving employment. As we have also seen, younger employees are much less likely to belong to a union than older workers, and this gap in membership rates by age has grown sharply in recent years. In 1975, 55 per cent of employees aged 18–64 were union members, but by 2001 this figure had fallen by 29 per cent. Membership rates were lower in both years for employees aged below 30. In 1975, union membership density was only 11 percentage points lower for younger people (48 per cent compared with 59 per cent), but by 2001 the gap had risen to 19 points (15 per cent compared with 34 per cent). Between 1979 and 2004, union density among young men fell by 39 percentage points and among young women by 23 points.

Metcalf (2005) has argued that the failure to recruit young workers is probably the main factor in explaining falling union density in workplaces where unions are recognised. Between 1983 and 1998, he points out, in workplaces where unions were recognised, the density of those aged 30 remained virtually unchanged at 70 per cent, but the density of those aged 18–25 almost halved from 67 per cent in 1983 to 41 per cent in 1998. One reason for the increasing gap between membership rates of younger and older workers is said to be the transmission of membership across generations. Blanden and Machin (2003) have shown that there is a

30 per cent higher probability of being a union member if your father is also a union member. Fewer parents are union members today than was previously the case, so – given the cross-generation correlation in trends of taking up union membership – fewer younger people are likely now, and in the future, to join trade unions.

However, as we discussed in Chapter 3, there are tentative signs that attitudes among new generations of workers may be more conducive to union organisation. Perceptions of inequality are increasingly stark and younger workers face particular challenges in terms of stagnant wages, the impact of new technology, job insecurity and rising costs of housing. In fact, as Vandaele (2018: 667) argues, evidence suggests that 'strong antagonistic attitudes towards unionism in principle are not at all common among young people'. Moreover, as we saw in Chapter 3, younger workers in the UK tend to have relatively positive attitudes to trade unions. Instead, the fundamental challenges reflect the contexts in which young workers enter the labour market and the wider lack of institutional presence of trade unions. In summary, although young people may like 'the idea' of trade unions these are seldom part of their experience of work.

Reflective activity 6.7

Why do you think that younger workers have been less likely to join trade unions than their older colleagues? To what extent do you think this is changing and what more could trade unions do to recruit younger workers?

Employer attitude and action

It is also argued that employers have become more hostile to unions. To examine this view one could look at plant closures, de-recognition activity and the new recognition of trade unions. There is no research evidence to support the hypothesis that union activity has resulted in a higher rate of plant closures among unionised workplaces relative to their non-union counterparts, nor that management embarked on the wholesale de-recognition of trade unions. Research by Machin (2000) and Blanden and Machin (2003), however, suggests that union decline is linked to the inability of unions to achieve recognition in newer workplaces. It shows that union recognition in workplaces with 25 or more employees fell from 64 per cent in 1980 to 42 per cent in 1998. In 1980, establishments less than 10 years old had a recognition rate of 0.59 – almost as large as the proportion of workplaces aged 10 or more years which recognised unions. They also show, however, that over the next 20 years, unions found it increasingly difficult to organise new workplaces. By 1998, just over a quarter of workplaces under 10 years of age recognised a trade union – only half the corresponding figure of older workplaces. This inability of unions to make an impact on new workplaces is not, as often thought, restricted to the private services sector. Only 14 per cent of manufacturing workplaces that opened between 1980 and 1998 recognised a trade union, compared with 50 per cent of those establishments opened in 1980 or before.

Blanden and Machin's (2003) research demonstrates that workplace age is a central factor in explaining the decline in union membership over the past 30 years. It also indicates that lower recognition rates in newer workplaces is not the end of the story, since even where union recognition was achieved, union density was 11 percentage points lower than in older workplaces. It could be argued that this is related to changed managerial attitudes to trade unions. According to WERS2011, four out of five managers said that 'they would rather consult directly with employees than with unions', a slight increase from 2004. However, this arguably reflects the spread of unitaristic perspectives among British managers, intensified and underpinned by the growth of HRM in which a focus on communication and engagement has replaced more traditional approaches to collective employment relations. In short, managers would rather not deal with trade unions and therefore in new workplaces and enterprises, managers are likely to avoid union recognition where possible.

Hostile terrain?

A fundamental challenge for trade unions has been the changing composition of industry and the labour market. What Blyton and Turnbull (2004) refer to as the 'Mountain Gorilla hypothesis' argues that, like the habitat of the mountain gorilla, the natural terrain that supports trade unions has progressively disappeared. The industries from which trade unionism grew – textiles, coal mining, iron and steel works, port transport, shipbuilding and car manufacturing – have been decimated through de-industrialisation, globalisation and, arguably, a lack of government support. These dangerous and physically demanding jobs, often in state-owned industries, in which trade union membership was extremely high, have been replaced by low-paid, unskilled service sector jobs with little tradition of trade union organisation and membership. At the same time, the growth of non-standard employment contracts has also hampered the ability of trade unions to recruit. Booth (1989) attributes over two-fifths of the decline in union membership in the 1980s to such compositional factors.

The challenge for trade unions – a lethal cocktail?

While it is difficult to attribute the rapid decline in trade union membership and density to a single explanation, together, the factors discussed here provide a potentially lethal cocktail for organised labour. The terrain in which they operate has been transformed and the environments in which union organisation thrived have all but disappeared. At the same time, the enterprises that have replaced them and their managers have embraced a unitarist perspective which reflects a preference for engaging directly with their employees. Therefore, in the absence of a regulatory framework which supports the role of trade unions in providing a source of collective voice, organisations often prefer to work without unions than with them. Where trade unions are not recognised, it is more difficult to demonstrate their potential effectiveness, and their lack of workplace presence means that potential members have little contact with, and are therefore less likely to join, trade unions. More broadly, trade unions are caught in a catch-22, in which falling density and presence reduces union bargaining power and, therefore, effectiveness, which in turn undermines the rationale for union membership.

 Reflective activity 6.8

Has trade union density and presence increased or reduced in your organisation? Why do you think this is? If your organisation does not currently recognise unions, can you see any circumstances under which it might do so?

6.6 The union response – strategies for survival, renewal and revitalisation

Given the scale of the challenge outlined in the previous section, developing strategies to survive in an increasingly hostile terrain and to renew workplace organisation has become a central issue for British trade unions. Some measures, such as mergers with other unions, have been, in part, forced by economic and practical necessity. However, the debate over the provision of services, workplace partnership and grassroots organising highlights questions over the fundamental purposes of unions.

Union mergers – efficiency and identity

As union membership declined, so did the revenue from subscriptions used to support organisational infrastructure. As with any other organisation, one response was to seek efficiencies by merging trade unions and so making significant savings on operational costs. In fact, mergers have been a constant part of trade union history, but over the last 40 years, as a result of trade union mergers, the number of unions affiliated to the TUC has fallen from 112 in 1979 to just 48 in 2024.

Furthermore, the trend in union mergers has been towards the formation of 'mega-unions' aspiring to represent whole sectors of the economy. This trend was confirmed by the merger in 2007 of Amicus (which itself was a result of a previous merger between Manufacturing Science and Finance, the AEEU (Amalgamated Engineering and Electrical Union) and two smaller unions, UNIFI and the GPMU) and the Transport and General Workers Union to form Unite, which now represents approximately 1.2 million members employed across the private and public sectors. The largest union in the UK, with approximately 1.4 million members, is UNISON, which was formed from NALGO, which traditionally represented local government officers, NUPE, which represented low-paid workers in the public services, and COHSE, which organised health service workers. A further aspiration underpinning the desire to merge trade unions was the potential of increased influence at both a national and international level with employers and government.

However, mergers have not been straightforward. Roger Undy's (2008) empirical study of union mergers found that potential transformative gains were difficult to achieve in practice, and that there was little impact in terms of union renewal. A key problem has been the resilience of different cultures and structures of constituent trade unions post-merger. Furthermore, it could be argued that the development of large super-unions not only created increased distance between members and the union but eroded the professional and occupational identities on which trade unions were built. Some potential members may see large unions as being too diffuse to represent their specific concerns. It is perhaps not surprising that new, smaller unions have emerged in recent years with more focus on specific parts of the workforce. We explore this in more detail below.

Workplace partnership – increased influence or collusion?

One of the main responses of trade unions to their declining fortunes was the development of workplace partnerships with employers. In some respects, this was underpinned by the importance placed on partnership by the Labour government elected in 1997. The Fairness at Work White Paper published in 1998 set out the new administration's philosophy. In relation to trade unions, it argued that:

> Trade unions can make the task of forging effective partnerships easier for employers and employees. In recent years they have changed to reflect change in business. Many trade unions now focus much more strongly on working with management to develop a flexible, skilled and motivated workforce. Trade unions can be a force for fair treatment, and a means of driving towards innovation and partnerships.

Partnership was also enthusiastically embraced by the TUC, which believed that more confrontational approaches to employment relations had failed to deliver benefits for unions or members. Perhaps more importantly, trade unions no longer had the industrial bargaining power to 'take on' employers; therefore, if unions were to rebuild, they had to do this by regaining their influence through constructive engagement. The message that underpinned this approach was that trade unions were 'good for business'. In 2002, the TUC published a report entitled *Partnership Works*, which argued that effective partnership working led to increased productivity and profitability at the same time as making work more rewarding and fulfilling. The report highlighted the work of the TUC's Partnership Institute in facilitating the development of partnerships across public and private sectors. The research detailed in the report claimed that partnership workplaces were one-third more likely to have financial performance that was 'a lot better than average'; and were a quarter more likely to have labour productivity that was also 'a lot better than average'.

The report also set out *six key principles* that make up a meaningful partnership agreement:

- a joint commitment to success of the enterprise;
- unions and employers recognising each other's legitimate interests and resolving difference in an atmosphere of trust;
- a commitment to employment security;
- a focus on the quality of working life;
- transparency and sharing information;
- mutual gains for unions and employers, delivering concrete improvements to business performance, terms and conditions, and employee involvement.

Reflective activity 6.9

What are the benefits and the potential drawbacks for trade unions of working in close partnership with employers? If you were a rank-and-file trade union member, how would you perceive 'partnership working'?

There is little doubt that partnership enabled trade unions to retain a foothold in organisations, and its supporters would argue that, as a consequence, unions were able to shape organisational decision-making (Tailby and Winchester, 2000). This in turn could demonstrate to members and potential members that unions had an influence that could have a demonstrable effect on their working lives.

However, unions did not enter partnership from a position of strength; instead, it reflected the weakness of union organisation. In entering into partnership in this way, it is not surprising that partnership tended to reflect managerial rather than union aspirations and was, arguably, a way of controlling potential union opposition to restructuring and change. Furthermore, it has been suggested that while partnership was seen as a necessity by senior full-time officials keen to retain a place at the negotiating table, it created a gulf between the unions' rank and file and their leadership (Wills, 2004). In this context, workers find it difficult to see tangible evidence that partnership has any demonstrable impact on increasing their job security or involvement with decision-making. Thus, while partnership strategies may consolidate union influence within a particular organisational setting, its impact on union renewal and revitalisation may be more questionable (Kelly, 2004; Stuart and Martinez Lucio, 2005).

REAL-WORLD EXAMPLE 6.1

Partnership at Deliveroo

In 2022, the GMB signed a partnership agreement with Deliveroo. As part of this arrangement, Deliveroo recognised the GMB as its official 'Rider Trade Union'. This followed legal action, which attempted to clarify the employment status of Deliveroo riders, and industrial action undertaken by riders. According to GMB, key elements of the agreement included:

- Two weeks of sick pay for riders
- A new parent grant of £1,000
- Free accident and third-party insurance
- The establishment of a Joint Council to agree policies relating to earnings, safety, diversity and benefits
- A right to be represented by GMB on issues at work.

For its part, Deliveroo welcomed the partnership saying that the GMB 'plays a vital role in shaping our ways of working at Deliveroo, and we share a common vision to make Deliveroo the best platform for riders to work'.

In 2024, the GMB, Deliveroo and a number of Deliveroo customer organisations set up a respect charter which developed a set of principles on the behaviour of riders and how they would be treated by customer organisations. Later, in May 2024, the GMB agreed increased minimum rates of guaranteed pay of £12 per hour plus expenses for bikes and e-bikes. However, the agreement came in the midst of an attempt by the IWGB union to push for recognition by Deliveroo. Part of this campaign was the ultimately unsuccessful legal challenge to establish the rights of Deliveroo riders as workers. The IWGB claimed that the partnership agreement with the GMB was part of an attempt by Deliveroo to undermine the recognition campaign. Furthermore, it is argued that relatively few Deliveroo riders are members of either union and that the GMB deal has not delivered significant benefits (McGurdy, 2024).

Notably, riders working for Deliveroo and UberEats, organised by another group, Job Delivery UK, staged unofficial industrial action on Valentine's Day, 2024. One of the organisers, writing in the *Guardian* on 14 February 2024, explained their experiences as follows:

> I have to spend about £3 on petrol, insurance, maintenance and other costs for every hour I work. So, if my account says I'm making £10 an hour, I'm actually making £7. I have to make nearly £14 just to earn the equivalent of the minimum wage. It's rare that I make that much nowadays… I get so exhausted that I have to go home for a nap between lunch and dinner. The apps talk about flexibility, but there's no flexibility at all: you have to work the peak hours, or you don't make anywhere near enough money… We've had enough. That's why we started organising this strike. Thousands of us across more than 90 areas went on strike on 2 February, and we're going to do it again today. Some might point out that Deliveroo riders have a union: the GMB signed a 'partnership' deal with the platform in 2022 and calls itself 'the union for riders'. But we are fighting for ourselves.

Reflective activity 6.10

What are the main characteristics of the approach outlined in Real-world example 6.1? What do you think the GMB's motivations were in entering into this partnership? To what extent does this offer a sustainable way of increasing union influence and extending organisation?

Nonetheless, partnership remains a central aspect of employment relations, and a number of commentators argue that, given an increasingly hostile environment for organising, it can provide an opportunity for trade unions to develop specific areas of influence and shape important issues that affect their members. One particular example of this has been the development of partnership to identify and address the learning needs of the workforce, through the union learning initiative. This has been embraced by trade unions who have developed networks of union learning representatives and drawn on government support through the Union Learning Fund to provide learning opportunities for their members. This not only provides benefits for workers but can also strengthen union organisation by establishing a connection between union membership and employability and strengthening relationships between the unions and their members (Rainbird and Stuart, 2011).

Research by Bennett (2014a) into learning partnerships in the north-west of England revealed that the collaborative work of managers and union learning representatives (ULRs) in the workplace not only increased the skills, knowledge and, therefore, effectiveness of the workforce, it also reduced individual and collective conflict within those organisations which had signed up to learning partnerships. Table 6.1 summarises the key findings.

Table 6.1 The effectiveness of learning partnerships: a summary of the findings

Impact of learning on workplace conflict	Key findings
Context for the conflict	• On-going government support for union learning projects • Pressure to deliver learning outcomes • Pressure of current economic climate and in particular job losses
Facilitative nature of the learning partnership	• Based on a learning agreement – Agreed funding arrangements – Time off for lead ULR – Support for learners • Clear joint objectives identified • On-site learning centre • On-going project worker support • Inter-union collaboration • Role of 'key players' in organisation
Managing individual conflict	• Encourages members to share workplace problems with their ULR • Pre-empts performance issues through early intervention in training • Addresses disadvantage • Engenders employee commitment • Promotes well-being • Supports career development
Managing collective conflict	• Facilitates systematic deployment of ULRs to manage redundancy and redeployment • Promotes better trust between partners • Develops inter-union co-operation • Enhances branch organisation

SOURCE: Bennett (2014a: 28)

The servicing agenda

The role and significance of servicing has become a central theme within the debate over the effectiveness of unions' renewal strategies. However, it is important to stress that providing 'services' to individual members in terms of advice and representational support over discipline, grievance and redundancy is not a new phenomenon and has always been an important element of union activity and particularly the work of local shop stewards and representatives.

Nonetheless, the erosion of collective bargaining and reduction of union influence over collective issues has meant that greater emphasis has been placed on individual representation. As we noted in Chapter 3, in the 1960s and 1970s, disputes relating to individual workers and employees were often resolved through collective channels and the threat of industrial action. Moreover, disciplinary and grievance issues were a major source of days lost through industrial stoppages (see Chapter 9 for further details). However, as the threat of industrial action became less acute and the scope of individual employment legislation expanded following the election of the Labour government in 1997, trade unions redirected efforts to enforcing these rights and the threat of employment tribunal litigation replaced that of industrial action (Dickens and Hall, 2010).

This has had important consequences for the role played by local representatives and the relationships between unions and their members. For many representatives, individual 'case-work' takes up the bulk of their time, arguably crowding out other activities, in particular recruitment and organising. Given the shrinking number of representatives (noted earlier), this places particular stress on the representative capacity of trade unions. Furthermore, it has been argued that this creates a passive relationship (Jarley, 2005; Saundry and McKeown, 2013) between the member and union in which the former does not necessarily see the union as a living and breathing entity of which they are a part, but as a provider of services. Given the limited resources of trade unions, some would argue that this is unsustainable.

In addition to the traditional services provided to union members, one response to declining membership was the development of a range of discounted benefits. While trade union members had long been able to access legal advice on work-related matters, they were now able to get discounted advice over other personal matters, cheap car and home insurance, and retail discounts. It is this aspect of servicing that critics often point to in arguing that it cannot provide a substantive basis for union renewal. In particular, it is claimed that such benefits are not among the main reasons why members join trade unions. The most cited evidence to support this contention is the seminal research conducted by Jeremy Waddington and Colin Whitson (1997), who surveyed over 11,000 new union members in 12 unions between 1991 and 1993. The key results of this survey (Figure 6.4) show that the main reason for joining was 'support if I had a problem at work', cited by almost three-quarters of respondents, followed by 'improved pay and conditions' (36.4 per cent).

Therefore, Waddington and Whitson argued that their findings confirmed 'the centrality of collective reasons for joining, and support among new members for traditional trade union activities' (1997: 520). Furthermore, the fact that individual benefits rank very low has been cited as evidence that trade unions should focus on traditional bargaining activities as opposed to narrow servicing strategies. However, 'support' for problems at work does not necessarily infer collective reasons and is consistent with individual representation for disciplinary, grievance, absence and

Figure 6.4 Reason for joining trade unions

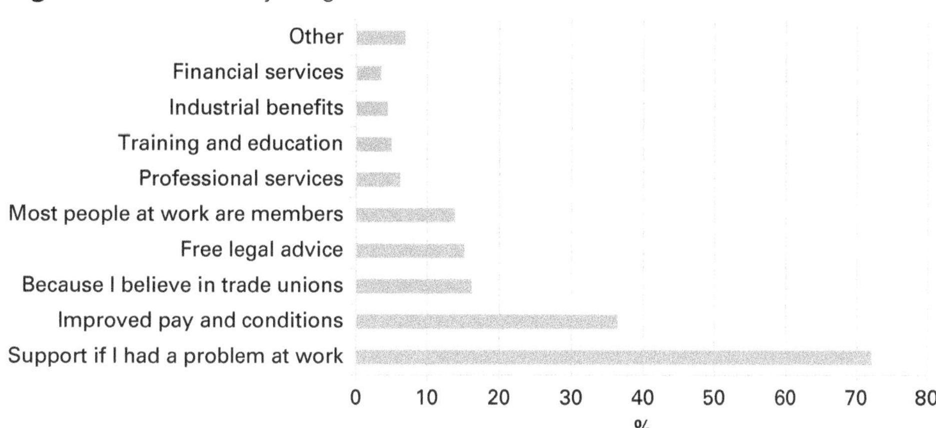

SOURCE: Waddington and Whitson (1997)

redundancy. Indeed, if unions were not able to provide effective representation over individual issues, both recruiting and retaining members would prove particularly challenging.

The importance of facility time

In this context the 'facility time' provided to trade union representatives is critical. Facility time refers to the extent to which an employer allows representatives to conduct their union work within normal working time, for which they are paid. This is underpinned by statutory rights contained in section 198 of the Trade Union and Labour Relations (Consolidation) Act 1998, which provides for employers to give officials of recognised unions reasonable paid time off for the purpose of carrying out trade union duties. Further clarification and guidance is provided by the Acas Code of Practice – Time off for Trade Union Duties (Acas, 2010).

PAID TIME OFF FOR TRADE UNION DUTIES

Examples of trade union duties which reps have the right to paid time off for are:

- negotiating pay, terms and conditions;
- helping union members with disciplinary or grievance procedures, including meetings to hear their cases;
- going with union members to meetings with their line manager to discuss flexible working requests;
- discussing issues that affect union members like redundancies or the sale of the business;
- training in connection with their role as a representative.

Union learning reps have the right to paid time off to:

- analyse the learning or training needs of union members;
- give information and advice about learning or training;
- arrange or encourage learning or training;
- discuss their activities as a learning representative with their employer;
- train as a learning representative.

In addition, trade union representatives have a right to unpaid time off to undertake union activities such as taking part in union meetings with other representatives and officials. Representatives are entitled to 'reasonable' time off; however, this is not specified in the legislation, although the Acas Code of Practice suggests that this should reflect the size of the organisation, the production process, the need to maintain a service to the public and the need for safety and security at all times. It is generally advisable for employers to negotiate agreements over facility time with recognised unions to avoid any unnecessary conflict.

Perhaps not surprisingly, some employers are reluctant to allow their staff to take significant amounts of time away from their day job to act as a union representative. Line managers in particular can object to vital members of the team being pulled away on union business. In recent years we have seen facility time restricted, and the Trade Union Act 2016 introduced a new requirement for public sector employers to report the level of facility time granted to union representatives and gave the Secretary of State the power to limit facility time where it was deemed to be unreasonable. However, there is good evidence to suggest that providing reasonable facility time to trade union representatives makes good sense for businesses and the UK economy (see the following box). As we argue in Chapters 9, 10 and 11, union representatives often play a constructive role in the resolution of conflict and they are particularly effective when there is a high degree of trust with the employer (see also Saundry et al, 2016). The provision of facility time provides space in which high-trust relationships between union representatives and managers can be built and also gives representatives time for the vital conversations with members that often resolve difficult workplace problems at the earliest possible stage.

THE CASE FOR FACILITY TIME

Research conducted by the government in 2007 (Department of Trade and Industry, 2007), found that the work of union representatives contributed to annual savings of between £322 million and £977 million due to lower levels of resignations, dismissals, employment tribunals and work-related injuries and illnesses.

Hoque and Bacon's (2015) analysis of WERS2011 found that the presence of union representatives was generally welcomed by managers and positively associated with partnership working. They concluded that the increased regulation of facility time was 'more likely to hinder rather than support public sector managers in their attempts to improve public service provision in the future'.

A major study funded by Acas found that high-trust relationships between union representatives and HR practitioners underpinned informal resolution; however:

> a lack of union capacity was increasingly causing delays to formal disciplinary and grievance proceedings and also making informal resolution more difficult... any legislative measures which further weakened union capacity would have a negative knock-on effect on the ability of organisations to manage and resolve conflict (Saundry et al, 2016: 31–32).

Research undertaken by NatCen commissioned by UNISON (Mitchell et al, 2012) found that:

- HR practitioners felt that working in partnership with trade unions improved employment relations and had a positive impact on the employers' reputation;
- Union representation made early resolution of disciplinary and grievances more likely;
- Union representatives played a valuable role during redundancy exercises, improving communication and reducing potential conflict.

Gall (2016) concluded that for every £1 spent on facility time, the accrued benefits have a value of between £2.31 and £6.24.

Reflective activity 6.11

Does your organisation recognise trade unions? If so, do you feel that trade union representatives play a positive role in helping to resolve workplace problems?

Union organising – a new approach

There is little doubt that the provision of individual representational services has become central to union strategies to recruit and retain members. Moreover, while few union organisers would claim that member benefits, such as those listed earlier, are primary reasons for joining trade unions, they may be important as added incentives to 'seal the deal' with new recruits. However, a reliance on individual services is unsustainable and counter productive in the longer run. These services have to be provided by an increasingly small group of (often older) union activists (see Charlwood and Terry, 2007; Charlwood and Angrave, 2014). Therefore, unions will find it difficult to meet the growing demands of their members. This in turn could lead to dissatisfaction and consequently problems in both recruiting new and retaining existing members if the union is unable to provide them with the support that they require. Perhaps more fundamentally, it has been argued that this servicing agenda has hollowed out union organisation, severing bonds between union officials and members (Jarley, 2005).

In response, an alternative approach seeks to focus on 'union organising'. While this covers a wide range of strategies and practices (Simms and Holgate, 2010), the essential components are to:

1. identify, recruit and develop new workplace union leaders and by doing this rebuild the representative capacity of local branches;
2. mobilise workers and develop collective consciousness around local concerns and issues;
3. encourage a culture of self-organisation through which members become more empowered and take responsibility for addressing and resolving issues;
4. increase membership density, strengthen bargaining power and consequently secure demonstrable improvements in terms and conditions.

Most organising strategies contain these elements; however, different unions place an emphasis on certain aspects. For example, Simms and Holgate distinguish between approaches which are based on the 'political imperative of worker self-organisation' (2010: 164) pursued in the UK by unions such as the GMB and Unite, compared with unions such as USDAW, who place a much greater emphasis on increasing membership density and strengthening existing representative structures.

Evidence from the UK is mixed – unions have been successful in some instances in securing recognition and it could be argued that the slowing of the rate of decline of union density and membership even during the recession following the financial collapse in 2008 is due, in some part, to more effective organising efforts (van Wanrooy et al, 2013). However, long-term increases in union density have been elusive (Gall, 2007) and an authoritative review of union organising in the UK conducted by Mel Simms, Jane Holgate and Ed Heery concluded 'that thirteen years of organising activity has made comparatively little impact on formal aggregate measures of union power' (2012: 163).

Debates over the effectiveness of union organising have tended to focus on the different approaches that unions have taken and the relationship between organising and the use of other servicing and partnership approaches (Heery, 2002). It can be argued that as organising is based on developing grass-roots campaigns around collective grievances with the employer, this is incompatible with workplace partnership. Therefore, the impact of organising is restricted by concerns that union officials have over maintaining relationships with the employer. It is certainly the case that most trade unions use partnership and organising strategies concurrently, even if they may adopt different approaches for different settings.

Saundry and Wibberley's (2014a) study of a major organising campaign in the public sector in the UK found that outcomes were improved where there were positive employer–union relationships which provided access to workers and workplaces.

However, the research found two main obstacles to successful organising. First, there is a tension between short-term pressures on unions to curb declining membership and the longer-term sustainable returns that an organising-led approach aims to achieve. Therefore, there is a danger that engagement, empowerment and the development of grass-roots leadership are sacrificed at the 'altar of quantitative recruitment goals' (Hurd, 2004).

Second, there are tensions between the competing visions of the servicing and organising approaches. While engaging and empowering rank-and-file members is undoubtedly a positive aspiration, the reality (at least in the short term) for many local representatives is that they face a demand for the representational services. Moreover, retaining members recruited through an organising campaign depends largely on whether the local union can respond effectively to that member's request for support. Unless they are seen to be able to defend their members effectively, there is little prospect of building a sense of engagement, which is arguably a prerequisite for the development of self-organisation.

It could be argued that whether organising prioritises the recruitment of new members or more relational approaches to stimulating grass-roots activism, it is important only in so far as it reflects the challenges posed by different organisational contexts. But within both approaches, the union must have the commitment and the resources to support the mentoring, development and training of new representatives and to provide a context in which strong, trusting relationships between members and the union, and crucially between union activists and officers, can be built.

A further criticism of union organising has come from US academic Paul Jarley, who argues that union organising can sometimes be insular and does not extend outside the workplace to the hard-to-reach groups with which unions must engage. Therefore he argues that union renewal strategies need to 'recreate community in the workplace' by focusing on people rather than issues and building 'personal relationships among all members of the work group in ways that create an emotional bond among the workers and between the workers and the union leadership' (Jarley, 2005: 12–13).

More recently in the UK, there has been a greater focus on 'community organising', whereby trade unions have attempted to develop strategic alliances with community groups (McBride and Greenwood, 2009; Wills and Simms, 2004; Holgate, 2015b). By forming networks in this way, it is hoped that unions can achieve key goals, for example increasing wages for the lowest paid, but also engage with groups of workers who otherwise are resistant to, or have little inclination towards, joining trade unions. One of the best-known examples was the successful campaign conducted by Citizens UK to persuade employers in the capital to pay the Living Wage – here trade unions such as UNISON joined a coalition of church and other groups to lobby major corporations to pay their lowest-paid workers in London a wage significantly above the national minimum wage. Importantly, many of the workers involved were migrants to the UK, often employed on a part-time or temporary basis and therefore typical of the groups that trade unions need to attract but often struggle to reach.

Jane Holgate's (2015a) international study of community organising found that there were opportunities for trade unions to extend organisation through building broader community alliances and importantly to find out the real needs, views and aspirations of their members and potential members. However, in the UK, there was a tendency for unions to adopt an instrumental attitude, looking for short-term organising gains, which hampered their ability to develop long-term and mutually beneficial relationships with community groups. Interestingly, a number of new smaller unions have also emerged, such as the IWGB (see Real-world example 6.2), which specifically organise among more precarious groups of workers. They tend to use legal action and adopt high-profile and disruptive campaigns to try to win improved conditions for their members. Some commentators have suggested that less bureaucratic and arguably more agile forms of union organisation have the potential to reach groups of workers who may be resistant to more conventional organising approaches (Bertolini and Dukes, 2021). However, whether this approach can be scaled up and replicated across wider sectors of the economy is questionable. Moreover, it has been argued that strategies that focus specifically on litigation to deliver radical improvements to workers' lives and experiences may have limitations (Adams, 2023).

REAL-WORLD EXAMPLE 6.2

IWGB – the future of trade unions?

One of the apparent trade union success stories in recent years is the growth of the IWGB (Independent Workers Union of Great Britain). The IWGB was set up in 2012 and now has more than 2,500 members. It developed out of campaigns to improve the conditions of low-paid and outsourced cleaners working at the University of London. It particularly represents workers in more precarious areas of the economy, including those working in the gig economy and outsourced services. A significant proportion of its membership are migrant workers for whom English is not their first language.

The IWGB is much smaller than other unions and claims to be a 'grass-roots' union operating with a lower cost base and less bureaucracy. It also has a robust approach to representing its members, using legal action in the courts to establish rights for gig economy workers, including those working for Uber, CitySprint and Addison Lee. In contrast to the partnership approaches preferred by some of the larger unions, it uses high-profile, visible and disruptive campaigns against employers, often aiming to inflict reputational damage – this has included targeting customers and clients of firms with whom they are in dispute – and making use of social media and crowdfunding to boost its campaigning.

Reflective activity 6.12

Some commentators have suggested that the IWGB offers an alternative model for the future development of trade unions in the UK. What are the features that distinguish the IWGB from some of the larger trade unions? What are the advantages and limitations of this model? Are there lessons that the wider trade union movement could learn from the IWGB?

A slightly more conventional set of recommendations was produced by the Fabian Society in 2017 in a report entitled *Future Unions: Towards a membership renaissance in the private sector* (Tait, 2017). This specifically targeted the problems faced by trade unions in organising private sector workers and those in younger age groups. The report suggested an 11-point plan as follows:

1. **Answer the 'what can you do for me?' question.** Unions need to be able to give prospective members a tangible idea of what they should expect as a member, using real-world examples and qualified promises to echo the marketing strategies of disruptive start-up businesses.
2. **Be representative of the workforce.** Unions need to set out plans to ensure their reps, committees, staff teams and leadership are as diverse as the industries in which they organise.
3. **Introduce discount membership rates.** Unions should offer discounted membership deals to under-35s and to workers in unrecognised workplaces – to bring in younger members and to acknowledge that workers in unorganised workplaces tend to get less from their membership.
4. **Provide 'instant breakdown cover' for workers with pre-existing problems.** Unions should follow the lead of the AA by committing to provide non-members with instant support for pre-existing issues in exchange for a fee and an upfront commitment to membership.
5. **Reach out to the workforce of the future.** Unions should understand the journey that brings workers into their industries and occupations and deliver outreach activities in key parts of this pipeline, in order to educate future employees about how unions can support them in their career.
6. **Invest in technology to reach hard-to-reach workers.** Unions should invest in the development of tools, apps and other tech-based solutions to make it economically viable to organise isolated and dispersed workers.
7. **Establish career development centres.** Unions must support workers who don't expect to be in their job or sector for life by helping them develop their careers – to help people prepare for the future, while also bargaining for the here and now.
8. **Make the most of available data.** Unions are sitting on an abundance of data, much of which can be put to better use to improve the effectiveness of campaigns, recruitment strategies and overall decision-making.
9. **Set standards across multiple workplaces.** Unions should consider establishing or promoting sectoral standards to improve work across multiple workplaces.
10. **Collaborate to increase bargaining power.** In the 150th anniversary of the foundation of the TUC, unions should come together to agree a new collective mission to reverse historic membership decline. This should involve giving the TUC a new role as a clearing house for union membership, through which workers can 'join the family' of the union movement.
11. **Build a new partnership with government and business.** Unions should extend a hand of friendship to good, responsible employers with a new cross-union kitemark scheme to reward good employment practice. In return, government and business should acknowledge the vital contribution unions can make, especially as the fourth industrial revolution gathers pace, and give

unions access to all workplaces and end union-busting. This new partnership should form the basis of a new industrial relations framework for the UK, complemented by sector-level forums for unions, employers and, where necessary, government to co-create plans to boost productivity, fill skills gaps and improve work for all.

SOURCE: Fabian Society. Available at: https://fabians.org.uk/11-steps-to-stem-trade-union-decline/

Reflective activity 6.13

Do you think that the Fabian Society's recommendations provide a coherent plan for the future of trade unions? Which of these suggestions would be most effective in boosting trade union membership and organisation?

The non-union alternative?

The decline of trade unions in the UK has created what Towers (1997) called the 'representation gap', with no union members in more than three-quarters of workplaces and no on-site union representatives in more than nine out of ten workplaces. However, a key question is, have alternative, non-union forms of representation expanded to fill this gap? The short answer to this is no. Although there has been some growth in the incidence of non-union representatives in large private sector organisations, from 6 per cent in 2004 to 11 per cent in 2011, non-union representatives could be found in just 7 per cent of British workplaces (van Wanrooy et al, 2013). These were more likely to be found in larger workplaces and, unlike union representatives, there was little difference in coverage between the public and private sectors, in which 13 per cent and 18 per cent of employees respectively had access to a non-union representative.

Interestingly, the roles played by union and non-union representatives appear to be very different. WERS2011 found that the three most common issues that union representatives spent time on were discipline and grievance (78 per cent), health and safety (69 per cent) and pay (61 per cent). In contrast, 44 per cent, 52 per cent and 50 per cent of non-union representatives spent time on these matters.

REAL-WORLD EXAMPLE 6.3

Non-union representatives in Marks & Spencer PLC

One of the foremost examples of non-union representation is operated by Marks & Spencer PLC. Marks & Spencer does not recognise trade unions and has actively resisted attempts by USDAW, Unite and the GMB to organise its employees. The company has a network of elected employee representatives, who form its Business Involvement Group (BIG).

According to Marks & Spencer:

> through the BIG network, the Company informs, involves and consults with its people on the matters that affect them. The Company's commitment to BIG means that colleagues have the chance to voice their opinions and ideas, get answers and have their views represented when the business considers changes that affect them. This means everyone has an opportunity to positively influence the business we work in.

BIG representatives are elected at business unit, regional and national level every five years. Formal consultative mechanisms at business unit, regional and national level are supplemented by regular informal meetings between employee representatives and managers. However, BIG representatives do not negotiate as such.

Importantly, unlike most non-union representatives, BIG representatives are trained by the company and have a relatively wide role, which includes accompanying employees at disciplinary or grievance hearings; representing employees' views, either by raising issues on the behalf of other staff, or by asking for colleagues' feedback as requested by management; and acting as a channel for communicating changes to employees. In addition, staff are encouraged to discuss their concerns with a representative before raising a grievance or appeal, and if they are facing disciplinary action.

Reflective activity 6.14

What are the advantages for Marks & Spencer of taking this approach to employee representation? Do you think it has any limitations, from the point of view of both the organisation and its employees?

The research to date also casts doubt on the effectiveness of non-union representation. One of the main difficulties facing non-union representatives is that, unlike their union counterparts, their rights to paid time off and protection against detriment or dismissal are limited to specific situations and contexts, which include:

- acting as a health and safety representative;
- representative duties in relation to health and safety;
- acting as a representative under the Information and Consultation of Employees (ICE) Regulations;
- membership of a European works council;
- representative duties in relation to pensions.

Therefore, non-union representatives have no rights to time off in regard to the core representative roles in discipline and grievance and also no rights in relation to day-to-day organisational consultative structures. Furthermore, if an employer took disciplinary action against or dismissed a non-union representative for activity that fell outside those contexts just outlined, they would not be protected.

This has three effects: first, it may deter employees from taking on a representative role; second, it means that non-union representatives are dependent on the support and patronage of the employer; and third, it will inevitably restrict the representative in their activities. The independence of non-union representatives is also questionable given the fact that fewer than 40 per cent are elected, with the majority either taking on the role unopposed or selected by the employer (Moore et al, 2008). In addition, while trade union representatives have potential sanctions such as strike action or litigation at their disposal to lever concessions from management, this is not the case for non-union representatives. If a non-union representative encouraged fellow employees to withdraw their labour, they would not have the immunity given to industrial action officially sanctioned by trade unions. In addition, they are in no position to support employees in taking legal action against their employer.

There is clear evidence from the WERS series of data that non-union representatives generally have more positive views about the state of employment relations in their organisations compared with their unionised counterparts. Furthermore, WERS2011 found that non-union representatives were more likely to trust managers to act with honesty and integrity (93 per cent) than their union counterparts (66 per cent) and mutual trust between managers and non-union representatives was much higher than between union representatives and managers (van Wanrooy et al, 2013). This could simply be because relationships are more positive in non-unionised workplaces or reflect the fact that trade unions are more likely to be organised in workplaces in which there are employment relations challenges. However, it could also reflect a greater acquiescence on the part of non-union representatives. Certainly, Charlwood and Forth (2009) found that non-union representatives appeared not to be valued and appreciated by the employees they covered.

Non-unionised channels of representation tend to be more effective when there is a threat of greater union presence (Gollan, 2006). For example, it could be argued that Marks & Spencer has made a serious commitment to its BIG representatives because of the consistent attempts by unions such as USDAW to organise its staff and so force recognition.

6.7 Summary

This chapter has focused in some detail on the challenges facing trade unions in the UK. This may seem questionable given the fact that they represent only one in four workers; however, they remain the main source of employee representation in British workplaces and retain significant influence in many larger organisations. Although there has been some increase in the prevalence of non-union forms of representation, these have not filled the gap left by union decline, and there are significant questions over their ability to provide effective and independent support for employees. The key problem is that the non-union employee 'voice' is currently almost totally dependent on the patronage of the employer, and representatives lack credibility and the power to threaten and enforce any realistic sanctions.

In the absence of the development of any alternative, the role of trade unions in providing effective representation remains a core issue in employment relations. As we argue throughout this book, representation does not just provide support to employees but can facilitate the management and resolution of conflict and underpin notions of justice and fairness which form the basis of employee engagement. The future of trade unions and employee representation is therefore an important question for both employees and employers. However, unions face significant challenges. The nature of work in the UK has changed rapidly in recent years away from the full-time, male, skilled manual workers who formed the bedrock of union organisation. The 'tradition' of trade union membership has also faded as future generations entering workplaces are often greeted with no visible signs of unionisation and have little familial link with the labour movement. Interestingly, evidence suggests that young workers are not necessarily anti-union and often exhibit a collective identity around shared problems (Tailby and Pollert, 2011). Indeed, there is growing evidence that post-pandemic, younger workers see trade unions as playing a positive role and are much less negative about unions taking industrial action than some older sections of the community. At the same time, the influence and visibility of trade unions is at its highest level (at the time of writing in 2024) for some time.

Unions have placed significant faith in renewal through rebuilding grass-roots organisation. However, while there are some examples where this has generated positive results, organising has tended to consolidate union density and influence where it was already relatively strong. The emergence of new smaller and more agile trade unions such as the IWGB offers an alternative model. But whether their success can be replicated in more conventional areas of the labour market is unclear. It is difficult to escape the conclusion that if unions are to have a future and if structures of employee representation are to survive in contemporary workplaces, it is likely to depend on the provision of statutory support for collective representation and bargaining. Even organisations such as the IMF and the OECD have recently pointed to the economic benefits of collective bargaining. In this context, it will be interesting to see whether the policies of the Labour government elected in July 2024 will provide a more conducive environment for union organisation and lead to a renewal of workplace representation.

KEY LEARNING POINTS

- Trade unions developed in response to the rapid industrialisation of Britain in the nineteenth century. They subsequently grew to represent the majority of workers in British workplaces by the end of the 1970s.
- The main functions of trade unions are to negotiate on behalf of their members in order to defend and improve their terms and conditions of work. They also provide support and representation to individual members who may have a problem at work. This latter role has come to dominate the work done by unions as the scale and scope of collective bargaining has been curtailed.

- The membership of trade unions and their influence in employment relations has been rapidly eroded in the last four decades. This is due to a combination of factors: de-industrialisation; more ambivalent (or even hostile) attitudes to trade unions on the part of government and employers; globalisation; and reduced power and effectiveness.
- Despite the decline of trade unions, there is substantial evidence that they play a key role, not just in representing the interests of their members, but in maintaining good employment relations and helping to resolve workplace conflict. Consequently, there is a strong case for employers, particularly in larger organisations, to invest in developing constructive relationships with trade unions.
- Trade unions have adopted a variety of approaches in an attempt to manage, arrest and reverse the decline in membership and density. This has included: union mergers to reduce costs and increase political influence; the provision of a wide range of member benefits and incentives; the development of workplace partnerships with employers; and investment in grass-roots organising in an attempt to build capacity and union activity. The evidence suggests that while a greater focus on organising may have slowed the rate of decline, it has not as yet significantly strengthened union power and influence.
- Non-union forms of representation have not filled the gap left by trade unions. Furthermore, research suggests that they often lack credibility with employees. This is in part due to the fact that they have relatively few statutory protections and lack independence from the employer. They also tend to be less well trained than their trade union counterparts.
- Perhaps the most significant developments in the representation of employee interests has come through the development of broad community alliances and in campaigns over issues such as the Living Wage. Trade unions are now placing greater emphasis on building coalitions with such groups and this may be one way that they can begin to rebuild some of the influence that they have lost.
- Despite the challenges facing unions, 2022 and 2023 saw an increase in union activity and influence. Membership and the union wage premium increased while there was evidence of increasing support for trade unions, particularly among younger people. The election of the Labour government in July 2024 also has the potential to create a much more conducive environment for trade union organising and worker representation.

Review Questions

1 What were the main reasons for the development of trade unions? To what extent does the rationale for trade unions still exist today?
2 Do you think that effective representation has benefits for employers? From the perspective of an employer, what are the main advantages and disadvantages of recognising, and managing with, trade unions?
3 What are the main reasons for trade union decline? Why do you think that employees in your workplace are not trade union members?
4 If you were employed as a marketing specialist by a trade union to enhance its image and boost its appeal to younger workers, what would be the main elements of your campaign?
5 Do you have non-union representatives in your workplace? If yes, how effective are they and why do you think this is?
6 Do you think that non-union representatives can fill the place left by trade unions?
7 What are the main barriers to trade unions successfully revitalising their workplace capacity and organisation? To what extent do you think that alliances with broader community groups offer a way forward for trade unions?

Explore further

Adams, Z (2023) Legal mobilisations, trade unions and radical social change: a case study of the IWGB, *Industrial Law Journal*, **52** (3), pp 560–94 https://doi.org/10.1093/indlaw/dwac031 (archived at https://perma.cc/C4LQ-22WA).

Bertolini, A and Dukes, R (2021) Trade unions and platform workers in the UK: worker representation in the shadow of the law, *Industrial Law Journal*, **50** (4), pp 662–88 https://doi.org/10.1093/indlaw/dwab022 (archived at https://perma.cc/C7EX-J9VS).

Freeman, R and Medoff, J (1984) *What Do Unions Do?* Basic Books, New York.

Gall, G (2016) *The Benefits of Paid Time off for Trade Union Representatives*, Trades Union Congress. Available from: https://www.tuc.org.uk/sites/default/files/Facility_Time_Report_2016.pdf (archived at https://perma.cc/U6TS-X9SM) [accessed 18 September 2019].

Gollan, P (2006) Representation at Suncorp – what do the employees want?, *Human Resource Management Journal*, **16** (3), pp 268–86.

Holgate, J (2015b) Community organising in the UK: a 'new' approach for trade unions? *Economic and Industrial Democracy*, **36** (3), pp 431–55.

Tait, C (2017) *11 Steps to Stem Trade Union Decline*, Fabian Society. Available from: https://fabians.org.uk/11-steps-to-stem-trade-union-decline/ (archived at https://perma.cc/3CDW-QZJA) (accessed 4 October 2019).

Vandaele, K (2018) How can trade unions in Europe connect with young workers?, in O'Reilly, J et al (eds) *Youth Labor in Transition: Inequalities, mobility, and policies in Europe*, New York, Oxford Academic, pp 661–88.

Websites

www.iwgb.org.uk (archived at https://perma.cc/J8Q6-PB29) – website of the IWGB trade union; provides details of aims, structures and current campaigns.

www.tuc.org.uk (archived at https://perma.cc/9NZC-ADXW) – the website of the trades union congress contains a wide range of information about national issues relating to work employment.

www.unison.org.uk (archived at https://perma.cc/R4BC-HKCT) – the website of UNISON, one of the largest unions in the UK mainly representing those working in the public sector.

www.unitetheunion.org (archived at https://perma.cc/8QUE-DQCN) – website of Unite providing details of current union activity, action and campaigns.

07 Equality, diversity and inclusion

Overview

This chapter explores the meaning and implementation of equality, diversity and inclusion within the study of employment relations. The concepts of equality, diversity and inclusion relate closely to notions of fairness and 'good work', while negative experiences of inequality and discrimination run counter to the aspiration that employers and HR professionals should 'do what's right', as promoted in the CIPD Profession Map. Nevertheless, there is substantial evidence of inequality in the UK, from the increasing gap between the highest and lowest earners to inequality between different groups of workers on the basis of sex, race, religion, disability and other differences. The chapter begins by discussing the evolution and meanings of the key concepts, from equal opportunities to diversity and inclusion. It continues by considering the significant contribution of a feminist and intersectional lens to bringing a far more diverse range of voices and experiences to the study of employment relations. The chapter then moves on to investigate evidence of labour market segregation and an evaluation of the key theoretical explanations for the shaping of labour market inequalities. The next section provides an overview of the legal context, with a particular focus on the Equality Act 2010, before exploring the different and competing rationales adopted by employers for developing strategies to tackle inequality and disadvantage. Finally, the chapter critically examines the available policy options.

LEARNING OUTCOMES

When you have completed this chapter, you should be able to:

- understand what is meant by the different concepts of equality, diversity and inclusion;
- critically evaluate the contribution of a feminist and intersectional lens to the study of equality and employment relations;
- explore the evidence of employment segregation in the labour market and critically analyse the main theories used to explain these patterns and outcomes;
- understand and critically assess the key principles of employment legislation relating to discrimination;
- review and critically evaluate organisational rationales for equality and diversity;
- understand and critically assess the different policy approaches available to employers.

7.1 Introduction

The early chapters of this book have already highlighted that the study and context of employment relations has changed significantly over the last few decades. There has been a move away from a focus on the collective to the individual, a fall in trade union membership, a recognition of the increasing importance of non-standard employees and a growing dominance of unitary HRM narratives. Within this changing context, it has been argued that equality is becoming key to much organisational thinking and public policy development (Holgate et al, 2012). However, claims that equality, diversity and inclusion (EDI) are now central to an organisation's mission are sometimes as misleading as organisations claiming that people are their greatest asset. The last Workplace Employment Relations Survey indicated that workplace policies on EDI had changed, but that there had been little change in practice since the previous survey in 2004 (van Wanrooy et al, 2013).

The concepts of equality, equal opportunities, diversity and inclusion are used frequently and often interchangeably with regard to the employment relationship. The espoused purpose of most employers is usually identified as benign, to indicate that the organisation wants all stakeholders to know that they believe in something positive and desirable. However, there are a number of stakeholders with different and conflicting interests in equality and diversity and this can obscure what is meant by these terms. To add to the confusion, the discourse around anti-discrimination often changes, reflecting the dominant ideology. Since the 1990s, diversity and inclusion have replaced equal opportunities as the most popular terms in the UK. This shift represents a step away from efforts to eradicate group-based disadvantage, often using the law as a scaffold, and towards an individualised and business-case rationale for equality initiatives (Özbilgin and Tatli, 2011; Oswick and Noon, 2014).

There is much debate about whether equal opportunities and diversity are distinctive concepts (Kirton and Greene, 2021). At least in theory, equality and equal opportunities refer to a commitment to treating people equally regardless of group membership (or identity) – or perhaps equitably, since it is sometimes necessary to treat people differently in order to treat them equally. For instance, failing to provide facilities for women to dispose of sanitary products, on the basis that men do not need them, might be equal but it is not equitable. Diversity, on the other hand, is generally viewed as valuing individual difference, while inclusion is concerned with welcoming people from all social groups. However, there is a fundamental lack of conceptual and practical clarity around the use of these terms, certainly at the level of the organisation. It is often far from clear what EDI policies are designed to achieve: same treatment or different treatment, equal treatment or equal outcomes – or indeed all or none of these. Crucially, if organisations are not clear about what they are intending to achieve, there can be no way of evaluating whether they have achieved it. In short, there are different conceptualisations of equality and diversity, all of which are disputed in some way, and there is no clear route for organisational policy and practice (Kirton and Greene, 2021).

7.2 The contribution of a feminist and intersectional lens to the study of employment relations

A feminist approach ensures that women are included in the employment relations terrain and that their voices and experiences are treated as legitimate and important. In particular, it acknowledges that the social reproduction system is just as significant as the production system, meaning unpaid work in the home is as important as paid work outside it. Historically, gender and equality concerns were marginal or absent from the mainstream of employment relations scholarship, which focused primarily on class, neglected the gendering of work ('men's jobs' and 'women's jobs') and ignored domestic work (see for instance Dickens, 2000; Wajcman, 2000; Holgate et al, 2006; Holgate et al, 2012; Hebson and Rubery, 2019). The institutions of employment relations may appear to be gender neutral, yet, as we discussed in Chapter 2, they are still gendered. Moreover, traditional employment relations research often failed to integrate the experiences of other labour market participants – people of colour, disabled people, LGBT+ workers and others – and the intersections of these groups.

More recently, however, gender and other forms of equality have moved to become one of the central themes of employment relations research. Three key developments have contributed to this. First, an increasing number of women participate in employment and trade unions; indeed, women are more likely to be members of a union than men (Department for Business and Trade, 2024) and a number of women play leading roles in the union movement. Second, trade unions campaign on many equality and diversity issues, including gender, seeking to influence organisations and government (see for instance Kirton, 2021). Third, a growing body of employment relations and human resource management scholarship recognises the importance of analysing gender and its intersections.

The concept of intersectionality was originally used in feminist and race studies. It recognises that discrimination, disadvantage and oppression do not take place in discrete categories and that membership of a minority group is not an exclusive or necessarily immutable activity. Many people belong to more than one minority group simultaneously and shift in their prioritisation of member group identification over time (Acker, 2006a). Intersectionality, therefore, allows us to explore the complexities of power and inequality in a more nuanced way (Bradley, 2013).

American academic Kimberle Crenshaw introduced the concept of intersectionality when she discussed the case of a Black woman who was trying to gain employment in a particular organisation. When taken to court, the organisation could demonstrate that they employed Black people and women. The argument against the organisation was that the Black employees were men, in manual jobs on the factory floor, and the women were all white secretaries. The Black woman in this case fell outside both of these groups. However, the court rejected the case, stating that the organisation was able to prove no discrimination against Black people and no discrimination against women. The law did not reflect the lived experience of discrimination, where the experience of African-American women was different from that of white women or Black men (Crenshaw, 1991).

Intersectionality helps us explore the nature of the interaction between simultaneous, multiple memberships by providing a way to combine 'sameness' and 'difference', which is essential for discovering shared oppressions and integrated interests (Holgate et al, 2012). Intersectionality also highlights the need for a more holistic view of equality, diversity and inclusion. While it is still important to focus policy on specific identity issues, such as race, this should not be to the detriment of the wider picture. For example, in 2023, women held 40 per cent of senior roles in the top 350 companies listed on the London stock exchange (FTSE, 2024); however, only around 3 per cent of board members in those same companies were women from Black, Asian or minority ethnic heritage.

Reflective activity 7.1: intersectionality and me

We all have a variety of identities and forms of difference which intersect with our other identities (sometimes called multiple positioning). For example, we all have a gender, an age, a race or ethnicity, a sexual orientation and a class, and intersectionality means taking into account differences among people from the same group. Thinking about yourself and your work colleagues and/or fellow students, what kinds of intersectionality exist? How does an intersectional perspective add to the complexity of analysing a group of people and thus in developing a more fine-grained understanding of it?

7.3 The labour market, employment segregation and inequality

In a hypothetical free market economy, wages and other conditions of employment would be determined by 'rational', unregulated interaction between supply and demand. In the UK, however, the employment relationship is subject to a range of influences, not least decisions made by governments, employers, employees and trade unions. Such decisions are not rational but 'irrational' and may be influenced by conscious or subconscious prejudice and stereotypes. As a result, labour market outcomes are mediated by sex, race and ethnicity, age, disability, sexual orientation and other differences.

There is substantial evidence of the marginalisation of, and discrimination against, women and other groups in the UK. In particular, the labour market is segregated, both horizontally and vertically, between different groups of workers. Vertical segregation refers to organisational levels: who makes the decisions and the people who are in high- or low-paid jobs. Horizontal segregation describes the different kinds of work carried out by people from different social groups. This section will therefore explore the employment patterns and outcomes of diverse social groups in the UK labour market. Labour market statistics published by the government (through the Office for National Statistics) and others are a valuable starting point in our understanding of and analysis of equality, inequality and diversity. However, the available data and information is limited in two ways. First, it varies from one group to another in terms of quantity and detail; second, it does not capture the experience of multiple discrimination, so precluding an intersectional approach. Crucially, too, changes in the data over time have been slow and incremental, rather than rapid and revolutionary (Kirton and Greene, 2021).

Gender employment rates

In the first quarter of 2024, 74.5 per cent of all people aged 16–64 were employed. However, the employment rate for men, at 77.4 per cent, exceeded that for women, 71.6 per cent of whom were in work (Office for National Statistics, 2024b). In 1971, the employment rate for women was just 53 per cent, demonstrating the relatively rapid feminisation of the workforce. However, women's increased participation in the labour market has not led to increased equality, and women are often to be found in the lowest-paid, lowest-status and most precarious jobs (Rubery, 2015) and/or in part-time work. Moreover, much of this increase has been through part-time employment, which again is often lower status, lower paid and more precarious. Data from the first quarter of 2024 provides a stark illustration of the gendered difference in labour market status: while just under 12 per cent of men worked part time and 3.5 per cent had more than one job, 35 per cent of women were employed part time and 5 per cent had two or more jobs. Given that the bulk of domestic work is still carried out by women (BBC, 2023b), it is perhaps not surprising that, while 9 per cent of men working part time did not want a full-time role, 35 per cent of women working part time did so out of choice.

Occupational segregation by gender

Men and women often do different kinds of work, at different levels within organisations. There have been some changes, albeit slow, but it remains the case that women dominate in some occupations and sectors and men in others: that is, horizontal segregation. Broadly speaking, women are more likely to work in catering, cleaning, caring, clerical work and retail – all jobs which reflect domestic tasks, which might involve emotional labour, and which are low paid, considered low status and frequently part time. Men, on the other hand, are more likely to work in the manual trades and technical work. Moreover, the workforce is also vertically segregated in terms of gender: as we have noted, women are less likely to be in senior roles.

REAL-WORLD EXAMPLE 7.1

Occupational segregation and equal pay

In 1968, nearly 200 women who worked as machinists making covers for vehicle seats at Ford's Dagenham plant went on strike for equal pay with the men in the factory, all of whom earned more than the women. The strike, which has been dramatised in the film *Made in Dagenham*, brought the factory to a halt and spread to the company's other UK plants, involving over 800 employees. Eventually, the women won a pay rise, although it was 1984 before they achieved full parity with their male colleagues. The action taken by the Ford women resulted in the passage of the Equal Pay Act 1970, which came into force in 1975.

Originally, the Equal Pay Act only required that men and women doing the same jobs, or equal work, be paid the same. In 1982, however, following legal action against the UK government by the European Commission, the Act was amended to incorporate the concept of equal value. That is, men and women who do work of equal value, even if they do different jobs, must be paid the same. The first equal value claim was lodged by Julie Hayward, a cook at the Cammell Laird shipyard in Liverpool. She argued that the training, skills and demands of her job were equal to those required of male colleagues who worked in the manual trades; for instance, in common with them she had undergone an apprenticeship. Her claim was successful, although it took some years.

At the time of writing, there are a number of outstanding claims for equal pay for work of equal value involving supermarket and other retail employees. The first group of such workers to lodge a claim were women working in Asda supermarkets: they claimed that working in the shops, where most employees are women, was of equal value to that of the predominantly male workforce in the warehouses, who were paid around £3 per hour more. Similar claims have been lodged against other retail chains, including Tesco, Sainsburys, Morrisons and Next.

Reflective activity 7.2

Thinking about the retail sector, why are the majority of shop workers female and the majority of warehouse and distribution workers male?

Does this matter? Should the men and women be paid the same?

Gender pay gap

The gender pay gap is not the same as unequal pay. Equal pay is about parity for women and men who work for the same employer and do the same jobs, equivalent jobs or work of equal value. The gender pay gap, on the other hand, is the average difference between men's pay and women's pay, whether within an organisation, a sector, a region or nationally. In 2023, the overall gender pay gap in the UK was 14.3 per cent: that is, men's average hourly earnings, excluding overtime, were 14.3 per cent higher than women's (Office for National Statistics, 2023d). This represented a decrease across all occupational groups compared with previous years. Looking at the details, however, a number of points stand out. There are, for instance, big age-related differences: the gap for workers over the age of 40 is much higher than that for younger people. Similarly, the gender pay gap is much larger for higher earners and those working in the skilled trades. Crucially, too, the gender pay gap for full-time workers, at 7.7 per cent, is very different from that for part-time workers, which is minus 3.3 per cent – that is, women working part time earn, on average, 3.3 per cent more than men who work part time. As we have seen, this reflects the dominance of women in part-time work.

Race and ethnicity

Race and ethnicity are particularly salient in the construction of identity because they fix people in a permanent and visible category. Data from the 2021 census, which includes residents of all ages, illustrates the diversity of England and Wales in terms of racial and ethnic origins. The percentage of people identifying as White is 81.7 (74.4 per cent White English, Welsh, Scottish, Northern Irish or British, and 6.2 per cent 'White: other'); 9.3 per cent are Asian, Asian British or Asian Welsh (an increase from 7.5 per cent in 2011); 4 per cent are Black, Black British, Black Welsh, Caribbean or African; 2.9 per cent are of 'mixed or multiple' ethnicity and 2.1 per cent identify as 'any other ethnic group'. One in ten households has members from two or more ethnic groups.

Labour market data shows that inequality on the basis of race or ethnicity persists, although there has been progress over the years. This is supported by research evidence of the persistence of bias in recruitment and selection, including bias based on location, and the prevalence of racial abuse and marginalisation (BITC, 2024). However, there are notable differences between ethnic groups, and of course other factors such as gender also have an impact. Therefore it is not possible – or indeed advisable – to draw general conclusions. On the whole, however, there can be little doubt that the experience of racial and ethnic minorities in the UK workplace is often one of inequality, discrimination, disadvantage and marginalisation. For example, statistics confirm continued differences in employment rates and there is clear evidence of occupational segregation, both horizontal and vertical,

Official statistics also demonstrate that, just as there is a gender pay gap, there is an ethnicity pay gap. At the time of writing, there is no legal requirement to report on this but government statisticians extrapolate data from a range of sources. This shows that, in 2022, the median gross hourly pay for White employees was £14.35, but for Black workers it was just £13.53. The pay gap varied from one ethnic group to another, but the average earnings of White people were higher than any other group. The widest pay gap was for people of 'mixed or multiple' ethnicity, who earned an average of 18.5 per cent less than White employees. In addition, country of birth was significant: in most groups, people born in the UK earned more than people who were born elsewhere (Office for National Statistics, 2023c).

Religious minorities

In contrast to gender and race or ethnicity, religion may or may not be a visible difference, depending on whether the individual belongs to a religion which has requirements relating to appearance such as clothing and personal decoration – and on whether that individual follows those practices. Similarly, while religion is often considered to be a matter of individual decision, there are many people for whom it is not experienced as choice. The 2021 census of England and Wales illustrates the diversity of religion; however, it should be noted that this question is not mandatory, and that 6 per cent of residents chose not to answer it. Less than half of the population (46.2 per cent) describe themselves as Christian, the largest group. 37.2 per cent have no religion, and there are substantial minorities of people who are Muslim (6.5 per cent), Hindu (1.7 per cent), Sikh (0.9 per cent), Jewish (0.5 per cent), Buddhist (0.5 per cent) and 'other religions' (0.6 per cent).

Religion is often – but not always – associated with race or ethnicity, so it can be difficult to confirm whether employment gaps and unequal outcomes are the result of religious identity, ethnicity or both. However, one major study has found that Muslims are severely disadvantaged in the labour market: Muslim men are up to 76 per cent less likely to be employed than White, male British Christians with the same qualifications and experience; the corresponding figure for Muslim women is up to 65 per cent. Jewish people, on the other hand, have the best job prospects, followed by White British Christians and White British people with no religion (Khattab and Johnston, 2015).

The experiences of disabled workers

The definition of disability varies, but data on disabled people's labour market experiences demonstrates consistent disadvantage. Disabled people are not only less likely to be employed than non-disabled people, but are also more likely to be working part-time, and more likely to be doing so because they cannot get a full-time job. However, the employment rate varies significantly depending on the nature of an individual's disability. Turning to pay, there is no legal requirement to report on disability pay gaps, but analysis by the Trades Union Congress shows that disabled people earn on average 14.6 per cent less than non-disabled workers, and that this gap has increased since 2013, when it was 13.2 per cent. Disabled women experience the widest pay gap, at 30 per cent less than non-disabled men. There are differences by region and industry, but no major difference by age: that is, people with disabilities experience a substantial pay gap throughout their working lives (TUC, 2023a).

Age and the labour market

Age discrimination happens at all ages. However, employment disadvantage is concentrated at the ends of the age distribution: among younger and older workers. While younger people's employment is of course affected by participation in full-time education, there is particular concern about the position of older people. Data from the first quarter of 2024 shows that, compared to the 74.5 per cent employment rate of all people aged 16–64, only 70.8 per cent of those aged 50–64 were employed. Women in this age group were less likely to be working, and both men and women over 50 are more likely to work part time, whether by choice or not. Moreover, a high proportion of unemployed people over 50 have been unemployed and looking for work for 12 months or more. There is no statutory retirement age, and the state pension age has been raised progressively, meaning that many people have to work for longer than they might have expected.

LGBT (lesbian, gay, bisexual and trans) experiences of work

There is more limited data available in respect of LGBT workers than for other diversity dimensions, although this is slowly changing as organisations begin to recognise that their employees need to feel confident that they can be themselves at work. However, around one in five LGBT employees do not feel able to be open with their colleagues about their sexuality or gender identity, and those who do 'come out' at work may be subject to discrimination and abuse. Trans people in particular have also been affected by the increasingly toxic public 'debate' about gender identity and face substantial discrimination, disadvantage and harassment, up to and including physical assault. Sexuality and gender identity also intersect with other group characteristics such as race or ethnicity, disability, religion or age. One study found that 19 per cent of LGBT people from ethnic minorities and 16 per cent of LGBT disabled people reported being denied jobs or promotion because of their identity, compared with 10 per cent of White, non-disabled LGBT people.

This section has demonstrated that the UK labour market can be an unrewarding environment for different groups of employees based on their demographic and identity characteristics and the intersections of these characteristics. Although there has been progress in reducing inequalities in some areas between different groups, the evidence is stark and uncomfortable: it is clear that labour market outcomes are mediated by our gender, race/ethnicity, religion, age, disability, sexual orientation and gender identities. It is a complicated picture, which is influenced by wider economic, social and political changes, including Brexit, migration, global crises and shifts in social attitudes towards different groups of people. The following section explores the most commonly cited theoretical explanations for this group-based employment segregation.

7.4 Theoretical explanations for labour market segregation

The key theoretical explanations for the shaping of labour market inequalities are derived from a number of academic disciplines, including economics and sociology. These theories give a range of insights into the processes which produce and reinforce inequality, disadvantage and discrimination in the workplace. This section gives an overview of the main theories; fuller discussion can be found in the relevant chapter in Kirton and Greene (2021).

Economic explanations

In neoclassical economic theory, the market is rational and efficient. Resources are allocated according to supply and demand; jobs are resources, so they are also allocated according to supply and demand. Therefore, prejudice, discrimination and disadvantage should not exist, since they distort the rational and efficient labour market (Kirton and Greene, 2021). However, and as we have seen in the previous section, there is substantial evidence of inequality, so theorists have sought to explain this. There are two sets of neoclassical economic theories: supply-side theories are concerned with workers and their characteristics, while demand-side theories are concerned with employers and their actions.

Supply-side theories are based on the view that the market is rational and that individuals have agency (the ability to act in a given environment). Individuals therefore make active, rational choices about work and employment. These theories draw on the concept of human capital. An individual's human capital is made up of the skills, qualifications and training they bring to the labour market and the experience and training they have acquired in the labour market. In supply-side theories, then, people make rational decisions based on their human capital and what they think they can achieve. Those decisions are based on individual agency (active preferences and choices) and rational decisions about how to invest one's human capital – and employers have to accommodate these choices and decisions. Hence people from some groups are more likely to be in certain occupations and in lower-paid positions because they have different, and 'inferior', human capital when compared with others. Supply-side theories 'tend to exonerate employers from inequalities in the labour market and instead focus on individual workers' circumstances in order to explain their position of disadvantage' (Kumra and Manfredi, 2012: 17).

One example of supply-side theories is preference theory, a controversial set of views about women and work developed by Hakim (1991). According to preference theory, women make their own destinies and have genuine choices about how they balance work and family: they might be 'work-centred', 'home-centred' or 'adaptive' (moving between the two). As a result, many women are satisfied to be in lower-status, lower-paid jobs because they want to be home-makers: employment is peripheral to their lives and they 'actively collude' in their own 'slavery', carrying out unpaid work at home and taking low-paid, low-status employment (Hakim, 1991).

Demand-side theories, on the other hand, are concerned with employers' preferences for a particular type (or types) of worker. In this approach, some groups of workers are seen as costing the employer more than others; it is therefore rational to avoid recruiting the more costly people. Furthermore, this works in a cycle: due to stereotypes, some groups of people are considered more costly to employ than others. Employers therefore discriminate against those they consider more costly, resulting in employment segregation which then reinforces the stereotypes.

Dual labour market theory focuses on the demand side. Here, the labour market is viewed as being divided into primary and secondary labour markets. Jobs in the primary, or core, labour market are skilled, well paid, secure and offer opportunities for progression. These are 'good' jobs, and often also 'male' and 'white' jobs. Jobs in the secondary, or peripheral, labour market, however, are low skilled, low paid, insecure and offer few opportunities for progression. These are 'poor' and 'bad' jobs, and often also 'female', 'black and ethnic minority', 'older' or 'disabled' jobs. Furthermore, it is difficult to move from the secondary to the primary labour market because people in the secondary labour market might not possess the necessary human capital. In addition, jobs in the secondary market may be stigmatised: people who have done these jobs might be seen as lacking the knowledge, skills and experience to compete in the primary market. Therefore, prejudice and stigma combine with the operation of the dual market to produce employment segregation; then, because of segregation, disadvantaged groups cannot develop their human capital, so segregation, stereotypes, prejudice and stigma are reinforced. Hence the dual labour market is entrenched, self-reinforcing and self-perpetuating.

Critics point out that although dual labour market theory explains vertical employment segregation, it does not explain horizontal employment segregation and fails to reflect the fact that some jobs have both primary and secondary characteristics. Marxist and/or critical theories of inequality focus on the impact of capitalism, again looking at demand for labour. In a capitalist economy, employers seek to maximise profits and minimise costs. It is in employers' interests to have segmented labour markets: if workers are divided, they are easier to control. Discrimination therefore helps to preserve the economic status quo, maximising both control and profits.

REAL-WORLD EXAMPLE 7.2

Racism and labour market inequality

A major piece of research commissioned by the TUC Anti-Racism Taskforce (TUC, 2022) exposed the extent of discrimination and disadvantage experienced by people from Black and other ethnic minorities (BME) in the British labour market. Among other findings, the report found that:

- Over 14 per cent of BME workers were in insecure jobs, compared to 11 per cent of White workers. Almost one in five had two or more jobs in order to make a living.
- BME workers were over-represented in the lowest-paid jobs and under-represented in the highest-paid occupations. BME workers were 321 per cent more likely to work in basic cleaning jobs than White people.

- Two in five BME workers had experienced racism or racial harassment at work in the previous five years. The majority did not report this to their employer; of those who did, the majority of reports did not result in any action being taken to prevent a recurrence.

The report highlighted the role of three kinds of racism in explaining these findings: everyday racism, institutional racism and structural racism.

- Everyday racism (or individual racism) describes repeated and systemic practices that discriminate against BME people. It includes slights, snubs, insults, so-called 'banter' and being 'othered': marked out as being different from the dominant group.
- Institutional racism was defined in the Macpherson Report into the Metropolitan Police's handling of the Stephen Lawrence murder. It is 'the collective failure of an organisation to provide an appropriate and professional service to people because of their colour, culture or ethnic origin. It can be seen or detected in processes, attitudes and behaviour which amount to discrimination through unwitting prejudice, ignorance, thoughtlessness, and racial stereotyping which disadvantage minority ethnic people' (Macpherson, 1999).
- Structural racism reflects wider political and social disadvantage which is derived from a history of domination and oppression. Structural racism means that some ethnic groups are disadvantaged in comparison with others; for instance, rates of household poverty are higher among BME people than White people.

Sociological explanations

Economic theories explain some aspects of inequality in the labour market, but they do not on their own explain why such inequality persists and is reproduced. Sociological theories, however, explore how inequalities are both caused by and reflect social structures and attitudes. Social identity theories and feminist socio-economic research provide greater insight.

Social identity theory explores how we, as individuals, define ourselves, how we are defined by others, the social groups we belong to and the 'in-groups' we belong to. Identity is both ascribed and achieved. Ascribed identities are given to us; they are based on accident of birth, are socially constructed and relatively fixed. Sex, race or ethnicity and socio-economic background are ascribed identities. Achieved identities, as the name suggests, are those we acquire or assume as we go through life; they are not fixed and may be self-directed. Age is an achieved identity. However, the distinction between the two is not always clear; in particular, religion, gender identity and sexuality may be ascribed or achieved identities. Crucially, however, ascribed identities are more likely to influence whether an individual is seen as acceptable, or 'fits', in a specific context. People who 'fit' are considered to be less costly and less trouble to employ; for instance, it is frequently assumed that disabled people will be more costly and will not 'fit', despite there being little evidence to support this. Social group stereotypes are therefore critical with regard to opportunities to enter and progress in many industries, occupations and organisations.

Social categorisation involves putting people into groups based on shared characteristics such as sex, age or ethnicity. People with whom we share one or more characteristics are members of our 'in-group' and we will tend to highlight the similarities between us. Those with different characteristics are members of an 'out-group'; here, we will emphasise the differences between us and them. People are, therefore, drawn towards others in their in-groups. This explains, for instance, why research tends to show that interviewers are likely to favour individuals who are like themselves. In addition, social attribution describes how the behaviour of an individual may be viewed as representative of a group. Here, then, if an individual from an out-group does something which is considered 'bad', that negative behaviour is considered typical of the whole group. However, when somebody from an out-group does something 'good', that positive behaviour is not seen as representative: instead, the individual is considered special, or lucky, or different from the rest of their group. This is known as fundamental attribution error.

Social identity theories explain how individual choices and preferences in the labour market are socially constructed. However, different social groups are very diverse and, of course, social group identities intersect with each other. There is no single identity group which is uniquely privileged or disadvantaged in comparison with all the others, and 'the white male is not the "common enemy" of all other groups of worker' (Kirton and Greene, 2021: 85).

Theories and concepts relating to specific social groups

Feminist socio-economic research has made substantial contributions to our understanding of inequality in the labour market. First, it has demonstrated how the politics of social reproduction and the household division of labour directly affects whether jobs are considered 'good' or 'bad'. Second, critical analysis of the link between wages and the social construction of skill demonstrates that jobs done predominantly by women are likely to be undervalued because women have historically been less able than men to establish high status for those occupations and sectors of female-dominated work. Consequently, for the same skill level the jobs occupied by women are more likely to be attributed periphery status and paid at a lower level than those carried out by men (Grimshaw et al, 2017). Moreover, jobs are often labelled differently according to whether they are done predominantly by women (e.g. cook) or men (e.g. chef) and assigned a higher level of skill when done by men. Employers and society fail to value caring roles and part-time work, seeing both as unskilled. Values are attributed to particular skills depending upon how they are gained (for instance by formal training, experience or learning in the home), who has them (men or women) and the context in which they are used (e.g. paid work or the home). A typical example is care work, which remains invisible, low status and exploited in most societies (Hebson et al, 2015). For the employer, the outcome of undervaluation is access to a higher quality of labour for a given wage (Grimshaw and Rubery, 2007).

A third crucial insight from feminist socio-economic research finds widespread evidence of significant 'motherhood pay gaps'. These cannot be explained by human capital depreciation, less experience, lower skill levels, women's concentration in jobs that offer family-compatible working hours or measures of employment commitment (Grimshaw and Rubery, 2015).

Feminist theorising has also focused on the way that gendered structures and stereotypes disadvantage women in the labour market. In this regard, Acker proposed three valuable concepts: gender regimes, gendered substructures and the concept of the 'ideal worker'. Gender regimes are the 'structures, processes and beliefs' and assumptions which result in men and women carrying out different tasks and holding different positions in organisations (Acker, 2006b). This concept was also expanded to incorporate race or ethnicity and social class, resulting in the intersectional theory of inequality regimes (Acker, 2006a, 2009). Similarly, gendered substructures are the processes by which assumptions based on masculinity and femininity are 'embedded' in organisations, thereby reproducing and maintaining inequality (Acker, 2012). Gender regimes and gendered subcultures might be visible or invisible, conscious or unconscious, but both underpin the notion of the 'ideal worker': a 'gender neutral, abstract worker who has no body and no obligations outside the workplace: this worker is unencumbered' (Acker, 2012: 218). Far from being gender neutral and having no body, however, this ideal is most likely to be met by a non-disabled man.

Turning to theories about other forms of discrimination, heteronormativity refers to the assumption that everybody is heterosexual ('straight'). Heterosexism is the view that everybody should be heterosexual and that heterosexual relationships are the ideal; heteronormativity builds upon this to cast heterosexuality as the 'norm', or in-group, and any other sexual orientation as the 'other', or out-group. Heteronormativity may be seen in the expectations and constraints placed upon employees by their employers and colleagues.

There are a number of ways of thinking about disability, all of which can have an impact on the way disabled people are treated at work and elsewhere. Disability may be viewed as a tragedy for the individual or, conversely, as the result of something they or their parents have done: that is, as somebody's fault. More commonly, though, disability is viewed as either a medical issue or a social issue. The medical model of disability focuses on what is 'wrong' with the individual: that is, on the impairment. The disabled person is not 'normal', they need care or treatment, and they are assumed to be inadequate and dependent, with little or no contribution to make. The social model of disability, on the other hand, rejects the medical approach and focuses instead on the barriers encountered by disabled people. Driven by disabled people, this approach starts from the view that disability is not the problem; instead, disabled people are disadvantaged by attitudes towards them, together with social structures, processes and a built environment which excludes them (Foster and Wass, 2012).

REAL-WORLD EXAMPLE 7.3

Gendered constructions of skill

A study carried out in the US examined popular management texts and the training programmes based on them. There was little or no mention of gender in these books, but it became clear that gender was read into them, regardless of whether the authors – usually academics – had intended this. Focusing on one programme, the study found that 'it (re) produces and encourages gendered behaviour and perpetuates stereotypes about gender and skill' (Blithe, 2019: 517). At the start of this programme, participants completed an assessment which identified their 'natural' strengths and talents with a view to enabling them and their employers to make the most of them. The assessment identified the top five strengths for each individual, classing them as, for instance, an achiever, a developer, empathetic, a good communicator, responsible, strategic and so on. During the training sessions using this approach, it became clear that the strengths were valued in different and unequal ways, and that this was related to gender. Men who were identified as having what they viewed as a 'feminine' strength would joke about it, argue that the assessment was wrong or suggest it was due to their upbringing, coming from, for example, a family consisting of a single mother with no male siblings. Similarly, women who had 'masculine' strengths attributed this to having deliberately worked on that skill or, again, to their upbringing. In addition, participants made gendered assumptions when they perceived a connection: for instance, empathy was considered a 'feminine' skill and command a 'masculine' strength. None of these statements or assumptions were challenged by other participants: indeed, most agreed with them. Throughout the programme, strengths were discussed by the participants in gendered terms; 'there was no critical reflection about how gendered skills would impact people in different and unequal ways, nor... how skills might be gender neutral' (Blithe, 2019: 527).

 Reflective activity 7.3

Thinking about an organisation you know well, what assumptions are made about men's and women's skills? What impact does this have on individuals? Does it affect their opportunities for progression?

7.5 The legal context

Equality is one of the most dynamic and complex areas of employment law. Many employers and HR professionals emphasise the need to avoid claims of discrimination because there is no limit on the compensation that can be awarded to successful claimants and because high-profile cases can lead to damaging publicity. However, most awards of compensation are relatively low (see 'Compensation for unlawful discrimination', later) and, as with most employment law, the legal requirements are minimum standards. Therefore, it is perhaps more important to see the eradication of discrimination, harassment and inequality as a fundamental part of developing a culture of fairness and trust and a climate of good employment relations. The law on discrimination in employment (and elsewhere) is set out in the Equality Act 2010, which draws together disparate pieces of anti-discrimination legislation made since the 1970s. The Act identifies nine 'protected characteristics', defines discrimination and outlaws discrimination on the basis of the protected characteristics. In terms of employment, the Equality Act makes it unlawful to discriminate in recruitment and selection, training, promotion, dismissal, pay and other terms and conditions of employment, and any other 'benefit, facility or service'.

EQUALITY ACT 2010: PROTECTED CHARACTERISTICS

Age: this applies to workers of all ages.

Disability: the Equality Act defines disability as 'a physical or mental impairment, [which] has a substantial and long-term adverse effect on [the] ability to carry out normal day-to-day activities'. A long-term adverse effect is one that is permanent, has lasted for at least 12 months or is likely to last for at least 12 months. Normal day-to-day activities mean anything we might do at work or elsewhere, such as shopping, eating, washing or walking.

Gender reassignment: this applies to anybody who is proposing to undergo, who is undergoing or who has undergone 'a process (or part of a process) to reassign their gender by changing physiological or other attributes of sex'.

Marriage and civil partnership: the protected characteristic applies only to people who are married or in a civil partnership.

Pregnancy and maternity: this protected characteristic applies to women who are pregnant and during the period of any statutory maternity leave.

Race: this is defined as colour, nationality, ethnic origins or national origins. The protected characteristic applies to people of all colours, nationalities and ethnic or national origins.

Religion or belief: The Act protects people against discrimination on grounds of their religion or belief, or lack of religion or belief. A religion must have a clear structure and belief system; denominations or sects within a religion (for instance, Sunni and Shia Muslim or Catholic, Protestant and Orthodox Christianity) are treated as religions in their own right. A 'belief' must be genuinely held and a weighty and substantial aspect of human life and behaviour. Religion or belief is not protected if it conflicts with the fundamental rights of others.

Sex: This protected characteristic applies to both men and women.

Sexual orientation: this applies to bisexual, gay or lesbian (homosexual) and heterosexual people.

The nine protected characteristics – age, disability, gender reassignment, marriage and civil partnership, pregnancy and maternity, race, religion or belief, sex, and sexual orientation – are wide-ranging, but the Equality Act 2010 does not protect against all forms of discrimination. For instance, single people – those who are not married or in a civil partnership – are not protected. Similarly, protection against discrimination on the basis of gender reassignment does not apply to people with differences in sex development (DSD), also known as intersex people. In addition, discrimination might occur on the basis of social class, appearance or other factors, but this is only unlawful if a protected characteristic is also involved.

One complex issue relating to discrimination law is the extent to which different protected characteristics might come into conflict with each other. For example, rights related to sexual orientation might clash with those of religion and belief, since some religious groups are opposed to homosexuality. The Equality Act accords equal standing to all nine protected characteristics. Nevertheless, there have been cases where employees have been dismissed for refusing to undertake certain duties on the basis that those duties went against their religious beliefs, and where those employees have brought cases for discrimination. Two notable cases involved a marriage counsellor, who objected to providing sex therapy for same sex couples, and a registrar who refused to conduct same sex civil partnership ceremonies. In both cases, the employee was unsuccessful: the two employers were entitled to require their employees to comply with equality and diversity policies.

However, employers are also required to conform with the Human Rights Act 1998, which incorporated the European Convention for the Protection of Human Rights and Fundamental Freedoms (the European Convention on Human Rights, or ECHR, 1950) into British law. Both the employees just mentioned, having had their claims rejected in the UK courts, appealed to the European Court of Human Rights in Strasbourg, stating that their rights to freedom of thought, conscience and religion under Article 9 of the ECHR had been breached. They were not successful, but their cases highlight the importance of ensuring that equality, diversity and inclusion, and anti-discrimination legislation, are taken into account when designing organisational policies on other issues.

Direct and indirect discrimination

Under the Equality Act 2010 there are three main types of discrimination: direct discrimination, indirect discrimination and harassment. In addition, it is unlawful to discriminate by perception or association. However, it may be lawful to discriminate if a specific protected characteristic is a requirement for the job, known as a genuine occupational requirement.

Direct discrimination occurs when an individual is treated less favourably because of their sex, race or other protected characteristic. Refusing a job to somebody on the basis of their ethnicity or dismissing an employee on the grounds of their age, would constitute direct discrimination. Crucially, however, the treatment must be less favourable: treating people differently is not necessarily unlawful.

Discrimination by perception occurs when somebody is assumed to have a protected characteristic and is treated less favourably on the basis of that assumed, or perceived, protected characteristic. Discrimination by association (or associative discrimination) refers to situations where individuals are discriminated against because they are associated with somebody or a group who has a protected characteristic. Both discrimination by perception and discrimination by association are forms of direct discrimination.

REAL-WORLD EXAMPLE 7.4

Discrimination by association or perception

Coleman v Attridge Law (2008) IRLR 722, ECJ

Coleman was the primary carer for her disabled son. She took voluntary redundancy from her job with Attridge Law, but claimed disability discrimination and constructive dismissal. She argued that she had been subjected to abusive and insulting comments about herself and her son and that she was described as lazy when she requested time off to care for him. In addition, she was denied flexible working hours and accused of trying to manipulate her working conditions. The case was heard under the law as it existed before the passage of the Equality Act 2010 and the employment tribunal queried whether that law (the Disability Discrimination Act 1995) was consistent with the European Equal Treatment Framework Directive (the Directive), which protects individuals from discrimination by association with a disabled person. Coleman's case was referred to the European Court of Justice, which ruled that discrimination by association was within the scope of the Directive. Therefore, the concept of discrimination by association was incorporated into British law.

English v Thomas Sanderson Blinds Ltd (2008) EWCA Civ 1421 CA

English had worked for Sanderson Blinds and argued that during his employment he had been subject to endless 'homophobic banter', mainly on the basis that he had attended a boys' boarding school and that he lived in Brighton. The alleged harassers knew that English was not gay. He resigned and claimed unfair constructive dismissal and discrimination on grounds of sexual orientation. The Court of Appeal ruled in his favour and argued that it was irrelevant whether Mr English was gay or not; the actions still constituted harassment on grounds of sexual orientation.

In most cases, there are only two defences against claims of direct discrimination: first, if the employer might show that no discrimination took place, or second, if an employer can demonstrate that a protected characteristic is a genuine occupational requirement for the role. A specific protected characteristic may be a requirement if a job involves:

- privacy and decency or the provision of personal or welfare services, for instance in care work;
- authenticity, for example in acting or serving in a specialised restaurant;
- promoting or representing a specific religion.

Indirect discrimination occurs if an employer applies 'a provision, criterion or practice which is discriminatory in relation to a relevant protected characteristic' and cannot show that this is a proportionate means of achieving a legitimate aim. In other words, when 'an apparently neutral provision, criterion or practice puts workers sharing a protected characteristic at a particular disadvantage' (EHRC, 2011: 61). One example of indirect discrimination might be a requirement that part-time workers must work 75 per cent of full-time hours: this could have a disproportionate effect on women, who are more likely to have childcare, caring and domestic responsibilities. Similarly, a job advertisement requiring a substantial number of years' experience might indirectly discriminate on the grounds of age unless the requirement can be justified in terms of the demands of the role; it might also be indirect sex discrimination, since women are less likely to have unbroken employment records due to maternity and childcare.

Harassment and victimisation

The third form of discrimination defined in the Equality Act 2010 is harassment, defined as:

> unwanted conduct related to a relevant protected characteristic, which has the purpose or effect of violating an individual's dignity or creating an intimidating, hostile, degrading, humiliating or offensive environment for that individual.

This means that employees can complain about offensive behaviour even if it is not directly aimed at them. It is also worth noting that employers may also be liable if their staff are subjected to harassment from customers or clients. However, harassment will not be shown to have occurred just because the behaviour complained of offends the claimant: the employment tribunal will need to be satisfied that it either has the purpose or effect of violating the dignity of the claimant or creating an intimidating, hostile, degrading, humiliating or offensive environment. The cases set out in Real-world example 7.5 illustrate this distinction.

REAL-WORLD EXAMPLE 7.5

Harassment – violating dignity?

Morgan v Halls of Gloucester UKEAT/0573/10/DA

Morgan, who is Black, worked for Halls of Gloucester as a delivery driver. He claimed that he was forced to resign, in part due to suffering serious racial harassment. This had involved being told by another employee to 'stop speaking that jungle talk' and also overhearing a number of instances in which another Black employee was referred to in racist terms or racist comments in general. Furthermore, he alleged that the company had done nothing to prevent this behaviour and had failed to discipline one employee who had expressed extreme racist views despite complaints being made by other staff. The company did have an equal opportunities policy, but it was kept in a cabinet and neither managers nor employees knew of its existence. The tribunal found that even though a number of the comments were not aimed at Morgan, they did violate his dignity and therefore the claim was successful, and the company was ordered to pay compensation.

Heafield v Times Newspaper Ltd EAT/1305/12

Heafield was employed as sub-editor for the *Times* newspaper and was also a practising

Roman Catholic. In 2011, the *Times* was working on a story regarding the alleged involvement of the Pope in a cover-up over the actions of a paedophile priest. As the deadline approached, another employee shouted to other colleagues across the newsroom, 'Can anyone tell me what's happening to the fucking Pope?' in an attempt to get some information on the progress of the story. He then repeated this request. Heafield was offended by this but did not complain at the time and instead raised the issue informally with a manager at a later point. The manager, after getting advice from a colleague, decided to take no further action on the basis that 'these things tended to sort themselves out if left alone'. Heafield brought a claim of discrimination on grounds of his religion or belief, arguing that the repeated comments about the Pope violated his dignity. While the tribunal accepted that the words represented unwanted conduct, they did not agree that the words had the purpose or effect of violating Mr Heafield's dignity. Instead, this was an inquiry about a story and the expletive had been used because of the pressure of the situation. The decision was upheld by the EAT.

Three forms of harassment are specifically outlawed:

- harassment related to relevant protected characteristics (age, disability, gender reassignment, race, religion or belief, sex or sexual orientation); this includes harassment by perception and harassment by association;
- sexual harassment;
- less favourable treatment of somebody who submits to or rejects sexual harassment or harassment related to sex or gender reassignment.

Victimisation is also a form of unlawful discrimination specified under the Equality Act 2010. Victimisation occurs when a person is subject to a detriment because they have made a complaint of discrimination under the Equality Act 2010, helped somebody else to make a complaint of discrimination (for instance, acting as a witness), alleged that the employer or somebody else is in breach of the Equality Act or done something else in connection with the Equality Act. This includes situations where an individual is believed to have made a complaint or to have supported a complaint, and where it is suspected that an individual might bring a complaint. However, if an employee gives false evidence or information or makes a false allegation (in bad faith), they are not protected.

Disability discrimination

Slightly different provisions apply to disability discrimination under the Equality Act. Protection is only afforded to people who are disabled and who have disclosed this to their employer. Direct and indirect discrimination on the grounds of disability are both unlawful, and the Act places a duty on employers to make reasonable adjustments for staff who may otherwise be placed at a disadvantage because of a disability. This might include adjustments to work equipment, the work premises or shifts and other working arrangements; many reasonable adjustments are 'simple and affordable' (Disability Confident / CIPD, 2024: 13). In addition, the Equality Act protects people from discrimination arising from their disability, defined as treating a disabled person unfavourably in connection with disability. Discrimination arising from disability occurs when:

- An employee is put at a disadvantage, whether or not this was intended, *and*
- The unfavourable treatment is connected with the employee's disability, *and*
- The treatment cannot be justified by showing that it is a proportionate means of achieving a legitimate aim.

REAL-WORLD EXAMPLE 7.6

Discrimination arising from disability (*McGraw v London Ambulance Service NHS Trust* ET/3301865/11)

McGraw, who worked as a paramedic, was dismissed for gross misconduct for attempting to steal Entonox, an anaesthetic which he had been abusing for a number of years, from his ambulance station. This act was committed while McGraw was absent from work suffering from depression. He was also found to be in breach of the Trust's policy in relation to drug abuse. Among other claims, McGraw argued that in dismissing him the Trust had discriminated against him for a reason arising from a disability. The trust argued that it could not tolerate substance abuse and that McGraw could not be relied upon to maintain a proper service to the public. The tribunal could find no link between McGraw's depression and any medication he was taking and the theft of the Entonox and concluded that the dismissal of McGraw was a proportionate means of achieving a legitimate aim. However, if, for example, the medication being taken by a worker with a disability resulted in poor performance, it could be unlawful to take disciplinary or other action against them.

Positive action and positive discrimination

Positive action refers to situations where an employer takes steps to remove obstacles to equality. *Positive discrimination*, on the other hand, involves discriminating in favour of a disadvantaged group. Under the Equality Act 2010, positive action is lawful in specific circumstances, but positive discrimination is unlawful.

Under Sections 158 and 159 of the Equality Act, employers can take positive action before or at the application stage of recruitment. For instance, if the workforce does not reflect the local population in terms of one or more protected characteristics, those groups can be particularly encouraged to apply. Similarly, the employer can provide training or other support to enable people from those groups to make an application; one example might be the provision of targeted training in CV writing or interview skills. In a situation where two candidates for recruitment or promotion cannot be separated on the basis of skills, qualifications, experience and similar, the Equality Act also permits an employer to appoint or promote the candidate from an under-represented or disadvantaged group: this is sometimes called the 'tie-break'.

Positive discrimination means treating someone with a protected characteristic more favourably to counteract the effects of past discrimination. It is only lawful where the duty to make reasonable adjustments might involve treating a disabled person more favourably. The use of quotas, where only people from a specific social group are recruited until the quota has been reached, is unlawful. However, setting targets for the employment of people with a specific protected characteristic is lawful.

Compensation for unlawful discrimination

There is no upper limit on the level of compensation which can be awarded for unlawful discrimination. Awards are calculated on the basis of compensation for financial loss (loss of earnings or future earnings), injury to feelings and any personal injury related to discrimination (for example, depression or anxiety caused by harassment). Aggravated damages may also be awarded if the employer has aggravated the injury to feelings, for instance by acting in a malicious or insulting way. Interest may also be added to the award. However, and despite some headline cases where compensation is in six or more figures, typical awards are much lower. For example, in 2022–2023 there was one award of £1,767,869 for disability discrimination but the average (mean) award was £45,435 and the median award £15,634. Similarly, one claimant won £84,723 for age discrimination but the mean award was £19,332 and the median £9,239.

Statutory codes of practice

The Equality and Human Rights Commission (EHRC) have published two statutory codes of practice under the Equality Act. The *Employment Statutory Code of Practice* (2011) and *Equal Pay Statutory Code of Practice* (2016) offer official guidance on how to comply with the law and can be used in legal proceedings. Both include comprehensive guidance and examples; they can be downloaded from the EHRC website.

Gender pay gap reporting

The Equality Act 2010 (Gender Pay Gap Information) Regulations 2017 require all organisations with 250 or more employees to report and publish specific data about their gender pay gap. Employers must both report this data to the government online, through the gender pay gap reporting service, and publish the data, along with a written statement, on their public-facing website. Failure to report on time, or reporting inaccurate data, can result in legal action. Employers with fewer than 250 employees are not required to report or publish gender pay gap data, but can do so voluntarily, thus sending a powerful message about the organisation's commitment to transparency and equality.

REAL-WORLD EXAMPLE 7.7

Age discrimination – not the same?

In contrast to the other eight protected characteristics, discrimination on the basis of age may be lawful if it is a 'proportionate means of achieving a legitimate aim'. For example, age discrimination might be lawful if there is a legitimate aim of opening up opportunities for young people, rewarding long service or facilitating the involvement of older workers.

In *Lockwood v Department of Work and Pensions* (2013) EWCA Civ 1195, Lockwood, who was 26 years old and had eight years' service, was awarded £10,849.04 compensation for voluntary redundancy. Had she been aged 35 or over, with the same length of service, the payment would have been £28,539.62. She claimed age discrimination but, in a case which took several years to complete, was unsuccessful at the Employment Tribunal and in appeals to the Employment Appeal Tribunal and the Court of Appeal. Although she had been discriminated against on the grounds of age, it was held that the discrimination was lawful: it was justified on the basis that an older woman might face more difficulty in finding a new job than a younger one.

More recently, two judgements in the Employment Appeal Tribunal have held that, although there is no legal retirement age, employers can impose a compulsory retirement age. However, the employer must show that this would meet a legitimate aim such as succession planning.

Reflective activity 7.4

Thinking about an organisation you know, examine the policies relating to pay and other conditions. Do employees receive a pay rise, or get additional holiday, relating to their length of service? If so, is this a proportionate means of achieving a legitimate aim?

The role of the Equality and Human Rights Commission

The Equality and Human Rights Commission (EHRC) was established in 2007, bringing together the work of the three commissions charged with ensuring sex, race and disability equality. The EHRC has a statutory duty to encourage and support the development of a society in which:

1 People's ability to achieve their potential is not limited by prejudice or discrimination;
2 There is respect for and protection of each individual's human rights;
3 There is respect for the dignity and worth of each individual;

4 Each individual has an equal opportunity to participate in society;
5 There is mutual respect between groups based on understanding and valuing of diversity and on shared respect for equality and human rights.

The EHRC can apply for judicial review of government decisions and intervene in court proceedings. In particular, the EHRC can support claimants in bringing cases under existing equality legislation where it feels that this is a way of meeting the duties we have just outlined. The EHRC also has powers to assess public authorities' compliance with their positive equality duties under the Equality Act 2010 and can issue 'compliance notices' if it finds a public authority is failing in its duties. It can also carry out investigations when there is a suspicion of unlawful discrimination. Finally, the EHRC provides a 'one-stop shop' for those seeking advice and information on equality issues, legal matters and diversity strategies. However, the ability of the EHRC to carry out its functions has been substantially diluted as a result of cuts in its budget and workforce over several years. Moreover, in relation to trans people and gender reassignment, questions have been asked about its impartiality and willingness to enforce some aspects of the law (BBC 2022, 2023a).

Enforcing equality rights

As with most employment law, the burden of enforcing equality rights rests with the individual who believes they have been discriminated against. This can be a lengthy, costly and stressful process.

For employers, the cost of dealing with complaints of discrimination and harassment can be very high compared with other workplace and legal issues, especially if complaints result in a claim to the employment tribunal. More evidence and witnesses may be required, and there is no cap on the compensation which can be awarded to a successful claimant. Discrimination cases are also very time-consuming, and the business risks of a claim are substantial. For the organisation, there is the risk of reputational damage, especially if the case receives media coverage. Such cases also pose issues for the individual manager(s): a claim can be personally embarrassing and distressing, particularly for any manager named in the case; and a manager found to have discriminated against or harassed an employee is likely to be subject to disciplinary action and might be dismissed, blighting their career.

7.6 The organisational rationale for equality and diversity

As the language of equality has shifted from equal opportunities to diversity and inclusion, the topic has risen up the corporate and HR agenda. Despite the lack of clarity about these concepts, most organisations have a clear policy or guidelines in place. The law, meanwhile, places wide-ranging duties on employers and others and encourages a general level of fairness, even if only to avoid the costs associated with failing to do so. Nevertheless, substantial numbers of employers feel able to ignore the law because, on the rare occasion that an employee makes a claim, the issue can be settled and everything can carry on as before (Women and Equalities Committee, 2019). However, there are positive rationales for the pursuit of equality, diversity and inclusion.

Social justice arguments

The social justice case rests on the view that inequality in employment is unjust and unfair and that employers have a duty to address discrimination and disadvantage. Essentially it is an ethical and moral issue and an end in itself; it is 'the right thing to do' (Johns et al, 2012; Green et al, 2018). This implies that employers should take into account the ways in which social processes, institutions and history combine to produce unequal and unfair outcomes for different social groups (Foster and Williams, 2011). In this respect, equality policy and practice has been viewed as contributing to organisational justice (Dahanayake et al, 2018). Critiques of the social justice case include its reliance on the law and formal policies which, it is argued, may be weak and/or inflexible. In addition, social justice arguments are held to focus on the negatives – discrimination, disadvantage and penalties for breaking the law – instead of making a positive case for change.

The business case

The business case for diversity came to prominence in the 1990s as a response to the changing political and economic environment and the widespread acceptance of neo-liberal market models of economic efficiency (Dickens, 2005). In essence, business case arguments emphasise the benefits to business of having a diverse and inclusive workforce: it is argued, for instance, that performance and productivity are enhanced, turnover reduced and the 'bottom line' benefited. Where social justice arguments focus on group differences, the business case is concerned with individual difference and how it might be harnessed to the benefit of the organisation. Noon (2007) suggests that business case arguments have engaged line managers with questions of diversity in a way that calls for social justice have not. However, critiques have focused on the business case as a top-down, managerialist approach which resonates with the dominance of unitary discourse in HRM and on the short-term need to satisfy shareholders, which conflicts with the need to develop strategies for equality in the medium to long term. Moreover, there is little evidence to support the view that diversity makes good business sense: research has found that the impact of diversity on organisational performance appears to differ according to industry or sector and other factors. While there is a correlation between diversity and corporate performance, it is not clear whether this is caused by diversity; similarly, some studies have found that team performance is improved with diversity, but others have found team performance worsening. Crucially, too, research has tended to focus on some characteristics and/or some outcomes; little or no attention has been paid to intersectional issues, or to whether individual outcomes are improved by diversity policies (Green et al, 2018; Ely and Thomas, 2020).

Social justice and *the business case?*

In recent years, the debate has moved on from the dichotomy of social justice or business case rationales, with academics and practitioners arguing that the two should work together. While business leaders and others might need a financial rationale, it is increasingly the view that the moral case for action on equality is a strong one (Green et al, 2018). Noon (2007) argued that equality cannot be 'depoliticised', and it has been argued that business case calls for diversity are simply a way to avoid confronting 'the elephant in the room' of racism, sexism, ableism and other forms of discrimination (Byrd and Sparkman, 2022). Increasingly, then, it seems that the future of equality and diversity will depend on a return to the understanding of inequality as arising from 'specific socioeconomic causes and institutions' and, therefore, on the need to develop policies and practices which will bring about real change (Vincent et al, 2024).

Reflective activity 7.5

Explore the website of your own organisation (or any with which you are familiar). Search for pages of (or mentions devoted to) equality or diversity. Which diversity strands are mentioned? What types of imagery are used? How is the rationale framed? Does it support a social justice case or a business case or both? Are there any contradictions? What evidence informed your conclusions?

7.7 Equality, diversity and inclusion policy

This final section will explore some of the issues involved in developing and implementing an equality, diversity and inclusion (EDI) policy. It is beyond the scope of this book to provide detailed advice on how to do EDI; however, it will explore some key sources of further information and guidance.

There is no legal requirement for organisational EDI policies, but most large employers have one. In addition, many highlight their commitment to EDI, along with kitemarks and other symbols for a range of campaigns and initiatives; moreover, a substantial number also sponsor or otherwise support major events such as Pride Month or Black History Month. It is sometimes questionable, however, how far such public commitment translates into meaningful action. For example, one study explored the government's 'Two Ticks' scheme to promote employment for disabled people, now called Disability Confident. The study found little evidence to suggest that employers who displayed the relevant symbol on their communications showed any greater adherence to the scheme's commitments than those who did not, and concluded that the symbol was little more than an 'empty shell' (Hoque et al, 2014; Hoque and Noon, 2004).

Reflective activity 7.6

In addition to those employers who do nothing to address EDI, Kirton and Greene (2021) identified three organisational types with regard to EDI policy and practice. Thinking about any organisation(s) you are familiar with, which type are they?

- A 'minimalist/partial' organisation might not have a formal EDI policy but will claim not to discriminate and might use the language of diversity and the business case. It is unlikely to have any specific measures in place and nobody will be required to take any action.
- A 'compliant' organisation will have a formal policy and comply with the law. Policy will be driven by a relatively narrow interpretation of the business case. Attention will be focused primarily on recruitment and selection and the organisation will seek to apply 'good practice' as laid out in guidance from Acas and the EHRC. Social group discrimination and disadvantage might be neglected in favour of an individual approach. Line managers might view EDI as 'interference' from HR.
- A 'comprehensive proactive' organisation will have a comprehensive EDI policy. It might emphasise the business case but will also be influenced by social justice arguments. It will comply with the law, but go further, developing 'best practice' approaches as well as monitoring outcomes and ensuring impact. EDI might be linked to corporate social responsibility and similar policies. A senior member will probably be an EDI champion, relevant objectives might be set for other employees and positive action will be taken where appropriate.

There are three main options for EDI policy: the liberal approach to equality, the radical approach to equality and the managing diversity approach. A liberal approach draws on social justice arguments and pursues equality regardless of difference. The main focus is on the individual, and the emphasis – for instance, in selection and promotion – is on merit, with positive action where appropriate. Critiques of this approach focus in particular on the concept of merit. Merit might be considered an objective measure, but in practice it is often assessed according to subjective requirements such as 'drive' or 'passion'. Crucially, too, notions of merit may be developed on the basis of the people who have done the job before, meaning that 'the status quo look[s] natural and therefore right, or best' (Dean and Liff, 2010: 427) and inequality persists. Liberal approaches dominate in the UK and have stimulated some success, but there are problems with the perceived gap between rhetoric and reality and the focus on equality of opportunity, rather than equality of outcomes.

Radical approaches, on the other hand, are based on the understanding that inequality is socially constructed and therefore aim both for equal treatment and equal outcomes. This is achieved not only through fair procedures but also by adopting targets and quotas, using positive discrimination to reverse the disadvantage experienced by social groups. As noted earlier, quotas and other forms of positive discrimination are generally unlawful in the UK, making radical approaches unworkable.

The managing diversity approach to EDI is based firmly on the business case and focuses on individual differences, which are to be nurtured and harnessed to the benefit of the organisation. In this context, difference is not restricted to the protected characteristics in the Equality Act 2010 but might include personal characteristics such as preferred styles of working. Little or no attention is paid to social group differences, and instead of relying on a top-down approach with formal procedures and processes, diversity is considered to be everybody's responsibility. In practice, however, employers are still bound by the law, which addresses group-based disadvantage, and indeed there are different ways of doing diversity (see for instance Liff, 1997).

Managing diversity approaches have been criticised for neglecting the wider realities of discrimination and disadvantage and for focusing on the people inside an organisation while ignoring those outside it. Moreover, and as just discussed, there is no conclusive evidence on the impact of the business case. The use of diversity language can sanitise the debate, avoiding uncomfortable discussions about inequality, discrimination and disadvantage (Byrd and Sparkman, 2022) and indeed there is a risk that it might reinforce and perpetuate stereotypes relating to, for example, the abilities of disabled people or the 'caring' nature of women.

Reflective activity 7.7

Find the EDI policy for your organisation, or one you are familiar with. What language is used? Which policy approach is reflected – liberal, radical, managing diversity or a mixture of two or more of these?

Ultimately, there is no single policy approach which will guarantee equality, diversity or inclusion. This is, at least in part, because there is often a lack of clarity about what EDI policies are designed to achieve: equal treatment, equal outcomes or both. However, just as the debate about the two rationales for EDI has moved on to encompass the view that both play a role, a combination of policy approaches appears most likely to support change.

Doing EDI: sources of guidance and advice

In additional to formal policy, EDI strategy is only effective if there is full commitment and support from the top of the organisation. It also requires that attention is paid to the full range of HR policies and procedures, including recruitment and selection, promotion, training and development, pay and other terms and conditions of employment, disciplinary and grievance procedures, dismissal and redundancy. There is, however, a wealth of guidance addressing both general and specific EDI matters. Details of key sources are provided in the following box.

GUIDANCE AND ADVICE ON EQUALITY, DIVERSITY AND INCLUSION

General guidance and advice, including the law

- Acas (the Advisory, Conciliation and Arbitration Service) publishes a range of advice and guidance on discrimination and bullying at work, including legal advice and advice on good practice, on its website at www.acas.org.uk/discrimination-and-bullying
- Acas also offers training, and a helpline for employers and employees: full details are available at www.acas.org.uk/contact
- The CIPD provides extensive resources on all aspects of diversity, including advice and guidance for HR practitioners; it also carries out and commissions research on specific EDI issues. Some items are only available to CIPD members. Website: www.cipd.org/uk
- The Equality and Human Rights Commission publishes the two statutory codes of practice, on employment and equal pay. The EHRC also provides guidance and advice on general EDI matters, as well as on specific protected characteristics. Website: www.equalityhumanrights.com
- The Trades Union Congress (TUC) provide resources and advice for trade union representatives, as well as carrying out and publishing relevant research. Website: www.tuc.org.uk. Individual trade unions also provide training and advice, while the larger ones also carry out and publish research.
- The UK government website has a large section devoted to equality issues, including guidance on the law, research and statistics. Website: www.gov.uk/society-and-culture/equality
- Most of the large business and employers' organisations also publish guidance and advice on EDI, but membership might be required to access this. Such organisations include:
    - The Confederation of British Industry www.cbi.org.uk
    - The Local Government Association www.local.gov.uk
    - The National Council for Voluntary Associations www.ncvo.org.uk
    - The NHS Confederation www.nhsconfed.org

Guidance and advice for specific protected characteristics or equality strands

- Business in the Community offers detailed advice, often based on its own research, on **age**, **race** and **sex**, as well as case studies. Website: www.bitc.org.uk/post_tag/diversity-and-inclusion

- The Fawcett Society is the leading membership organisation focusing on **women** in the UK. It provides extensive guidance on women's equality, including intersectional issues and equal pay. Website: www.fawcettsociety.org.uk
- The Runnymede Trust carries out research and analysis on **race** in the UK, including on employment and the wider economy, and publishes reports. Website: www.runnymedetrust.org/publication-categories/employment-economy
- Stonewall promotes the rights of **lesbian, gay, bisexual, trans, questioning** and **asexual (LGBTQ+)** people, and runs the Diversity Champions, Workplace Equality Index and Worldwide Workplace Equality Index schemes, as well as providing training. Its website has extensive resources and toolkits for creating inclusive workplaces: www.stonewall.org.uk/resources-creating-lgbtq-inclusive-workplace

Reflective activity 7.8

Find and read one source of information and guidance from those discussed above (if your chosen document is a long one, focus on one protected characteristic). How does practice in your organisation match up? Could your organisation do more with regard to the issues covered?

7.8 Summary

Despite some significant changes since the 1970s, the British workplace remains stubbornly segregated, both horizontally and vertically, with discrimination disproportionately affecting specific social groups based on their demographic and identity characteristics. Young people, disabled people and Muslims have consistently lower employment rates and there is clear evidence of pay gaps with regard to gender, race or ethnicity and disability. Bullying and sexual harassment remain widespread, with young women, Black and other minority ethnic groups, LGBT workers and people from religious minorities at greatest risk.

This chapter opened by exploring the different concepts in equality, diversity and inclusion (EDI) and the contribution of a feminist and intersectional lens to the study of employment relations. It then presented some of the evidence of inequality and employment segregation before examining some of the theoretical explanations for inequality. The law, in the form of the Equality Act 2010, was then outlined and explained. Finally, the chapter examined the key rationales for EDI in the workplace and discussed the policy options open to employers.

Throughout, the chapter has highlighted the fact that there is no single concept, law, rationale or policy option which will guarantee change. Instead, the pursuit of equality requires a thoughtful, critical and nuanced approach based on the facts of inequality; an understanding of the needs of different individuals and groups based on their views and experiences; action on all aspects of employment and HRM and commitment and support from everybody at work.

KEY LEARNING POINTS

- Concepts and shared understandings of equality, diversity and inclusion are always changing, and terminology is susceptible to phases of popularity. Key distinctions revolve around whether priority is given to the individual, the social group or both, and whether the focus is on equal opportunities, equal outcomes or both.
- A feminist lens ensures that the lives, voices and experiences of women and other minority groups are included and validated in employment relations research.
- An intersectional lens highlights the intersections between differences, especially those of gender, race and class. An intersectional approach ensures that policy and practice is not over-generalised.
- Inequality and disadvantage persist in the UK labour market, which is segregated horizontally and vertically by gender, race or ethnicity and other factors.
- The law plays an important role in seeking to eliminate discrimination.
- Neither social justice arguments nor the business case for diversity constitute a comprehensive rationale for action on EDI. Contemporary commentators suggest that a combination of the two is most likely to be effective in bringing about change.
- There are options for employers and HR professionals in terms of policy and strategy for EDI, but there are no quick fixes.

Review Questions

1 Critically evaluate the role of the law in tackling inequality and disadvantage in your organisation and wider society.

2 What are the main barriers to creating inclusive and diverse workplaces? To what extent can these be overcome by organisations without additional action from the government.

3 Design a workshop for line managers on their role in promoting equality and diversity among

staff. What challenges do you think you would face in securing buy-in and engagement and how could these be overcome?

4 Critically evaluate the arguments for and against your organisation adopting a rationale for EDI which incorporates both social justice arguments and the business case.

5 Prepare a short report for your senior management on the benefits of employing disabled people.

Explore further

BITC (2024) *Voices from the Race at Work Surveys*, Business in the Community, London Available at https://www.bitc.org.uk/wp-content/uploads/2024/03/bitc-report-race-voices-from-race-at-work-survey-march24.pdf (archived at https://perma.cc/PXZ6-ELSM)

Blithe, S (2019) 'I always knew I was a little girly': the gendering of skills in management training, *Management Learning*, **50**(5), pp 517–33

Byrd, M and Sparkman, T (2022) Reconciling the business case and the social justice case for diversity: a model of human relations, *Human Resource Development Review*, **21**(1), pp 75–100

Disability Confident / CIPD (2024) *Recruiting, Managing and Developing People with a Disability or Bealth Condition: A practical guide for managers*, Department for Work and Pensions, London. Available at https://www.gov.uk/government/publications/disability-confident-and-cipd-guide-for-line-managers-on-employing-people-with-a-disability-or-health-condition (archived at https://perma.cc/4R87-M73J)

Green, M, Bond, H, Miller, J and Gifford, J (2018) *Diversity and Inclusion at Work: Facing up to the business case*, CIPD, London

Holgate, J, Abbott, S, Kamenou, N, Kinge, J, Parker, J, Sayce, S, Sinclair, J and Williams, L (2012) Equality and diversity in employment relations: Do we practise what we preach? *Equality, Diversity and Inclusion: An International Journal*, **31**(4), pp 323–39

Khattab, N and Johnston, R (2015) Ethno-religious identities and persisting penalties in the UK labour market, *Social Science Journal*, **52**, pp 490–502

Kirton, G and Greene, A-M (2021) *The Dynamics of Managing Diversity and Inclusion: A critical approach*, 5th edn, Routledge, Abingdon

TUC (2022) *Still Rigged: Racism in the UK labour market*, TUC Publications, London

Vincent, S, Lopes, A, Meliou, E and Özbilgin, M (2024) Relational responsibilisation and diversity management in the 21st century: the case for reframing equality regulation, *Work, Employment and Society*, online first, DOI https://doi.org/10.1177/09500170231217660 (archived at https://perma.cc/AGS8-2NF4)

Websites

www.acas.org.uk (archived at https://perma.cc/3EYY-VZWD) – provides extensive guidance in relation to the management of equality and diversity.

www.cipd.co.uk (archived at https://perma.cc/G2WK-XMA2) – gives access to information relating to the law of discrimination and equality and also a wide range if useful research papers.

www.equalityhumanrights.com/en (archived at https://perma.cc/Y6NQ-W6T6) – comprehensive information on all aspects of equality law, research and practice.

www.fawcettsociety.org.uk (archived at https://perma.cc/V83N-FXPC) – website of the Fawcett Society, the UK's leading charity campaigning for gender equality and women's rights.

08 Health, well-being and the employment relationship

Overview

This chapter explores the nature and complexity of health and well-being in the workplace. It begins by discussing the development of health and safety protection for employees, from its earliest days to the more recent legislative processes which have placed a 'duty of care' on employers and employees. The next part of the chapter then charts the way in which legislation and good practice have developed to encompass not only the physical well-being of workers but also their mental health. We also critically reflect on the increasing impact of workplace stress on employees, the causes and consequences of poor mental health and the potential solutions for this growing problem. The chapter then focuses on debates over the theory and practice of workplace well-being. Several influential conceptualisations and their practical implications are considered as part of this discussion. From here, the chapter turns to the practical means by which employers can successfully facilitate 'good work'. Finally, the chapter closes with a number of examples of how specific characteristics or experiences of certain groups of workers can impact adversely on their health and well-being and how these issues might be addressed.

LEARNING OUTCOMES

When you have completed this chapter, you should be able to:

- critically reflect on the development of health and well-being legislation and good practice;
- explain and critically analyse the processes through which health and safety legislation, and its enforcement, informs good practice in the workplace;
- describe the nature, extent and causes of workplace stress and critically evaluate the development of procedures to address its impact;
- understand and critique the role of policymakers, managers and union representatives in operationalising health and well-being policy and practice;
- understand and critically assess the business case for enhancing well-being;
- identify and critically assess the different challenges and possible solutions to successfully enacting both physical and mental health policy and practice in the workplace.

8.1 Introduction

Since the introduction of the first welfare officers in enlightened companies around the start of the twentieth century, and the formation of the early trade unions, the health and safety of workers has been an acknowledged aspect of good employment relations. More recently, a more holistic approach to the well-being of employees has been promoted. In particular, organisations have increasingly realised that in order to create an engaged and effective workforce, there is a need to develop policy and practice which protects the well-being of individuals both in and outside work (Acas, 2018). Similarly, a recent CIPD/Simplyhealth (2023: 31) survey-based report argued that:

> The attention of senior leaders needs to be firmly focused on health and wellbeing. Even if it already is, HR professionals should continue to build the business case for ongoing commitment and investment from the board by demonstrating the impact of their health and wellbeing activity.

This chapter offers a working definition of well-being and explains how health and safety forms a key element of the obligation of employers to recognise the broader needs of their workforce. To this end, we will critically consider the impact of work on the physical, mental, psychological and emotional state of people in employment. This recognises that the relationship between work and health is both multi-layered and complex in nature. To put this into context, there were approximately 36.8 million working days lost in Great Britain due to work-related injury or illness, with 1.8 million people currently at work suffering from ill health which is believed to be work-related (Health and Safety Executive, 2023a).

THE SCALE OF ILL HEALTH IN UK WORKPLACES, 2022–23

- **1.8 million** working people suffering from a work-related illness (2021/22);
- **135** workers killed at work (2021/22);
- **600,000** workers sustaining a workplace non-fatal injury in 2021/22;
- **36.8 million** working days lost due to work-related ill health and non-fatal workplace injury in 2021/22;
- **£20.7 billion** annual costs of workplace injury and new cases of work-related ill health in 2019/20, excluding long latency illness such as cancer.

SOURCE: HSE (2023a: 9)

This clearly demonstrates the scale of this key employment relations issue and the challenge it poses to practitioners. What is less clear is how we first identify and then start to address the many elements of work-related illness. In particular, there is a growing awareness that health and safety at work extends beyond physical injury and illness to the increasing incidence of poor mental health. Donaldson Feilder (2012: 2) explains this as follows:

> Traditionally, measures of health and work-related risk to health were largely focussed on physical safety, for example, accidents, injury, slips, trips, and hazardous chemicals; and interventions were mainly aimed at preventing harm. Over the last 20 years, however, there has been an increasing recognition of the importance of the psychosocial environment (i.e. the psychological and social elements of jobs and the workplace) and the risks presented for mental health, as well as the need to address the issues associated with physical and long-term illness.

This has led to a greater emphasis on promoting well-being rather than simply addressing the causes of work-related ill health. However, before we turn to the nature and practice of promoting well-being in the workplace, we must first consider the more traditional focus on health and safety at work.

8.2 The development of health and safety regulation in the UK

Prior to 1974, there was no clear health and safety law. As Bill Callaghan, a former head of the Health and Safety Executive (HSE), explains, following the government-sponsored review of health and safety legislation by Lord Robens in the early 1970s, the 'vision was to sweep away previous prescriptive legislation and replace these with simpler regulations under the framework of the Act' (Callaghan, 2007: 10). The Health and Safety at Work Act (HASAWA) 1974 subsequently became an enabling Act under which more detailed regulations, including many implementing European Directives, were and are still made. Nonetheless, it provided for the first time a 'clear statement of general principles of responsibility for health and safety' covering all activities at work. Crucially, in section 2, it set out the guiding principle of health and safety legislation:

> It shall be the duty of every employer to ensure, as far as is reasonably practicable, the health, safety, and welfare at work of all employees.

Significantly, this duty of care extended beyond employees to contractors, clients, visitors and the public. Therefore, since the 1970s, employers have had a legal obligation under the Health and Safety at Work Act 1974, and more latterly the Management of Health and Safety at Work Regulations 1999, to carry out risk assessments in relation to work activities; and then to take necessary measures to control any consequent health and safety risks. This relates to potential causes of both physical and mental ill health, with stress increasingly seen as a major cause of worker ill health and absence from work.

Interestingly, despite the introduction and development of this apparently robust legal framework for the protection of workers, by the late 1990s, critical writers on the labour process, such as Nichols (1997), have argued that many workers were still subjected to 'structures of vulnerability'. Work intensification, a strengthened management prerogative, weaker union influence and the continuing dominance of neo-liberal market-driven praxis has created an environment in which it is more difficult to challenge unsafe management practices and therefore contributed to a rise in industrial injury rates.

Similarly, Tombs and Whyte have criticised the approach of successive Labour governments between 1997 and 2010. Specifically, they point to the recommendations of the Hampton Report, which New Labour had originally commissioned to 'consider the scope to reduce administrative burdens on business by promoting more efficient approaches to regulatory inspection and enforcement without reducing regulatory outcomes' (Tombs and Whyte, 2010: 12). For Tombs and Whyte, this resulted in several negative outcomes. Crucially, it advocated more self-regulation by businesses rather than independent inspection. But more fundamentally, it was philosophically driven, framing regulation as an economic 'burden' or 'cost' that contravened 'market forces': as opposed to a check on the duty of care, business has to put health and safety before profits. We will assess the validity of this charge in the course of our discussion (for instance, the impact of a reduction in the number of inspectors). However, it is important to note that health and well-being, as all of our topics of focus in the book, can never be seen in isolation from the fundamental power dynamics and differing perspectives that inform the employment relationship and its management.

Reflective activity 8.1

To what degree do you think that 'the balance of power' in organisations and society as a whole impact on health and safety in the workplace?

To what extent are workers or trade unions in your organisations involved in the development of well-being policy and practice?

8.3 Key elements of the law

The Act and the 'six pack'

The Health and Safety at Work Act created the Health and Safety Commission (HSC) and the Health and Safety Executive (HSE). In 2008 these bodies merged to become a single, integrated, policy and enforcement body. Health and safety regulations are legally binding. In order to encourage adherence to legislation, approved codes of practice (ACOPs) and/or guidance notes are often issued alongside new regulations. Failing to follow ACOPs or guidance notes is not an offence in itself; however, it can be taken into account when cases are heard. For example, the safe use of lifting equipment has an ACOP.

More specifically, the key duties of the employer under the HASAWA 1974 include:

- providing and maintaining plant and systems at work so that they are safe and without risks to health;
- ensuring the safe use, handling, storage and transport of articles and substances;
- providing health and safety information, instruction, training and supervision;
- maintaining the place of work (where it is in the employer's control) so that it, and access to and exit from it, are safe and without risks to health;
- providing and maintaining a safe working environment and adequate welfare facilities.

These obligations to ensure satisfactory health and safety in the workplace are also informed by the so-called 'six pack' of regulations which came into force due to a European law called the 'framework directive', the aim of which was to harmonise health and safety legislation throughout Europe. This came into effect in the UK in 1999 through a series of regulations introduced under the Health and Safety at Work Act covering:

- management of risk assessment
- provision and use of personal protective equipment (PPE)
- manual handling operations
- display screen equipment
- physical working conditions
- guarding of machinery.

As noted earlier, the law expects employers to take 'reasonably practicable' steps to ensure the health and safety of their staff, but what does this actually mean? It is extremely difficult to eliminate all risks and make every aspect of work and the workplace completely healthy and safe. Nonetheless, all risk assessment and subsequent action involves taking a considered view of all the circumstances. That is, the employer should do as much as they can to try to eliminate risks, and in doing so they should take into account the gravity of the risk, its likelihood and steps needed to avert it.

Duties of employees

The Health and Safety at Work Act also explicitly sets out the duties of the employee, which are:

- to take responsibility for their own health and safety and any health and safety problems they might cause to colleagues;
- not to recklessly interfere with or misuse any machinery, equipment or processes;
- to co-operate with employers about health and safety initiatives.

It is important to note that in most circumstances, employers are vicariously liable for the actions of their employees. Therefore, it is expected that reasonable processes of supervision and management are put in place. In addition, this will include ensuring that staff are made aware of risks and provided with suitable training. Furthermore, 'a duty of care' is implied into the contracts of all employees. In practice this means that if an employee commits a serious breach of health and safety standards or processes, this could be considered as gross misconduct with the potential for summary dismissal. At the same time, an identical implied term applies to employers. Therefore, if employers force employees to work in a way that endangers their health and safety, employees could see this as grounds for constructive dismissal.

Enforcing the legislation

In the UK, the Health and Safety Executive (HSE) and local authority environment health officers (EHOs) are responsible for enforcing health and safety law in workplaces. Currently, there are approximately 950 front-line HSE inspectors and 1,100 local authority EHOs. Critics have argued that this is a small resource given the scale of the duties necessary to effectively monitor health and safety compliance across the UK economy. Crucially, where employers are accused of breaches of health and safety law, the onus is on them to show that they could not have done more. That is, the 'burden of proof' rests with the employer. Therefore, if an employer does not comply with health and safety regulations, they will be committing an offence.

The most recent enforcement statistics for the UK reveal that in 2022/23, the HSE completed 216 criminal prosecutions with a 94 per cent conviction rate (Health and Safety Executive, 2023c). In comparison, in 2017/18, the HSE secured a conviction in 493 cases with a conviction rate of 95 per cent (Health and Safety Executive, 2019a). Furthermore, for 2018/9, where duty holders were found guilty of health and safety offences, they received fines totalling £72.6 million, an average penalty of around £147,000 per case resulting in conviction, which is a slight increase compared with the average fine of just under £126,000 per case resulting in conviction in 2016/17.

HSE – ENFORCING HEALTH AND SAFETY

- Completed 216 criminal prosecutions with a 94 per cent conviction rate;
- Issued over 8,000 notices, including approximately 6,000 notices for improvement and 2,000 notices prohibiting work activity placing people at risk of death/serious injury;
- Completed 86 per cent of fatal investigations within 12 months of receiving primacy against a target of 80;
- Delivered over 16,800 proactive inspections.

SOURCE: Health and Safety Executive (2023c)

The role of the HSE and its inspectors

The role of the inspector is varied but includes seizing, rendering harmless or destroying any article or substance considered to be a cause of imminent danger or serious injury. In terms of the seriousness or potential seriousness of an offence, inspectors are also tasked with issuing appropriate guidance or stipulations to an employer. The main actions are as follows:

- to issue advice (verbally or in writing)
- to issue an improvement notice
- to issue a prohibition notice
- to initiate a prosecution (summary or indictment).

HSE inspectors or appropriate officers from local authorities enforce the health and safety laws relating to all businesses and organisations in the UK. Their role is to investigate when an accident occurs or a complaint has been made and find whether workers are at risk in that workplace and, if so, why. They will offer employers advice as to how they can comply with the law and on the measures that employers can take to avoid injury or illnesses among the workforce. If necessary, they can take enforcement action to ensure that organisations comply in properly controlling risks to health and safety. From an enforcement perspective, the inspector can compel the employer to take appropriate action if they fail to comply with legislation. As outlined above, this can range from offering verbal or written advice through to initiating criminal prosecutions if they consider that people are in danger. Crucially, inspectors have a legal right to enter any employer's premises and meet with employees and workplace safety representatives. The role and duties of HSE inspectors are set out in more detail on the HSE website (www.hse.gov.uk).

Inspectors typically enforce health and safety standards by giving advice to an employer on how to comply with the law. Sometimes, it is necessary to formalise this by issuing them with a notice: either an improvement notice, which allows time for the recipient to comply, or a prohibition notice, which prohibits an activity until remedial action has been taken. The details of the nature of the orders can be found on the HSE website at www.hse.gov.uk/enforce/enforcementguide/notices/notices-types.htm.

However, it has been argued that the ability of the HSE to properly regulate the activities of employers and take necessary enforcement action has been constrained by the erosion of the inspectorate. Prospect, the union that represents HSE inspectors, claims that 'numbers (regardless of grade role or division) have fallen from a total figure of 1,651 in 2023, to 1,187 in 2010, to the current figure of 974 (a 41 per cent reduction over 20 years)' (Prospect, 2023: 8). In addition, the number of local authority inspectors halved over a similar period (British Safety Council, 2018a). While the impact of these reductions is not clear, we would argue that unless there is significant investment from government in this vital function, ensuring the health and well-being of UK employees, not to mention achieving the wider aspirations of 'good work', will be difficult. Prospect argues that the number of inspections has fallen from an average of 25,000 per year prior to 2010 to 16,000–17,000 in 2023. Furthermore, they suggest that even this number is likely to fall as the number of inspectors continues to decline (Prospect, 2023: 9).

Other key legislation

It is beyond the scope of this chapter to cover the full breadth and complexity of UK health and safety legislation. However, it is incumbent on us to highlight key legislation and direct the reader to the HSE website for more detailed guidance.

The Reporting of Injuries, Diseases and Dangerous Occurrences Regulations 1995 (RIDDOR)

RIDDOR puts duties on employers, the self-employed and people in control of work premises (the responsible person) to report certain serious workplace accidents, occupational diseases and specified dangerous occurrences (near misses). These responsibilities include reporting: death and injuries caused by workplace accidents; occupational diseases; carcinogens, mutagens and biological agents; specified injuries to workers; dangerous occurrences; and gas incidents.

The Control of Substances Hazardous to Health Regulations 1988 (COSHH)

COSHH is the law that requires employers to control substances that are hazardous to health and includes nanomaterials. You can prevent or reduce workers' exposure to hazardous substances by: finding out what the health hazards are; deciding how to prevent harm to health (risk assessment); and providing control measures to reduce harm to health.

The Working Time Regulations 1998

The enactment of the Working Time Regulations aimed to address a culture of long hours in the UK. Unlike elsewhere in the EU, legal regulation of working time has traditionally been very limited. However, our membership of the EU obliged the

British government to implement the European Working Time Directive. This said, it was not implemented in the UK until 1998, and remains subject to highly controversial 'opt-out' provisions. However, and despite the UK subsequently leaving the EU, following a consultation with employers, there are currently no plans to revise the legislation.

KEY RIGHTS PROVIDED BY THE WORKING TIME REGULATIONS

- A limit of an average 48 hours a week on the hours a worker can be required to work, though individuals may choose to work longer by 'opting out'; the average is calculated over a 17-week reference period;
- Paid annual leave of 5.6 weeks a year;
- 11 consecutive hours' rest in any 24-hour period;
- A 20-minute rest break if the working day is longer than six hours;
- One day off each week;
- A limit on the normal working hours of night workers to an average eight hours in any 24-hour period, and an entitlement for night workers to receive regular health assessments.

Corporate Manslaughter and Corporate Homicide Act 2007 (CMCHA)

Since 2007, companies can now face an unlimited fine, a remedial order and/or a publicity order if found to have caused death through gross negligence or failures in their safety systems.

Public Interest Disclosure Act 1998 (PIDA)

Under the Public Interest Disclosure Act 1998 (PIDA), sometimes referred to as the 'whistleblowing legislation', if an employee feels that they need to disclose some wrongdoing at work – such as contravening health and safety duties – which they 'reasonably believed' was in the 'public interest', they have a right to protection under the law, and in particular any dismissal connected to a protected disclosure under the Act will be automatically unfair. However, legislation and case law in this area is particularly complex and it is advisable to seek expert advice should a case arise.

The role of the health and safety representative

Employers must consult their employees in relation to health and safety matters. They can do this directly or through safety representatives who are elected by the workforce or appointed by recognised trade unions. The duties and rights of trade union safety representatives are covered by the Safety Representatives and Safety Committee Regulations 1977, and the role of employee representatives is set out in the Health and Safety (Consultation with Employees) Regulations 1996, to represent employees not covered by the 1977 Regulations.

Employers have a duty to consult about the following issues:

- the introduction of any measure which may substantially affect health and safety at work, such as new equipment or new systems of work;
- arrangements for getting competent people to help them comply with health and safety laws;
- information on the risks and dangers arising from the work, measures to reduce or get rid of these risks and what employees should do if they are exposed to a risk;
- the planning and organisation of health and safety training;
- the health and safety consequences of introducing new technology.

Although the law does not specify when employers should consult over health and safety matters, it should be in good time. We would recommend that the most effective way to ensure regular consultation is through a health and safety committee. In fact, if at least two health and safety representatives request, in writing, that a safety committee is set up, the employer has a legal duty to do so within three months.

It is also important to note that health and safety representatives have a right to reasonable paid time off to undertake their duties and activities and the employer must also provide them with the facilities they need to undertake their role – this could include access to a telephone, email and a photocopier among other things. Their activities are also protected under the law – therefore if a health and safety representative is dismissed in connection with undertaking their duties under the law, this is likely to be automatically unfair.

In our experience, health and safety is an area of employment relations which benefits from close partnership working. Health and safety managers can create a highly effective climate of awareness and good practice within the organisation by developing good relationships with union or employee health and safety representatives. To this end, the top five hazards that most concerned reps reported in a survey conducted by the TUC in 2022/23 captures both the mental, emotional and physical elements of health and safety (Table 8.1). Furthermore, it highlights the increasing impact of stress on well-being in the wake of the Covid pandemic.

Table 8.1 Hazards cited by health and safety representatives as top-five concerns

Stress	59%
Bullying/harassment	45%
Covid 19 exposure	39%
Slips, trips, falls	29%
Back strains	29%

SOURCE: TUC (2023b: 8)

8.4 Mental health, stress and well-being

There is growing evidence of the impact of mental health issues related to work. In 2018, research by the CIPD and Mind reported that in a survey of over 40,000 employees, 48 per cent were experiencing some form of mental health problem at work. Furthermore, half of those experiencing mental health issues felt unable to talk to their employer about these issues. This suggested that many workers in the UK with work-related mental health problems are suffering in silence. Interestingly, more recent survey data found that mental ill health remains the most common cause of long-term absence (CIPD/Simplyhealth, 2023).

There is a long and influential literature on the notion of work as a cause of stress and, therefore, ill health. This has particularly come to the fore since 2003 when, for the first time, the HSE issued a stress-related enforcement notice under the Health and Safety at Work Act 1974 to West Dorset Trust to undertake a risk assessment of its work practice following complaints from staff (Carvel, 2003). The TUC's (2018) *Mental Health in the Workplace* workbook, designed for union representatives working with their managers and HR colleagues, provides some valuable guidance and explains the nature of work-related stress and a range of other mental health problems that can be caused by, or affect, experience of work. In this context, Wright et al's study found that while employees felt that their employers treated health and well-being as an important issue, over half those participating in the research reported 'stress, anxiety or depression caused by, or made worse by work, with findings amplified for women' (2022: 26).

THE NATURE OF WORK-RELATED STRESS

Stress is not a mental health diagnosis and is not a recognised mental health condition. Most people with work-related stress will have anxiety, depression or what is termed 'generalised anxiety disorder'. Common mental health problems include:

- anxiety – about one in ten people in the UK
- depression – about one in ten people
- mixed anxiety and depression – about one in ten people
- post-natal depression – 8–15 per cent of women
- obsessive compulsive disorder – 3 per cent of people
- phobias (and panic attacks) – 1–3 per cent of people.

In contrast, severe mental health problems are:

- psychosis – 1 in 200 people in the UK
- bipolar disorder – 1–2 per cent of people
- schizophrenia – 1–2.4 per cent of people.

Other types of mental health problems include:

- eating disorders
- attention deficit hyperactivity disorder
- alcohol and substance dependency – 3 per cent of adults
- dementia – 5 per cent of people over 65 and 1 in 1,000 people aged under 65 in the UK.

SOURCE: TUC (2018: 5–6)

Reflective activity 8.2

Have you, or has someone you know, suffered from any of these conditions? What impact did this have on your/their ability to work and how was this managed by your employer?

While employers are more likely to be faced with the more common mental health problems outlined here, it is important to acknowledge the impact of 'severe mental health problems' on some employees and the type of support they need. For example, a long-standing mental health condition which has a significant and adverse impact on an employee is likely to be defined as a disability under the Equality Act 2010. In such cases, not only must the employer ensure that employees are not subject to discrimination as a result of their condition, but also that the employer must make reasonable adjustments to accommodate that worker in their role. This could include allowing an employee to work from home or work shorter or more flexible working hours.

It is beyond the scope of this book to discuss the specific support needed for different conditions. However, the current CIPD/Mind guide (2022) offers very useful advice on general good practice. It points out that no two people will experience a mental condition in the same way. Symptoms, and the way that different people cope with their conditions, can vary considerably. This means that managers need to support their employees flexibly and on an individual basis – the confines of rigid process and procedure may be particularly unhelpful and often more flexible responses will be needed. Furthermore, many mental health conditions are 'hidden' disabilities, which employees may be reluctant to disclose to their employer, particularly if they are unsure whether they would be protected under the terms of the Equality Act 2010. In our experience, HR practitioners and line managers are more likely to provide support to an employee if they believe that an employee's condition is likely to meet the definition of a disability, particularly if this is backed up by an opinion from a health professional. However, CIPD/Mind advise that all employees with poor mental health should be supported by their employer and treated in the same way, irrespective of the legal context or implications.

 Reflective activity 8.3

How does your organisation support employees with poor mental health? Do you think that managers handle these situations well and, if not, what could they or their organisations do?

Turning now to stress-related mental health issues, Ivan Robertson offers practical guidance for alleviating stress as a means of improving workplace well-being. His 'six essentials of workplace well-being model' usefully sets out the key areas that employers need to address as having the 'potential to cause stress at work' (2016: 19).

SIX ESSENTIALS OF WORKPLACE WELL-BEING

- **Resources and communications** – employees need adequate information, training and equipment to do their job.
- **Control and autonomy** – don't limit workers' autonomy to do the job their way.
- **Balanced workloads** – a balanced workload with a good work–life balance is crucial.
- **Job security and change** – the impact of change on workers' needs and any consequent training they need should be assessed.
- **Work relationships** – employees need to be treated with respect.
- **Job conditions** – employers should provide the best working conditions, including pay and benefits, that they can.

SOURCE: Robertson (2016: 19)

It would be hard to argue with the above list in terms of best practice, and these key areas of workplace policy and procedure form an important backdrop to our discussion. The HSE (2019b) also offer a helpful template which can be used to conduct a stress risk assessment (see Figure 8.1).

Using this approach, you can build up a list of hazards, set out how each is being addressed and indicate when those actions have been completed. This can be done regularly with respect to existing workplace practices and employees' roles. It should form a key element of assessing the implications of any planned changes to workplace practices. For example, if your organisation is going through a redundancy or restructuring exercise, the risks to those employees who remain (such as increased workloads) should be assessed and necessary action taken.

Figure 8.1 Risk assessment template

What are the hazards?	Who might be harmed and how?	What are you already doing?	Do you need to do anything else to control this risk?	Action by whom?	Action by when?	Done

SOURCE: HSE (2019b)

However, it is salutary to note that many employers do not adhere to this type of model. Carter et al's (2013) study shows that when proper risk assessment of the introduction of new working practices is not carried out, there can be negative implications for workers. They highlight several issues in relation to health and well-being in the workplace that are worthy of deeper consideration. The apparently innocuous introduction of 'lean' management techniques to a back-office clerical environment at HRMC offices in the UK subsequently resulted in higher levels of both physical and mental illness among staff. This included higher incidents of musculoskeletal disorders – such as stiff shoulders, back, arm and wrist pains – and increased stress.

In an attempt to address situations like this, the Health and Safety Executive (2023b) has produced a succinct but focused set of management standards to help employers address the effects of stress on their employees. Crucially, the HSE argues that these standards:

- demonstrate good practice through a step-by-step risk assessment approach;
- allow assessment of the current situation using pre-existing data, surveys and other techniques;
- promote active discussion and working in partnership with employees and their representatives, to help decide on practical improvements that can be made;
- help simplify risk assessment for work-related stress by:
  - identifying the main risk factors;
  - helping employers focus on the underlying causes and their prevention;
  - providing a yardstick by which organisations can gauge their performance in tackling the key causes of stress.

HSE MANAGEMENT STANDARDS

The standards identify six components of work design that, if not properly managed, can lead to poor employee health, lower productivity and increased accident and sickness absence rates:

- **demands:** this includes issues such as workload, work patterns and the work environment;

- **control:** how much say the person has in the way they do their work;
- **support:** this includes the encouragement, sponsorship and resources provided by the organisation, line management and colleagues;
- **relationship:** this includes promoting positive working to avoid conflict and dealing with unacceptable behaviour;
- **role:** whether people understand their role within the organisation and whether the organisation ensures that they do not have conflicting roles;
- **change:** how organisational change (large or small) is managed and communicated in the organisation.

SOURCE: Health and Safety Executive (2023b)

Reflective activity 8.4

Examine each of the standards outlined here in relation to the way that work is designed in your organisation. What more could you, and your employer, do to take action in each of these six areas to reduce the risk of stress and poor mental health within the workforce?

Applying the standards in order to reduce stress-related mental health conditions

The HSE management standards capture the challenge facing HR practitioners, managers and employee representatives in understanding the support needed by staff when their mental health is negatively affected by the nature of their work. This section focuses on the increasing realisation that stress, depression and anxiety (SDA) can often be a result of poor work practices and conditions which fall within the employer's obligation to address under the Health and Safety at Work Act 1974.

There is a growing recognition across industry in the UK of the duty of care of employers to protect the mental well-being of employees. In 2023, a CIPD/Simplyhealth survey revealed that stress was one of the top three causes of short- and long-term absence. Significantly, respondents were not convinced that managers had the skills and confidence necessary to support employees with mental health needs. Paradoxically, 'management style also remains among the most common causes of stress at work' (CIPD/Simplyhealth, 2023: 18).

This reflects our discussion in Chapter 4 and suggests that the way in which the employment relationship is managed can have a major impact on the well-being of employees. Gallie et al's analysis of the Fair Treatment at Work Survey also concludes that along with employment insecurity, the way in which employees are treated by managers is a significant cause of anxiety at work:

> While job tenure insecurity refers to anxiety about the loss of employment, job status insecurity relates to anxieties about the threat of loss of valued features of the job. The concept implies that there are certain features of jobs that are very widely regarded as aspects of a good quality job. While there are individual differences in the extent to which some features of work are valued, previous research has shown that there is a high degree of consensus among British employees about the importance of personal treatment by one's superiors, the ability to use one's skills, opportunities for initiative or task discretion, task interest and the level of pay (Gallie et al, 2017: 37).

Therefore, we would argue that skilled line managers who communicate effectively with their staff and, importantly, provide them with a significant degree of input into decision-making play a key role in creating more healthy environments at work. In addition, as Whitehouse (2019) suggests, a clear sickness policy is a basic necessity which will help line managers deal with these challenging issues in a fair and consistent way. It should outline the processes in relation to sick pay, medical assessments, contact points and review meetings. In this way the employee can be aided more effectively back into work. However, it is also important to build managerial capability – Whitehouse cites the example of a local authority which encouraged managers to become mental health first-aid champions. It was hoped that this would build confidence so that managers addressed issues at an early stage.

8.5 Well-being at work

So far in this chapter, we have focused on the 'traditional' aspects of health and safety in the workplace. Our discussion now turns to a more recent acknowledgement of how these and other elements of work can be better understood within the broader notion of employee well-being. For instance, new research in the NHS has revealed that well-being can be impacted by issues such as the culture of the organisation, demands for greater job flexibility by employees, workplace conflict and line managers' capability and capacity to undertake their roles (Bennett et al, 2023). Significantly, a recent survey by the Chartered Managers Institute also highlighted that poor or 'accidental' managers can have a negative effect on staff well-being (Chartered Management Institute, 2023).

The origins of well-being

The role of people management with respect to the well-being of workers is not a new concept. From a collective perspective, the early trade unions of the nineteenth century were formed specifically as 'friendly societies', which, through subscriptions from members, could cover the basic needs of often itinerant workers, or 'journeymen', as they sought work from town to town. Similarly, they provided a collective means of saving money to fund workers and their families when work was hard to obtain. Personnel or staff welfare officers were employed by larger and more enlightened organisations from around the turn of the twentieth century. These individuals were tasked with facilitating the employer's perceived obligation to their workforce to ameliorate the more negative elements of the employment relationship. This included the provision of washing, rest and recreational facilities, first aid and protective clothing (Clegg, 1976). By 1945, there were approximately 5,000 personnel specialists.

The growth of HRM, with its focus on delivering business imperatives and driving organisational performance, saw the traditional functions of 'personnel' increasingly seen (and arguably denigrated) as peripheral and transactional. Welfare was certainly not seen as part of the strategic mission of HR. However, increased awareness over the implications of work intensification for mental health and greater emphasis on the idea of 'good work' has started to change the narrative. More recently, the need to develop a more holistic approach that accepts that well-being and all aspects of mental health – mental, psychological and emotional – are central to decent work and organisational performance, has been increasingly recognised (Bevan and Cooper, 2022; Black, 2008). Furthermore, from an organisational development perspective, drawing on the analysis of data from an extensive global survey of well-being and its link to career development, Clifton and Harter (2021: 430) underline the importance of building managerial capability and argue that organisational leaders need to:

- ensure everyone in the organisation knows their strengths
- remove abusive managers
- upskill managers
- make well-being part of career development conversations.

Defining and conceptualising well-being

From a conceptual perspective, the term subjective well-being (SWB) is used to cover a number of different aspects of a person's subjective mental state and has been argued by the OECD to include 'all of the various evaluations, positive and negative, that people make of their lives, and the affective reactions of people to their experiences' (Bryson et al, 2014: 11). In the context of this chapter, we favour the following definition of well-being as being a mental state that:

> enables people to cope with the stresses of life, to realize their abilities, to learn well and work well, and to contribute to their communities. Mental health is an integral component of health and well-being and is more than the absence of mental disorder (World Health Organization, 2024).

Kowalski and Loretto (2017) argue that we cannot fully understand well-being without considering its context, in terms of working environment, sector, occupation and job role. As we note elsewhere in the book, when that environment is compromised by crisis, as was the case of the Covid outbreak, this can have an impact on the nature of work across sectors and, consequently, on the health and well-being of workers (Spencer, 2022). This presents real challenges for managers and unions. Also, as Cheese stresses, the increase in remote and hybrid working in the wake of the pandemic means that 'employers must take a wider view of how they support and protect people's wellbeing beyond the workplace' (2021: 339). Significantly, a recent review of nearly 2,000 academic articles on home working, teleworking and other types of hybrid working revealed major health benefits for workers, including reduced levels of stress (Hall et al, 2024).

Moreover, a number of commentators agree that good work and job quality are critical in shaping health and well-being at work (Black, 2008; Gallie et al, 2017; Kowalski and Loretto, 2017). Donaldson Feilder (2012: 2) concurs with this approach, noting that:

> Commentators increasingly link well-being at work with innovation, productivity, creativity, quality, and reliability and ultimately to levels of growth at a national level, as well as our ability to compete on the global stage. A growing body of evidence also suggests that the key to making a positive connection between well-being, creativity and productivity is to recognise the value of 'good work' in people's lives.

The link between well-being, organisational performance and HR action is captured by contrasting conceptual framings of the relationship between these key notions. The first conceptualisation is captured in two complementary but differing perspectives of how we may understand the nature of SWB (Ryan and Deci, 2001), where, as Bryson et al highlight (2014: 12 – our emphasis):

> *Hedonic* approaches focus on the type of affective feelings that a person experiences (e.g. anxiety or contentment) and also on the adequacy of those feelings (e.g. whether the person is satisfied with certain aspects of their life). In contrast to these hedonic approaches, the *eudemonic* approach to SWB focuses on the extent to which a person experiences feelings that are considered to demonstrate good mental health (e.g. the extent to which they feel a sense of purpose.

For Bryson and his team, most research has tended to adopt a more hedonic viewpoint, focusing for instance on job-related aspects as a measurement of SWB; whereas the eudemonic approach to SWB has been less frequently operationalised in organisational research, and therefore less studied. Guest (2017), in his analysis of the role of HR, also acknowledges the distinction between hedonic and eudemonic forms of well-being. He argues that hedonic well-being is usually represented by job satisfaction, while eudemonic well-being reflects the extent to which workers find fulfilment, meaning and purpose from their employment. The distinction for others between 'eudemonic' and 'hedonic' is seen as the contrast between 'feeling good' and 'functioning well' (Huppert, 2009).

Guest's critical analysis of the extant literature identifies the key antecedents of well-being in the workplace. He argues that investing in people through engaging work, a positive physical and social environment, and giving employees voice and organisational support can result in increased individual and organisational performance. Positive employment relationships, based on trust, fairness, security, a fulfilled psychological contract, and a high quality of working life, are critical in positively shaping a worker's psychological, social and physical well-being (Guest, 2017). From this, he subsequently identifies a number of key HRM strategies to enable this to happen in practice.

PROVISIONAL HR PRACTICES DESIGNED TO PROMOTE EMPLOYEE WELL-BEING

- Investing in employees
- Recruitment and selection
- Training and development
- Mentoring and career support
- Providing engaging work jobs designed to provide autonomy and challenge
- Information provision and feedback
- Skill utilisation
- Positive social and physical environment with health and safety a priority
- Effective equal opportunities and diversity management
- Zero tolerance for bullying and harassment
- Required and optional social interaction
- Fair collective rewards/high basic pay
- Employment security/employability
- An effective voice with extensive two-way communication
- Employee surveys
- Collective representation
- Organisational support through participative and supportive management
- Involvement climate and practices
- Flexible and family-friendly work arrangements
- Developmental performance management.

SOURCE: Guest (2017: 31)

Reflective activity 8.5

Check through the list of strategies above. Which of these does your organisation currently have?

Performance versus well-being: 'conflicting outcomes' or 'mutual gains'?

However, is a well-being strategy as straightforward as introducing all or a package of these HR initiatives in practice? In answer to this question, Kowalski and Loretto (2017) highlight the potential mediating effect on the impact of HR initiatives depending on the choice, design, delivery and evaluation of those practices on well-being and the employees' perception of this relationship. Guest (2017) also notes that if such strategies are not sufficiently thought out, they could potentially have a negative effect on well-being. For example, if initiatives are developed without the involvement of staff or which managers do not have the skills to enact, perceptions of trust and fairness are likely to be undermined. Although we would argue that employee well-being is consistent with high performance, it is important to recognise that organisations often see a route to efficiency through downsizing and work intensification, which can have a negative impact on those workers affected (Hudson, 2016).

In some respects, this reveals a tension between an optimistic 'mutual gains' approach (see Guest, 2017) and a more pessimistic 'conflictive outcomes' perspective. The former emphasises the way in which good HR practice, together with employee voice, can protect well-being in the face of business and organisational demands for efficiency. The latter implies that the well-being of employees is ultimately incompatible with the inescapable logic of profit maximisation or cost minimisation.

Reflective activity 8.6

Which of these perspectives do you share? To what extent do you think that employee well-being is consistent with the objectives of your organisation? Can HR practitioners have a positive impact on employee well-being, or is there a need for more fundamental changes in the way that we view work?

In reality, this is probably not a binary issue. Kowalski and Loretto (2017) argue that, given the multi-dimensional nature of well-being and workplace performance, there is not a simple causal relationship between HR strategy, productivity and well-being. Inevitably the key actors within employment relations have to tread a difficult line between the interests of the employer and their employees. However, strong arguments can be made that a greater focus on well-being can contribute, at least in the long term, to improved organisational outcomes, and that short-term approaches which prioritise work intensification are ultimately unsustainable. At a very practical level, the relatively simple process of assessing the risks of a particular strategy can have a powerful effect. For example, an organisation may have no realistic choice but to propose redundancies. However, if it assesses the risks associated with downsizing, it will be better placed to protect the well-being of staff in the future. Furthermore, different managerial approaches to achieving organisational goals will have different outcomes in respect of well-being. In this context, a study by Franco-Santos and Doherty (2017), which uses the model of conflicting outcomes against mutual gains to examine developments in the higher education sector, found that conflicting outcomes are more likely when a more 'directive' performance management approach is adopted by the employer. In contrast, a more 'enabling' approach realised tangible mutual gains in terms of both well-being and organisational performance.

Well-being in practice: the need for a more strategic approach and the key role of the line manager

The most recent CIPD/Simplyhealth survey into health and well-being in UK organisations, published in 2023, painted a mixed picture of how organisations were putting the rhetoric around well-being into practice. It reported that nearly half of respondents (48 per cent) agreed that their organisation was taking a continuous improvement or feedback loop approach to improve their well-being programmes. However, less than one-quarter agreed that their organisation critically assessed the quality of well-being outcomes for those who participate in activities/interventions. In addition, around one in three organisations did not provide their managers with training or even guidance on supporting staff about ill health. Once again, the research found that a lack of skills and confidence among line managers was the 'top challenge' for organisations. This echoed the previous year's report which argued that:

> As a priority, organisations need to ensure their line managers have the confidence and capability to nurture trust-based relationships with those they manage, so individuals feel they can talk about any work or wellbeing issues. To perform this role effectively, managers need the behaviours, education, and skills they will only gain from receiving effective training, support, and expert guidance. They also need the time and space to devote to people management, which should be a core part of their role (CIPD/Simplyhealth, 2022: 31).

A key strategic aim must be that line managers are better equipped to recognise early signs of stress and mental ill health as they are often the first port of call for struggling staff. Similarly, the British Safety Council published a report in 2018 (British Safety Council, 2018b) stressing that organisations need a more coherent and long-term approach to managing employee well-being. Some of their key recommendations include:

- Senior management needs to ensure that health and well-being are a central part of corporate strategy, including investment in that aspect of strategy.
- Line managers should have mental health awareness training in order to be able to effectively support employees.
- To these ends, organisations should regularly evaluate the efficacy of their employee well-being policy and practice.
- Employees should be involved in initiatives to enhance their well-being in the workplace.

- Fundamentally, employers must acknowledge that well-being is not only dependent on a safe and healthy workplace; rather, the whole nature of a worker's wages, career prospects, job satisfaction and relationships with managers and colleagues also impact on that well-being.

As these findings and recommendations make clear, there is a pressing need for line managers to be trained to handle the complex and difficult well-being issues that they are increasingly faced with. Furthermore, by developing skilled line managers, the potential for workplace stress and the development of mental health issues can be minimised. However, for this to happen, it is apparent that there is still a need for senior managers to more fully recognise that staff well-being (and employment relations more generally) should be a key part of business strategy. It is of note, therefore, that its latest long-term workforce development plan for the largest organisation in the UK, the NHS, stresses the strategic need to address employee well-being (NHS England, 2023). Crucially, this is intended to positively impact on a key organisational aim of more effective recruitment and retention across the service. Importantly, the plan explicitly recognises the key role of the line manager. Furthermore, it is stressed that this 'health and wellbeing support' is premised on addressing the needs of full-time workers, those who work more flexibly (home workers) and those on less regular contracts, such as bank staff or portfolio workers.

The myth of 'resilience'

Greater focus on well-being has been mirrored by growing attention given to the idea of resilience. This has spawned a body of academic research, as well as a range of online materials and training courses. While the idea of resilience has proved popular with practitioners, research has cast doubt on the efficacy of typical resilience-building interventions (Fleming, 2023; Spicer, 2024). The central focus of resilience is that workers can develop ways of handling the problems that they encounter in the workplace and develop strategies and coping mechanisms in the face of pressure and stress. Lewis et al (2011: 5) have commented that 'a consistent theme among the definitions of resilience is a sense of recovery and rebounding despite adversity or change'. This tends to point towards a shift of responsibility from the employer to the individual, suggesting that negative outcomes in terms of health, safety and well-being can be avoided if workers and employees can learn to cope better with work intensification.

In fact, it would appear that a range of consultants and providers are effectively selling resilience as a solution to workplace stress (Robertson, 2013). This flies in the face of a basic principle of health and safety legislation that it is the employer who has the responsibility, where reasonably practicable, to remove or minimise hazards in the workplace that could impact negatively on their workers. There is a danger, therefore, that too much focus on resilience could simply get employers 'off the hook'. Furthermore, as Teoh et al (2023) argue, any organisational interventions targeting well-being, including resilience training, are not generic. They are context-dependent, need staff involvement and senior leadership buy-in, and should be iterative and long-term in their execution.

However, this does not mean that helping employees manage difficult work situations cannot be useful in addition to pursuing the more fundamental task of addressing the sources of workplace stress. It can also be argued that there are some practical aspects of proposed changes to lifestyle that can potentially pay dividends for workers and their employers. In particular, there may be issues that are out of the control of the employer, but which impact on the well-being of employees at work, such as relationship, financial and health problems. The CIPD and the TUC, among others, have highlighted a range of measures that can support workers in improving their quality of working life as part of a broader strategy for well-being. None of these initiatives are panaceas, but as part of the support strategy are valuable to consider. They include:

- counselling
- employee assistance programmes
- occupational health support.

Reflective activity 8.7

Do you think that workers and employees in your organisation could be more 'resilient'? If so, what can they or the organisation do to achieve this?

Are there any potential dangers of developing strategies which focus on resilience?

Counselling

Counselling, ideally free to the employee, can offer a short-term intervention that can help employees manage mental health issues. It is confidential and voluntary. The approach may be person-centred or use cognitive behavioural therapy (CBT), or one of several other disciplines. The role of the counsellor is not to give advice but rather, through listening, questioning and discussion, to help the employee identify a way forward. It is often part of an employee assistance programme (EAP). It can be usefully utilised to support employees who are experiencing bereavement and loss, relationship and family difficulties, substance misuse and other stress-related issues.

Employee assistance programmes (EAPs)

As noted above, EAPs can be an additional or alternative support mechanism utilised by an organisation to offer assistance to employees. Typical EAP services provide advice and guidance on issues including:

- financial problems
- drug and alcohol concerns
- medical worries
- bereavement

- housing
- stress and anxiety
- domestic abuse.

Occupational health

Occupational health (OH) has a long tradition, particularly in the manufacturing sector, in supporting employers with work-related health issues. The service can be in-house or bought in from external providers. It is essentially an advisory service, providing advice to both employee and employer. Cooper (2017) usefully summarised its key functions and objectives. It aims to try to identify and help prevent illness caused by work, which can be physical or mental. OH practitioners will work closely with health and safety specialists and HR practitioners in monitoring the incidence of particular problems and developing effective responses. One of the main roles taken on by OH practitioners is to advise on the fitness of an employee to do their job. This will include working with the employee to understand the nature of the problem and to develop a plan to keep them in work or get them back into work. This could include reduced hours or staged returns after a period of absence. OH practitioners, often in conjunction with medical specialists, are also expected to provide the employer with an opinion as to whether an employee has a disability under the terms of the Equality Act 2010. If this is the case, OH practitioners would play a key role in helping to develop a package of reasonable adjustments.

8.6 Well-being, equality and inclusion

A key theme of this book is the importance of diversity and inclusion. Although the Equality Act 2010 provides certain safeguards for workers with protected characteristics, there is a need for employers to take a broader view of ensuring the well-being of workers who may be vulnerable to discrimination. In the following section we illustrate this challenge with reference to three specific cases: the mental health of older workers; the impact of the menopause; and the effects of domestic violence on experiences of work and employment.

Age and disability

Although age is a protected characteristic and some employers have developed specific programmes to recruit and retain older workers, it is not always clear that employers consider some of the more nuanced ways in which older workers might be disadvantaged. MacKenzie (2019), in an article in *People Management*, argued that older workers were being left behind as employers enthusiastically promoted well-being initiatives and encouraged greater openness and disclosure around mental health. In particular, older workers may feel more inhibited about discussing such issues and consequently targeted approaches may be needed.

MENTAL HEALTH AND OLDER EMPLOYEES

- For older workers there is still a significant stigma and taboo around mental health.
- Older workers are less likely to disclose that they are suffering with poor mental health.
- They will tend to avoid difficult conversations with managers and are more likely to leave the organisation rather than voice their concerns and problems.
- Older workers may feel that their employer would be unlikely to prioritise the mental health of those who might be nearing retirement.
- Employers need to develop a culture in which all workers feel valued and in which open and honest conversations are encouraged.
- There should be regular one-to-ones and opportunities to raise issues.
- Managers need to be made aware that older staff, in particular, may be more likely to conceal mental health issues.
- Good communication is needed to raise awareness of available support and to normalise the idea that good mental health is a priority – this will help to break the stigma felt by older people.

SOURCE: MacKenzie (2019)

Reflective activity 8.8

How are older workers treated in your organisation? Do you think that the needs and perspectives of older staff are taken into account when policies and initiatives are developed?

Managing the menopause

A key area in which issues of gender, age and well-being intersect is the impact of the menopause. Although this has been ignored for many years, there is increasing awareness about the implications of the menopause for the working experiences of women. Furthermore, a growing number of organisations are developing targeted policies and strategies designed to raise awareness and prevent unfair treatment. For instance, the TUC argues that:

> Employers have been slow to recognise that women of menopausal age may need special consideration and for too long it has simply been seen as a private matter.

> As a result it is very rarely discussed and many managers will have no awareness of the issues involved. This means many women feel that they have to hide their symptoms and will be less likely to ask for the adjustments that may help them. (TUC, 2013: 3)

In a survey of 500 safety representatives undertaken by the TUC, nearly half of respondents reported that managers did not recognise the issues relating to menopause. A third reported that staff were criticised by management for taking sick leave related to the menopause. A significant minority cited problems with staff discussing the menopause with their employers. The types of symptoms of the menopause most likely to be made worse by work were:

- hot flushes (53 per cent)
- headaches (46 per cent)
- tiredness and a lack of energy (45 per cent)
- sweating (39 per cent)
- anxiety attacks (33 per cent)
- aches and pains (30 per cent)
- dry skin and eyes (29 per cent).

The study highlighted that the working environment was responsible for making these symptoms worse. For instance, representatives reported 'high workplace temperatures', 'poor ventilation', and 'poor or non-existent rest facilities or toilet facilities' or a 'lack of access to cold drinking water'. Job-related stress and working hours were also cited as a problem for women working through the menopause. More recently, the TUC (2021b) argued that to address these adverse effects on women, employers have a responsibility to take into account the difficulties that women may experience during the menopause under health and safety legislation and the 2010 Equality Act. In response to such concerns, the government has made a number of recommendations to employers, including raising awareness among staff, and providing flexible working arrangements and specific training for line managers (Department for Work and Pensions, 2022). Furthermore, the EHRC (2024b) has published guidance to employers to make reasonable adjustments for menopausal women or risk claims of discrimination under the Equality Act.

Reflective activity 8.9

In what ways do you think that existing management and HR processes could disadvantage women going through the menopause? Taking into account your answer to this question, what could your organisation do to address these issues?

REAL-WORLD EXAMPLE 8.1

Menopause and employment rights

There are no specific employment rights related to the menopause or menopausal systems, however case law is developing in this area to provide protection for employees.

Farquharson v Thistle Marine (ET Scotland – Case no. 4101775/2023)

Farquharson had worked as an office manager for Thistle Marine for 27 years. She was a dedicated member of staff and was a 'strong and forceful character'. She informed her employer in August 2021 that she had a range of serious menopausal symptoms which sometimes impacted on her work. However, she did not ask for specific measures to be taken. In December 2022, Farquharson informed her employer that she would work from home as she was suffering from severe menopausal symptoms. On her return to the office the following day her manager greeted her with sarcastic and abusive remarks suggesting that the menopause was her 'excuse for everything' and said that this was just 'aches and pains'. He also referred to her as 'a biddy'. Farquharson left the office and was signed off sick. She filed a grievance, however this was not even acknowledged and her access to company systems was cut off. In response, Farquharson resigned and made a claim for unfair constructive dismissal and sex discrimination (harassment). Her claim was successful, and she was awarded total compensation of £37,000.

In addition, in a further case taken by Maria Rooney, a social worker, against Leicester City Council for disability discrimination, a preliminary judgement by an employment tribunal decided that her menopausal symptoms amounted to a disability under the Equality Act. Therefore, this demonstrates that government warnings in relation to the potential consequences of employers adopting discriminatory attitudes and practices to women with menopausal symptoms are very real.

The impact of domestic abuse in the workplace

Our final example is based on research undertaken to raise awareness about the damaging psychological, physical and emotional impact that domestic abuse can have on individuals and the implications for organisational performance. Fundamentally, domestic violence is not a private issue. The scale and scope of domestic violence has long been recognised in the UK, with at least 27 per cent of women and 13 per cent of men suffering from domestic violence during their lifetime (Office for National Statistics, 2018).

More recently, survey data revealed that 2.1 million people aged 16 years and over in England and Wales experienced domestic abuse in the year ending March 2023, equating to a prevalence rate of 4.4 per cent (Office for National Statistics, 2023b). Furthermore, Refuge (2024) reports that two women are killed each week by a current or former partner in England and Wales. This is at a time when councils are reducing their funding to refuges who could shelter those victims and give them support (Bryant, 2023). It is important to note also that abuse can be experienced by individuals immaterial of gender, sexuality, age or ethnicity. What is less well documented is the impact of domestic violence on employees and workplaces, although 'over one in ten of those who experience domestic abuse report that the abuse continues in the workplace' (TUC, 2020: 4).

Research has shown that the stigma surrounding domestic abuse continues to make it very difficult for employees to disclose their experiences. This can result in disciplinary sanctions against many victims (EHRC/CIPD, 2013), as poor performance, attendance and other workplace problems are often misinterpreted. Crucially, in the unionised workplaces reported on in the following box, there is clear evidence that enlightened partnership working between managers and union representatives, supported by HR colleagues, can start to positively address, sensitively and practically, this devastating experience, both for individuals and their organisation.

A significant move by the UK government is the enactment of the Domestic Abuse Act 2021. A key aim of this new legislation is to challenge the underlying attitudes and norms that underpin all aspects of abuse. However, while the legislation has potential implications for employers there are no specific provisions relating to the impact of domestic abuse in the workplace.

REAL-WORLD EXAMPLE 8.2

Addressing the effects of domestic violence in the workplace

Tony Bennett, Gemma Wibberley and Carol Jones (University of Central Lancashire) conducted qualitative interviews with over 55 union officers and reps in the north of England to explore the nature, extent and impact of domestic violence in the workplace. There were several key findings. Fundamentally, disclosure of abuse tends only to happen when the employee is faced with serious discipline or absence sanctions. Best practice in these situations saw union representatives and line managers, with the support of HR colleagues, recognising the real reason for these performance issues and then working together to agree appropriate adjustments to support the employee to remain and perform effectively in their job. This could involve a change of work location, a change in work patterns, and more understanding and support if the abuse meant that the victim on occasion was prevented from getting to the workplace. This also helped to ensure that the perpetrator did not victimise the employee while in the workplace. Another key finding was the value of raising awareness among both trade unions and line managers of the effect that domestic violence can have and of ways in which they could deal with the consequences when they arise. For instance, the ability to be able to signpost a victim for more specialised help was seen as crucial by all respondents. Crucially, a clear ethical argument emerged by which the unions articulated the key moral, legal and business drivers for effective domestic abuse policy and practice.

From a business perspective, producing a detailed domestic violence policy offers clear guidance to all employees on how the organisation manages fairly and with understanding of the impact of domestic violence on employees in their workplaces. Other practical actions for organisations include:

- the initiation of awareness training for all HR practitioners and line managers on how to proceed when a member of staff discloses that they are a victim of domestic abuse;
- carrying out an audit of all employee performance practices and policies to ensure that they align with and do not contradict domestic violence policy and practice;
- where present, a partnership approach with unions is of great value;
- policies should be integrated with existing HR policies, such as absence and performance management, and effectively communicated to all staff.

SOURCE: Wibberley et al (2016, 2018); Bennett et al (2019, 2021); Bennett and Wibberley (2023)

The GMB's Employer's Charter (2023) offers an excellent and succinct guide to how an employer and its unions can negotiate a meaningful agreement for introducing a domestic abuse policy and practice.

WORK TO STOP DOMESTIC ABUSE: GMB EMPLOYER CHARTER

As an employer who cares about the impact of domestic abuse on our employees, we pledge to:

1. Support employees who are experiencing domestic abuse to access support services and information confidentially.
2. Ensure that those experiencing domestic abuse will not be disadvantaged within the terms and conditions of their employment and will take all reasonable measures to facilitate any needs in the workplace.
3. Commit to working/participating with other organisations to facilitate best support for those experiencing domestic abuse.
4. Provide all employees with access to toolkits, information and our policies on domestic abuse, in a format that is easily and discreetly accessible within the workplace.
5. Ensure that we have employees trained across our organisation, to provide adequate access to support within the workplace for all employees. Staff trained should be representative of our workplace and will include line managers and trade union representatives.

Reflective activity 8.10

Using the GMB template as a possible model for your organisation, you are tasked with organising a joint workshop of HR and union colleagues to discuss the introduction of a domestic abuse policy. How would you address the following key questions in order to make the policy work in practice? To what degree does the charter work for your organisation? What might you add and why? How would you raise awareness of its existence in the organisation? To what degree would you need to look at and amend existing people management policy and practice and why? What is the role of line managers, senior managers and union representatives in making the policy a success? Where would you go for guidance in formulating this policy and practice?

8.7 Summary

As with so many of the areas we consider in this and other chapters, there are clear business, moral and legal imperatives for addressing the negative aspects of the employment relationship. We would argue that our discussion in this chapter has clearly highlighted why the well-being of employees should be central to employment relations and organisational strategy. Morally, and as good corporate citizens, all employers have a duty of care to their staff. Furthermore, the law, particularly the Health and Safety at Work Act 1974 and the Equality Act 2010, expects employers to minimise risk and to make reasonable adjustments for employees with a disability. However, it can also be argued that there is also a solid business case for ensuring the physical, mental, psychological and emotional well-being of your staff – not least avoiding the cost and reputational damage of potential litigation, but also in terms of improved productivity, motivation and commitment. As Professor Dame Carol Black argues in her government-commissioned report on improving occupational health in the UK:

> Good health improves an individual's quality of life, and a focus on their well-being can also add value to organisations by promoting better health and increasing motivation and engagement of employees, in turn helping to drive increases in productivity and profitability. In other words, the benefits of health and well-being extend far beyond avoiding or reducing the costs of absence or poor performance (Black, 2008: 52).

The notion and practice of well-being has developed considerably from the more 'ad hoc' work of the early welfare campaigners and trade union activists to a strategy which seeks to encompass the physical, mental, emotional and psychological issues confronting employees. Certainly, these developments have benefitted from the establishment of legal protections. However, we have already pointed out the limitations of enforcement of individual employment rights in the UK and this is accentuated for those employees in poor health as a consequence of their working environment. Furthermore, the potential for enforcement of health and safety legislation has been undermined by a lack of resources for the HSE. While government action to remedy this situation and to provide a solid legislative framework is essential, there is also a strong case for placing the idea of health, safety and well-being at the centre of HR and organisational strategy. Crucially, this includes ensuring that line managers have the capability and capacity to create and sustain healthy workplaces.

KEY LEARNING POINTS

- The legislative underpinning for health, safety and well-being at work is the Health and Safety at Work Act 1974. This places a duty on employers to 'ensure, as far as is reasonably practicable, the health, safety and welfare at work of all employees'. The Act is also supplemented by the 'six pack' of regulations which, among other things, provide for employers to remove or reduce potential hazards through risk assessment.
- A key challenge in maintaining high standards of workplace health and safety is enforcement. Unfortunately, the system of inspection and enforcement undertaken by the HSE and local authorities has been eroded in recent years.
- Employers have a legal duty to consult with their employees over health and safety matters. Workplace health and safety representatives play a key role in this and provide a vital channel through which workers can voice any concerns. The rights and duties of representatives are underpinned by law. However, proactive approaches by employers to establish safety committees and work in close partnership with representatives can have a positive impact on health, safety and well-being.
- There is growing evidence of the extent of poor mental health connected to work and the potential impact of this on well-being of staff and organisational performance. Many commentators argue that this is closely linked to the changing nature of work and particularly the intensification of the labour process. In addition, there is growing evidence that this has been exacerbated by the Covid pandemic.
- Stress is not a mental health diagnosis and is not a recognised mental health condition. Most people with work-related stress will have anxiety, depression or what is termed 'generalised anxiety disorder'. Other common mental health problems include: mixed anxiety and depression, post-natal depression, obsessive compulsive disorder and phobias (and panic attacks). Severe mental health problems include psychosis, bipolar disorder and schizophrenia.
- The use of stress risk assessments and having robust policies and processes around sickness are important in minimising poor mental health, but also in managing staff with mental health issues in a fair and sensitive way. However,

line managers play a key role creating environments in which the mental well-being of staff is protected – good communication, involvement in decision-making and the ability to deal sensitively with complex issues can all have a positive effect.

- In recent years, increased attention has been given to the wider notion of well-being. This has been defined by the World Health Organization (2022) as a mental state that 'enables people to cope with the stresses of life, to realize their abilities, to learn well and work well, and to contribute to their communities. Mental health is an integral component of health and well-being and is more than the absence of mental disorder.'
- However, the nature of the employment relationship means that there are inevitable tensions between staff well-being and the short-term goals and objectives of organisations. It can be argued that in the longer run, approaches that take into account the well-being of staff will create sustainable improvements in organisational performance. This reflects the important notion of 'good work'. However, if fair and decent work is to be delivered, well-being must be at the centre of organisational strategy. This will require a change of mindset on the part of both senior leaders and HR practitioners.

Review Questions

1. Having considered the discussion in the chapter, to what degree do you think current health and safety legislative obligations in the UK are effectively monitored and enforced?
2. What are the main challenges in your organisation in respect of health, safety and well-being? What short-term actions could your organisation take to start to address these problems?
3. You have been asked by your HR manager to facilitate a workshop for line managers on the significance of effective health and well-being policy and practice in the workplace. Using the model of the moral, legal and business arguments for well-being, briefly outline the itinerary for the event.
4. Your board members have noticed the growing interest in the notion of good work in your sector. Devise a short paper that sets out the key arguments for pursuing such a policy in relation to staff well-being and explain how it could be implemented in your own organisation.
5. Critically reflect on the statement that 'with the right type of training and development, workers can build up the necessary resilience to avoid stress that might occur from carrying out their workplace tasks'.

Explore further

Acas (2024) *Supporting Mental Health at Work: Managing employees' wellbeing*. Available from: https://www.acas.org.uk/supporting-mental-health-workplace/managing-your-employees-mental-health-at-work (archived at https://perma.cc/B45T-T7BJ) [accessed 1 July 2024]

Bennett, T and Wibberley, G (2023) Making the ethical case for effective domestic abuse policy and practice: The role of trade unions, *Employee Relations Journal*, **45**(3), pp 637–52

Bryson, A (2016) Health and safety risks in Britain's workplaces: where are they and who controls them? *Industrial Relations Journal*, **47**(5–6), pp 547–66

CIPD/Simplyhealth (2023) *Health and Wellbeing at Work*, CIPD, London

Guest, D (2017) Human resource management and employee well-being: towards a new analytic framework, *Human Resource Management Journal*, **27**(1), pp 22–38

TUC (2018) *Mental Health and the Workplace: A TUC education workbook*, TUC Publications, London

Websites

www.acas.org.uk/health-and-wellbeing (archived at https://perma.cc/FU4E-QCCN) – Acas provides detailed information on health and safety at work and particularly in relation to mental health at work.

www.hse.gov.uk (archived at https://perma.cc/W3NQ-U5Y7) – the HSE website gives access to legislation, guidance and advice in relation to all aspects of health and safety.

www.mind.org.uk (archived at https://perma.cc/ 5MVY-ZAA2) – the mental health charity Mind provides research and guidance for employers in relation to mental health in the workplace.

09 The management of workplace conflict

Overview

This chapter examines the management of workplace conflict and in doing so provides a foundation for the next section of the book, which goes on to explore some of the practical challenges faced by employment relations professionals in responding to disciplinary issues, employee grievances and redundancy situations. The chapter defines conflict and sets out a basic conceptual framework, which we then use for exploring the nature and pattern of workplace disputes. This includes tracing the incidence of collective industrial action and employment tribunal applications and discussing the factors that shape individual conflict in the workplace. The changing legal context of conflict management is then discussed, with a particular focus on the ways in which governments have sought to reduce the risks of litigation faced by employers. Finally, the chapter looks at the way in which conflict is managed in the workplace and at how changes to the nature of the HR function and employee voice have exposed the critical and often problematic role of frontline management.

LEARNING OUTCOMES

When you have completed this chapter, you should be able to:

- understand and explain the definition of workplace conflict;
- identify and critically assess the key factors that shape the nature and pattern of workplace conflict and employment disputes;

- explain and critically evaluate the development of the legal framework underpinning employment dispute resolution;
- critically analyse the changing role of HR practitioners, line managers and employee representatives in the management of conflict;
- describe the key elements of integrated conflict management systems.

9.1 Introduction

For the last four decades, a key feature of UK employment relations has been the reduction in the scale and scope of collective industrial action and the increased emphasis on individual employment disputes and litigation. Consequently, the resolution of individual workplace conflict became a focus of policy and practice, primarily driven by concerns over the cost of defending employment tribunal claims and the perceived burden that this placed on employers. In reality, the growth of individual workplace conflict during the 1990s and 2000s was triggered by the erosion of union organisation and bargaining power. This made industrial action less likely but also led trade unions to focus their attention on individual representation (Dickens and Hall, 2010). Furthermore, the growing representation gap has narrowed the informal pathways through which conflict has been traditionally resolved in the workplace.

However, 2022 and 2023 saw collective industrial action increase to its highest level since 1989, as workers across a range of sectors sought to defend real wages and improve working conditions. This upsurge in collective conflict was largely driven by rapid increases in the cost of living in the context of tight labour market conditions, which substantially boosted union bargaining power. In addition, some commentators have suggested that increased worker resistance is linked to the Covid pandemic, changing attitudes to work and a growing sense of unease about income inequality.

It is far too early to say whether this upsurge in collective action will be sustained. Nonetheless, it illustrates the inevitability of workplace conflict and underlines the importance of the political, economic and social context in shaping how this is expressed. It also shows that HR and employment relations practitioners need to be able to manage and resolve conflict in both collective and individual arenas.

9.2 Defining and conceptualising workplace conflict

Before considering how conflict is managed, we need to briefly examine how it is understood. Often, in both policy and practice, 'conflict' and 'disputes' are used interchangeably, while within academic literature the 'links between wider processes of conflict and overt disputes are rarely discussed' (Edwards, 1995: 434). Furthermore, there is often little distinction between different types of disputes.

Dix et al (2009) define conflict as 'discontent arising from a perceived clash of interests'. The root cause of this 'clash of interests' depends on your perspective of the employment relationship. In Chapter 2 we discussed the unitarist, pluralist and radical frames of reference. These produce very different views as to the basic cause of conflict and its potential resolution. From a unitarist perspective, the interests of employer and employee are identical. Therefore, conflict is either a function of miscommunication by management or due to agitation by individuals deliberately 'making trouble'. A radical perspective sees that the interests of capital and labour are irreconcilable within a capitalist system – not only is conflict between employers and employees inevitable, but any settlement or resolution is only a 'sticking plaster'. A pluralist frame of reference also sees conflict as an inherent part of the employment relationship but emphasises that different interests can be accommodated, and resolutions reached, through negotiation and consultation.

Irrespective of the underlying causes, conflict can be triggered by a wide range of different factors, as shown in the box below, but, as the definition above suggests, this 'discontent' is not always visible and can be expressed in informal and often covert ways. For example, individuals or groups of workers may choose not to voice concerns and/or may indirectly articulate them through absence, quitting or lower levels of performance. Furthermore, these consequences can also be seen through petty theft (pilfering), mischief or misbehaviour, where rules are deliberately breached, and even through industrial sabotage.

TRIGGERS FOR WORKPLACE CONFLICT

Issues that can lead to workplace conflict include:

- poor management
- changes to terms and conditions
- low levels of pay
- unfair treatment
- lack of communication or miscommunication
- poor working conditions
- inequality in treatment and opportunity
- bullying and harassment
- work intensification.

Conflict may also be expressed through more formal channels. Dix et al (2009) draw a crucial distinction between conflict and the disputes which are 'manifest expressions' of that discontent. At an individual level, these normally take one of two forms: a grievance brought by the employee, or disciplinary action taken by the organisation against an employee. Discontent can also develop into collective disputes in the form of industrial action. This can take a wide variety of forms, such as strike action where a group of workers remove their labour by stopping work for a limited or an indefinite period. Other forms include refusal to work overtime or working 'to rule', whereby workers refuse to work beyond the terms of their contract. Workers may also choose not to undertake a particular part of their contractual duties.

Whether conflict escalates into individual employment disputes, collective industrial action or is expressed through more informal action, it is likely to depend on a number of critical factors, which are summarised below and represented in Figure 9.1:

1. Political and legal context – if the regulatory framework underpins employment rights and provides a clear route through which rights can be enforced, discontent is likely to be converted into disputes. Whether this is in the form of individual grievances and litigation will depend on the extent to which collective action is supported or constrained by legislation.
2. Organisational processes – if there are accessible processes through which employees can raise concerns and managers can deal with issues of conduct and capability, discontent is likely to be expressed through formal grievances and disciplinary action. Where such processes are not present, conflict is more likely to be expressed through informal and indirect channels such as quitting, absence and poor performance.
3. Employee voice – while formal processes may act as channels for employee voice, access to representation may be critical in mobilising discontent and articulating this as an individual or collective grievance.
4. Personal characteristics and emotional contexts – emotional contexts can influence conflict escalation. Issues outside the workplace often shaped by economic circumstance may affect how individuals respond to conflict. Both manager and managed will rely on 'attributions' to make sense of the situation they find themselves in.

Figure 9.1 The dynamics of individual employment disputes

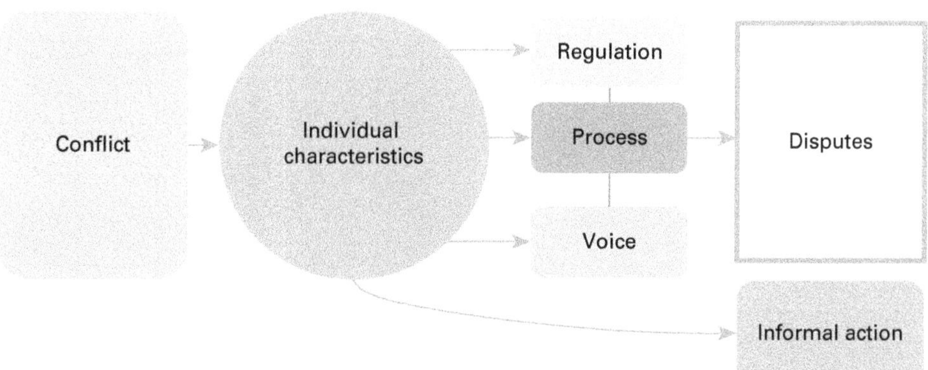

Reflective activity 9.1

What are the main sources of conflict in your workplace? How is this conflict expressed?

9.3 The pattern of workplace disputes in the UK

The conceptual framework just outlined provides us with a way of understanding the changing pattern of workplace disputes in the UK. Between 1979 and 2022, the most distinctive feature of this was the significant reduction in the incidence and scale of collective industrial action and the increase in the prominence of employment tribunal applications. While this was seen as reflecting the individualisation of workplace conflict, the evidence suggests a more complex picture revolving around changes in the nature of employee voice mechanisms and the regulatory framework of dispute resolution. Indeed, the significant upsurge of industrial action in 2022 reinforces this argument – in short, while the scope and shape of conflict may change, it is an inevitable aspect of organisational life.

Strike action in the UK

Collective grievances can be expressed in a number of ways – groups of workers can take strike action where they withdraw their labour completely for a limited or an indefinite period. In addition, they can take industrial action, short of strike action, by refusing to work overtime, declining to complete certain parts of their normal duties or by strictly limiting their work to the terms of their employment contracts – sometimes known as 'working to rule'.

Figure 9.2 Days lost due to industrial action, 1970–2023

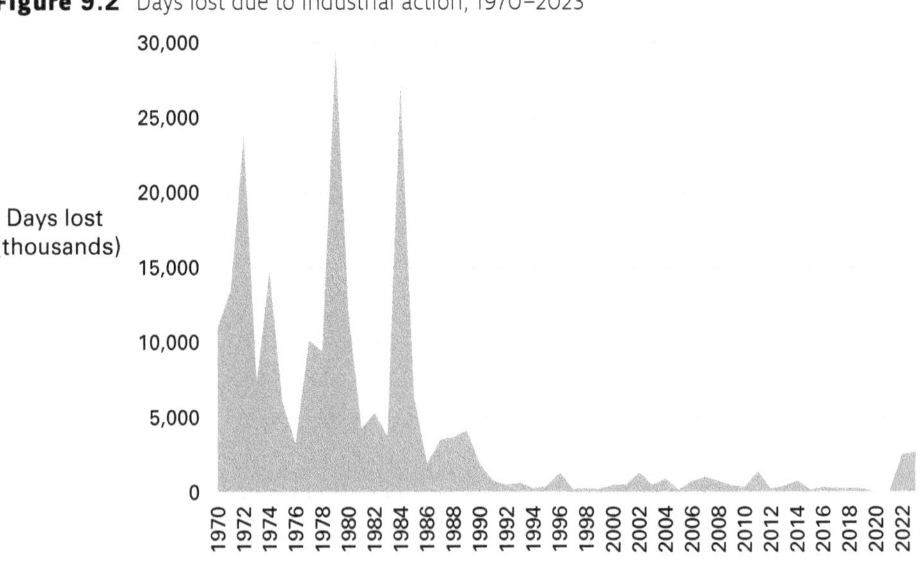

SOURCE: Office for National Statistics

As Figure 9.2 illustrates, one of the defining features of UK employment relations over the last 50 years has been the dramatic reduction in the incidence and scale of industrial action. During the 1970s, an average of nearly 13 million working days were lost each year due to industrial action. This fell to just over 7 million per year during the 1980s and an average of just 600,000 between 1990 and 2019.

Reflective activity 9.2

How would you explain the historical reduction in levels of industrial action since the 1980s?

The factors that triggered the reduction in strike activity have been widely discussed. It may be suggested that this reflects a broader reduction in discontent and improving employment relations as organisations have focused on high-involvement work practices and employee engagement. However, this is not supported by the evidence, which shows that the sharp decline in levels of strike action during the late 1980s and early 1990s coincided with a general deterioration in perceptions of employee relations and attitudes to work (Dix et al, 2009). Therefore, while discontent was higher, for some reason this was not translated into industrial disputes.

Following the model in Figure 9.1, a key factor may be the nature of the regulatory framework. It could be argued that the introduction of legislation restricting the ability of trade unions to win support for and prosecute industrial action suppressed strike activity during this period. Although these measures undoubtedly made it more difficult for trade unions to organise and enforce industrial action, strike activity fell in other countries, where similar legislative changes were not made. Therefore, it is unlikely that the changing legal framework was the main, or even a major, factor in triggering the rapid decline in the incidence of industrial action.

Even if individuals and groups of workers are unhappy about their pay and conditions, whether they are prepared to withdraw their labour and go on strike will be affected by their own personal circumstances in the context of the broader economic climate. For example, during periods of high unemployment and low inflation, such as the UK economy experienced in the 1980s and 1990s, the incentive for those in work to go on strike may be reduced. Workers may be more concerned about keeping their jobs and prepared to put up with a squeeze on their pay or changes to their working conditions. Consequently, the threat of unemployment may also deter workers from taking industrial action. This may well have been the case in the 1980s and in subsequent periods of recession. But, if this was the main factor, we might have expected to see greater militancy during periods of falling unemployment between 1997 and 2007.

The relative absence of collective disputes during this period could be explained by three related factors. First, rapid industrial restructuring and the increased globalisation of production contributed to the decline of industries that had traditionally experienced relatively high levels of strikes and other industrial action (including coal mining, shipbuilding and motor manufacturing). Second, the increased mobility of capital meant that the threat of organisations relocating production, sometimes referred to as coercive comparisons, made workers and trade unions less likely to take industrial action. Third, these forces combined to create a more hostile environment for trade union organisation, as union density and collective bargaining structures were progressively eroded (Charlwood and Terry, 2007).

Overall, in terms of the this model, it could be argued that fundamental changes to the structure of employee voice mechanisms within British workplaces meant that it was much less likely that discontent could be mobilised into collective action (Kelly, 1998). Moreover, the relative resilience of trade union organisation in the public sector (and those which were previously state owned and managed) is arguably a major reason why there were more than twice as many days lost to labour disputes in the public sector between 1996 and 2023.

However, in 2022 and 2023 there was an upsurge in industrial conflict, and days lost increased to their highest level since 1989 – 2.5 million in 2022 and 2.7 million in 2023. Superficially, the bulk of these disputes revolved around pay, driven by a rapid increase in inflation and interest rates in the wake of the war in Ukraine but also the economic policies of the Conservative government, during the brief premiership of Liz Truss in late 2022. For the first time since the late 1970s, the rising cost of living was accompanied by labour shortages boosting the bargaining power of trade unions. However, it is important to note that the incidence and impact of this wave of industrial action was still modest in historical terms. Nonetheless, it involved a wide variety of occupational groups and trade unions including some which had not previously been involved in this type of activity, such as the Criminal Bar Association and the Royal College of Nursing. Moreover, many of the disputes reflected discontent about wider issues related to working conditions and experience. It could be argued that this is linked to changing attitudes to work linked to the Covid pandemic that we discussed in greater detail in Chapter 3.

REAL-WORLD EXAMPLE 9.1

Even the lawyers are on strike...

In April 2022, around 2,500 criminal barristers started to refuse to substitute for colleagues who were involved in late-running cases. This informal action was rooted in long-standing concerns over the under-funding of the UK's criminal justice system. A large part of the work done by criminal barristers is paid for through legal aid. However, barristers claimed that reduced funding meant that their income from this work had been cut by 35 per cent over the previous decade. It was also argued that a lack of government support had contributed to a backlog of cases which increased from just over 40,000 in 2017 to more than 60,000 in 2022. However, the trigger for the action was the failure of the government to increase rates for legal aid. The low level of fees particularly affected newly qualified barristers who claimed that their hourly pay could fall below the National Minimum Wage at the same time as working long hours.

In June 2022, members of the Criminal Bar Association voted to step up their campaign by taking strike action in pursuit of a 25 per cent pay increase. The action involved a series of two-, three- and four-day strikes, culminating in a full week of action in mid-July. There were also widely publicised demonstrations outside courts across the UK as the action created significant disruption and delay. In September 2022, after pay talks had stalled, CBA members voted overwhelmingly for an indefinite strike. Finally, in October 2022, 57 per cent of CBA members voted to accept a deal which included a 15 per cent rise in fees for government-funded defence work and increases in payments for preparation work.

Reflective activity 9.3

What does Real-world example 9.1 suggest about the changing nature of industrial conflict in the UK? What are the implications of this for the future management of employment relations?

The individualisation of workplace conflict

Despite the upsurge in collective action in 2022 and 2023, a critical feature of contemporary employment relations has been the increased emphasis on individual expressions of conflict and particularly on employment litigation. The sustained decline in strike action in the UK through the 1990s and 2000s was mirrored by a growth in the number of employment tribunal applications. The number of registered employment tribunal applications grew from 34,697 in 1989/90 to a high point of 236,100 two decades later (Dix et al, 2009). There was then a rapid decline to just over 60,000 following the introduction of employment tribunal fees in 2013 and a steady increase in the wake of their abolition in July 2017 (Ministry of Justice, 2019). Changes in the way that the data is gathered and reported means that we should be cautious in analysing recent data (together with complications caused by the Covid pandemic). Nonetheless, as Figure 9.3 illustrates, it is clear that the incidence of claims has settled at a lower level compared to the peak of 2010 (Ministry of Justice, 2023).

Understanding employment tribunal volumes is important as it has become a focus of government employment relations policy and a key justification for radical reform of the UK's system of dispute resolution. The evidence suggests that the increase in litigation during the 1990s and 2000s was related to changes to workplace structures of industrial relations and, once again, the erosion of trade union voice. For example, Burgess et al (2000) found that increasing employment tribunal volumes were positively linked to falling union density. This suggests that as union influence and presence was reduced, workers were less able to resolve conflict through collective channels. In addition, it could be argued that this also had a negative effect on informal processes of resolution through which management and union representatives negotiated settlements on individual issues. The decline of collective bargaining meant that trade unions were forced to rely on the legal enforcement of individual

Figure 9.3 Employment tribunal applications, 2003–2023

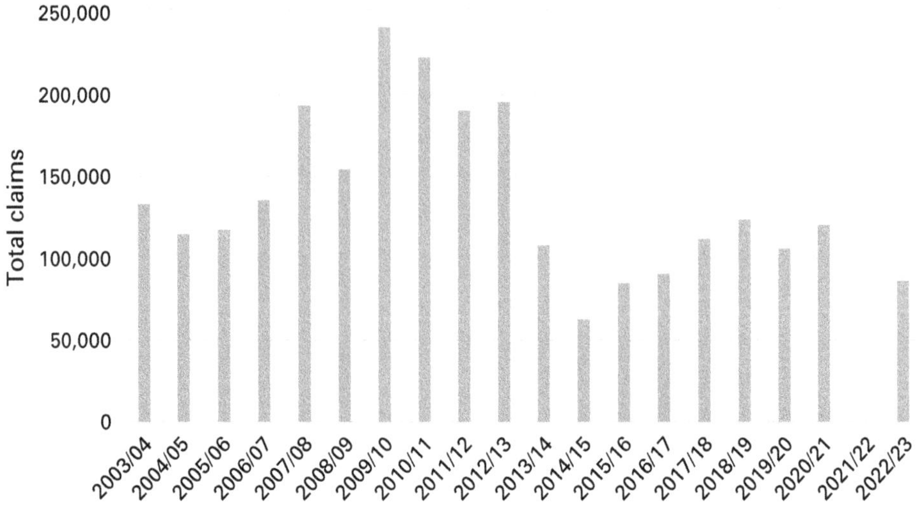

SOURCE: Ministry of Justice

rights to represent their members' interests. Furthermore, employees who were not union members had little alternative but to turn to the law.

Therefore, in terms of the conceptual framework set out at the start of this chapter, the pattern of employment disputes has been shaped by fundamental changes to the structure of employee voice. It could also be argued that regulatory change had a crucial impact. Between 1997 and 2010, under the Labour government, the scope of employment protection was widened, extending the opportunities for litigation. This was partly due to domestic measures such as the reduction in qualifying periods for claiming unfair dismissal from two years to one year. However, much more influential was the signing of the Social Chapter and the consequent increased influence of European law. By 2012, employment tribunals had the authority to make decisions on more than 60 different types of claim or jurisdiction. Critically, between 2013 and 2015, there was a dramatic fall in the number of employment tribunal applications from 191,541 to just 61,308 in the wake of a range of measures introduced by the government (including tribunal fees) to reduce the risk of employment litigation. Perhaps not surprisingly, the lifting of fees following a legal challenge mounted by the trade union UNISON increased access to the employment tribunal system and saw a significant increase in applications.

Reflective activity 9.4

What do you think are the main factors that influence the volume of employment tribunal applications? If you felt that your employment rights had been breached, what issues would you take into account in deciding whether or not to pursue legal action?

Moreover, while perceptions of high employment tribunal volumes have shaped organisational and government policy, it could be argued that the scale of this 'problem' has been somewhat inflated. The peaks in employment tribunal applications were closely linked to waves of co-ordinated claims brought by large numbers of employees relating to issues such as equal pay, redundancy and working time. For example, in 2009/10, more than 130,000 claims (56 per cent of the total) were made in respect of breaches of the working time regulations and equal pay legislation. In addition, there has been a growth in individuals bringing claims under more than one jurisdiction – for example claiming unfair dismissal, sex discrimination and unfair deduction of wages. This would be registered as three claims although they would relate to a single claimant and normally a single set of circumstances. This also suggests that many employment tribunal claims are actually triggered by collective issues. Therefore, it could be argued that it is not conflict that has become more individualised – after all, the issues are fundamentally the same – but the collective channels through which that conflict can be expressed, managed and resolved have been progressively blocked (Saundry and Dix, 2014).

This discussion suggests the need for a more nuanced analysis of the incidence of workplace conflict and the interplay between individualised and collective expressions of discontent. In particular, conflict may be suppressed due to employee concerns over recriminations or job security, particularly at times of recession or high unemployment. In addition, the way in which conflict becomes manifest will be shaped by the channels that are open to workers – in larger, unionised workplaces, discontent is more likely to be channelled through collective action. However, where workers lack representative voice, conflict may lead to sickness absence, resignation and in a small minority of cases legal challenge. In fact, a substantial proportion of workers take no action in response to workplace conflict, although this may still have negative organisational impacts in terms of reduced engagement and productivity.

Reflective activity 9.5

Do you think that conflict is increasing in your workplace? What are the main factors that influence the level of discontent in your organisation and do these escalate into visible disputes?

The contours and costs of individual workplace conflict

While the UK government collects reliable data regarding strikes and employment tribunal claims, there is a lack of up-to-date information on potential disciplinary issues and employee grievances. This data was traditionally gathered through the Workplace Employment Relations Survey (WERS), however, the last of these was conducted in 2011 (van Wanrooy et al, 2013). Although dated, its findings suggest that employment tribunal applications represent a small proportion of individual workplace conflicts. In fact, there are 7 times as many grievances, 8 times as many dismissals and more than 30 times as many disciplinary sanctions. Therefore, it is important not to over-emphasise the importance of litigation – in most workplaces it is rare and the real challenge for HR professionals is addressing issues that are much closer to the ground.

Research has also found that the main factor shaping the contours of individual conflict is the nature of the organisation. For example, grievances and disciplinary action are both more likely to occur in workplaces with larger numbers of employees (Knight and Latreille, 2000; Antcliff and Saundry, 2009; Wood et al, 2017). This could reflect the more impersonal nature of employment relations in big organisations. It could be further argued that in smaller workplaces conflict is more likely to be resolved informally, and there is good evidence that in smaller and medium-sized enterprises managers are more likely to use disciplinary warnings than dismissals (Forth et al, 2006). Similarly, we know that those working in smaller workplaces have more positive perceptions of employment relations. However, the relative absence of disputes in smaller organisations may simply reflect the fact that conflict could be suppressed due to the highly personal nature of employment relations in such environments. Disciplinary sanctions and dismissals are also less likely in public sector organisations, even when other factors such as unionisation, procedural formality and size are taken into account. This possibly suggests that the history and culture of organisations and/or the extent to which they are shielded from competitive pressures could be important in shaping managerial attitudes to discipline and grievance.

However, as we have pointed out, much of this data is more than a decade old. It also tends to focus on the more formal expressions of individual conflict. Therefore, it is helpful to look at more recent research conducted by the CIPD (2020) based on representative data collected by the polling organisation YouGov. This found that more than one-third of UK employees experience conflict at work – almost 10 million workers. One in five employees and 26 per cent of employers surveyed by the CIPD also agreed that conflict was a 'common occurrence'. The most common reason for conflict was difference in personality or working styles, closely followed by individual competence or performance. More than one-quarter (27 per cent) of non-managerial employees reported that their most serious conflict was with their manager. This reinforces qualitative research that has suggested that conflict at work often revolves around the (mis)management of performance and underlines the importance of managerial capability (Saundry et al, 2016).

The research conducted by CIPD also provides insights into the impacts of conflict and the way in which those involved respond. This has allowed us to paint a much more detailed picture of the impact of workplace conflict. In 2021, Saundry and Urwin used this data to explore the cost of conflict. Some of the findings are outlined in Real-world example 9.2.

REAL-WORLD EXAMPLE 9.2

The cost of conflict

- The vast majority of employees who experience conflict stay with the organisation – just 5 per cent resign. A slightly higher proportion of respondents take time off as sickness absence (9 per cent). However, 40 per cent report being less motivated and more than half (56 per cent) reported stress, anxiety and/or depression.
- An average of 485,800 employees resign each year as a result of conflict at a cost of £14.9 billion. A further 874,000 employees are estimated to take sickness absence each year as a result of conflict, at an estimated cost to their organisations of £2.2 billion.
- The vast majority of those who suffer from stress, anxiety and/or depression due to conflict continue to work. This 'presenteeism' has a negative impact on productivity with an annual cost estimated between £590 million and £2.3 billion.
- One in five employees take no action in response to the conflict in which they are involved, while around one-quarter discuss the issue with the other person involved in the conflict. Just over half of all employees discuss the matter with their manager, HR or union representative. In total, informal discussions cost UK organisations an estimated £231 million each year.
- There are an estimated 374,760 formal grievances and 1.7 million disciplinary cases each year. Together, these cost around £2.4 billion. Approximately 428,000 employees are dismissed each year and replacing them costs UK organisations an estimated £13.1 billion. Employment litigation costs UK employers an average of £776 million.
- The largest proportion of the costs of conflict is connected to an ending of the employment relationship – either through resignation or dismissal. Costs in the early stages of conflict are relatively low – these start to mount if employees continue to work while ill and/or take time off work through sickness absence. The use of formal processes pushes costs higher, however costs escalate very quickly as soon as employees either resign or are dismissed.
- The overall total annual cost of conflict to employers (including management and resolution) is £28.5 billion. This represents an average of just over £1,000 for every employee in the UK each year, and just under £3,000 annually.

SOURCE: Saundry and Urwin (2021)

The analysis conducted by Saundry and Urwin has a number of important consequences for policy and practice. First, it demonstrates that the most significant costs of conflict are incurred when the employment relationship ends, either through resignation or dismissal (see Figure 9.4).

Figure 9.4 The escalating costs of conflict (£ billion)

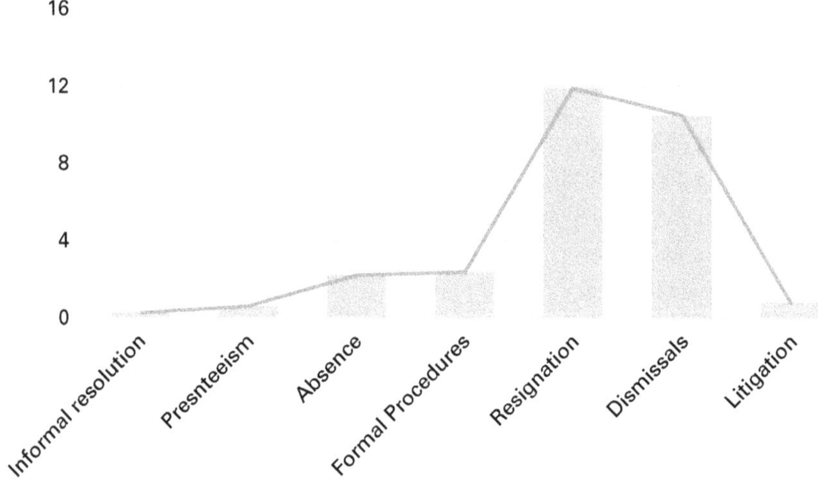

SOURCE: Saundry and Urwin (2021)

This suggests a need to move the policy focus away from employment litigation and towards improving employment relationships. Second, it underlines the importance of early conflict resolution that revolves around repairing and maintaining employment relationships. Third, as we have already argued in this book, this demonstrates the need to give managers the skills, space and support they need to prevent, contain and resolve conflict.

 Reflective activity 9.6

Thinking about a conflict you have witnessed or been involved in – what were the key factors that led to its escalation and resolution?

9.4 The legal context of conflict management

Of all the different aspects of employment relations, workplace conflict has arguably attracted the most attention from government. Concerns over its impact on efficiency, employment and economic growth have led successive administrations to attempt to develop regulatory frameworks which minimise and/or help to resolve workplace conflict. As we discussed in Chapter 3, the UK has generally moved from a 'voluntaristic' approach, which essentially placed the responsibility for the resolution of conflict in the hands of employers and trade unions, to one which imposes regulatory constraints on trade unions in respect of collective disputes and on employers in terms of individual employment rights. While a settled political consensus appears to have developed over legislative restrictions on collective industrial action, the thrust of recent policy towards the resolution of individual conflict has seen a return to what might be described as a neo-voluntaristic agenda, which provides employers with greater freedom to manage but in a context in which trade union organisation and structures of free collective bargaining are absent from most workplaces.

Regulating industrial action

From the end of the Second World War until the 1980s, conflict was essentially managed through structures of collective bargaining. This took place within a legal framework which was based on a system of immunities protecting unions from employer claims under common law if they called on their members to take industrial action. For the Conservative government elected in 1979, trade unions and their ability to maintain and increase wages through collective bargaining represented a major impediment to the operation of the free market. This provided the rationale for a sustained programme of legislation designed to restrict trade union activity and behaviour (outlined in the following box).

RESTRICTING THE ROLE OF TRADE UNIONS – LEGISLATION BETWEEN 1980 AND 1993

- The Employment Act (1980) removed the unions' immunity if their members engaged in picketing premises other than their own place of work.
- The Employment Act (1982) narrowed the definition of a trade dispute, outlawed the practice of pressuring employers not to include non-union firms on tender lists, and enabled employers to sue trade unions for an injunction or damages where they were responsible for unlawful industrial action.
- The Trade Union Act (1984) introduced pre-strike ballots.
- The Employment Act (1988), among other things, effectively outlawed the closed shop.
- The Employment Act (1990) removed unions' immunity if they organised any type of secondary action in support of an individual dismissed for taking unlawful action.
- The Trade Union and Labour Relations (Consolidation) Act (1992) brought together in one piece of legislation much of the law relating to collective provision.
- The Trade Union Reform and Employment Rights Act (1993) made some amendments to existing requirements, most particularly in relation to ballots for industrial action.

 Reflective activity 9.7

Do you think that legislation to restrict or regulate industrial action is necessary? Does current legislation go too far or are further measures needed?

Despite opposition from trade unions and those on the left of the political spectrum, a political consensus developed around these measures. Requiring unions to hold a ballot of their members prior to taking industrial action has become part of the employment relations landscape. However, the election of a majority Conservative government in 2015 again put the restriction of trade union activity firmly on the political agenda. The Trade Union Act 2016 further constrained the ability of trade unions to organise industrial action, limit facility time for trade union representatives and make it more difficult for trade unions to make political donations. The key measure was the insistence that at least 50 per cent of eligible members have to vote in a ballot for it to be used as a lawful basis for industrial action. In essential public services, at least 40 per cent of the total constituency must also vote in favour. Proponents of such measures argue that this prevents industrial action being pursued with only weak support from members. Against this, trade unions point out that current legislation restricts them from using electronic and other forms of voting that may boost participation, and also that minimum voting thresholds are not applied in political life.

TRADE UNION ACT 2016 – MAKING INDUSTRIAL ACTION IMPOSSIBLE?

- In order for industrial action to retain immunity, it must be supported by a majority of those voting and the turnout must be at least 50 per cent of those entitled to vote. There is an additional requirement that 40 per cent of all relevant members vote in favour where the workers involved provide an important public service. This would include teachers, some hospital workers and firefighters.
- Unions must provide additional information on the ballot paper to make clear the issues involved in the dispute and which issues remain unresolved, the precise type of industrial action being considered and an indication of the date of the action. Furthermore, the mandate for a ballot will automatically expire six months after the ballot (or nine months with the agreement of the employer). This is designed to prevent ballots being used for a prolonged series of one-day strikes.
- Unions must provide information regarding any industrial action and any political expenditure in trade unions' annual returns to the Certification Officer,

who will also have wide-ranging powers to make enquiries 'as he sees fit' into complaints made by members and to investigate issues in relation to financial affairs or breaches of duties in relation to the register of members, even where no complaint has been made. The Certification Officer can also impose financial penalties on trade unions for a failure to meet these and other reporting obligations.

- The period of notice that unions must give before industrial action can commence has been extended from 7 to 14 days.
- New union members have to opt in to pay into the political fund of a trade union.
- All public sector employers must publish details of trade union facility time in order to 'promote transparency and public scrutiny of facility time; and to encourage those employers to moderate the amount of money spent on facility time in light of that scrutiny'. Government ministers have the power to place a cap on the amount of facility time that a union representative might receive.

Reflective activity 9.8

To what extent do you think that placing a threshold on industrial action ballots is justified?

Government concern over the increased incidence of strike action in the public sector led to the introduction of the Strikes (Minimum Service Levels) Act in July 2023. In short, this legislation gave the government the ability to force unions to ensure that minimum levels of service are provided during periods of strike action in the following sectors:

- Health services
- Fire and rescue services
- Education services
- Transport services
- Decommissioning of nuclear installations and management of radioactive waste and spent fuel
- Border security.

However, the idea of minimum service levels was met with widespread criticism from unions and employers seemed reluctant to use the legislation, possibly due to the potential to further inflame conflict. There are also signs that the Labour government elected in July 2024 will attempt to loosen restrictions on industrial action. The Labour Party has made clear that it will repeal the Strikes (Minimum Service

Levels) Act and pledged to repeal the 2016 Trade Union Act, to support electronic and workplace balloting and remove 'unnecessary restrictions on industrial action' (Labour Party, 2024). While we await enactment of these policies, this undoubtedly represents a shift away from the previous consensus over trade union legislation.

Individual disputes – formality, flexibility and fairness

The relatively low level of collective industrial action in the last four decades has focused public policy attention on individual employment disputes and litigation. In this context a significant source of concern has been the growing formality of dispute resolution in the UK and increased influence of the law and the tribunal system. In fact, these developments have their roots in the report of the Donovan Commission (Donovan, 1968), published in 1968, and the subsequent introduction of the right to claim unfair dismissal and the development of employment tribunals as 'an accessible, speedy, informal and inexpensive' system through which disputes could be resolved. The traditional composition of employment tribunals reflected this approach, comprising three members: an employment judge (a solicitor or barrister of seven years' qualification), an employer representative and an employee representative (usually a trade union representative). The tribunal, therefore, was seen as representing an 'industrial jury' capable of understanding the reality of the environments within which employment disputes originate.

The UK's system of dispute resolution was further developed by the introduction in 1977 of the Acas Code of Practice on 'Disciplinary Practice and Procedures' to provide guidance for employers and employees. This code, while not legally binding, defined good practice. Perhaps more importantly, it was used by employment tribunals as a guide to what could be expected of a reasonable employer. Paragraph 11 summed up the essence of procedural fairness as follows:

> Before a decision is made or imposed the individual should be interviewed and given the opportunity to state his or her case and should be advised of any rights under the procedure, including the right to be accompanied.

Therefore, although there was no legal compulsion to implement disciplinary and grievance procedures, the code of practice became a key benchmark of what organisations needed to do in order to avoid claims for unfair dismissal. As a result, procedures spread rapidly. By 1990, they were present in approximately 90 per cent of workplaces employing 25 employees or more (Millward et al, 1992), but growth was much slower in smaller non-unionised organisations, perhaps reflecting a general hostility towards regulation.

The importance of written procedures for dealing with disciplinary and grievance issues was also increased by the decline in union presence. Consequently, informal relationships between trade union representatives and managers which could help in managing individual conflict were less likely to be found. Instead, decisions over workplace discipline and on employee grievances were increasingly made unilaterally by management. Crucially, disciplinary and grievance procedures were and are subject to negotiation with trade unions in a minority of unionised workplaces (van Wanrooy et al, 2013).

At the same time, the employment tribunal system became 'increasingly complex, legalistic and adversarial' (Gibbons, 2007: 21). Tribunals were tasked with hearing cases from an array of jurisdictions and the development of case law in both domestic and European courts added a further layer of complexity to many issues and made legal representation increasingly important. It is slightly ironic that the formalisation of workplace dispute resolution took place during a period when successive Conservative administrations were promoting a more de-regulated approach to employment policy. For example, the Thatcher government increased the qualifying period for claiming unfair dismissal from one to two years, providing employers with greater freedom to dismiss employees and contributing to a small fall in employment tribunal applications between 1980 and 1988 (Dix et al, 2009).

This measure was reversed by the incoming Labour government, elected in 1997. Nonetheless, continued standardisation of dispute resolution procedures was seen as an important way of combating rising employment tribunal applications. In particular, the government felt that a major problem was the lack of basic employment practices in smaller workplaces and organisations. Findings from WERS2004 confirmed that while formal procedures were widespread in larger workplaces, in very small workplaces a significant minority still had no formal grievance (37 per cent) or disciplinary procedure (31 per cent) (Forth et al, 2006).

In an attempt to fill this gap, the Employment Act 2002 introduced minimum compulsory procedures for dealing with dismissals and employee grievances. These regulations stipulated that employers (and employees) should follow three key steps when dealing with a dismissal or employee grievance. First, the issue should be set out in writing; second, there should be a hearing or meeting to discuss and decide on the issue; and third, the employee should have the right to an appeal. If an employer dismissed an employee without following the necessary three steps, the dismissal was deemed to be automatically unfair. In addition, if either the employer or employee failed to follow the minimum procedure, compensation in the event of a finding of unfair dismissal could be increased or reduced by between 10 and 50 per cent. The government argued that these measures were designed to ensure basic procedural standards and that parties in dispute exhausted all possibilities of resolution before litigation. However, some commentators (for example, Hepple and Morris, 2002) pointed out that the majority of workplaces operated procedures which were more extensive and offered employees greater protection. Therefore, there was a danger that there would be a levelling down of overall standards. Either way, the main driver behind these measures was the desire to reduce employment tribunal volumes.

Reflective activity 9.9

Why do you think that disciplinary and grievance procedures are necessary? Do you think they are designed to protect the interests of employees or employers? Do you believe that they help to resolve conflict and disputes or do they make things worse?

The Gibbons Review – from litigation to early resolution

In fact, there was little evidence that the introduction of statutory procedures had the desired effect of reducing the volume of employment tribunal applications. In particular, they were unpopular with employers, who complained that the regulations increased the associated administrative burden and made it more likely that conflict would escalate into formal disputes. In response to these criticisms, the government commissioned a review chaired by Sir Anthony Gibbons to 'identify options for simplifying and improving all aspects of employment dispute resolution' (Gibbons, 2007: 7). He argued that the three-step procedures encouraged employers to adopt defensive positions in disputes and to turn to formal processes at an early point to avert the threat of legal action. Having to put issues in writing was counter to the personal nature of employment relations in small workplaces and so helped to escalate rather than defuse disputes.

There were two main aspects to the recommendations of the Gibbons Review. The first was to urge the government, employers and trade unions to promote the greater use of mediation to resolve workplace disputes (mediation is examined in greater depth in Chapter 13). Second, it called for the repeal of the statutory dispute resolution procedures and the development of 'clear, simple, non-prescriptive guidelines' for employers and employees in relation to grievances, discipline and dismissal. The government accepted the need for a greater focus on the early resolution of disputes and repealed the statutory dispute resolution procedures as part of the Employment Act 2008. At the same time, a revised Acas Code of Practice on Disciplinary and Grievance Procedures (Acas, 2015) was introduced in 2009. This was much shorter than the previous version and provided employers with a greater degree of flexibility and discretion in handling individual employment disputes backed by more detailed non-statutory guidance. Importantly, the government increased the influence of the Code by allowing tribunals to adjust tribunal awards by up to 25 per cent if either party acted unreasonably in not complying with its provisions.

Reflective activity 9.10

You can find the Acas Code of Practice on Disciplinary and Grievance Procedures on the Acas website (www.acas.org.uk). Do you think that it provides clear guidance for employers? How much flexibility do you think it provides employers when handling disciplinary and grievance issues?

Neo-voluntarism and de-regulation?

The Gibbons Review and the repeal of the Dispute Resolution Regulations arguably marked a return to a more voluntaristic approach to the management and resolution of individual conflict. From the perspective of employers, this was needed, given what they saw as the burdensome nature of the existing system of dispute resolution. This inevitably revolved around the issue of employment litigation.

Employers' organisations argued that the existing employment tribunal system encouraged weak and speculative claims from employees. The fact that legal costs were rarely awarded to the successful party in employment litigation meant that employees without strong cases could pursue claims in the hope that employers would agree to a financial settlement rather than incur the costs associated with defending a claim through the tribunal system. Moreover, it was argued that the fear of facing a possible employment tribunal application discouraged employers from taking on new employees and also from dealing with conflict in informal ways.

There is general consensus that employment tribunals, which were originally conceived as industrial juries, providing an accessible and relatively informal source of workplace justice, had become 'increasingly complex, legalistic and adversarial' (Gibbons, 2007: 21). However, the argument that the system was unfairly weighted in favour of claimants is questionable. Although tribunals rarely awarded costs to the successful party, their powers to do so had been significantly expanded in that respect. Prior to 2001, costs awards (of up to a maximum of £500) were generally limited to cases where an application or actions of a party were 'frivolous' or 'vexatious'. But in 2001, the maximum costs award was increased to £10,000 and extended to cases where 'the bringing or conducting of the proceedings by a party has been misconceived'. This meant that tribunals now had an explicit power to award costs where cases were without merit. However, there has been little sign of a substantial and sustained increase in the use of these powers. Ewing and Hendy (2012) argue that the system is in fact weighted against the employee. They point out that only a very small proportion of cases are successful and even then, levels of compensation are generally low. In 2020/21 just 8 per cent of all unfair dismissal claims disposed of were successful at hearing, while a further 24 per cent resulted in Acas conciliated settlements. In 2022/23, the median compensation for an unfair dismissal claim was £6,201 (Ministry of Justice, 2023).

Nonetheless, in October 2013, employment tribunal fees of up to £1,200 were introduced to 'prevent poorly conceived claims from progressing through the system, wasting time and cost for all' (BIS, 2011: 28). Moreover, the government sought to streamline the hearing system itself by providing for employment judges to sit alone on most unfair dismissal cases. While these changes were generally welcomed by employers' organisations, trade unions warned that they would reduce access to justice. Subsequently in July 2017, the trade union UNISON was successful in a legal challenge which claimed that the introduction of fees was unlawful, and they were abolished by the UK government.

Interestingly, while the 'problem' identified by policymakers has been the growing complexity of the regulatory system and the threat of appearances before the employment tribunals, there has been little detailed consideration of radical reform to the nature of adjudication over employment cases. Although the Acas Arbitration Scheme (launched in 2001 and still in operation) was not intended to replace the employment tribunal system, it offers an alternative means of deciding claims of unfair dismissal and those relating to requests to work more flexibly. To date, the voluntary nature of the scheme, its jurisdictional reach and a lack of incentives for potential users (among other factors) has limited its use and significance (see Dickens, 2012b). Nonetheless, it potentially provides a model for a less adversarial and more accessible means by which workplace disputes can be decided.

Employment tribunals in practice

So far in this section, we have discussed the development of the system of dispute resolution in the UK. We now look at how the employment tribunal system operates in practice. Before an employment tribunal application can be brought, an individual intending to make a claim must submit an early conciliation notification form to Acas. This asks for details about the individual, their representative, their employer and their dates of employment, but it does not ask for any details of the complaint itself. Acas will then contact the potential claimant and the employer and offer to conciliate. Normally, claimants have three months in which to bring employment tribunal claims (six months in cases regarding redundancy pay and equal pay); however, this period is suspended while early conciliation takes place. There is then normally one month in which to conciliate, although this period can be extended by a further 14 days if Acas feels there is a good prospect of the case being settled.

The process is completely voluntary. The role of Acas is to help find a solution and assist the parties to settle their differences on their own terms. If either party does not wish to conciliate or no agreement can be reached, Acas will issue an early conciliation certificate, which indicates the end of early conciliation, and the claimant is then able to make a claim to the employment tribunal. This is done by completing an ET1 form, which is normally submitted online. Importantly, the ET1 asks claimants to set out the nature of their claim and also the grounds on which it is made.

The ET1 is then sent to the employer (the respondent), who has 28 days in which to respond to the claim. This is done on a specified form, the ET3, on which the respondent is asked whether they wish to defend the claim and to outline their reasons for resisting any application. The completion of the ET3 is extremely important for employers when defending claims, as the arguments made in both the ET1 and ET3 will be presented at any future hearing and will be scrutinised against any additional evidence which is brought. Therefore, it is important that any details in the ET3 are accurate and consistent with the evidence that will be presented later.

Once the tribunal has received both the ET1 and the ET3, an employment judge will go through a sifting process whereby the tribunal can dismiss a claim or the response made by the employer in full or in part, either because the tribunal has no jurisdiction (for example because the claim is out of time or the claimant does not have the necessary qualifying service) or because they feel that the claim has no reasonable prospect of success. Before such a decision is confirmed, the parties will have a chance to make written representations. If the claim passes this initial hurdle, an employment judge has powers to manage the proceedings in order to ensure the smooth and efficient running of the case. They can issue directions on any matter that they think is appropriate, either from the parties' application/response or at a pre-hearing review.

Either party may make an application – or the tribunal may order – that one or other party must provide further and better particulars of any grounds upon which they rely, or any facts or contentions relevant to their claim. The essence of further particulars is to enable a party to know in advance the nature of the case that they must meet at the hearing. The tribunal can also order either party to disclose relevant documents. As with further particulars, 'discovery' is an important step in the process of enabling the parties to know the nature and extent of the case they will have to respond to.

In preparing for the hearing, parties will be expected to provide written statements for all the witnesses they intend to call and to agree on a 'bundle' of documents for use during the hearing. This responsibility generally falls to the respondent (employer) because it is considered that they will have the appropriate administrative resources and, in the majority of cases, will have in their possession all, or most of, the documents. Typical 'bundles' will comprise the following:

- ET1, ET3 and any correspondence with the tribunal;
- contract of employment of claimant;
- relevant policies, procedures and collective agreements;
- correspondence (including emails) relating to the case (in chronological order);
- other relevant documents – this could include personnel records, performance appraisal documentation, etc.

Parties may appear before a tribunal without representation or may be represented by a lawyer, a trade union official or any other person of their choice. If they are unrepresented, the tribunal does what it can to assist them while ensuring that there is no bias.

Although there is no specific rule that dictates the order in which evidence is given, it usually depends on who has the burden of proof. In unfair dismissal cases where dismissal is admitted, the respondent employer begins. If dismissal is not admitted, or it is incumbent upon the applicant to prove their case – for example, in constructive dismissal – the applicant begins. In order to speed up the process of evidence-giving, witness statements are generally exchanged prior to the hearing. This helps both parties with their preparation and can avoid lengthy cross-examination. Witnesses give their evidence under oath, but most witness statements are 'taken as read'. They may then be cross-examined by the other side and may also have to answer questions put to them by the tribunal members. Witnesses may also be re-examined by their own representative if any points need to be clarified.

When the parties have called all their witnesses, they are given an opportunity to make their final submissions. Generally, the party who presented their evidence first will have the final word. After this, the tribunal will withdraw to make its decision. It will usually indicate whether it can announce its decision on the day of the hearing or whether it will be given in writing to the parties afterwards. When the applicant is successful, there will often be a need for the parties to make further submissions in respect of the size of any compensation payment or the type of relief to be granted.

Decisions of the employment tribunal can be appealed to the Employment Appeal Tribunal. Appeals must be made within 42 days of the date that either the decision or the reasons for the decision was sent to the parties. You cannot simply appeal because you disagree with the decision of the tribunal or because you feel that it made a factual mistake. However, you can appeal if you can show that the tribunal:

- applied the law incorrectly;
- failed to follow proper tribunal procedure in a way that affected the final decision;
- had no evidence to support its decision;
- was unfairly biased towards the other party.

Decisions of the Employment Appeal Tribunal can be appealed to the Court of Appeal and those adjudications can be appealed to the Supreme Court.

Awards and compensation

A key element of the employment tribunal process is the determination of remedy. Those claiming unfair dismissal may ask for reinstatement, re-engagement or compensation; however, in reality reinstatement and re-engagement are very rarely awarded. For unfair dismissal compensation there are two elements: the basic award and the compensatory award. The basic award is calculated in the same way as statutory redundancy payment. It is made up of:

- 1.5 weeks' pay for each complete year of employment when you were 41 or over;
- 1 week's pay for each complete year of employment when you were between the ages of 22 and 40 inclusive;
- half a week's pay for each complete year of employment when you were below the age of 22.

The maximum number of years' service one can include is 30 and, as from 6 April 2024, the maximum week's pay is £700. The compensatory award is based on actual and future financial loss. Therefore, the tribunal will take into account any earnings between the date of dismissal and the tribunal, and also whether the claimant is in employment at the time of the judgement. At the time of writing, the maximum unfair dismissal award was the lower of a year's salary or £115,115. However, for claims of discrimination on the basis of a 'protected characteristic', there is no limit to compensation and the tribunal can also make an award in relation to 'injury to feelings'.

As mentioned earlier, awards can be increased by 25 per cent if the employer has not followed the Acas Code of Practice on Discipline and Grievance. However, they can also be reduced by 25 per cent if the employee has not followed the Code, for example, if they have not appealed a decision. In addition, awards can be reduced for three other reasons:

- If the employee has failed to mitigate their loss – employees who have been dismissed are expected to look for work following dismissal. If the tribunal finds no or little evidence that they have done so, the compensatory award can be reduced.
- If the dismissal is due to a procedural flaw – the tribunal can reduce compensation by an amount to reflect the probability that the claimant would have been dismissed if a fair procedure had been used. This reduction can be up to 100 per cent.
- The basic award can be reduced if the claimant has received a statutory redundancy or other ex gratia payment.

Statistics in relation to employment tribunal awards in 2022/23 are provided in Table 9.1. There is a significant difference between the maximum and median, which illustrates the danger in exaggerating the potential for employment tribunal proceedings to generate substantial compensation. Those claims which result in very significant payments to the claimant are extremely rare.

Table 9.1 Employment tribunal compensation, 2022/23

	Maximum award	Median award	Average award
	£	£	£
Unfair dismissal	184,200	6,201	11,914
Race discrimination	452,474	11,400	23,070
Sex discrimination	995,128	11,177	37,607
Disability discrimination	1,767,869	15,634	45,435
Religious discrimination	92,039	9,239	19,332
Sexual orientation discrimination	82,168	26,247	31,623
Age discrimination	84,723	5,675	14,210

SOURCE: Ministry of Justice (2023)

Of course, employment tribunals may have a negative reputational effect and employers may incur significant costs in defending claims. It is important to remember that costs can only be awarded in employment tribunal proceedings where participants act vexatiously, abusively, disruptively or otherwise unreasonably, or where a case was misconceived or had no reasonable prospects of success. Despite giving tribunals greater discretion to award costs, this occurs in less than 1 per cent of cases. Moreover, the median cost of legal representation is around £5,000 per case, although this increases significantly if a case goes to a full hearing. As we have noted, this leads some employers to argue that it is cheaper to settle cases even where they feel the claim is relatively weak. However, there is no compulsion for employers to be legally represented – and the tribunal system provides for parties to represent themselves. In these circumstances, the tribunal may take a less formal and more inquisitorial approach to proceedings. In our experience, a competent and well-prepared employment relations professional is more than capable of representing their organisation in cases in which the legal issues are relatively straightforward.

Reflective activity 9.11

You are asked by a line manager who is due to give evidence at an employment tribunal hearing for some guidance on what to expect. What would you advise and how would you prepare her for the experience?

Mediation and conciliation

In addition to the reform of employment tribunals, the other area of policy attention in recent years has been the promotion of mediation and conciliation as a way of resolving workplace conflict. The Gibbons Review urged a greater focus on workplace mediation, which we examine in more detail in Chapter 13. While the government has stopped short of concrete measures to increase its use, it has promoted the idea of mediation across a range of activities, and there is evidence that mediation is becoming an increasingly important part of the management of employment relations.

Perhaps the most significant development has been the introduction of 'early conciliation' conducted by Acas. In fact, Acas already had an existing statutory duty to conciliate between employment tribunal claimants and respondents in order to promote settlement. In most cases, once a claim had been registered with the tribunal, Acas would be provided with details and a conciliator would contact both parties to explore the possibility of settlement. This approach was remarkably effective, with around four out of every ten cases being settled and only around 20 per cent of cases referred to Acas proceeding to a full hearing (Peters et al, 2010).

In April 2014, in a further attempt to reduce tribunal volumes, the structure of individual conciliation was revised to provide 'early conciliation' in respect of all tribunal applications. In most respects, the role of the conciliator, and the methods used, are unchanged. The key difference is the timing of the intervention – instead of referring cases to Acas after claims had been lodged, all tribunal applications have to be first sent to Acas, which attempts to facilitate a settlement before the claimant decides whether to lodge a complaint with the employment tribunal. The rationale of early conciliation is that matters are more likely to be resolved before the parties are forced to set out their cases more formally. Perhaps more cynically, it could be argued that it could also reduce the recorded number of applications by conciliating before a written claim is submitted. Evaluations of the early conciliation service have generally been positive, with high levels of satisfaction shown by workers and employers in relation to the process and the role of Acas (Downer et al, 2015).

The statistics for early conciliation outcomes between 2015 and 2022 are set out in Table 9.2. In some respects, these provide a more useful indication of the level of individual disputes than employment tribunal case volumes. Indeed, this would suggest a relatively high and fairly stable pattern of disputes. This data also shows that over the last five years the proportion of cases that are settled is consistent at 10–11 per cent with around 30 per cent of cases proceeding to a full employment tribunal claim.

Table 9.2 Acas early conciliation, 2015–2022

	2015	2016	2017	2018	2019	2020	2021	2022
Early conciliation notifications	92,172	92,251	109,364	125,975	130,326	118,672	103,938	102,728
Settled	16%	18%	16%	10%	10%	14%	11%	11%
Did not proceed	65%	63%	56%	63%	63%	56%	61%	60%
ET1	19%	19%	28%	27%	26%	30%	27%	29%

SOURCE: Acas Annual Reports

However, a key feature of the UK system is that a significant proportion of cases that enter early conciliation do not result in a formal agreement or settlement but do 'not proceed', normally because the complainant decides not to pursue an application, or the parties reach a private agreement outside the auspices of early conciliation.

REAL-WORLD EXAMPLE 9.3

Early conciliation – to proceed or not to proceed

Acas commissioned an evaluation of early conciliation in 2019 (Pedley et al, 2020). The evaluation found high levels of satisfaction with the early conciliation process from both claimants and respondents. Most participants in the evaluation would use the service again if they found themselves in a similar situation. Participants were generally driven to engage with early conciliation because it offered a faster resolution and a means of avoiding the cost, stress and delay of an employment tribunal.

A key finding in the evaluation relates to the reasons why claimants decided not to proceed with claims to the employment tribunal. It could be argued that creating an extra step of early conciliation was designed to create a deterrent effect, particularly in the context of employment tribunal fees (Rahim et al, 2017). However, the 2019 evaluation found that almost half of those who did not reach an Acas negotiated settlement but who decided not to proceed with a claim, did so because they felt the issue had been resolved. This suggests that early conciliation provides a space where the parties can independently reach some type of resolution. Nonetheless, just over a quarter of claimants decided not to take their case any further because they did not feel they would be successful.

There is little doubt that the introduction of early conciliation has had a significant impact on employment tribunal volumes and has reduced the number of employment tribunal claims. Of course, early conciliation notifications cannot simply be equated with employment tribunal claims under the previous system – notification is a much less onerous process. However early conciliation has introduced a type of triage for claims, where weaker cases are more likely to be dropped, as well as creating a space for resolution.

Reflective activity 9.12

If you felt you had been unfairly dismissed or your employment rights infringed in another way, what would be your main considerations in deciding whether to pursue an employment tribunal claim? What would be your attitude to early conciliation?

9.5 The management of conflict in UK workplaces

Interestingly, the policy debate over conflict and dispute resolution in the UK has almost entirely focused on the potential of reform of the regulatory framework. Much less attention has been given to the way in which conflict is managed within the workplace. While the government has acknowledged that a lack of capability and competence among line managers is a barrier to early and effective interventions to address and manage workplace conflict, there has been little detailed consideration of this issue and the way in which managers interact with HR practitioners and employee representatives.

HR practitioners and their role in conflict management

The traditional role played by personnel managers within the management of conflict was interventionist. In short, personnel, or later HR, staff were generally called on to resolve or handle disputes. Therefore, workplace conflict was seen as an issue for HR or personnel, who were generally expected to provide solutions to problems that had often arisen between workers and operational managers.

This tended to be seen as reactive and was commonly stereotyped as 'fire-fighting'. Furthermore, conflict-handling came to be seen as a largely administrative and low-status function, while there was a perception that personnel managers lacked the training and expertise necessary to fulfil this role effectively. Whatever the truth of this, there is less doubt that as the role of personnel managers in collective issues and negotiations diminished along with union presence and influence, they became increasingly responsible for the management of individual employment disputes. While operational managers may have had decision-making power, they were largely dependent on 'personnel' or 'HR' to manage disciplinary, grievance and other individual issues.

Nonetheless, it is easy to underestimate the important role played by many personnel and HR managers in maintaining and negotiating relationships with key organisational actors such as managers and trade union representatives. These relationships underpinned more informal processes of discussion, mediation and resolution. HR practitioners were therefore involved in negotiating informal resolutions, investigating disputes and ensuring the implementation of formal procedures. In some workplaces this was a complex and challenging role, often treading a very delicate line between building and maintaining trust with union representatives while providing support and advice to operational managers. In addition, HR professionals were often viewed as playing a neutral and impartial role, ensuring equity, consistency and fair treatment. In particular, they were often relied upon by trade union representatives as an honest broker in disputes.

More recently, two related developments have had a fundamental impact on the role played by HR practitioners within the management of conflict. First, the HR function has attempted to develop a more strategic focus, more closely aligned with 'business' goals and objectives. Second, as we discussed in Chapter 4, responsibility for the day-to-day management of people, and particularly conflict, has been increasingly devolved to line and operational managers. In relation to conflict management this has seen HR practitioners attempt to adopt a more arm's-length advisory service, leaving managers with direct responsibility for handling difficult issues.

The extent to which HR practitioners have been successful in distancing themselves from the operational management of conflict varies greatly from organisation to organisation. In some cases, a lack of managerial confidence and competence has meant that there is still a significant degree of dependence on HR professionals. Nonetheless, HR practitioners and employment relations specialists still play an important role (Hunter and Renwick, 2009) in developing, maintaining and ensuring the consistent application of workplace procedures. Moreover, they are routinely seen as a source of expert advice in relation to employment law. In addition, it would be mistaken to characterise HR practitioners as simply ensuring procedural and legal compliance. They can also play a key role in coaching and developing managers through conflict situations and (in unionised environments) acting as a link between managers and trade union representatives. For example, regular meetings between employment relations professionals and union representatives can help to identify potential areas of conflict, while informal 'off the record' discussions can explore potential resolutions (Saundry and Wibberley, 2014b).

THE ROLE OF HR PRACTITIONERS IN THE MANAGEMENT OF CONFLICT

Virginia Fisher, Sue Kinsey and Richard Saundry conducted the first detailed study in the role played by HR practitioners in managing conflict in 2018. Funded by Acas, their research made a number of important findings:

- Conflict management was a consequence, but not part of, strategic considerations. Work related to employment relations and the handling of conflict was seen as operational, 'day-to-day' and transactional. But this was too simplistic – employment relations specialists provided guidance over issues with complex legal implications, were vital in building managerial competence and played a mediating role between employees, managers and trade unions.
- Expertise in conflict management and employment relations was not seen as a path to career success for most HR practitioners. Instead progression was associated with leaving such work behind. This raises the possibility that the ghettoisation of employment relations could lead to a shrinking body of skills and expertise.
- High-trust relationships between key stakeholders underpinned effective conflict resolution. However, more centralised and remote systems of advice and guidance resulted in more compliance-focussed advice and encouraged cultures of avoidance among line managers.

- The separation between HR business partners and practitioners specialising in employment relations made early resolution of conflict less likely. Conflict management was a second-order activity, whereby HR business partners would 'commission' employment relations advice if conflict occurred. Therefore, responses to conflict were inevitably reactive, late and focussed on the management of risk.
- A lack of confidence and capability among line managers meant that many HR practitioners were not able to 'let go'. In most organisations, there was evidence of informal processes being formalised and the widespread use of management tools – such as checklists, flowcharts and templates.
- While most HR practitioners rejected their role in 'handholding', this has been replaced by longer 'reins'. A number of respondents also argued that real devolution was unrealistic given the expectations and pressures placed on some line managers. There was a view from some respondents that, while upskilling and empowering line managers was important, HR should maintain an active role in managing employment relations issues.
- HR practitioners at all levels need to see building the competence of line and operational managers as a principal goal. Proximity between HR and the line is vital. High-trust relationships provide a foundation for more informal and nuanced solutions to workplace problems. However, our research has also shown that the coaching role of HR practitioners is essential in building the confidence of line managers to address the difficult issues that they will inevitably face.

SOURCE: Saundry et al (2021)

However, the development of HR structures threatens to make this more difficult. Many organisations, in seeking to increase the efficiency of their HR function, have moved to centralise certain HR services. These shared service centre models have generally been employed to handle issues such as payroll and other HR administration. But, in some cases this has included employee relations advice, with operational managers at local level relying on online guidance and an employment relations specialist on the end of a telephone. This poses a number of possible challenges. First, we noted earlier the importance of high-trust relationships in underpinning more informal channels of discussion, negotiation and resolution. This may be more difficult in remote settings – in fact, some remote employment relations advice services actively discourage managers from asking for specific individual advisers. Second, remotely located advisers may not have the contextual knowledge of the workplace and workforce that could lead to more nuanced and creative approaches to employment disputes. Finally, the centralisation and (in some cases) outsourcing of employee relations advice suggests that managing conflict is a transactional issue which does not require specialist knowledge or skill.

Reflective activity 9.13

In organisations in which you have worked, what has been the role played by HR practitioners in handling workplace conflict? Have they helped in attempts to resolve issues informally or focused on ensuring that policy and procedure have been followed?

Line managers and conflict – a question of confidence?

The ability of HR professionals to develop a more arm's-length advisory role depends on whether line and operational managers have the skills and the confidence to deal with their new responsibilities. Unfortunately, the signs are not encouraging – the government has argued that 'it is clear that many more problems could be prevented from escalating into disputes if line managers were better able to manage conflict' (BIS, 2011: 17). At the same time, CIPD research found that 'conflict management' and 'managing difficult conversations' were the two skills that line managers found most difficult to put into practice (CIPD, 2013b). In fact, this is consistent with a large amount of research evidence which points to a lack of confidence among UK line managers (Hutchinson and Purcell, 2010; Teague and Roche, 2012).

Traditionally, operational managers have tended to prefer to manage conflict informally, relying on instincts and 'gut feeling' (Rollinson et al, 1996: 51) rather than having to abide by written rules and procedures. This could just reflect a reluctance to take on the administrative burden that inevitably accompanies disciplinary and grievance processes. However, line managers could argue that operational imperatives may need a more flexible approach to such issues. For example, they may be less strict in applying rules in order to maintain morale. Similarly, they may be more lenient in dealing with members of staff who they see as important to the team. Although this is perhaps understandable, one problem of giving managers discretion in this way is that it is open to favouritism, discrimination and potential breaches of organisational procedures that have legal implications.

More recent research has suggested that instead of dealing with conflict informally, many managers take shelter behind the rigid application of process and procedure (Saundry et al, 2022). This may reflect the lack of confidence and skill just noted, particularly given the potential for litigation. However, line managers may also come under pressure from their managers to meet short-term operational objectives. Thus, they may not have the time and space to resolve issues through discussion and communication. Importantly, competences in relation to conflict management (and people management in general) rarely feature in the recruitment, development and promotion of managers.

Reflective activity 9.14

What are the key challenges facing front-line managers in handling workplace conflict? What do you think organisations can do to overcome these problems?

Employee representation and voice – the key to early resolution?

In the context of the changes outlined in the previous two sections, it has been argued that the growing 'representation gap' in British workplaces has in turn created a 'resolution gap' (Saundry and Wibberley, 2014b). Employee representatives play a very important role in the management and outcomes of workplace conflict. For example, the decline of collective regulation in general and trade union organisation in particular has seen a dramatic reduction in collective industrial action but has also been influential in the growing number of employment tribunal applications.

As we have noted, there is a clear statistical relationship between falling trade union density and the rapid growth of employment tribunal applications during the 1990s and 2000s. At the same time, workplaces in which trade unions are recognised and union density is high tend to have lower rates of disciplinary sanctions and dismissals. Conversely, employee grievances are perhaps more likely to occur in unionised settings. Why is this? One explanation could be that stronger trade unions are more likely to challenge managerial decisions, deterring them from taking disciplinary action or supporting their members in bringing legal claims through the tribunal system.

However, research has shown that the role of employee representatives is much more complex and nuanced. Union representatives, for example, can play a crucial role in resolving disputes in a constructive way, in helping to maintain and repair employment relations – they can help to manage the expectations of their members, make the potential implications of certain behaviours and conflict clear, and negotiate with managers to resolve issues or minimise sanctions (Saundry et al, 2008). In fact, managers in unionised environments tend to be very positive about the role played by representatives in identifying problems and exploring potential resolutions (Saundry and Wibberley, 2014b). This also depends on the quality of employer–union relationships. Where these are negative, representatives may be more likely to adopt adversarial approaches in defending members – here a grievance or a disciplinary issue may become something that is either 'won' or 'lost' rather than an issue that needs to be resolved. In contrast, high levels of trust give managers, HR and unions the confidence to discuss issues 'off the record' in order to try to find informal solutions to difficult workplace problems. Where there are positive relations, a virtuous circle can develop whereby high trust enables the parties to resolve an issue informally, which in turn further strengthens working relationships, facilitating constructive approaches in the future.

Therefore, the decline of employee representation potentially shuts down these informal channels of conflict management and resolution. Of course, this gap could potentially be filled by non-union employee representatives. However, while there is evidence of isolated attempts to develop roles for non-union employee representatives within discipline and grievance processes in companies such as Marks & Spencer PLC, there is little evidence as to their impact. Furthermore, while improved employee engagement may prevent or slow down the development of workplace conflict, it does not provide representational structures through which conflict can be mediated when it does occur.

 Reflective activity 9.15

What is your experience of the role played by employee representatives in disciplinary and grievance processes? Do you think they play a constructive role or make the process more adversarial? If you were facing disciplinary allegations, would you seek the support of a representative and, if so, what would you expect?

Developing a strategic approach – from dispute resolution to conflict management

Growing concerns over the cost and impact of workplace conflict have seen increased attention being given to alternative approaches to dispute resolution and conflict management. Much of the innovation in this area originated in the United States and revolves around the idea of integrated conflict management systems (ICMS). The essential idea behind ICMS is that organisations need to move away from using individual dispute resolution tools in a fragmented and isolated way. Instead, organisations need a combination of rights-based processes (such as disciplinary and grievance procedures) and interest-based processes such as workplace mediation. Moreover, this needs to be developed as part of a strategic approach.

Importantly, this also involves a much broader change in the organisational 'mindset' with regards to workplace conflict and how it should be managed (Lipsky and Seeber, 2000: 23). Lynch (2001) argues that this involves a change in philosophy from dispute resolution where managers apply processes in an ad hoc manner to resolve specific disputes to conflict management which aims to address underlying sources of discontent. In this way an environment is developed in which organisations do not simply wait for disputes to escalate before attempting to resolve them, but rather managers are expected to prevent, manage, contain and resolve all conflict at the earliest time and lowest level possible. In this way ICMS creates a 'conflict-competent culture' where all conflict may be safely raised and where persons will feel confident that their concerns will be heard, respected and acted upon (Lynch, 2001: 212–13).

In relation to the design of an ICMS, Lynch points out the importance of an organisational champion to drive the development of conflict management. Furthermore, while integrated approaches may be triggered by 'crisis', the need for regulatory 'compliance' and a desire to reduce 'cost', they may also be developed in the pursuit of 'cultural transformation' in order to underpin their broader strategies and seek 'competitive advantage' (Lynch refers to these as the 5Cs). In the US, Lipsky et al's (2012) study of Fortune 1000 companies suggests organisations are increasingly adopting more strategic and proactive approaches to managing conflict. Overall, a third of the corporations in the sample had adopted features associated with conflict management systems. Furthermore, there was evidence of a wide range of practices, beyond mediation and arbitration, such as 'early case assessment' and 'peer review' (a process by which disputes are adjudicated by a panel of co-workers).

In contrast, in Great Britain and Ireland, there has been very little sign of this type of innovation being commonly used. Roche et al (2018) have identified three distinct patterns of conflict management innovation in the Republic of Ireland. 'Improvisers' turn to conflict management in reaction to a particular problem or specific shock, but then fail to develop or embed this new approach. Other organisations ('incrementalists') extend or adapt their use of conflict management as it proves effective and in certain cases that may become aligned with wider strategic goals. 'Strategists' proactively invest in systems of alternative dispute resolution (ADR), driven 'top-down' by commercial and organisational objectives. Other evidence would seem to suggest that 'strategists' are a rare breed. An earlier study conducted by Paul Teague and Liam Doherty (2011) found that senior managers in a sample of non-unionised companies were extremely unwilling to concede that 'conflict' should be accepted as a part of organisational life. In fact, they found that managers were resistant to even talk about the issue of conflict let alone see it as an important strategic issue. This perhaps explains some of the pressures experienced by front-line managers – if the management of conflict is not seen as a strategic imperative, this will be reflected in the time that managers are able to devote to it, the extent to which they are trained and supported, and also whether it is seen as a core competency in the recruitment and promotion of managers.

Nonetheless, there are examples of organisations adopting more proactive and co-ordinated approaches. The case of Northumbria Healthcare Trust is particularly interesting (see Real-world example 9.4).

REAL-WORLD EXAMPLE 9.4

More than just a mediation scheme – the case of Northumbria Healthcare NHS Foundation Trust

Northumbria Healthcare Trust's approach to conflict management began with the development of an in-house mediation service in 2006. One of the main drivers for this was stress management standards by the Health and Safety Executive in 2005, which included the promotion of 'positive working to avoid conflict and dealing with unacceptable behaviour' and the need for organisations to: have systems in place to respond to individual concerns; promote positive behaviours at work to avoid conflict and ensure fairness; have agreed policies and procedures to prevent or resolve unacceptable behaviour; and systems to enable and encourage managers to deal with unacceptable behaviour.

Consequently, the establishment of an internal mediation service was supported at a high level by senior management. Initially a cohort of 12 staff were trained, drawn from a range of posts within the organisation, including consultants, managers, nurses, HR staff and trade union representatives. This reflected a deliberate attempt to embed the service in different areas of the organisation. Subsequently, a further seven mediators were trained in 2011. The champion of the service was a consultant clinical psychologist in NHCT's occupational health department and there was also palpable commitment from senior management.

Crucially, this reflected an acceptance that managing conflict more effectively was central to the well-being and engagement of staff and also standards of patient care. As a result, conflict management was a specific strand of the organisation's HR strategy. Subsequently, existing 'rights-based' policies were rewritten to emphasise the role of mediation and the importance of conflict resolution. In addition, training for managers, in 'holding difficult conversations', was rolled out along with more specialised conflict resolution training. Furthermore, people management attributes became a core competence under a new values-based system.

A broader approach to managing conflict and its consequences has been developed through a partnership between occupational health psychologists, trade unions, HR and senior management. A Health and Well-being Steering Group identifies conflict stress 'hotspots' within the organisation by analysing a range of key indicators. A range of interventions are then considered and deployed, including individual mediation, targeted training, stress risk assessments, team facilitation and conflict coaching.

SOURCE: Latreille and Saundry (2015)

The case of Northumbria Healthcare Trust highlights a number of principles that arguably underpin effective conflict management:

- The management of conflict needs to be seen as a strategic issue – critical in underpinning well-being, engagement and performance.
- Conflict resolution and people skills should be viewed as a core competence for front-line managers.
- Working in partnership with organisational stakeholders is crucial in facilitating early and informal resolution of conflict.
- Organisations need to combine traditional disciplinary and grievance procedures with a range of alternative dispute resolution (ADR) approaches and tools.
- Conflict management intervention needs to be flexible and based on systematic analysis of data.

9.6 Summary

In this chapter we have provided an overview of the nature and pattern of workplace conflict and examined the key factors that shape the ability of organisations to manage it effectively. It is almost impossible to say whether there has been any reduction or increase in workplace conflict in recent years. However, the last 20 to 30 years have seen a fundamental shift in the channels through which workplace conflict is expressed. The decline of trade unions and the collective regulation of employment have seen a significant reduction in the use of strike action and a relative increase in individual employment disputes. The most visible example of this has been employment tribunal claims, which increased rapidly during the 1990s and early 2000s. Although there was a sharp increase in the incidence of collective industrial action in 2022 and 2023, most workers' experiences of conflict are individualised and often go unseen and unrecognised.

Conventionally, the application of policy and procedure has been seen as central in managing conflict and avoiding unnecessary employment disputes. However, the Gibbons Review marked an important turning point, with the conclusion that formality could block early resolution of disputes and in some situations make litigation more likely. Gibbons saw mediation as one way to deal with this problem. However, while the use of mediation has become more prominent, government policy has instead revolved around employment legislation. Conservative governments have generally sought to reduce the threat of litigation by minimising the risks faced by employers while Labour administrations have strengthened rights to encourage good management practice.

Unfortunately there is a danger that a policy focus on the law masks some of the underlying problems with conflict management 'competence' in UK workplaces. Barriers to effective conflict resolution are not simply a function of unduly formal procedures or bad employers. Instead, the main problem is the inability or unwillingness of many organisations to recognise the inevitability of conflict and develop clear strategies to manage it.

In the following chapters we look at different processes through which conflict is managed and disputes resolved. First, we examine the management of workplace discipline. Second, we explore the nature and pattern of employee grievances and how these can be addressed and handled. Third, we focus on the management of redundancy, and finally we examine the theory and practice underpinning workplace mediation.

KEY LEARNING POINTS

- There has been a substantial and possibly permanent decline in the incidence of industrial action. This has largely been caused by the erosion of trade union organisation and the reduction of the bargaining power of labour, which in turn has blunted the potency of strike action.
- These changes coincided with a rapid growth in employment tribunal volumes. However, it is questionable whether this represents an individualisation of conflict. Many of the main sources of tribunal claims are collective in character and much of the growth was driven by multiple applications.
- Government policy has revolved around employers' concerns over the burden of employment regulation in general and on the costs of litigation in particular. While there is little evidence that employer perceptions reflect the actual burdens of employment legislation, these perceptions have shaped the way that conflict has been managed and have encouraged more formal approaches.

- The capacity of organisations to manage conflict has been restricted by three related factors: the changing nature of the HR function; the erosion of workplace structures of employee representation; and a lack of confidence among front-line managers in handling difficult issues. Consequently, informal processes whereby conflict is resolved through discussion and negotiation have been increasingly replaced by rigid procedural adherence.
- There is limited evidence of organisational innovation in conflict management in the UK. There has been some growth in interest in workplace mediation and there is evidence that this can have a range of benefits. However, it tends to be used as a last resort rather than as part of a strategic approach to the management of conflict.

Review Questions

1. What are the main reasons for the reduction in strike action in the UK over the past four decades? To what extent does this represent a permanent change in employment relations?
2. What were the main recommendations of the Gibbons Review? Evaluate the impact of these recommendations on UK policy and on organisational practice.
3. What are the implications of the devolution of responsibility for people management from HR to the line for conflict management and the ability of organisations to resolve difficult issues in an early and informal manner?
4. Does your organisation have a conflict management system? What are the main barriers to the adoption of strategic approaches to conflict management by UK organisations?

Explore further

CIPD (2020) Managing conflict in the modern workplace. Available from: https://www.cipd.co.uk/knowledge/fundamentals/relations/disputes/managing-workplace-conflict-report (archived at https://perma.cc/UE6L-WDJY)

Latreille, P and Saundry, R (2015) *Towards a System of Conflict Management?* Acas Research Papers, 03/15

Pedley, K, Clemence, M, Writer-Davies, R and Spielman, D (2020) *Evaluation of Acas Individual Conciliation 2019: Evaluations of early conciliation and conciliation in Employment Tribunal applications*, Acas, London

Roche, W, Teague, P, Gormley, T and Currie, D (2018) Improvisers, incrementalists and strategists: how and why organizations adopt ADR innovations, *British Journal of Industrial Relations*, 57(1), pp 3–32

Saundry, R, Fisher, V and Kinsey, S (2021) Disconnected Human Resource? Proximity and the (mis)management of workplace conflict, *Human Resource Management Journal*, **31**, pp 476–92

Saundry, R, Fisher, V and Kinsey, S (2022) Line management and the resolution of workplace conflict in the UK, in *Research Handbook on Line Managers*, eds K Townsend, A Bos-Nehles and K Jiang, Edward Elgar, Cheltenham, pp 258–69

Saundry, R, and Urwin, P (2021) *Estimating the Costs of Workplace Conflict*, Acas, London

Wood, S, Saundry, R and Latreille, P (2017) The management of discipline and grievances in British Workplaces: the evidence from 2011 WERS, *Industrial Relations Journal*, **48**(1), pp 2–21

Websites

www.acas.org.uk (archived at https://perma.cc/JEA5-LEY6) – this is the website of the Advisory, Conciliation and Arbitration Service, where you can find a wide range of guidance, advice and research.

www.cipd.org/uk/topics/conflict-management/ (archived at https://perma.cc/V34B-6NWN) – CIPD resources on conflict management.

10 Workplace discipline

Overview

In this chapter we explore the challenges faced by employment relations professionals when managing employee behaviour and performance. This includes the principles of discipline-handling, the characteristics of a fair and effective disciplinary procedure, the legal aspects of discipline and dismissal, and the monitoring and evaluation of disciplinary procedures. The chapter stresses the importance of focusing on improving or changing behaviour, rather than punishing employees who fall below expected norms and standards. It also underlines the need to consider the well-being of those involved in disciplinary proceedings. It sets out the key elements of the Acas Code of Practice on Disciplinary and Grievance Procedures and explains in detail the steps that managers should follow in order to manage disciplinary issues in a fair, consistent and effective manner.

LEARNING OUTCOMES

When you have completed this chapter, you should be able to:

- explain and critically reflect on the purpose of disciplinary procedures;
- understand the importance of, and draft, clear rules;
- explain the importance of informal resolution and understand the roles played by managers, employment relations specialists and union representatives in this regard;
- design effective disciplinary procedures;
- give advice in regard to the management of disciplinary issues in accordance with the principles of natural justice and in compliance with UK law.

10.1 Introduction

As we have noted earlier in this book, responsibility for many employment relations issues has been devolved from HR practitioners to line managers. Perhaps the most important of these is the management of workplace discipline. Front-line managers are now expected to: address issues of poor performance or behaviour; explore informal resolutions; enact and conduct disciplinary procedures; and take decisions over possible sanctions. As we discussed in the previous chapter, many managers find this extremely daunting. Therefore, the employment relations professional plays a critical role in providing advice at all stages of the process and often in coaching managers, who may lack confidence. Furthermore, they can help to ensure that disciplinary matters are handled fairly and consistently across the organisation.

10.2 Discipline – improving behaviour?

Discipline is an emotive word and dictionaries offer several definitions, ranging from 'punishment or chastisement' to 'systematic training in obedience'. There is no doubt that discipline at work can be one of the most difficult issues that a manager has to deal with. In our view, discipline should be used as an opportunity to improve conduct and performance, rather than punish employees for falling short of organisational expectations. Organisations should seek to learn the underlying reasons for a breach of discipline rather than simply to apportion blame. In many cases apparent misconduct and misbehaviour are a symptom of deeper organisational and systemic problems. The prime objective should always be to keep the employee in the organisation wherever possible and to seek to develop their potential. We have noted earlier in this book that changes to the framework of employment rights have reduced the risks associated with 'hiring and firing' staff. However, such an approach not only means that investment in recruitment and training is lost but also undermines perceptions of organisational justice, which, as John Purcell (2014) has argued, is one of the main pillars of employee engagement. Moreover, in the previous chapter we discussed research that has estimated the annual cost of disciplinary action to organisations in the UK at £12.5 billion (Saundry and Urwin, 2021).

Therefore, it is important for managers, at all levels, to appreciate that organisational effectiveness can be damaged if issues relating to conduct, capability and performance are not addressed at the earliest possible point and handled fairly and consistently. It is also vital to learn the wider lessons from any disciplinary situation and be prepared to make difficult decisions. It is important to understand that this does not just reflect a set of prescriptive rules and guidelines. Taking into account the context of the organisation and the circumstances of each situation is critical to the effective management of discipline.

REAL-WORLD EXAMPLE 10.1

Managing discipline – context and challenge

In 2024, Acas published research conducted by researchers at the Universities of Westminster and Sheffield (Saundry et al, 2024) that explored the challenges facing managers in handling disciplinary issues. The findings of the research were:

- Managers were reluctant to initiate formal procedure and when managing poor performance and minor disciplinary issues, wanted to give staff as much opportunity as possible to improve. However, this could result in perpetual informal discussion.
- Managers worried about the threat of litigation, which could be reinforced by advice and training, which focussed on risk management. Formalising issues could create greater work pressure, more conflict and increased stress.
- In some cases, HR practitioners did not trust managers to implement policy or good practice when managing poor performance or misbehaviour. This could lead to HR restraining managers from moving towards more formal action. This potentially undermined managerial authority and encouraged avoidant behaviours.
- Managers found the clarity of disciplinary procedure helpful. It was also important in ensuring equity and fairness for employees and helped to legitimise disciplinary decision-making. However, procedures could have negative impacts on the well-being of all those involved. Moreover, implementing procedures could also be extremely stressful for managers themselves.
- Formal investigations could be a source of delay and unnecessary complexity. This could have negative impacts – investigations took up significant managerial time that could otherwise be used for informal resolution and delays added to the stress and anxiety felt by employees involved. While the Acas Code specifies that nature and scope of investigations is dependent on the circumstances of the particular case, nonetheless, it appeared that this flexibility was not always used by managers and their organisations.

As Real-world example 10.1 shows, employment relations professionals should also be aware that many managers are reluctant to address problems with conduct and capability because they believe that disciplinary procedures are cumbersome and ineffective and fear that any attempt to manage 'difficult issues' could result in legal challenge or internal criticism. Furthermore, managers often lack necessary training and sometimes the support of senior colleagues. This can result in problems being ignored and/or procedures being implemented in a rigid and inflexible way. Providing sound and sensible advice and coaching for inexperienced managers in handling disciplinary issues is, therefore, a critical aspect of the HR function.

Reflective activity 10.1

To what extent do the research findings outlined in Real-world example 10.1 reflect your own experience within your organisation? How do you think your organisation could improve the way that it manages disciplinary issues?

10.3 Disciplinary procedures

Having a written disciplinary procedure is essential for any organisation. It establishes clear standards and provides a transparent process through which disciplinary issues can be managed. It helps to ensure consistency, particularly in large organisations, and underpins fairness and equity. The starting point for any disciplinary procedure is the Acas Code of Practice on Disciplinary and Grievance Procedures. Not only does the Code provide a clear benchmark of 'good practice', but it is taken into account by employment tribunals when considering claims of unfair dismissal. While a breach of the Code of Practice is itself not unlawful, managers can be reassured that if they follow the terms of the Code and their own procedure, they will normally be seen by an employment tribunal to have used a fair process. Furthermore, tribunals are able to adjust any awards made in relevant cases by up to 25 per cent if they consider that any party has unreasonably failed to follow the guidance set out in the Code. The Code is also supported by guidance entitled *Discipline and Grievances at Work* (Acas, 2019a), which provides more detailed advice for dealing with discipline and grievances in the workplace. All managers and HR practitioners should be familiar with this guide.

The disciplinary process

Disciplinary procedures traditionally observed a specific sequence, as follows:

1. Oral warning;
2. Written warning if the required improvement was not forthcoming;
3. Final written warning if conduct or performance was still unsatisfactory;
4. Dismissal.

Under this type of procedure employers routinely issued oral warnings that were anything but 'verbal'. More often than not, such warnings were followed up in writing and placed on an employee's personnel record – thus, in effect, making them a written warning in everything but name. Acas guidance recognises this contradiction and suggests that cases of minor misconduct or unsatisfactory performance are dealt with informally. In the informal stage, which effectively replaces the oral warning, managers are seeking an agreement with the employee on how to ensure that the misconduct (perhaps in timekeeping) is not repeated or that steps are taken to overcome the performance issues. There is no reason why, if agreement is reached on the way forward, that it is not confirmed in writing. For example, some organisations have systems of 'improvement notes', which are not disciplinary warnings but reminders of the standards expected if more formal steps are not to be considered.

This also reflects an increased emphasis in Acas guidance on the importance of addressing issues at an early stage before they have escalated. By doing this, disciplinary sanctions can be avoided; the chances of improving behaviour and repairing the employment relationship are much greater if difficult issues are not left to fester. In doing this, good relationships between HR practitioners, line managers and also employee and union representatives can be extremely helpful. Research conducted by Saundry and Wibberley (2014b) into the management of workplace conflict found that, in large organisations, regular meetings between HR practitioners and employee representatives were vital in identifying emerging problems and trying to find ways of 'nipping them in the bud' before there was a need to launch formal disciplinary proceedings. Managers can be wary of having 'difficult conversations' with their staff and are also sometimes concerned that informal discussions will cause legal and other problems (Saundry et al, 2016). However, this is where the HR practitioner can play a key role, by providing managers with the confidence to look for more creative solutions to problems and brokering relationships with trade union and other employee representatives.

Reflective activity 10.2

When do you think it is appropriate to advise managers to resolve a disciplinary matter through informal discussion? How can you help managers to use their discretion and common sense while maintaining a consistent approach?

It is only if the informal approach does not work, or matters are too serious for such an approach, that employers are recommended to move into the formal stage. The essential components of the formal stage, which could result in a written warning, final written warning or dismissal, are clearly set out in the Code of Practice.

THE ACAS CODE OF PRACTICE

The Acas Code of Practice on Disciplinary and Grievance Procedures (Acas, 2015) is a statutory Code of Practice which sets out the basic principles for handling disciplinary and grievance issues. In terms of discipline and dismissals, failing to follow the Code does not in itself open an organisation to legal challenge. But this will be taken into account by an employment tribunal considering a claim of unfair dismissal, and adhering to the Code will provide employers with substantial protection in the event of litigation. Furthermore, tribunals can adjust awards by up to 25 per cent if they consider either the employer or employee has unreasonably failed to follow the Code.

The Code essentially sets out five key steps that an employer must take.

Establish the facts of each case – carry out an investigation without unreasonable delay. Where practical, different people should carry out the investigation and any subsequent hearing.

Inform the employee of the problem – if it is decided that there is a case to answer, the employer should write to the employee explaining the basis for this decision, providing any relevant evidence and setting out the arrangements for a disciplinary hearing.

Hold a meeting with the employee to discuss the problem – a hearing should be held at which the complaint against the employee is explained and relevant evidence presented. The employee should be given the chance to answer allegations, ask questions and present evidence.

Decide on appropriate action – the employer should decide whether disciplinary action is warranted and inform the employee accordingly in writing.

Provide employees with an opportunity to appeal – where an employee feels that disciplinary action taken against them is wrong or unjust, they should be given the opportunity to appeal against the decision. This should be heard, wherever possible, by a manager who has not previously been involved in the case.

In addition to the key steps outlined above, the Acas Code also sets out a number of principles that should underpin effective disciplinary procedures. These are important in two respects: first, they reflect the key tenets of natural justice that tribunals will consider in deciding whether a procedure used in dismissing an employee is fair; second, they underpin procedural justice, which in turn is a key factor in generating high-trust employment relations. These are set out in the following box.

DISCIPLINARY PROCEDURES – KEY PRINCIPLES

Disciplinary procedures should:

- be in writing;
- not discriminate;
- provide for matters to be dealt with without undue delay;
- provide for proceedings, witness statements and records to be kept confidential;
- clearly indicate the disciplinary actions which may be taken;

- specify the levels of management which have the authority to take the various forms of disciplinary action;
- provide for workers to be informed of the complaints against them and, where possible, to see all relevant evidence before any hearing;
- give employees time to prepare the case before the hearing;
- provide workers with an opportunity to state their case before decisions are reached;
- provide workers with the right to be accompanied;
- ensure that, except for gross misconduct, no worker is dismissed for a first breach of discipline;
- ensure that disciplinary action is not taken until the case has been carefully investigated;
- ensure that workers are given an explanation for any penalty imposed;
- provide a right of appeal – normally to a more senior manager – and specify the procedure to be followed.

Reflective activity 10.3

Try to design a simple disciplinary procedure, either for your organisation or for one you are familiar with. Make sure that it reflects the principles given here.

The importance of rules

The basis of workplace discipline is the set of rules which define and make clear exactly what standards of behaviour are expected in the workplace. If these are not clear, it will be impossible to manage disciplinary issues in a fair and consistent way. It will also be very difficult to resolve issues through informal discussion. Typically, rules cover the following areas:

- Timekeeping
- Absence
- Health and safety
- Misconduct
- Use of company facilities
- Confidentiality
- Discrimination.

Normally, these will be contained in an employee handbook or a range of different policies. However, the most important consideration is that they are clear and not open to (mis)interpretation. In addition, it is important that they distinguish between ordinary misconduct and gross misconduct. It is no good having a very clear procedure, laying down the type and number of warnings that an individual should receive, if the rules that are being applied are imprecise or do not reflect the attitudes and requirements of the organisation.

For example, vague statements about whether a breach of a specific rule 'may' be treated as gross misconduct can leave room for doubt and confusion. If an employee stole a large sum of money from the company, there is little doubt that they would be charged with gross misconduct and, if the allegation was proved, dismissed without notice. What, though, would happen if the alleged theft was of items of company stationery or spare parts for machinery? Employment relations professionals have to be aware of these potential contradictions when helping to frame rules that govern the employment relationship. Allowing different managers to take a different view about the seriousness of certain acts of theft brings inconsistency into the process. Therefore, a clear rule in relation to theft may be:

> Stealing from the company, its suppliers or fellow employees is unacceptable, whatever the value or amount involved, and will be treated as gross misconduct.

Using this style of wording should help to ensure that every employee in the organisation knows the consequences of any dishonest action on their part. Ensuring that managers apply the sanction consistently is another problem, and one that we will examine later in the chapter.

Reflective activity 10.4

How often are the rules in your organisation reviewed, and when were they last updated? Can you think of a rule that is vague and difficult to enforce? How could this be changed to make it more effective?

It is also important to make sure that rules reflect current industrial practice, as illustrated in Real-world example 10.2.

REAL-WORLD EXAMPLE 10.2

***Hewtson v Ofsted* (2023) EAT 109 (07 August 2023)**

Hewtson was an Ofsted inspector. During a school inspection, he was alleged to have brushed water off the head and shoulder of a pupil. The school complained to Ofsted after a teacher reported the incident and that the pupil concerned 'looked uncomfortable/embarrassed when this happened and commented he was unhappy to another student'. The pupil also completed an incident form to corroborate this. After an investigation, Hewtson was summarily dismissed because these actions were seen as 'inappropriate and were contrary to Ofsted core values, professional standards and the Civil Service Code'. Hewtson made a claim for unfair dismissal, however the employment tribunal decided that although it was possibly harsh, the decision to dismiss was fair. In particular they pointed out that Hewtson was:

> aware of his behaviour in respect of which he was being investigated and subsequently disciplined. The claimant was an inspector and a senior member of the respondent's staff, and in the circumstances the claimant should have been aware of the consequences of inappropriate touching.

However, this decision was overturned by the Employment Appeal Tribunal (EAT). One of the main reasons for this was that Ofsted did not have a specific 'no touch' policy and it was not made clear to Hewtson, either through policy, guidance or training that this type of behaviour could be seen as gross misconduct and could result in dismissal. The EAT concluded that:

> It is not fair to dismiss an employee for conduct which he did not appreciate, and could not reasonably have been expected to appreciate, might attract the sanction of dismissal for a single occurrence.

There may be certain types of conduct, such as theft or violence which would normally be accepted to be viewed as gross misconduct. Indeed, it would not be possible to list every possible example of gross misconduct in a disciplinary procedure. However, if an employer wishes to set a particular standard of behaviour, it needs to be clear about the consequences if this standard is not met. The message is very clear: if something is not allowed, say so.

A contemporary example is the growth of the use of social media through sites such as Facebook, X and Instagram. The most obvious problem for employers is the use of social media for non-work purposes during working hours. However, in many occupations, workers are now encouraged to use social media for marketing, public relations and recruitment activities, which further complicates the development of clear policies and rules. Furthermore, social media can be a cause of conflict that spills over into the workplace. Research commissioned by Acas and conducted by the Institute of Employment Studies identified some of the key challenges facing employers and concluded that:

> A good and clear policy on what constitutes an unacceptable use of social media in a particular organisation will help both the employer and the employee to understand where the boundaries between acceptable and non-acceptable use lie (Broughton et al, 2011: 30).

Acas advises that policies should clearly define what is regarded as acceptable and unacceptable behaviour in the use of social media at work. In addition, an organisation should be clear about what employees can comment on in relation to work.

Finally, it should make a clear distinction between using social media in relation to business and using it privately. This includes setting limits as to how social media can be used for private use while in work.

A sample policy for a company in which the use of social media for work purposes is encouraged is set out in the following box.

SOCIAL MEDIA POLICY

Policy

This policy provides guidance in relation to employees' use of social media. This may include blogs, social networking sites, online forums and message boards and chat rooms. The company accepts that employees may need to use social media in the course of their work and to achieve the goals and objectives of the business. This policy covers the use of social media for both business and personal reasons. While social media can have a positive impact on the operations of the company, it can also have a negative and detrimental effect on the image and reputation of the company and its employees. This policy should be read in conjunction with the employee handbook and, in particular, the company's disciplinary and grievance policies.

Procedure

1. The company reserves the right to observe any content made publicly available by employees through social media.
2. The following are some examples of social media use that would normally be prohibited:
   a. posting comments or material that could be considered defamatory, pornographic, proprietary, harassing, libellous, or that can create a hostile work environment;
   b. comments that are critical of the company, its employees or customers and which could have a negative impact on its image or reputation;
   c. material or information that is considered confidential or commercially sensitive, including personal information related to other employees of the company.
3. Legitimate professional use of social media can create interest from the wider media or public. Any such enquiries should be referred to the employee's line manager in the first instance.
4. Employees should get appropriate permission before referring to or posting images of current or former employees, customers, suppliers, associates or members of the public. Employees should get appropriate permission to use a

third party's copyrights, copyrighted material, trademarks, service marks or other intellectual property.
5 Employees' use of social media should not have a negative impact on their performance or their work responsibilities.
6 Where social media use is consistent with fulfilling employees' job responsibilities, the use of the company's computer systems during working hours is permitted, but personal use is discouraged and could result in disciplinary action.
7 If employees refer to their employment with the company in relation to personal use of social media, it should be made clear that views expressed are not those of the company.
8 Personal and private use of social media out of working hours that are in breach of other company policies and/or have a negative impact on the reputation or business operations of the company could result in disciplinary action.
9 Where practical, employees should keep company-related social media accounts separate from personal accounts.

Reflective activity 10.5

Policies need to reflect the particular circumstances of the organisation. Would this policy work in your organisation? If not, how would you amend it?

As we have stated, there are a number of variables – such as technological developments – in the drafting of company rules, and employment relations professionals should try to ensure that in their organisation these are regularly monitored and reviewed so that they properly reflect the organisation's current values and requirements.

Gross misconduct

Clear rules are vital when dealing with issues of potential gross misconduct. It is important to note that it can be fair to summarily dismiss an employee (without notice) if they have been found to have committed an act of gross misconduct. But what is 'gross misconduct'? Acas very helpfully provides a list of actions that would normally fall into this category.

POTENTIAL ACTS OF GROSS MISCONDUCT

- Theft or fraud
- Physical violence or bullying
- Deliberate and serious damage to property
- Serious misuse of an organisation's property or name
- Deliberately accessing websites containing pornographic, offensive or obscene material
- Bringing the organisation into serious disrepute
- Serious incapability through alcohol or the influence of illegal drugs
- Causing loss, damage or injury through serious negligence
- A serious breach of health and safety rules
- Serious acts of insubordination
- Unlawful discrimination or harassment
- A serious breach of confidence.

While that is quite an extensive list, a number of items are still open to interpretation. For example, what is an act of serious insubordination? Would it cover the refusal to carry out instructions received from a supervisor? What is serious negligence or serious incapability through alcohol? Although attitudes have changed and people tend not to socialise so much during their breaks, drinking at lunchtime still happens. How do you decide when a lunchtime drink crosses the threshold? One of the difficulties managers face in dealing with this type of disciplinary issue is ensuring that they do not impose their own moral standards on other people. Furthermore, the culture of the organisation is relevant to deciding whether a particular behaviour constitutes gross misconduct.

One way in which a distinction can be drawn is by reference to the relationship of trust that has to exist between employer and employee. In all contracts of employment there is an implied term of mutual trust and confidence between employer and employee. If an employer breaches this, perhaps by bullying an employee or treating them with a lack of respect, this may constitute constructive dismissal. But if an employee acts in a way that undermines the ability of the employer to trust them in the future, this may justify summary dismissal. One of the purposes of disciplinary action is to bring about a change in behaviour, and if, for instance, the offence is one of poor timekeeping, there is usually no question of a total breakdown of trust: the expected outcome of disciplinary action is of improved timekeeping and a rebuilding of the relationship. Conversely, if the cause of the disciplinary action is a serious assault on another employee, perhaps a manager, a disciplinary sanction might bring about a change in behaviour or ensure that the offence is not repeated, but there is a high probability that the relationship of mutual trust and confidence might be damaged beyond repair, and it could be impossible for the employment relationship to be maintained.

Nonetheless, in matters of gross misconduct there will sometimes be a lack of clarity over when somebody has 'overstepped the mark'. The potential difficulties caused by this lack of clarity mean that whatever procedure you establish, it reflects the organisation's structure and culture – the norms and beliefs within which an organisation functions. This is where the writing of clear company rules is so important. Not only do they help to distinguish between ordinary and gross misconduct, they provide employees with clear guidelines on what is acceptable in the workplace, in terms of both behaviour and performance.

Reflective activity 10.6

You are an HR manager for a mid-sized engineering firm. The company recognises trade unions and employs a mainly male skilled and semi-skilled workforce. The company has a basic disciplinary procedure. The culture on the shop floor is fairly 'robust' – in this part of the company all the employees are male and the majority are aged between 18 and 30. Swearing and banter are part and parcel of daily work. You have discussed this with the supervisors, but they argue that it's simply 'the way things work around here' and that to impose strict rules would be bad for morale. However, this morning you received a phone call from Terry Clawson, the machine shop manager, who reports to you that two of his staff – Ged Byrne and Lee Smith (both members of the union) – had been fighting. This is listed in your disciplinary procedure as an example of gross misconduct. They are both now sitting in the foreman's office. He asks you how he should proceed. He tells you that he doesn't care if Ged is sacked as he has terrible attendance. However, he really doesn't want to lose Lee, who is not only a good worker but is also very popular with the rest of the workforce.

Taking into account what we have said so far in this chapter, what advice would you give to Terry on the next steps he should take?

Suspension

In some cases (usually involving serious misconduct) it may be appropriate to suspend an employee on full pay while an investigation is carried out. However, there is a danger that suspension becomes a default response in cases of potential gross misconduct. This is particularly in occupations in which misconduct can pose a threat to health, safety and well-being. Here, employers can feel that the safest option is to suspend. However, being suspended can be extremely challenging for those involved. It can have particularly severe and negative impacts on well-being and mental health.

In response to concerns over the impact and over-use of suspension, Acas published new guidance in 2022 (Acas, 2022). Acas advises that employers should never use suspension automatically and instead should:

- consider the well-being and mental health of anyone they are thinking of suspending;
- only suspend someone if there is no other option;
- plan what support they will provide to anyone they suspend.

Before making a decision to suspend, employers should do some initial fact-finding and only consider suspension if there is the potential that the person could damage evidence, influence witnesses or if they pose a genuine risk to the organisation, its customers or its employees. Employers should also consider alternatives – these could include changing shifts, moving departments, working from home or limiting access to certain systems. A common dilemma is where an employee makes a complaint about the behaviour of a colleague, and the organisation decides an investigation is needed. It may be appropriate to separate the complainant and the alleged perpetrator. In this situation it is important that the complainant is not moved or negatively affected to facilitate the investigation. If an employer decides to suspend, Acas advises that they should:

- make clear the suspension does not mean they have decided that person has done something wrong;
- make sure the suspension is as brief as possible;
- keep in touch with the suspended person and support their mental health and well-being.

GOOD PRACTICE DURING A SUSPENSION

1 Keep the employee updated about the progress of the investigation.
2 Discuss with the employee how they would like you to contact them and how regularly they would like this to happen.
3 Make sure the employee knows who they can contact if they have any concerns, for example their manager or someone in HR.
4 Where possible, signpost the employee to sources of support – this could be a trade union representative, occupational health, an employee assistance programme or a mental health champion within the organisation.
5 Where practicable, keep the suspension confidential. Where other people need further information, the employer and employee should discuss how this will be done and what will be said.
6 Discuss with the employee what they can and can't say to their colleagues about their situation. Remember that suspension can be a very isolating experience – contact which maintains confidentiality and protects the credibility of the investigation is perfectly reasonable.

It is also important to note that line managers are often unsure about how to deal with suspensions – both in making the decision whether to suspend and how to communicate with employees if a suspension comes into force. Therefore, HR practitioners play an important role in providing advice and support, and, if necessary, coaching managers through these situations. It may even be useful to build the advice outlined here into your organisation's policies and procedures – for example by prompting managers to consider whether suspension is really necessary.

Using warnings to improve behaviour

Most disciplinary offences do not warrant dismissal, and it is important to note that even in cases of gross misconduct, employers can, and should, still consider whether a lesser sanction might be appropriate. The use of warnings can be a way of helping employees to improve their behaviour or their performance and fulfil their potential in the organisation. The most important consideration is that when employees are issued with a warning, the nature of the problem and the expected improvement is made clear. Where appropriate, this may also be backed up by training, support, mentoring and ongoing review. However, it is also crucial that a warning has a finite 'life', which indicates the length of time that a specific disciplinary sanction will stay on the record. 'Live' warnings can trigger more serious action. For example, if an employee receives a first warning for poor timekeeping which lasts for a period of six months, a failure to improve within that period could legitimately lead to a final written warning. However, if the employee improves their timekeeping initially but then this deteriorates again after the six months has elapsed, the employer would normally have to return to the start of the procedure. Many organisations will have different timescales for different levels of warning. For example, a written warning might only be live for six months, whereas a final written warning might be live for 12 months.

Although it is to be hoped that any disciplinary problems within an organisation can be resolved at the earliest opportunity, and without recourse to all levels of the procedure, the world of work is not so simple. Many managers complain that employees may initially respond to a warning by improving their behaviour or performance, only for the issue to resurface once the warning ceases to be 'live'. To avoid such a situation, two points must be considered. First, it is important that the life of the warning is appropriate. If it is for too short a time, there is the risk of only achieving short-term changes in behaviour. On the other hand, a sanction that remains on an employee's record for an excessive period of time can act as a demotivating influence. Second, the Acas Code of Practice makes it clear that the procedure may be implemented at any stage. Therefore, it is usually reasonable to take the past disciplinary record into account before deciding whether to issue a first or a final written warning. For example, if an employee had a history of first warnings for absenteeism, followed by initial improvement which was not sustained, the employer could consider moving straight to a final written warning.

A more contentious question is whether expired warnings can be taken into account when reaching a decision to dismiss. In the case of *Airbus v Webb* (2008), Webb was one of five employees found watching television when they should have been working. While they were all disciplined, Webb was the only one to be sacked because he had had a previous warning, although expired, for a similar matter. The Court of Appeal ruled that although employers should not rely on expired warnings 'as a matter of course', they could be one factor to be taken into account in deciding whether the employer had acted reasonably or not. In broad terms this suggests that employers can take the wider personnel record of an employee into account in arriving at a decision. However, they should not use spent warnings as a reason for dismissal in themselves.

 REAL-WORLD EXAMPLE 10.3

***Stratford v Auto Trail VR Ltd* UKEAT/0116/16**

Mr Stratford was an employee of approximately 12 years' service. He had an extensive disciplinary history including a nine-month warning for failing to make contact while off sick in December 2012 and a three-month warning for using company machinery and time to prepare materials for personal purposes in January 2014. At the time of his dismissal, there were no live warnings on Mr Stratford's file.

In October 2014, Stratford was seen with his mobile phone on the shop floor, which was strictly prohibited in accordance with the company's employee handbook. Mr Stratford was dismissed on the following grounds:

1 The employee was aware of the correct procedure regarding the use of mobile phones and emergency contact and had ignored it on this occasion. The employer concluded that this is an offence which would usually attract a final written warning and not gross misconduct.
2 Despite various informal conversations, this was now the 18th time that Mr Stratford had been subject to formal action. While the company accepted that Stratford had not always acted intentionally, he did not appear to appreciate the consequences of his actions and it decided that his behaviour would not change, even if a last chance was given.

The ET found that the dismissal was fair; however, Stratford appealed on the grounds that it was not reasonable to use earlier misconduct as a reason for dismissal when warnings for that misconduct were no longer live. The EAT dismissed the appeal, ruling that expired warnings can be taken into account as part of the overall circumstances of a dismissal.

In fact, it is arguably more contentious if employers seek to use live warnings for a different type of disciplinary offence to justify dismissal. The EAT in *Wincanton Group PLC v Stone* (UKEAT/0011/12/LA) provided some guidance to employers faced with this situation. This suggested that in most situations, warnings should not be relied upon until internal processes have been exhausted. In addition, employers should act consistently and also consider the similarity in the circumstances giving rise to the initial warning and the decision to dismiss.

10.4 Handling disciplinary issues

The way in which managers and employment relations professionals approach disciplinary issues will be subtly different, depending on the nature of the problem. Most organisations will have some form of disciplinary procedure, and probably some company rules as outlined earlier, but the use and application of the procedure may vary from company to company and from manager to manager. In some organisations disciplinary action is very rarely taken, either because standards are clear and accepted by employees or because standards are vague and applied haphazardly. In others, standards are maintained by an over-reliance on procedures, which usually acts as a demotivating influence on the workforce. The purpose of any disciplinary procedure should be to promote good employment relations and fairness and consistency in the treatment of individuals. It should also provide managers with a clear framework for handling disciplinary issues. However, in addition any procedure should allow for a sensible degree of flexibility so that managers are able to react and respond appropriately to the circumstances of each situation.

Reflective activity 10.7

Is your organisation's disciplinary procedure clear? Does it set out the time for which individual warnings will remain 'live', and is it capable of ensuring consistent and fair treatment for all employees? Are there any ways in which your disciplinary procedure could be improved?

Capability and performance

Many HR and employment relations professionals find that conventional disciplinary procedures are more suited to the handling of issues of conduct rather than the capability of employees. Although capability is potentially a fair reason for dismissal, it is often more nuanced than misconduct. Furthermore, many organisations are managing the performance of their staff much more closely than in the past as they seek to reduce costs and increase efficiency. A major Acas-funded study looking at the management of conflict in UK workplaces found that discussions over performance were the most common trigger for individual employment disputes. Furthermore, what often started as relatively minor concerns over employee capability could quickly escalate into complaints of bullying and harassment, particularly when these issues were poorly handled by line managers (Saundry et al, 2016).

This is not helped if organisations use disciplinary procedures (and potential sanctions) to address problems with an employee's performance. Many managers feel that this is often inappropriate and has a negative and demotivating effect on the employee concerned, who has done nothing wrong but simply has a performance issue that needs to be addressed. Furthermore, unlike conduct, it is very difficult to devise clear and unambiguous rules and standards relating to performance. Consequently, many companies now include a section on capability within their disciplinary procedures (see the following box for an example) or have a separate and dedicated capability procedure.

CAPABILITY

We recognise that during your employment with us your capability to carry out your duties may vary. This can be for a number of reasons, the most common ones being that either the job changes over a period of time and you have difficulty adapting to the changes, or you change (most commonly because of health reasons).

Job changes

1. If the nature of your job changes and we have concerns regarding your capability, we will make every effort to ensure that you understand the level of performance expected of you and that you receive adequate training and supervision. This will be done in an informal manner in the first instance and you will be given time to improve.
2. If your standard of performance is still not adequate, you will be warned, in writing, that a failure to improve and to maintain the performance required will lead to disciplinary action. If this were to happen, the principles set out in paragraph 1 above will apply. We will also consider a transfer to more suitable work, if possible.
3. If we cannot transfer you to more suitable work and there is still no improvement after you have received appropriate warnings, you will be issued with a final warning that you will be dismissed unless the required standard of performance is achieved and maintained.

Personal circumstances

1. Personal circumstances may arise which do not prevent you from attending work but which prevent you from carrying out your normal duties (e.g. a lack of dexterity or general ill health). If such a situation arises, we will normally need to have details of your medical diagnosis and prognosis so that we have the benefit of expert advice. Under normal circumstances this can be most easily obtained by asking your own doctor for a medical report. Your permission is needed before we can obtain such a report, and we will expect you to co-operate in this matter should the need arise. When we have obtained as much information as possible regarding your condition, and after consultation with you, a decision will be made as to whether any adjustments need to be made in order for you to continue in your current role or, where circumstances permit, a more suitable role should be found for you.
2. There may also be personal circumstances which prevent you from attending work, either for a prolonged period or periods or for frequent short periods.

> Under these circumstances we will need to know when we can expect your attendance to reach an acceptable level, and again this can usually be most easily obtained by asking your own doctor for a medical report. When we have obtained as much information as possible regarding your condition, and after consultation with you, a decision will be made as to whether any adjustments need to be made in order for you to continue in your current role or, where circumstances permit, a more suitable role should be found for you.

Informal and early resolution – difficult conversations?

If managers are only concerned with legal compliance, it could mean that they miss potential opportunities to resolve issues informally and at an early stage. In short, the best way of avoiding litigation and an unwelcome visit to an employment tribunal is to address problems before they escalate. Good managers have nothing to fear from the laws relating to individual employment rights. Furthermore, reaching for the disciplinary or capability procedure should be the last resort. Instead, managers and HR practitioners should always consider whether some other route would be more appropriate. Maintaining good standards of discipline and maximising productivity within an organisation is not just about applying the rules or operating the procedure. It is about the ability to achieve standards of performance and behaviour without using a 'big stick'.

Many serious issues start with lower-level problems, particularly related to poor performance or minor lapses in timekeeping and attendance. Advising line managers who are dealing with these issues is a crucial part of the HR practitioner's role. It is not unusual for the employment relations professional to be told by a manager that a particular employee is not 'up to the job' and that they need help to 'get rid of them'. However, we saw in the previous chapter that ending the employment relationship is by far the most significant cost of conflict. Therefore, persuading a line manager not to launch into a formal process without considering what other options are open to them is very important. In the event of a dismissal, an employment tribunal would want to satisfy itself that an employee knew what standards were expected of them, that they had been given an opportunity to achieve them, and that all this had happened before any formal procedures had begun. Another option might be the provision of alternative work, training or mentoring for the employee concerned, if they were having difficulties coping with their current tasks.

Whatever options are taken, the employee is entitled on grounds of fairness to be told exactly what is required of them, what standards are being set, and the timescale in which they are expected to achieve them. During the period of time that an individual is being given to reach the desired standards, a good manager ensures that they are kept informed of progress. This process is made easier if there is a structured performance management process, through which managers meet with employees on a reasonably regular basis to discuss their needs for training and development and identify and discuss any areas in which they may need to improve.

This often involves a line manager, sometimes with little experience or training, having to have a difficult conversation with one of their team. This can be extremely daunting, particularly for those line managers who have recently been promoted from the ranks and who may now have to address problems with people with whom they used to work side by side. A persistent theme of this book is the need to develop the people skills of line managers, and HR practitioners have a key role to play both in securing resources for proper training and in coaching managers in order to build their confidence.

HAVING A DIFFICULT CONVERSATION

Prepare

- Plan your approach to the meeting.
- Think about the outcome that you want and how to achieve that without escalating the situation.
- Make sure you have the information you need to support what you're going to say.
- Sketch out a plan or guide that you can refer to.

Start the meeting

- Explain the purpose of the meeting straight away – don't prevaricate.
- Strike the right note – calm, professional and business-like. Try to avoid being aggressive or defensive.
- Reassure the employee that the meeting and discussion is confidential.
- Focus on the issue that you need to resolve and not the person.

Outline the issue

- Outline the problem and give specific examples and illustrations – try to be as specific as possible.
- Explain why it is a problem in terms of the impact on the individual, team and the organisation – again, focus on the issue and not the person.
- Ask for their perspective – listen to what they have to say and don't interrupt. Acknowledge their position and probe for any mitigating circumstances.
- Explore the issues together rather than imposing an explanation, but...
- Keep in control of the discussion and try not to lose sight that there is still a problem that needs to be addressed.

Develop a resolution

- Ask the employee how the situation could be resolved and explore the options – focus on the future.
- Make a decision – remember that you are in control.
- Agree a plan with specific actions and review points, including a follow-up meeting.
- Be clear about the potential consequences if the situation is not resolved.
- Confirm in writing.

However, managers and HR practitioners can help an individual, in a non-threatening way, to come to terms with a particular problem. The problem may be about performance, about timekeeping, about drug or alcohol abuse, or about another employee. In a situation, for example, involving potential drug or alcohol abuse, managers may not have the necessary skills to fully address such a sensitive issue, but even if they conclude that specialist assistance is required, they can still help to bring the problem out into the open. In other cases, provided the problem is approached in a systematic way, this type of intervention may avoid disciplinary action. The steps contained in the box above provide a basic framework for preparing for, and conducting, such difficult conversations.

Reflective activity 10.8

You manage a team of 20 staff working in a telemarketing company. You are under pressure to hit specific sales targets and your staff are paid by results. On the whole your department is successful and you have managed to develop a positive environment and a good team ethic, partly by ensuring that bonuses reflect the collective performance of the team. However, a number of your employees have complained that one of their colleagues, Steve, who is normally a high performer, is not pulling his weight. His timekeeping has been erratic and he has been spending a lot of time on social media on his phone. He also seems to be less talkative than normal and a little withdrawn. How would you address this problem?

In addition, developing constructive relationships with trade union and employee representatives may be extremely useful in providing an environment in which early and informal resolution takes place. In many cases, representatives can act as an 'early warning system' of escalating conflict. Crucially, a worker or employee who is embroiled in a disciplinary issue is much more likely to confide in, and trust, their representative rather than their manager or an HR practitioner, and this can be invaluable in helping to find creative solutions to what may seem like intractable problems.

As we discussed at the start of this chapter, the first question facing a manager in addressing a potential disciplinary issue is whether informal discussion and potential resolution is appropriate. Even cases of serious misconduct can often be complex and multi-faceted. A sensitive and informal approach in the first instance may reveal underlying causes which can be resolved, helping the worker change their behaviour, retaining valuable skills and avoiding the costs involved in disciplinary action and potential dismissal. Accusations of bullying and harassment are one area in which early informal resolution can be effective. Of course, if this involves serious mistreatment, disciplinary action may be warranted. However, some complainants simply want the offending behaviour to cease. At the same time the alleged harasser or bully often does not realise that their behaviour or actions are causing offence or fear. Sitting down with an individual and explaining to them that some of their words or actions are causing distress to another employee can often be very effective. It is important not to leave it there but to monitor the situation, ensure that the behavioural change is permanent, and see that the complainant is satisfied with the action taken and the eventual outcome. Moreover, as discussed in Chapter 13, techniques such as workplace mediation may also be invaluable if used at an early point in the process.

Reflective activity 10.9

Accusations of bullying and harassment are increasingly prevalent in UK workplaces. In what circumstances would it be appropriate to try to resolve such an issue informally, and when should a formal disciplinary procedure be enacted?

Using the disciplinary procedure

If informal attempts to resolve the problem are not successful, it may be necessary to initiate the disciplinary procedure. However, starting down the disciplinary path can, ultimately, lead to a dismissal. Therefore, it is important to remember the requirement that, in taking a decision to dismiss somebody, you should act reasonably and in accordance with natural justice.

Investigation

In all cases of alleged misconduct it is vital that a proper investigation is carried out. Such an investigation should take place in a timely and sensitive fashion and must be seen to be fair. Where possible and practicable, the investigation should be undertaken by a person different from the one who might hear any consequent disciplinary case. The purpose of an investigation is to establish the facts and not to build a case against the employee. The law only requires that a 'reasonable' investigation is conducted (see Real-world example 10.4). What is reasonable will depend on the circumstances of each case. As the Acas Code of Practice points out, in some instances, investigatory meetings with the employee and any other witnesses may be needed. If so, it is vital to keep clear notes of any interviews and, if possible, agree the contents with the interviewee. However, in other cases, and particularly where the facts are not in dispute, gathering existing documentation and information may be all that is needed.

REAL-WORLD EXAMPLE 10.4

A reasonable investigation? *Sainsburys Supermarkets Ltd v Hitt* (2002) EWCA Civ 1588

Hitt was employed by Sainsbury's as a baker from April 1991. He was suspended on full pay pending an investigation in early September 1999 for allegedly stealing a box of razor blades from his place of work. A box of razor blades was found in his locker. He claimed the stock had been planted, naming other employees whose locker keys fitted his own. Only one of these was in the store at the time and he denied leaving his work area. The employer's investigation showed that Hitt had had the opportunity to take the stock and had left his work area twice that day. A disciplinary hearing took place whereby Mr Hitt argued that the razor blades had been planted. It was adjourned for two weeks to enable the store manager to investigate the matter further, including an investigation into locker keys. The disciplinary hearing recommenced on 30 September 1999 and Mr Hitt was dismissed for gross misconduct. Mr Hitt appealed and attended an appeal hearing before the district manager for the south-west region, who upheld the decision of the disciplinary hearing. Mr Hitt claimed unfair dismissal, alleging that his employers had failed to carry out a reasonable investigation. In particular he argued that they should have interviewed all employees with keys fitting his locker and also fully investigated the possibility that the razor blades had been planted by the manager. The employment tribunal concluded that there had been inadequate investigation, and that Sainsbury's should have investigated all their staff with a key fitting Mr Hitt's locker who could have been near his locker at the relevant time. Sainsbury's should also have ascertained the whereabouts of the bakery manager at the time of the theft to eliminate the possibility that he had put the razor blades in Mr Hitt's locker. However, the Court of Appeal overturned the decision, arguing that the investigation was one that could have been undertaken by a reasonable employer in the circumstances.

This case underlines the fact that an investigation only needs to be reasonable in the circumstances. Moreover, neither legislation, case law nor Acas guidance prescribes a particular format for investigations. In fact, in the case of *Sunshine Hotel v Godard* (2009), the EAT made it clear that there was no requirement for separate investigation meetings and disciplinary hearing in every case. Nonetheless, those circumstances can include the seriousness of the case and its implications for the employee – the judgement of the Court of Appeal in *Salford Royal NHS Foundation Trust v Roldan* (2010) EWCA Civ 522 suggested that employers would be expected to ensure that an investigation was particularly even-handed and fair where someone's career and professional reputation is at stake.

Accompaniment and representation

One of the key principles is that workers should have the opportunity to be accompanied at a disciplinary hearing by either a union representative or a work colleague. If an employer refuses to allow this, it is likely to render any subsequent dismissal unfair. In fact, under the Employment Relations Act (1999), all workers have a statutory right to be accompanied at disciplinary and grievance hearings by either a work colleague or a trade union representative. The right does not extend to family members, friends or legal representatives unless they happen to be a work colleague. It is important to note that the right to be accompanied applies to every individual, not just union members, and it does not matter whether the organisation recognises unions or not. The right applies where the worker is required or invited by their employer to attend a disciplinary hearing at which a sanction may be levied and when they make a reasonable request to be accompanied. Importantly the onus is on the worker to request accompaniment; however, it is good practice for employers to remind workers of this right.

Companions are able to provide advice and support to the worker and can address the hearing to put the case on behalf of the employee, sum up the case, and ask questions. They can also respond to any views expressed at the hearing. However, they are not permitted to answer questions on behalf of the worker, or address the hearing, if the worker does not want the companion to do so. In reality, some employers may find it useful for companions to answer for workers, who may find it difficult to express themselves, particularly in the stressful environment of a disciplinary hearing.

The right only applies to hearings or meetings which could result in a sanction being levied or confirmed. Therefore, it does not apply to an informal discussion, counselling session, facilitated meeting or investigatory interview. However, in some unionised organisations, it is common practice for workers to be offered representation during investigations. Whether this is advisable largely depends on the context of the organisation and the nature of relationships between management and unions. There is a danger that representation at an early stage can escalate matters unnecessarily and encourage defensive and adversarial attitudes. This said, research has shown that where relationships between representatives and managers are good, representatives can play an important role during the disciplinary process (Saundry et al, 2011). Not only can they ensure that processes are implemented fairly, they can help to manage the expectations of workers, uncover mitigating circumstances and act as a broker in negotiating potential resolutions.

Research conducted on behalf of Acas suggested that non-union companions, who are generally work colleagues with limited experience or training, tend to play little role in disciplinary hearings apart from offering moral support (Saundry et al, 2008). In most cases, they have little idea of what they are able to do and, therefore, we would suggest that managers, where possible, brief companions prior to the hearing. The same research also suggested that in most unionised organisations, managers were very positive about the role played by union representatives during disciplinary hearings. Having representatives present helped to ensure that issues were explored and that the process was fair. In addition, representatives were able to explain the implications of the process and manage the expectations of the worker, often reducing tensions and unnecessary confrontation. However, this was dependent on high-trust relationships between employers and unions. Where employee relations were poor or, in non-unionised companies with little experience of unions, managers perceived union representatives to be adversarial, and found their legal and procedural knowledge daunting. This suggests that good employment relations are crucial in providing the basis for managing discipline in an effective and constructive manner.

Reflective activity 10.10

What are the main advantages for employers if employees facing disciplinary issues are represented? What can HR practitioners do to ensure that they develop constructive relationships with trade union representatives?

Preparing for the disciplinary hearing

If the outcome of any investigation is that the disciplinary procedure should be invoked – as with all management activities – preparing properly is extremely important. There are various steps that must be taken, in line with the Acas Code of Practice:

1 **Prepare carefully** and ensure that the person who is going to conduct the disciplinary hearing has all the facts and details of the investigation. In almost all cases the person who will make the decision at a disciplinary hearing must not have been involved in the investigation. If the investigation and decision is not separated in this way, any decision to dismiss is likely to be unfair. The only exception to this may be in micro-organisations where there are only one or two managers – even here the employer should see if they can find a third party who could conduct the investigation.

2 **Write to the employee inviting them to a disciplinary hearing.** The letter should cover the following elements:

   - **The date and time of the hearing** – this should allow the employee time to prepare their case. The question here is how much time should be allowed. It is important that issues of discipline are dealt with speedily once an employee has been advised of the complaint against them, but it is important for the employee not to feel unfairly pressured in putting together any defence that they have. A good tip is to state clearly in the letter that if the employee has any concerns over the arrangements, they should raise them as soon as possible.

- **The venue** – try to find a location where there will be no disturbances and, if possible, where the employee will have some privacy and will not have to see or 'bump into' their colleagues. It is also beneficial if a room can be found that is relatively neutral ground, i.e. not the manager's office or in the HR department; however, this is not always easy in a smaller organisation.
- **The nature of the complaint and the potential outcome** – the employee must know what they are up against. If there is a possibility that the hearing could result in dismissal, the employee needs to be forewarned, normally in the invitation letter to the hearing. This again sounds straightforward but is often the point at which things begin to go wrong. For example, it would not be enough to tell an employee that they are to attend a disciplinary hearing in respect of their poor performance. It is good practice to provide the employee with any evidence that could be relied on during the disciplinary hearing, including copies of witness statements.
- **The process to be followed** – it is always wise to provide the employee with a new copy of the disciplinary procedure – not least because they may have never read the disciplinary procedure and, even if they have, it may have been revised.
- **The right to be accompanied** – where individuals work in a unionised environment this tends to be automatic, with an invitation to attend the meeting sent directly to the appropriate union official. However, in non-unionised environments, people are not always sure who would be an appropriate person to accompany them or whether they want to be accompanied at all. It is sensible to encourage somebody to be accompanied, but if they refuse, this should be respected. It is important to understand that it is up to the employee to choose who accompanies them as long as it is either a co-worker, union representative or union official. If the employee's companion is not available on the date of the hearing, the hearing should be postponed until a suitable date can be found, provided that this does not mean an unreasonable delay. The Acas Code cites a period of five working days after the date originally proposed, but in order to avoid problems and maintain good relationships with trade unions, we would suggest that the employer should be as accommodating as possible.

3. **Determine the composition of the disciplinary panel.** This may be set out in the disciplinary procedure, but it is crucial to make sure that the person chairing the hearing has the authority to make any potential decision, for example, if a dismissal is possible. It is always useful for the chair to be accompanied because of the possible need at some future time to corroborate what was said. If the organisation has an HR function, having an HR practitioner present to provide advice and to make sure that the process is fair is advisable. It is also important to make sure that there is someone present to take notes of proceedings.
4. **Consider whether witnesses should be called.** The Acas Code of Practice advises that employees should be given a reasonable opportunity to call

relevant witnesses. In our experience, this is quite rare and most employers wait for employees to raise this issue, but if the Code is followed strictly, the employee should be asked if they wish witnesses to be invited. The employer may also request witnesses to attend. If so, it should be explained to them that the employee would have the opportunity to question them and the employee should be informed so that they can prepare any questions.

5 **Consider the evidence and whether any further investigation is necessary.** If there are any loose ends to the investigation or if it seems that there may be additional relevant information, the manager should follow this up. It is not uncommon for an employee to withhold information in relation to mitigating circumstances, particularly if this is of a personal nature. In such circumstances, good relationships with union and employee representatives can be vital. Employees may often confide in their representative and, therefore, an off-the-record discussion with that representative may reveal information that will help to ensure a fair decision and potentially avoid dismissal.

6 **Make sure that the chair knows the process.** Experienced managers who are confident in dealing with disciplinary issues will usually know the procedure to be followed. However, as we have already noted, many managers lack confidence in dealing with difficult issues. Therefore, they are often nervous and over-reliant on HR advice. As we have noted in Chapters 4 and 9, we found in our research that this can result in the use of scripts, checklists and flowcharts, which make it difficult to create a context in which the employee feels that they are being treated fairly (Saundry et al, 2016). Consequently, we believe that it is important that the manager is coached and supported so that they are able to manage the hearing in a confident and professional manner.

The disciplinary hearing

Good preparation underpins the third part of the process – conducting the disciplinary hearing. There are a number of points to remember at this stage:

1 **Introduce those present** – not just on grounds of courtesy, but because an employee facing a possible sanction is entitled to know who is going to be involved in any decision. In a small workplace this may be unnecessary, but it can be important in larger establishments.

2 **Explain the purpose of the meeting and how it will be conducted.** This builds on the need to ensure that the employee fully understands the nature of the complaint against them and the procedure to be followed. As with any hearing, however informal, what it is for, what the possible outcomes are, and the method by which it is to be conducted are important prerequisites for demonstrating adherence to natural justice. If it is apparent that, for whatever reason, the employee does not fully understand the nature of the complaint against them, you must halt the proceedings until they are clear – even if this means postponing to another day.

3. **If the employee is accompanied, it may be useful to define the role of the companion.** This may not be necessary if the employee is accompanied by an experienced trade union representative. But if they are accompanied by a work colleague, it should be explained that, by law, they are able to address the hearing, confer with the employee and ask any relevant questions, but they are not permitted to answer questions on behalf of the employee. That said, in some situations it may be advisable to be relatively flexible about how the right to accompaniment is applied. Employees can be nervous and upset, and therefore may find it difficult to answer questions clearly or put their case confidently. Here, experienced representatives can be very helpful in making sure that all points of view are taken into account.
4. **Set out precisely the nature of the complaint and outline the case by briefly going through the evidence.** This may seem like overkill, but it is important to ensure that there are no misunderstandings. It is important to ensure that the employee and their representative or companion, if they have one, have already seen witness statements and any other relevant documentation. If they have not, they should be provided with copies and given a proper opportunity to read them, even if this means adjourning the hearing.
5. **Give the employee the right to reply.** Put simply: no right of reply – no natural justice, and any decision to dismiss will almost certainly be unfair.
6. **Allow time for general questioning.** If witnesses have been called, it is important that you allow the employee and/or the representative time to question them. If this did not happen, it would be difficult to persuade a tribunal that the test of reasonableness had been achieved.
7. **No matter how carefully you prepare, or how well you are conducting a disciplinary hearing, things might not always proceed smoothly.** People can get upset or angry and the whole process might become very emotional. In such circumstances it might be advisable to adjourn and reconvene at a later date. Again, the representative or companion can play a key role here. It is perfectly reasonable to use an adjournment to hold discussions with the representative or companion with a view to ensuring a fair outcome or a possible resolution.
8. **Sum up the key points and give the employee an opportunity to make any final representations.**
9. **Adjourn so that a properly considered decision can be made.** If this is not done, no matter how clear the issues, it will suggest that the decision has been pre-judged, something that can render a dismissal unfair.

Most unfair dismissal cases that succeed do so because of a procedural flaw, but if the employer follows these steps and makes sure that they adhere to the Acas Code of Practice, they will minimise the chances of a legal challenge.

REAL-WORLD EXAMPLE 10.5

Judge, jury and executioner? (*Whitbread plc v Hall* (2001) IRLR 275)

Hall was employed as manager of a pub. He had been employed by the company for 13 years. The pub was considered to be a flagship pub and Hall had received a number of congratulatory letters and awards from his employers. However, during the course of his employment, there had been a range of stock control problems. In May 1997, he was given a final written warning. Hall's wife was suffering from terminal cancer and she died in June 1997. Hall took two weeks' compassionate leave. On his return from leave the pub was still doing well, but the relationship between Hall and his area manager, Hayes, deteriorated. While Hall was taking his Christmas vacation, Hayes arranged and conducted a stock control audit at the pub, which revealed some problems. Subsequently, Hayes convened a disciplinary hearing (which she also chaired) after which she decided to dismiss Hall for gross misconduct. Hall admitted to the misconduct in question; however, he argued that dismissal was too harsh in the circumstances. No other course of action was considered. He appealed to a more senior manager but this appeal was dismissed and he took a claim to the employment tribunal.

Reflective activity 10.11

Hall won his claim for unfair dismissal – what procedural defects can you identify in this case?

Making the decision

As we have outlined, all disciplinary decisions need to be taken with care. This is particularly true when considering possible dismissal. If a former employee makes a claim for unfair dismissal, the employment tribunal will look at whether the decision to dismiss is fair or unfair. Section 98(4) of the Employment Rights Act states that this depends on:

> whether in the circumstances (including the size and administrative resources of the employer's undertaking) the employer acted reasonably or unreasonably in treating it as a sufficient reason for dismissing the employee, and… shall be determined in accordance with equity and the substantial merits of the case.

Importantly, the tribunal will ask whether the decision to dismiss falls within the range of responses that would have been made by a reasonable employer. This will require an employer to show that it has considered: the seriousness of the offence; mitigating circumstances; the previous record and service of the employee; alternatives to dismissal; and whether warnings have been used appropriately. This 'band of reasonable responses' test is designed to provide an objective measure of fairness such that the tribunal doesn't attempt to second-guess or put itself 'in the shoes of the employer'. However, some legal commentators have argued that it essentially allows for employers to justify overly harsh decisions and provides a very low 'hurdle' over which employers have to jump (see Collins, 2000).

Therefore, all the evidence should be reviewed and alternative courses of action considered. The law is an important factor, and providing advice in relation to this is a key function of the employment relations professional. However, the most important thing is to ensure that decisions are fair, consistent and, where appropriate, employees are given an opportunity to improve their behaviour or performance. The following steps provide a useful guide:

1 **Decide whether the accusation is proved.** In some cases this will be straightforward – the employee may admit to misconduct or the evidence may be incontrovertible. Nevertheless, particularly where misconduct is involved, you may have to weigh up conflicting accounts. In doing this, the courts have provided some useful guidance. The 'Burchell test' relates to a case that was decided in 1978 involving an incident of alleged theft (*British Home Stores v Burchell* (1978) IRLR 379). This provides three conditions that employers must meet when considering whether an employee is guilty of alleged misconduct:

   - The employer must have a genuine belief in the reason for dismissal.
   - The belief that the employee committed the offence must be based on reasonable grounds – that is, that on the evidence before it, the employer was entitled to say that it was more probable that the employee did, in fact, commit the offence than that they did not.
   - These grounds must be based on a reasonable investigation in the circumstances.

   If any one of these conditions is not met, a claim for unfair dismissal will normally succeed. It is important to note that the standard of proof in employment cases is the 'balance of probabilities' – is it more likely than not that the employee committed the alleged misdemeanour(s)? This is weaker than in criminal prosecutions, which are based on proof 'beyond a reasonable doubt'. This means that it is entirely possible for an employee to be fairly dismissed for an act of misconduct over which they have faced previous criminal investigation and been acquitted.

2 **The next question is what type of sanction to impose.** If this is likely to be short of dismissal, the main considerations should be whether the sanction will have the desired effect on the behaviour or performance of the individual and whether this is fair and consistent given the facts of the case and previous practice within the organisation. However, if dismissal is a possibility, a range of questions must be asked. First, are there any alternatives to dismissal? For example, would a final written warning or a demotion be more appropriate? Remember, dismissal should be a last resort. Second, what is the record of the employee concerned? Matters such as length of service, performance, previous disciplinary infractions and absence should be considered. Here it may be appropriate to take a more lenient approach if the employee has an otherwise exemplary record. Third, are there any mitigating factors? If so, it may be important to explore whether these circumstances are likely to be ongoing and whether the support of the organisation could help the situation.

If a claim for unfair dismissal is brought, the 'dismissing officer' will have to account for their reasoning behind the decision, so having considered each of the issues listed here will be crucial in demonstrating 'reasonableness'.

3 **Once the decision has been made, the meeting should be reconvened and the decision explained clearly to the employee.** If the decision is to warn the employee, the period of the warning, the required improvements and the consequences if improvements are not forthcoming should be clearly set out. If the decision is to dismiss, the reasons for this should be given. In either event, the employee should be offered the right to appeal and provided with details of the process. This should be confirmed in writing.

REAL-WORLD EXAMPLE 10.6

A reasonable response? (*Post Office v Foley* (2000) IRLR 827)

Foley was employed by the Post Office as a postal worker. He was on a late shift when his wife telephoned him saying she was in a bad state of nerves and required his attention. His immediate line manager, Mr Martin Joyce, gave him permission to leave work early. He left between 7.30 and 7.45pm. At about 8.47pm another manager, Mr Simon Kowalski, who was off duty, reported that he saw Mr Foley at the Innisfree Public House in Harrow Road, Wembley, which was about 12 minutes away from the depot, and notified Mr Joyce on his mobile phone. The late-shift manager, Ms Susan Johnson, sent two managers (the indoor patrol) to the pub, but Mr Foley could not be seen.

On 11 and 12 June a disciplinary hearing was conducted by Ms Johnson. Mr Foley was accompanied by his trade union representative. There was a dispute about the timing of the events on 16 May. Mr Foley's case was that he was not in the pub at the time when Mr Kowalski said he had seen him. He had gone into the pub at about 8.00pm to phone for a taxi as he wished to get home early and the bus would not arrive for another 18 minutes. The taxi came at 8.20pm. According to Mrs Foley, he arrived home at 8.40pm. The owner of the pub, Mr Mulvaney, supplied a letter saying that he had called a minicab for Mr Foley at 8.00pm and that it had arrived at 8.20pm and the minicab company supplied a document from driver number 98 indicating a time of 8.00pm. Ms Johnson didn't follow up this evidence. Ms Johnson dismissed Mr Foley, who had a clean conduct record, for the alleged misconduct. The Post Office Conduct Code stated that the possible penalties for 'unauthorised absence for all or part of duty' were 'warning or dismissal'.

Mr Foley appealed. His appeal, at which he was accompanied by his trade union representative, was heard by the appeals manager, Miss Susan Little. Little reviewed the evidence given by Mr Kowalski and investigated the documentation in relation to the licensee of the pub and the minicab company. She could see no reason for disbelieving Mr Kowalski and concluded that Mr Foley was in the pub after 8.20pm. She attempted unsuccessfully to obtain more information from the minicab company about the time of the pick-up. There was uncontradicted evidence in the chairman's notes of evidence that, like Ms Johnson, she considered alternatives to dismissal before concluding that dismissal was the appropriate remedy.

Reflective activity 10.12

Would you have dismissed Mr Foley in this situation? Do you think that the decision to dismiss fell within the 'band of reasonable responses'?

Appeals

Every disciplinary procedure must contain an appeals process – otherwise, it is almost impossible to demonstrate that the organisation has acted reasonably within the law. In common with every other aspect of the disciplinary process, it is important to ensure fairness and consistency within an appeals procedure, which should provide for appeals to be dealt with as quickly as possible. An employee should be able to appeal at every stage of the disciplinary process, and common sense dictates that any appeal should be heard by a different manager, who is senior to the person who has imposed the disciplinary sanction. However, this will not always be possible, particularly in smaller organisations.

The appeals procedure generally falls into two parts: action prior to the appeal and the actual hearing itself. Before any appeal hearing the employee should be told what the arrangements are and what their rights under the procedure are. It is also important then to obtain, and read, any relevant documentation. At the appeal hearing the appellant should be told its purpose, how it will be conducted, and what decisions the person or persons hearing the appeal are able to make. Any new evidence must be considered and all relevant issues properly examined. Although appeals are not regarded as an opportunity to seek a more sympathetic assessment of the issue in question, it is equally true that appeals are not routinely dismissed. Overturning a bad or unjust decision is just as important as confirming a fair decision. It is an effective way of signalling to employees that all disciplinary issues will be dealt with consistently and objectively.

Many organisations fall into the trap of using their grievance procedure in place of a proper appeals process. This is to be avoided wherever possible. The grievance procedure should be reserved for resolving problems arising from employment that the employee has highlighted – and is covered in the next chapter. Finally, not only should appeals be dealt with in a timely fashion, but the procedure should specify time limits within which appeals should be lodged.

10.5 Summary

In this chapter we have explained why managing discipline is such a key area for the employment relations professional and the line manager. For most practitioners in large organisations and for most front-line managers, responding to issues that may have disciplinary implications is a regular part of the job. However, if issues related to conduct and performance can be dealt with at an early stage, the need for formal disciplinary action may often be averted. Employment relations professionals have an important role to play in giving line managers the skills to have difficult conversations with staff and the confidence to pursue more informal resolutions. Good relationships with trade union representatives can also be helpful in identifying problems and finding possible solutions. It is also important to remember that formal disciplinary investigation and action should be a last resort – disciplinary processes are incredibly challenging for everyone involved and organisations are increasingly looking at ways of reducing the impacts on managers and staff.

If disciplinary action is inevitable, this chapter has set out the key steps that managers need to follow in order to ensure that matters are dealt with fairly and consistently. Although managers often complain that procedure is cumbersome and inflexible, an effective process is simple and straightforward: employees must be provided with the details of the problem; invited to a meeting to discuss the problem; and if a sanction is imposed, they must be given a right to appeal. Along with ensuring that matters are properly investigated, and that individuals are allowed to be accompanied to disciplinary hearings, these simple steps are the basis of natural justice. These principles are not only important in avoiding legal challenge, they are a key ingredient in ensuring organisational justice and maintaining trust and commitment. Furthermore, irrespective of the alleged offence, it is critical that workers subject to discipline are supported by the organisation and treated with compassion.

KEY LEARNING POINTS

- Managing discipline is about acting with just cause, using procedures correctly, acting consistently and following the rules of natural justice.
- A fair and effective disciplinary procedure is one that concentrates on improving or changing behaviour and helping all parties to learn from the situation. It should not revolve around blame and punishment, and is not one that relies on the principle of punishment. It should allow all employees to understand what is expected of them in respect of conduct, attendance and job performance, and set out rules by which such matters will be governed.
- It is important to discuss any emerging problems in relation to conduct or performance at the earliest possible point. In unionised workplaces, representatives can also be helpful in trying to resolve issues informally and avoid the need for formal action.
- Suspension, investigation and formal disciplinary proceedings should only be used as a last resort. Formal procedures have a significant impact on all those involved and damage employment relationships. If triggering a disciplinary procedure cannot be avoided, it is vital that employees are supported and kept informed of progress.
- Employees are entitled to know the details of allegations against them and to be able to respond to these allegations at a disciplinary hearing. They have a right to accompaniment and must be offered the opportunity to appeal against any disciplinary sanction levied against them.

Review Questions

1 Using research into the contemporary policy and practice of organisations, identify at least three factors that can affect the way discipline is handled in the workplace.

2 A senior manager wants you to brief supervisors about the different purposes of a disciplinary policy. The manager would like you to emphasise that discipline is not simply a matter of punishment. Using examples from your own organisation, outline what you would say, and why.

3 You have been asked to investigate an allegation of cyber-bullying. What steps would you take to investigate this issue? If you find that the allegations have substance, how would you recommend that this be dealt with?

4 An employee is regularly late back from lunch – as often as three or four times a week. The line manager has mentioned several times to them that this is unacceptable, usually in passing or during a conversation about something else. Provide the line manager with advice on how to progress the matter.

5 An employee in your organisation has submitted expenses for travelling and entertaining over a four-week period which do not tally with their record of customer visits. Their line manager says they are 'on the fiddle' and should be dismissed. You are responsible for advising line managers on how to deal with difficulties like this. Explain how you would handle this situation.

Explore further

Acas (2015) *Code of Practice on Discipline and Grievance Procedures*. Available from: https://www.acas.org.uk/media/1047/Acas-Code-of-Practice-on-Discipline-and-Grievance/pdf/Acas_Code_of_Practice_on_Discipline_and_Grievance.PDF (archived at https://perma.cc/27UC-HBZT)

Acas (2019) *Discipline and Grievances at Work: The Acas guide*. Available from: https://www.acas.org.uk/media/1043/Discipline-and-grievances-at-work-The-Acas-guide/pdf/DG_Guide_Feb_2019.pdf (archived at https://perma.cc/DN45-SREW)

Acas (2022) *Suspension from Work*. Available from: https://www.acas.org.uk/suspension (archived at https://perma.cc/GX5H-RNYH)

Saundry, R, Latreille, P, Saundry, F, Urwin, P, Bowyer, A, Mason, S and Kameshwara, K (2024) *Line manager handling of discipline and grievance – a barrier to resolution?*, London, Acas

Websites

www.acas.org.uk (archived at https://perma.cc/3D89-NK8K) – provides a wealth of information in relation to the management of discipline.

www.gov.uk/disciplinary-procedures-and-action-at-work (archived at https://perma.cc/KZX9-N5XW) – gives access to basic guidance and advice relating to the legislation relevant to discipline at work.

www.cipd.co.uk (archived at https://perma.cc/G2WK-XMA2) – gives access to CIPD resources relating to workplace discipline and employment law.

11
Managing employee grievances

Overview

This chapter explores the management of employee grievances. It begins by discussing how employees conceive of, and characterise, mistreatment, and the implications of managerial responses. We then provide an analysis of recent data to give an overview of the incidence of individual employee grievances in British workplaces and the development of process and procedure. The next part of the chapter sets out the business case for adopting a proactive approach to grievance management and outlines key aspects of informal processes of resolution. However, this is not always either successful or appropriate. Consequently, we move on to explain in some detail the main elements of effective grievance procedures and the ways in which these processes can be managed fairly and consistently and with a view to negotiate outcomes that are acceptable to all parties. Finally, the chapter briefly examines the place of specialist procedures for dealing with specific types of employee grievances, such as complaints related to dignity at work.

LEARNING OUTCOMES

When you have completed this chapter, you should be able to:

- explain and critically analyse the processes through which employee grievances escalate;
- describe the nature and pattern of employee grievances in British workplaces and examine the development of workplace procedures;

- describe the key stages of informal and formal processes to manage and resolve grievances;
- discuss and evaluate the main strategies and skills needed to implement a grievance procedure and negotiate fair and acceptable outcomes;
- identify and critically assess the limitations of conventional grievance procedures and how these issues can be addressed through specialist processes.

11.1 Introduction

The Acas Code of Practice on Disciplinary and Grievance Procedures defines grievances as 'concerns, problems or complaints that employees raise with their employers'. For some commentators, a complaint is the informal expression of discontent to the line manager; whereas a grievance is the more formal manifestation. Furthermore, grievances can revolve around individual issues or those which are collective in nature (Dundon and Rollinson, 2011). Irrespective of the definition we may use, finding quick and effective resolutions is vital. To the individual concerned, their grievance is of immediate importance. In addition, an organisation cannot ignore employee grievances, since the mishandling of an individual's grievance could lead to an escalation of the dispute, which will have implications for the well-being and performance of the complainant but could also impact on the team or unit they work in. The objective of grievance management is to address grievances by:

- thoroughly investigating the situation;
- identifying the cause of the employee's complaint;
- taking appropriate action to resolve the complaint to the mutual satisfaction of the employee and the management;
- resolving the grievance as quickly as possible.

A key aspect of fairness at work is the opportunity for the individual employee to complain about, and receive redress for, unfair treatment. As we have already discussed in this book, the main responsibility for the management and resolution of employees' concerns and grievances increasingly rests with line managers. However, these issues can be complex and challenging. HR professionals, therefore, have a key role to play in developing effective policies that provide managers with a clear framework to operate within. In addition, they will be called on to provide advice and guidance and coach managers through particularly difficult situations. Therefore, in this chapter, we also explore the knowledge, skills and techniques that line and operational managers can employ to manage employee grievances fairly, consistently and effectively. Moreover, we discuss innovative ways in which organisations can encourage early and informal resolution.

 Reflective activity 11.1

In your experience, what are the main reasons for a grievance being raised in your organisation? How do managers in your organisation respond to complaints and grievances and in what ways can this be improved?

11.2 Perceptions of mistreatment and the escalation of grievances

Before we discuss the nature and management of employee grievances in British workplaces, it is important to examine the dynamic processes through which grievances escalate. To do this, we draw on research into the causes and the consequences of unresolved grievances undertaken in the US. This work highlights the need for employment relations practitioners to adopt a more nuanced, rather than merely procedural, approach when dealing with grievances in the workplace. Olson-Buchanan and Boswell (2008) present a model that focuses on the way in which employee perceptions of mistreatment and the managerial response can combine to produce specific outcomes. In particular, they explore how complainants: 'characterise' mistreatment; perceive the severity of that mistreatment; and the negative implications for the employment relationship if the individual feels that justice has not been fully served.

Characterisation of mistreatment

For Olson-Buchanan and Boswell, the nature or character of the mistreatment as perceived by the individual can affect how that individual may react, particularly in terms of the degree to which they may feel maligned. In earlier work, Boswell and Olson-Buchanan (2004) make the distinction between whether the complainant feels that they have been mistreated due to the discretionary actions of another individual ('personalised') and when they believe they are a victim of the application of an organisational procedure or administration of a work policy ('policy-related'). Significantly for any assessment of the causes, consequences and, crucially, successful resolution of grievances, this study alerts us to the distinction that mistreatment related to enactment of organisational policy is less likely to be internalised and thus not seen as a personal attack by the employee. In contrast, perceived 'personalised mistreatment' can have a far more negative impact on their emotions, and lead to greater 'job withdrawal'. It is clear that these perceptions, founded or otherwise, have real implications for managers charged with addressing and trying to resolve employee grievances fairly.

 Reflective activity 11.2

Can you think of a situation at work in which you felt aggrieved? In this case, was this personalised (because of something another individual had done) or policy-related (something that the organisation had done)? Did this shape how you responded and resolved the problem?

Severity of mistreatment

A second key dimension of the grievance is the degree of 'severity' or 'seriousness' the individual attributes to their perceived mistreatment. Todor and Owen also note that the severity of the dispute is 'perhaps the central factor in determining the responses of the parties involved' (1991: 44). Conceptually, for Olson-Buchanan and Boswell (2008), these 'individual perceptions of injustice' can be located across a continuum of severity, from minor to severe, as perceived by the complainant. The harsher the employee feels the treatment to have been, the more likely there will be a higher level of negativity in response. This is also the case if the individual feels that the mistreatment was intentional in nature or due to some 'socially unacceptable reasons', which could include discrimination or harassment.

The outcomes

If the complaint is not seen to have been managed fairly or the basis of the grievance has not been addressed or heard, the long-term performance and engagement of the complainant will be inevitably undermined. To illustrate this point, Olson-Buchanan and Boswell (2008: 92) cite the example of an individual who experiences retaliation for voicing their grievance and may choose:

> to not pursue voicing the mistreatment further, and instead may withdraw from his or her job, ultimately lowering job performance. This lowered performance may be noticed by the supervisor, resulting in a lower performance evaluation, possibly triggering another perception of mistreatment.

This example of a potential vicious circle clearly highlights the need for all managers, supported by HR colleagues, to respond quickly and effectively to all perceptions of mistreatment. In contrast, if an employee perceives that they have achieved a positive resolution of their complaint, they are more likely to feel greater allegiance to the organisation and feel generally more positive. Therefore, the effective management of grievances can build perceptions of organisational justice, deepen trust and even extend employee engagement.

REAL-WORLD EXAMPLE 11.1

A problem with Facebook 'friends'

You are an HR adviser at an SME employing around 170 staff that operates in the financial services sector. One Monday morning, you receive an urgent email from a member of staff who claims that he is being 'picked on' by members of his team and he needs your help. He is part of the sales team based in a small call centre in the company's main office in town. The email goes on to outline that for the last three weeks, but particularly over the last weekend, he has experienced increasing criticism and insulting comments from other members of the team on Facebook. People who he had considered 'friends' are now openly 'attacking' his sales ability and say that 'he is not up to the job'. He explains that previously he has raised the issue with his line manager. However, she did not see it as an issue because it is happening outside working hours.

You have agreed to speak to the member of staff but first need to establish what information you need for that discussion. The issue is not helped by the fact that your company has not, as yet, got a social media policy, although different forms of social media are used quite extensively in the firm, not least by sales staff when chasing up leads on potential clients.

In preparation for your first discussion with the member of staff who has raised the grievance, use the Olson-Buchanan and Boswell model, outlined earlier, to establish the potential character, severity and outcomes of the grievance. Then, set out a plan of action for addressing and resolving this problem. Finally, think about what you and the organisation can learn from this situation.

11.3 The nature and pattern of employee grievances

This section examines key trends in the nature and extent of employee grievances. Unfortunately, the data collected on this issue is patchy. The last Workplace Employment Relations Survey, which traditionally measured the incidence of grievances at work was conducted in 2011. However, the CIPD's 2020 *Managing Conflict in the Modern Workplace* report provides valuable additional and more recent data which helps us deepen our understanding of this issue.

The incidence of formal grievances

The data suggests that formal grievances tend to be less common than disciplinary cases. Nonetheless Saundry and Urwin (2021) have estimated that there are over 374,000 grievances in the UK every year. The CIPD (2020) found that just under 14 per cent of employers surveyed had experienced grievances. Among these organisations, the average number of grievances in the last 12 months was six and the median was two. This suggests that grievances tend to be concentrated in certain types of organisations. Wood et al's (2017) analysis clearly points to grievances being more likely in larger organisations. In addition, the presence of an HR practitioner tends to be associated with higher grievance rates. It would be a mistake to interpret this as suggesting that HR practitioners cause conflict. Instead, it is more likely that employees feel more able to voice concerns where there is an HR function. Moreover, Wood et al found that good HR practice can play a positive role, with high-involvement work practices being significantly associated with lower levels of grievances.

It is important to note that formal grievances may just be the tip of the conflict iceberg. A CIPD study (2020) found that although almost four out of every ten employees had experienced conflict of some sort, only 9 per cent responded by using a formal grievance, discipline or complaints procedure. Therefore, higher levels of grievances do not necessarily reflect more conflictual working environments but may be a sign of a more open and inclusive culture. In reality, many employees do not feel confident in raising concerns with their employer – the CIPD found that less than half the employees surveyed agreed that their organisation had 'effective procedures for resolving interpersonal conflict'. Furthermore, around one-third of those who had experienced conflict felt satisfied with the way their organisation had handled it. This creates an interesting organisational dilemma – while it is undoubtedly good practice to provide channels through which employees can raise concerns, in the short term this may increase the amount of visible conflict.

Reflective activity 11.3

Do you feel that your organisation is a safe environment for employees to raise concerns?

How could your organisation create more accessible channels to voice employee concerns?

The cause of individual grievances

Grievances from individual employees can centre on a wide range of issues (Faragher, 2018). While the CIPD study mentioned above does not specifically explore the causes of grievances, it does provide an insight into the causes of individual conflicts

Figure 11.1 Causes of conflict

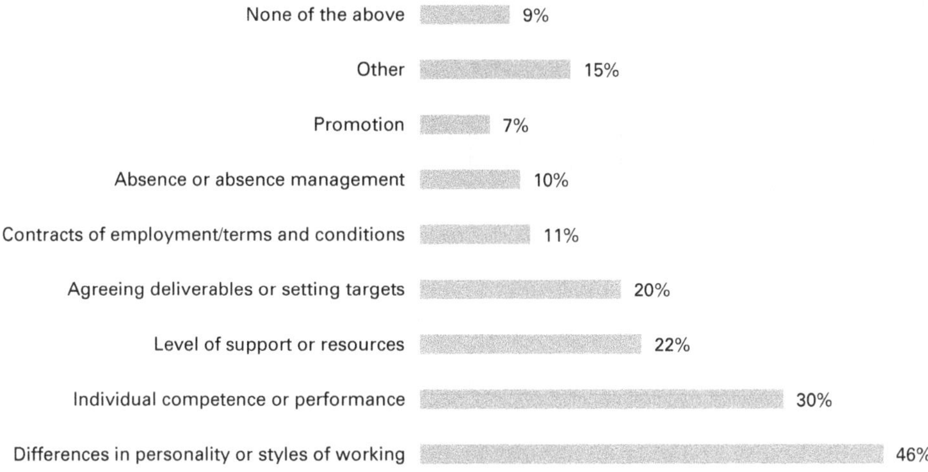

SOURCE: CIPD (2020)

at work. As Figure 11.1 shows, the main cause revolves around differences in personalities or ways of working. Respondents could select one or more causes of conflict, and the next three most widely cited all relate to the management of people – performance, support and targets, which once again underlines the crucial role played by supervisors and line managers. This also points to the complex nature of grievances in that quite often they are interrelated with potential disciplinary issues, in particular where the way that a manager seeks to address poor performance or capability is seen by the employee as unfair and unreasonable.

Overall, the CIPD data points to the growing importance of the way that people are managed and how that is received. Figure 11.2 shows the main behaviours that those involved in conflict experience; again, respondents could cite more than one behaviour. Sixty-six per cent of respondents reported a lack of respect and 35 per cent reported bullying, intimidation and harassment. Interestingly, four in ten of those who reported being bullied identified their manager as the alleged bully. Overall, this underlines the complexity of grievances whereby employee complaints of bullying or mistreatment may lead to disciplinary action, but also may be a response to attempts by managers or colleagues to raise concerns over capability and performance.

Figure 11.2 Behaviours in conflict

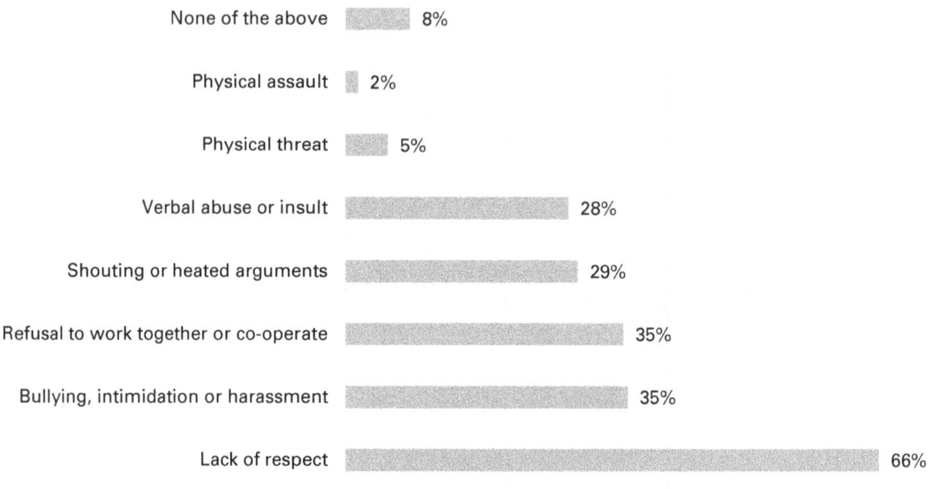

SOURCE: CIPD (2020)

The extent of grievance procedures

Turning to the role of formal procedures in resolving grievances, Wood et al (2017) found that by 2011, written grievance procedures had become ubiquitous in the UK. By 2011, all workplaces with 50 or more employees had a formal grievance procedure in place. Interestingly, the greatest rate of increase was in the smallest workplaces and those without union recognition. In the smallest workplaces, i.e. those with between 5 and 9 employees, more than 8 out of 10 were covered by a written grievance procedure. This reflects a gradual formalisation and filling in of 'procedural gaps' in UK organisations. At the same time, procedural adherence in relation to grievances lagged substantially behind that for disciplinary issues. This could reflect the greater scope for resolution within grievance processes or alternatively the added pressures of compliance when considering dismissals.

Collective grievances

Employee grievances can also be collective in that a group of employees have a common complaint relating to their employment or an individual has a grievance which has collective implications. The main causes of grievances raised by a group of employees typically include:

- the interpretation and application of an existing agreement;
- pay and bonus arrangements;
- organisational change;
- new working practices;
- grading issues.

Traditionally, collective disputes have been handled through joint negotiation with recognised trade unions. The process used was often codified through a formal collective disputes procedure. However, such procedures are not now as widespread as individual grievance procedures. WERS2011 found that just over a third of workplaces had an internal procedure for handling collective disputes, compared with 40 per cent in 2004 (van Wanrooy et al, 2013). In workplaces with no recognised union, only a quarter had such arrangements compared with three-quarters of workplaces with recognised unions. Therefore, the contemporary reality is that most workplaces have no process, whether formal or informal, for handling collective grievances. As a consequence, where there are no channels for collective negotiation, it is likely that discontent that is collective in character will be expressed through individual disputes and/or through other manifestations, such as high staff turnover, absenteeism, low morale and reduced performance.

Reflective activity 11.4

To what degree are collective grievances raised in your organisation? Do you think that individual grievances reflect collective concerns and issues?

11.4 The benefits of effective resolution

Employee grievances on a wide variety of issues (including discrimination, harassment and bullying) arise even in organisations that enjoy positive employment relations. If grievances are not dealt with or handled quickly, they are likely to fester and harm the employment relationship. A grievance may be felt by a group as well as an individual and, if left unresolved, may develop into a major collective dispute and even industrial action. However, whether individual or collective, unresolved grievances can have a wide range of damaging effects, including:

- employee frustration;
- deteriorating interpersonal relationships;
- low morale;
- poor performance, resulting in lower productivity and/or a poorer quality of output or service;
- disciplinary problems, including poor performance by employees;
- resignation and loss of good staff (increased labour turnover);
- increased employee absenteeism;

- the withdrawal of employee goodwill;
- resistance to change – if employees feel they have been treated badly, they are likely to oppose the introduction of change.

Clearly this will also have a negative impact on organisational performance and efficiency. In addition, unresolved grievances can lead to employees feeling that they no longer have any trust and confidence in their employer, resigning and seeking to make a claim for unfair constructive dismissal to an employment tribunal. A reputation for employee dissatisfaction also gives an organisation a negative image in the labour market, which will make it more difficult to recruit and retain staff. As noted in Chapter 9, it can be argued that a sense of procedural justice underpins employee engagement – therefore responding quickly and effectively to employee grievances not only helps to ensure fairness and equity, it also makes good business sense (Purcell, 2012b).

11.5 Handling employee grievances

As we noted earlier in this chapter, the way that managers respond to the concerns of their employees will have a significant effect on whether discontent escalates into a formal grievance and on employees' perceptions of equity and justice. Ideally, skilled and confident managers will seek to address and resolve issues at the lowest possible point. However, in some cases it will be necessary to enact a grievance procedure, which needs to be applied and managed in a transparent, consistent and fair manner.

The potential for early resolution

Most employees' complaints over management behaviour do not reach the formal grievance procedure for many reasons. First, as noted earlier, the employee may merely want to get their dissatisfaction 'off their chest'. Second, on reflection, the employee may feel that the issue is not serious enough to go through the potential stress of a formal process. Third, in times of high levels of unemployment, individuals are often reluctant to raise grievances formally, fearing that management may hold it against them and react by denying them promotion or access to training. Fourth, employees may, in some cases, see little point in raising their grievance since they have little faith in the process itself. Finally, some individuals are unwilling to express their dissatisfaction with management for fear of offending their immediate superior, who may see the complaint as a criticism of their competency.

Reflective activity 11.5

One of the problems facing organisations in addressing employee grievances is creating a culture in which staff feel able to raise concerns and grievances. If you experienced a problem with one of your colleagues or your manager, would you feel able to make a complaint? If not, why is this and what could the organisation do to improve the situation?

This underlines the importance of managers developing an 'open culture' within their teams with clear channels for communication and consultation. In this way problems and concerns can be voiced, discussed and settled as a matter of course. We would argue that whenever possible, managers should seek to resolve issues raised by employees informally. Sometimes an employee simply wishes to make their feelings or concerns known and for them to be properly recognised by the employer. Depending on the issue, good management practice is to discuss those concerns and genuinely commit to addressing them. The first step should always be to explore whether the issue can be resolved at an early stage without the need for the time, anxiety and potential for further conflict that formal grievance proceedings often involve. The first point of call is normally either a manager or a member of the HR team. As we saw in Chapter 4, many managers lack the confidence and the skills to have these difficult conversations, and this can even be difficult for HR specialists. Nonetheless, by following some basic steps and using some simple techniques, managers can start the process of resolution.

INFORMAL GRIEVANCE RESOLUTION – KEY TIPS

- Always try to have face-to-face discussions.
- Make sure the employee knows that the conversation is confidential.
- Listen carefully and attentively – make and maintain eye contact.
- Recognise the legitimacy of the concern – it is their perception that counts.
- Ask questions – try to examine and explore the underlying cause of the problem.
- Where possible, probe for details and potential evidence of the problem.
- Rephrase or reinterpret what's been said so that the individual concerned can see the issue from an alternative perspective.
- Ask the individual how they want to resolve the issue.
- Try to move the focus of the individual on to their interests, not positions and personalities.
- Encourage a 'future focus'.

After such discussions, it is important to keep a note of what was said in the event that the conflict escalates. It may also be appropriate to involve others. A more senior manager or HR practitioner may be useful in a facilitated discussion to try to provide an objective view of the particular problem. If a more structured approach is needed, mediation could be considered. This can be particularly effective if the issue involves the deterioration of a relationship between two colleagues. We look at this in greater detail in Chapter 13.

Some organisations have gone much further in attempting to encourage the early and informal resolution of grievances and developed specific policies and processes.

While these may change the language around 'grievance' they maintain channels through which complaints can be investigated formally, if necessary. However, they provide a much greater focus on informal resolution. Real-world example 11.2 looks at an innovative approach developed by East Lancashire Hospitals Trust.

REAL-WORLD EXAMPLE 11.2

East Lancashire Hospitals Trust – early and informal resolution

Prior to 2016, conflict management at the Trust was risk-averse and revolved around the rigid application of procedure. Grievances tended to escalate quickly and often became locked into long and complex processes. Managers lacked the skills and confidence needed to address problems and therefore tended to avoid addressing difficult issues. Although the Trust had an internal mediation service, it was under-resourced and difficult to access.

To address these issues, the Trust introduced a new Early Resolution Policy. This replaced existing grievance and bullying and harassment policies. Formal complaints could still be made, however early resolution must be considered first. Employees can use a variety of channels to voice concerns: line managers, freedom-to-speak guardians, trade unions, HR practitioners, occupational health, or a combination of these. This was designed to trigger conversations between the individual(s) and key stakeholders themselves and create space for a wider range of interventions which can include mediation, training, coaching or team facilitation.

The Trust also reinforced its support for mediation – new mediators were trained and a full-time co-ordinator was appointed. Mediators were provided with dedicated time and space. The service was also relocated from HR to Occupational Health underlining the link between dispute resolution and well-being.

An evaluation of the Early Resolution Policy (Saundry et al, 2023) found that it helped to clarify informal resolution in practical terms to managers and staff. It also placed a clear expectation on managers that they should use informal approaches to conflict resolution wherever possible and appropriate. Between 2019 and July 2022, 223 cases had been referred to the Early Resolution Policy and 188 had been concluded. Of these, nearly three-quarters were resolved informally and only 22 per cent progressed to formal procedures. However, a lack of confidence among some line managers within the Trust remained a barrier to early resolution. This also resulted in a tendency for problems that could have been addressed by managers being referred to mediation.

As this case suggests, early or informal resolution policies can move the emphasis away from procedural compliance and towards resolution. Furthermore, as we saw in the previous chapter, managers can benefit from having a clear map to follow when responding to conflict at work. Nonetheless, the case also points to several key ingredients for success if organisations are going to adopt such an approach.

EARLY AND INFORMAL RESOLUTION POLICIES – KEY SUCCESS FACTORS

- Invest in building the confidence and competence of line and middle managers to manage conflict.
- Develop multiple channels of resolution, which should include rights-based procedures through which employees can bring formal complaints alongside interest-based processes such as mediation.
- Adopt a systematic and integrated approach to conflict management clearly targeted at strategic goals such as well-being and engagement.
- Communicate the policy in a clear and transparent way to engage those involved in operationalising dispute resolution, particularly line managers.

Of course, informal resolution may not be appropriate in some cases. For example, if it appears that a potential complaint suggests mistreatment or serious bullying, formal action may be the correct course of action to ensure that such behaviour is not allowed to continue and to clearly signal that it will not be tolerated by the organisation. Furthermore, when the concerns raised by an individual are symptomatic of a wider problem within a team, even if the immediate issue is resolved, it may still be necessary to provide additional training, support and/or coaching to the manager.

Reflective activity 11.6

Has the grievance procedure in your organisation been activated in the last 12 months? If it has, what were the issues and groups of workers involved and what was the outcome? Why weren't these issues resolved informally?

Grievance procedures

If attempts to resolve the issue through informal means are not successful or appropriate, a systematic grievance procedure should be followed. The purpose of a grievance procedure is to:

- ensure the fair and consistent treatment of employees;
- reduce the risk of 'unpredictable' action;
- clarify the manner in which grievances will be dealt;
- maintain a good employment relations environment;
- help the employer to avoid disputes or costly legal action.

The form of grievance procedures varies immensely. In a small non-union establishment, the procedure is likely to be relatively short and is often written into the employee's contract of employment. In larger organisations, grievance procedures will often be more detailed and may have been negotiated with trade union representatives. The grievance procedure is likely to be available on the organisation's intranet, typically via the HRM pages on the site, and reproduced in the company handbook, or made available as a separate document. However, irrespective of the size of the organisation, the Acas Code sets out three key principles that should be adhered to:

1 The employee sets out the nature of their complaint.
2 A meeting is held to discuss the complaint (at which the employee can be accompanied) and a decision is made.
3 The employee has the right to appeal against that decision.

It can be useful to define the purpose of the policy at the outset. An example of this is provided in the following box.

PURPOSE OF THE POLICY

We seek to ensure that if you wish to raise a work-related grievance, it will be treated in a fair and equitable manner. Every effort will be made to settle grievances to the satisfaction of all concerned, using the procedure set out in this policy. If you have a grievance relating to your working conditions, your pay and benefits, working hours, treatment at the hands of your fellow workers, or if you are concerned about your health and safety or a breach of your statutory employment rights or any other issue affecting your employment, you should first talk the matter over with your immediate team leader/manager. In some instances it may not be appropriate to approach your manager, in which case you should bring the matter to the attention of the head of HR. This procedure complies with the ACAS statutory Code of Practice on grievance.

It is also important to explain the scope of the policy – setting out who the policy applies to (normally all staff) and the types of concerns that staff can make a complaint about. For example, it may be necessary to distinguish between individual and collective issues. In many unionised organisations, there will be a separate collective disputes procedure for the latter. In addition, procedures for managing employee complaints relating to health and safety provision, job grading, bullying and harassment, dignity at work and 'whistle-blowing' are often separate from the general grievance procedure (particularly in larger organisations). The role of more specialist procedures is discussed in greater detail later in the chapter.

The purpose statement above implies that employees should try to resolve issues informally as a first step. However, it may be useful to set this out in greater detail and explain what informal resolution means and how this will be attempted. Some organisations, particularly those who have their own trained mediators, also include a provision for issues to be referred to mediation. An example of this is provided in the following box.

RESOLVING GRIEVANCES: MEDIATION

- At any stage in this procedure any party may request that this matter be dealt with via referral to mediation.
- Mediation offers support to resolve interpersonal disputes between parties; it cannot mediate between an individual and the company. Mediation is voluntary and will only take place if all parties agree. However, it is hoped that complainants will be amenable to any suggestion made by the company to refer grievances to the mediation service and it is hoped that complainants co-operate with all efforts to resolve their complaint.

Underlying principles of grievance procedure

Importantly, all grievance procedures should reflect a number of principles – fairness, transparency, consistency, representation and promptness. More specifically, procedures should:

- prevent management from dismissing the employee's complaint out of hand on the grounds that it is trivial, too time-consuming and/or too costly;
- ensure that there is a full investigation by an unbiased individual to establish the facts of the case;
- provide the employee with adequate time to prepare their case and to question management witnesses;
- allow for the case to be heard by individuals not directly involved in the complaint;
- provide for the right of appeal to a higher level of management and, in some cases, to an independent external body.

A grievance procedure with a clearly demarcated number of stages and standards of behaviour at each stage provides consistency of treatment and reduces the influence of subjectivity. When a complaint is raised, the procedure should provide the individual with the right to be accompanied by a work colleague or trade union representative in accordance with the Employment Relations Act 1999 (as set out in the previous chapter). This legal right only extends to a formal grievance hearing. However, some organisations feel that it is reasonable to extend this. The promptness principle is achieved by the procedure having a small number of stages, each of which has time limits for their completion. This enables the grievance to be resolved as quickly and as simply as possible. Remember, an unreasonable delay in hearing and resolving a grievance could amount to a fundamental breach of an implied term of the employment contract and lead to a claim for unfair constructive dismissal (Lewis et al, 2023).

Reflective activity 11.7

Compare your organisation's grievance procedure with the checklist just discussed. Does it have all these elements?

Stages

There are a number of stages in a typical grievance procedure. At each stage, the procedure will normally:

- spell out the details of who hears the case (e.g. the departmental manager, the managing director) and the individuals to be present (e.g. the HR manager, the line manager and the employee concerned), including who may represent the employee (e.g. a colleague, a friend or a shop steward);
- explain the appeal mechanisms available to employees;
- define the time limits by which the stage must be complete;
- explain what will happen if the grievance is not resolved or remains unsettled.

This is illustrated in the typical three-stage grievance procedure presented here.

A BASIC THREE-STAGE GRIEVANCE PROCEDURE

Stage 1

If you wish to raise a formal grievance, you should, in the first instance, raise it orally or in writing with your immediate supervisor or manager. The supervisor/manager will normally respond within five working days.

Stage 2

If the matter is not resolved at Stage 1 or within five working days, you may refer it in writing within three working days to the next level of management, who may also involve a representative of the personnel department. You should set out the grounds for the complaint and the reasons for your dissatisfaction with the Stage 1 response.

A meeting will normally take place to consider the matter within seven working days of the request being made. You will have the right to be accompanied by a work colleague or trade union representative.

Stage 3

If the matter is not resolved at Stage 2 or within seven working days, you may refer it in writing within three working days to the next level of management, who may involve a representative of the personnel department. You should set out the grounds for the complaint and the reasons for your dissatisfaction with the Stage 2 response. A meeting will normally take place to consider the matter within 10 working days of the request being made. You will have the right to be accompanied by a work colleague or trade union representative. The decision of the divisional executive is the final stage of the procedure and will be given in writing.

While defined stages are essential, there is no ideal number of stages. The number is a function of many factors, including the size of the organisation. However, natural justice principles would point to a minimum of two stages, because this at least ensures one level of appeal from the first immediate decision. Nor should the procedure contain too many stages, since this makes the process unduly cumbersome and helps neither the complainant nor the organisation.

Reflective activity 11.8

Do you have a grievance procedure in your organisation? If not, why not? If you do, how effective do you think it is and how could it be improved?

Employee representation and accompaniment

It is important to remember that making a formal complaint under a grievance procedure is an extremely serious step. In essence, the individual employee, often someone with relatively little power and status, is challenging their employer. As a result of this power imbalance, representation in grievance proceedings is particularly important. We noted earlier that employees may have little faith in grievance procedures; however, the availability of representation will help to build confidence in, and legitimise, the process. Representation can also be helpful to the employer in both managing grievances and finding creative resolutions. Off-line discussions between representatives and managers can explore issues and potential solutions in an informal manner and in a way that may not be possible in the formal environment of a grievance hearing. In addition, the representative can help to manage employee expectations of the process. The Employment Relations Act (1999) gives workers a statutory right to be accompanied by a fellow worker or trade union official where they are required or invited by their employer to attend certain categories of grievance hearings and when they make a reasonable request to be so accompanied. As is the case in disciplinary hearings, companions can address the hearing, ask questions and confer with the worker – but they have no statutory right to answer questions on the worker's behalf.

Analysis of WERS2011 undertaken by Wood et al (2017) found that almost all workplaces allowed employees to have a companion at formal meetings to discuss individual grievances. However, there was significant variation in how this was applied, with some employers moving beyond the statute. For example, around one in three workplaces allowed anyone chosen by the employee and around one in ten were prepared to allow legal representatives to accompany employees. Furthermore, approximately one in five workplaces allowed accompaniment from friends or family members. While, in exceptional circumstances, it may be reasonable to allow friends or family members to accompany an employee, research and our own experience suggests that this should generally be avoided. Friends and family members may find it difficult to provide the objectivity and distance from the issue that marks effective representation.

Although the statutory right to accompaniment only applies to a grievance hearing, some organisations routinely provide access to representation at all stages of the process. Whether this is appropriate in a particular setting depends on the nature of employment relations. In some circumstances, offering representation at a very early stage may formalise the situation and make an early resolution more difficult. For example, if the employee feels confident to raise their concerns with the other party directly, that should be encouraged. However, where there are good relationships between representatives and managers or HR practitioners, early discussions involving representatives may help to avoid formal proceedings. Our research has often found that in organisations with effective approaches to conflict resolution, it is routine to alert the trade union representative of any potential or actual grievances or for the representative to contact management if a member has first come to them with a complaint.

Reflective activity 11.9

What is the involvement of employee representatives in grievances in your organisation? Do they help to facilitate resolution? Do you think that representation is important in grievance processes and, if so, why?

The role of the employment relations professional

Grievance procedures are an integral part of the way in which an organisation is managed. They directly affect line management at all levels. As we have noted already in this book, recent years have seen the progressive devolution of responsibility for handling disciplinary and grievance issues from HR to the line. However, many line managers lack the confidence to manage grievances in a proactive and effective way. Consequently, the relationship between the employment relations professional and the line manager is crucial. While it is important that the employment relations professional does not take direct responsibility for managing grievances, they need to build trust and rapport with managers, guiding, advising and sometimes coaching them through the process.

Furthermore, the employment relations professional should:

- identify line management training and development needs with regard to managing grievances – it is important to train line managers both to listen to grievances properly and to deal with them in a consistent manner;
- devise and implement a training and development programme so that line managers can acquire and develop the skills necessary to become effective managers of employee grievances;
- ensure that line managers have a clear understanding of the way in which grievance procedures are intended to operate;
- devise a grievance procedure which conforms with 'good practice' and spells out what has to happen at each stage, and why;
- promote awareness among line managers of 'good practice' in managing grievances;
- Ensure that employees are aware of their rights under the procedure.

The HR practitioner also has an important role to play in monitoring and reviewing the operation of the grievance procedure, and in recommending revisions to its design or operation. Following the revisions to the Acas Code of Practice in 2009, many organisations sought to revise their procedures accordingly, placing a greater emphasis on informal resolution and possible alternative approaches such as mediation (Rahim et al, 2011). This also involves reviewing the outcomes of the grievance decisions and assessing whether these outcomes have been those intended and desired by the management – and if not, why not. For example, is it because line managers are not undertaking a thorough investigation of the complaint? Alternatively, it may be that line managers are missing opportunities to 'nip issues in the bud' and are instead hiding behind the process (Saundry et al, 2016). The answers to these questions may identify the areas of competence and confidence that the employment relations professional needs to develop through training and coaching.

REAL-WORLD EXAMPLE 11.3

How not to handle a grievance (*Ms C Bickerstaff v The Royal British Legion*, ET, 2017)

Carolyn Bickerstaff was employed by the Royal British Legion as a case worker. In July 2015, one of her colleagues went on long-term sick leave. Bickerstaff was concerned about her workload and raised this in an email to her line manager. Bickerstaff received what she considered to be an unsupportive reply, which said there was little that could be done and suggested that it might be useful for a more senior manager to shadow her in the future. She then emailed the HR department raising concerns about her workload. She marked the email confidential and specifically said that she was worried that there would be repercussions if her line manager found out she had gone to HR. HR simply forwarded the email to her line manager. Bickerstaff then met with her line manager in September; however, at the meeting he read from a pre-prepared document and did not allow any interruption. Bickerstaff found his attitude to be confrontational and aggressive. She also raised concerns about the work of other colleagues.

Bickerstaff was then absent due to sickness for some time. HR asked her whether she wanted to raise a grievance and she said that she intended to on her return and that she did not want to be managed by her current line manager. Nonetheless, her manager attempted to contact her while she was off work.

When she returned to work she was assigned a new line manager and she submitted a written grievance. However, before this could be heard, another matter arose when she drew attention to the fact that blank cheques, signed by her new line manager, were being left in an unlocked drawer. Her new line manager then asked Bickerstaff not to come into the office or attend any meetings until the matter was resolved. This went on for 11 weeks until Bickerstaff was eventually signed off work suffering from stress. She resigned in December 2016 after claiming that no resolution had been put in place to allow her to come back to work and her original grievance had still not been heard.

Among other things she claimed unfair constructive dismissal. The employment tribunal upheld her claim, concluding that the actions of the employer amounted to a breach of mutual trust and confidence.

Reflective activity 11.10

How could the employer have handled this issue more effectively and, in particular, what steps could HR have taken to avoid this outcome? If you were acting as a consultant to the employer, what measures should now be taken to make sure that there is no repeat of this situation?

The role of the line manager

As we have already established, the front-line manager is the key player in the operation of a grievance procedure and in resolving issues at the earliest stage. However, the reality is that many grievances are brought against line managers and this can be seen as reflecting badly on their managerial competence. In these circumstances it is understandable that many managers will react defensively, which will make a resolution of the issue much less likely. Therefore, if grievance procedures are to operate effectively, senior management must reassure front-line managers that their managerial competence may not be the main cause of the dispute. On the contrary, front-line managers should be encouraged by their own managers to hear and listen properly to their employees' concerns. The front-line manager has little executive authority, and this limits their ability (as well as confidence) to make decisions without reference to a more senior manager. If a front-line manager or team leader frequently refers grievances up to a superior, the employee will realise that a possibly quicker way of having their problem resolved is to short-circuit the manager and go directly to their superior. If this happens, the legitimate authority of the front-line manager becomes undermined. Moreover, this also removes the grievance from its source of origin, which can slow down the process, cause confusion and create bad feeling. To avoid this happening, the employment relations professional must ensure that:

- everyone knows, within the procedure, the limits of their own and others' authority;
- the procedures are operated consistently by line managers;
- front-line managers have the authority to settle grievances;
- front-line managers are trained in conflict resolution;
- proper support is provided to front-line managers.

Furthermore, it is vital that senior managers try to provide line managers with space and time to resolve potential grievances at the earliest possible stage. Informal resolution can be time-consuming and is often not very visible, but it can provide significant long-term benefits to the organisation.

It is equally important that front-line management continues to be involved in the settling of grievances, even if the complaint proceeds beyond the stage at which they are formally involved. This can be achieved by their attendance at subsequent meetings or at the very least by being kept informed of the outcome as the grievance proceeds through subsequent stages of the procedure. In addition, it may be the case that the grievance is with the individual's direct manager, and in this case an alternative route through which the grievance can be made is useful. This is one reason why organisations have developed specialist procedures for dealing with complaints of bullying and harassment, which we explore at the end of this chapter.

Reflective activity 11.11

Do line managers in your organisation receive compulsory training in grievance handling and resolution? If not, identify the training needs of your line managers and draw up a development plan to improve their conflict competence.

Keeping records

When a grievance progresses to a higher stage in the procedure, documentation of what happened at the previous stage is needed by those managers who now become involved for the first time and are not familiar with the issues involved. In practice, the extent to which records of grievances are kept varies widely. The Acas Code of

Practice advises employers to keep a written record of any grievance cases with which they deal. Records should include the nature of the grievance, what was decided, the action taken, the reason for the action, whether an appeal was lodged, the outcome of the appeal, and any subsequent developments. Records have to be treated as confidential. Summaries or transcriptions of meetings should be given to the employee, including copies of any formal minutes that may have been taken.

Grievance records serve useful purposes for management. If there is a failure to agree at any stage, a written record clarifies the complaint and the arguments put forward about it by the individual employee and/or their representative. Such a record is also helpful to those managers involved in the next stage of the procedure. Grievance record forms assist the personnel/HRM function to keep in touch with the progress of unresolved grievances and to analyse trends in the use and outcomes of the grievance procedure.

Reflective activity 11.12

Does your organisation keep records and statistics in relation to employee grievances? If not, why not? Can you think of a way in which you could improve the documentation and analysis of grievances?

11.6 Managing the grievance procedure

As we have outlined, ideally most grievances are resolved informally through discussion or mediation before formal proceedings are needed. However, inevitably some grievances will need to be managed through the procedure. Management must deal with all grievances in a competent and systematic manner, which involves a number of stages:

- hearing the grievance;
- preparing for the meeting with the employee and/or their representative;
- meeting with the employee and/or their representative;
- confirming the common ground between the employee and the management;
- resolving the grievance;
- reporting the outcome.

The grievance meeting

The grievance meeting enables an individual to state their complaint, and for management to examine the issue, explore any potential resolution and come to a decision about what action to take. Good management practice in preparation for a grievance meeting is to check on the employee's employment record with the organisation and conduct any initial investigations that might shed light on the complaint. As suggested earlier, if the individual is to be represented at the meeting, an informal discussion with the representative in advance of the meeting may be useful.

In conducting the meeting itself, the focus should be on providing the employee with an opportunity to explain their complaint. The manager needs to use good watching, listening and questioning skills in order to gather information about the employee's grievance. Although the issues may be sensitive, it is important to ascertain the details of 'who, what, when and why' to ensure that a fair decision can be reached. Furthermore, the manager must explore what the employee wants the organisation to do if their grievance is found to have substance, as this will inform any potential resolution. On the basis of the information collected from the grievance interview, the manager then makes an assessment of the complaint/problem.

At the end of the meeting, management may conclude that the grievance is unfounded. However, all grievances are important to the individual concerned – so, if managers receive a complaint which they judge to be without substance, it is not good practice to dismiss it in an arbitrary manner. They should find out why, and how, it happened and also explain clearly why it is a complaint which merits no action. This not only sets the record straight but also allows everyone to see that all complaints are handled seriously. It is important that the issue is handled in a way which avoids the individual feeling ignored or snubbed.

Even if the grievance is unfounded, there may be a need to put measures in place to repair relationships between the complainant and other colleagues. For example, an employee may feel that their manager is placing undue pressure on them and treating them unfairly. Even if as a result of the grievance meeting it is concluded that the complaint has not been substantiated, there is clearly an issue between the employee and their manager which needs to be resolved, possibly through further discussion or even mediation.

On the other hand, the manager hearing the grievance may decide at the end of the grievance meeting that further investigation is needed before a decision can be made. For example, do any agreements cover the area of dispute and what do they say? What is company policy on the issue? Are there any witnesses or other people with relevant information who should also be interviewed? In such circumstances management will make arrangements with the employee and their representative for a further meeting. Alternatively, following the meeting, management may decide that the employee's grievance is genuine. In this situation management informs the employee of the decision but will also try to make arrangements for a further meeting with the employee and their representative to resolve the issue.

Reflective activity 11.13

Losing patience...

You are the owner of a small firm. An employee has been complaining that she is being given too much work and cannot complete it on time. You have told the employee that her predecessor had no problem completing the same amount of work and that things got easier with experience. During this conversation, you lost your temper and raised your voice and as a result the employee became extremely upset. The employee is not happy and has put her grievance to you in writing. You invite the employee to a meeting to discuss the grievance. The meeting reveals that the employee has been working on a computer that is different from the one used by her predecessor and that the computer she has been using is slower and uses an older version of the software required to carry out the work. How should you deal with this grievance and what are the risks associated with the complaint?

Resolving the grievance

If the grievance is upheld, either in full or in part, the key task for the manager is to decide how the issue can be resolved. In some situations, if the grievance involves serious misconduct by another member of staff, disciplinary proceedings may be initiated. However, many grievances are not clear-cut but have the potential to escalate into litigation or collective disputes. In these cases, the manager will need to meet the complainant and their representative again to try to negotiate a settlement to the individual's grievance. In essence the techniques and skills used to negotiate a resolution in this context are similar to those needed in negotiating a pay claim or any other terms of employment.

There are normally three main stages to preparing for such a meeting:

- analysis (or the research stage);
- establishment of the aims as to how the grievance can be resolved while at the same time protecting management's interests;
- planning the strategy and tactics to achieve the established aims.

Analysis

The analysis stage involves the manager collecting and analysing relevant information to substantiate their proposals for resolving the individual employee's grievance. It also includes developing the argument(s) to be put to the employee and their representative to support the objective(s) that the manager is seeking to achieve. In managing grievances, the main sources of relevant information are the colleagues and employees who are regarded as likely to have factually useful information (for example, they witnessed the incident about which the employee is complaining) relevant to the issue that is the subject of the complaint.

The analysis stage also involves the managers checking whether the subject matter of the grievance has been complained about previously by employees, and if so, what the outcome was. Knowledge of such outcomes enables management to know whether any precedent exists for dealing with the employee's grievance. It is also important to explore whether there are any relevant company rules, custom and practice, personal contracts or collective agreements.

Any agreement on a resolution may be reached by the parties 'trading off' the details surrounding the issue but retaining certain principles. In making a decision about which 'details' to trade, management assess their value to the employee and anticipate which 'details' they will be prepared to trade in return.

For example, let us consider a complaint from a member of staff that their manager prevented them from accessing Facebook during work hours and in doing so insulted them in an abusive way. At the same time it was common practice for members of the team (including the manager) to access social media. The grievance meeting found that the complaint was based on fact but that this was related to concerns over the performance of the member of staff which had not been addressed. In developing a potential resolution, the manager handling the grievance would need to consider what the organisation's social media policy stated. They would also need to think about whether disciplinary action of any sort or an apology from the manager was warranted and the potential implications of this on team dynamics. If appropriate, they may ask whether the parties would be prepared to agree to mediation. A fundamental question would be what the employee wanted and whether they were prepared to take further action if the issue was not resolved.

 Reflective activity 11.14

If you were dealing with the issue above, how would you seek to resolve this and what would be your approach to negotiate a positive outcome?

Establishing a strategy

In order to achieve a satisfactory conclusion, it is important that clear management objectives are set prior to any meeting taking place. For example:

- How would they ideally like the grievance to be resolved?
- How do they think the grievance can realistically be resolved?
- What is the least that management will settle for (the fall-back position)?

As part of the objective-setting process it might be appropriate to construct an aspiration grid. A possible aspiration grid for the example just discussed is shown in Figure 11.3. It shows that management would ideally like the issue to be resolved through an apology to the team member. However, management have assessed this as an unrealistic position, partly because the line manager concerned does not think she has done anything wrong and because the complainant has threatened that, unless some formal action is taken against her, she will resign and claim constructive dismissal. They have established a 'realistic' position of a compromise resolution centring on an informal reprimand for the manager and an agreement to resolve the issue through mediation. Their fall-back position is to commence formal disciplinary action against the manager (with a likely outcome of a written warning) but they are concerned that this could lead the manager (who is generally well respected) to resign and have a negative impact on the team as a whole.

Figure 11.3 Aspiration grid

Possible resolution to grievance	MANAGEMENT			EMPLOYEE		
	Ideal	Real	Fall-back	Fall-back	Real	Ideal
Disciplinary action against manager	X	X	O	O	O	X
Informal reprimand against manager	X	O	O	O	X	X
Mediation	X	O	O	O	X	X
Apology	O	O	O	X	X	X

Key: **O** means prepared to trade; **X** means not prepared to trade.

Using an aspiration grid can help identify if there is a basis for a resolution to the employee's complaint and can help when meeting with the individual employee and their representative. At this point you would expect to present a broad picture of your proposals for resolving the grievance subject to discussion and negotiation between the parties.

Resolving the issue

If a resolution to a grievance is found – but before finally accepting that the resolution has been agreed – management must:

- be convinced that the employee understands what has been agreed;
- 'play back' to the employee what management understands the resolution of the grievance actually means, to prevent any misunderstanding from arising.

Once management has an oral agreement for the resolution of the employee's grievance, it should be written up. In many grievances this will take the form of an internal memo or letter to another manager and to the employee recording what has been agreed. For example, if the complaint was one of denial of access to a training opportunity, and it is upheld via the grievance-handling process, a manager will write to the personnel or the appropriate department reporting it has been agreed that the individual concerned should attend the next available appropriate training course. On the other hand, 'writing up' can, depending on the issue, take the form of a signed agreement by the manager concerned, the individual employee and their representative. The outcome is then reported to the appropriate interested parties. Clarity is important, and the manner of recording what has been agreed should leave no room for doubt.

Reflective activity 11.15

Outline the skills required of managers in successfully handling grievances. Which do you consider to be the most important – and why?

The appeal meeting

Where an employee feels that their grievance has not been satisfactorily resolved (i.e. they are unhappy with the decision) at the grievance meeting, they have the right of appeal. The employee should inform the employer of the grounds for their appeal without unreasonable delay and in writing. Appeals should likewise be heard without unreasonable delay, and at a time and place that should be notified to the employee well in advance. The appeal has to be handled with impartiality and by a more senior manager than the one who dealt with the original grievance. This senior manager must not previously have been involved in the case. Employees have a statutory right to be accompanied at any such appeal hearing. The outcome of the appeal must be communicated without unreasonable delay.

REAL-WORLD EXAMPLE 11.4

An appealing case (*Blackburn v Aldi Stores Ltd* UKEAT/0185/12)

Mr Blackburn worked for Aldi as a lorry driver. He lodged a formal grievance claiming that he had been mistreated by the deputy transport manager, who he argued had sworn at him; he also claimed there had been a lack of training and breaches in health and safety. The grievance was heard by the regional managing director, Mr Heatherington, who accepted certain parts of the grievance but rejected the allegations that Blackburn had been abused. Blackburn appealed against the decision. Mr Heatherington heard the appeal but dismissed it after a hearing which only lasted 20 minutes. Importantly, the company's procedure did not specify that the appeal should be heard by an impartial party. Blackburn resigned and brought a claim for constructive unfair dismissal, arguing that Aldi had breached the implied term of trust and confidence by effectively denying him a proper appeal against the grievance decision, because Mr Heatherington had heard both the original grievance and the appeal.

The EAT found in favour of Blackburn and concluded that failing to have a different person hearing the appeal could amount to a breach of the implied term of trust and confidence, entitling the employee to resign and claim constructive unfair dismissal. It was 'not easy to see' why an organisation of Aldi's size was unable to provide an impartial hearing by a manager not previously involved. As the tribunal had failed to make a proper assessment of the seriousness of the breach, the EAT sent the case back to the tribunal to reconsider.

In small organisations, even when there is no senior manager available, another manager should, if possible, hear the appeal. If this is not possible, consider whether the owner or, in the case of a charity, the board of trustees, should hear the appeal. Whoever hears the appeal should consider it as impartially as possible. As with the first meeting, the employer should write to the employee with a decision on their grievance as soon as possible. The employer should also tell the employee if the appeal meeting is the final stage of the grievance procedure. Some larger organisations do permit a further appeal to a higher level of management, such as a director.

Dignity at work

Harassment based on gender, race and disability, and bullying at work have received increasing attention in recent years as organisations and worker representative bodies have become more concerned about the dignity of individuals in the workplace. As we have seen in this chapter, bullying and harassment is a major cause of employee grievances. For example, in the National Health Service, around a quarter of all employees reported being bullied or harassed by other staff in 2018. Furthermore, Roger Kline and Duncan Lewis (2019) have calculated that bullying and harassment in the NHS costs the taxpayer over £2 billion every year due to absence, presenteeism, lost management time and reduced productivity.

It is important to distinguish between bullying and harassment, because as we observed in Chapter 7, harassment (when related to a protected characteristic) has a specific legal definition under the Equality Act 2010:

A person (A) harasses another (B) if:

1. A engages in unwanted conduct related to a relevant protected characteristic, and
2. the conduct has the purpose or effect of:
   i. violating B's dignity, or
   ii. creating an intimidating, hostile, degrading, humiliating or offensive environment for B.

There are two things to note here: first, the word 'unwanted' firmly establishes that it is the perception of the victim of harassment that is key. Second, even if an individual's conduct is not meant to harass or cause someone distress, if it has that *effect*, it will be unlawful.

However, bullying is much less clear cut and it is important to understand that, at present, there is no legislation that specifically makes bullying in the workplace unlawful. Instead, the only legal option for an employee who is bullied is to resign and claim unfair constructive dismissal, although in most cases a tribunal would expect the claimant to have first attempted to raise a complaint through internal organisational procedures. It is therefore not surprising that many victims of bullying choose not to raise their concerns.

Bullying is defined by Acas (2023b) as:

> unwanted behaviour from a person or group that is either: offensive, intimidating, malicious, or insulting, an abuse or misuse of power that undermines, humiliates, or causes physical or emotional harm to someone.

However, it is argued that there is a continuum of behaviour (Evesson et al, 2015; Fevre et al, 2012). This can range from clumsy management, where an employee feels that their performance is being unfairly criticised or scrutinised, to verbal abuse and even to physical violence. Acas (2023b) give the following examples of behaviour that could constitute bullying or harassment:

- Constantly criticising someone's work;
- Spreading malicious rumours about someone;
- Constantly putting someone down in meetings;
- Deliberately giving someone a heavier workload than everyone else;
- Excluding someone from team social events;
- Putting humiliating, offensive or threatening comments or photos on social media.

Reflective activity 11.16

Have you or has someone that you know been subject to any of the behaviours outlined here? What impact did this have and how was the issue raised and/or resolved?

Bullying and/or harassment can make someone feel anxious and humiliated. Feelings of anger and frustration at being unable to cope may also be triggered. Some employees may try to retaliate in some way. Others may become frightened and demotivated. Stress and loss of self-confidence and self-esteem caused by bullying and/or harassment can lead to job insecurity, illness, absence from work and even resignation. Almost always, job performance is affected and relations in the workplace suffer.

Employers are responsible for preventing bullying and harassing behaviour. It is in their interests to make it clear to everyone that such behaviour will not be tolerated. As shown in the example of the National Health Service earlier, the costs to the organisation may include poor employment relations, low morale, lower productivity and efficiency, and potentially the resignation of staff. An organisational statement to all staff about the standards expected can make it easier for all individuals to be fully aware of their responsibilities to others. Furthermore, if an employer fails to take action to prevent or address such behaviours, they may be vulnerable to a claim of discrimination and/or unfair constructive dismissal.

While bullying and harassment are complex and are inevitably shaped by differing perceptions, they essentially reflect an imbalance of power. Consequently, in many, if not all, cases, the recipient of such behaviour has less power than the bully or the harasser. This poses significant problems for organisations and raises important questions about the suitability of grievance procedures, as invariably these are controlled and managed by senior managers, with little impartial external scrutiny. The recent case of bullying and harassment at the Houses of Parliament brings this tension into sharp focus.

REAL-WORLD EXAMPLE 11.5

Bullying and harassment at Westminster

In 2017, serious allegations began to emerge of widespread bullying and harassment of staff working for Members of Parliament. These ranged from unreasonable behaviour and excessive pressure to accusations of sexual harassment and assault. A key problem for those working for MPs was that they are directly employed by those MPs and therefore were not covered by the wider HR policies and practices of other staff working at Westminster. In addition, many felt that it was impossible to complain because of the potential impact on their career. Furthermore, many of those working for MPs had very strong political and personal loyalties, which created a further barrier to raising concerns.

A cross-party working group was then established to develop an independent complaints and grievance policy, which reported in February 2018. It recommended the introduction of a code of behaviour, an independent complaints and grievance scheme and the provision of third-party HR advice. Due to continuing concern, an inquiry chaired by Gemma White QC was set up in July 2018. Her findings, published on 10 July 2019 (White, 2019), made for sobering reading. It contained many first-hand accounts from MPs' staff, including the following comments:

> 'My time working for [MP] was the most stressful and hostile period of my life. My entire sense of self was crushed, and by the end, I felt incapable and incompetent, despite all of the work I had done in that office.'

> 'Working in the Houses of Parliament is meant to be an honour, but the actions of some MPs and Staff Members destroys any sense of pride. We are expendable staffers, with no independent HR service, and therefore no recourse. Responding to this inquiry is the only action I have ever taken to report what I have seen, and so expect a vast majority of other cases are lurking below the surface elsewhere.'

> '[The MP] absolutely crushed my confidence and made me feel worthless. Getting away from [them], that office and (I am sad to say it, but) Parliament was the best move for me. It is only in my more recent jobs that I realise actually how inappropriate [their] behaviour was and how little scrutiny process is in place.'

White concluded that ex-members of staff should be allowed to make complaints about historical actions before 2017, and also that the system of HR help and advice, introduced in 2018, should be extended. White argued that MPs should not be seen as small businesses. Instead, the report called for each member to be required to adopt and follow employment practices and procedures aligned with those followed in other public sector workplaces and for the introduction of a properly resourced and staffed HR department in the House of Commons to support members and their staff.

However, some commentators have questioned whether greater external scrutiny is needed if the treatment of staff is to be improved in the long term. Furthermore, it remains the case that MPs cannot be dismissed if they are found guilty of serious misconduct but merely suspended and potentially subject to recall.

Reflective activity 11.17

Do you think the measures outlined here will have a positive impact in addressing the problem of bullying and harassment at Westminster? To what extent does this example provide lessons for the way that employers outside Westminster should manage these issues?

A particular tension within most standard grievance procedures is that the line manager plays a key role. The reality in many bullying and harassment cases is that managers are often the alleged perpetrators. Therefore, many organisations have developed specific policies and procedures which offer increased protection and support to complainants.

In organisations where a bullying and harassment policy exists, it is normal for a dual system to operate. The initial action is usually confined to the specifics of the complaint within the procedure laid down for managing harassment and/or bullying. If the problem cannot be resolved within the limits of the policy and is proved to be an issue that merits disciplinary proceedings, the disciplinary procedure is triggered. In addition, specialist dignity-at-work policies make it possible for a complaint to be made to someone other than the line manager, as they are often the subject of many complaints of this type. In addition, complainants are commonly provided with sources of support and advice, in addition to union or employee representatives.

In dealing with allegations of harassment and/or bullying, the manager dealing with the complaint first conducts a thorough investigation to establish whether there is a *prima facie* case of harassment and/or bullying for the accused employee to answer. If the manager decides, on the basis of the investigation, that there is a case to answer, disciplinary proceedings may be instigated against the accused employee. However, as we have seen, many cases are not clear-cut. The definition of 'bullying' in particular is inevitably subjective. In recent years, researchers have noted an increase in the numbers of bullying claims related to processes of performance management. In essence, employees believe that they are being bullied by their manager, while the manager believes that they are simply trying to 'manage' the employee. In some situations, therefore, complaints of bullying may reflect a breakdown of relationships between colleagues and particularly between employees and their line managers. Here, there may be significant scope for early and informal resolution. In fact, there tends to be a greater emphasis on the potential of workplace mediation in 'dignity at work' policies and procedures than in more generic grievance procedures.

In Chapter 9 we provided the example of Northumbria Healthcare Trust, which developed an integrated conflict management system designed, in part, to address the problem of bullying and harassment. The use of mediation to resolve bullying cases, where appropriate, is a key element of this approach. This is also reflected in Manchester University's well-respected 'Dignity at Work and Study Procedure'. For a harassment or bullying case, four options open to complainants are set out in the procedures.

EXTRACT FROM MANCHESTER UNIVERSITY'S DIGNITY AT WORK PROCEDURE

- Many complaints can be resolved informally and this approach is encouraged where possible.
- Mediation is also available at any stage of the procedure and offers a less adversarial method of dispute resolution.
- However, if complainants do not feel able to follow either the informal procedure or mediation, or if the incident is too serious for such approaches, they should proceed straight to the formal stage.
- As a general principle, the decision of whether to progress a complaint is up to the individual. However, the University has a duty to protect all staff and may pursue the matter independently if it considers it appropriate to do so.

It is important to reinforce the point that mediation will not be appropriate in all cases of bullying and harassment and care must be taken in deciding whether this is a viable option. Fundamentally, it is up to the complainant to decide on the course of action they want to take and to activate the formal procedure at any point. At Manchester University, the complaint is not made to the victim's line manager, but to an HR manager, who acknowledges receipt of the complaint and will refer the matter to an appropriate investigating officer. The university also provides harassment advisors to advise and support employees through the process.

Different organisations define their acceptable standards of behaviour differently, particularly with respect to gross misconduct. In many organisations, harassment and/or bullying is regarded as gross misconduct, carrying the threat of summary dismissal if proved. If this is the case, this should be clearly spelled out to employees in the organisation's policy statement on harassment and/or dignity at work. Of course, this needs to be underpinned by training and other initiatives to raise awareness of bullying and harassment and to provide staff with the skills and knowledge they need to address such behaviour.

There are, therefore, good reasons for dealing with harassment and/or bullying complaints outside of the general grievance procedure. First, there is a reasonable chance that the person who is the subject of the complaint is the line manager of the employee making the complaint. This can make it difficult to resolve the grievance as near to the point of its origin as possible. Second, there is a link between grievance, discipline and harassment. The role of the employment relations professional in harassment/bullying complaints is to act as a back-up for line managers in managing the issue, by providing them with general expertise and support, advising them on the appropriate course of action, and ensuring that they have access to training programmes to handle dignity-at-work issues. However, one area that is particularly challenging relates to the dividing line between harmless 'banter' and bullying and harassment. Managers will understandably want to create a good atmosphere and build morale within their team, but employees will have different views on what is acceptable. As we have pointed out in cases of bullying and harassment, the most important perspective is that of the person who feels that their dignity is being violated or that they are working in an intimidating, hostile, degrading, humiliating or offensive environment. Real-world example 11.6 is an extreme example: however, the tribunal decision clearly shows that many of those involved did not accept that their behaviour was unusual or unacceptable. In short, a toxic and racist culture had been allowed to develop which was ignored in favour of hitting performance targets.

REAL-WORLD EXAMPLE 11.6

K Sidhu v Exertis (UK) Ltd and Others 1400943/2017

Sidhu was a British national of mixed Scottish and Indian descent. He is heterosexual and a Sikh and a Christian. He was employed by Exertis as a Brand Manager. He worked in an open-plan office with a team which was highly sales-driven. According to the tribunal, 'a culture existed in the claimant's workplace where crude sexual innuendo and express sexual reference was considered entertaining and, in order to fit in to the culture, it was necessary to enter into jokes and discussions of that nature'. According to another Exertis employee, 'It's a male orientated environment. There is banter, on the limit, over the limit. If you are of a more sensitive disposition you may struggle.' One example of Sidhu's treatment was that his name would be regularly changed to 'Sidoku', although it was also the case that other members of the team were referred to by nicknames. A range of other behaviours were reported by the claimant including:

- Pretending to Sidhu that a company event was black tie, causing him to buy and arrive in a tuxedo;
- Hiding his laptop and other equipment;
- Sticking a gigolo business card on his monitor;
- Referring to the area where Sidhu lived as looking like a terrorist war zone and comparing it to Aleppo in Syria;
- One of Sidhu's colleagues was alleged to have said to him, 'How does it feel being the only ethnic on the team, mate? Without you retail is 100 per cent white and that's not a bad thing';
- One colleague sang, 'Sidhu, Sidhu, Sidhu he is bigger than me and he has a bomb in his shoe'.

Although Sidhu initially put up with this behaviour, he eventually complained to his manager but the tribunal found that the manager showed little interest. While he was aware of what was going on, he did little about it apart from having what the tribunal described as 'one ineffective conversation with the team'. Eventually Sidhu lodged a formal grievance, however, the tribunal found that the investigation into the grievance was limited to interviewing those people against whom Sidhu had made allegations. The subsequent grievance outcome 'shied away from making a proper decision' on the basis that in respect of many of the allegations there was little independent corroboration. The tribunal concluded that Sidhu had been subject to direct race discrimination and harassment and been unfairly constructively dismissed.

The Sidhu case underlines the need for organisations to establish very clear expectations around acceptable behaviour and to put robust policies and procedures in place. However, policies alone are not enough; they need to be reflected in the way that people are managed. Moreover, it reinforces the importance of creating channels through which workers and employees can voice concerns and have these properly investigated and addressed.

Reflective activity 11.18

If you were an HR practitioner who received a similar complaint to the one made in the Sidhu case, how would you deal with the situation? What sort of guidance would you put in place to ensure that this type of situation did not occur in the future?

11.7 Summary

This chapter began by examining the dynamic process through which grievances are formed and escalate. This discussion highlighted the critical importance of the way that managers respond to initial complaints of mistreatment. Perhaps most importantly, it suggests that if managers deal with such concerns quickly and appropriately, trust can be rebuilt and commitment to the organisation strengthened. Unfortunately, many managers lack the confidence to do this and, as a result, grievances often become intractable and extremely damaging for the individual involved and the organisation.

Managers should ideally attempt to resolve grievances informally at an early stage and, as we saw in respect of disciplinary issues in the previous chapter, employment relations professionals have a key role to play in providing the support and advice that line managers need. In addition, good relationships with union and employee representatives are valuable in providing channels through which resolutions can be found. It is also important to note recent research that suggests that managers need greater clarity about the meaning of informal resolution. Therefore, it is worth considering whether policies can include more detailed guidance on informal processes and possibly signpost alternative approaches such as mediation.

Of course, not all grievances can be resolved in this way and, for more serious complaints, there is little alternative to formal procedure. If this is the case, the chapter sets out sound advice as to how grievance procedures can be implemented in a fair and effective manner. Importantly, unlike disciplinary issues, grievance outcomes are not clear-cut and rest on the wishes of the complainant. Therefore, there is the potential to negotiate outcomes which are satisfactory to the employee and also serve to rebuild the employment relationship.

Grievances relating to bullying and harassment pose particular challenges for organisations. There is growing evidence that this is becoming an increasing problem, particularly as organisations seek to manage performance more closely in order to cut costs and increase efficiency. Bullying and harassment covers a wide range of negative behaviours and therefore organisations need to develop a flexible approach to its management. In some instances, this may involve the careful use of mediation, but robust procedures that provide increased support and protection for victims are vital. Many employers talk about having a 'zero-tolerance' approach to bullying and harassment, but if this is to be made a reality, they must ensure that all staff have confidence not only to raise these issues, but that these will be acted on.

KEY LEARNING POINTS

- The extent to which employee grievances escalate and their implications for the organisation are dependent on the adequacy of the managerial response. Recognition of the issue and prompt action to seek a resolution can rebuild the employment relationship and the complainant's commitment to the organisation, but a failure to address the complaint can deepen the seriousness of the grievance with damaging consequences.
- Most employee complaints against management behaviour do not reach the formal grievance procedure. Often, this is due to the inadequacy of procedures or a lack of confidence in management's capacity to react reasonably.
- The grievance procedure ensures that employees are treated in a fair and consistent manner and they know where they stand and know what to expect. In managing employee complaints, management should be guided by a number of principles: fairness, transparency, consistency and promptness.
- In managing grievances, management's objective is to settle the employee's complaint as near as possible to the point of its source. Early and informal resolution can be supported through a consistent employment relations approach and high-trust relationships with union and employee representatives. However, managers may need clear guidance on what informal resolution entails.

- Where a grievance is well founded, the manager must decide on the appropriate response. In some cases this will be clear cut and disciplinary proceedings will need to be started if there has been serious misconduct. Where the issues are more complex, a process of negotiation can be used to find a mutually acceptable outcome.
- Bullying and harassment are a growing problem for many organisations and need a targeted response. This means training for staff and managers; the possible use of workplace mediation; and the development of bespoke, robust policies and procedures that can win the confidence of organisational stakeholders.

Review Questions

1. Frank has been given the most unpopular job in his department for three weeks in a row. He thinks this is unfair and that the supervisor should be sharing it among all the employees in his department. You are the HR representative, and Frank has approached you and voiced his discontent. How should you deal with the situation?
2. You are responsible for conducting workshops for new line managers on employment relations techniques. One of the topics you have been asked to deal with is managing employee complaints in the workplace. Explain, and justify, the key areas of knowledge and skills that you would cover in your workshop.
3. Explain the principles that underpin a grievance procedure.
4. Explain, and justify, the criteria you would use to evaluate whether a grievance procedure was operating effectively.
5. An employee has approached you as her HR adviser. She feels that she is being bullied by her line manager and asks for your advice. She reports that the line manager constantly shouts at her in front of colleagues. She also alleges that he has made sexual innuendos towards her. What advice do you give the employee, and how will you deal with the situation?

Explore further

Acas (2015) *Code of Practice on Discipline and Grievance Procedures*. Available from: https://www.acas.org.uk/acas-code-of-practice-on-disciplinary-and-grievance-procedures/html (archived at https://perma.cc/K7J5-CAMR)

Acas (2020) *Discipline and Grievances at Work: The Acas guide*. Available from: https://www.acas.org.uk/acas-guide-to-discipline-and-grievances-at-work (archived at https://perma.cc/GR52-L3FD)

Acas (2023b) *Discrimination and Bullying*. Available from: https://www.acas.org.uk/discrimination-and-bullying (archived at https://perma.cc/4WME-JZZ4) [accessed 4 June 2024]

Evesson, J, Oxenbridge, S and Taylor, D (2015) *Seeking Better Solutions: Tackling bullying and ill-treatment in Britain's workplaces*, Acas Policy Paper. Available from: https://www.acas.org.uk/media/4498/Seeking-better-solutions-tackling-bullying-and-ill-treatment-in-Britains-workplaces/pdf/Seeking-better-solutions-tackling-bullying-and-ill-treatment-in-Britains-workplaces.pdf (archived at https://perma.cc/HH9T-6H8E)

Lewis, D, Sargeant, M and Schwab, B (2023) *Employment Law: The essentials*, 16th edn, Kogan Page, London

Olson-Buchanan, J and Boswell, W (2008) An integrative model of experiencing and responding to mistreatment at work, *Academy of Management Review*, **33**(1), pp 76–96

Saundry, R Wibberley, G, Wright, A and Hollinrake, A (2023) *Mediation and Early Resolution in East Lancashire Hospitals NHS Trust*, Acas Research Paper. Available from: https://www.acas.org.uk/early-resolution-in-east-lancs-hospitals-NHS-trust/html (archived at https://perma.cc/37DB-KDBM)

Websites

www.acas.org.uk (archived at https://perma.cc/U7C7-PK53) is the website of Acas and will give you access to the Acas Code on Grievance and Disciplinary Procedures and other guidance for employers on the management of grievances and bullying and harassment.

www.gov.uk/handling-employee-grievance (archived at https://perma.cc/X4C9-5H4W) is the government website which gives advice to employers on how to manage grievances.

www.worksmart.org.uk (archived at https://perma.cc/52US-VQJG) is from the TUC and gives access to its guidance on understanding grievance procedures.

12 Managing redundancies

Overview

The earlier chapters of this book have highlighted the dynamic context of employment relations – the intensification of global competition, rapid advances in automation and artificial intelligence, and in the UK, the impact of Brexit and the pandemic. In this environment, HR practitioners need to respond effectively to organisational change and inevitably this will mean at some point managing redundancies. The starting point of this chapter is an exploration of the organisational and personal impact of redundancy and the importance of looking for alternatives wherever possible. Of course, all redundancies have damaging effects, but these can be ameliorated where organisations handle the process in a sensitive and equitable way. To this end, we examine the case for robust redundancy policies and procedures and consider research into experiences of the managers who handle redundancies. This highlights the need for support and training to be provided to those who have to take on this difficult role. Consideration of alternatives is an important element of redundancy consultation, and we examine the legal obligations of employers relating to collective consultations and the need for employers to consult with individuals to ensure that any redundancy dismissals are deemed reasonable and fair. We then discuss the importance of adopting fair selection criteria when employers are forced to make compulsory redundancies. We close the chapter by examining how organisations can look after the well-being of the employees who remain in employment after the redundancy. This covers topics such as counselling, outplacement and the issue of 'survivor syndrome'.

LEARNING OUTCOMES

When you have completed this chapter, you should be able to:

- understand and critically evaluate the connection between redundancy and the management of change;
- critically assess the roles played by managers tasked with making staff redundant;
- explain how to produce a redundancy policy and associated procedures;
- understand and provide advice on the legal framework in respect of redundancy, in particular the requirements on consultation;
- evaluate the long-term implications of redundancy for organisational survivors and identify appropriate measures for managing this issue.

12.1 Introduction

Redundancy and restructuring would appear to be an inevitable part of organisational life in a market economy. At the end of 2023, just under one in five employers reported that they were intending to make redundancies in the first three months of 2024 (CIPD, 2024d). If one takes a historical view, there is an overall downward trend in the rate of redundancies per 1,000 employees (see Figure 12.1) from more than 8 in 1995 to 3.3 in 2023. However, within that time there have been significant peaks, coinciding with the 2008/09 financial crash and the Covid pandemic.

Figure 12.1 Redundancy rate (UK), 1995–2023

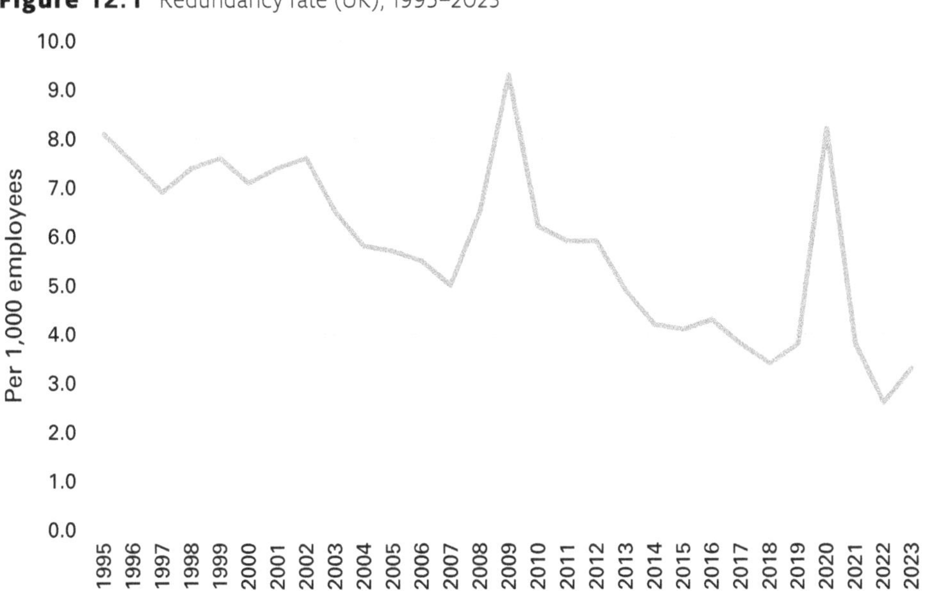

SOURCE: Office for National Statistics

Significantly, how we handle redundancy is crucial for long-term business and organisational success. However, the rapid pace of technological change underlines the challenge of managing fundamental changes in the structure of work and employment. For example, Pakes (2019: 10) reports OECD estimates that:

> More than 1 in 10 UK jobs face a more than 70 per cent probability of complete automation and another 3 in 10 are likely to see significant change to tasks and content as a result of AI [artificial intelligence] and robotics

Therefore, in this chapter, we look at not only the legal obligations with which employers have to comply when considering redundancies, but the ways in which organisations can try to ensure that the redundancy process is managed fairly and equitably.

12.2 Defining redundancy

Redundancy is defined in section 139 of the Employment Rights Act (1996) as follows:

- **a** The fact that [the] employer has ceased or intends to cease –
  - i. To carry on the business for the purposes of which the employee was employed by him, or
  - ii. To carry on that business in the place where the employee was so employed, or
- **b** The fact that the requirements of that business –
  - i. For employees to carry out work of a particular kind, or
  - ii. For employees to carry out work of a particular kind in the place where the employee was employed by the employer, have ceased or diminished or are expected to cease or diminish.

To put this in everyday language: redundancy occurs when the employer closes down completely, moves premises, requires fewer people for particular jobs or requires no people for particular jobs. Redundancy can also occur when an individual has been laid off or kept on short-time working for a period. However, there are certain situations in which employees may perceive that they have been made redundant but employers could argue that the definition of redundancy is not met. For example, an employee may have a clause in their contract which provides for them to work at more than one site. If one site closes, the employer could argue that there is no redundancy. Therefore, it is important, when drawing up the employee's statement of terms and particulars of employment as required by the Employment Rights Act (1996), to identify whether 'the employee is required or permitted to work at various places' (section 1(4)(h)).

Even if an employee has no mobility clause in their contract, in a redundancy situation, they could be offered alternative employment at another location. If the employee refuses 'suitable alternative employment', there will be no redundancy and therefore they will not qualify for a redundancy payment. Whether the offer was suitable would depend on the distance of relocation and the ease of travelling to the new location. Location is not the only consideration. An employee could also argue that alternative employment that involves a substantial change in role, responsibility or terms and conditions is not 'suitable' and consequently that they retain their right to refuse the offer and be paid a redundancy payment. If an employee is unsure about the suitability of alternative employment, they can opt for a trial period of four weeks, after which time, if the job is not suitable, a redundancy payment is still payable.

REAL-WORLD EXAMPLE 12.1

***Stevenson v Mid Essex Hospital Services NHS Trust* (2021) UKEAT**

The three claimants were employed as Head of Human Resources across three separate NHS Trusts. However, a decision was made to develop an integrated HR function working across the three Trusts in which they were employed. This made their posts redundant, but they were instead offered the role of Senior HR Lead on the same grade, pay, hours of work and working at the same location. However, the claimants initially declined this offer due to a range of concerns including reduced status, lack of role clarity and job insecurity. The HR Director met the claimants to discuss possible changes to the role descriptor to allay these concerns, but these suggestions were not sent in writing to the claimants before their employment ended. The employer then refused to pay a redundancy payment on the grounds that they had unreasonably refused offers of suitable alternative employment and that they would not be entitled to redundancy payments.

An employment tribunal found in favour of the employer and dismissed the claim for redundancy payments. The tribunal concluded that the offer was a suitable alternative. In addition, the refusal to accept was unreasonable because they had a closed mind to the offer. In part this was due to the prospect of substantial redundancy payments and negative feeling towards the HR Director. However, the Employment Appeal Tribunal overturned the decision and remitted the claims to a fresh hearing. It concluded that the tribunal had not examined the practical impact of all the differences that the claimants had highlighted.

12.3 Redundancy and the management of change

The fluctuating nature of the economic cycle means that we become used to hearing the words 'downturn', 'slowdown' and 'downsize'. However, redundancies, or more specifically the way they are managed, are not simply a function of external factors and shocks. In investigating changes in organisational ownership, Goyer et al (2016) found that downsizing was driven, in part, by growing financialisation whereby shareholder value is prioritised above all else and particularly the interests of employees. Furthermore, redundancies were more likely in economies with a more 'permissive' institutional culture, with fewer legal restraints and weaker trade unions.

Therefore, the inherent short-termism within the structure of the UK economy runs the risk of ignoring the value of retaining the skills and knowledge of workers as part of an alternative longer-term strategy for organisational success. In short, organisations have choices in how they respond to challenging economic conditions and HR practitioners have a key role in shaping strategy in this respect. Interestingly, there is some evidence that, in response to the 2008/09 recession and the subsequent economic turmoil, organisations did seek alternatives to redundancy, often working with unions and staff to avoid job losses. Forty-one per cent of workplaces introduced a wage freeze, while 19 per cent reduced overtime in response to recessionary pressures, compared with just 13 per cent who made staff compulsorily redundant and 7 per cent who sought voluntary redundancies. Similarly, commentators also pointed to the co-operation between unions, employers' organisations and the government in developing responses to the Covid pandemic (Coulter, 2020). The development of the Coronavirus Job Retention Scheme (CJRS) not only showed what genuine partnership working could achieve but also that active government policy can also play a key role in minimising and reducing the impact of redundancy. In total nearly 12 million workers were furloughed during the pandemic at a cost of £70 billion. While redundancies increased significantly during the pandemic, research conducted by the House of Commons Library argued: 'It is clear that many of the workers on furlough would have been made redundant if the scheme had not been in place, and that the CJRS has limited the impact of the pandemic on the labour market' (Francis-Devine et al, 2021: 6). It is, therefore, a lost opportunity that partnership working between government, employers and trade unions was not maintained as the UK returned to business as usual.

Reflective activity 12.1

Is redundancy the only option? If your organisation was faced with the possibility of redundancies, what realistic alternatives could be considered? As an HR professional, what strategies would you use to avoid redundancies?

Decisions on redundancy, because they are often made to address an immediate and short-term problem, can be counterproductive. They can engender a mood of disillusionment and cynicism that can destroy any of the short-term financial gains of a redundancy exercise. Stevens (2022) has developed an eight-stage model that aims to attenuate the negative impacts of downsizing for individuals and organisations.

1. Organisations should define their goals – there needs to be a clear alignment between the rationale for redundancies and organisational strategy, vision and culture.
2. There needs to be a transparent and demonstrable effort to contain costs and make savings with the aim of minimising or avoiding redundancies.
3. Organisations should analyse the wider implications of redundancies and develop a clear implementation plan, in consultation with key stakeholders.

4 The managers and other key players who will have the responsibility to implement the plan need proper training in order to respond to employees with sensitivity, maintain morale and minimise risks of legal challenge.
5 After training has been completed, it is important to develop a strategy as to how the redundancies will be implemented in practice. This will mean deciding whether compulsory redundancies will be necessary and the skills that the organisation will need to retain.
6 The organisation will then need to develop a clear and transparent approach to communicating with staff. This is vital in reducing stress, maintaining morale and retaining staff.
7 Support should be put in place for both potential victims and survivors. In that, the way that those subject to a redundancy are treated will shape the attitudes of those that retain their jobs. This can include career guidance and advice and support for mental health.
8 The organisation needs to recognise the potential impact on the survivors of redundancy. This will include recognising negative effects and taking clear steps to address concerns. There should be a particular focus on the contribution of staff to organisation success and sustainability.

This model underlines the importance of developing a systematic approach to redundancy and one which includes key stakeholders at all times.

Reflective activity 12.2

Have there been any redundancies where you work in the past two years? How was this handled and what impact did it have on the organisation and the remaining employees? To what extent did your organisation follow the eight-step model outlined here?

12.4 Managing redundancy – the role of the 'envoy'

A critical role in managing redundancy is played by those managers and HR professionals tasked with 'delivering the news' to employees. Ian Ashman (2012, 2014) conducted a study for Acas into what he termed downsizing 'envoys'. Crucially, the research identified the skills and experience those envoys need to do that job effectively. Fundamentally, for Ashman, the 'primary endeavour of the task' reflected in the envoy's role includes: 'tact, diplomacy and the maintenance of constructive and co-operative relationships among victims and survivors rather than simply and coldly dismissing employees' (2016: 153). In this context, he set out the key considerations in the management of the redundancy process:

- The message must be communicated accurately and with sensitivity.
- A balance is needed between strategic intent, procedural fairness and humane treatment.

- People leaving the organisation do so with dignity (especially given the moral and PR implications).
- Workers being redeployed are transferred into roles for which they are suited.
- Survivors experience and witness a just process and can feel comfortable in their task of taking the organisation forward.

Importantly, organisations often underestimate the difficulties facing envoys who are rarely trained or prepared for the role. Adjectives that envoys used to describe the emotional impact of the role included: 'traumatic', 'nerve wracking', 'dreadful', 'very upsetting', 'hideous', and ultimately, 'stressful'. A more recent study into the role of envoys conducted by Stevens and Hannibal (2023) argues that it is important to take into account that they are asked to manage redundancies fairly infrequently. Therefore, this involves a change in focus from maintaining and developing the employment relationship to ending it. This exacerbates the negative impacts on managers, which can also extend to other key stakeholders such as employee and trade union representatives.

Ashman found that envoys coped with this challenge in a number of ways which ranged from emotional hardening and cognitive distancing (separating the 'downsizing me' from the 'real me') to using procedures as a psychological support that de-personalises individuals and events. Despite the heightened emotional burden, the envoys always felt it right and proper that they should take responsibility for delivering the news of downsizing to their subordinates and colleagues because they knew them best and wanted to provide support.

Reflective activity 12.3

Have you had to deliver the news of redundancy? If so, what was the impact on you and how could you have been supported to carry out this task?

Significantly, the research highlighted the unique relationship between the line manager and the HR practitioner as joint envoys and raises several important issues for us to consider in any redundancy situation. For line managers, the role of envoy became additional to their normal role and therefore led to role overload. They also often felt isolated because they could not talk to other managers in a similar position. In contrast, HR envoys had access to others in their organisation and in the HR community to share their experiences and were able also to incorporate the role into their normal workload.

Both Ashman and Stevens and Hannibal point to the need for HR interventions to provide envoys with training, support and guidance. The ability of the envoy to manage that pressure effectively will come with more experience of the role. However, organisations need to do more to help envoys prepare. This could include mentoring, role-playing in CPD training and greater understanding of the psychological and emotional impact of organisational change. Petzer (2020) also argues that, in addition to training, envoys should be given access to counselling and the chance to meet and share their experiences with other envoys. Similarly, ensuring that people 'buy into' rather than feel coerced into the role, and providing support to deal with the inevitable emotional stress they themselves will encounter, are essential. This is particularly the case when having to deal with colleagues with whom they have worked, often for a long time.

Reflective activity 12.4

Imagine that you are an HR practitioner tasked with supporting a manager who is about to meet 25 staff to inform them that there needs to be a reduction of six posts. How would you advise that they handle this situation? What skills do you think managers need to deliver bad news such as redundancy?

12.5 Redundancy policy and procedures

For HR professionals, job security policies and the avoidance of redundancy are an increasingly important part of the employment relations framework. Organisational change leads to the inevitable weakening of employees' confidence in their employer's ability to maintain job security. If redundancy is unavoidable, 'good practice' dictates that organisations have policies and procedures in place that enable them to deal with a difficult situation with sensitivity and equity. Policies and procedures are important not only because the law has certain requirements but also because there is a good business case for making sure that redundancies are managed in a consistent way.

A statement of policy on redundancy might in some ways be better classified as an organisation's statement of intent in respect of its commitment to maintaining employment. For an example policy, see the following box. Such a policy statement does not make any commitment to no compulsory redundancies, but it is an important first step in recognising people as an important asset and can be a key plank in building a partnership between management and workforce.

Reflective activity 12.5

Does your organisation have a redundancy policy? If it does, what does it say about job security? What other policies is it linked to and why?

Redundancy procedures should be written and designed to cater for the individuality of each organisation. Draft procedures can be obtained from professional bodies such as the CIPD or from commercial organisations, but they should always be treated as guidelines or templates and be amended to meet individual organisations' requirements. The following are some extracts from a redundancy policy that indicate some of the steps which have to be taken when redundancies do arise.

1. Policy statement

1.1 The company is committed to working in partnership with its employees in order to ensure its success and sustainability. In doing so, it will make every effort to ensure security of employment for its employees. However, there may be situations where a change in the overall level of employment or the structure of employment cannot be avoided. In such circumstances, the company will consult with trade unions and employees to find ways, where possible, of avoiding or reducing the need for redundancies and minimising the impact on employees.

2. Scope and principles

2.1 This procedure will apply to any situation in which the company proposes to dismiss an employee due to redundancy. For the purposes of this procedure, redundancy is defined in accordance with Section 139(1) of the Employment Rights Act 1996 or any legislation that may supersede this.

2.2 In applying this procedure, the following principles will be followed:

a. Before reaching any decision to make an employee, or employees, redundant, the company will consult with recognised trade unions and affected employee(s). In doing so, it will comply with all duties imposed by legislation.
b. The company will do everything possible to avoid compulsory redundancies, reduce the number of redundancies and minimise the impact on employees.
c. Employees may be accompanied by a trade union representative or work colleague at any meeting under this procedure.

3. Voluntary redundancy, early retirement or reduced hours

3.1 In the event of a proposal for redundancies, the company will make every effort to secure staff reductions through voluntary redundancy, early retirement and/or a change in working hours.

4. Redundancy consultation

4.1 Before reaching any decision to make an employee, or employees, redundant, the company will consult with recognised trade unions and affected employee(s). Consultation will be undertaken as early as possible. The company will provide recognised trade unions with details of the proposals, which will include: the reasons for the proposals; the number and types of employees affected; the level of potential redundancy payments; and any measures for avoiding or mitigating redundancies.

4.2 The company will consider any alternative proposals put forward. Consultations will be meaningful and will seek to reach agreement on ways in which redundancies can be avoided or any impact mitigated. If necessary, the company will also consult over any selection criteria in the event of compulsory redundancies.

4.3 If the company is proposing that 20 or more employees are made redundant, minimum consultation periods will apply in accordance with existing legislation:

- 20 to 99 proposed redundancies over a period of 90 days or fewer – at least 30 days' collective consultation before the first dismissal;
- 100 or more proposed redundancies over a period of 90 days or fewer – at least 45 days' collective consultation before the first dismissal.

These periods can be extended by mutual agreement

4.4 Following the conclusion of collective consultation, individual employees at risk of compulsory redundancy will also be consulted. The employee will be invited to an initial meeting with their manager, at which they are entitled to be accompanied by their trade union representative or a work colleague. At the meeting the manager will explain how the employee could be affected and, if relevant, the selection process. They will also outline the payments that the employee will receive in the event of their redundancy and the assistance available to help employees affected by redundancy. The employee will have the opportunity to make any representations as to how their redundancy may be avoided or the effects of the potential redundancy minimised. They will also be able to provide any feedback on the proposed selection criteria.

4.5 A further meeting will be held at which the employee can be accompanied by a trade union representative or a work colleague. At this meeting the employee's manager will inform the employee if they are to be dismissed on grounds of redundancy and the basis for this decision. The employee will be given a full opportunity to make any further representations regarding any aspect of the decision. In the event of a decision to dismiss, the employee will be given a right to appeal (see below).

5. Selection criteria

5.1 Careful consideration will be given in identifying essential selection criteria to ensure that they are objective and relevant to the requirements of the role. Part of this will be to ensure that the criteria do not either directly or indirectly disadvantage any individual with a protected characteristic as defined within the Equality Act 2010. Selection criteria will be subject to consultation, as outlined above.

6. Alternative employment

6.1 The company will make every effort to identify and secure suitable alternative employment for affected employees through individual consultation.

The rest of the procedure goes on to set out provisions in relation to appeals against dismissal, the company's process in relation to redeployment, redundancy payment terms and outplacement support. It also provides a mechanism for review of the procedure.

12.6 Redundancy consultation

A key part of the redundancy procedure outlined here is the process for consultation. If there is a possibility that employees will be made redundant, employers need to consider their legal obligations regarding consultation.

Collective consultations and the law

As this procedure outlines, under section 188 of the Trade Union and Labour Relations (Consolidation) Act 1992, consultation on large-scale redundancies must start 'in good time' and must begin:

- at least 30 days before the first dismissal takes effect if 20 to 99 employees are to be made redundant at one establishment over a period of 90 days or less;
- at least 45 days before the first dismissal takes effect if 100 or more employees are to be made redundant at one establishment over a period of 90 days or less.

In addition, the same timeframe should be applied to notifying the government of the proposed redundancies using an HR1 form.

An important question is, when should consultations begin? The broad consensus on this issue is that the duty to consult arises when the employer has developed proposals that are likely to result in redundancies. However, these proposals should still be at a 'formative stage' so that there is an opportunity for amendment and change. In most cases, starting to consult after a firm decision has been made to make redundancies will be unlawful. This can be quite a complex issue for employers – if they start to consult too early, there is a danger that this will cause unnecessary alarm; however, it is crucial that consultations take place so that the views of representatives can be properly taken into account and used to shape the decision-making process. This is another area in which high-trust relationships with trade unions can be very helpful in minimising the impact of redundancies and in avoiding any legal problems.

Collective consultations must be conducted with trade unions if they are officially recognised. Where this is not the case, there is a duty to consult with elected employee representatives. Where employees decide that they want some form of collective representation in such circumstances, it is for the employer to arrange for the election of representatives. The number of representatives and their period of 'office' should be sufficient to represent all employees properly, for example by having representatives for different sections of the workforce. Representatives must themselves be affected by the proposed redundancy and all those affected should be given a vote. The ballot must be secret, and each person may cast as many votes as there are representatives to be elected.

Collective consultations can only really begin once employees or their representatives have been provided with certain information:

1 The reasons for the employer's proposals;
2 The numbers and descriptions of the employees to be dismissed;
3 The method of selection the employer proposes for dismissal;
4 The method of carrying out the dismissals the employer proposes, having due regard to any procedure agreement that might be in existence;
5 The period of time over which the programme of redundancies is to be carried out;
6 The method the employer intends to use in calculating redundancy payments, unless the statutory formula is being applied.

It is difficult to give precise guidance on what, and how much, detail must be provided, but vague and open-ended statements will not be acceptable. For the employment relations specialist, there has to be an acceptance that every case must be decided on its merits.

Consultation must also be meaningful and be undertaken 'with a view to reaching agreement' with employee representatives. We argue that three things have to happen. An examination has to take place on ways to avoid dismissals. If avoidance is impossible, ways to reduce the numbers to be dismissed should be looked at. Finally, ways should be found of mitigating the consequences of any dismissals. However, the employer is under no obligation to negotiate. Instead, they must approach the discussions with an open mind and, where possible, take account of any proposals put to them by the representatives.

It is important to note even if the numbers of staff proposed for redundancy fall below the threshold outlined here, a failure to consult with recognised trade unions is likely to be seen as unreasonable, rendering any subsequent dismissals potentially unfair. Moreover, a recent judgement from the Employment Appeal Tribunal (see Real-world example 12.2) suggests that employers who do not recognise unions should consult collectively with those affected at a formative stage as a matter of good employment relations practice.

REAL-WORLD EXAMPLE 12.2

Joseph de Bank Haycocks v ADP RPO UK Ltd (2023) EAT 129

ADP RPO is a subsidiary of a US firm which employed 50–60 people. The claimant worked with 15 others to recruit staff for a client, Goldman Sachs. In May 2020, as a consequence of the Covid pandemic, the demand from Goldman Sachs for new staff fell by around 50 per cent. As it was clear that there would need to be a reduction in ADP RPO staff, the claimant's manager was asked to score staff. This was carried out in early June 2020 and was done in good faith, but the claimant was scored last. On 18 June, a decision was made that there was a need to cut the size of the team from 16 to 14. The company put a timetable in place for the redundancy process – staff were to be informed of the proposal in an initial meeting on 30 June, there would then be two weeks of consultation with redundancies confirmed at a meeting on 14 July.

The claimant was called to an individual meeting on 30 June and informed of the proposals. He was invited to ask questions and to suggest alternatives to redundancy. He was invited to further meetings on 8 and 14 July, after which he was handed a letter of dismissal. He was not given information about his score or those of his colleagues. He appealed against dismissal on the grounds that his score was too low and that the criteria were subjective. He was then provided with his score but not those of his colleagues. His appeal was denied. The employment tribunal dismissed the claimant's application that the process used was unfair and found that the appeal process was 'carried out conscientiously' and there was no evidence that the claimant should have been ranked more highly. The ET did not directly consider the broader issue of consultation.

The EAT overturned this decision on the basis that there was 'a clear lack of consultation at the formative stage… the absence of meaningful consultation at a stage when employees have the potential to impact on the decision is indicative of an unfair process'. Moreover, the judgement makes it clear that in unionised workplaces a fair process would involve some element of collective consultation even if the numbers affected fell below the thresholds for statutory consultation. The principle of workforce consultation should also apply to non-unionised workplaces, particularly given changes in UK employment relations.

Notwithstanding the legal considerations, consultation with the workforce and their representatives is likely to minimise the negative long-term implications for organisations. Bergström and Arman (2017) have argued that the way in which redundancy is implemented can have a significant impact on organisational commitment in the longer term. In examining a case where commitment was found to have increased after a redundancy exercise, they highlighted the importance of involving worker representatives and effective communication with staff. Good communication and consultation can lead to better discussions, keep employees motivated and engaged, protect employee well-being, help the business survive and plan for the future, potentially minimise job losses and ultimately provide cost savings for the organisation. At the same time, alarming speculation about redundancies can be extremely damaging for employees and the organisation, so taking great care in the way that employees and their representatives are informed about potential redundancies is crucial.

A prime example of the importance of constructive management–union relationships is the following case (Real-world example 12.3) which explores the role played by employer and union learning partnerships in addressing some of the negative elements of a downsizing programme.

REAL-WORLD EXAMPLE 12.3

Learning partnerships in the NHS

In one NHS trust, large-scale redundancies due to technological change were managed through the learning partnership between management and unions identifying retraining to redeploy those at risk and so avoiding compulsory redundancy. The local union branch secretary involved explained this as follows:

> A prime example of why it was necessary to work together in partnership… Medical records were going to shut completely. There were about 50-odd people working in medical. Now as a result of the technological change all that was going to change, there'd be no need to store the record. It's all stored electronically. So as a result of that their jobs are going to disappear, what do you do with them? Luckily enough there was a lead-in time for this, and what it gave both the union and the employer time to do was to sit down and think how we were going to manage that situation. If we'd have done nothing, that place would have closed and the staff would have been redundant. So we developed a plan… and that was where retraining [to enable redeployment] was part of that.

SOURCE: Bennett (2014a: 27)

Findings from this research suggest that if downsizing is perceived to be handled fairly by staff, and the learning strategy is timely and effectively applied, the negative effects of survivor syndrome can be reduced. Also, people who leave the organisation are more likely to feel that they have been fairly treated and supported through the process.

Alternatives to redundancy

One of the main purposes of consultation is to establish whether any potential job losses can be achieved by means other than compulsory redundancies. Factors that would normally be considered at this point include:

- A ban on recruitment (unless unavoidable);
- Retraining of staff;
- Redeployment of staff;
- Restricted use of subcontracted labour, temporary and casual staff;
- Reduced amount of overtime working;
- Voluntary redundancy;
- Early retirement;
- Depending on the nature of the business, other considerations might include temporary lay-offs, short-time working, pay cuts/freezes or even job-sharing.

One of the first considerations for organisations when faced with the need for redundancies is to explore whether it is possible to avoid compulsory redundancies by asking for volunteers for either early retirement or voluntary redundancy. There are obviously a number of advantages in adopting the voluntary approach. First, it can help to avoid some of the demotivating effects that redundancy inevitably has on an organisation. Second, it can be cost-effective. While persuading people to go, rather than forcing them, will probably require higher individual payments, the financial benefits of a redundancy exercise can begin to impact much earlier if a costly and time-consuming consultation process can be avoided.

However, there is a danger that more people will volunteer than was originally envisaged. This raises two immediate problems: first, if all those volunteering are accepted, those left behind will be put under particular pressure to make up for staffing shortages; second, if the organisation wants to maintain certain levels of staffing, it may need some sort of process through which applications for voluntary redundancy are approved or rejected. This may be both time-consuming and can also have a demotivating impact on those employees whose applications are turned down. Moreover, there is a danger that voluntary redundancy exercises can lead to a 'talent drain', as those high-performing staff with more marketable skills may be more likely to apply as they know that they can get alternative employment. Therefore, it is important to carry out a comprehensive human resource planning exercise in order to assess future labour requirements. Furthermore, it is vital that managers make a proper and objective analysis of the skills and staffing levels that they need to retain. This is where the employment relations professional, in their role as objective adviser, can make a valuable contribution.

Reflective activity 12.6

You are an HR practitioner working in a large organisation that is facing difficult market conditions. Morale among the staff is poor and there is a significant amount of concern about the future of the company. The board of directors has informed you that it believes that staffing across the company needs to be reduced by 20 per cent. Board members are worried that compulsory redundancies could generate bad publicity and cause reputational damage. Consequently, they have agreed to an enhanced redundancy package for any volunteers. What are the potential advantages and disadvantages of this approach and what should the organisation do to manage this situation as effectively as possible?

It may also be appropriate to ask for volunteers for early retirement. This is only an option if the business has its own regulated pension scheme which allows for the payment of pensions early on grounds of redundancy. It is possible, however, that the employer might have to make a substantial payment into the pension fund – more than a redundancy payment, in many cases – to ensure that there is no detriment to the early-retired employee. Alternatively, the employer might have to provide a one-off lump sum that will take the employee up to an agreed date for receiving their pension. It is important that these financial considerations are taken into account by employment relations professionals when they are asked, as they often are, to cost the available options for reducing the workforce. Furthermore, to allow early retirement on redundancy grounds or to enhance the value of an individual's pension are not management decisions; they are trustee decisions. This means that the question of whether early retirement as an alternative to compulsory redundancy is an option must be carefully costed and researched.

Penalties for failing to consult

If there has been a failure to follow the proper consultation process, an application can be made to an employment tribunal for a declaration to this effect, and for a 'protective award' to be paid. This is an award requiring the employer to pay the employee remuneration for a protected period. The legislation relating to protective awards is quite complex, but some of the important elements are:

- The affected employee receives payment at the rate of one week's gross pay for each week of the 'protected period'.
- Unlike some compensatory awards, there are no statutory limits on a week's pay.
- Subject to certain maximums, the length of a protected period is at the employment tribunal's discretion; the test is, 'what is just and equitable having regard to the seriousness of the employer's default'.
- The maximum periods are 45 days when 45 days should have been the consultation period, and 30 days when 30 days should have been the consultation period; in any other case the maximum is 28 days.

The financial implications of protective awards can be quite significant because there are often substantial numbers of employees involved. It is unlikely that employers with well-established redundancy procedures will come into conflict with the law over a failure to consult. Notwithstanding this, the prudent employment relations specialist will keep the procedure under review in the light of any relevant tribunal decisions. The real problems arise for those organisations that do not have a procedure, or that try to put together a process in a hurried and casual manner when redundancies are imminent. Such organisations might find that the price they pay for a lack of preparedness is extremely high. Employment tribunals have shown an increasing tendency to take a very narrow view of any special pleading by employers that there was no time to consult.

REAL-WORLD EXAMPLE 12.4

***GMB and Others v Susie Radin Ltd (2004)* EWCA Civ 180**

Susie Radin was a clothing manufacturer that recognised the GMB union for collective bargaining purposes. In March 2000, the employer informed the union that the factory faced closure. On 6 April 2000 staff were informed that they would be made redundant, and they were sent letters of dismissal less than two weeks later. The employer finally met with the union on 13 June to discuss the possibility of saving the factory, but there were no further discussions before it was closed; on 14 July it was closed with no further delay. According to legislation at the time, there was a duty to start consultations with the union at least 90 days before any dismissals took effect. The GMB made an application to the employment tribunal arguing that it had not received necessary information to enable representatives to take part in consultations and that the consultations themselves had not been meaningful. The claim was successful and the tribunal awarded the maximum protective award period of 90 days. The claim was upheld by the EAT and the Court of Appeal, which found that if an employer fails to collectively consult on redundancies, the starting point should be an award that reflects the maximum protected period. Although the employer argued that consultation would have made no difference, the Court of Appeal concluded that the award should reflect the seriousness of the employer's breach and only be reduced if there were clear extenuating circumstances.

Unfair dismissal and redundancy

Irrespective of the duty to consult over collective redundancies, a failure to consult in any redundancy will leave an employer vulnerable to a claim of unfair dismissal. Many managers have fallen into the trap of assuming that when only one or two individuals are to be made redundant there is no obligation to consult or that consultation can be cursory. As we have already seen, this is incorrect. The Employment Rights Act (1996) identifies redundancy as a fair reason for dismissal provided that the employer has acted 'reasonably'. This requirement opens the door for an employee to claim unfair dismissal on the grounds that the employer, by failing to consult, had not acted reasonably. It is also important to note that consulting collectively with a trade union does not mean that an employer can ignore the importance of consulting with individuals, as the following case emphasises. In these situations, tribunals will look at the adequacy of the consultation process as a whole in deciding whether an employer has acted reasonably in making an employee redundant.

REAL-WORLD EXAMPLE 12.5

***Mugford v Midland Bank PLC* (1997) EAT/760/96**

Mugford was a bank manager and had been employed by the respondents for 25 years. In 1995, a substantial restructuring exercise was planned which included the potential redundancy of 858 managers, around 1 manager per branch. The employer recognised the trade union BIFU for collective bargaining purposes and engaged in statutory collective consultations over the redundancy programme. On 22 March 1995, Mugford attended a divisional meeting at which managers were briefed on the proposals and the method of selecting individuals for redundancy. The area manager then assessed Mugford against the criteria and recommended him for redundancy. Mugford was not made aware of this but on 11 May he was informed that he was in a potential redundancy position and his employment would end on 30 September unless suitable alternative employment could be found. Mugford objected to this and had a series of meetings with the area manager – these were related to possible redeployment and Mugford was provided with details of his assessment which was used as the basis for the redundancy decision. No alternative work could be found, and his employment ended on 30 September. His appeal was unsuccessful. Mugford claimed unfair dismissal – one of the main grounds was that there was no consultation. It was found that while there was no consultation between March and May, there was consultation with the trade union throughout. Furthermore, there was an opportunity for individual consultation open to Mugford, as evidenced by the meetings with his area manager during May. While the tribunal was critical of a lack of individual consultation before Mugford was identified for redundancy, it concluded that overall, the Bank 'fulfilled its obligations as to consultation'. Mugford appealed to the EAT, which upheld the tribunal decision arguing that the tribunal in examining the consultation process as a whole had applied the law correctly. However, in reaching its decision it also gave the following guidance:

- Where no consultation has taken place with either the trade union or employee, the dismissal will normally be unfair.
- Consultation with a trade union does not of itself relieve the employer from consulting individually with the employee being identified for redundancy.

It is important to manage issues reasonably and in accordance with the principles of natural justice, whether or not the employee concerned has the potential to bring an employment tribunal claim against you. By far the best option for employers is to recognise that good employment relations dictates a systematic approach to consultation, whether the proposed redundancies are going to affect 5 people or 50 people. This means that you should always allow enough time for a proper consultation exercise, immaterial of the number of the people that are to be made redundant. You should give very careful consideration to the possibilities of alternative employment, even lower-paid alternative employment. You must allow people time and an opportunity (normally through individual meetings) to:

- consider their options
- challenge the need for redundancy
- propose their own alternatives
- comment on selection criteria
- provide feedback on or challenge selection decisions.

The employer does not have to go along with any alternatives proposed by an employee facing redundancy but must be able to demonstrate that they have given careful and objective consideration to any suggestions made. Furthermore, it is important for the employer to be proactive in looking for ways of avoiding redundancies. It is particularly important not to assume what the employee concerned may be prepared to consider. For example, if it is possible to redeploy someone at risk of redundancy to another role, this should be explored, even if it involves a reduction in seniority or pay. If such a possibility is not discussed with the employee, the employer could be open to a claim of unfair dismissal.

Reflective activity 12.7

What are the organisational benefits of consulting over redundancies? Design an action plan for a process of consultation for your own workplace that could be used in the event of redundancies.

12.7 Compulsory redundancy

If the voluntary option is not feasible, the next step would have to be compulsory redundancies. At this point in the procedure there should be an acknowledgement that the organisation would, as far in advance of any proposed termination date as possible, notify all those employees at risk of compulsory redundancy.

Selection criteria for redundancy

As we have outlined, the method of selection should be part of the consultation process and ideally agreed with representatives or, where statutory consultations are not required, with the affected individuals. Employers should be careful when choosing the criteria against which selections are made.

Particular care should be taken if using criteria which may be discriminatory – for example, using length of service would likely discriminate indirectly on the basis of both age and sex. This does not necessarily mean that length of service cannot be used, but to do so, employers must show that the inclusion of the length of service criterion is a proportionate means of achieving a legitimate aim. For example, in the case of *Rolls-Royce PLC v Unite the Union* (2009) (EWCA Civ 387), it was found that the aim of rewarding loyalty was a legitimate aim. Nonetheless, it was only seen as proportionate because it was one of a large number of criteria and was not on its own a determining factor. Even if length of service is seen as a reasonable criterion, over-reliance on this may mean that organisations will lose their youngest employees or those with the most up-to-date skills. For this reason, many organisations have adopted a selection system that is based on a number of criteria, such as attendance records, range of work experience, disciplinary records and performance appraisals. Where possible, employers should use criteria which are transparent and objectively measured.

Creating a score

Once management has determined what criteria should be used, it is suggested that each employee should be scored by an appropriate number of points for each criterion (usually on a scale of 10). Using attendance as a criterion must also be treated with some caution as this could be seen to discriminate on grounds of disability. Consequently, employers should generally ignore any periods of absence related to a condition defined as a disability under the Equality Act 2010. Similarly, employers should take great care to ensure that part-time workers or those who are on, or have been on, maternity or paternity leave are not disadvantaged by selection criteria or their ability to take part in the consultation process (Wynn-Evans, 2019). Clear guidance should be given to the managers who are asked to decide on the number of points each individual receives. Some thought should also be given to weighting each criterion by a factor that would take into account the importance of that factor to the employer. For example, you could decide which particular attribute or criterion is the most important and then multiply that score by a factor of, for example, 5. The criterion that has the lowest importance might be multiplied by a factor of, for example, 1. A specimen matrix and score sheet is set out in Figure 12.2.

It is important that great care is taken in setting scoring guidelines. There may be certain employees who are engaged in particular projects or have certain skills that are critical to the organisation. If that is the case, this should be reflected in the

Figure 12.2 A specimen selection matrix and score sheet

Matrix and score sheet

Name:	Age:
Date of birth:	Years of service:
Department:	Job role:

Employee assessment			
Criteria	Score out of 10	Weighting (maximum × 5)	Total
		X	
Skills		X	
Attendance		X	
Flexibility		X	
		X	
		X	
		X	
Grand total			

Assessed by:.................... Checked by: ....

criteria. Alternatively, such individuals should be removed from the pool for selection. Consideration should also be given to how the scoring is conducted. In order to avoid accusations of bias, it is sensible that more than one person is involved in scoring and that at least one of those scoring should (where possible) not be known to the individual concerned. For example, a panel of three individuals could be set up – the line manager, a manager from another department and a representative from the HR department.

When all the scores have been calculated, those at risk of redundancy will be the ones selected for redundancy. There should then be further consultations. It is important to give individuals selected for redundancy the opportunity to receive details of the scoring and the opportunity to provide feedback to the employer and, if necessary, challenge the scoring decisions made. This can be done through individual meetings or by providing an appeal process. The failure to do this may render any subsequent dismissal on grounds of redundancy unfair, as the employment tribunal finding in Real-world example 12.6 demonstrates.

REAL-WORLD EXAMPLE 12.6

***John Brown Engineering Ltd v Brown* (1997) IRLR 90**

Brown was selected for redundancy following a selection process whereby each candidate in the selection pool had been scored against certain criteria. Brown was unhappy with this; however, the employer refused to disclose details of individuals' scores to either employees or representatives. It was claimed that, as a result, consultation had not been effective and the dismissal was unfair. The EAT found that, in this case, the failure to disclose individual assessments carried with it a risk of unfairness. Hence it upheld an earlier tribunal decision in favour of Brown.

Assistance for redundant employees

Once the selection of individuals has been confirmed, it is important that the employer makes reasonable efforts once again to look for alternative employment. The individual consultation process can be used here to discuss with the individual other roles that they would be prepared to consider. Of course, alternative employment is not always possible, nor is it always desired by those to be made redundant. Nevertheless, as discussed earlier, it is incumbent on the employer to make every effort to look for alternatives, and where they exist, to consider redundant employees for suitable vacancies.

One way of dealing with this is to draw up a redeployment procedure which sets out the basis on which employees will be interviewed for any vacancies and the terms and conditions on which alternative jobs will be offered. It is common for employees facing redundancy to be placed on a 'redeployment list or register' and provided with the opportunity to apply for a vacancy before other candidates are considered.

Some organisations go so far as guaranteeing an interview to all 'redeployees' as long as they meet the essential criteria for a job. In addition, the organisation will need to decide whether it offers any protection in the event of someone being redeployed into a role with inferior pay and conditions compared with their current job. Whatever the terms of the redeployment policy, the employment relations professional will have to work closely with managers to ensure that it is applied fairly, as managers can be resistant if they feel that they are being forced to take someone into their team. Trial periods can be one way of providing the redeployed employee time to see if their new post is suitable.

REAL-WORLD EXAMPLE 12.7

Consulting on redundancy?

Northtown College is a large college of further education based in the north-east of England. It employs a total of 250 staff (of which 160 are teaching/lecturing staff) across four locations within a 20-mile radius of the city of Gateley. It recognises UCU and UNISON for collective bargaining purposes.

In recent years universities have been lowering their admission requirements. This has had a significant impact on the college and student admissions have fallen significantly. This has had a knock-on effect on the finances of the college. About 12 months ago the senior managers of the college decided that redundancies were inevitable; however, they have been waiting for the right time to announce them in order to minimise bad publicity and opposition from staff. However, it has now been decided by college management to announce that 58 lecturing staff and 42 support and administrative staff will be made redundant, with the first of these taking effect in one month's time. The redundancies are spread equally across the four sites. Redundancy notices have been drawn up and are to be sent out just as the redundancies are to be announced.

Staff have been selected on the basis of a number of factors: contractual status (whether full-time or part-time); length of service; absence record; qualifications and skill; disciplinary record; performance. Heads of department were asked to score each member of staff out of 10 on each criterion and come up with a total score. These were then compared across the whole college, with the lowest scores selected for redundancy. These were done about three months ago in utmost secrecy – as management didn't want to cause staff any unnecessary worry.

You are an HR practitioner who has been asked to comment on the college's plans. What advice would you give?

It would also be normal practice for a redundancy procedure to set out what steps the organisation proposed to take in assisting the redundant employee who could not be found alternative employment within the business. Such steps should include provisions for paid time off to attend interviews, to seek retraining opportunities or to attend counselling sessions. This latter point will be dealt with in more detail later in the chapter.

Statutory rules on payment

All those employees with a minimum of two years' service will (with certain exceptions) qualify for a statutory redundancy payment. The key rules on the nature of redundancy payment are covered in depth on the government website (search www.gov.uk). However, payments are calculated as follows:

For each complete year of service up to a maximum of 20, employees are entitled to:

- for each year of service under age 22 – half a week's pay;
- for each year of service at age 22 but under 41 – one week's pay;
- for each year of service at age 41 or over – one and a half weeks' pay.

Length of service is capped at 20 years and weekly pay is currently (as at July 2024) capped at £700. Therefore, the maximum statutory redundancy pay is £21,000. However, this is reviewed annually, and current rates can be found at www.gov.uk/staff-redundant/redundancy-pay. Employers can also pay redundant staff in excess of the statutory minimum. Importantly, redundancy payments are generally not taxable up to a maximum of £30,000.

Notice of redundancy

It is important that employers do not issue notices terminating employment on grounds of redundancy until collective and individual consultation has been completed. If this is done, a tribunal is likely to conclude that the consultation has been a 'sham' and therefore in breach of legal requirements. Notices can only be given before the end of the minimum period if the consultation is genuinely complete. In this case, it is important to note that the dismissal itself cannot take effect until the minimum period of consultation has expired and individual notice periods have been observed. The date on which a dismissal 'takes effect' is the date on which the notice expires, not the date on which it is given. However, employment can be terminated before the end of the notice period where an employee has agreed to take a payment in lieu of notice. This can be a way of enhancing the overall package available to redundant employees; however, it is important to note that payments in lieu are normally taxable.

The employer must give at least the minimum statutory notice period. This is:

- one week's notice if the employee has been employed by the employer continuously for one month or more, but for less than two years; or
- one week's notice for each year employed if the employee has been employed by the employer continuously for two years or more, up to a maximum of 12 weeks.

For example, if an employee has worked for five years, they are entitled to five weeks' notice.

12.8 Transfer of undertakings

When the ownership of a business transfers, there is always the possibility that redundancies will be one of the results that flow from such an action. Under the Transfer of Undertakings Protection of Employment (TUPE) Regulations 2006, all employees who are covered by employment protection legislation receive additional protection in respect of job security if the identity of their employer changes. TUPE applies when an organisation, or part of it, is transferred from one employer to another. In general, this means when its main assets (such as employees, equipment or premises) have transferred to the new employer and its activities remain the same or are similar. TUPE can also apply where a service is transferred to a new provider – this could be through outsourcing, insourcing or retendering. However, TUPE doesn't apply to contracts that only apply to the supply of goods or to a short-term or specific task. In addition, for TUPE to apply, the service must be provided by an 'organised grouping of employees'. For example, if an organisation decides to switch the company which runs the staff canteen which employs five people, this transfer would probably fall under TUPE.

Before the transfer any redundancies that relate specifically to the transfer itself will be automatically unfair. This could include situations whereby the original employer tries to cut staff to attract a new buyer or where the new employer asks the original employer to make staff redundant. However, if the new employer is planning 20 or more redundancies within 90 days of the transfer they could start collective consultations before the transfer takes place, as long as they have the consent of the original employer.

After the transfer, staff can only be made redundant if there is a genuine redundancy situation and this is because of an economic, technical or organisational reason such as essential cost savings, introduction of new equipment or process or necessary restructuring. It is very important to note that transferred staff should be treated in the same way as existing staff and should not be disadvantaged in any selection process.

Should employers find that, on the transfer of a business, there is a redundancy situation, the existing law regarding redundancy applies. This means if any employees are made redundant and they have the requisite period of service with their old employer to qualify for a redundancy payment, the new employer cannot avoid making a redundancy payment to them. In the context of consultation, all the issues of representation and the right to information that we have discussed with respect to collective redundancies apply equally to transfers of undertakings.

12.9 Fire and rehire

It is important to understand that the law in relation to redundancy also applies to situations in which employers are proposing to terminate existing contracts and offering new terms and conditions – so-called 'fire and rehire'. In principle, if an organisation wants to substantially revise terms of employment, this has to be done by agreement with the relevant employees, often through union negotiation. If an employer simply imposes an inferior contract, an employee can potentially resign and claim unfair constructive dismissal. Of course, this places the employee in a weak bargaining position as they are faced with a choice of keeping their job or challenging their employer. When an employer is contemplating changing collective agreements, they should try to negotiate those changes – however if they propose to 'fire and rehire' they have a duty to collectively consult. However, the case of P&O Ferries (Real-world example 12.8) shows the weakness of that legislation.

REAL-WORLD EXAMPLE 12.8

Fire and rehire – P&O in the dock

On 17 March 2022, 800 people employed by P&O Ferries across the UK were dismissed with immediate effect, with many informed in a three-minute video call. There had been no warning of this and no consultation with trade unions recognised by the company. Some of the affected staff were on board ships at the time and were asked to leave. The company suspended its operations while new crew could be recruited – initially, these were agency staff recruited outside the UK and paid below the minimum wage. This is possible as minimum wage legislation does not apply to ships operating in international waters and registered outside the UK. However, P&O pays workers on domestic UK routes in accordance with UK law.

The decision sparked widespread protests. While P&O claimed that the decision was necessary to protect the viability of the business, the decision was condemned as 'one of the most shameful acts in the history of British industrial relations' by the RMT union, which represented many of the affected staff. The actions of the firm were also criticised by the Conservative government, which called on the company to reverse its decision or face the prospect of legal action or new legislation. In addition, the chairs of the House of Commons transport and business select committees demanded that the P&O chief executive be struck off and called on the government to prosecute the company.

Subsequently the company offered dismissed staff enhanced redundancy payments alongside agreements to sign non-disclosure agreements (NDAs). According to reports, the vast majority of sacked staff accepted the settlement and signed an NDA. Some workers took up new employment on inferior terms and conditions, often through employment agencies. In a report in the *Guardian* in May 2023, one former P&O employee explained that he had accepted the redundancy payment because 'If you didn't sign, you had a lot to lose' (Topham, 2023).

In evidence to the transport committee and business, energy and industrial strategy committee on 24 March 2022, P&O chief executive, Peter Hebblethwaite said, 'There is absolutely no doubt that we were required to consult with the unions. We chose not to do so… It was our assessment that the change was of such a magnitude that no union could possibly accept our proposal.' In fact, the government did not go on to take legal action against P&O. The only legal action was taken by one P&O worker who refused the redundancy package and made a claim for unfair dismissal – P&O admitted unfair dismissal and paid the worker a significant sum in compensation. At a subsequent hearing of the business and trade select committee, Hebblethwaite confirmed that P&O staff are now supplied through agencies and are paid a minimum of £4.87 per hour, which he claimed was above minimum international standards for seafarers.

The difficulty for workers who are fired and then offered terms on inferior terms and conditions is that any legal redress is (at the time of writing) reactive – in short, the employees and trade unions can take legal action on the grounds that the employer is in breach of a duty to consult and that the dismissals are unfair. However, the compensation they can win is limited and success at a tribunal is not guaranteed. What is guaranteed, is that the workers will have lost their jobs. Employers can also take action similar to P&O and offer financial settlements which preclude any litigation – unfortunately for some organisations this may be seen as a rational response – an 'efficient breach' of the law. However, it ignores the long-term damage to organisational reputation, employee engagement and consequently quality and productivity.

Acas research (2021) suggested that while fire and rehire was not a new phenomenon, its use widened during the Covid pandemic. Rather than being concentrated in large, unionised workplaces, the tactic was increasingly being used by smaller non-unionised organisations. There was also concern by some participants in the research that the threat of fire and rehire was being used as a negotiation tactic by some employers. In fact, a survey of employees conducted for the TUC in 2021 found that 9 per cent of workers (and 18 per cent of 18–24-year-olds) had been told to re-apply for their jobs on inferior terms since March 2020 (TUC, 2021a).

In response to the concern over the use of fire and rehire, the government published a draft Code of Practice on Dismissal and Re-engagement (see the following box). At the time of writing this is set to be introduced in the summer of 2024. An unreasonable failure to comply with the Code will not be unlawful; however, it will be taken into account by employment tribunals and could lead to an increase in compensation of up to 25 per cent.

DRAFT CODE OF PRACTICE ON DISMISSAL AND RE-ENGAGEMENT

- Fire and rehire should only be used as a last resort and should not be used as a negotiating tactic.
- Employers should engage with employees and/or their representatives as early as reasonably possible and should share as much information as is reasonably possible.
- Consultations should continue for as long as reasonably possible although this will depend on the circumstances.
- Where agreement cannot be reached, employers should carefully re-examine their proposals in light of consultations.
- Employers should contact Acas for advice before discussing the potential for dismissal and re-engagement with their staff.
- If employers decide to dismiss and re-engage, they should act responsibly and should consider providing staff with longer periods of notice than provided for in contracts or by statute.
- Employers should consider the provision of practical support to employees and reviewing the impact of changes, including feedback from staff.

However, the draft Code lacks specifics and reflects a generalised statement of good practice. Although this was welcomed by the CIPD and Acas, trade unions have argued strongly that the Code will be insufficient to change employer behaviour. Importantly, it is likely that the Labour government elected in July 2024 will go further. Labour have pledged to strengthen protections to effectively 'outlaw' hire and fire in three respects:

- Improving information and consultation procedures to make employers consult and reach agreements about contractual changes.
- Reforming unfair dismissal and redundancy legislation to prevent workers being dismissed for failing to agree a worse contract.
- Revising legislation so that trade unions are able to take lawful industrial action where fire and rehire tactics are being implemented.

Reflective activity 12.8

To what extent do you think 'fire and rehire' can be justified? What are arguments for and against legislation to prevent organisations from using this tactic?

12.10 The aftermath of redundancy

Following the completion of the redundancy procedure, good employers will need to consider the welfare of their staff leaving the organisation, but also those who 'survive'. In this section we look at the growth in both counselling and outplacement services and, in addition, the position of those employees who remain in employment and who may consequently suffer so-called 'survivor syndrome'. Crucially, as Petzer (2020) argues, there is a substantial body of evidence that suggests that redundancy and restructuring often have a number of negative long-term implications for organisations including reduced profits, lower productivity and reduced staff commitment. However, she also contends that these impacts can be minimised by the way in which the organisation treats both the victims of restructuring and those left behind.

Counselling

Although redundancy has become part of everyday life, the loss of one's job usually comes as a tremendous personal blow. Even when 'the writing is on the wall' and job losses are inevitable, individuals still hope that they will not be affected. There can be a tendency for employers to want a redundancy exercise to be forgotten as quickly as possible. This can appear uncaring. The employment relations specialist should be reminding managerial colleagues that they have a continuing responsibility for those staff leaving the organisation. Redundant employees can feel anger, resentment and even guilt – emotions which, if not carefully managed, can inhibit an employee from moving forward to the next phase of their career. In addition, this will transmit to their colleagues who remain in the organisation. This is where effective counselling becomes crucial. However, it is important to proceed cautiously.

Not every redundant employee will agree to or want counselling, but nevertheless it is important to understand its key purpose. The objective of counselling is to bring all these emotions out into the open and to help individuals to make decisions about their future. It is not a panacea – it will not stop people being angry or feeling betrayed – but it might help them to view their future constructively.

Because redundancies are often cost-cutting exercises, many organisations are reluctant to hire counsellors to help with the aftermath. But a study in 2003 by Professor John McLeod of the School of Social and Health Sciences at the University of Aberdeen suggests that it might be an investment worth making (Blyth, 2003). His review of more than 80 studies on workplace counselling showed that 90 per cent of employees are highly satisfied with the process and outcome. Moreover, evidence suggested that counselling helps to relieve work-related stress and reduces sickness absence rates by up to half.

Outplacement

Outplacement is a process in which individuals who have been made redundant by their employer are given support and counselling to assist them in achieving the next stage of their career. There are a large number of organisations that offer outplacement services, but the range and quality of their services varies greatly, and the employment relations specialist must carefully research prospective suppliers if a decision to use outplacement is taken. Broadly, outplacement consultancies offer services on a group or individual basis which fall into the following general categories:

- CV preparation
- Researching the job market
- Communication techniques
- Interview presentation
- Managing the job search.

Each organisation operates differently, but in the best organisations the process would probably start with a personal session with a trained counsellor. Once this has been carried out, the next step would be the preparation of the CV. This involves identifying key skills and achievements so that the job-hunter can market themselves from a position of strength. Step three would be to make decisions about job search methods (cold contact, advertisement, recruitment consultants and so on and contact development – for example, networking. Step four would be to ensure that the key communication skills of letter-writing, telephone techniques and interview presentation were of a sufficiently high standard to enhance and progress the job search. Where skills have to be improved, the better consultancies provide the necessary training at no extra cost.

REAL-WORLD EXAMPLE 12.9

Rolls-Royce

When aero engine company Rolls-Royce had to axe 4,800 jobs worldwide in the wake of the 11 September attacks on targets in the US, it was well placed to deal with the crisis. Here in Britain, the company had set up six resource centres in early 2000 to handle an anticipated downturn in the market.

The centres, one at each of the company's main UK sites, provide a three-day career transition training programme and continuing, open-ended support and advice. The centres take CIPD good practice as a model. Each is staffed with a manager, a counsellor, several other dedicated Rolls-Royce personnel and a flexible team from the company's two external outplacement providers, Capita Grosvenor and Winchester Consulting. The providers give access to national jobs databases with online search facilities.

Since the centres opened, hundreds of employees affected by cutbacks have used them for careers guidance, advice on writing CVs, training and so on. Eighty-five per cent have found new employment, typically after some weeks.

'One of the challenges was the reputation that resource centres have in other organisations,' says John McKell, Rolls-Royce head of employment policy. 'They are renowned for providing minimal provision to lower-paid workers in pokey surroundings, while managers get executive packages. But at Rolls-Royce, the service is gold-plated for everyone.'

The company has involved employees and unions from the start. In response to a proposal from union officers, it set up a resourcing committee by means of which employee and union representatives could review redundancy support. Several improvements, such as better communications, have resulted.

SOURCE: Blyth (2003)

The final step is managing the actual job search, setting personal targets, keeping records of letters and phone calls, maintaining notes of interviews and carrying out a regular job search evaluation. Running alongside these basic services is a range of support services, such as secretarial help, free telephone and office space and financial planning advice. What an individual gets will depend on the particular package that the former employer purchases on their behalf.

Of course, not every employer will be able to afford the cost of outplacement, particularly if large numbers of employees are affected by the redundancies. In such circumstances, organisations must consider what they can do to help from within their own resources, or by using a mixture of internal and external resources. The TUC (2009) has also recognised the value of good advice being made available to workers facing redundancy. It has produced a guide on how employees can make the best use of the Government's Rapid Response Service (RRS). RRS was established in 2003 and aims to help workers affected by major redundancies. Operated through local Job Centre Plus centres, it aims to help people into new jobs before they lose their current ones by providing specialist advice services.

Reflective activity 12.9

Does your organisation have any sort of policy on counselling and outplacement? Having considered the arguments in the previous sections, what sort of proposals could you put in place to improve the experiences of staff involved in downsizing?

Survivor syndrome

When people are forced to leave employment because of redundancy, those that are left behind can be affected just as much as those that have left. Disenchantment, pessimism and stress are the likely result of even a small-scale redundancy exercise. Survivor syndrome, as it is called, can be minimised if, as we have argued, those who are to be made redundant are treated fairly and equitably and there is a decision made to invest in an effective post-redundancy programme. Further research suggests that if the conflict, both for individuals and the collective group, which arises out of redundancy is properly managed through fair and transparent consultation processes, this negative element of redundancy can be attenuated (Bennett, 2014a). This usually means a time commitment from senior managers and a good communications process. The impact can be significant, as a 2009 IRS survey with respect to survivor syndrome reveals (see Table 12.1).

The feelings referred to in Table 12.1 are the result of two factors. The first is that the remaining employees are often asked to 'pick up' the work of their former colleagues, either directly or indirectly. In one local authority, individuals had to re-apply for their own jobs three times in three years, following a series of redundancies and reorganisations. The second factor concerns communication. Evidence suggests that

Table 12.1 The impact of redundancy on the survivors

Impact	Percentage
Low morale and commitment	67
Increased stress	65
Reduced motivation	53
Breakdown of trust in management	50
Lower productivity	19
Increased absence	17
Staff retention problems	17
Poorer performance	16
Greater risk avoidance	15

SOURCE: Murphy (2009)

in many organisations the remaining employees are not always communicated with effectively, thus providing the opportunity for rumour and disenchantment to thrive. Haddon (2017) points out that good communication is key to rebuilding teams and reassuring survivors with respect to where their new role subsequently fits within the organisation. Getting the message across about why redundancies were necessary and what happens next is vitally important. As Haddon argues:

> When staff feel like their concerns are important, when they feel consulted, listened to and when they are provided with further information about the direction of the company, they are less likely to be fearful of the future.

Petzer (2020) outlines six key interventions that can help to support the survivors of redundancy. These measures provide the basis for a strategic approach to rebuilding trust and engagement.

Provision of training – redundancy survivors may well see their roles change as the organisation adapts to coping with fewer staff. Therefore, it is important that they are provided with the skills and support they need to make this transition.

Increased support – it is common for workloads to increase in the wake of a redundancy exercise. Employers need to recognise this, and also to provide support to staff to help them deal with the increased pressure – this may mean more careful planning and job redesign.

Workshops – peer support can be crucial in helping survivors adapt and also manage feelings of envy towards those who have left the organisation, particularly if colleagues have left with generous financial settlements.

Counselling – while counselling can be important for those facing redundancy it can also help those left behind deal with complex and negative emotions. Moreover, the offer of counselling in itself demonstrates that the employer recognises the challenges faced by survivors.

Reward and recognition – as soon as possible, the employer should consider how it can recognise and reward those staff who have had to pick up the pieces after downsizing. Even if finances are tight, recognising their contribution will help to rebuild trust.

Communication – regular and effective communication from senior leaders and line managers is crucial in demonstrating the future vision of the organisation and combatting uncertainty about the future.

Crucially, the key to minimising the effects of survivor syndrome lies not in simply reacting after the redundancies have been completed, but in the way the organisation handles the process from start to finish.

12.11 Summary

Redundancy is one of the most emotive issues that any manager can be faced with. Calling an individual into your office and informing them that their job is at risk is never easy. For the employment relations specialist, steering an organisation through a redundancy exercise can also be extremely challenging. No matter how experienced you are, managing redundancy is never straightforward, but in this chapter we have attempted to set out the process in a systematic way. Most redundancies occur because organisations need to change, and although we recognise this, we nevertheless feel that it is important that employment relations specialists understand that there should be alternatives to reducing an organisation's headcount. In particular, businesses are unlikely to retain their competitive advantage if their employees are constantly looking over their shoulders, fearing for their jobs.

One of the challenges that all managers, whether or not they are HR practitioners, face in the twenty-first century is how to reconcile the need for organisational change with the individual's need for contentment and security at work. We believe that the notion of 'good work', even when confronted by the continuing challenges of rapid economic and technical change, should remain a lodestar for HR strategy. To this end, it remains crucial that while the employment relations specialist must understand the need for organisations to change, this should also be accommodated within a well-developed legal framework that directs and constrains their actions. Importantly, the obligation to consult provides opportunities to avoid or minimise the impact of redundancy and to deal equitably with those employees who are directly affected.

Finally, as we discussed in the closing section of the chapter, redundancy leaves 'survivors' in its wake. They often experience a psychological state that is not unlike bereavement, and inevitably suffer a loss of trust in their organisation and sometimes in their immediate manager. In order to counter this, it is not only vital to ensure that communication with staff is frequent, open and honest, but also that effective training and support is provided to the envoys in the organisation who must deliver the message.

KEY LEARNING POINTS

- The definition of when redundancy occurs is important because it determines an individual's right to consultation, fair treatment and compensation.
- Redundancy should always be a last resort, and it is therefore important to have effective policies and procedures for dealing with a redundancy situation. The employment relations professional has a key role to play in this process in advising management colleagues on the scope and extent of any policy, and in advising them on how to manage the redundancy process.
- Employers must ensure that they fulfil their statutory obligation to consult collectively if proposing to dismiss 20 or more employees. This consultation must be meaningful with a view to reaching an agreement. In all cases of redundancy the employer must also consult with any individual worker they are proposing to dismiss – a failure to do this is likely to result in a claim for unfair dismissal.
- When redundancy is unavoidable, 'good practice' dictates that the organisation has in place policies and procedures that enable it to deal with a difficult situation with sensitivity and equity. In addition, the managers tasked with 'delivering the news' need proper support and training.

- An important element in the management of a redundancy situation is the need to provide effective counselling and support for the redundant employee, as well as giving support in terms of job security and outplacement. It is also important to communicate with, and support, those who remain in employment. Ignoring the 'survivors' is likely to produce a demotivated workforce and create the conditions for higher levels of workplace conflict.

Review Questions

1 Your organisation needs to reduce the workforce by 20 per cent. Your CEO, who is fully aware of the statutory need to consult with the workforce, wants, in achieving this, to act in a fair, reasonable and consistent way. You have been asked to advise her on how the required redundancies can be achieved. What would you advise?

2 You are employed as head of HR at an organisation employing some 750 staff who will now have to be cut back drastically. It will mean a 50 per cent reduction in the size of the present workforce. You have been asked to produce a position paper for the senior management team explaining how the workforce reduction might be achieved while minimising any adverse impact on morale. Drawing on contemporary research and policy and practice, justify what you would include in your position paper.

3 You are the HR adviser for a retail chain of 34 shops. The area manager has asked your advice on a possible redundancy situation. He has identified one shop that will probably have to close sometime in the next few months. The shop in question has 27 people. The organisation is non-unionised but there is an employee consultation forum. He does not know how to initiate the process and has asked your advice about what he should do, and why. How would you respond?

4 Your HR director is concerned that with a sudden downturn in the economy, the company needs to review its redundancy policy. She would like you to brief her on the things that a redundancy policy should include as a minimum, and what else could be considered good employment practice. Prepare an outline of the briefing you will give her, justifying what you will include.

Explore further

Acas (2021) *Dismissal and Re-engagement (Fire-and-Rehire): A fact-finding exercise.* Available from: https://www.acas.org.uk/fire-and-rehire-report/html#annex:-survey-data-provided-to-acas-on-the-prevalence-of-fire-and-rehire (archived at https://perma.cc/L8FH-QEAD) [accessed 14 May 2024]

Coulter, S (2020) All in it together? The unlikely rebirth of covid corporatism, *The Political Quarterly*, **91**(3), pp 534–41
Petzer, M (2020) *How to Limit 'the Sinking Ship Syndrome' during Redundancies*, CIPD. Available from: https://www.cipd.org/uk/views-and-insights/thought-leadership/the-world-of-work/sinking-ships-syndrome-redundancies/ (archived at https://perma.cc/B4SN-67KM) [accessed 14 March 2024].
Stevens, M (2022) *Strategic Redundancy Implementation: Re-focus, re-organise and re-build*, Routledge, London.
Stevens, M and Hannibal, C (2023) The smiling assassin?: Reconceptualising redundancy envoys as quasi-dirty workers, *International Journal of Human Resource Management*, **34**(5), pp 879–911
Topham, G (2023) One year on, has P&O Ferries got away with illegally sacking all its crew?, *The Guardian*, 17 March. Available from: https://www.theguardian.com/business/2023/mar/17/one-year-on-has-po-ferries-got-away-with-illegally-sacking-all-its-crew (archived at https://perma.cc/74VC-7HN4) [accessed 14 May 2024]

Websites

www.acas.org.uk (archived at https://perma.cc/ U7C7-PK53) is the website of Acas, and gives access to Acas publications, including guides and information on redundancy management.

www.cipd.co.uk (archived at https://perma.cc/ G7MM-9S96) is the website of the CIPD, and gives access to the CIPD's wide range of publications and information on redundancy, as well as its *Labour Market Outlook* surveys.

13 Workplace mediation

Overview

The chapter is structured in two parts. Part one begins by defining workplace mediation in contrast to other alternative dispute resolution processes. The key benefits of workplace mediation are then discussed, followed by a critical review of the extant literature and current research on the topic. The chapter then turns to discuss workplace mediation as an alternative to more formal and conventional methods of resolving employment disputes, such as grievance and discipline procedures. Like any other method of resolving disputes, it is argued that mediation is not a panacea. Nonetheless, when the process is better understood by all parties, and depending on the issue and the outcomes sought by the disputants, mediation can help to rebuild employment relationships that have become fractured. Furthermore, in terms of the exercise of power and control in the management of workplace conflict, we ask whether mediation offers greater equality of access to justice. Part two of the chapter focuses on the practice of mediation, by examining the nature of the process and the role played by HR practitioners and employment relations specialists. This is followed by a more detailed discussion of the stages of mediation, from referral to resolution, and an exploration of the knowledge, skills and attitude needed to be an effective mediator and how these skills can be employed by line managers. The chapter closes by reflecting on the future prospects for workplace mediation.

LEARNING OUTCOMES

When you have completed this chapter, you should be able to:

- understand and describe the term 'workplace mediation' and its main functions;

- critically assess the key benefits that mediation can bring to an organisation;
- identify and critically analyse the limitations of mediation and barriers to its use;
- understand and critically evaluate the key theoretical concepts developed in the study of workplace mediation;
- provide an analytical account of mediation's relationship with more formal dispute resolution practices;
- explain and evaluate the role of the key players in the process;
- identify, describe and explain the process of initiating, managing and concluding a mediation case.

13.1 Introduction

As we identified in Chapter 9, there has been a growing trend to consider alternative approaches to resolving disputes instead of the more traditional channels of grievance, discipline and performance management (Latreille, 2011; Liddle, 2023). However, as subsequent discussions in Chapters 10 and 11 have demonstrated, 'rights-based' procedures remain the main way in which conflict disputes are handled in the vast majority of UK workplaces. Nevertheless, there is growing evidence to support the argument that, for certain types of disputes, organisations are increasingly turning to different methods of resolution. The focus of this chapter is on one increasingly popular alternative method for resolving disputes between individuals – workplace mediation. Mediation is not a new concept. It has its origins in the resolution of family and community disputes and has been used successfully for many years in the United States, particularly in addressing employment disputes in the public sector (Mareschal, 2003). Its long-standing use and success within the US Postal Service is a particularly impressive example of a large-scale conflict management strategy (Bingham and Pitts, 2002).

Mediation is argued by its advocates to be a model of dispute resolution which lends itself particularly well to situations where the parties have become entrenched in their positions (CIPD, 2024e). From a practical perspective, it is a method of resolving workplace disputes that seeks to avoid a more formal and often more confrontational route, such as grievance and discipline procedures; rather than attributing blame, it looks to rebuild damaged relationships for the future. In the UK, the publication of the Gibbons Review in 2007 marked the start of government support for mediation as a dispute resolution strategy to reduce 'the burden' on the employment tribunal system (Gibbons, 2007). Further evidence of continued government interest in the strategic role of workplace mediation was provided in its consultation on workplace dispute resolution policy and practice (BIS, 2011).

However, evidence of the scale of mediation use in the UK is mixed. According to the Workplace Employment Relations Survey, in 2011 it was used to resolve disputes in only 7 per cent of all workplaces but 17 per cent of those that had experienced formal employee grievances. However, the same data suggested that mediation was included in almost two-thirds of written disciplinary and grievance procedures

(Wood et al, 2017). A more recent survey suggested that mediation use was more widespread. In 2015, the CIPD found that in-house mediation was used in 24 per cent of organisations, and external mediation in 9 per cent. However, by 2020, its use had fallen back slightly – 23 per cent of employers reported using internal mediators and 7 per cent external mediation (CIPD, 2020). Furthermore, we have to be a little careful when interpreting the data in relation to mediation, given a likelihood that respondents may impose their own definition of mediation, which may include less structured facilitated conversations conducted by HR and line managers.

13.2 What is workplace mediation?

Mediation is one of a number of dispute relation processes that have been developed in recent times as alternatives to the more traditional processes for resolving disputes in the workplace. Alternative dispute resolution (ADR) can be defined as 'the use of any form of mediation or arbitration as a substitute for the public judicial or administrative process available to resolve a dispute' (Lipsky and Seeber, 2000: 37). In the US, in particular, ADR mechanisms have been increasingly integrated into newly developed conflict management systems.

In some ways, in order to understand the potential role of mediation, it is useful to first define it in terms of how it differs from other ADR processes. For instance, it is not the same as conciliation: this is, rather, 'a process whereby a third party, such as Acas, will *guide* the parties in dispute to try and reach a compromise that suits both parties' (Ridley-Duff and Bennett, 2011: 109 – our emphasis). Similarly, it is unlike arbitration, which as Aubrey-Johnson and Curtis explain, involves 'an independent and impartial expert determining the outcome of the problem. Arbitration differs from conciliation and mediation because the arbitrator acts like a judge. Making a firm decision on a case' (2012: 315). In contrast, a useful definition of mediation is given in the following box.

DEFINING MEDIATION

Mediation is a voluntary process where a third party provides impartial facilitation with the intention of trying to resolve a disagreement between individuals. The mediator should be independent of the individuals and issues, although this does not mean that they must be external to the organisation. In some situations, an internal mediator can be helpful (in part because of their understanding of the organisational context). In certain cases, HR professionals may act as mediators although it is important to avoid any tensions with their other responsibilities in a dispute situation. Whatever the background, it is important to make sure that the mediator is appropriately trained.

SOURCE: CIPD (2024e)

The decision as to which of these different resolution processes are used often turns on the type of dispute, the stage of the dispute and, crucially, what type of resolution is being sought. For example, if a dispute has escalated to the stage where an employee submits a claim against their employer to an employment tribunal (ET), the employee must first notify Acas to give it an opportunity to conciliate between the parties to settle that dispute before it proceeds to the ET. If the parties wish to avoid the time demands and stress of going through litigation, and the employment relationship is so far compromised as to be beyond 'repair', an independent arbitrator can be assigned to the case under the Acas Arbitration Scheme. It is of note, however, that this option is very seldom used. However, if the parties feel that the relationship is worth rebuilding, for instance if the dispute turns largely on personality issues, mediation could be the most appropriate route to resolution.

Nevertheless, the choice of mediation does not preclude other channels. The mediation process is confidential and does not, therefore, prejudice any subsequent decision to turn to other means of resolution if mediation is not successful (Saundry et al, 2018). Mediation can be and is used at any point in the course of resolving a dispute. However, it can be at its most effective when the mediation begins at the earliest stage in the dispute, as discussed further throughout this chapter.

Reflective activity 13.1

Thinking about disputes in which you have been involved at work, would mediation have been an appropriate course of action? If your answer is yes, why would mediation have been useful?

Facilitative mediation is the most common model utilised in the UK. The facilitative method is based on an approach of avoiding 'positions', looking beyond parties' legal entitlements to a negotiated settlement that reflects their underlying needs and interests. Essentially it is a process of joint problem-solving, where the disputants identify, evaluate and agree suitable solutions to the problems they face. A key facet of facilitative mediation is to promote communication between the parties, so that they can candidly 'air their differences' but, at the same time, identify shared interests and look for common ground that may lead to a settlement. Because, in facilitative mediation, the mediator is neutral, they can assist the disputants to communicate with each other in a way that would not be possible through other dispute resolution channels. It is, therefore, a model that lends itself to situations where the parties have become entrenched in their positions. The following box outlines the key principles of facilitative mediation.

FACILITATIVE MEDIATION

1. Mediation is a confidential and voluntary process in which a neutral person helps people in dispute to explore and understand their differences so that they can find their own solution.
2. Mediation is based upon the principles of it being: voluntary, impartial, confidential and binding in honour.
3. The key skills and qualities of a successful mediator are: fairness, being non-judgemental, empathy, building rapport and facilitating agreements through questioning, active listening, summarising but not leading and adhering to practice standards.
4. The mediation process is normally made up of:
   - a separate first contact meeting with each client;
   - a subsequent joint meeting with the parties in dispute in order to: set the scene; explore the issues; build agreement; reach closure and agree follow-up.
5. Mediation is about being clear and honest with disputants with respect to:
   - what can and cannot be achieved;
   - how the process works;
   - what is expected of each person in terms of: setting ground rules for behaviour; respecting the other party; commitment to the process; commitment to seeking and agreeing a joint solution;
   - the facilitative role of the mediator;
   - looking for ways to maintain an ongoing and future relationship rather than apportioning blame for actions in the past.

SOURCE: Ridley-Duff and Bennett (2011)

Workplace mediation in the UK is generally accessed in two ways. First, organisations can employ an 'external' mediator from one of a number of specialist mediation and conflict management providers. Second, larger organisations may want to invest in 'in-house' mediation capacity. This can range from training one or two HR specialists to the development of an in-house mediation service, in which a number of employees are trained as mediators. They are then allocated cases by a mediation co-ordinator who has overall responsibility for administering the service. The key advantages and disadvantages of internal and external mediation are discussed later.

Interestingly, to date, other than Acas's (2013) survey of the commissioners of its mediation service and the participants in those mediations, little is known about the experiences and perception of the key player in the process, the disputant. Saundry et al's (2018) cross-sectoral research, however, gives some initial insight into this important issue. Their findings are summarised in the following box.

MEDIATION – WHAT DO THE DISPUTANTS ACTUALLY THINK?

- Many of the disputes within the sample were complex – for example, approximately half the cases involved allegations by one party of bullying or unfair treatment following attempts by the other party to manage performance or raise performance concerns. Therefore, issues tended to involve both potential grievances and discipline issues.
- The initial trigger for mediation mostly came from either senior managers or HR practitioners. Problematically, it tended to be used as a last resort for particularly difficult issues.
- Attitudes to taking part in mediation were mixed. While some respondents welcomed the opportunity to voice concerns within a safe environment, managers were more sceptical, particularly where the mediation involved a challenge to their decisions or attempts to address performance.
- Respondents were generally very positive about the role played by mediators.
- Most respondents felt that they had benefited from taking part in mediation but they also found the process extremely challenging.
- In the majority of cases, mediations resulted in agreement. However, this often did not lead to any fundamental change in behaviour and/or attitude, and in around half of cases within the sample was not ultimately sustained.
- Perceptions of 'success' were nuanced – in some cases, even where there was no significant change in attitude and behaviour, mediation paved the way for a degree of pragmatism allowing the parties to continue to work together in some form. Moreover, for employees who had complained of unfair treatment, the opportunity to air their views could be cathartic and empowering, even if mediation did not deliver the justice that they sought.
- Crucially, almost all respondents would either recommend mediation to others or consider taking part again in the right circumstances.

SOURCE: Saundry et al (2018)

Reflective activity 13.2

If you were considering introducing an internal mediation service into your organisation, what lessons would you draw from the research findings outlined here?

13.3 A theoretical approach to workplace mediation

To further understand workplace mediation, it is useful to consider Ridley-Duff and Bennett's (2011) conceptual model of dispute resolution. This explores whether mediation offers an alternative and *more equitable* means of dispute resolution than conventional procedural approaches (see Figure 13.1). They argue that most organisations handle conflict by imposing and enforcing consistent standards of 'fairness' which revolve around the culpability of individuals. An alternative perspective is that workplace conflict and individual employment disputes stem from relationship and communication issues, not personality characteristics or failings. Thus, through mediation, the object of investigation is the relationship between two people, and the goal is increasing the capacity of disputants to maintain and develop that relationship. Thinking back to Fox's (1974) frames of reference discussed in Chapter 2, it is argued that:

> Mediation errs not just towards pluralism, but towards the Marxian perspective on emancipation and transformation. Traditional discipline and grievance practices operate within a framework of line management and a unitary ideology. While they may permit discussion of an issue or person, they prevent discussion about the nature of the relationship, or the legitimacy of hierarchical power (Ridley-Duff and Bennett, 2011: 115).

Both in theory and in practice, there are fundamental differences that underpin disciplinary procedures, arbitration, conciliation and the various forms of mediation potentially available to disputants. If we recognise these differences, mediation begins to challenge the process-driven approaches of discipline and grievance. From this perspective, it can be argued that mediation can empower employees and allow them to challenge managerial authority.

Furthermore, Ridley-Duff and Bennett (2011) claim that traditional disciplinary and grievance procedures are underpinned by managerial and organisational notions of appropriate behaviour. Mediation, on the other hand, does not accept this framework in an uncritical way. It gives that authority to the disputants to best decide how their dispute is resolved. Moreover, they suggest that mediation is a dispute resolution mechanism based on direct, rather than representative, democracy, which seeks solutions that best suit the disputants but that cannot necessarily be fully shared within the public domain. Critics may see this as a weakness. However, it is argued that, conceptually and practically, direct representation, free of public expectations to follow set procedures and fully disclose outcomes, allows the realisation of solutions that better maintain long-term relationships and give a *greater sense of equity* than more traditional approaches. It is this that makes it a more radical alternative.

In contrast, other commentators have argued that, rather than empowering employees, mediation can offer a means of controlling dissent and asserting control (Colling, 2004; Latreille and Saundry, 2014). By using mediation in certain cases, the responsibility for unfair treatment can be shifted to the employee and the employer can evade the responsibility for changing practices and holding managers to account.

Figure 13.1 A theoretical framework for understanding dispute resolution

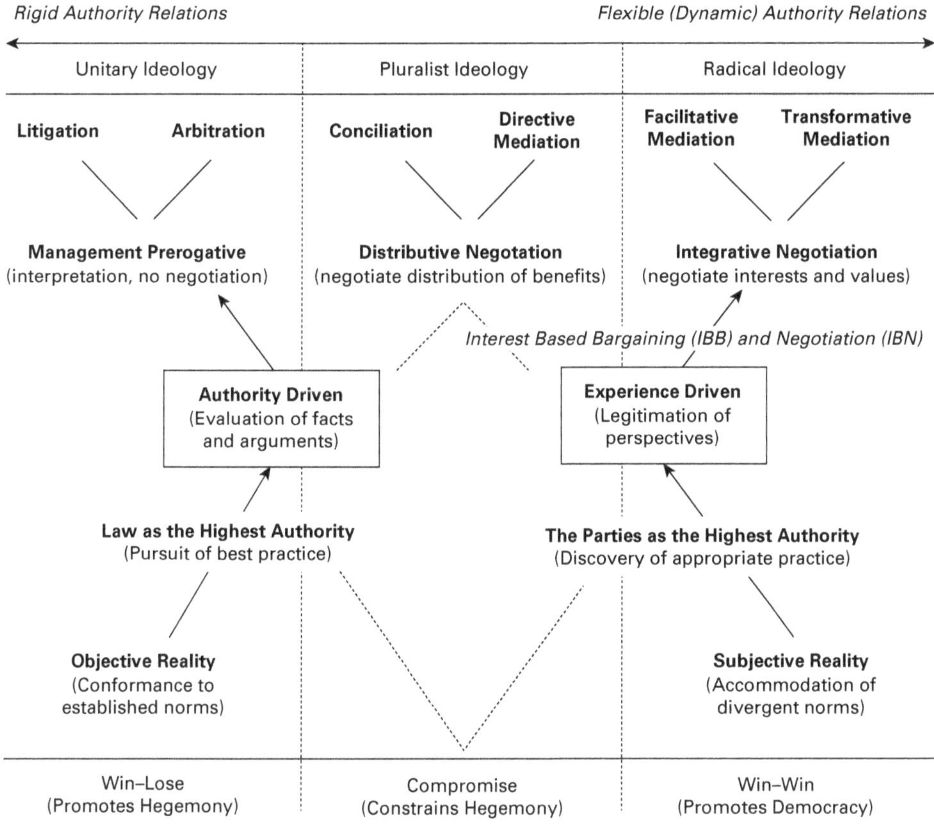

SOURCE: Ridley-Duff and Bennett (2011)

Keashly and Nowell (2011) point out that because mediation focuses on the future, it has no means of addressing or 'punishing' past behaviour. Therefore, some writers have questioned whether mediation is appropriate in addressing sensitive and power-based disputes over bullying and harassment.

Reflective activity 13.3

Critically reflect on the appropriateness of referring bullying and harassment cases to mediation. What are the advantages and disadvantages of using mediation for these types of cases?

The way in which mediation is used can also vary among and within sectors depending on the context. Organisational and managerial drivers will also impact, to some degree, on the mediation process. For example, Bennett's (2014a, 2017) research into the use of mediation in higher education revealed that mediators saw a key strength of mediation as being its ability to address inequality and 'power imbalance' between disputants, characteristics which were seen as particularly important in that sector. The key findings from this study are outlined in Real-world example 13.1.

REAL-WORLD EXAMPLE 13.1

'Managing academics is like herding cats' – the use of mediation in higher education

The study of a cross-section of universities in the north of England uncovered a number of interesting findings in terms of how conflict and its management are predicated on specific elements of the context, culture and type of workers in that sector.

- Watson's (2006) observation that 'managing people was like herding cats' was echoed by a number of HR managers as a metaphor for the challenges presented to them and line managers in managing professional workers such as academics and the sources of conflict that could arise.
- The unique nature of the academic role, the need to be critical and to challenge, the competitive nature of academia and the largely unchallenged sanctity of academic freedom were all reported causes of conflict and barriers to its resolution.
- The 'reluctant' academic manager, rewarded through promotion but with no real desire to manage others, could be an equal cause of conflict that higher education (HE) mediators were called to address.
- For many respondents to the research the ethos of the HE sector – in terms of developing academic but also life skills in students and staff, and also framed in a culture of mutual respect – lent itself well to this type of dispute resolution process. However, for many critics, in reality, disputes occurred more often because of poor management skills or inappropriate 'Taylorist' approaches to managing staff.
- Many of the universities were part of a mediation network between HE institutions in the region.
- A number of universities extended their service to their client group, their students, with a high measure of success.

SOURCE: Bennett (2014a, 2017)

Reflective activity 13.4

University lecturers are not unique among professional workers in 'jealously guarding' their independence. What other occupations might fall into the same category? What challenges for managing conflict might that raise for you as an HR practitioner?

13.4 The direct benefits of mediation

Advocates of mediation highlight a number of important benefits. First, it is an opportunity to intervene early and resolve specific disputes, thereby avoiding grievance and disciplinary procedures, the long-term absence of those involved, and, in some cases, employment tribunal proceedings (see Real-world example 13.2). Furthermore, it provides an opportunity to repair and restore the employment relationship. Therefore, for employers, mediation offers significant financial savings compared with other more conventional routes. Second, it could be argued that disputants find mediation a more acceptable approach to resolving their differences and, therefore, are more likely to commit to any final agreement. Research also suggests that mediation provides an opportunity for individuals to approach a complaint or grievance in a less confrontational manner than is possible through conventional processes. Consequently, staff who would otherwise leave are able to make their concerns known while remaining with their employer.

Third, mediation allows employees to have 'their day in court', where they can express their views and emotions can be clearly shown, but without the procedural limitations of organisational grievance and disciplinary processes. Through the mediator, the disputants also consider what they can get from a possible solution by focusing on common ground, not their differences. Because the process is facilitated by a neutral mediator to create a non-threatening environment, people are more likely to listen to the other person's viewpoint and experiences, and to understand how their behaviour is affecting the other person. The aim of mediation is to change that behaviour. It is also argued that people are more likely to commit to a solution if they have been a party to finding that solution. So, if the disputants feel that it has not been imposed upon them, it can be argued that there is a feeling of a greater ownership of the outcome. The confidential nature of mediation is another important benefit of the process. The parties are reassured that anything that they say will not be put on record or be used later should the mediation process prove unsuccessful.

REAL-WORLD EXAMPLE 13.2

Mediation and the cost of conflict

Richard Saundry and Peter Urwin explored the cost of workplace conflict in a research paper commissioned by Acas and published in 2021. Their analysis pointed to the potential benefits of early resolution and workplace mediation. Using CIPD (2020) data, they calculated that there were just under 500,000 mediations in 2018/19 – although this may include less structured facilitated discussions. The total cost of mediation for employers was estimated to be £140 million per year. This compares to a cost of £360 million per year spent on handling grievances, £2.2 billion spent on sickness absence as a result of conflict and a cost of £11.9 billion on resignations due to workplace conflict.

In order to compare the costs of a mediated resolution and a case which remains unresolved and escalates to litigation, they examined a scenario in which an employee complains that they have been unfairly treated by a colleague. They go to their line manager who suggests a meeting with an HR practitioner and employee representative to try to resolve the issue. The outcome of this meeting is a mediation between the employee and their colleague, which results in a satisfactory resolution. The average cost of this process in the UK was estimated at £1,918. In contrast, if the issue is not mediated and escalates to a formal grievance, there is a strong likelihood that one or more of the employees involved would take time off work. Saundry and Urwin estimated the average cost to an employer to be £8,775.32. Furthermore, if the complainant resigned and claimed constructive dismissal, the cost would increase to £44,961.32.

SOURCE: Saundry and Urwin (2021)

13.5 Mediation – increasing conflict competence?

While most organisations turn to mediation to find resolutions to specific disputes, there is some evidence that it can also have a positive impact on the way that organisations manage conflict more generally. For example, Gibbons saw mediation as one element in developing 'culture change, so that parties to employment disputes think in terms of finding ways to achieve an early outcome for them, rather than in terms of fighting their case at a tribunal' (2007: 38). Moreover, the government argued in 2011 that mediation could lead to improved 'employer–employee relationships, the development of organisational culture and the development of "high-trust" relationships' (BIS, 2011: 3).

There is certainly evidence that managers, employees and mediators who are involved with mediation feel that they gain additional skills and often a new perspective on handling conflict. Perhaps not surprisingly, mediation training is seen to have a very positive impact on conflict-handling skills and enhances 'creative problem-solving' (Kressel, 2007: 747). Some have claimed that this can be 'transformational'. A study of the introduction of mediation into an NHS organisation, carried out by Saundry, McArdle and Thomas (2013), cited the case of the self-styled 'grievance king', a union representative who had developed a very adversarial approach to workplace conflict. For this individual, taking part in mediation training significantly changed his approach and attitude towards his members' problems and convinced him of the need to look for informal resolutions rather than reverting to formal procedure. A recent study on the views of union representatives on mediation suggested that 'UK unions are likely to be more supportive... (albeit conditionally) and less hostile than some employers and mediation advocates might assume' (Branney, 2016: 206). However, as Branney argues, union support is far more likely and sustainable when the unions are fully involved in the process of introducing a mediation service from the start. This is a point that the case of the 'grievance king' clearly substantiates.

REAL-WORLD EXAMPLE 13.3

The 'grievance king'

An Acas-commissioned case study of East Lancashire Primary Care Trust highlighted the potential of the introduction of internal mediation capacity to have a broader effect on employment relations.

Prior to the introduction of a mediation service, employment relations had become highly adversarial – in a climate of rapid and substantial change, trust between managers and union representatives had been substantially eroded. As a result, employee grievances had become a battleground. The unions encouraged formal grievances as a way of highlighting wider issues, while management reacted defensively. Cases became mired in complex and time-consuming procedures. At the centre of this was a senior shop steward who was referred to as the 'grievance king'.

In setting up an internal mediation scheme, an acting HR director persuaded the 'grievance king' to train as a mediator. He was not convinced but agreed to attend the training to sabotage the whole process:

> I thought they were looking to convince me. I went in with the attitude… I thought if anything I'll come in and I'll kibosh it. I will get my voice heard that there is no other better way than a grievance procedure.

In fact, the experience had a profound effect. Managers, HR professionals and union representatives were trained together and gained a new understanding of each other's perspectives. Subsequently, the 'grievance king' became one of the mediation scheme co-ordinators. Union support for the scheme was based on a belief that the outcomes for members were, in most cases, much better than those possible through formal grievance procedures. Furthermore, working together in the mediation scheme rebuilt trust between union representatives and management, which in turn underpinned informal routes to conflict resolution.

SOURCE: Saundry et al (2013)

Of course, not all staff can be trained in mediation, but research has suggested that participating in mediation can develop communication and conflict management skills (Bush and Folger, 2004). Recent research in the UK has also found that managers who go through the mediation process often reflect on their own behaviours and practice, encouraging them to address issues at an earlier stage (Saundry et al, 2023). The most significant evidence of the transformative impact of mediation comes from analysis of the REDRESS programme introduced by the US Postal Service. This found that supervisors who underwent mediation training and/or mediation 'listen more, are more open to expressing emotion, and take a less hierarchical top-down approach to managing conflict' (Bingham et al, 2009: 43).

Reflective activity 13.5

You have been tasked by your manager to produce a short presentation to the HR team comprising a critical review of the merits of mediation in the workplace. What key aspects of the process would you include and why? What sources would you use to support your arguments?

13.6 Barriers to workplace mediation

Despite its potential benefits, recent research in the UK (Latreille, 2011; Saundry and Wibberley, 2014b; Saundry et al, 2018) has pointed to a number of barriers to the use of mediation and the development of internal mediation services. For smaller organisations with no in-house mediation capacity, an important deterrent is cost; bringing in an external mediator normally costs between £2,000 and £2,500. Although there is convincing evidence that this can represent good value for money in the long term compared with the costs of formal disciplinary and grievance procedures and litigation (Saundry and Urwin, 2021), this is sometimes not immediately apparent. Smaller organisations can also be resistant to bringing in an 'outsider' to 'wash their dirty laundry'. There is fairly strong evidence that mediation is more likely to be found in larger workplaces and organisations. Research undertaken by Acas found that just 5 per cent of private sector businesses had used mediation, falling to just 4 per cent in small and medium-sized enterprises (SMEs) (Williams, 2011). Furthermore, Wood et al (2017) found a statistically significant relationship between mediation use and organisational size.

In larger organisations, the main opposition has come from line and operational managers, who find their authority threatened by the ability of employees to ask for mediation. This is particularly acute in cases involving performance management, where managers felt that attempts to manage performance could be effectively challenged through employees referring issues to mediation (Latreille and Saundry, 2014). Managers are also reluctant to refer cases to mediation as they are concerned that this could be seen within the organisation as an admittance of failure. With in-house schemes, this appears to be exacerbated when the provision of the mediation service is located within the HR function, as managers might be reluctant to signal that they are incapable of handling a specific problem. In addition, where only HR professionals are trained as mediators, the diffusion of skills, referred to earlier, is inevitably limited.

REAL-WORLD EXAMPLE 13.4

'A fear of failure'

Saundry and Wibberley's (2012) case study of Qualco, a large private sector organisation, highlighted a number of the key benefits of mediation, but also some of the barriers to it becoming embedded within managerial practice.

The researchers found that the success rate of mediation was high and that those who had used mediation were highly satisfied. Mediation had been used to resolve a wide range of disputes, including employment tribunal claims. This was seen to have retained staff and resuscitated employment relationships that had seemed irretrievably broken. There was also evidence that managers who had been through the mediation process had reflected on, and subsequently changed, their approach to conflict.

However, at the time of the research, awareness of the service was limited and managers were also reluctant to refer cases to mediation. In particular, bringing in help from outside their workplace, in the form of a trained mediator, was seen as an admission of failure. This was made more acute by the fact that the mediation service was located in the HR department and the mediators were mostly senior HR professionals. Therefore, there was a concern in individual units that referring cases could invite scrutiny and possible criticism from 'head office'. According to one operational manger:

> there's a bit of a barrier around I think just admitting that there is an issue and we try and resolve things in-house because sometimes we don't want other [parts of the business] to know there is a problem.

In their eyes, a referral to the mediation scheme had become a formal 'last resort' to be considered only when all other procedures had been exhausted.

A further problem facing internal mediation services is sustainability – mediators often find it hard to find time to combine mediation with normal duties. Consequently, there can be a high turnover of mediators. The viability of mediation can therefore become dependent on a small number of key individuals. This fragility means that the understanding and support of senior managers is crucial.

There can also be resistance from employees and their representatives. For employees, mediation is often perceived as a relatively formal process, and sitting in a room without representation and challenging their manager or another work colleague can be extremely daunting. This illustrates concerns that power inequalities in the workplace are inevitably felt within the mediation process. Keashly and Nowell (2011) question whether mediation participants can actually negotiate on equal terms. In contrast, research into the views of disputants in the UK by Saundry et al (2018) found that it was managers who felt most uncomfortable in being challenged by their subordinates.

Mediation has also been viewed with suspicion by trade union representatives, who have concerns that it may be a way of restricting their traditional role and their ability to contest decisions made by the employer – importantly, employee representation is not normally permitted within the mediation 'room'. Even where trade union representatives can see the potential benefits of mediation for their members, they are sometimes reluctant to become actively involved as, for example, mediators, due to concerns that this could lead to a conflict of interest.

Finally, and crucially, there is the key question of the sustainability of any agreement arising from a mediated dispute. This turns initially on the original decision to refer a dispute for mediation. The HR manager, line manager and, where there is an internal mediation service, the co-ordinator, need to be sure that mediation is appropriate for the outcomes expected by the disputants. If they want, for instance, a finding that will be made public, the dispute should be referred to another route. Furthermore, it is crucial for all parties to realise that they are committing to an ongoing process. It is not a 'one-off meeting'. Instead, it is a process that begins with individual meetings with the disputants to understand their concerns and expectations. It then progresses to a joint meeting, or meetings, to seek to resolve those differences. Fundamentally, if successful, it culminates in an agreement to put the solutions identified into practice on an ongoing basis. If this is not realistic, the 'commissioner' of mediation, the disputants or the mediator should, on reflection, look to alternative, more formal, means of resolution open to them within the organisation's conflict management systems and structures.

For instance, as Saundry et al (2018) discovered in their research, agreements were often short-lived. This was because the parties were not fully committed to the process or that the agreed outcomes were not really achievable. Typically this is due to underlying problems being outside the gift of the disputants to resolve. In reality, workplace mediation takes place within the context and therefore the constraints of the dominant management style and the strategy of the organisation. Consequently, a settlement made inside the 'mediation room' may be very difficult to enforce and sustain outside it.

Reflective activity 13.6

What barriers do you think you would encounter if you suggested that your organisation should make use of mediation?

What arguments would you use to persuade sceptics that mediation could make a positive contribution?

13.7 Mediation in practice

Having critically reflected on the context of workplace mediation, and the key theoretical and conceptual considerations that its study and practice have raised, this part of the chapter will focus on the practical aspects of mediation in terms of the process, its objectives and the role of the mediator.

Developing an internal mediation service

For larger organisations, which may have to deal with complex conflict on a fairly regular basis, it may be worthwhile to consider investing in their own internal mediation service. This will normally involve training a number of staff as accredited mediators who can be deployed to mediate cases as part of their normal duties. Establishing an internal mediation service can be costly and requires a significant commitment from the organisation. However, it has a number of important advantages:

1. In the long term, it is much more cost-effective than engaging external mediators and, if cases are resolved, it is both cheaper and faster than using conventional disciplinary and grievance procedures.
2. Internal mediators may be much better placed to understand the specific organisational context, which may help participants to find a sustainable resolution.
3. Training a cohort of mediators can be one way of diffusing key conflict-handling skills and changing the culture of conflict management, particularly if mediators are selected strategically.
4. Trained mediators can be deployed flexibly to a wide range of conflict management situations – for example, in facilitated meetings, team discussions, training provision and as conflict coaches.

Even if an organisation has its own internal mediation service, if senior and well-known figures in the organisation are in dispute, it may be necessary to look to an external provider in order to ensure impartiality. Another alternative is to develop a network or sharing agreement between a number of organisations, whereby mediators can be deployed on a reciprocal basis.

KEY FEATURES OF SUCCESSFUL INTERNAL MEDIATION

In developing and designing an internal mediation service, research has pointed to a number of important considerations:

Organisational support and commitment – the backing of senior management is vital if internal mediation is going to be sustainable (Saundry et al, 2023). This does not just mean approving the initial start-up costs of training, but also ensuring that mediators are given time and encouragement in undertaking their role and developing their skills. It is also crucial that the scheme has a champion, or champions, who occupy an influential position within the organisation.

Locating the scheme – as suggested earlier, try to avoid locating the service within the HR department. Good relationships between HR and any internal mediation service are vital, but if mediation is seen as a department of HR, managers may be more reluctant to use it. There are interesting examples of this in the

NHS – in East Lancashire Primary Care Trust, joint co-ordinators were appointed. The involvement of the union provided the service with a greater degree of legitimacy and increased take-up by union members (Saundry et al, 2013).

Selecting your mediators – it may be tempting to simply select HR practitioners as mediators, but evidence suggests that when mediators are drawn from different parts of the organisation, it is more likely that support for, and awareness of, the service will increase and that an emphasis on early resolution will be encouraged. This will particularly be the case if influential individuals are trained – this may include senior managers, trade union representatives or simply members of staff who come into contact with large numbers of other colleagues through their normal role.

Review your procedures – examine your existing disciplinary, grievance and dignity at work procedures and see whether mediation can be built into the early stages. Furthermore, placing a greater emphasis on the importance of conflict resolution more generally may increase the use of mediation.

Use your mediators flexibly – think about different ways in which trained mediators can be used in addition to conventional mediation. For example, they could be used to train managers, assist in facilitated meetings and also to coach managers in teams where there is a particular problem (see Latreille and Saundry, 2015).

Evaluate the results – try to make sure that resources are in place to evaluate mediations but also to follow this up at a later point to see whether the solution has been sustained. Evaluations will also help to establish the value of the service.

Reflective activity 13.7

Do you think an internal mediation service would be effective in your organisation? If so, how would you seek to secure the support of senior leaders?

Co-ordinating mediation

Internal mediation services normally have a dedicated co-ordinator, whose job it is to manage the overall mediation service for the organisation. All referrals are channelled in the first instance to the co-ordinator. They then 'triage' each case, usually through an informal conversation with each party in dispute, to establish if mediation is the best route to resolving their dispute. If this is felt to be the case, then, depending on whether the service is provided externally or internally, the provider is contacted or one of the team of internal mediators is allocated to the case.

The basis for that choice varies across organisations but is typically around availability or finding a mediator with no direct knowledge of the disputants (in a university this would mean, for instance, allocating a mediator from another school or faculty). In some circumstances, disputants may feel more comfortable with a mediator of a particular gender or who has a certain degree of seniority. Of course, such requests can only be accommodated if both parties are happy. Interestingly, in the higher education sector, some universities are able to draw on a network of mediators based in other institutions to mediate in disputes where an internal mediator may not be suitable.

In organisations without in-house capacity, engaging external mediators is normally the responsibility of the HR professional or manager dealing with that case. It is critical that someone liaises between the external mediator and the participants. Research in the UK found that in some circumstances, once the external mediator was employed, the organisations provided very little support to those involved, and in more than one case left it to the participants to organise the mediation themselves (Saundry et al, 2013).

The role of HR practitioners, line managers and representatives

Unsurprisingly, the role of the line managers is very different in mediation than in grievance or disciplinary procedures. In some cases, they will be one of the disputants, as a breakdown in relationships between employees and their manager is a common occurrence. If they are not party to the dispute, they may have referred a dispute to the mediation service or advised members of their team to go to mediation. In any case, this is where their involvement ends in the process until they are advised by HR that the dispute has been resolved or not. Only with the full agreement of the disputants will the nature of the resolution be shared with the line manager.

The same considerations apply to HR practitioners, who can also refer cases to mediation. In organisations with internal mediation schemes, HR advisers and business partners will normally be fully briefed on the mediation process and are able to signpost cases they think are appropriate. Furthermore, some HR practitioners may be part of the mediation team. Research has indicated that this varies among organisations (Saundry et al, 2023; Bennett, 2013). It can be of significant benefit as involvement in the scheme can encourage buy-in from senior HR practitioners. However, as we have noted, if mediation is seen as being a function of HR, there is a danger that this could deter referrals.

In general, the involvement of employee and union representatives is crucial in winning support for mediation and in developing a culture of early and informal dispute resolution. However, in the UK, representation within the mediation room itself is not generally permitted or encouraged. As the basis of mediation is that the participants develop their own solutions, many mediators feel that representation would disturb this balance. Of course, that does not mean that representatives cannot play a vital role in supporting and advising employees, both before and after the mediation takes place.

 Reflective activity 13.8

Your organisation has chosen to establish an internal mediation service. The head of HR has asked for a short report outlining both the merits and drawbacks of the HR department co-ordinating the service and encouraging business partners to train to be internal mediators. What would be your conclusions?

Is mediation the right choice?

A critical question is whether mediation is the right response to a particular issue or dispute. Typically, mediation is seen as appropriate where there are breakdowns in relationships, poor management and communication problems (CIPD, 2024e; Bennett, 2013, 2017). Mediation is also more likely to be employed to resolve grievances brought by employees. However, workplace conflict is complex and presents difficult choices for those considering mediation.

Mediation is often employed to resolve complaints that emerge from attempts by managers to manage performance. Therefore, a manager may seek to address a problem with performance, behaviour or attendance. But, the employee may argue that this and/or the approach used by the manager could constitute bullying or harassment. In such cases mediation is a relatively common response, and reference to mediation can increasingly be found in bullying and harassment and dignity at work policies.

Nonetheless, both managers and employees can have reservations about the use of mediation in such cases. Managers argue that, while mediation can resolve relationship issues, it does nothing to address the underlying performance issue. Conversely, for some employees, as discussed earlier, mediation can be perceived as an inadequate response to mistreatment, effectively denying them access to 'justice' (Saundry et al, 2018). As Figure 13.2 shows, just over one in five employees surveyed by the CIPD agreed that mediation 'lets the perpetrators of bullying and harassment get away with it', while at the same time just over one-third would not be 'willing to mediate with someone I had thought had bullied or harassed me' (CIPD, 2020).

This shows that support for mediation is not a given and that HR practitioners need to build support for its use. It also underlines the importance of participation being voluntary and mediation only being used when appropriate. However, generalised rules are not particularly helpful and each case should be treated on its merits. Crucially, mediation is most likely to be appropriate where a central element of the dispute involves a breakdown in the relationship between two (or sometimes more) people and critically where both parties are prepared to attempt to rebuild and maintain that relationship. In contrast, mediation may not be the best way forward:

- if either (or both) party (parties) is/are unwilling to engage in the process;
- when either party is incapable of taking part or can't keep an agreement;

Figure 13.2 Employee perspectives on mediation

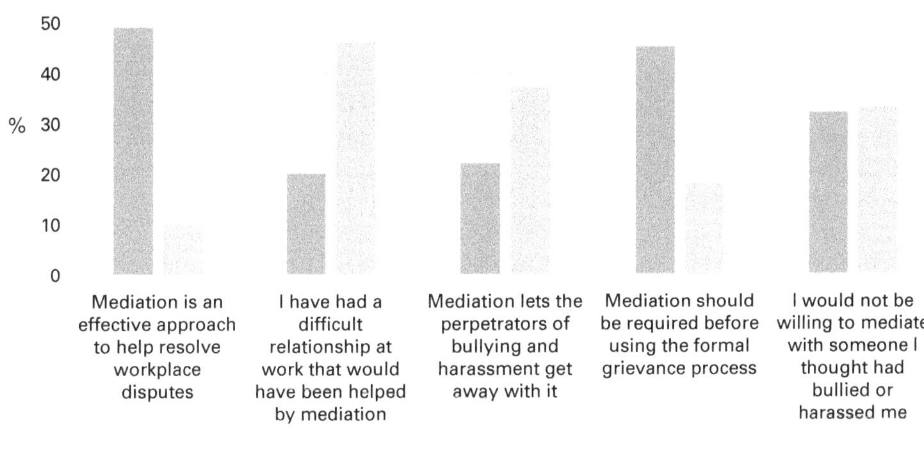

SOURCE: CIPD (2020)

- if it is not in the interests of one party to settle;
- if the dispute needs a public judgement (Liebmann, 2000).

In such cases, the utilisation of formal procedures may be necessary or inevitable. Furthermore, if an employee has 'broken the rules', such as committing an act of gross misconduct, disciplinary action will often be more appropriate. This could include accusations of mistreatment and serious bullying and harassment. Here, organisations may also wish to adopt a formal response to make clear that such behaviour is not acceptable. Furthermore, as noted, mediation cannot resolve underlying performance problems, so ultimately, disciplinary or capability procedures may need to be enacted.

Reflective activity 13.9

You are an HR practitioner in a large organisation which has its own internal mediation service. One of your employees has made an informal complaint about the behaviour of their line manager. They have claimed that during a performance appraisal, the manager became angry and the employee felt threatened. They claim that this type of behaviour has been going on for some time. Informal enquiries show that similar complaints have been made in the past and that the employee has a history of poor performance. Do you think that mediation is appropriate in this case? If not, what other courses of action would you recommend?

Single or dual mediation

Whether to use single or dual mediation (using two mediators) is also a key consideration for organisations in providing a mediation service. In Bennett's (2014b) research in higher education, a number of the universities studied utilised dual mediation as a matter of best practice. In other institutions it was felt that it was more difficult to effectively manage dual mediation because of the difficulties of securing time off for mediators or on the basis of costs. Ultimately, however, for many co-ordinators in this sector, given the fairly limited number of cases they were managing, dual mediation was seen as a useful way to offer their mediators ongoing opportunities to practise.

13.8 The five stages of the mediation process

Having considered the role of the main players in workplace mediation and the key issues in designing an internal scheme, this section explains the mediation process in detail.

Stage 1: Separate meetings with the parties

In the pre-stage of the process, the mediator contacts the parties separately and, having gained their agreement to take part, arranges a separate meeting with each disputant. This is the first time the mediator will meet each party in person. The mediator and disputant will introduce themselves, and the mediator will explain their role and outline the process and objectives of mediation. In particular they will stress their neutral position, their non-judgemental approach and that all conversations are in total confidence. At this stage, the mediator uses questions and listening to try to understand the situation, the context of the dispute and the perceptions of each party as to the causes and consequences of the dispute. The mediator will also explain the potential outcomes of mediation. This is the first opportunity for the mediator to build a rapport with each of the parties and gain their trust. Each party is encouraged to talk about themselves, their job role and their relationship with others, including the other disputant. Through this process of openness and empathy to the concerns and feelings of each party, the mediator seeks to get the agreement of each party to continue the process and crucially to move to the next stage, which is the joint meeting.

Stage 2: Hearing the issues

The second stage in the process is about setting the scene for the mediation and hearing the issues with both the parties present. The joint meeting opens with a welcome from the mediator and an introduction to the parties. This takes the form of the mediator outlining the process and the purpose of the joint meeting and explaining how the meeting is to be conducted. A key aspect of this part of the meeting is the need to establish ground rules for the meeting and the rest of the process. For example, the mediator will stress the need to respect the other's point of view, to use appropriate language and not to interrupt the other party while they are giving their account of the dispute. Each party then gets the opportunity to 'tell their side of things', to put their case and for the other party to reflect on the feelings of, and impact on, the other person. When both sides have put their case, the mediator summarises the points raised by both parties and suggests an agenda for discussion. If this agenda is agreed by both parties, the process moves to the third stage.

Stage 3: Exploring the issues

This is the stage that gives an opportunity for both parties to express in more detail how they feel about the issues causing the conflict and the impact that it is having on them in the workplace. The mediator will direct questions to each party to check their understanding of the issues. Crucially, this stage in the process offers participants the chance to acknowledge their differences, accept different perspectives on issues and seek to move on from those differences. Throughout this stage, the mediator's role is to maintain the agenda or, if new issues arise, to negotiate with the parties to table these for further discussion. A key aspect of the mediation process, particularly when utilising the facilitative model, is to change the focus of the relationship between the two disputants from the past to the future. The mediator manages this by getting the parties to express their feelings about past events, articulate 'the history' of their relationship, but then to emphasise the positive aspects of looking to a settlement which can seek to repair or restore their relationship in the future. When the mediator decides that discussion has progressed sufficiently, they will summarise the areas of consensus and disagreement between the two parties. This allows the mediator to demonstrate the progress that has been made and then allows a focus on the issues that remain to be addressed.

Stage 4: Building and writing agreements

In this stage, the mediator helps the parties to suggest options for resolving the issues that lie between them. They then assess which options may be most acceptable or practical. At this juncture, the process of negotiation may start in earnest as the mediator encourages the parties to offer a concession on an issue in return for an offer from the other party. A key aim at this point is to get the two parties to prioritise their resolution and to jointly look for a settlement. The role of the mediator here is to highlight gestures of conciliation made by the parties. This stage closes by the mediator summarising the actions that have been agreed between the two parties, including issues that may still need to be discussed or where differences have been conceded. The mediator then records the agreement made between the two parties. Finally, the mediator writes up the agreement for the parties.

Stage 5: Closure and follow-up

This is the final stage in the process and the point at which the mediator congratulates the parties on the progress they have made and reiterates what has been achieved through the mediation process. This statement acts as a summary, but also aims to reconfirm the two parties' commitment to the agreement and their relationship.

Closure is then achieved through the parties signing the agreement and taking their copies. The mediator at this point will also ask the parties if they want a follow-up or review meeting before formally leaving. If no agreement is reached, the mediator will close by summarising the situation and outlining what alternative action the parties have decided to take and the possible next steps.

13.9 The skills and knowledge needed for effective mediation

There are a number of key skills, qualities and knowledge required to be an effective mediator in the workplace. For a more detailed discussion, Crawley's (2012) practical guide to workplace mediation is helpful, where, in particular, he advocates skills such as 'being a good listener', having 'empathy' and being 'self-aware' and 'reflective' as crucial for effective mediation. Table 13.1 sets out the key skills, qualities and knowledge needed for effective mediation.

Table 13.1 Effective mediation – key skills, qualities and knowledge

Skills	Qualities	Knowledge
• active listening • good written and communication skills • questioning • observing • understanding of body language and people's behaviour • effective summarising and ability to review and evaluate • ability to reflect and be self-aware • influencing skills • ability to build rapport • assertiveness • facilitation • analysis of information and problem solving • planning and time management • negotiation skills	• empathy • approachability • impartiality and fairness • ability to be non-judgemental • professionalism • honesty and integrity • credibility, creativity and flexibility	• theory of conflict resolution • causes and consequences of conflict • dispute resolution techniques • the mediation process • principles and practice standards • legal context of mediation • equal opportunities and diversity issues • dynamics of power and conflict • context of the particular dispute

The attitude and approach needed to be an effective mediator

The mediator makes a priority of building rapport with the client, establishing empathy and demonstrating their impartiality. All of these actions are fundamental aspects of what a mediator does. In addition, there are a number of other approaches that the mediator undertakes in any intervention.

The mediator should always aim to be fair and non-judgemental. They need to be patient to ensure that each participant is able to fully make their case. Communication skills, including picking up on non-verbal cues, are crucial, as is the ability to time-manage the process, allowing sufficient space for both parties to feel that they are being fully heard but judging when to summarise a discussion and move onto the next issue or issues. The mediator must clearly introduce the parties to the process and establish the issues. They must set ground rules for all meetings, summarise when appropriate and look to gain agreement when the parties are disposed to do so. The mediator must be able to encourage the parties to agree solutions when judged to be in their best interests and felt by the mediator to genuinely offer a potential resolution to their conflict.

In encouraging people to participate in mediation, the mediator can adopt a particular strategy to engage with the disputants. The mediator stresses that there is no compulsion to participate and that mediation does not preclude them from raising a grievance or taking further action should the mediation not succeed. By stressing the neutrality of the process and setting clear ground rules, the mediator hopes to allay any fears that participants may have. The skilled mediator will discuss the alternatives and balance their potential efficacy against that of mediation in terms of time, costs, loss of control and chances of success.

The mediator remains realistic with the two parties as to what is possible and emphasises that success is dependent on all parties being committed to the process. In this respect, there are a number of things that a mediator cannot do. These must be made clear to the two parties to avoid misunderstandings and misconceptions. It is not the role of the mediator to judge clients or the case that they make. Neither is it their role to offer advice to the parties, offer solutions or take sides. The mediator's role is to facilitate discussion between the clients that will allow them to make informed choices between possible solutions generated through their own discourse. Even if they see merit in an argument or the case of one party, it is the role of the mediator to assist the disputants to weigh up the merits of their cases and seek solutions through dialogue and informed negotiation. It is not the task of the mediator to apportion blame. Rather it is their role to move the parties away from the past and blaming one another to seek a solution that will hold for the future. Finally, the mediator must never break the confidentiality of either party unless there has been agreement to do so.

Reflective activity 13.10

What sort of managing conflict training do you have in your organisation for line managers? Would managers in your organisation benefit from a workshop on basic mediation skills? If the answer is yes, what would the main advantages be?

Figure 13.3 The CCS model for managing workplace conflict

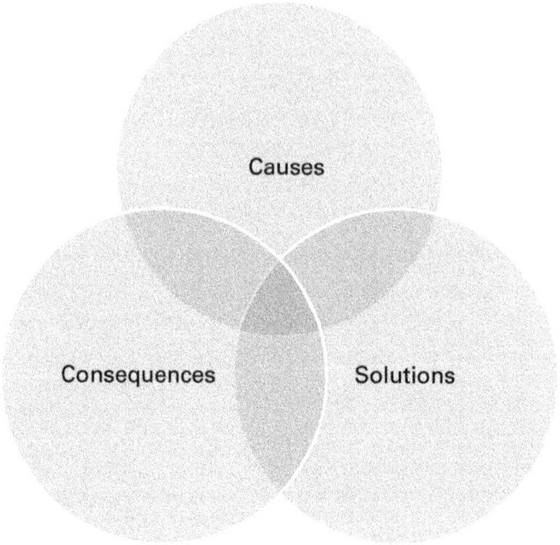

Mediation skills for management?

A major theme of this textbook is that there is no panacea for the successful prevention or resolution of conflict in the workplace. Rather, there are many key variables that will 'mediate' that process (for instance, the balance of power, the presence of a union and the framework of employment legislation and regulation).

Similarly, the process of mediation discussed in this chapter remains one of several options available to organisations in managing workplace conflict. However, it can be further argued that the knowledge, skills and approach utilised for successful mediation can provide managers with useful additional tools in resolving disputes within their team, before the issue reaches more 'formal' channels.

Through training events, members of this writing team have delivered learning on the value, process and limitations of mediation; this has allowed us to raise awareness of how mediation works but also equip delegates with new skills to take back to the workplace. The following section offers some practical insight into how those skills and knowledge can be developed and used. From a practical perspective, our starting point, as illustrated in Figure 13.3, is to recognise the interrelated nature of conflict, its causes, its consequences and the solutions available (the CCS model).

 Reflective activity 13.11

In our conflict resolution workshops, we first ask delegates to identify the common causes and consequences of conflict in the workplace. Complete the following grid in respect of your own workplace or experience.

Causes	Consequences
E.g. Personality clash between team members	Reduced morale and effectiveness of the team

Then we ask delegates to consider what strategies, processes and procedures do we typically have in an organisation for dealing with workplace conflict. How effective do they think these potential solutions are and why?

Process or procedure	When effective?	When less effective?
In the example above, line manager applies 'mediation' skills	Potentially in example above	If dispute proves to have deeper rooted causes – potential to refer to mediation
		If the behaviour of parties requires formal procedure – go to grievance or discipline

These activities allow us to reflect on the extent to which mediation is a potential solution for resolving a dispute that has escalated beyond the abilities of the manager. However, they also suggest ways in which managers might draw on the knowledge, skills and perspectives offered by mediation to resolve conflict within their teams in a more informal way.

Therefore a line manager who is confronted with two members of their team who are in dispute can use a basic 'mediative' process to try to address the issue at an early stage. Holding separate and joint meetings, using the idea of uninterrupted time and using questioning, listening and summarising skills to explore potential solutions can help managers develop a proactive approach to conflict. In this way, managers can apply the key approaches of mediation but can adapt them to their role as a manager and leader to direct team members away from conflicting 'positions' to an acceptable resolution based on their common 'interests'.

A BASIC MEDIATIVE MODEL FOR MANAGERS

- Hold separate meetings with the individuals concerned.
- Use questioning and listening techniques to recognise their concern and understand the nature of the problem.
- Explore the resolutions that they are looking for – try to explore their longer-term interests and needs.
- Ask whether they would be prepared to take part in a joint meeting.
- Hold a joint meeting with the parties.
- Explain the process and establish ground rules.
- Allow each party uninterrupted time to give their side of the story.
- Try to establish common ground by focusing on overlapping interests.
- Use reframing and rephrasing techniques to create a more constructive narrative.
- Explore potential resolutions.
- Agree on a set of actions and a process of review.

This mediative model was a key part of a unique research project conducted by academics based at the Universities of Westminster and Sheffield. The Skilled Managers project sought to explore whether developing conflict resolution skills could boost the conflict confidence of managers. Moreover, it looked at whether these skills could be carried over into the workplace to encourage early conflict resolution.

REAL-WORLD EXAMPLE 13.5

Skilled Managers – boosting conflict confidence?

Researchers from the Universities of Westminster and Sheffield designed an online training intervention (called Skilled Managers) which was aimed at first line managers who otherwise would be unlikely to have the time or resources to take part in more conventional conflict management training. The intervention was made up of four modules: these examined key communication skills, having difficult conversations about performance and conduct, decision-making in conflict situations and resolving team-based conflicts. In short, the course revolved around the basic skills that underpin workplace mediation. The intervention used bite-size videos, scenarios and simulations and could be completed in around three hours and accessed via a tablet or smartphone.

The impact of the intervention was assessed in three ways: first managers were asked to complete questionnaires at the start and end of the course to measure their conflict management style. This gave them a score (out of five) across five dimensions: problem-solving, obliging, compromising, dominating and avoiding. Second, the research team asked for feedback from managers on their experience of the course. Third, the researchers measured the engagement of staff through an online 10-item pulse survey. In the larger organisations, a randomised controlled trial approach was used where the impacts on staff of (treatment by) groups of managers who received the training were measured against a control group of managers who were not trained. Overall, the research involved over 70 different organisations and trained over 1,000 managers.

The key findings of the research were:

- There were positive changes to the conflict style of managers after completing the intervention – there were statistically significant increases in problem-solving scores and even larger reductions in avoiding scores. This pointed to the development of more collaborative and proactive styles.
- Among a sample of small and micro-organisations more than 90 per cent of managers said that the training had increased their confidence and 80 per cent agreed that they intended to change the way that they managed their team.
- Analysis of pulse survey data showed positive changes in most of the organisations where managers had been trained.

SOURCE: Urwin et al (2024)

This research shows that using mediative skills as a basis for managerial training can have a positive impact and encourage early resolution. Moreover, if organisations can develop the conflict confidence of their line managers, more straightforward issues will be resolved close to source, meaning that structured mediation can focus on more complex issues when a trained mediator is really needed. Finally, as Latreille and Saundry (2015) found in their evaluation of internal mediation in the NHS, organisations can use their mediators to train and develop their line managers. In addition, research into employee relations in the NHS revealed that mediation figured extensively in dispute resolution. Furthermore, 'mediation was also seen as a key aspect of changing the culture of managing conflict, such as the encouragement to use facilitated conversations by both HR colleagues and line managers before more formal actions or mediation is chosen' (Bennett et al, 2023: 6).

13.10 Developing a model of good practice

Having reviewed both the process and some of the key findings from current research on mediation, the main generic elements of workplace mediation are mapped out in Figure 13.4. This allows us to consider how a model for mediation can be applied in practice. First, there are key variables that will inform the successful implementation of the initiative, such as a champion at the senior level, the culture of the

Figure 13.4 A practical model of workplace mediation

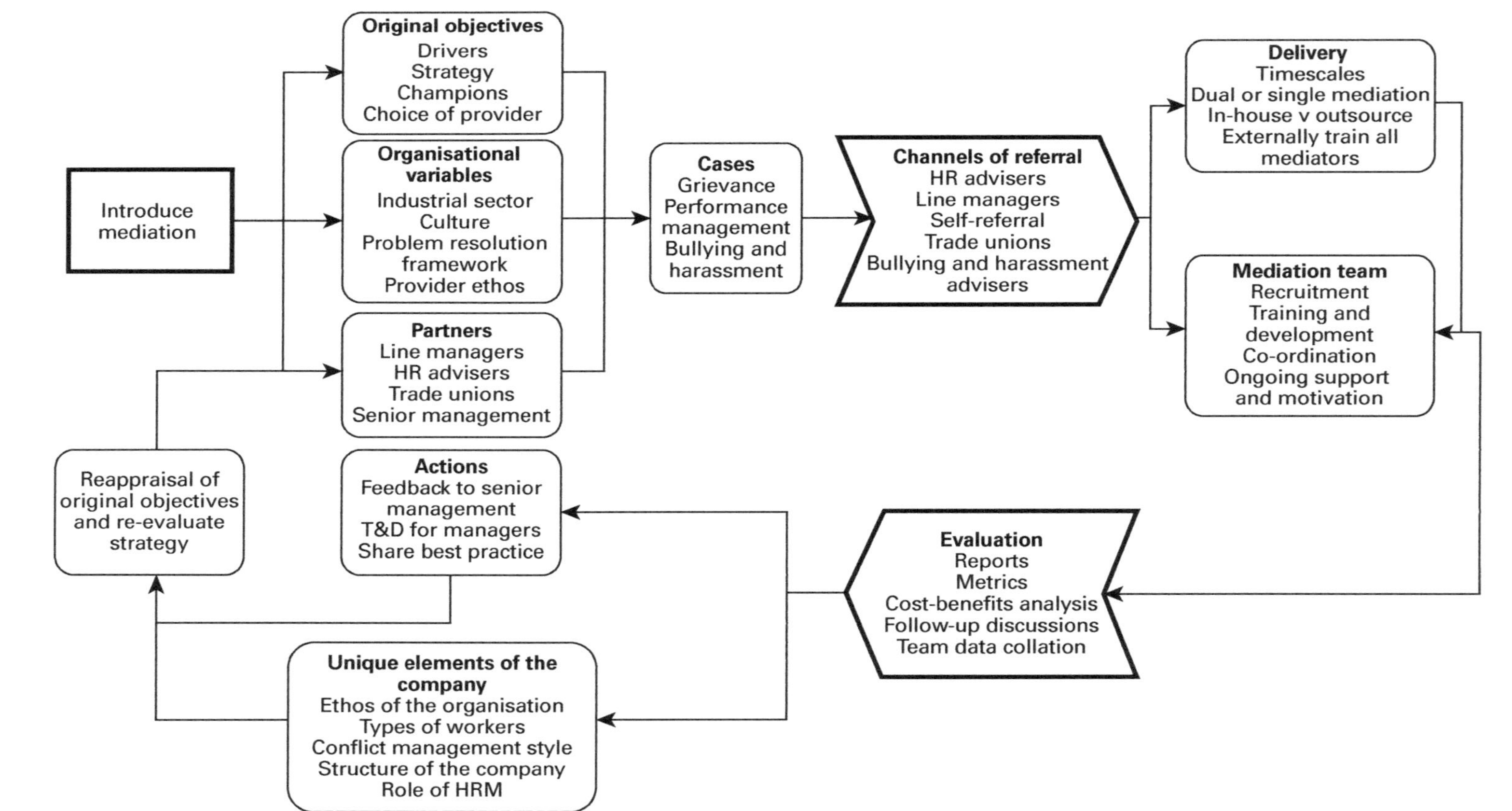

organisation and the key partners to be involved in the process. Second, in terms of managing the system, evidence suggests that developing clear and multiple channels of referral, managed by a single co-ordinator, is the most effective approach. This also helps in making decisions over the appropriateness of the dispute for mediation and whether the mediation should be conducted by an internal or external mediator. Third, as in any HRM process, evaluation is a key element captured in the model. This allows appropriate feedback to senior management to demonstrate its effectiveness and, crucially, for action to be taken to address any limitations in the service. This can then feed into a broader reappraisal of the strategic objectives of the initiative.

13.11 Summary

There is growing interest in the potential of mediation to offer an effective alternative process for the resolution of individual employment disputes. However, we do not suggest that mediation is a panacea for all disputes. Rather, depending on the reasons for the dispute and the outcomes expected by the parties, mediation can offer the potential to rebuild and maintain an employment relationship that has become compromised without resort to more formal disciplinary and grievance procedures. While these are often necessary, they are costly, time-consuming and rarely provide positive experiences or outcomes for those involved. In contrast, mediation can also empower employees, allowing them an opportunity to challenge managerial prerogative in a way that is not possible through conventional dispute resolution procedures. Furthermore, given the problems faced by line managers in addressing and resolving 'difficult issues', the skills and techniques used in workplace mediation have the potential to provide the basis for the development of much needed conflict competence and confidence. More broadly, mediation has the potential to play a part in reshaping workplace environments to emphasise the importance of resolution and conciliation in managing the employment relationship.

KEY LEARNING POINTS

- Unlike more formal routes for resolving disputes, mediation is confidential, and the process and outcome are determined by the disputants. The mediator acts only to facilitate the overall process.
- Mediation is an alternative dispute resolution process. However, unlike conciliation, the disputants are not 'guided' through the process towards a solution. Equally it is not like arbitration, where the arbitrator acts as a judge and finds for one party or the other. The mediator should remain neutral at all times.
- Mediation is not a panacea for all disputes. However, where this involves a breakdown in the relationship between two or more parties, it can provide an

effective means of rebuilding and restoring relations to allow the parties to continue to work effectively.

- The knowledge, skills and approach used in mediation can also potentially inform and enhance the more general practice of managers and HR professionals in managing conflict.
- Dispute resolution is more likely to be successful if the mediation takes place at an early stage in the conflict. However, it is important that mediation does not replace or supplant managerial responsibility in addressing difficult issues at an early stage. However, if the line manager cannot resolve an issue, mediation may be used before formal procedures are enacted.
- The introduction of in-house mediation capacity can have a positive impact on the way that organisations manage conflict more broadly. However, for this to occur, mediation should be seen as a central element of HR strategy.
- The mediation process and the essential skills involved in mediation can provide a model for line managers which can be used to address conflict at an early stage.

Review Questions

1. In what types of situation, where workplace conflict has occurred, do you feel that mediation may be most appropriate and why?
2. Why do you think that the take-up of workplace mediation in the UK is relatively low? What could be done by policymakers and practitioners to extend its use?
3. To what extent does mediation allow organisations to evade responsibility for workplace mistreatment?
4. What do you feel are the key issues to be taken into account if you are considering the introduction of an internal mediation service in your organisation?
5. As an HR practitioner, what sort of role do you think you might take up in such a service?
6. To what degree do you think that mediation genuinely offers a more equitable approach for workers in dispute than more conventional methods of resolution?

Explore further

Bennett, T (2014) The role of workplace mediation: a critical assessment, *Personnel Review*, 43 (5), pp 764–79

CIPD (2020) *Managing Conflict in the Modern Workplace*. Available from: https://www.cipd.co.uk/knowledge/fundamentals/relations/disputes/managing-workplace-conflict-report (archived at https://perma.cc/ZQ5K-EEND) [accessed 13 May 2024]

CIPD (2024e) *Mediation: An approach to resolving workplace issues*. Available from: https://www.cipd.org/uk/knowledge/guides/workplace-mediation/#what-is-mediation (archived at https://perma.cc/R33E-DZCC) [accessed 12 June 2024]

Latreille, P and Saundry, R (2015) *Towards a System of Conflict Management?* Acas Research Paper, 03/15

Liddle, D (2023) *Managing Conflict: A practical guide to resolution in the workplace*, 2nd edn, Kogan Page, London

Saundry, R, Wibberley, G, Hollonrake, A and Wright, A (2023) *Mediation and Early Resolution in East Lancashire Hospitals NHS Trust*, Acas. Available from: https://www.acas.org.uk/early-resolution-in-east-lancs-hospitals-NHS-trust (archived at https://perma.cc/Q5VW-QJQT) [accessed 13 May 2024]

Websites

www.acas.org.uk (archived at https://perma.cc/U7C7-PK53) gives access to guides and research reports on conflict management and workplace mediation. This is a really valuable source of both current research and practical guides to how mediation works in practice.

www.cipd.co.uk (archived at https://perma.cc/G7MM-9S96) gives access to CIPD guides and reports on conflict management and workplace mediation. Very useful source for reports on CIPD members and their experiences of mediation, through reports and survey results. Excellent source of practical guides on the subject.

14
Conclusion – the future of employment relations

The eighth edition of *Managing Employment Relations*, like previous versions of the book, attempts to integrate theory, policy and practice to provide a valuable resource for all students of employment relations. In particular, it is aimed at aspiring or practising HR professionals who need to be able to critically analyse and evaluate contemporary trends and debates within HRM and employment relations. They must also be able to convert this knowledge into viable and effective strategy, policy and advice. The dynamic and volatile context of work and employment in the UK means that the challenges facing HR practitioners are more complex than ever. Automation, persistent low productivity, the rapid advance of artificial intelligence and growing inequalities have seen a new emphasis on the role that work plays and increasingly vocal demands for greater fairness and equity. These features have arguably been accentuated by the Covid pandemic and contributed to an environment in which employers face more resistance than at any time in the last three decades. This not only means that employment relations is more relevant than ever, but that HR professionals urgently need to develop their knowledge and skills in order to navigate these new challenges. In this concluding chapter, we offer our thoughts for the future and identify the key issues which we believe will shape work and employment in the UK over the next five years.

14.1 Pandemic and protest – a new world of employment relations?

The last edition of this book was written at a time when the UK government was attempting to negotiate a Brexit agreement with the EU. This had the potential to fundamentally reset employment relations with the possibility that a wide range of employment protections could be under threat. The fact that the then Conservative government did very little, if anything, to take advantage of its new-found 'freedom' arguably reflects widespread (and growing) support for basic employment rights. It is also notable that the Labour Party's 'New Deal for Working People' which we have discussed earlier in the book, provoked relatively little opposition from employers. In fact, research conducted by the Chartered Management Institute found that more than 7 out of 10 managers supported the measures, while more than 8 out of 10 felt that strengthening workers' rights can have a positive impact on productivity (Institute of Employment Rights, 2024).

In reality, Brexit has been one component of a significant shift in the context of employment relations in the UK over the past five years. By curtailing the free movement of EU labour, organisations in a range of sectors have been faced with staff shortages, increasing the bargaining power of workers and trade unions. At the same time, external shocks, including the war in Ukraine, increased the cost of living. The combination of high levels of union bargaining power and high inflation created, for the first time since the 1980s, the perfect conditions for collective industrial conflict. Not only did the UK experience the highest levels of strike action for more than 30 years, trade unions demonstrated an ability to have a positive impact on the working lives of their members. For example, they won improved pay for their members, reversing the downward trend in the union wage premium. This was particularly the case in the private sector where employers had greater freedom to make commercial decisions about the relative costs of pay increases against those of industrial conflict. Interestingly, there is evidence of growing support for the work of trade unions among younger workers and perhaps most crucially 2023 saw an increase in membership among 16–24-year-olds.

Given the recent history of UK employment relations, it is perhaps tempting to believe that these developments are just a 'blip'. It is entirely possible that managerial approaches influenced by hard unitarist perspectives will prevail and the broad trend of declining collective regulation will be reasserted. However, that doesn't take into account the existential impact of the Covid pandemic. While some of the immediate effects of Covid, such as the 'great resignation', may have been temporary, others, such as the spread of remote and hybrid working, are more likely to be sustained. But the impact of the pandemic has arguably been more profound, as the experiences of working people during this time have reinforced a sense of anger and frustration about increased employment insecurity and income inequality. This has the potential to provide the basis for a more sustained change in attitudes, which may shape the nature of employment relations in the coming decade.

14.2 Automation and AI – insecurity, inequality and innovation

The deep concerns over job insecurity and income inequality are also fuelled by the rapid advance of automation and artificial intelligence. The impact of what some have called the fourth industrial revolution is complex. In previous eras, new technology has reshaped the nature of work without any fundamental changes to the employment relationship. However, the spread and development of platform and gig working has created clear challenges for how employment is conceptualised and regulated. To date, legislators have failed to engage with the changing nature of work, leading to dissatisfaction and discontent and creating the conditions for collective organisation.

It is important to note that these sectors remain a relatively small part of the labour market. Nonetheless, it is almost certain that the next two to three decades will see the impact of automation and AI reach into more conventional areas of employment. While there may be greater demand for certain very highly skilled technical jobs, a range of roles that involve routine and predictable tasks, and which can be easily replicated through computerisation, will disappear. This will include not only manual and unskilled employment, but also more highly paid jobs which are currently seen as comparatively skilled or requiring technical expertise. This will inevitably require policymakers to examine radical approaches to rebalancing societal attitudes to work, leisure and welfare. This can already be seen in debates over measures such as a universal basic income and a four-day working week.

In addition, automation is already increasing the pace and intensity of work while providing employers with more sophisticated ways of monitoring their employees and reinforcing their control over the labour process. This is arguably reinforced by the growth of homeworking as employers seek to expand their reach into the personal lives of workers. However, this is also an area of potential conflict and resistance, as workers seek to preserve their autonomy and also their levels of income even as their jobs are being de-skilled. This can be seen in increasing demand for collective organisation and representation among gig and platform workers, and those employed in organisations at the forefront of the information economy, such as Amazon and Apple. In many cases these employers have actively resisted any attempt at union organisation; however, the sustainability of anti-union strategies is now much more questionable.

It also possible that we will see an increased value placed on those roles which require well-developed social skills, which will be difficult to replace and therefore in greater demand. This places a greater premium on the type of managerial capabilities we have discussed at length in this book and discuss in the next section. It also has the potential to change the way we think about work that is currently seen as low status and consequently tends to be low paid, such as personal care. While this sector is only going to become more important in the next decade, poor pay and challenging conditions (together with the impact of Brexit and the pandemic) have created an acute staffing crisis. In this context, it is notable that the Labour government has proposed the development of a Fair Pay Agreement in adult social care. This implicitly supports the idea that trade union organisation and collective bargaining have a role to play in negotiating better terms and conditions which will help to recruit and retain staff and improve standards. Whether management and unions have the skills they need to take advantage of this approach is something we discuss in the following sections.

14.3 Job quality, managerial capability and the productivity puzzle

Debates over the impact of automation inevitably turn to the importance of job quality and good work. It is often tempting to look at these issues in terms of ways in which a particular role is designed. While this is undoubtedly important, it tends to neglect the contemporary relevance of employment relations and the way that people are managed. The best designed work will not deliver positive experiences unless it is embedded in a context in which fairness and equity are located front and centre. This in turn is inextricably linked to the quality of management in the UK. According to the Chartered Management Institute most employees find that their manager has a 'deep impact on... their motivation, satisfaction, and likelihood of leaving the job' (CMI, 2023).

The importance of effective line management was a golden thread running through the previous edition of this book. We reported compelling evidence that poor management is one explanation for the UK's 'long tail' of low-productivity firms and that 'large, persistent gaps in basic managerial practices... were associated with large, persistent differences in firm performance' (Sadun et al, 2017: 123). The problem of a lack of managerial proficiency was also beginning to be acknowledged by the UK government (HM Government, 2017).

One might hope that in the years since, progress would have been made in this area. Unfortunately, the evidence, and our own experience, suggests that this remains a major obstacle to creating healthy, effective and productive workplaces. In fact, in 2023, 4 in 10 people moving into management positions had no formal management or leadership training (CMI, 2023). At the same time, the onus on operational managers to handle employment relations issues is increasing as HR functions continue to try to devolve people management to the line. Moreover, the rapidly changing context of work and employment is likely to place an even greater value on people-related skills, such as listening, questioning, negotiating and mediating, which cannot be computerised or automated.

Given that this issue is now widely acknowledged, it is difficult to understand why it is not being addressed. We suggest that there are a number of reasons. First, organisations still have a tendency to focus on leadership at the expense of managerial competence (Sadun et al, 2017). Core managerial competences are often perceived as being low-level and basic compared to the aspirational allure of leadership development. Second, the consequences of poor management – disengagement and conflict – are rarely seen as strategic priorities. In part this is due to the complexity of measuring and attributing the cost of conflict. For example, Saundry and Urwin's (2021) analysis of the cost of conflict estimated that dismissals and resignations cost UK businesses around £23 billion annually, however it is likely that this would be seen as inevitable rather than a direct result of poor management. This means that management training is often not prioritised and lacks the support of senior leaders. Third, even when organisations invest in training, managers are not provided with the space and support to put this into practice. Time spent in managing employment relations is rarely acknowledged or rewarded and senior management, preoccupied with short-term operational targets and objectives, will often see time spent on employment relations issues as wasted.

Therefore, while training is necessary, it is not always sufficient. Instead, organisations need to see the management of people in general, and employment relations more specifically, as central to developing and retaining engaged and productive staff. We would also suggest that government has a role to play by supporting and incentivising organisations to invest in high quality management. In fact, managerial capability is even more important in light of the new Labour government's intention to strengthen employment rights. The historic weakness of employment legislation in the UK has traditionally meant that organisations and their managers can simply resort to hire and fire as a short-term response to challenging people management situations. However, if the government does enact the right to claim unfair dismissal from day one, this will be much more difficult.

The most effective organisational response is to equip managers to prevent, contain and resolve the issues that have the potential to escalate into claims of unfair dismissal and discrimination. In this way, the 'New Deal for Working People' could nudge employers to create fairer, more effective and productive workplaces. This could include providing managers with the training and support they need and prioritising good people management. However, if managerial quality is not addressed, there is a danger that organisations will simply hide behind a wall of process and procedure and HR will revert to the policing role it has spent last 40 years trying to escape.

14.4 Voice, representation and bargaining

While the development of more skilled and effective line managers has the potential to increase the voice of employees in the workplace, the imbalance in the employment relationship requires collective mechanisms of representation. Notwithstanding the increased profile of trade unions during and after the Covid pandemic, channels of collective voice in terms of employee representation, consultative committees and collective bargaining have been critically eroded since 1979. This has negative consequences for workers and their employers – employee silence erodes any sense of organisational justice, fuels disengagement and encourages poor decision-making. More broadly, as organisations such as the OECD and the IMF have pointed out, fragmented pay determination and growing income inequality do not provide a stable basis for economic growth and improved productivity.

These arguments underpin the policy programme of the new Labour government, elected in July 2024. It argues that:

> collective bargaining can help companies and workers respond to demographic and technological change and adapt to the new world of work... strong collective bargaining rights and institutions are key to tackling problems of insecurity, inequality, discrimination, enforcement and low pay... Our existing framework for industrial relations and collective bargaining is rife with inefficiencies and anachronisms that work against cooperation, compromise and negotiation (Labour Party, 2024).

It is easy to dismiss this as rhetoric, while commentators and critics are understandably sceptical about whether this ambition will be reflected in reality. Nonetheless, Labour's plans and the arguments that underpin them mark a radical departure and go substantially beyond anything envisaged within the 14 years of Labour government under Tony Blair and Gordon Brown. We believe that a reset of this kind is urgently needed given the radical changes in the context of employment relations outlined earlier. Indeed, these challenges and the fundamental weakness of UK employment relations were cruelly exposed by the waves of industrial unrest in 2022 and 2023.

Strikes in the NHS alone were estimated to cost £1.5 billion up to January 2024 and the pay dispute with junior doctors was still unresolved when this book was written in July 2024. This is not to suggest that strike action is illegitimate – to the contrary, it is an expression of frustration and discontent and reflects the underlying conflict at the heart of the employment relationship. However, it does represent a complete failure of negotiation and points to a more fundamental lack of understanding of employment relations. It remains to be seen whether the Labour government will deliver on its promise to rebuild collective employment relations in the UK. Nonetheless, this new approach has the potential to create the conditions for genuine partnership and co-operation.

14.5 Rebuilding employment relations?

However, the scale of the challenge should not be understated. As we have discussed in this book, employment relations in the UK has been hollowed out in 45 years since the election of Margaret Thatcher. A crucial and often overlooked consequence of this has been a dramatic loss of collective knowledge of the practice of negotiation, consultation and conflict resolution – in short, the practice of employment relations. It is often forgotten that the HR profession was founded on the idea of managing the employment relationship. The first incarnation of the CIPD, the Institute of Labour Management, was set up in 1931 to 'assist in the management of recruitment, discipline, dismissal and industrial relations at plant level amongst unionised male workers' (CIPD, 2017a). As the profession developed, the collective regulation of employment and conflict resolution was a core part of its mission and HR practitioners were generally seen as neutral, honest brokers who stood between management and employees and who were there, in part, to resolve conflict and promote co-operative relationships.

However, the increasing dominance of HRM underpinned by unitarist perspectives has seen HR practitioners abandon this role in favour of one more closely aligned with 'business' imperatives. At the same time, employment relations has become increasingly marginalised – seen by many HR practitioners as a day-to-day, transactional activity well outside the strategic priorities of either organisations or even the HR function. Moreover, employment relations is seen as outmoded and 'counter aspirational', leading to a shortage of employment relations skills and expertise within the HR profession. The consequence of this is that the HR profession and many UK organisations are not equipped to respond in a positive way to the challenges of the current environment – whether this is resistance from workers, newly energised trade unions or the policy agenda of the Labour government.

This problem is not unique to the HR profession – trade unions have spent the last 40 years finding ways to survive in increasingly hostile terrain. This has meant moving away from traditional collective approaches with an increased focus on protecting and enforcing individual rights. In addition, they have devoted much greater time and resources into trying to rebuild grassroots organisation. This implicitly requires an approach which focuses on identifying and mobilising the concerns of workers, and challenging the positions and interests of employers. This is also driven by the demands of members (and potential members) who are understandably disenchanted by the erosion of pay and working conditions. Furthermore, new unions are emerging that are more prepared to confront employers in a more robust and assertive manner. In this climate, there is a danger that the traditional skills of negotiation and dispute resolution are crowded out.

It is also important to question whether the government itself, which after all is the largest employer in the UK, has the necessary capabilities to navigate the employment relations challenges it will undoubtedly face. There would seem to be little point in developing structures of bargaining and negotiation if the key players lack the capability needed to negotiate and bargain successfully. All key stakeholders have a responsibility to acknowledge and address this problem – nonetheless for HR, there is an acute need to place employment relations at the centre of its identity once again.

For us, the employment relationship is the main building block of 'good work', and therefore its effective management is more important than ever. This book aims to provide HR practitioners with the ability to guide and advise managers and senior leaders on how to handle a wide range of difficult and complex issues. It also attempts to convince HR practitioners that an emphasis on the employment relationship is central to delivering fair and decent work. Moreover, we hope it provides them with the arguments they require to persuade senior leaders of the need for structures and processes through which the interests of employees can be voiced and represented, and of the importance of equipping managers with the skills to build high-trust and engaged workplaces.

REFERENCES

Acas (2010) *Code of Practice: Time Off for Trade Union Duties*. Available from: https://www.acas.org.uk/acas-code-of-practice-on-time-off-for-trade-union-duties-and-activities/html (archived at https://perma.cc/C9X4-Z9ZZ) [accessed 19 May 2024]

Acas (2013) *Individual Mediation: Feedback from participants and commissioners*, Acas research paper, 7/13

Acas (2014) *Frontline Managers' Booklet*, Acas, London

Acas (2015) *Code of Practice on Discipline and Grievance Procedures*. Available from: https://www.acas.org.uk/acas-code-of-practice-on-disciplinary-and-grievance-procedures (archived at https://perma.cc/G63C-MGA3) [accessed 1 July 2024]

Acas (2018) *Wellbeing in the Workplace: Rhetoric or reality?* Available from: http://www.acas.org.uk/index.aspx?articleid=5031 (archived at https://perma.cc/N8VW-JLKS) [accessed 19 September 2018]

Acas (2019a) *Discipline and Grievances at Work: The Acas guide*. Available from: https://www.acas.org.uk/media/1043/Discipline-and-grievances-at-work-The-Acas-guide/pdf/DG_Guide_Feb_2019.pdf (archived at https://perma.cc/FG7N-W8FF) [accessed 14 September 2019]

Acas (2019b) *Leading People*. Available from: https://www.acas.org.uk/sites/default/files/2021-03/guidance-leading-people.pdf (archived at https://perma.cc/MV6G-ERRP) [accessed 6 June 2024]

Acas (2021) *Dismissal and Re-engagement (Fire-and-Rehire): A fact-finding exercise*. Available from: https://www.acas.org.uk/research-and-commentary/fire-and-rehire/report (archived at https://perma.cc/PS45-3ZAQ)

Acas (2022) *Suspension from Work*. Available from: https://www.acas.org.uk/suspension (archived at https://perma.cc/WJ75-J2MA) [accessed 12 June 2023]

Acas (2023a) *Annual Report and Accounts, 2022-2023*, Acas, London

Acas (2023b) *Discrimination and Bullying*. Available from: https://www.acas.org.uk/discrimination-and-bullying (archived at https://perma.cc/XJK7-REWB) [accessed 4 June 2024]

Acker, J (2006a) Inequality regimes: gender, class and race in organizations, *Gender and Society*, **20** (4), pp 441–64

Acker, J (2006b) The gender regime of Swedish banks, *Scandinavian Journal of Management*, **22**, pp 195–209

Acker, J (2009) From glass ceiling to inequality regimes, *Sociologie du Travail*, **51**, pp 199–217

Acker, J (2012) Gendered organisations and intersectionality: problems and possibilities, *Equality, Diversity and Inclusion: An International Journal*, **31** (3), pp 214–24

Adam, D, Purcell, J and Hall, M (2014) *Joint Consultative Committees under the Information and Consultation of Employees Regulations: A WERS analysis*, Acas research paper, 04/14

Adams, Z (2023) Legal mobilisations, trade unions and radical social change: a case study of the IWGB, *Industrial Law Journal*, **52** (3), pp 560–94

Alfes, K, Truss, C, Soane, E, Rees, C and Gatenby, M (2010) *Creating an Engaged Workforce: Findings from the Kingston Employee Engagement Consortium Project*, CIPD, London

Ali, V, Corfe, S, Norman, A and Wilson, J (2023) *Hybrid Work Commission 2023*, Public First. Available from: https://www.publicfirst.co.uk/wp-content/uploads/2023/08/Hybrid-Work-Commission-report-Embargoed-until-13th-Sept-2023.pdf (archived at https://perma.cc/9PU9-BSMJ) [accessed 17 May 2024].

Anguiano, D and Beckett, L (2023) How Hollywood writers triumphed over AI – and why it matters, *The Guardian*, 1 October. Available from: https://www.theguardian.com/culture/2023/oct/01/hollywood-writers-strike-artificial-intelligence (archived at https://perma.cc/SY8C-S9EW) [accessed 1 July 2024]

Antcliff, V and Saundry, R (2009) Accompaniment, workplace representation and disciplinary outcomes in British workplaces: just a formality? *British Journal of Industrial Relations*, **47** (1), pp 100–121

Armstrong, M (2021) *Armstrong's Handbook of Strategic Human Resource Management*, 7th edn, Kogan Page, London.

Ashman, I (2012) *Downsizing Envoys: A public/private sector comparison*, Acas research paper, 11/12

Ashman, I (2014) The face-to-face delivery of downsizing decisions in UK public sector organizations: the envoy role, *Public Management Review*, **17** (1), pp 108–28

Ashman, I (2016) Downsizing: managing redundancy and restructuring, in *Reframing Resolution: Innovation and change in the management of conflict*, eds R Saundry, P Latreille and I Ashman, Palgrave Macmillan, London

Aubrey-Johnson, K and Curtis, H (2012) *Making Mediation Work for You: A practical handbook*, Legal Action Group, London

Bacchetta, M, Ernst, E and Juana, P (2009) *Globalisation and Informal Jobs in Developing Countries*, WTO Publications, Geneva

Bach, S, Givan, R and Forth, J (2009) The public sector in transition, in *The Evolution of the Modern Workplace*, eds W Brown, A Bryson, J Forth and K Whitfield, Cambridge University Press, Cambridge

Bacon, N (2013) Industrial relations, in *Contemporary Human Resource Management: Text and cases*, 4th edn, eds A Wilkinson and T Redman, Pearson Education, Harlow

Bajorek, Z (2020) *The Squeezed Middle: Why HR should be hugging and not squeezing line managers*, Institute for Employment Studies. Available from: https://www.employment-studies.co.uk/resource/squeezed-middle-why-hr-should-be-hugging-and-not-squeezing-line-managers (archived at https://perma.cc/TUF5-7T6C) [accessed 1 July 2024]

Balogun, J, Hope Hailey, V and Stuart, R (2014) *Landing Transformational Change*, CIPD, London

Barrientos, S and Smith, S (2007) Do workers benefit from ethical trade? Assessing codes of labour practice in global production systems, *Third World Quarterly*, **28** (4), pp 713–29

BBC (2022) *Rights watchdog 'should lose status' over trans row*, BBC News, 11 February. Available from https://www.bbc.co.uk/news/education-60331962 (archived at https://perma.cc/Y6K8-YQJU) [accessed 1 July 2024]

BBC (2023a) *Equality watchdog head Baroness Falkner investigated over complaints*, BBC News, 24 May. Available at https://www.bbc.co.uk/news/education-65694666 (archived at https://perma.cc/ER25-WTTG) [accessed 1 July 2024]

BBC (2023b) *Women still do more housework, survey suggests,* BBC News, 21 September. Available from https://www.bbc.co.uk/news/uk-66866879 (archived at https://perma.cc/2HQD-SC68) [accessed 1 July 2024]

Behrend, H (1957) The effort bargain, *Industrial and Labour Relations Review*, **10** (9), pp 503–15

BEIS (2017) *Good Work: The Taylor review of modern working practices*. Available from: https://assets.publishing.service.gov.uk/government/uploads/system/uploads/attachment_data/file/627671/good-work-taylor-review-modern-working-practices-rg.pdf (archived at https://perma.cc/3ZS6-VGM8) [accessed 13 September 2019]

Bennett, T (2010) Employee voice initiatives in the public sector: views from the workplace, *International Journal of Public Sector Management,* **23** (5), pp 444–55

Bennett, T (2013) Workplace mediation and the empowerment of disputants: rhetoric or reality? *Industrial Relations Journal*, **44** (2), pp 189–209

Bennett, T (2014a) Do union–management learning partnerships reduce workplace conflict? *Employee Relations*, **36** (1), pp 17–32

Bennett, T (2014b) The role of workplace mediation: a critical assessment, *Personnel Review*, **43** (5), pp 764–79

Bennett, T (2017) Reflections on the role of a workplace mediator, *Journal of Mediation and Applied Conflict Analysis*, **4** (1), pp 117–30

Bennett, T and Wibberley, G (2023) Making the ethical case for effective domestic abuse policy and practice: the role of trade unions, *Employee Relations*, **45**(3), pp 637–52

Bennett, T, Wibberley, G and Jones, C (2019) The legal, moral and business implications of domestic abuse and its impact in the workplace, *Industrial Law Journal*, **48** (1), pp 137–42

Bennett, T, Wibberley, G and Paterson, A (2021) *It's Not Just a Private Matter: Developing effective policy and procedure for addressing the impact of domestic abuse in the workplace*. CIPD Applied Research Conference 2023 paper, CIPD

Bennett, T, Wright, A, Wibberley, G and Lawler, M (2023) *The State of Employee Relations in the NHS in 'the New Normal'*, CIPD Applied Research Conference 2023

Bergström, O and Arman, R (2017) Increasing commitment after downsizing: the role of involvement and voluntary redundancies, *Journal of Change Management*, **17** (4), pp 297–320

Bertolini, A and Dukes, R (2021) Trade unions and platform workers in the UK: worker representation in the shadow of the law, *Industrial Law Journal*, **50** (4), pp 662–88

Bevan, S and Cooper, C (2022) *The Healthy Workforce: Enhancing wellbeing and productivity in the workers of the future*, Emerald Publishing, Bingley

Bingham, L and Pitts, D (2002) Highlight of mediation at work: studies of the national REDRESS evaluation project, *Negotiation Journal*, **18** (2), pp 135–46

Bingham, LB, Hallberlin, CJ, Walker, DA and Chung, WT (2009) Dispute system design and justice in employment dispute resolution: mediation at the workplace, *Harvard Negotiation Law Review*, **14**, pp 1–50

BIS (2011) *Resolving Workplace Disputes: Government response to the consultation*, Department for Business, Innovation and Skills, London

BITC (2024) *Voices from the Race at Work Surveys*, Business in the Community, London. Available from: https://www.bitc.org.uk/wp-content/uploads/2024/03/bitc-report-race-voices-from-race-at-work-survey-march24.pdf (archived at https://perma.cc/Z87H-C4CN) [accessed 1 July 2024]

Black, C (2008) *Working for a Healthier Tomorrow: Dame Carol Black's review of the health of Britain's working age population*, The Stationery Office, London

Blanden, J and Machin, S (2003) Cross-generation correlations of union status for young people in Britain, *British Journal of Industrial Relations*, **41** (3), pp 391–415

Blithe, S (2019) 'I always knew I was a little girly': the gendering of skills in management training, *Management Learning*, **50** (5), pp 517–33

Bloodworth, J (2019) *Hired: Six months undercover in low-wage Britain*, Atlantic Books, London

Bloom, N and Van Reenen, J (2007) Measuring and explaining management practices across firms and countries, *Quarterly Journal of Economics*, **122** (4), pp 1351–408

Blyth, A (2003) The art of survival, *People Management*, **9** (9), pp 39–40

Blyton, P and Turnbull, P (2004) *The Dynamics of Employee Relations*, 3rd edn, Macmillan, Basingstoke

Booth, A (1989) *What Do Unions Do Now?* Discussion Papers in Economics, No. 8903, Brunel University

Bos-Nehles, A, Van Riemsdijk, M and Looise, J (2013) Employee perceptions of line management performance: applying the AMO theory to explain the effectiveness of line managers' HRM implementation, *Human Resource Management*, **52** (6), pp 861–77

Boswell, WR and Olson-Buchanan, JB (2004) Experiencing mistreatment at work: the role of grievance-filing, nature of mistreatment, and employee withdrawal, *Academy of Management Journal*, **47**, pp 129–39

Boxall, P and Purcell, J (2022) *Strategy and Human Resource Management*, 5th edn, Bloomsbury, London

Boxall, P, Guthrie, J and Paawe, J (2016) Editorial introduction: progressing our understanding of the mediating variables linking HRM, employee well-being and organizational performance, *Human Resource Management Journal*, **26** (2), pp 103–11

Boys, J (2022) *The Great Resignation – Fact or fiction?* CIPD. Available from: https://www.cipd.org/uk/views-and-insights/thought-leadership/cipd-voice/great-resignation-fact-fiction/ (archived at https://perma.cc/Y8N2-FMMB) [accessed 16 May 2024]

Bradley, H (2013) *Gender*, 2nd edn, Polity Press, Cambridge

Branney, V (2016) Workplace mediation and UK trade unions: the missing link?, in *Reframing Resolution: Innovation and change in the management of workplace conflict*, eds R Saundry, P Latreille and I Ashman, Palgrave Macmillan, Basingstoke

Bratton, J and Gold, J (2015) Towards critical human resource management education (CHRME): a sociological imagination approach, *Work, Employment and Society*, **29** (3), pp 496–507

Bratton, J, Gold, J, Bratton, A and Steele, L (2022) *Human Resource Management: A critical approach*, 7th edn, Bloomsbury Academic, London.

Braverman, H (1974) *Labor and Monopoly Capital: The degradation of work in the twentieth century*, Monthly Review Press, New York

Brione, P (2017) *Mind Over Machines: New technology and employment relations*, Acas Research Paper, 02/17

British Safety Council (2018a) *News: Report reveals dramatic fall in local authorities' inspections for health and safety*. Available from: https://www.britsafe.org/publications/safety-management-magazine/safety-management-magazine/2018/report-reveals-dramatic-fall-in-local-authorities-inspections-for-health-and-safety/ (archived at https://perma.cc/4VRL-BX49) [accessed 24 April 2019]

British Safety Council (2018b) *Not Just Free Fruit: Wellbeing at work*. Available from: https://www.britsafe.org/campaigns-policy/not-just-free-fruit-wellbeing-at-work/ (archived at https://perma.cc/7CFH-7T66) [accessed 19 September 2019]

Brookes, M and Brewster, C (2022) The allocation of HRM responsibilities: where is it most likely to happen? in *Research Handbook on Line Managers*, eds K Townsend, A Bos-Nehles and K Jiang, Edward Elgar Publishing, Cheltenham

Broughton, A, Higgins, T, Hicks, B and Cox, A (2011) *Workplaces and Social Networking: The implications for employment relations*, Acas Research Paper, 11/11

Brown, W, Bryson, A and Forth, J (2008) *Competition and the Retreat from Collective Bargaining*, NIESR Discussion Paper, No. 318, August

Bryant, M (2023) Women 'forced to return to violent homes' as shortage of UK refuge places leads to crisis, *The Guardian*, 18 June. Available from: https://www.theguardian.com/society/2023/jun/18/women-forced-to-return-to-violent-homes-as-shortage-of-uk-refuge-places-leads-to-crisis (archived at https://perma.cc/R324-X9K2) [accessed 12 June 2024]

Bryson, A (2016) Health and safety risks in Britain's workplaces: where are they and who controls them? *Industrial Relations Journal*, **47** (5–6), pp 547–66

Bryson, A and Forth, J (2017) *The Added Value of Trade Unions*, Trades Union Congress. Available from: https://www.tuc.org.uk/added-value-trade-unions (archived at https://perma.cc/Z45B-Y8TG) [accessed 18 September 2019]

Bryson, A, Forth, J and Stokes, L (2014) *Does Worker Wellbeing Affect Workplace Performance?* Department for Business, Innovation and Skills. Available from: https://assets.publishing.service.gov.uk/government/uploads/system/uploads/attachment_data/file/366637/bis-14-1120-does-worker-wellbeing-affect-workplace-performance-final.pdf (archived at https://perma.cc/3JRK-N9FD) [accessed 19 September 2019]

Budd, J and Bhave, D (2008) Values, ideologies, and frames of reference in industrial relations, in *The Sage Handbook of Industrial Relations*, eds P Blyton, E Heery, N Bacon and J Fiorito, Sage, London

Burgess, S, Propper, C and Wilson, D (2000) *Explaining the Growth in the Number of Applications to Industrial Tribunals 1972–1997*, Employment Relations Research Series, No. 10, Department of Trade and Industry

Bush, RA and Folger, JP (2004) *The Promise of Mediation: The transformative approach to conflict*, Jossey-Bass, San Francisco

Byrd, M and Sparkman, T (2022) Reconciling the business case and the social justice case for diversity: a model of human relations, *Human Resource Development Review*, **21** (1), pp 75–100

Callaghan, B (2007) *Employment Relations: The heart of health and safety*, Warwick Papers in Industrial Relations, No. 84

Cant, C (2019) *Riding for Deliveroo: Resistance in the new economy*, Wiley, Oxford

Carter, B, Danford, A, Howcroft, D, Richardson, H, Smith, A and Taylor, P (2013) Stressed out of my box: employee experience of lean working and occupational ill-health in clerical work in the UK, *Work, Employment and Society*, **27** (5), pp 747–67

Carvel, J (2003) HSE investigates staff stress at leading hospital, *The Guardian*, 5 August

CBI (2013) *On the Up: CBI Accenture Employment Trends Survey, 2013*, CBI, London

Charlwood, A and Angrave, D (2014) *Worker Representation in Great Britain 2004–2011: An analysis based on the Workplace Employment Relations Study*, Acas Research Paper, 3/14

Charlwood, A and Forth, J (2009) Employee representation, in *The Evolution of the Modern Workplace*, eds W Brown, A Bryson, J Forth and K Whitfield, Cambridge University Press, Cambridge

Charlwood, A and Terry, M (2007) 21st-century models of employee representation: structures, processes and outcomes, *Industrial Relations Journal*, **38** (4), pp 320–37

Chartered Management Institute (2023) *Taking Responsibility – why UK PLC needs better managers*. Available from: https://www.managers.org.uk/wp-content/uploads/2023/10/CMI_BMB_GoodManagment_Report.pdf (archived at https://perma.cc/546E-QP9Y) [accessed 21 May 2024]

Cheese, P (2017) What is 'good work' and can it be encouraged? *The New Statesman*, 14 August

Cheese, P (2021) *The New World of Work*, Kogan Page, London

CIPD (2007) *Managing Conflict at Work*, CIPD, London

CIPD (2013a) *Organising HR for Partnering Success,* CIPD, London

CIPD (2013b) *Real-life Leaders: Closing the knowing–doing gap*, CIPD, London

CIPD (2016) *HR Outlook: Views of our profession, winter 2016–17*. Available from: https://www.cipd.org/globalassets/media/knowledge/knowledge-hub/reports/hr-outlook_2017_tcm18-17697.pdf (archived at https://perma.cc/T7NU-ZS6Q) [accessed 19 March 2017]

CIPD (2017a) *Our History*. CIPD, London. Available from: www.cipd.co.uk/about/who-we-are/history (archived at https://perma.cc/H6M2-8U2J) [accessed 30 March 2017]

CIPD (2017b) *To Gig or Not to Gig? Stories from the modern economy*, CIPD, London

CIPD (2020) *Managing Conflict in the Modern Workplace*. Available from: https://www.cipd.co.uk/knowledge/fundamentals/relations/disputes/managing-workplace-conflict-report (archived at https://perma.cc/RQ8D-J2CN) [accessed 12 June 2024]

CIPD (2024a) *The Profession Map*. Available from: https://www.cipd.org/uk/the-people-profession/the-profession-map/ (archived at https://perma.cc/62M7-V6JP) [accessed 26 April 2024]

CIPD (2024b) *The Core Purpose*. Available from: https://peopleprofession.cipd.org/profession-map/core-purpose (archived at https://perma.cc/A8TN-MK46) [accessed 25 April 2024]

CIPD (2024c) *Good Work Index – Survey Report*. Available from: https://www.cipd.org/globalassets/media/knowledge/knowledge-hub/reports/2024-pdfs/8625-good-work-index-2024-survey-report-web.pdf (archived at https://perma.cc/7977-QHV9) [accessed 10 June 2024]

CIPD (2024d) *Labour Market Outlook – View from Employers*, Winter 2023/24. Available from: https://www.cipd.org/globalassets/media/knowledge/knowledge-hub/reports/2024-pdfs/2024-labour-market-outlook-winter-2024-8552.pdf (archived at https://perma.cc/H38Y-SS3L) [accessed 2 June 2024]

CIPD (2024e) *Mediation: An approach to resolving workplace issues*. Available from: https://www.cipd.org/uk/knowledge/guides/workplace-mediation/#what-is-mediation (archived at https://perma.cc/H22L-WXV2) [accessed 12 June 2024]

CIPD/Mind (2022) *Supporting Mental Health at Work: Guide for managers*, CIPD, London

CIPD/Simplyhealth (2022) *Health and Wellbeing at Work 2022*. Available from: https://www.cipd.org/globalassets/media/comms/news/ahealth-wellbeing-work-report-2022_tcm18-108440.pdf (archived at https://perma.cc/9ZQU-XVJC) [accessed 12 May 2024]

CIPD/Simplyhealth (2023) *Health and Wellbeing at Work 2023*. Available from: https://www.cipd.org/globalassets/media/knowledge/knowledge-hub/reports/2023-pdfs/8436-health-and-wellbeing-report-2023.pdf (archived at https://perma.cc/4L49-DJAS) [accessed 14 May 2024]

Clegg, HA (1976) *The System of Industrial Relations in Great Britain*, Camelot Press, Southampton

Clifton, J and Harter, J (2021) *Wellbeing at Work: How to build resilient and thriving teams*, Gallup Press, Washington

Cole, N (2008) Consistency in employee discipline: an empirical exploration, *Personnel Review*, **37** (5), pp 109–17

Colling, T (2004) No claim, no pain? The privatization of dispute resolution in Britain, *Economic and Industrial Democracy*, **25** (4), pp 555–79

Collins, H (2000) Recent case note: finding the right direction for the 'industrial jury': Haddon v Van den Bergh Foods Ltd / Midland Bank plc v Madden, *Industrial Law Journal*, **29** (3), pp 288–96

Cooke, H (2006) Examining the disciplinary process in nursing: a case study approach, *Work, Employment and Society*, **20** (4), pp 687–707

Cooper, J (2017) What is occupational health? A guide for HR and line managers, *Personnel Today*. Available from: https://www.personneltoday.com/hr/what-is-occupational-health-a-guide-for-hr-and-line-managers/ (archived at https://perma.cc/J4S3-ZC8H) [accessed 3 July 2019]

Coulter, S (2020) All in it together? The unlikely rebirth of Covid corporatism, *The Political Quarterly*, **91** (3), pp 534–41

Cox, A, Marchington, M and Suter, J (2007) *Embedding the Provision of Information and Consultation in the Workplace: A longitudinal analysis of employee outcomes in 1998 and 2004*, Employment Relations Series No. 72, DTI, London

Cox, A, Zagelmeyer, S and Marchington, M (2006) Embedding employee involvement and participation (EIP) at work, *Human Resource Management Journal*, **16** (3), pp 250–67

Crawley, J (2012) *From Argument to Agreement: Resolving disputes through mediation*, John Crawley Mediation

Crenshaw, K (1991) Mapping the margins: intersectionality, identity politics and violence against women of color, *Stanford Law Review*, **43** (6), pp 1241–99

Cullinane, N and Dundon, T (2006) The psychological contract: a critical review, *International Journal of Management Reviews*, **8** (2), pp 113–29

Cunningham, I and Hyman, J (1999) Devolving human resource responsibilities to the line: beginning of the end or a new beginning for personnel? *Personnel Review*, **28** (1/2), pp 9–27

Curtice, J (2023) *Secular or Cyclical? 40 years of tracking public opinion*, British Social Attitudes 40. Available from: https://natcen.ac.uk/sites/default/files/2023-09/BSA%2040%20Overview%20-%20Secular%20or%20Cyclical.pdf (archived at https://perma.cc/LST6-E3BN) [accessed 17 May 2024]

Curtice, J and Scholes, A (2023) Role and responsibilities of government – have public expectations changed? British Social Attitudes 40. Available from: https://natcen.ac.uk/sites/default/files/2023-09/BSA%2040%20Role%20and%20responsibilities%20of%20government.pdf (archived at https://perma.cc/VWL8-DV2J) [accessed 17 May 2024]

Dabla-Norris, E, Kochhar, K, Suphaphiphat, N, Ricka, F and Tsounta, E (2015) *Causes and Consequences of Income Inequality: A global perspective*, International Monetary Fund. Available from: http://www.imf.org/external/pubs/ft/sdn/2015/sdn1513.pdf (archived at https://perma.cc/6MZL-E7EB) [accessed 20 September 2019]

Dahanayake, P, Rajendran, D, Selvarajah, C and Ballantyne, G (2018) Justice and fairness in the workplace: a trajectory for managing diversity, *Equality Diversity and Inclusion*, **37** (5), pp 470–90

Darlington, R (2009) Leadership and union militancy: the case of the RMT, *Capital & Class*, **33** (9), pp 3–32

Dean, D and Liff, S (2010) Equality and diversity: the ultimate industrial relations concern, in *Industrial Relations: Theory and practice*, eds T Colling and M Terry, 3rd edn, Wiley, Oxford

Demougin, P, Gooberman, L, Hauptmeier, M and Heery, E (2019) Employer organisations transformed, *Human Resource Management Journal*, **29** (1), pp 1–16

Department for Business and Trade (2024) *Trade Union Membership, UK 1995-2023: Statistical Bulletin*. Available from: https://assets.publishing.service.gov.uk/media/665db15a0c8f88e868d334b8/Trade_Union_Membership_UK_1995_to_2023_Statistical_Bulletin.pdf (archived at https://perma.cc/B4S2-34D2) [accessed 12 June 2024]

Department of Trade and Industry (2007) *Consultation Document: Workplace Representatives: A review of their facilities and facility time*, URN 06/1793

Department for Work and Pensions (2022) *Menopause and the Workplace: How to enable fulfilling working lives*. Available from: https://www.gov.uk/government/publications/menopause-and-the-workplace-how-to-enable-fulfilling-working-lives-government-response/menopause-and-the-workplace-how-to-enable-fulfilling-working-lives-government-response (archived at https://perma.cc/9YQ7-A4YB) [accessed 12 June 2024]

Dickens, L (2000) Collective bargaining and the promotion of gender equality at work: opportunities and challenges to trade unions, *Transfer*, **6** (2), pp 193–208

Dickens, L (2005) Walking the talk: equality and diversity in organizations, in *Managing Human Resources: Personnel management in transition*, ed S Bach, Blackwell, Oxford

Dickens, L (ed) (2012a) *Making Employment Rights Effective: Issues of enforcement and compliance*, Hart Publishing, Oxford

Dickens, L (2012b) Employment tribunals and ADR, in *Making Employment Rights Effective: Issues of enforcement and compliance*, ed L Dickens, Hart Publishing, Oxford

Dickens, L and Hall, M (2010) The changing legal framework of employment relations, in *Industrial Relations: Theory and practice*, eds D Colling and M Terry, Wiley-Blackwell, Oxford

Disability Confident/CIPD (2024) *Recruiting, Managing and Developing People with a Disability or Health Condition: A practical guide for managers*, Department for Work and Pensions, London. Available from: https://www.gov.uk/government/publications/disability-confident-and-cipd-guide-for-line-managers-on-employing-people-with-a-disability-or-health-condition (archived at https://perma.cc/NST8-9UKT) [accessed 1 July 2024]

Dix, G, Forth, J and Sisson, K (2009) Conflict at work: the changing pattern of disputes, in *The Evolution of the Modern Workplace*, eds W Brown, A Bryson, J Forth and K Whitfield, Cambridge University Press, Cambridge

Donaldson Feilder, E (2012) *The Future of Health and Wellbeing in the Workplace*, Acas, London

Donovan (Lord) (1968) *Report of the Royal Commission on Trade Unions and Employers' Associations*, HMSO, London

Downer, M, Harding, C, Ghezelayagh, S, Fu, E and Gkiza, M (2015) *Evaluation of Acas Early Conciliation*, Acas Research Paper, 04/15

Drent, E, Renkema, M and Salojarvi, S (2022) Reconceptualizing the HRM role of the line manager in the age of artificial intelligence, in *Research Handbook on Line Managers*, eds K Townsend, A Bos-Nehles and K Jiang, Edward Elgar Publishing, Cheltenham

Dromey, J (2014) *MacLeod and Clarke's Concept of Employee Engagement: An analysis based on the Workplace Employment Relations Study*, Acas Research Paper, 08/14

Dromey, J (2018) *Power to the People: How stronger unions can deliver economic justice*, Discussion Paper, IPPR Commission on Economic Justice. Available from: https://www.ippr.org/articles/power-to-the-people (archived at https://perma.cc/ 3KUP-WC4W) [accessed 19 September 2019]

Duggan, J, Carbery, R, McDonnell, A and Sherman, U (2023) Algorithmic HRM control in the gig economy: the app-worker perspective, *Human Resource Management*, **62**, pp 883–99

Dundon, T and Rollinson, D (2011) *Understanding Employment Relations*, 2nd edn, McGraw-Hill Higher Education, London

Dundon, T, Martinez Lucio, M, Hughes, E, Howcroft, D, Keizer, A and Walden, R (2020) *Power, Politics and Influence at Work,* Manchester University Press, Manchester

Dundon, T and Wilkinson, A (2013) Employee participation, in *Contemporary Human Resource Management: Text and cases*, 4th edn, eds A Wilkinson and T Redman, Pearson, Harlow

Dundon, T, Wilkinson, A and Ackers, P (2023) Mapping employee involvement and participation in institutional context: Mick Marchington's applied pluralist contributions to human resource management research methods, theory and policy, *Human Resource Management Journal*, **33** (3), pp 551–63

Dunlop, JT (1958) *Industrial Relations Systems*, Holt, New York

Dunn, C and Wilkinson, A (2002) Wish you were here: managing absence, *Personnel Review*, **31** (2), pp 228–46

Dutta, D, Mishra, SK and Tyagi, D (2023) Augmented employee voice and employee engagement using artificial intelligence-enabled chatbots: a field study, *International Journal of Human Resource Management*, **34** (12), pp 2451–80, DOI: 10.1080/09585192.2022.2085525

Earnshaw, J, Marchington, M and Goodman, J (2000) Unfair to whom? Discipline and dismissal in small establishments, *Industrial Relations Journal*, **31** (1), pp 62–73

Eaton, J (2000) *Comparative Employment Relations*, Polity Press, Cambridge

Edwards, P (1986) *Conflict at Work: A materialist analysis of workplace relations*, Blackwell, Oxford

Edwards, P (1994) Discipline and the creation of order, in *Personnel Management: A comprehensive guide to theory and practice in Britain*, ed K Sisson, Blackwell, Oxford

Edwards, P (1995) Strikes and industrial conflict, in *Industrial Relations: Theory and practice in Britain*, ed P Edwards, Blackwell, Oxford

Edwards, P (2003) The employment relationship and the field of industrial relations, in *Industrial Relations*, 2nd edn, ed P Edwards, Blackwell, Oxford

Edwards, T and Walsh, J (2009) Foreign ownership and industrial relations in the UK, in *The Evolution of the Modern Workplace*, eds W Brown, A Bryson, J Forth and K Whitfield, Cambridge University Press, Cambridge

EHRC (2011) *Employment Statutory Code of Practice: Equality Act 2010*, Equality and Human Rights Commission, London

EHRC (2016) *Equal Pay Statutory Code of Practice*, Equality and Human Rights Commission, London

EHRC (2024b) *Menopause in the Workplace: Guidance for employers*. Available from: https://www.equalityhumanrights.com/guidance/menopause-workplace-guidance-employers (archived at https://perma.cc/3WBS-ZFJ8) [accessed 12 June 2024]

EHRC/CIPD (2013) *Managing and Supporting Employees Experiencing Domestic Abuse*, Equality and Human Rights Commission, London

Ely, R and Thomas, A (2020) Getting serious about diversity: enough already with the business case, *Harvard Business Review*, November–December 2020

Evans, S (2015) Juggling on the line: frontline managers and their management of human resources in the retail industry, *Employee Relations*, **37** (4), pp 459–74

Evans, S (2017) HRM and frontline managers: the influence of role stress, *International Journal of Human Resource Management*, **28** (22), pp 3128–48

Evesson, J, Oxenbridge, S and Taylor, D (2015) *Seeking Better Solutions: Tackling bullying and ill-treatment in Britain's workplaces*, Acas Policy Paper. Available from: https://www.acas.org.uk/media/4498/Seeking-better-solutions-tackling-bullying-and-ill-treatment-in-Britains-workplaces/pdf/Seeking-better-solutions-tackling-bullying-and-ill-treatment-in-Britains-workplaces.pdf (archived at https://perma.cc/6VY9-YTWG) [accessed 12 September 2019]

Ewing, K and Hendy, J (2012) Unfair dismissal law changes – unfair? *Industrial Law Journal*, **41** (1), pp 115–21

Faragher, J (2015) Trade union bill provokes anger from unions. Available from: https://www.personneltoday.com/hr/trade-union-bill-introduced-anger-unions/ (archived at https://perma.cc/6BP9-3KBK) [accessed 1 July 2024]

Faragher, J (2018) The ultimate guide to disciplinaries and grievances, *People Management*, 13 December. Available from: https://www.peoplemanagement.co.uk/long-reads/articles/ultimate-guide-disciplinaries-grievances (archived at https://perma.cc/SH33-3K92) [accessed 8 July 2019]

Fayol, H (1990) General principles of management, in *Organization Theory*, 3rd edn, ed DS Pugh, Penguin, London

Federation of Small Businesses (2024) *Annual report and financial statements 2022-23*, Federation of Small Businesses, London

Fernie, S and Metcalf, D (2005) *Trade Unions: Resurgence or demise,* Routledge, London

Fevre, R, Lewis, D, Robinson, A and Jones, T (2012) *Trouble at Work*, Bloomsbury Academic, London

Fisher, V, Kinsey, S and Saundry, R (2017) *The Myth of Devolution? The role of HR practitioners in the management of workplace conflict*, CIPD, Applied Research Conference, Glasgow, December

Flanders, A (1970) *Management and Unions: The theory and reform of industrial relations*, Faber, London

Fleming, W (2023) Employee well-being outcomes from individual-level mental health interventions: cross-sectional evidence from the United Kingdom, *Industrial Relations Journal*, **55** (2), pp 162–82

Forth, J, Bewley, H and Bryson, A (2006) *Small and Medium-sized Enterprises: Findings from the Workplace Employment Relations Survey 2004*, Routledge, London

Foster, D and Wass, V (2012) Disability in the labour market: an exploration of concepts of the ideal worker and organisational fit that disadvantage employees with impairments, *Sociology*, **47** (4), pp 705–21

Foster, D and Williams, L (2011) The past, present and future of workplace equality agendas: problems of intersectionality in theory and practice, in *Reassessing the Employment Relationship*, eds P Blyton, E Heery and P Turnbull, Palgrave Macmillan, Basingstoke, pp 318–41

Fox, A (1974) *Beyond Contract: Work, power and trust relations*, Faber, London

Fox, A (1985) *Man Mismanagement*, 2nd edn, Hutchinson and Co, London

Francis, H and Keegan, A (2006) The changing face of HRM: in search of balance, *Human Resource Management Journal*, **16** (3), pp 231–49

Francis-Devine, B, Powell, A and Clark, H (2021) *Coronavirus Job Retention Scheme: Statistics*. House of Commons Library, 21 December. Available from: https://researchbriefings.files.parliament.uk/documents/CBP-9152/CBP-9152.pdf (archived at https://perma.cc/5TDT-7T7T) [accessed 14 May 2024]

Franco-Santos, M and Doherty, N (2017) Performance management and well-being: a close look at the changing nature of the UK higher education workplace, *International Journal of Human Resource Management*, **28** (16), pp 2319–50

Franklin, A and Pagan, J (2006) Organization culture as an explanation for employee discipline practices, *Review of Public Personnel Administration*, **26** (1), pp 52–73

Fredman, S (2011) The public sector equality duty, *Industrial Law Journal*, **40** (4), pp 405–27

Freeman, R and Medoff, J (1984) *What Do Unions Do?* Basic Books, New York

Freeman, R and Pelletier, J (1990) The impact of industrial relations legislation on British union density, *British Journal of Industrial Relations*, **28** (2), pp 141–64

Frey, C and Osborne, M (2013) *The Future of Employment: How susceptible are jobs to computerisation?* Available from: http://www.oxfordmartin.ox.ac.uk/downloads/academic/The_Future_of_Employment.pdf (archived at https://perma.cc/Q9ZE-6XCH) [accessed 6 September 2019]

Frobel, F, Heinrichs, J and Kreye, O (1980) *The New International Division of Labour*, Cambridge University Press, Cambridge

Frost, S and Alidina, R (2019) *Building an Inclusive Organization: Leveraging the power of a diverse workforce*, Kogan Page, London

FTSE (2024) *FTSE Women Leaders Review: Achieving gender balance*. Available from: https://ftsewomenleaders.com/latest-reports/ (archived at https://perma.cc/XRW6-EXA6) [accessed 1 July 2024]

Gall, G (2007) Trade union recognition in Britain: an emerging crisis for trade unions? *Economic and Industrial Democracy*, **28** (1), pp 97–109

Gall, G (2016) *The Benefits of Paid Time Off for Trade Union Representatives*, Trades Union Congress. Available from: https://www.tuc.org.uk/sites/default/files/Facility_Time_Report_2016.pdf (archived at https://perma.cc/XJ6P-EMA5) [accessed 18 September 2019]

Gallie, D, Felstead, A, Green, F and Inanc, H (2017) The hidden face of job insecurity, *Work, Employment and Society*, **31** (1), pp 36–53

Gallup (2024) *State of the Global Workforce*. Available from: https://www.gallup.com/workplace/349484/state-of-the-global-workplace.aspx (archived at https://perma.cc/MA9C-4YTW) [accessed 6 June 2024]

Gibbons, M (2007) *A Review of Employment Dispute Resolution in Great Britain*, DTI, London

GMB (2023) *Work to Stop Domestic Abuse: GMB Employer Charter*. Available from: https://www.gmb.org.uk/campaigns/domestic-abuse-charter (archived at https://perma.cc/T85R-WHCK) [accessed 19 May 2024]

Gollan, P (2006) Representation at Suncorp: what do the employees want? *Human Resource Management Journal*, **16** (3), pp 268–86

Gooberman, L, Hauptmeier, M and Heery, E (2018) Contemporary employer interest representation in the United Kingdom, *Work, Employment and Society*, **32** (1), pp 114–32

Goodwin, J (2019) *Hear My Voice! Supporting a fair and inclusive employee voice for older local government workers*, Paper for the BUIRA Conference at Newcastle University Business School, 1–3 July

Gourlay, S, Alfes, K, Bul, E, Petrov, G and Georgellis, Y (2012) *Emotional or Transactional Engagement: Does it matter?* Research insight, CIPD, London

Goyer, M, Clark, I and Bhankaraully, S (2016) Necessary and sufficient factors in employee downsizing? A qualitative comparative analysis of lay-offs in France and the UK, 2008–2013, *Human Resource Management Journal*, **26** (3), pp 252–68

Green, M, Bond, H, Miller, J and Gifford, J (2018) *Diversity and Inclusion at Work: Facing up to the business case*, CIPD, London

Greer, I and Hauptmeier, M (2016) Management whipsawing: the staging of labor competition under globalization, *ILR Review*, **69** (1), pp 29–52

Grimshaw, D and Rubery, J (2007) *Undervaluing Women's Work*, Equal Opportunities Commission Working Paper Series No. 53, EOC, Manchester

Grimshaw, D and Rubery, J (2015) The motherhood pay gap: a review of the issues, theory and international evidence, *ILO Conditions of Work and Employment Series,* **57**, International Labour Office, Geneva

Grimshaw, D, Fagan, C, Hebson, G and Tavora, I (eds) (2017) *Making Work More Equal: A new labour market segmentation approach*, Manchester University Press, Manchester

Guest, D (1987) Human resource management and industrial relations, *Journal of Management Studies*, **24** (5), pp 503–21

Guest, D (1991) Personnel management: the end of orthodoxy? *British Journal of Industrial Relations,* **29** (2), pp 149–75

Guest, D (2004) The psychology of the employment relationship: an analysis based on the psychological contract, *Applied Psychology*, **53**, pp 541–55

Guest, D (2017) Human resource management and employee well-being: towards a new analytic framework, *Human Resource Management Journal*, **27** (1), pp 22–38

Guest, D and King, Z (2004) Power, innovation and problem-solving: the personnel managers' three steps to heaven? *Journal of Management Studies*, **41** (3), pp 401–23

Haddon, J (2017) *Survivor Syndrome: How redundancies affect the staff that remain*. Available from: https://www.peoplemanagement.co.uk/experts/advice/survivor-syndrome-redundancies (archived at https://perma.cc/SE89-SQ2D) [accessed 1 June 2019]

Hakim, C (1991) Grateful slaves and self made women: fact and fantasy in women's work orientations, *European Sociological Review*, **7** (2), pp 101–18

Haldane, A (2018) *The UK's Productivity Problem: Hub no spokes*, Speech given at the Academy of Social Sciences Annual Lecture, London, 28 June

Hall, CE, Brooks, SK, Mills, F, Greenberg, N and Weston, D (2024) Experiences of working from home: umbrella review, *Journal of Occupational Health*, **66** (1) doi: 10.1093/joccuh/uiad013

Hall, M, Hutchinson, S, Purcell, J, Terry, M and Parker, J (2013), Promoting effective consultation? Assessing the impact of the ICE regulations, *British Journal of Industrial Relations*, **51**, pp 355–81. Available from: https://doi.org/10.1111/j.1467-8543.2011.00870.x (archived at https://perma.cc/5Z5U-2PVZ) [accessed 1 July 2024]

Hall, P and Soskice, D (2001) Introduction, in *Varieties of Capitalism: The institutional foundations of comparative advantage*, eds P Hall and D Soskice, Oxford University Press, Oxford

Health and Safety Executive (2019a) *Health and Safety Statistics*. Available from: http://www.hse.gov.uk/statistics/ (archived at https://perma.cc/M3T4-A8UY) [accessed 3 July 2019]

Health and Safety Executive (2019b) *Stress Risk Assessment*. Available from: http://www.hse.gov.uk/stress/risk-assessment.htm (archived at https://perma.cc/37K8-BLJ8) [accessed 3 July 2019]

Health and Safety Executive (2023a) Health and safety at work – summary statistics for Great Britain 2022. Available from: https://www.hse.gov.uk/statistics/ (archived at https://perma.cc/8KMW-5CRU) [accessed 5 June 2024]

Health and Safety Executive (2023b) *What are the Management Standards?* Available from: https://www.hse.gov.uk/stress/standards/ (archived at https://perma.cc/K7BR-WN7X) [accessed 3 June 2024]

Health and Safety Executive (2023c) *Annual Report and Accounts, 2022-23*. Available from: https://assets.publishing.service.gov.uk/media/64b52a5461adff000d01b138/hse-annual-report-and-accounts-2022-2023.pdf (archived at https://perma.cc/7FLN-A58V) [accessed 12 June 2024]

Heath, O and Bennett, M (2023) *Social Class*. British Social Attitudes 40. Available from: https://natcen.ac.uk/sites/default/files/2023-09/BSA%2040%20Social%20class.pdf (archived at https://perma.cc/NX5N-Q77Z) [accessed 17 May 2024]

Hebson, G and Rubery, J (2019) Employment relations and gender equality, in *The Routledge Companion to Employment Relations*, eds A Wilkinson, T Dundon, J Donaghey and A Colvin, Routledge, London

Hebson, G, Rubery, J and Grimshaw, D (2015) Rethinking job satisfaction in care work: looking beyond the care debates, *Work, Employment and Society*, **29** (2), pp 314–30

Heery, E (2002) Partnership versus organising: alternative futures for British trade unionism, *Industrial Relations Journal*, **33** (1), pp 20–35

Heery, E (2016) *Framing Work: Unitary, pluralist, and critical perspectives in the twenty-first century*, Oxford University Press, Oxford

Hepple, B (2005) *Labour Laws and Global Trade*, Blackwell, Oxford

Hepple, B (2013) Back to the future: employment law under the coalition government, *Industrial Law Journal*, **42** (3), pp 203–23

Hepple, B and Morris, G (2002) The Employment Act 2002 and the crisis of individual employment rights, *Industrial Law Journal*, **30** (1), pp 245–69

Hesketh, I and Cooper, C (2019) *Wellbeing at Work: How to design, implement and evaluate an effective strategy*, Kogan Page, London

Hirsch, B (2004) What do unions do for economic performance? *Journal of Labor Research*, **25** (3), pp 415–55

HM Government (2017) *Industrial Strategy: Building a Britain fit for the future*. Available from: https://assets.publishing.service.gov.uk/government/uploads/system/uploads/attachment_data/file/664563/industrial-strategy-white-paper-web-ready-version.pdf (archived at https://perma.cc/DV4H-CYGH) [accessed 7 September 2024]

Holgate, J (2015a) An international study of trade union involvement in community organizing: same model, different outcomes, *British Journal of Industrial Relations*, **53** (3), pp 460–83

Holgate, J (2015b) Community organising in the UK: a 'new' approach for trade unions? *Economic and Industrial Democracy*, **36** (3), pp 431–55

Holgate, J, Hebson, G and McBride, A (2006) Why gender and difference matters: a critical appraisal of industrial relations research, *Industrial Relations Journal*, **37** (4), pp 323–39

Holgate, J, Abbott, S, Kamenou, N, Kinge, J, Parker, J, Sayce, S, Sinclair, J and Williams, L (2012) Equality and diversity in employment relations: do we practise what we preach? *Equality, Diversity and Inclusion: An International Journal*, **31** (4), pp 323–39

Holmes, C and Mayhew, K (2012) *The Changing Shape of the UK Job Market and its Implications for the Bottom Half of Earners*, Resolution Foundation, London

Hoque, K and Bacon, N (2015) *Workplace Union Representation in the British Public Sector: Evidence from the 2011 Workplace Employment Relations Survey*, Warwick Papers in Industrial Relations, No. 101, August

Hoque, K, Bacon, N and Parr, D (2014) Employer disability practice in Britain: assessing the impact of the Positive About Disabled People 'Two Ticks' symbol, *Work, Employment and Society*, **28** (3), pp 430–51

Hoque, K and Noon, M (2004) EO policy and practice in Britain: evaluating the empty shell hypothesis, *Work, Employment and Society*, **18** (3), pp 481–506

Howell, C (2000) From New Labour to no labour? The industrial relations project of the Blair government, *New Political Science*, **22** (2), pp 201–29

Hudson, M (2016) *The Management of Mental Health at Work*, Acas Research Paper, 11/16

Hunter, W and Renwick, D (2009) Involving British line managers in HRM in a small non-profit organisation, *Employee Relations*, **31** (4), pp 398–411

Huppert, FA (2009) Psychological well-being: evidence regarding its causes and consequences, *Applied Psychology: Health and Well-being*, **1**, pp 137–64

Hurd, R (2004) *The Rise and Fall of the Organising Model in the US*. Available from: http://digitalcommons.ilr.cornell.edu/articles/301/ (archived at https://perma.cc/9H6P-MA8S) [accessed 19 October 2015]

Hutchinson, S and Purcell, J (2010) Managing ward managers for roles in HRM in the NHS: overworked and under-resourced, *Human Resource Management Journal*, **20** (4), pp 357–74

Hyman, J and Mason, B (1995) *Managing Employee Involvement and Participation*, Sage, London

Hyman, R (1975) *Industrial Relations: A Marxist introduction,* Macmillan, Basingstoke

Hyman, R (1987) Strategy or structure? Capital, labour and control, *Work, Employment and Society*, **1** (1) pp 25–55

IMF (2024) *World Economic Outlook, April 2024*. Available from: https://www.imf.org/en/Publications/WEO/Issues/2024/04/16/world-economic-outlook-april-2024#:~:text=A%20slight%20acceleration%20for%20advanced,in%20both%202024%20and%202025 (archived at https://perma.cc/63NK-VDTK) [accessed 15 May 2024]

Institute of Employment Rights (2024) *More than 70 per cent of managers support Labour's changes to employment law.* Available from: https://www.ier.org.uk/news/more-than-70-per-cent-of-managers-support-labours-changes-to-employment-law/#:~:text="Organisations%20need%20to%20ditch%20the,work%20and%20life%20responsibilities%20effectively (archived at https://perma.cc/3SPY-FP86) [accessed 25 June 2024]

International Trade Union Confederation (2023) *2023 ITUC Global Rights Index*. Available from: https://www.ituc-csi.org/ituc-global-rights-index-2023 (archived at https://perma.cc/U4T3-MBJ9) [accessed 15 May 2024]

Jarley, P (2005) Unions as social capital: renewal through a return to the logic of mutual aid, *Labor Studies Journal,* **29** (4), pp 1–26

Jaumotte, F and Osorio Buitron, C (2015) Power from the people, *Finance & Development*, March, pp 29–31.

Jiang, K, Shi, W and Wen, X (2022) Implications of frames of reference for strategic human resource management research: opportunities and challenges, *Industrial Relations,* **61**, pp 303–13

Jirjahn, U, Laible, MC and Mohrenweiser, J (2024) Management practices and productivity: does employee representation play a moderating role? *Human Resource Management Journal*, **34** (1), pp 236–54

Johns, N, Green, A and Powell, M (2012) Diversity in the British NHS: the business versus the 'moral' case, *Equality, Diversity and Inclusion: An International Journal*, **31** (8), pp 768–83

Kaufman, R (ed) (2004) *Theoretical Perspectives on Work and Employment Relationships*, Cornell University Press, Ithaca, NY

Keashly, L and Nowell, B (2011) Conflict, conflict resolution and bullying, in *Bullying and Harassment in the Workplace: Development in theory, research and practice*, 2nd edn, eds S Einarsen, H Hoel, D Zapf and C Cooper, CRC Press, Boca Raton, FL

Keegan, A and Francis, H (2010) Practitioner talk: the changing textscape of HRM and emergence of HR business partnership, *International Journal of Human Resource Management*, **21** (6), pp 873–98

Kehoe, R and Han, JH (2020) An expanded conceptualization of line managers' involvement in human resource management, *Journal of Applied Psychology*, **105** (2), pp 111–29

Kellner, A, Townsend, K, Wilkinson, A, Lawrence, S and Greenfield, D (2016) Learning to manage: development experiences of hospital frontline managers, *Human Resource Management Journal*, **26** (4), pp 505–22

Kelly, J (1998) *Rethinking Industrial Relations: Mobilization, collectivism and long waves*, Routledge, London

Kelly, J (2004) Social partnership agreements in Britain: labor cooperation and compliance, *Industrial Relations: A Journal of Economy and Society*, **43**, pp 267–92

Kerr, C, Dunlop, J, Harbison, F and Myers, C (1960) *Industrialism and Industrial Man*, Harvard University Press, Cambridge, MA

Kersley, B, Alpin, C, Forth, J, Bryson, A, Bewley, H, Dix, G and Oxenbridge, S (2006) *Inside the Workplace: Findings from the 2004 Workplace Employment Relations Survey,* Routledge, London

Khan, M, Mowbray, P and Wilkinson, A (2023) Employee voice on social media – an affordance lens, *International Journal of Management Reviews*, **225**, pp 687–706

Khattab, N and Johnston, R (2015) Ethno-religious identities and persisting penalties in the UK labour market, *Social Science Journal*, **52**, 490–502

Kim, J-Y and Kehoe, R (2022) The underappreciated role of line managers in human resource management, in *Research Handbook on Line Managers*, eds K Townsend, A Bos-Nehles and K Jiang, Edward Elgar Publishing, Cheltenham

Kirton, G (2021) Union framing of gender equality and the elusive potential of equality bargaining in a difficult climate, *Journal of Industrial Relations*, **63** (4), 591–613

Kirton, G and Greene, A-M (2021) *The Dynamics of Managing Diversity and Inclusion: A critical approach*, 5th edn, Routledge, Abingdon

Kirton, G and Healy, G (2013) Commitment and collective identity of long-term union participation: the case of women union leaders in the UK and USA, *Work, Employment and Society*, **27** (2), pp 195–221

Kline, R and Lewis, D (2019) The price of fear: estimating the financial cost of bullying and harassment to the NHS in England, *Public Money & Management*, **39** (3), pp 166–74

Knight, K and Latreille, P (2000) Discipline, dismissals and complaints to employment tribunals, *British Journal of Industrial Relations*, **38** (4), pp 533–55

Kougiannou, NK, Wilkinson, A and Dundon, T (2022) Inside the meetings: the role of managerial attitudes in approaches to information and consultation for employees. *British Journal of Industrial Relations*, **60**, pp 585–605

Kowalski, THP and Loretto, W (2017) Well-being and HRM in the changing workplace, *International Journal of Human Resource Management*, **28** (16), pp 2229–55

Kressel, K (2007) The strategic style in mediation, *Conflict Resolution Quarterly*, **24** (3), pp 251–83

Kumra, S and Manfredi, S (2012) *Managing Equality and Diversity: Theory and practice* Oxford University Press, Oxford

Kuruvilla, S and Verma, A (2006) International labor standards, soft regulation and national government roles, *Journal of Industrial Relations*, **48** (1), pp 41–58

Labour Party (2024) *Labour's Plan to Make Work Pay: Delivering a new deal for working people.* Available from: https://labour.org.uk/updates/stories/a-new-deal-for-working-people/ (archived at https://perma.cc/RF4N-8HKC) [accessed 28 May 2024]

Latreille, P (2011) *Mediation: A thematic review of ACAS/CIPD evidence*, Acas Research Paper, 13/11

Latreille, P and Saundry, R (2014) Mediation, in *The Oxford Handbook on Conflict Management*, eds W Roche, P Teague and A Colvin, Oxford University Press, Oxford

Latreille, P and Saundry, R (2015) *Towards a System of Conflict Management?* Acas Research Paper, 03/15

Leat, M (2006) *Exploring Employee Relations: An international approach,* Butterworth Heinemann, Oxford

Legge, K (2005) *Human Resource Management: Rhetorics and realities,* Palgrave, London

Lewis, D, Sargeant, M and Schwab, B (2023) *Employment Law: The essentials*, 16th edn, Kogan Page, London

Lewis, R, Donaldson-Feilder, E and Pangallo, A (2011) *Developing Resilience*, CIPD Research Insight, May. Available from: https://www.cipd.co.uk/Images/developing-resilience_2011_tcm18-10576.pdf (archived at https://perma.cc/ET4B-88S5) [accessed 19 September 2019]

Liebmann, M (2000) History and overview of mediation in the UK, in *Mediation in Context*, ed M Liebmann, Jessica Kingsley Publishers, London

Liddle, D (2023) *Managing Conflict: A practical guide to resolution in the workplace*, 2nd edn, Kogan Page, London

Liff, S (1997) Two routes to managing diversity: individual differences or social group characteristics, *Employee Relations*, **19** (1), pp 11–26

Lipsky, DB, Avgar, AC, Lamare, JR and Gupta, A (2012) *The Antecedents of Workplace Conflict Management Systems in U.S. Corporations: Evidence from a new survey of Fortune 1000 companies*, Mimeo

Lipsky, DB and Seeber, RL (2000) Resolving workplace disputes in the United States: the growth of alternative dispute resolution in employment relations, *Alternative Dispute Resolution in Employment*, **2**, pp 37–49

Local Government Association (2024) *Employment Relations*. Available from: https://www.local.gov.uk/our-support/workforce-and-hr-support/employment-relations (archived at https://perma.cc/A7CG-9NSP) [accessed 12 May 2024]

Logan, J (2021) Crushing unions, by any means necessary: how Amazon's blistering anti-union campaign won in Bessemer, Alabama, *New Labor Forum*, **30** (3), pp 38–45

Lynch, JF (2001) Beyond ADR: a systems approach to conflict management, *Negotiation Journal*, **17** (3), pp 207–16

Machin, S (2000) Union decline in Britain, *British Journal of Industrial Relations*, **38** (4), pp 631–45

MacKenzie, J (2019) Are you considering the mental health needs of older employees? *People Management*. Available from: https://www.peoplemanagement.co.uk/voices/comment/considering-mental-health-needs-older-workers (archived at https://perma.cc/77NE-2JZR) [accessed 10 June 2019]

MacLeod, D and Clarke, N (2009) *Engaging for Success: Enhancing performance through employee engagement: a report to government*, Department for Business, Innovation and Skills, London

Macpherson, W (1999) *The Stephen Lawrence Inquiry*, Home Office, London

Marchington, M (2015) Analysing the forces shaping employee involvement and participation (EIP) at organisation level in liberal market economies (LMEs), *Human Resource Management Journal*, **25** (1), pp 1–18

Marchington, M, Cox, A and Suter, J (2007) *Embedding the Provision of Information and Consultation in the Workplace,* DTI, London

Marchington, M, Goodman, J, Wilkinson, A and Ackers, P (1992) *New Developments in Employee Involvement,* Employment Department Research Series, No. 2

Marchington, M and Wilkinson, A (2005) Direct participation and involvement, in *Managing Human Resources: Personnel management in transition*, ed S Bach, Blackwell Publishing, Oxford

Marchington, M and Wilkinson, A (2012) *Human Resource Management at Work*, 5th edn, CIPD, London

Marchington, M, Wilkinson, A, Ackers, P and Dundon, T (2001) *Management Choice and Employee Voice*, CIPD, London

Mareschal, P (2003) Solving problems and transforming relationships: the bifocal approach to mediation, *American Review of Public Administration*, **33**, pp 423–48

Marginson, P and Meardi, G (2010) Multinational companies: transforming national industrial relations, in *Industrial Relations: Theory and practice*, 3rd edn, eds T Colling and M Terry, John Wiley, Chichester

Marginson, P and Sisson, K (2004) *European Integration and Industrial Relations*, Palgrave, Basingstoke

Marsden, R (1982) Industrial relations: a critique of empiricism, *Sociology*, **16** (2), pp 232–50

McBride, J and Greenwood, I (2009) *Community Unionism: A comparative analysis of concepts and contexts*, Palgrave Macmillan, Basingstoke

McCurdy, C and Murphy, L (2024) *We've only just begun: Action to improve young people's mental health, education and employment,* Resolution Foundation, February 2024. Available from: https://www.resolutionfoundation.org/app/uploads/2024/02/Weve-only-just-begun.pdf (archived at https://perma.cc/K24S-W5KC) [accessed 16 May 2024]

McGurdy, C (2024) Deliveroo-GMB deal: have GMB delivered? *The Social Review.* Available from: https://www.thesocialreview.co.uk/2024/02/25/deliveroo-gmb-deal-2/ (archived at https://perma.cc/FA2M-P3UF) [accessed 21 May 2024]

Meltz, NM (1991) Sectoral realignment in Canada: shifting patterns of output and employment and the consequences for labour-management relations, in *Industrial Restructuring and Industrial Relations in Canada and the United States*, ed EB Willis, Industrial Relations Centre, Queen's University, Kingston, Ontario

Metcalf, D (2005) Trade unions: resurgence or perdition? An economic analysis, in *Trade Unions: Resurgence or demise*, eds S Fernie and D Metcalf, Routledge, London

Millward, N, Bryson, A and Forth, J (2000) *All Change at Work*, Routledge, London

Millward, N, Stevens, M, Smart, D and Hawes, W (1992) *Workplace Industrial Relations in Transition*, Dartmouth Publishing, Aldershot

Ministry of Justice (2019) *Tribunal Statistics Quarterly: April to June 2019*. Available from: https://www.gov.uk/government/statistics/tribunal-statistics-quarterly-april-to-june-2019 (archived at https://perma.cc/P9DB-YALY) [accessed 13 September 2019]

Ministry of Justice (2023) *Tribunal Statistics Quarterly: April to June 2023*. Available from: https://www.gov.uk/government/statistics/tribunal-statistics-quarterly-april-to-june-2023 (archived at https://perma.cc/H46Q-GFYH) [accessed 12 June 2024]

Mintzberg, H (1990) The manager's job: folklore and fact, in *Organization Theory*, ed DS Pugh, Penguin Group, London

Mitchell, L (2023) Two fifths of HR leaders do not believe their business partner colleagues are ready for future requirements of the role, survey reveals, People Management, 5 July. Available from: https://www.peoplemanagement.co.uk/article/1828950/two-fifths-hr-leaders-not-believe-business-partner-colleagues-ready-future-requirements-role-survey-reveals (archived at https://perma.cc/22VN-9SJV) [accessed 1 July 2024]

Mitchell, M, Coutinho, S and Morrell, G (2012) *The Value of Trade Union Facility Time: Insight, challenges and solutions*, NatCen Social Research. Available from: https://www.unison.org.uk/content/uploads/2013/06/NatCen-Value-trade-union-facility-time-full-report-RV.pdf (archived at https://perma.cc/TQ88-5XU5) [accessed 1 July 2024]

Monks, K and Conway, E (2022) The future of work: implications for the frontline manager's role in HR implementation, in *Research Handbook on Line Managers*, eds K Townsend, A Bos-Nehles and K Jiang, Edward Elgar Publishing, Cheltenham

Moore, S, Tasiran, A and Jefferys, S (2008) *The Impact of Employee Representation upon Workplace Industrial Relations Outcomes*, Employment Relations Research Series, No. 87, BERR, London

Morris, G (2012) The development of statutory employment rights in Britain and enforcement mechanisms, in *Making Employment Rights Effective: Issues of enforcement and compliance*, ed L Dickens, Hart Publishing, Oxford

Mowbray, P, Wilkinson, A and Tse, H (2022) Strategic or silencing? Line managers' repurposing of employee voice mechanisms for high performance, *British Journal of Management*, **33**, pp 1054–70

Muller, F and Purcell, J (1992) The Europeanization of manufacturing and the decentralization of bargaining: multinational management strategies in the European automobile industry, *International Journal of Human Resource Management*, **3** (1), pp 15–24

Muller-Jentsch, W (2004) Theoretical approaches to industrial relations, in *Theoretical Perspectives on Work and Employment Relationships*, ed R Kaufman, Cornell University Press, Ithaca, New York

Mullins, LJ (2010) *Management and Organizational Behavior*, 9th edn, FT Prentice Hall, Harlow

Murphy, N (2009) Managing the survivor syndrome during and after redundancies, *IRS Employment Review*, Industrial Relations Services, London

Nechanska, E, Hughes, E and Dundon, T (2020), Towards an integration of employee voice and silence, *Human Resource Management Review,* **30** (1), 100674

Ngai, P (2005) Global production, company codes of conduct, and labour conditions in China: a case study of two factories, *The China Journal*, **54**, pp 101–13

NHS England (2023) *Long Term Workforce Plan*. Available from: https://www.england.nhs.uk/publication/nhs-long-term-workforce-plan/ (archived at https://perma.cc/JW22-THW9) [accessed 4 June 2024]

Nichols, T (1997) *The Sociology of Industrial Injury*, Mansell, London

Nondo, N (2023) *Facing disturbing content daily, online moderators in Africa want better protections and a fair wage*. CBC Radio, 19 May. Available from: https://www.cbc.ca/radio/thecurrent/content-moderators-union-social-media-ai-1.6848949 (archived at https://perma.cc/BD9B-SD3R) [accessed 15 May 2024]

Noon, M (2007) The fatal flaws of diversity and the business case for ethnic minorities, *Work, Employment and Society*, **21** (4), pp 773–84

OECD (2018) *Multinational Enterprises and Global Value Chains*. Available from: https://www.oecd.org/en/data/datasets/multinational-enterprises-and-global-value-chains.html (archived at https://perma.cc/9AN4-94KA) [accessed 1 July 2024]

Office for National Statistics (2015) *Labour disputes in the UK: 2015*. Office for National Statistics, London. Available from: https://www.ons.gov.uk/employmentandlabourmarket/peopleinwork/workplacedisputesandworkingconditions/articles/labourdisputes/2015 (archived at https://perma.cc/3QCQ-S78C) [accessed 1 July 2024]

Office for National Statistics (2018) *Domestic Abuse: Findings from the Crime Survey for England and Wales: year ending March 2018*, Office for National Statistics, London

Office for National Statistics (2021) *Coronavirus and Redundancies in the UK Labour Market: September to November 2020*. Available from: https://www.ons.gov.uk/employmentandlabourmarket/peopleinwork/employmentandemployeetypes/articles/labourmarketeconomicanalysisquarterly/december2020 (archived at https://perma.cc/PCQ2-KVGT [accessed 16 May 2024]

Office for National Statistics (2023a) *Characteristics of Homeworkers, Great Britain: September 2022 to January 2023*. Office for National Statistics. Available from: https://www.ons.gov.uk/employmentandlabourmarket/peopleinwork/employmentandemployeetypes/articles/characteristicsofhomeworkersgreatbritain/september2022tojanuary2023 (archived at https://perma.cc/US57-Z5CX) [accessed 17 May 2024]

Office for National Statistics (2023b) *Domestic Abuse in England and Wales Overview: November 2023*. Available from: https://www.ons.gov.uk/peoplepopulationandcommunity/crimeandjustice/bulletins/domesticabuseinenglandandwalesoverview/november2023 (archived at https://perma.cc/N4YQ-7QRM) [accessed 13 June 2024]

Office for National Statistics (2023c) *Ethnicity Pay Gaps, UK: 2012 to 2022*. Available at https://backup.ons.gov.uk/wp-content/uploads/sites/3/2023/11/Ethnicity-pay-gaps-UK-2012-to-2022.pdf (archived at https://perma.cc/P36K-2PHG) [accessed 25 May 2024]

Office for National Statistics (2023d) *Gender Pay Gap in the UK: 2023*. Available from: https://www.ons.gov.uk/employmentandlabourmarket/peopleinwork/earningsandworkinghours/bulletins/genderpaygapintheuk/2023 (archived at https://perma.cc/GS4R-332A) [accessed 25 May 2024]

Office for National Statistics (2024a) *EMP13: Employment by Industry*. Available from: https://www.ons.gov.uk/employmentandlabourmarket/peopleinwork/employmentandemployeetypes/datasets/employmentbyindustryemp13 (archived at https://perma.cc/5R7P-ZUX3) [accessed 10 May 2024]

Office for National Statistics (2024b) *UK Labour Market: Employment and employee types* Office for National Statistics. Available from: https://www.ons.gov.uk/employmentandlabourmarket/peopleinwork/employmentandemployeetypes (archived at https://perma.cc/9SE8-2Q2C) [accessed 10 May 2024]

Olson-Buchanan, J and Boswell, W (2008) An integrative model of experiencing and responding to mistreatment at work, *Academy of Management Review*, **33** (1), pp 76–96

Op de Beeck, S, Wynena, J and Hondeghem, A (2016) HRM implementation by line managers: explaining the discrepancy in HR-line perceptions of HR devolution, *International Journal of Human Resource Management,* **27** (17), pp 1901–19

Oswick, C and Noon, M (2014) Discourses of diversity, equality and inclusion: trenchant formulations or transient fashions? *British Journal of Management*, **25**, pp 23–39

Özbilgin, M and Tatli, A (2011) Mapping out the field of equality and diversity: rise of individualism and voluntarism, *Human Relations*, **64** (9), pp 1229–53

Pakes, A (2019) A strong voice, in *People Power: Building an industrial strategy with workers at its heart*, eds O Bailey and K Murray. Available from: https://fabians.org.uk/publication/people-power/ (archived at https://perma.cc/994C-JP4F) [accessed 13 September 2019]

Pass, S, Court-Smith, J, Liu-Smith, Y-L, Popescu, S, Ridgway, M and Kougiannou, N (2023) *Engage for Success UK Employee Engagement Levels 2022: Exploring the impact of the pandemic on employee engagement.* Engage for Success. https://doi.org/10.17631/rd-2023-0001-drep (archived at https://perma.cc/QR2X-GTEQ)

Pedley, K, Clemence, M, Writer-Davies, R and Spielman, D (2020) *Evaluation of Acas Individual Conciliation 2019: Evaluations of early conciliation and conciliation in employment tribunal applications*, Acas. Available from: https://www.acas.org.uk/sites/default/files/inline-files/IC-evaluation-2019-Final-accessible.pdf (archived at https://perma.cc/NF9P-M6Q3) [accessed 7 June 2024]

Perrigo, B (2022) Inside Facebook's African sweatshop, *Time*, 17 February. Available from: https://time.com/6147458/facebook-africa-content-moderation-employee-treatment/ (archived at https://perma.cc/K33R-VBSN) [accessed 16 May 2024]

Peters, M, Seeds, K, Harding, C and Garnett, E (2010) *Findings from the Survey of Employment Tribunal Applications 2008*, Employment Relations Research Series, 107, BIS

Petzer, M (2020) *How to Limit 'the Sinking Ship Syndrome' during Redundancies*, CIPD. Available from: https://www.cipd.org/uk/views-and-insights/thought-leadership/the-world-of-work/sinking-ships-syndrome-redundancies/ (archived at https://perma.cc/SN47-G3EY) [accessed 14 March 2024]

Powell, A, Francis-Devine, B and Harriet, C (2022) *Coronavirus: Impact on the labour market*, House of Commons Library. Available from: https://researchbriefings.files.parliament.uk/documents/CBP-8898/CBP-8898.pdf (archived at https://perma.cc/T52L-DS4J) [accessed 16 March 2024]

Prikshat, V, Malik, A and Budhwar, P (2021) AI-augmented HRM: antecedents, assimilation and multilevel consequences, *Human Resource Management Review*, **33** (1),100860. https://doi.org/10.1016/j.hrmr.2021.100860 (archived at https://perma.cc/ML88-6UTT)

Primark (2023) *Our Supplier Code of Conduct*. Available from: https://corporate.primark.com/en-gb/primark-cares/our-approach/our-supplier-code-of-conduct (archived at https://perma.cc/66PL-PP9L) [accessed 16 May 2024]

Pritchard, K (2010) Becoming an HR strategic partner: tales of transition, *Human Resource Management Journal*, **20** (2), pp 175–88

Prospect (2023) *HSE under Pressure: A perfect storm*, Prospect the union. Available from: https://library.prospect.org.uk/id/2023/April/24/HSE-under-pressure-perfect-storm (archived at https://perma.cc/7HJ2-ZSVD) [accessed 12 June 2024]

Prowse, P, Prowse, J and Snook, J (2019) *The Living Wage: A regional study of care homes in Yorkshire: evidence to the Low Pay Commission*, Sheffield Hallam University

Purcell, J (1987) Mapping management styles in employee relations, *Journal of Management Studies*, **24** (5), pp 533–48

Purcell, J (2012a) *The Limits and Possibilities of Employee Engagement*, Warwick Papers in Industrial Relations, No. 96, April

Purcell, J (2012b) The management of employment rights, in *Making Employment Rights Effective: Issues of enforcement and compliance*, ed L Dickens, Hart Publishing, Oxford

Purcell, J (2014) Disengaging from engagement, *Human Resource Management Journal*, **24** (3), pp 241–54

Purcell, J and Hutchinson, S (2007) Front-line managers as agents in the HRM-performance causal chain: theory, analysis and evidence, *Human Resource Management Journal*, **17** (1), pp 3–20

Purcell, J and Sisson, K (1983) Strategies and practice in the management of industrial relations, in *Industrial Relations in Britain*, ed G Bain, Blackwell, London

Rahim, N, Brown, A and Graham, J (2011) *Evaluation of the Acas Code of Practice on Disciplinary and Grievance Procedures*, Acas Research Paper, 06/11

Rahim, N, Piggott, H, Davies, M, Cooper, E and Day, F (2017) *Early Conciliation Decision-making: Exploring the behaviours of claimants who neither settle nor proceed to an employment tribunal*, Acas Research Paper, 7/17

Rainbird, H and Stuart, M (2011) The state and the union learning agenda in Britain, *Work, Employment and Society*, **25** (2), pp 202–17

Rainnie, A (1989) *Industrial Relations in Small Firms*, Routledge, London

Ram, M, Edwards, P, Gilman, M and Arrowsmith, J (2001) The dynamics of informality: employment relations in small firms and the effects of regulatory change, *Work, Employment and Society*, **15** (4), pp 856–61

Ramsay, H (1996) Involvement, empowerment and commitment, in *The Handbook of Human Resource Management*, 2nd edn, ed B Towers, Blackwell, Oxford

Ravenswood, K and Markey, R (2018) Gender and voice in aged care: embeddedness and institutional forces, *International Journal of Human Resource Management*, **29** (5), pp 725–45

Refuge (2024) *Facts and Statistics*. Available from: https://refuge.org.uk/what-is-domestic-abuse/the-facts/ (archived at https://perma.cc/UQP7-6WHL) [accessed 12 June 2024]

Renwick, D (2013) Line managers and HRM, in *Contemporary Human Resource Management: Text and cases*, 4th edn, eds A Wilkinson and T Redman, Pearson, Harlow

Rhodes, C and Sear, D (2015) *The Motor Industry: Statistics and policy*, House of Commons Library Briefing Paper, Number 00611, August

Riddell, R, Ahmed, N, Maitland, A, Lawson, M and Taneja, A (2024) *Inequality Inc. – How corporate power divides our world and the need for a new era of public action*, Oxfam International. Available from: https://oi-files-d8-prod.s3.eu-west-2.amazonaws.com/s3fs-public/2024-01/Davos%202024%20Report-%20English.pdf (archived at https://perma.cc/6ULN-YBNQ) [accessed 15 May 2024]

Ridley-Duff, R and Bennett, T (2011) Mediation: developing a theoretical framework for understanding alternative dispute resolution, *Industrial Relations Journal*, **42** (2), pp 106–23

Robertson, H (2013) A case of pointing the finger and missing the point, *Hazards Magazine*, July–September. Available from: http://www.hazards.org/stress/resilience.htm (archived at https://perma.cc/YD4E-AUNT) [accessed 1 July 2019]

Robertson, I (2016) The six essentials of workplace wellbeing, *Occupational Health and Wellbeing*, **68** (10), pp 18–19

Robinson, D and Hayday, S (2009) *Engaging Managers*, Institute of Employment Studies, London

Roche, W, Teague, P, Gormley, T and Currie, D (2018) Improvisers, incrementalists and strategists: how and why organizations adopt ADR innovations, *British Journal of Industrial Relations*, **57** (1), pp 3–32

Rollinson, D (2000) Supervisor and manager approaches to handling discipline and grievance: a follow-up study, *Personnel Review*, **29** (6), pp 743–68

Rollinson, D, Hook, C and Foot, M (1996) Supervisor and manager styles in handling discipline and grievance: part two – approaches to handling discipline and grievance, *Personnel Review*, **25** (4), pp 38–55

Rousseau, D (1995) *Psychological Contracts in Organisations: Understanding written and unwritten agreements*, Sage, Thousand Oaks, CA

Rowsell, J (2024) Why we're working hard to get the unions on side, *People Management*, February–April. Available from: https://www.peoplemanagement.co.uk/article/1861291/why-cardiff-council-working-hard-unions-side (archived at https://perma.cc/WF7J-CW23) [accessed 10 June 2024]

Roy Bannya, A and Bainbridge, H (2022) Front line managers and human resource management: a social exchange theory perspective, in *Research Handbook on Line Managers*, eds K Townsend, A Bos-Nehles and K Jiang, Edward Elgar Publishing, Cheltenham

Rubery, J (2015) Change at work: feminization, flexibilization, fragmentation and financialization, *Employee Relations*, **37** (6), pp 633–44

Ruck, K, Welch, M and Menara, B (2017) Employee voice: an antecedent to organisational engagement? *Public Relations Review*, **43** (5), pp 904–14

Ryan, RM and Deci, EL (2001) On happiness and human potentials: a review of research on hedonic and eudaimonic well-being, *Annual Review of Psychology*, **52**, pp 141–66

Sadun, R, Bloom, N and Van Reenen, J (2017) Why do we undervalue competent management? *Harvard Business Review*, **95** (5), pp 120–27

Saks, A (2006) Antecedents and consequences of engagement, *Journal of Managerial Psychology*, **21** (7), pp 600–619

Saundry, R, Adam, D, Ashman, I, Forde, C, Wibberley, G and Wright, S (2016) *Managing Individual Conflict in the Contemporary British Workplace*, Acas Research Paper, 02/16

Saundry, R, Antcliff, V and Jones, C (2008) *Accompaniment and Representation in Workplace Discipline and Grievance*, Acas Research Paper, 06/08

Saundry, R, Bennett, T and Wibberley, G (2018) Inside the mediation room: efficiency, voice and equity in workplace mediation, *International Journal for Human Resource Management*, **29** (6), pp 1157–77

Saundry, R and Dix, G (2014) Conflict resolution in the UK, in *The Oxford Handbook on Conflict Management*, eds W Roche, P Teague and A Colvin, Oxford University Press, Oxford

Saundry, R, Fisher, V and Kinsey, S (2019) *Managing Workplace Conflict: The changing role of HR*, Acas Research Paper, London.

Saundry R, Fisher, V and Kinsey, S (2021) Disconnected Human Resource? Proximity and the (mis)management of workplace conflict, *Human Resource Management Journal*, **31** (2), pp 476–92

Saundry, R, Fisher, V and Kinsey, S (2022) Line management and the resolution of workplace conflict in the UK in *Research Handbook on Line Managers*, eds K Townsend, A Bos-Nehles and K Jiang, Edward Elgar Publishing, Cheltenham

Saundry, R, Jones, C and Antcliff, V (2011) Discipline, representation and dispute resolution: exploring the role of trade unions and employee companions in workplace discipline, *Industrial Relations Journal*, **42** (2), pp 195–211

Saundry, R, Latreille, P, Saundry, F, Urwin, P, Bowyer, A, Mason, S and Kameshwara, K (2024) *Line Manager Handling of Discipline and Grievance – a barrier to resolution?*, Acas, London

Saundry, R, McArdle, L and Thomas, P (2013) Reframing workplace relations? Conflict resolution and mediation in a primary care trust, *Work, Employment and Society*, **27** (2), pp 213–31

Saundry, R and McKeown, M (2013) Relational union organising in a healthcare setting: a qualitative study, *Industrial Relations Journal*, **44** (5–6), pp 533–47

Saundry, R and Urwin, P (2021) *Estimating the Costs of Workplace Conflict*, Acas. Available from: https://www.acas.org.uk/costs-of-conflict (archived at https://perma.cc/TY95-SS8N) [accessed 12 June 2024]

Saundry, R and Wibberley, G (2012) *Mediation and Early Resolution: A case study in conflict management*, Acas Research Paper, 12/12

Saundry, R and Wibberley, G (2014a) Contemporary union organizing in the UK: back to the future, *Labor Studies Journal*, **38** (4), pp 281–99

Saundry, R and Wibberley, G (2014b) *Workplace Dispute Resolution and the Management of Individual Conflict: A thematic analysis of 5 case studies*, Acas Research Paper, 06/14

Saundry, R Wibberley, G Wright, A and Hollinrake, A (2023) *Mediation and Early Resolution in East Lancashire Hospitals NHS Trust*, Acas Research Paper. Available from: https://www.acas.org.uk/early-resolution-in-east-lancs-hospitals-NHS-trust/html (archived at https://perma.cc/3KAT-5F8S) [accessed 2 June 2024]

Schein, E (1978) *Career Dynamics,* Addison Wesley, Reading, MA

Shaw, J (2021) The resource-based view and its use in strategic human resource management research: the elegant and inglorious, *Journal of Management,* **47** (7), pp 1787–95

Shone, E (2024) *Where Labour and the Tories Got their Money From in 2023*, Open Democracy, 13 March. Available from: https://www.opendemocracy.net/en/dark-money-investigations/labour-conservative-party-donations-2023-spending-analysis/ (archived at https://perma.cc/N8SY-8B8R) [accessed 16 May 2024]

Silverman, M, Bakhshalian, E and Hillman, L (2013) *Social Media and Employee Voice: The current landscape*, CIPD, London

Simms, M and Holgate, J (2010) TUC Organizing Academy 10 years on: what has been the impact on British unions? *International Journal of Human Resource Management*, **21** (3), pp 355–70

Simms, M, Holgate, J and Heery, E (2012) *Union Voices: Tactics and tensions in UK organizing*, Cornell University Press, Ithaca, New York

Sisson, K and Purcell, J (2010) Management: caught between competing views of the organisation, in *Industrial Relations: Theory and practice*, 3rd edn, eds T Colling and M Terry, John Wiley, Chichester

Smith, R (1983) Work control and management prerogatives in industrial relations, in *Industrial Relations and Management Strategy*, eds K Thurley and S Wood, Cambridge University Press, Cambridge

Smythe, P (2024) *Amazon is Holding Special Union-Busting Seminars for Workers,* Novara Media, 8 May. Available from https://novaramedia.com/2024/05/08/amazon-is-holding-special-union-busting-seminars-for-workers/ (archived at https://perma.cc/J6M2-5XQJ) [accessed 4 June 2024]

Spencer, D (2022) *Making Light Work*, Polity Press, Cambridge

Spicer, A (2024) Work 'wellness' programmes don't make employees happier – but I know what does, *The Guardian*, 17 January. Available from: https://www.theguardian.com/commentisfree/2024/jan/17/work-wellness-programmes-dont-make-employees-happier-but-i-know-what-does (archived at https://perma.cc/7KPZ-TY7S) [accessed 13 June 2024]

Standing, G (2011) *The Precariat: The new dangerous class*, Bloomsbury Academic, London

Stephens, C (2015) Are HR business partners a dying breed? *People Management*, February, pp 36–37

Stevens, M (2022) *Strategic Redundancy Implementation: Re-focus, re-organise and re-build,* Routledge, London

Stevens, M and Hannibal, C (2023) The smiling assassin?: Reconceptualising redundancy envoys as quasi-dirty workers. *International Journal of Human Resource Management*, **34** (5), pp 879–911

Streeck, W (1997) Industrial citizenship under regime competition: the case of the European works' councils, *Journal of European Public Policy*, **4** (4), pp 643–64

Stuart, M and Martinez Lucio, M (eds) (2005) *Partnership and Modernisation in Employment Relations*, Routledge, London

Suff, R (2022) *Collective Employee Voice: Recommendations for working with employee representatives for mutual gain*, CIPD, London

Tailby, S and Pollert, A (2011) Non-unionized young workers and organizing the unorganized, *Economic and Industrial Democracy*, **32** (3), pp 499–522

Tailby, S and Winchester, D (2000) Management and trade unions: towards social partnership? in *Personnel Management: A comprehensive guide to theory and practice*, 3rd edn, eds S Bach and K Sisson, Blackwell, Oxford

Tait, C (2017) *Future Unions: Towards a membership renaissance in the private sector*, Fabian Society. Available from: https://fabians.org.uk/publication/future-unions/ (archived at https://perma.cc/796E-8ERD) [accessed 13 September 2019]

Taylor, P and Bain, P (1999) An assembly line in the head: work and employee relations in the call centre, *Industrial Relations Journal*, **30** (2), pp 101–17

Teague, P and Doherty, L (2011) Conflict management systems in non-union multinationals in the Republic of Ireland, *International Journal of Human Resource Management*, **21** (1), pp 57–71

Teague, P and Roche, W (2012) Line managers and the management of workplace conflict: evidence from Ireland, *Human Resource Management Journal*, **22** (3), pp 235–51

Teoh, K, Dhensa-Kahlon, R, Christensen, M and Frost, F, Hatton, E and Nielsen, K (2023) *Organisational Wellbeing Interventions: Case studies from the NHS*, Technical Report, Birkbeck, University of London

Thompson, P and McHugh, D (2009) *Work Organisations: A critical approach*, 3rd edn, Palgrave, Basingstoke

Tilly, C (1978) *From Mobilization to Revolution*, Addison-Wesley, Reading, MA

Timms, P (2018) *Transformational HR: How human resources can create value and impact business strategy*, Kogan Page, London

Todor, WD and Owen, CL (1991) Deriving benefits from conflict resolution: a macrojustice approach, *Employee Responsibilities and Rights Journal*, **4** (1), pp 37–49

Tombs, S and Whyte, D (2010) *Regulatory Surrender: Death, injury and the non-enforcement of law*, The Institute of Employment Rights Publications, Liverpool

Topham, G. (2023) One year on, has P&O Ferries got away with illegally sacking all its crew? *The Guardian,* 17 March. Available from: https://www.theguardian.com/business/2023/mar/17/one-year-on-has-po-ferries-got-away-with-illegally-sacking-all-its-crew (archived at https://perma.cc/ED2R-LKEH) [accessed 14 May 2024]

Towers, B (1997) *The Representation Gap: Change and reform in the British and American workplace*, Oxford University Press, Oxford

Townsend, K, Dundon, T, Cafferkey, K and Kilroy, J (2022) Victim or master of HRM implementation: the frontline manager conundrum, *Asia Pacific Journal of Human Resources*, **60**, 79–96

Townsend, K and Hutchinson, S (2017) Line managers in industrial relations: where are we now and where next? *Journal of Industrial Relations*, **59** (2), pp 139–52

Trullen, J, Stirpe, L, Bonache, J and Valverde, M (2016) The HR department's contribution to line managers' effective implementation of HR practices, *Human Resource Management Journal*, **26** (4), pp 449–70

Truss, C, Shantz, A, Soane, E, Alfes, K and Delbridge, R (2013) Employee engagement, organisational performance and individual well-being: exploring the evidence, developing the theory, *International Journal of Human Resource Management*, **24** (14), pp 2657–69

TUC (2002) *Partnership Works*, Trades Union Congress, London

TUC (2009) *The Jobcentre Plus Rapid Response*. Available from: https://www.tuc.org.uk/research-analysis/reports/jobcentre-plus-rapid-response (archived at https://perma.cc/234E-8FVQ) [accessed 16 September 2019]

TUC (2013) *Supporting Working Women through the Menopause: Guidance for union representatives*, TUC Publications, London

TUC (2018) *Mental Health and the Workplace: A TUC education workbook*, TUC Publications, London

TUC (2019) *Improving Line Management: Why better line management will help improve work for everyone*, TUC Publications, London

TUC (2020) *Support in the Workplace for Victims of Domestic Abuse: TUC response for BEIS call for evidence.* Available from: https://www.tuc.org.uk/research-analysis/reports/support-workplace-victims-domestic-abuse (archived at https://perma.cc/PV4T-H9QG) [accessed 14 June 2024]

TUC (2021a) *'Fire and Rehire' Tactics Have Become Widespread during Pandemic – Warns TUC.* Available from: https://www.tuc.org.uk/news/fire-and-rehire-tactics-have-become-widespread-during-pandemic-warns-tuc (archived at https://perma.cc/3H6V-J2PJ) [accessed 14 May 2024]

TUC (2021b) *Menopause and the Workplace: TUC response to the Women and Equalities Select Committee inquiry.* Available from: https://www.tuc.org.uk/research-analysis/reports/menopause-and-workplace (archived at https://perma.cc/FE8Y-TR47) [accessed 12 June 2024]

TUC (2022) *Still Rigged: Racism in the UK labour market 2022*, TUC Publications, London

TUC (2023a) *New Analysis Shows Pay Gap between Non-disabled and Disabled Workers is Now 14.6% – Bigher than it was a decade ago* TUC news release, 14 November Available from: https://www.tuc.org.uk/news/tuc-slams-zero-progress-disability-pay-gap-last-decade (archived at https://perma.cc/KU4D-JCSP) [accessed 1 July 2024]

TUC (2023b) *Trades Union Health and Safety Reps Survey Report.* Available from: https://www.tuc.org.uk/research-analysis/reports/trades-union-health-and-safety-reps-survey-report (archived at https://perma.cc/S4QY-DYEW) [accessed 20 May 2024]

Turner, L and Windmuller, JP (1998) Convergence and diversity in international and comparative industrial relations, in *Industrial Relations at the Dawn of the New Millennium*, eds MF Neufeld and JT McKelvey, Cornell University Press, Ithaca

Ulrich, D (1997) Human resource champion: the next agenda for adding value and delivering results, *Harvard Business Review*, **76** (1), pp 124–34

Ulrich, D (2015) The new HR operating model is all about relationships, not partners, *People Management*, 24 March

Ulrich, D and Brockbank, W (2005) *The HR Value Proposition*, Harvard Business School Press, Cambridge, MA

Undy, R (2008) *Trade Union Merger Strategies: Purpose, process and performance*, Oxford University Press, Oxford

Urwin, P, Saundry, R, Saundry, F, Latreille, P, Kameshwara, K and Bowyer, A (2024) *Managerial Capability and Staff Engagement – Findings from the Skilled Managers research programme*, Acas Research Papers

Vandaele, K (2018) How can trade unions in Europe connect with young workers?, in *Youth Labor in Transition: Inequalities, Mobility, and Policies in Europe*, eds J O'Reilly et al, Oxford Academic, New York, pp 661–88

Van Wanrooy, B, Bewley, H, Bryson, A, Forth, J, Freeth, S, Stokes, S and Wood, S (2013) *Employment Relations in the Shadow of Recession: Findings from the 2011 Workplace Employment Relations Study*, Palgrave Macmillan, London

Vermeeren, B (2014) Variability in HRM implementation among line managers and its effect on performance: a 2-1-2 mediational multilevel approach, *International Journal of Human Resource Management*, **25** (22), pp 3039–59

Vincent, S, Lopes, A, Meliou, E and Özbilgin, M (2024) Relational responsibilisation and diversity management in the 21st century: the case for reframing equality regulation, *Work, Employment and Society.* Online first, DOI https://doi.org/10.1177/09500170231217660 (archived at https://perma.cc/7NZ4-2MKB)

Waddington, J and Whitson, C (1997) Why do people join unions in a period of membership decline? *British Journal of Industrial Relations*, **35** (4), pp 515–46

Wajcman, J (2000) Feminism facing industrial relations in Britain, *British Journal of Industrial Relations*, **38** (2), pp 183–201

Wakeling, A (2020) *Consultation: A voice lost in the crowd*, Acas. Available from: https://www.acas.org.uk/research-and-commentary/consultation-a-voice-lost-in-a-crowd/paper (archived at https://perma.cc/3FG9-76CT) [accessed 25 May 2024]

Walton, R (1985) From control to commitment in the workplace, *Harvard Business Review*, **63** (2), pp 77–84

Watson, T (1995) *Sociology, Work and Industry*, 3rd edn, Routledge, London

Watson, T (2006) *Organising and Managing Work*, 2nd edn, FT Prentice Hall, London

Wedderburn, Lord (1995) *Labour Law and Freedom*, Lawrence and Wishart, London

Weyman, A, Glendinning, R, O'Hara, R, Coster, J, Roy, D and Nolan, P (2023) *Should I Stay or Should I Go? NHS staff retention in the post COVID-19 world: Challenges and prospects (1.0)*, Zenodo. Available from: https://doi.org/10.5281/zenodo.7611657 (archived at https://perma.cc/FF4T-VU6W)

White, G (2019) *Bullying and Harassment of MPs' Parliamentary Staff: Independent Inquiry Report*, 11 July, HC 2206 2017-19

Whitehouse, E (2019) How to cure the long-term sickness problem, *People Management*. Available from: https://www.peoplemanagement.co.uk/long-reads/articles/how-cure-long-term-sickness-headache (archived at https://perma.cc/U4UP-F7AA) [accessed 31 January 2019]

Whittaker, S and Marchington, M (2003) Devolving HR responsibility to the line: threat, opportunity or partnership, *Employee Relations*, **23** (3), pp 245–61

Whittington, R, Angwin, D, Regnér, P, Johnson, G and Scholes, K (2023) *Exploring Strategy*, 13th edn, Pearson Education, Harlow

Wibberley, G, Jones, C, Bennett, T and Hollinrake, A (2016) Domestic violence: management challenge: how trade unions can help, in *Overcoming Challenges to Gender Equality in the Workplace: Leadership and innovation*, eds P Flynn, K Haynes and M Kilgour, Greenleaf Publishing, Sheffield

Wibberley, G, Jones, C, Bennett, T and Hollinrake, A (2018) The role of trade unions in supporting victims of domestic violence in the workplace, *Industrial Relations Journal*, **49** (1), pp 69–85

Wilkinson, A, Gollan, PJ, Kalfa, S and Xu, Y (2018) Voices unheard: employee voice in the new century, *International Journal of Human Resource Management*, **29** (5), pp 711–24

Williams, M (2011) *Workplace Conflict Management: A poll of business*, Acas Research Paper, 08/11

Williams, S (2014) *Introducing Employment Relations: A critical approach*, 3rd edn, Oxford University Press, Oxford

Williams, S and Adam-Smith, D (2010) *Contemporary Employment Relations: A critical introduction*, Oxford University Press, Oxford

Wills, J (2004) Trade unionism and partnership in practice: evidence from the Barclays-Unifi agreement, *Industrial Relations Journal*, **35** (4), pp 329–43

Wills, J and Simms, M (2004) Building reciprocal community unionism in the UK, *Capital and Class*, **82**, pp 59–84

Women and Equalities Committee (2019) *Enforcing the Equality Act: The law and the role of the Equality and Human Rights Commission*, Tenth report of Session 2017–19, 30 July

Wood, S, Saundry, R and Latreille, P (2017) The management of discipline and grievances in British workplaces: the evidence from 2011 WERS, *Industrial Relations Journal*, **48** (1), pp 2–21

World Health Organization (2022) *World Mental Health Report: Transforming mental health for all*, World Health Organization, Geneva

World Health Organization (2024) *Mental Health*. Available from https://www.who.int/health-topics/mental-health#tab=tab_1 (archived at https://perma.cc/UK27-RAXE) [accessed 8 July 2024]

Wright, A, Lawler, M, Ellison, G and Bennett, A (2022) *Work in Lancashire – Understanding Job Quality and Productivity in the Region*. Available from: https://www.uclan.ac.uk/assets/pdf/research-pdfs/work-in-lancashire-understanding-job-quality-and-productivity-in-the-region.pdf (archived at https://perma.cc/BWM5-83GY) [accessed 12 June 2024]

Wright, C (2008) Reinventing human resource management: business partners, internal consultants and the limits to professionalization, *Human Relations*, **61** (8), pp 1063–86

Wright, P and Ulrich, M (2017) A road well traveled: the past, present, and future journey of strategic human resource management, *Annual Review of Organizational Psychology and Organizational Behavior*, **4**, pp 45–65. https://doi.org/10.1146/annurev-orgpsych-032516-113052 (archived at https://perma.cc/VL6Y-GJ48)

Wynn-Evans, C (2019) Redundancy when on maternity leave: a matter of communication, *Personnel Today*. Available from: https://www.personneltoday.com/hr/redundancy-when-on-maternity-leave-a-matter-of-communication/ (archived at https://perma.cc/U6WA-TGL9) [accessed 21 August 2019]

Yang, L, Holtz, D, Jaffe, S et al (2022) The effects of remote work on collaboration among information workers, *Nature Human Behaviour*, **6**, pp 43–54 https://doi.org/10.1038/s41562-021-01196-4 (archived at https://perma.cc/9P7Z-E459)

Zeitlin, M (1989) *The Large Corporation and Contemporary Classes*, Polity Press, Oxford

INDEX

Note: Page numbers in *italics* refer to tables or figures.